The Impact of
PLAGUE
in Tudor and Stuart England

Paul Slack

Fellow and Tutor in Modern History
Exeter College, Oxford

Routledge & Kegan Paul
London, Boston, Melbourne and Henley

First published in 1985
by Routledge & Kegan Paul plc

14 Leicester Square, London WC2H 7PH, England

9 Park Street, Boston, Mass. 02108, USA

464 St Kilda Road, Melbourne,
Victoria 3004, Australia and

Broadway House, Newtown Road,
Henley on Thames, Oxon RG9 1EN, England

Set in Linotron Ehrhardt, 10 on 12 pt
by Input Typesetting Ltd, London
and printed in Great Britain
by Hartnoll Print,
Bodmin, Cornwall

© Paul Slack 1985

Library of Congress Cataloging in Publication Data

Slack, Paul.

The impact of plague in Tudor and Stuart England.
Bibliography: p.
Includes index.
1. Plague—England—History. 2. Plague—England—Case
studies. 3. Plague—social aspects—England. 4. Great
Britain—History—Tudors, 1485–1603. 5. Great Britain—
History—Stuarts, 1603–1649. I. Title.
RA644.P7S65   1985   942.05   84–27574

British Library CIP data available

ISBN 0–7102–0469–8

This book is to be returned on or before
the last date stamped below.

The Impact of
PLAGUE
in Tudor and Stuart
England

For Jill

Contents

Tables

Figures

Preface

My interest in plague began where this book finishes: not with the disease itself, but with what I have called the social response – the ways in which people tried to control, interpret and come to terms with it in the past. I was particularly intrigued by the adoption in England in the sixteenth and seventeenth centuries of an ambitious code of health regulations designed to control plague, and by the intellectual controversies and popular opposition which that code aroused. These subjects were not new: they had attracted the attention of Daniel Defoe in the 1720s, and of several commentators and historians after him. But it seemed to me that they justified more extensive historical investigation than they had yet received. Part III of this book is devoted to them.

It soon became clear, however, that in order fully to understand social reactions, some study was needed of the historical phenomenon of plague. I needed to know how frequent epidemics were, which social groups and localities they most often affected, how high mortality was, and whether there were any changes in the shape of the phenomenon over time which might have helped to determine the changing social response to it. Part II of this book is therefore given over to an examination of the incidence of plague, largely through local case studies. Part I tries to set the scene for the rest by describing the history of plague, the ways in which it can be approached by historians, and the ways in which it could be fought and understood by Englishmen in the sixteenth and seventeenth centuries. By the end of the book, I hope I have shown why Englishmen battled against plague in the manner that they did, and with what results.

The writing of the book has taken me into many areas of inquiry, and I can claim expertise in few of them. I have been trained as an historian and my knowledge of the medical background to my subject has been gained at second hand. No doubt I have failed also to appreciate some of the subtleties of the several historical topics I have had to consider – the history of population and of urban economies, the social topography of towns and their political and administrative structures, the processes of policy-making in central and local government, the history of medical and religious thought and of popular and crowd behaviour. I hope that those more expert than me in these areas will pardon oversimplifications and find something to interest or provoke them in what follows. I am particularly aware that the studies in Part II will seem primitive to some readers, in the age of family reconstitution and the computer manipulation of demographic data. These chapters rest essentially on my own aggregative analysis of burials in rather more than 400 parish registers. I have gratefully used the publications of members of the Cambridge Group for the History of Population and Social Structure where I could; but my main concern has been to examine the immediate impact of plague in chosen localities by looking at as many registers as possible. There was no time for more sophisticated calculations.

I hope that the organisation of the chapters is sufficiently clear to allow readers to pick out discussion of the themes which interest them most. Those who find numbers tedious will spend little time on Part II, for example. I also hope, however, that the interrelationship between the various parts of the book will become evident. The incidence of plague, popular attitudes towards it, political and administrative constraints on the formation of policy, and intellectual presuppositions, all had an impact on one another. 'Public health' had – and has – manifold repercussions; and the most exciting and challenging part of my work has been the making of connections, however tentative, between areas of history which are often treated as discrete.

It is a pleasure to acknowledge the help which I have received along the way. First, my thanks must go to the many archivists and librarians who have provided my source materials: particularly to the staffs of the Bodleian Library and the British Library, the Wellcome Historical Medical Library, and the Guildhall Library, London; to the archivists of the Record Offices of Bristol, Cheshire, Devon, Essex, Hampshire, Kent, Norfolk and Norwich, Staffordshire, Wiltshire, the Corporation of London and the Greater London Council; and to those who had charge of the records of the towns of Beverley, Chester, Colchester, Exeter, Hull, Leicester, Plymouth, Salisbury, Winchester and York. Parish records are now, thankfully, being collected in county or diocesan repositories, but I was welcomed most generously by incumbents and churchwardens in Bristol, Exeter, Norwich and Salisbury, when I needed to examine documents then in their care. I owe a debt too to the many local historians and local record societies, on whose publications over the past century and a half I have been able to draw.

Some parts of this book embody revised versions of work which has appeared elsewhere. I am grateful to *Local Population Studies* for permission to use in Chapter 5 (ii) work published originally in *The Plague Reconsidered* (Local Population Studies Supplement, 1977); and to Cambridge University Press and the editors of the volumes for permission to use in Chapter 12 (i) parts of my essay in J. Walter and R.S. Schofield (eds), *Death and the Social Order* (Cambridge, forthcoming), and to use some of the material from my essay in C. Webster (ed.), *Health, Medicine and Mortality in the Sixteenth Century* (Cambridge, 1979).

I have accumulated a good many debts of a more personal kind over the years. Keith Thomas first kindled my interest in social history, when I was an undergraduate and he was my tutor; he suggested this subject to me; and he has provided encouragement and stimulus ever since. W.G. Hoskins supervised my first steps in historical research and gave me the benefit of his unrivalled knowledge of English local archives. Joan Thirsk and Roger Schofield were generous and constructive examiners of the D.Phil. thesis from which this book has grown. Much of the spade-work was done while I was a Junior Research Fellow of Balliol College, and I owe a great deal to the Master and Fellows corporately, and individually to Christopher Hill and Richard Cobb (from whom I have taken more than the title of Chapter 11). Something of my debt to these historians will, I hope, be evident in the pages that follow.

Many other colleagues and friends have given me references and encouraged me by their interest. I have tried to acknowledge specific obligations in the notes, but I must thank more generally here Gerald Aylmer, Peter Clark, Gordon Forster, Dwyryd Jones, Jennifer Loach, Stephen Macfarlane, John Maddicott, David Palliser, Charles Phythian-Adams, Conrad Russell, Jim Sharpe, David Vaisey, John Walsh and Charles Webster. Finally, I owe most of all to my wife – for tolerating being shut up with the plague for so long, and never giving up hope of seeing the end of it.

Exeter College, Oxford   P.A.S.

Conventions

In dates, the Old Style has been retained except that the year has been taken to begin on 1 January.

Spelling, punctuation and capitalisation in quotations from contemporary sources have been modernised.

Part I

Perspectives

Chapter 1

Disease and society

Pestilence meaneth . . . all manner of afflictions or calamities which cut and cancel the life of man, whether it be either in the deprivation of health for the weakening of the body, or in the loss of friends or goods for the vexation of the mind, whether it be sword, fire or famine, or whatsoever, all are the plagues of God. . . . Yet privately, for the particular understanding thereof, we do universally understand and comprehend by this word plague a common and sudden mortality of men, and . . . a special disease, manifestly differing from all other diseases, not only for the speediness thereof in death, but also for the outrage thereof in those that feel the same.

Anon., Sermon on Plague, *c.* 1600.[1]

Plague, the epidemic disease whose ravages in the past are the subject of this book, was both a personal affliction and a social calamity. Decimating communities, destroying families, bringing grief and pain to individuals, it deserves study in its own right as a fundamental part of man's experience in history. If we are to attempt a rounded understanding of our predecessors, their sufferings and misfortunes ought to command as much attention as their joys and achievements. Yet the history of plague is more than a sad tale of the diverse ways in which men were the playthings of fortune or providence, at the mercy of a harsh environment. For they had to react to their environment. They struggled to explain epidemic disease and to control it, and the ways in which they did so have much to tell us about the society in which they lived: its intellectual assumptions, its coherence and solidity, its political and administrative flexibility, and its capacity for change. The impact of plague is to be found in the social response to it no less than in the problems which it brought. This book has been designed to explore these two themes in sixteenth- and seventeenth-century England.

(i) The functions of disaster

Sudden disastrous events such as epidemics illuminate many facets
of the societies with which they collide. They create situations of
stress which test the institutions, and the habits of mind and behaviour,
which normally hold society together. That is one reason why catas-
trophes have proved to be attractive subject-matter for novelists and
journalists, anthropologists and sociologists, as well as historians.
There has been a flourishing genre of sociological 'Disaster Studies',
for example, analysing the response to such modern calamities as
tornadoes, hurricanes, earthquakes, and, in 1945, nuclear bombing.[2]
How people interpret these crises, with what precise mixture of superstition and science, reveals a great deal about their intellectual background. How governments deal with them demonstrates their authority and adaptability. When, in the greatest crises, the formal structures of government fail altogether, the spotlight turns on informal
ties of family and community which face new challenges and meet
them more or less successfully.

The stresses brought by disaster can also create, for a time, new
forms of behaviour and new patterns of thought. The popular assumption that catastrophe leads to panic is not, in fact, supported by history
or experience.[3] Except in a few individual cases, behaviour remains
rational. In critical circumstances, however, reason imposes hard
choices: between loyalty to family and loyalty to neighbours or
community; between official responsibilities and care for one's own
relatives or property. Flight from, or brutality towards, the victims of
disaster may then be common, whatever the obligations imposed by
prevailing moral values. Other usual modes of thought can similarly
be distorted by stress. Disasters may provoke a rejection of seemingly
useless and unfeeling deities, and equally, and apparently more often,
lead to religious revivals, sometimes with a distinct millenarian
character. They may also give rise to social tensions of various kinds.
Shared suffering binds together some sub-groups in a population, but
it may increase their distance from others if the suffering is not shared
equally. Authorities who seek to control or to mitigate the effects of
a disaster may appear ruthless and bureaucratic to its victims, and
thus upset the normal balance of paternalism and deference between
the rulers and the ruled. People look around for scapegoats who can
be blamed for the community's sufferings. Sudden disaster can thus
be divisive in an infinite number of ways.[4] Again, however, extreme

reactions tell us something about normality. The divisions occur along pre-existing fissures in the social fabric, and the social norms which are broken or exaggerated leave people's most fundamental loyalties and assumptions exposed to view.

It is not surprising that a subject with such wide ramifications should appeal to historians, who are often concerned to establish connections between apparently discrete social phenomena. A study of the Lisbon earthquake of 1755, for example, has thrown light not only on Portuguese government and society but on European attitudes towards religion at a crucial point in the history of the Enlightenment.[5] Major epidemics of infectious disease are obvious candidates for similar treatment. Recent historical work on cholera has advanced our understanding of religious and scientific assumptions, political and administrative conventions, and social relationships and social conflicts, in the nineteenth century.[6] A study of bubonic plague, cholera's predecessor as the cause of sudden surges in mortality, can be even more instructive. Plague caused far greater mortality than cholera in the towns and villages which it attacked, and thus subjected them to far greater stresses; it persisted for longer, from the fourteenth century to the eighteenth; and it tested a pre-industrial Europe whose social, intellectual and political order is more distant and hence less easily investigated than that of the nineteenth century.[7]

Before we can adopt these wider perspectives, however, it is necessary to examine with some care the phenomenon which caused the catastrophe. For studies of past and present disasters have also shown that the nature of the challenge helps to determine the character of the response. If the catastrophe occurs suddenly and without warning, reactions will be more spontaneous and less deliberate than if it can be seen approaching. If it is random in its impact, it might be expected to lead to less social division and more social cohesion than if its incidence is biased towards one social class or group. The duration and degree of severity of a disaster may be equally significant variables.[8] The attempts to measure the dimensions of the crises caused by plague which appear in Part II of this book are therefore a necessary preliminary to the description of the social response in Part III.

Epidemics of infectious disease have special features not common to all disasters, of course, and two of them may be noted here, since they suggest further perspectives from which to approach bubonic plague. In the first place, epidemics are obviously more common phenomena in most parts of the world than earthquakes or floods. There can thus be some continuity and some development in the social response to them, especially since the perception of any particular disease, even one so devastating as plague, is influenced by familiarity with others. Every society has customary methods of explaining and treating illness, which reflect its general assumptions about the social and natural order.[9] Some diseases are so common as scarcely to be regarded as disease at all; others are so unusual that they are thought to be outside the normal course of nature, the direct product of supernatural agencies. Most epidemic diseases fall between the two stools. Natural causes and remedies are attributed to them, but they are often explained simultaneously in terms which imply that they are a judgment on individuals or societies.[10] Whatever the precise view adopted in any given society, however, it always has historical roots and it generally changes over time.

Epidemic disease is also different from many other forms of disaster in its causation. It is not, like an earthquake or a tornado, a wholly autonomous, natural event, unshaped by human intervention. To a degree the incidence and severity of epidemic disease is socially determined. This is most obvious at the roots of disease, in the biological interactions between micro-organisms and human hosts which continuously evolve, and which can be influenced by external factors such as changes in the density of populations or in the frequency of contact between one population and another. Consequent transformations in disease patterns usually occur over far longer stretches of time than the two centuries considered in this book.[11] But even in the short term, the spread of an epidemic can be encouraged by ready transport facilities for the relevant vector, by bad hygiene and overcrowding, by poverty and malnutrition; and its severity may be alleviated by improvements in standards of living or by direct controls such as quarantine and the isolation of the sick. The importance of social factors in any particular instance depends on the aetiology of the disease under consideration; but the incidence of plague, as of many other epidemics, may be expected to reflect the different environments of town and country, and the different living standards of rich and poor.

In examining the impact of plague, therefore, we shall not be engaging simply in a static analysis of particular 'disaster situations', which gave rise to spontaneous and unco-ordinated responses. We shall be dealing with development and change, both in the nature of plague and in the nature of contemporary reactions to it. The first subject will lead us to look at what Louis Chevalier has termed the 'biological bases' of social history:[12] variations in the levels of mortality and morbidity in different places and at different times, and the reasons for them. The second will involve an examination of policies for public health, and the intellectual attitudes and political and social conditions which made them possible. These various topics will necessarily be discussed separately in the following pages; but it is hoped that they have a coherence, since they were intimately connected with one another. The aim will be to investigate one important instance of the interaction between social problems and social policies, and one small part of the relationship between man and his environment.

(ii) Plague and its history

It is necessary to begin with some explanatory account of plague itself. The bacillus reponsible for the disease is *Pasteurella pestis*, or *Yersinia pestis* as it is now more commonly called, after Yersin who first described it in 1894.[13] This micro-organism is primarily an internal parasite of rodents and particularly of rats, who themselves suffer from the disease, and it is carried initially to man by fleas deserting dying or dead animals and seeking nourishment on live humans. Some species of flea have a 'proventriculus', a sort of valve at the entrance to the stomach, which can become blocked by ingested bacilli. If such 'blocked' fleas bite human hosts, the blood which they suck cannot pass the blocked proventriculus and it is regurgitated along with plague bacilli back into the wound. Fleas without a proventriculus can also transmit the disease, however, since contamination can occur, not only through biting, but through the flea's excrement if it is deposited on scratches on the skin.

Once it reaches man, the bacillus proves remarkably toxic. Case fatality rates vary from epidemic to epidemic, but normally between 60 and 80 per cent of those infected die. The incubation period is short, usually less than six days, and half the deaths occur within eight days of infection, though some victims may die after an interval of a month or more. The disease also runs its course in a whole community quite quickly. Since it depends on fleas, it thrives in a humid and warm climate which allows fleas to breed and flourish. Although it can and often does persist through the winter months, thanks to fleas surviving in the warm 'micro-climate' of rodent nests, human mortality is always heaviest in the summer and autumn in temperate climates, and in Europe it is usually concentrated in the period from July to October.

The clinical symptoms of the disease are as striking as the speed with which it develops. Cells are rapidly destroyed and nervous tissues inflamed. The victim's temperature rises, to around 40°C, and he suffers headaches, vomiting, pain and delirium before sinking into a final coma. At the same time the unmistakable signs of the disease appear on the skin. A blister forms at the site of the original flea-bite and develops into a gangrenous blackish carbuncle. The lymph nodes, usually in the groin but sometimes in the armpit or the neck, swell and suppurate, forming the buboes which give *bubonic plague* its name. Finally fresh carbuncles appear, along with blisters and large subcutaneous spots which can change colour between orange and black, blue and purple. These spots were described by historical observers as the 'tokens' of plague, and they and the other clinical manifestations made cases of bubonic plague easily recognisable. John Ward, for example, who gathered information about the plague of 1665, noted that 'the Plague ordinarily begins with vomiting; there are in it Buboes that appear in the Emunctories [lymphatic glands]; Carbuncles which come anywhere; the Blanes which are things like blisters; and the tokens which are spots of bright flaming red colour.'

In a minority of cases, the normal clinical features of bubonic plague are absent. Sometimes the disease assumes a mild 'ambulatory' form, which manifests itself in a simple swelling of the lymph nodes without other dramatic symptoms. John Ward again described exactly this ambulatory plague: 'When the sickness was declining one might observe persons in London streets halting and holding their arms very strangely, which persons they concluded to have the sores upon them.' At the other extreme, and usually at the beginning of an epidemic, there can be cases of sudden death with, as Ward noted, 'no tokens nor sores'.[14] These are cases of what is sometimes termed *septicaemic plague*, when the bacilli invade the blood stream quickly and cause death before buboes have had time to develop. But septicaemic plague is simply an acute form of bubonic plague, not separable from it.

A third variety of plague, *pneumonic plague*, is clinically and epidemiologically much more distinct. It may begin with a case of bubonic plague complicated by pneumonia, but it can then take off as the disease is spread by bacteria coughed out in the sputum of the victim and inhaled by people around him. They develop primary pneumonic plague and in turn communicate the disease by coughing or sneezing. In this form plague is not dependent on fleas and it is highly infectious. It is not only the method of transmission which distinguishes pneumonic from bubonic plague. The incubation period is shorter in the former case, from one to three days; the symptoms are different, a cough and the spitting of blood being the most common; and the case fatality rate is much higher, being virtually 100 per cent if the victims are left untreated. With its dependence on lung involvement and not on fleas, pneumonic plague tends also to be associated with cold rather than warm climates and with winter rather than summer in Europe. However, it is highly unlikely than pneumonic plague played any substantial role in the epidemics of the sixteenth and seventeenth centuries which we shall consider. It was probably important in some parts of Europe in the fourteenth century, and perhaps even in the early fifteenth. There were descriptions of bloody sputum, heavy mortality sometimes continued through the winter months, and plague spread very rapidly from one community to another, all of which suggest that pneumonic plague had joined forces with bubonic plague in late medieval European epidemics.[15] But these indications were absent after 1500. There probably continued to be odd cases of secondary pneumonic plague, developing from original bubonic infection,[16] but there is no sign that primary pneumonic plague spread independently as an epidemic disease.

We can be sure, therefore, of the predominance of plague in its bubonic form and of its general clinical picture in our period. But certainty ends there. There is considerable controversy both among medical authorities and among historians about two aspects of the epidemiology of plague relevant to this study. Each concerns the mode of transmission of the disease: first within small communities and households, secondly across long distances between towns and countries.

In the first case the argument revolves around the role of fleas in the transmission of bubonic plague. Once the disease has been passed via the rat's flea from rat to man, can it then be transmitted by fleas directly from man to man without the intervention of the rat? Can the sequence man–flea–man replace rat–flea–man? In general, English epidemiologists, resting their case on studies of plague in modern South and South-East Asia, have thought not. For them the main rat flea, *Xenopsylla cheopis*, is the most efficient vector of plague (although another rat flea, *Nosopsylla fasciatus*, may also play a role); and *X. cheopis* prefers to feed off the black rat, *Rattus rattus*, deserting that rodent for men only when the rat is infected and dies. A contrary view has been taken by French epidemiologists, whose earliest studies related to modern outbreaks of the disease in North Africa. They have suggested that the human flea, *Pulex irritans*, can transmit the disease when it moves between human hosts, despite the fact that it has no proventriculus. Its efficiency as a vector is admitted to be inferior to that of *X. cheopis*, and it would need to feed on an acute septicaemic case of plague if its chances of transmitting the disease were to be high. They argue, however, that it has often acted as a carrier when present in sufficient numbers and in association with acute human cases of plague. Moreover, there were often multiple cases of plague in single households in North Africa, whereas in India and other areas of Asia, one plague case per household was the general rule. This suggested that while the first case in a household might have its origin in a rat death, succeeding cases were caused by human fleas communicating plague directly from one member of a family to another.[17]

Historians have not failed to notice the relevance of these arguments about modern North African epidemics for their studies of plague in medieval and early modern Europe.[18] In the past there were certainly swarms of human fleas, and there was no shortage of cases of septicaemic plague. In European epidemics plague was also conspicuously concentrated in households, many of which lost three, four or even all their members, as we shall see. It would be unwise, however, to jump to the conclusion that *Pulex irritans* played the major part in European epidemics in the past and the rat only a minor role, for there is evidence which points firmly in the other direction. First, there is the concentration of plague mortality in towns and, within towns, in separate neighbourhoods, often on the outskirts and not in the centre where the chances of contact between infected and non-infected humans might be expected to be greatest. This clearly suggests that in major urban epidemics the disease was dependent on infected colonies of rats.[19] Secondly, despite the frequency of multiple cases of plague within single households, it has not yet been shown that mortality rates were related to size of household, as one might expect if the human flea was the significant vector.[20] Finally, these clusters of cases in households need not necessarily imply direct transmission between humans: their temporal distribution suggests that they could be explained by successive and multiple deaths of rats.[21]

Neither the historical evidence nor the findings of modern epidemiology permit a final answer to this problem. But they do suggest that in the present state of our knowledge we must strike a balance between the two theories of transmission, and allow each a role – though not an equal one – in past European epidemics of bubonic plague. While the man–flea–man sequence may have been responsible for sporadic cases of infection, it is likely that rodent infection was the necessary foundation for a major epidemic.

There is no reason to doubt that the disease was sometimes passed from one person to another by fleas, both *Pulex irritans* and *X. cheopis*, either jumping directly, or carried in bedding and clothing.[22] Contemporary references to plague being caught from clothes and sheets, and contemporary stress on the need to air these personal belongings of plague victims, are too common to be ignored. In 1610, for example, 'a poor man' called Dobson, living on the outskirts of the parish of Westerham in Kent, had an 'inmate' or lodger who died of plague. He sold 'a coat of the said inmate, not well aired or purified, unto one Wexe of Westerham town, a poor man also, who by that coat was infected and died of the pestilence'. A few further cases of plague followed among the neighbours who came to prepare Wexe's corpse for burial: perhaps there were still infected and infective fleas around.[23]

At the same time, however, it is probable that infection was often communicated by fleas from an initial victim, like Wexe, to a rat; and that there was then a rodent epizootic which became the foundation for later human cases and so for a serious epidemic. This sequence did not happen at Westerham, where cases of plague were few, and where there had already been a serious outbreak of the disease, which may have killed the susceptible rodents, a few months before the Wexe incident. But rodent infection was a likely event in towns and in large villages from which plague had been absent for several years; and it was probably a necessary condition, not indeed for sporadic cases like those in Westerham, but for major urban mortalities of the kind described in later chapters. It is true that references to rats in connection with plague are almost entirely absent from contemporary records: so for that matter are references to fleas in the same context. Nevertheless, the rats themselves were not absent. Black rats must have been common between the floors and in the roofs of wooden or wattle-and-daub houses. Unlike grey rats, which did not appear in England until the eighteenth century, they prefer to nest close to man because of the food and warmth which human habitations provide. When they died, their corpses may have remained out of sight in their nests, leaving their fleas to wander. There are certainly several significant cases of people who caught plague after being in an environment where rats might be expected. In Portsmouth in 1563, for example, plague victims included a man who worked in a bakehouse and another who had charge of naval stores. In Chelmsford a plague epidemic in 1625 may have begun when the daughter of one 'ratcatcher' and the wife of another were buried in December 1624.[24]

These illustrative incidents also raise the second controversial problem concerning the transmission of plague: whether it was carried over long distances mainly by men or by rodents. In the case of the Portsmouth plague of 1563, the disease probably came, as contemporaries thought, from Le Havre, with English ships and soldiers returning from a military expedition there. In a similar way, we shall see that plague often reached London directly by ship from foreign ports, and moved from there along main transport routes to other towns. There has been some debate among epidemiologists about the precise mode of transport which is important: whether the infective fleas are carried on rats in ships and carts of grain; without rats or any other hosts in bales of cloth, wool and cotton; or on the backs of men themselves. Again the historical evidence suggests that all of these played a role. There are persuasive contemporary references to plague being caught from clothes, as in Wexe's case, or from boxes and bales of cloth and clothes, as in Eyam in Derbyshire in 1665, and to its being carried from one place to another by individuals, apparently without baggage.[25] In all these cases, however, human transport of one kind or another provides the essential vehicle of rapid transmission, and it is human transport which explains the movement of plague along major routes of trade and commerce, to major ports, cities, market towns, and eventually to a few villages, usually on main roads and navigable rivers.

Yet there is an alternative means of transport for plague: via wild rodents in the countryside who may catch plague from the domestic black rats of a human settlement and pass it on to another rat colony some distance away. According to one epidemiologist, plague might often move 'forward step by step, borne by field rodents, from field to field, from burrow to burrow, in thin epizootic trails winding across the countryside, infecting village rats in passing, and thus setting off murine epizootics which led in turn to human infection'.[26] It seems unlikely that this was the commonest mode of transmission in pre-industrial Europe. Plague spread too rapidly from one major centre of population to another for it to be explained by anything other than human transport. Nevertheless, once established in an area, plague sometimes spread sporadically and slowly from one village to another, and it is possible that rodents were then the agents.[27] One would like to know whether the ratcatchers whose relatives died in Chelmsford in December 1624 had caught infected field rather than infected domestic rodents: they may have done. It may be significant also that Dobson of Westerham, Kent, lived on the edge of the parish: his lodger may have caught plague from a field rodent before it was transmitted via his fleas and his coat to the centre of the township.

These different means of long-distance transmission are related to one final question concerning the epidemiology of plague. How far was it endemic in England in the past? Was it always present in some place or other, flaring up into serious epidemics whenever climatic conditions were favourable? Or were epidemics always preceded by the introduction of a virulent strain of the bacillus from abroad? The available evidence points towards the hypothesis of importation rather than endemicity, although it is once more necessary not to be wholly exclusive. Studies of plague in Europe show that major epidemics in London and then in other English towns were the consequence of waves of infection sweeping across the whole Continent and coming into England from outside. When it arrived in the country, however, the disease could linger for a decade or even longer before disappearing. By being carried from place to place either by rodents or by men it could set up, temporarily, what has been called an 'area-wide endemicity'.[28] The Westerham case in 1610 will serve again as an example. That outbreak came towards the end of a series of English epidemics which had begun in ports on the east coast in 1602 and had disastrous effects in London in 1603. But the disease remained in London in less serious form for the rest of the decade, as it did also in Kent. It could persist in black rat populations in London through the winters, and perhaps also among wild rodents in the countryside. After an epidemic in a parish like Westerham, it might appear again and infect a few more households, like Dobson's, in the following spring, and then move on. This series of outbreaks did not end until 1612. Yet after 1612, plague seems to have been absent from England until 1624, when it was again imported from the Continent and a fresh sequence of a similar kind began.[29]

So far as England is concerned, therefore, plague was an invader. It came in waves at irregular but frequent intervals, causing high mortality to begin with and only slowly dying away. The same might be said about Europe and the Mediterranean lands as a whole. Plague menaced them from the East, probably from the Steppes of Eurasia, and its movement can often be traced from port to port and country to country. There were also longer-term ebbs and flows of infection which can be observed across the centuries of European history. Individual epidemic waves were gathered into groups, between which there were long periods of remission. The first invasion of the West of which we have precise knowledge began in the sixth century, with the plague of Justinian, and ended in the eighth century. There was then a long interval until 1348, when a new series started, finishing in England in the 1660s and in western Europe only in the 1720s. A third world-wide dispersal of plague began at the end of the nineteenth century and continued into the twentieth, although its effects in Europe were slight.

It is convenient and conventional to describe these clusters of epidemics as 'pandemics'. The term is a description and not an explanation, however. The reasons for the secular advances and retreats of plague remain obscure. The retreat of the eighth century, for example, may have been due to changes in climate, to the absence as yet of large populations of commensal rodents in Europe, or to a disruption of communications between the Mediterranean and the endemic foci of plague in Asia; we do not know.[30] As for the withdrawal of plague in the eighteenth century, that has been attributed variously to improved living standards, the adoption of quarantine measures, and a change in the disease itself. We shall need to examine these hypotheses at the end of this book.[31] For the moment, however, it is sufficient to note that the plagues with which we are concerned formed the second half of a series of epidemics which had begun in the middle of the fourteenth century and which ended in the later seventeenth. In England the last of the series was the so-called 'Great Plague' of London, beginning in 1665. The first was the Black Death of 1348–9.

That initial outbreak of plague, which affected almost the whole of Europe between the beginning of 1348 and the end of 1352, had a more profound impact than any of those which followed it. This was partly because of its novelty. After a gap of more than 500 years, there was no memory to guide its interpretation or its treatment. Old texts had to be ransacked for appropriate references before plague could even be described; and only the sophisticated towns of Italy were able tentatively to embark on those practices of isolation and quarantine which were to be widely adopted in the following centuries. A rational response had to be invented almost from scratch.[32] As a result, in parts of Europe social reactions to plague took an extreme form which was to have no parallel later. Some people sought scapegoats for the Black Death and persecuted the Jews; others found the sins which had brought such a scourge on society in themselves, and there was a dramatic resurgence of the flagellant movement.[33] These were temporary phenomena. The return of plague also played a part in more permanent transformations. It has been suggested that it pushed Italian painting in new directions, towards more formal styles as well as more religious subjects. It was certainly one reason for the general popularity of themes connected with death in the painting, sculpture and literature of the later Middle Ages: the memento mori, the Dance of Death, or those macabre decaying cadavers on the tombs of the period.[34] To say that the age was obsessed with death is an exaggeration. But the problems of morbidity and mortality were given new relevance and fresh force by the series of plagues which began in 1348.

It was not only the novelty of the Black Death which made it unique, but also its severity. It is not unlikely that a third of the population of whole countries was swept away by this one disaster. Some of the best evidence for the extent of mortality comes from England. The king's tenants-in-chief, who could afford to keep away from infected localities, still lost 27 per cent of their number, while the clergy suffered a death rate of 40 to 45 per cent, to judge by the number of vacant benefices. Most persuasive of all are calculations of local mortality based on manorial records: they show that between one-third and two-thirds of the tenants on manors in different parts of England died during this first epidemic of plague.[35] To say that a third of the population of England perished in the course of 1348 and 1349 is therefore a minimum estimate. Further epidemics followed, the first in 1361, and although none was as severe as the initial outbreak, perhaps because pneumonic plague played a decreasing role in them, they were frequent and extensive enough to keep the population low until the middle of the fifteenth century.[36] Stretching as they did over most of western Europe, these epidemics had pronounced social and economic effects. Land went out of cultivation; industries and trade declined. A contraction in demand for goods and services of all kinds produced the depressed European economy of the later Middle Ages.

Towards the end of the fifteenth century, however, the situation began to change. Populations started to rise, economic depression lifted, and epidemics provided only a temporary brake on growth. In England outbreaks of plague declined in frequency after an epidemic in 1479, and it is probable also that their geographical range was narrowing.[37] Although the reasons for this are not at all clear, epidemics became more localised and their effect on gross national mortality was reduced. As we shall see, plague was never confined wholly to towns; but by the second half of the sixteenth century it affected a minority rather than a majority of villages. Coupled with a rise in fertility, which seems also to have occurred towards the end of the fifteenth century,[38] this meant that the population of England could grow. In contrast to the demographic stagnation of the later Middle Ages, the English population doubled in the sixteenth and seventeenth centuries.

The plagues of sixteenth- and seventeenth-century England, which form the subject of this book, therefore had less profound effects than those which had preceded them in the first half of the pandemic. Yet their impact was still far from small. If plagues did not occur as often as they had between 1348 and 1479, they happened often enough, especially in towns. If gross mortality over the whole country was less than it had once been, death rates were extraordinarily high in the many towns and villages where plague did strike. Plague very often killed 10 per cent of the population of a community in less than a year. In the worst epidemics the total approached one-third, as in Norwich in 1579, and occasionally may even have exceeded it, as in Newcastle in 1636 and in Colchester in 1666.[39] The social and economic consequences of these disasters for individual communities can scarcely be exaggerated. Furthermore, such disasters had still to be explained and dealt with. If people were more familiar with plague in 1500 than they had been in 1348, in England at least they had yet to develop organised means of fighting it; that was an achievement of the sixteenth and seventeenth centuries, as we shall see. Most important of all, plague continued to inflict extraordinary stresses on ordinary men and women and on their social relationships. This most immediate impact of epidemic disease will often be in the background in the following pages. But we ought to put it firmly in the foreground, in the last section of this chapter, before we proceed.

(iii) Social repercussions

The collective and individual strains imposed by epidemic disasters arose naturally from the nature of plague. Most obviously, it caused an enormous number of deaths in a small area in a very short space of time. In large cities and major epidemics hundreds of victims had to be hurriedly buried in winding sheets in common graves. Only the more prosperous could afford their own coffin, and in any case coffins were officially frowned upon in plague-time because there was no room for such final privacy in overcrowded graveyards. Sudden death left corpses in the streets, avoided by most passers-by, but taken away in the end by reluctant parish officials, in carts, like so much refuse, to be thrown into plague pits and covered in quicklime. 'A poor body that died in Chancery Lane' and a 'poor woman that lay in the street all night' are typical entries in the burial registers of London during epidemics. Two Londoners even 'died in the stocks of the plague'.[40] Death could be seen and smelt. It could also be heard, in the peals of bells from churches which marked the passing of a parishioner or his funeral. Small wonder that literary descriptions of plague celebrated *The Triumph of Death*,[41] for it was all around. As an observer of the London epidemic of 1665 noted:

> Death stares us continually in the face, in every infected person that passeth by us, in every coffin which is daily and hourly carried along the streets: the bells never cease to put us in mind of our mortality.[42]

Plague was a reminder of the transience of everything connected with life. It stopped work and destroyed wealth. The sickness or death of a quarter or a third of a town's labour force impoverished the whole community of which they were the essential foundation. Even the finances of the state could suffer, as we can see from the sudden drop in government revenues from customs, excise and the hearth tax after the plague of 1665.[43] But the effects were worst at the level of the household. When wage-earners – children as well as adults – fell ill, savings were used up, household goods pawned, and the family forced onto charity.[44] The family itself, of course, was broken up. In pre-industrial England the normal high death rates left many widows and orphans, but plague added substantially to their number. In the towns, Orphans' Courts were always busy after epidemics, patching together the affairs of deceased freemen. John Brooke of Exeter and two of his children died in 1590, for example, leaving a son and a widow who was worn out by the burden and cost of nursing an infected family. The Court had to pick up the pieces.[45] Social ties of every kind were ruptured by plague. Richard Smyth made a list of those of his acquaintance who died in seventeenth-century London. In 1665, 155 of them were buried; in 1664 there had been only forty-five deaths.[46] After a plague, ties of family and friendship had to be re-formed. They can never have seemed secure.

Insecurity extended to the very top of pre-industrial English society. It did not touch people here so directly, since the social elite, as we shall see, generally escaped infection. But they could not avoid fear of it, or stop it disrupting their normally busy and successful lives. Essential parts of the machinery of government – the legal term in London, the Assizes and Quarter Sessions in the country – ground to a halt during epidemics, as did the humbler meetings of leet juries and ward inquests.[47] Critical political circumstances sometimes compelled parliament to meet during an outbreak of plague, but the threat of disease then heightened the feeling of crisis. In the summer of 1641, as the Long Parliament moved toward irreparable division and civil war, many members stayed away from vital debates for fear of infection. Seven members in fact died suddenly during these months, some of smallpox but one or two perhaps of plague.[48] In 1625 and again in 1665 the two Houses moved to Oxford to escape disease in London. There were no casualties among members on these occasions, but plague followed them to Oxford in 1625 and their minds were concentrated on the issues of political corruption and social decay by the physical danger they felt themselves to be in.[49]

Monarchs themselves were not untouched. In 1603 and again in 1625 major epidemics of plague coincided with that precarious moment for the body politic when sovereignty passed from one person to another. The new kings had to be crowned, but the celebrations and processions which set the convincing seal of public approval to a coronation were severely curtailed. Access to the Court and the presence of the king or queen was similarly restricted during epidemics.[50]

Though temporary, these limitations on the appeal of monarchy sapped confidence. In much the same way, at a lower level, the cancellation of the Lord Mayor's Show in London or of the feasts of officeholders and companies in many infected towns did nothing to encourage social cohesion or deference to authority.[51] Occasionally plague might be associated directly with subversive sentiments. Anthony Wood noted the delight of the Cavaliers when an epidemic broke out in Chester in 1654, soon after Oliver Cromwell became Protector; they were able to turn the tables on their opponents, the 'fanatics', who said 'that King James and King Charles I brought the plague with them when they were first crowned'. More often, however, plague must simply have inculcated a more general pessimism, as in the man who thought that the epidemic of 1593 made successful resistance to a Spanish invasion impossible.[52]

Like other disasters, therefore, like famine or civil war itself, plague undermined any assurance men might normally find in family and friends, business and property, or even in government and nation. It also had its own special, pernicious horrors because it was a calamity which passed invisibly but rapidly from person to person. The precise means of transmission was unknown, but everyone knew that plague was infectious. It could be seen gathering momentum – moving from town to town, from house to house, and from one member of a household to another. Every effort was made to escape it. People with houses or friends in the country fled from infected towns, only to meet with suspicion and hostility wherever they went. John Evelyn remembered the 'strict watches and examinations upon the ways' when, in 1625, at the age of four, he had joined the mass exodus from London.[53] Inns and alehouses were avoided by the educated because they were potent sources of infection. Everything connected with the sick, down to their pots and pans, was thrown away, once plague was suspected.[54] Above all, the sick themselves were shunned. Fear of plague produced fear of its victims. A minister ejected from his living in 1665 'died of the plague between Shrewsbury and Oswestry upon a little straw, none daring to come near him because of the infection'. Parish authorities shunted sick servants, labourers and paupers across parish boundaries for fear of the costs and danger if they died in their jurisdiction. Corpses of travellers were refused burial in churchyards and interred in the road instead. In the country some of those 'suspected to die of the plague' were buried in their own gardens; there was no welcome for them anywhere else.[55]

In short, plague was especially destructive because it was divisive. For most men the impulse to preserve self and family necessarily triumphed over other loyalties and obligations. As we shall see, some magistrates and ministers obeyed the call of duty and stayed in infected towns, but they sent away their wives and children first; and there were more who left with their families. Calculation was inevitably introduced into all human relationships, as with the French girl in London in 1577 who sensibly broke off her engagement when her lover fell ill and the doctor pronounced it plague. A Jacobean preacher concluded that plague was 'more destructive than discord or hunger', because 'comfort and company' were denied the sick, and then 'the comfort of nature, the expectation of love among those that are left alive, is utterly dissolved'.[56]

How then did those who were infected and those who were left alive cope? The historical record only hints at a range of possible answers. Some – perhaps the majority – strove to go on with life as normal. In 1625 William Lilly's master fled from London, leaving him to look after his house. Among other duties, Lilly had to do the potentially dangerous job of paying weekly pensions to poor almspeople in the churchyard of St Clement Danes. He continued to work, and in his spare time he learnt how to play the bass-viol and went bowling in Lincoln's Inn Fields. But he also went regularly, perhaps more regularly than usual, to church, seeing the sick and dead in the streets on the way, and listening to a multitude of plague and funeral sermons when he got there.[57] Some people certainly turned deliberately to religion for consolation during epidemics. In 1665 John Rawlet penned spiritual reflections in 'A Consolatory Letter . . . to his mother upon his apprehension of dying by the plague'. A century earlier, in 1563, the Tudor musician Thomas Whythorne similarly fought the 'fear of death' in London by examining his conscience, composing devotional verses and continuing with his autobiography, which from this point onwards becomes markedly religious in tone. When some of his own household caught plague, he tells us,

> I looked every minute of an hour when I should be visited as the rest were. I doubting the worst, . . . did now gather so many comfortable places of the Scriptures as I could find, the which I did always think upon . . . as the chief physic for my soul.[58]

Devout resignation to the inevitable impelled a few people towards heroic self-sacrifice. The most famous example, but by no means the only one, was William Mompesson, rector of Eyam in Derbyshire, who kept the whole village isolated from the rest of the county when plague struck in 1665–6. He had sent his children away early, but his wife died of plague and he wrote a farewell letter to his patron, Sir George Savile, describing himself (wrongly as it turned out) as a 'dying man': 'This is the saddest letter that ever my pen did write, the destroying Angel having taken up his quarters within my habitation.' Nevertheless, he found 'God more good than ever I thought or imagined'.[59]

These, however, were all literate men with access to books, familiar with elite ideals, and able to express their opinions for the edification of contemporaries and posterity. Most victims suffered – so far as the historian can tell – in silence. Their heroism is not trumpeted in the records, though heroism it must often have been. We know of only one suicide directly attributable to plague. Richard Sandell caught plague in Nottinghamshire in 1544 and, 'being barely of sound mind by reason of his sickness and instigated by the devil, he struck and cut his chest with a knife . . . of which wound he immediately died'.[60] A few people who had soldiered on described their feelings after the event, when depression born of a host of misfortunes took them to consult Richard Napier, a practitioner of astrological medicine in Buckinghamshire. Mary Frankling, for example, aged twenty-five, 'took a flight and fright' in 1608 'by a fire which took the next house by, and that fear disquieted her; also the fear of a house visited with the plague where she was, and for that cause was let blood and since hath felt herself the worse'. An older man, William Stone, complained in 1605 of 'much grief from time to time: had a wife long sick who died after much physic; lost much cattle which died; had the plague in his house; two children died; himself had it, with heaviness under his throat with red spots in his hands and legs. Not well since.'[61] For such people plague could be the worst in a string of personal calamities, the ultimate demonstration of the precariousness of life in pre-industrial England.

In the following chapters we shall be looking coldly and analytically at the cause of these disasters, and at the ways in which different authorities and social groups publicly confronted them. But both subjects ultimately owe their importance to the largely unrecorded private feelings of inarticulate individuals. At the heart of the conflict between disease and society lay the sufferings and struggles of ordinary men and women.

Chapter 2

Attitudes and actions

For what is the cause that this pestilence is so greatly in one part of the land and not in another? And in the same city and town, why is it in one part, or in one house, and not in another? And in the same house, why is it upon one, and not upon all the rest, when they all live together, and draw in the same breath, and eat and drink together, and lodge in the same chamber, yea sometimes in the same bed? What is the cause of this, but that it pleaseth the Lord in wisdom, for some cause to defend some for a time, and not the rest? Therefore let us believe that in these dangerous times God must be our only defence.

Nicholas Bownd, *Medicines for the Plague* (1604)

And it is now as clear as the sun, that the last increase [of plague] came by the carelessness of the people, and greediness to receive into their houses infected goods. To this add great defect in the inferior governors, with great want among the poor, by reason of so many base tenements ... and you have all the causes under God himself of the present infection.

William Laud to Thomas Wentworth, 1637[1]

Despite the crippling burdens which plague imposed on some of them, Englishmen as a whole did not react passively to it in the sixteenth and seventeenth centuries. They sought to understand it and to fight against it. They found some slight reassurance in the face of mortality and disease when they could account for them in recognisable terms, when they could interpret them as part of the natural order of the universe as they saw it. They also drew from that interpretation various prescriptions which they used, with more or less confidence, in an attempt to avoid the disease or to mitigate its effects.

The explanatory system within which plague was set had been handed down from the past. In essentials it had been established at the time of the Black Death. It was conservative. It was not, however, a straitjacket which prohibited change. It was an eclectic collection of assumptions which could both incorporate new perceptions and permit new departures in action. In the end it allowed the development of a corpus of public-health regulations enforced by government whose repercussions will be described in Part III. This chapter is intended to explain the coherence and resilience of traditional, commonplace attitudes towards plague, and to show why they nevertheless contained the potential for change.

(i) Eclectic assumptions

Assumptions about plague were publicised and passed from one generation to another by various means. They were embodied in sermons by divines, and they informed the treatment and advice of doctors. They were referred to in letters between acquaintances and no doubt also in everyday conversation in plague-time. They are articulated most clearly for the historian, however, in the many printed medical tracts of the period which discuss plague and disease in general. Although often ostensibly written for the poor, these works were in fact handbooks for middle-class households and for unqualified medical practitioners in a society in which doctors were few. They thus expressed and influenced the views of the literate and articulate classes. But their contents and their popularity suggest that they also reflected some of the more pervasive assumptions and anxieties about disease in early modern England.[2]

At the beginning of our period, in the early days of printing, such works were naturally few; but the output of popular medical compendia increased enormously after the middle of the sixteenth century. During Elizabeth's reign an average of three or four medical books came out each year, and they were especially numerous whenever epidemics occurred. The very first printed work on medicine in English was a *Little Book* on plague, whose publication in 1486 was apparently inspired by a recent outbreak of the 'sweating sickness'.[3] Several similar treatises appeared after an epidemic of influenza in 1558–9, and after visitations of plague in 1577, 1592–3 and 1603. In all, 153 different books on medicine written in English were published between 1486 and 1604: twenty-three of them were exclusively concerned with plague, and many others included chapters on that disease. Beginning in the second half of the sixteenth century, there

was also a growing number of religious tracts and sermons describing
the origins of pestilence and offering consolation to its victims. In
1603 and 1604, for example, twenty-eight books dealing in some way
or other with plague were published, of which fifteen were of a
religious character. Between 1625 and 1627, when the disease again
spread over England, the total number of relevant publications was
thirty-six, and no less than twenty-one of them were works by divines.[4]
There was clearly no shortage of printed advice and explanation, and
no lack of demand for it.

The growth in religious publications on the subject was a new
development whose implications we shall need to consider later. But
in other respects the literature before the middle of the seventeenth
century was almost entirely conventional and derivative. Authors
borrowed extensively from one another, usually without acknowledgment, and often word for word. The most comprehensive of Tudor
plague tracts, Thomas Lodge's *Treatise* of 1603, was itself a translation
of a French original published forty years before.[5] The conservatism
of the literature was also a function of the fact that there were few
new discoveries to disrupt medical conventions. The contagionist ideas
of Fracastor were reflected in some writings of the later sixteenth
century; Paracelsian remedies also made their appearance; but both
were relatively easily absorbed into the traditional medical framework.
There was little that was novel in theoretical approaches to epidemic
disease until the work of Sydenham and his contemporaries after
1650. Some writers claimed that their own observation led them to
original deductions. As early as 1472 an Oxford surgeon based his
recommendations on 'experience', which was 'more profitable than all
the books that be compounded or written from the beginning of the
world to this . . . day'. Yet his prescriptions were no different from
those in many contemporary manuscripts and later printed books.[6]
Until the middle of the seventeenth century the prevailing intellectual
tradition was still that of the plague tractates of the fourteenth and
fifteenth centuries.[7] There were some additions to the authoritative
work of John of Burgundy, but there was no remodelling of a general
approach which had its roots even further back in time, in Hippocrates,
Galen, Avicenna and the Bible.

The plague literature of the sixteenth and early seventeenth
centuries can therefore be taken as a whole and plundered for
evidence of the conventional view of epidemics held by Englishmen
at the beginning of our period. The resounding impression is one of

a coherent but extremely catholic set of assumptions which had to serve, and which succeeded in serving, several different purposes. Most obviously, it had to account for the infinitely diverse ways in which epidemic disease manifested itself. Again and again writers stressed the novel and unpredictable forms which epidemics took: the 'strange and unknown diseases that swarm among us'; the 'sundry sicknesses and strange diseases' which seemed so frequent 'in these our days' that they had perhaps been 'long hidden and not come to light before this time'.[8] Although some optimists argued that epidemics after the Reformation were less serious than those before it, it was much more common to interpret the frequency and variety of epidemics, and the 'new' diseases of the later fifteenth and sixteenth centuries, such as syphilis and the sweating sickness, as symptoms of the general decay of the universe. Mankind was evidently moving 'from bad to worse' in 'these declining times of the world'.[9]

Faced with such a bewildering array of epidemic diseases, contemporaries naturally had some difficulty in distinguishing between them. There was little appreciation that individual diseases were separable entities before 1600.[10] For most of the period and for most writers bubonic plague was merely the most extreme form of epidemic infection – 'a pernicious and contagious fever' distinguishable from others only by the exceptional pain it caused its victims and by their slim hopes of recovery.[11] In a sense it was the quintessential pestilence, for while some diseases might be given distinguishing labels, plague was often simply 'The Sickness', with stress on the definite article. Other infectious illnesses were related to it, and might adopt its features from time to time. During a plague, said Bishop Hall, all sicknesses 'have some tincture of the Pestilence'. The sweat was 'one of the kinds of the plague or pestilence', and spotted fever and smallpox might also be transformed into it while 'the naughty influence' of plague persisted.[12]

Any attempt at diagnostic clarity was further impeded by the variable symptoms of plague itself. A few writers, like the astrologer Simon Forman, declared that there were different kinds of plague, but their efforts to specify them carried little conviction. As Paré noted, plague seemed never to occur 'after one sort: so that in so great variety it is very difficult to set down anything general and certain'.[13] All writers described some of the characteristic signs of the disease: buboes and carbuncles, headaches, a rapid pulse and delirium, a great thirst and a desire to sleep, the spots on the chest or back which were 'God's tokens'. There might also be a 'cough and foul spitting', possibly an indication of secondary pneumonic plague. But they also appreciated that none of these symptoms might appear, 'such is the uncertainty of this disease'. Men might drop dead without warning, presumably as a result of septicaemic plague, and at most be 'sensible of a blow suddenly given them on the head, neck, back or side'.[14]

Since the disease apparently took so many different forms, it is not surprising that a complex chain of explanation and a large variety of remedies were provided for it. Neither is it surprising that so severe and unpredictable a disease was universally assumed to have a supernatural origin. An affliction which spared some communities and individuals and struck others savagely, spreading from 'one to another by ways and means, neither visible nor sensible' so that 'no man knows where he shall be safe', was the expression of 'the will of God, rightfully punishing wicked men'.[15] Whether he used good or bad angels as his agents,[16] God sent plague just as he sent any other form of natural disaster against the sins of mankind. Particular epidemics were therefore to be explained by national vices, such as swearing, negligence in attending church, atheism, play-going, covetousness and extravagant female fashions. They could also be attributed to recent Catholic, Protestant or Laudian changes in religion, or to the sins of Parliamentarians or Royalists in the Civil War, depending on which side one was on.[17] If King David had brought plague down on Israel by numbering the people, England's pride in her population had just as surely produced a similar epidemic in 1603 – or so some observers argued, referring perhaps to the ecclesiastical census of that year.[18] Even the local incidence of the disease could be accounted for in the same way. Both sin and epidemic disease were concentrated in towns, and in London it was the suburbs which were 'most polluted' by spiritual 'filthiness' as well as by pestilence.[19]

Although God was the first cause of plague, however, he normally worked through secondary causes, 'by that constant course of order which he hath appointed unchangeable from the beginning'.[20] This natural machinery could be studied and profitable lessons learned. Particular conjunctions of stars caused the multiplication of 'stinking vapours by the which the air is putrefied'.[21] They thus created a 'miasma' which explained the prevalence of epidemic disease over large areas. Changes in the heavens or in the weather were an omen of plague to come and astrology might predict future epidemics. The comet of 1577, by attracting 'noisome exhalations and pestilent vapours' from the earth, caused epidemics in the following year. Conjunctions of Saturn and Jupiter, as in 1425, 1485 and 1583, or of Saturn and Mars, as in 1436, were particularly to be feared.[22] By the end of the sixteenth century there were critics of astrological predictions, some citing the failure of previous attempts, others the pre-eminence of divine providence or the inherent benevolence of the stars themselves.[23] But such scepticism had little effect on most of the popular accounts of plague. Predictions of future epidemics continued, and two astrologers successfully foretold the plague of 1665.[24] Over the whole period heavenly fluctuations were commonly regarded both as an omen of epidemics and as a direct, though intermediate, cause of them. Like divine providence itself, they provided an element of certainty in the explanation of a superficially uncertain phenomenon.

The stars were not the only cause of miasma, however. As Galen had pointed out, unburied corpses and stagnant pools polluted the atmosphere, and the stink of graveyards was thought to be a threat throughout the period. Experience added to these dangers the environment of the poor, which might create disease through 'much people in small room living uncleanly and sluttishly'.[25] In 1631 the king's physician thought the 'miserable poverty and nastiness' of Irish vagrants was in itself 'enough to engender the plague without any former contagion'. The 'fruiterers, poor people and stinking lanes' of St Sepulchre's parish in London similarly explained the prevalence of plague there, and the 'noisome stench' of starch-making infected many towns.[26] It was only a short step from these accounts to the concept of contagion, whether by touch or at a distance. 'The reek or smoke' of plague sores, according to the *Little Book* of 1486, was 'venemous and corrupteth the air' around. One person might thus infect another. But the miasma could also be transported in clothes or bedding, and be retained there for long periods of time.[27] Domestic animals, especially dogs, cats and pigs, might similarly carry it on their bodies from house to house.

The exact mechanism of contagion was never closely analysed in this literature. It was accepted because it accorded with the evidence of experience, and it was enough to acknowledge its existence in general terms and to draw practical conclusions. Even the clearest attempts at a definition lacked precision. For Stephen Bradwell, writing as late as 1636, for example, contagion was 'that which infecteth another with his own quality by touching it, whether the medium of the touch be corporeal or spiritual or an airy breath'. He quoted Fracastor on the subject, and described the infecting agent as a 'seminary tincture full of a venomous quality, that being very thin and spirituous mixeth itself with the air, and [pierces] the pores of the body'.[28] As this quotation suggests, there was no suggestion or perception of any conflict between theories of miasma and contagion. In the more sophisticated intellectual climate of Venice in the 1570s, the advocates of the one denied the existence of the other; but this did not happen in England before the end of the seventeenth century. Although there was an increasing emphasis on contagion as the actual movement of plague from place to place was observed, writers were happy to combine the two theories, as almost all authorities since 1348, including Fracastor himself, had done. After all, both miasma and contagion were thought to arise from ill-defined processes of corruption and putrefaction, either in the heavens, in the air or in terrestrial or human bodies, and they thus had the same root.[29]

The miasmatic theory did, however, raise the problem of why some people were infected and others were not in a locality where a pestilential miasma predominated. This could be accounted for by the doctrine of predisposing causes: some individuals were, or made themselves, more susceptible to infection than others. According to humoral theory, those of a sanguine constitution were most vulnerable to plague, but an abundance or deficiency of any humour was dangerous. Famine similarly left the body empty so that it drew in 'stinking commixed vapours of the air'. More mechanically, frequent hot baths, excessive exercise, work or sexual indulgence opened the pores to infection.[30] Psychological states might have a comparable effect. Fear of the plague, according to Bradwell, 'enforces the vital spirits to retire inward to the heart' and thus weakens the body's defences. 'To be merry in the heart is great remedy for health of the body', commented the *Little Book*.[31] More generally, any disorderly activity should be avoided, because sickness was by definition one expression of disorder both in the macrocosm of the universe and in the microcosm of man. An individual laid himself open to plague by 'the abuse of things not natural, that is to wit of meat and drink, of sleep and watching, of labour and ease, of fullness and emptiness of the passions of the mind, and of the immoderate use of lechery'. Sickness came from 'diverse and sundry disorder committed many ways'.[32]

The argument thus came full circle. For all these unnatural activities – gluttony, avarice, idleness, anger, lust – were sinful as well as unhealthy; and the two qualities were inseparable. The corruption which lay at the root of plague was not only a physical process but also a moral one. Plague arose from the 'filthy corruption which we carry continually about us'. Infected air, according to Bishop Hooper, could never cause disease, 'except man . . . be first corrupted by sin'.[33] Far from being distinct, therefore, supernatural and natural explanations for epidemic disease were interlocking parts of a single interpretative chain. Disorder of any kind weakened man's defences against plague, and it also provoked God to despatch it. Consequently, when alehouses were closed, or plays and popular games prohibited in time of plague, both the spiritual and the physical dangers inherent in them were emphasised. At entertainments of this kind, 'God is dishonoured, the bodies of men and women by surfeiting, drunkenness and other riots and excesses disposed to infection, and the contagion dangerously scattered'.[34] Similarly, when harlots and other 'lewd' persons were identified as the 'instruments the Lord used' to bring plague into a village, as they sometimes were, their physical movement was not the only relevant fact which was being commented on.[35]

Natural and supernatural explanations of plague thus reinforced one another in a manner which had an understandable appeal. Both could be employed to explain the timing of an epidemic and its incidence in one individual or area rather than another. Taken together, they could account for the variability of the phenomenon. They also satisfied contemporaries because they embodied all the cosmological assumptions which prevailed before the scientific innovations of the seventeenth century. Most important of all, perhaps, they had a firm hold because they buttressed conventional morality. The association of sin with disease could be used as a sanction against activities which were disapproved of for more than medical reasons. It appealed to a society much more anxious than our own about pervasive threats to order and discipline, and much more concerned than ours with the need for social control.

The interrelated elements in this account of the origins of plague, extending from theology through astrology and humoral theory back to theology, led naturally to a variety of recommendations to those threatened or affected by it. Religious remedies were normally placed first. Repentance and prayer 'should be preferred above all other medicines', in order to pacify the first cause of epidemics.[36] Before the Reformation there were special masses against plague, and special prayers to St Roch, St Sebastian and the Virgin, and English Catholics continued to use them into the seventeenth century.[37] For their part, Protestants had new official forms of prayer for use on nationally appointed days of public fasting in every major epidemic from 1563 onwards.[38] There could be disagreement about the details. Protestants thought prayers to the saints superstitious; some Puritans alleged that fasts without sermons were ineffectual.[39] But all accepted the basic premise that there must be some public as well as private display of repentance if the visitation was to end.

Secular recommendations also followed from the accepted theories of causation. From the start it was universally recognised that the best way of avoiding plague was by flight from the infected place and from the miasma which pervaded it. If one had to stay, however, precautions could be taken. Windows ought to be kept shut if they faced the enervating south wind. Fires should be lit in the streets to dispel infected air. Burning incense or rosemary might have the same effect in a house, and perfumes about the person and pomanders held to the nose could protect an individual. Contagion ought to be avoided as well as miasma. Men should keep away from close contact with the infected, and the clothes and bedding of the sick should be burned.[40] The latter recommendation at least would have done something to limit transmission of plague via fleas, as, more obviously, did the suggestion in some tracts that people should change their clothes and especially their linen regularly in plague-time. There was similar empirical sense in the suggestion that clean sheets be used in cases of sickness.[41]

Methods of escaping plague took up less space in the literature than medicines for use when they failed, however. Most writers treated plague as a poison which could be drawn or driven out of the body, or conquered within it, in a variety of ways. Bleeding remained the surest way of restoring the balance of the humours, although there was some debate about the timing and extent of blood-letting by the later sixteenth century;[42] and if buboes did not discharge their poison readily special irritant dressings should be applied to aid the process. Easily the most popular internal medicines for victims of plague were theriac, commonly called 'treacle', and mithridatium: the two renowned antidotes ever since the time of Galen. Part of their appeal may have lain in the opium which they contained, but their reputation seems to have been based on their history rather than on their constituents. In theory, they were 'the enemy to all infectious diseases' because their chief ingredient was viper's flesh, and this poisonous substance should destroy the poison of plague. Like cured like. But they might be compounded out of as many as 100 different simples, and even the College of Physicians agreed that 'London treacle', manufactured in the early seventeenth century in an effort to break an Italian monopoly, need not contain vipers at all.[43] Another ingredient was rue, whose synonym, 'herb of grace', indicated the mystical powers attached to it. As one of the commonest English herbs, it was included in many plague remedies, and like walnuts, vinegar and onions, it was thought to owe its efficacy against sharp fevers to its bitterness: 'all that is sharp and sour doth replenish the pipes and conduits of the body'. A roasted onion with treacle in it was perhaps the medicine most often recommended for the infected.[44]

Yet these were only the commonest prescriptions. The most conspicuous feature of all printed medical compilations is the large number of remedies they contained. One tract alone had no less than sixteen medicines for plague.[45] Some were based on the doctrine of analogies and sympathies between different parts of creation. Precious stones were a valuable protective, for example, especially if worn on the fourth finger of the left hand, which 'hath great affinity with the heart'. Several writers thought the application of a live hen or cock to a plague bubo would draw out the poison, because these fowl ate toads and other 'virulent beasts'. The supposed medical properties of human waste were not ignored. According to one writer, the poor who could not afford more elaborate medicines should 'drink twice in the day a draught of their own urine'.[46] Some antidotes, like unicorn's horn, owed their fame to their antiquity; others rested on the prestige of their supposed patrons or inventors. 'Carduus benedictus' had first been imported from India by the Emperor as a remedy for many diseases. One compound of rue and other herbs was taught to Henry VII by his doctors. Another was sent to the mayor of London by Henry VIII. A famous recipe for mithridatium had been concocted by Hugh Morgan, Queen Elizabeth's physician.[47]

It is scarcely surprising, therefore, that the new chemical and Para-celsian remedies of the later sixteenth century were as acceptable as any others to the readers of popular medical tracts. Oil of vitriol was simply one more suggested remedy which might be tried, and 'potable gold' was yet another 'precious' antidote, although its neo-Platonic affinity with the sun might now be stressed. A new mineral remedy praised by Paracelsus could be introduced with ease, because it was described as vaguely, and alleged to be as universally effective, as mithridatium itself.[48] Of the Paracelsian remedies for plague, only the wearing of arsenic amulets close to the skin aroused criticism. Was not arsenic 'an opposite, professed and perpetual enemy to our nature'? As its defenders pointed out, however, the efficacy of this poison was to be explained in precisely the same way as the efficacy of viper's flesh in treacle. Even William Perkins, who attacked the charms and spells thought to be popular among the 'common people', allowed that the use of amulets was 'grounded upon some good natural reason', for certain materials hung around the neck might well draw poison from the body.[49]

There was thus no lack of choice in precautions and remedies against plague and no lack of advertisement for them. The difficulty is to know how widely they were adopted. Much plainly depended on social status. The earl of Bedford could afford to build himself a refuge from plague in 1630 in a grotto at Woburn, facing north so that he might be shielded from the infectious southerly winds. Fellows of Oxford and Cambridge colleges regularly moved to their manors in the country during epidemics, and donors gave them property specifically for the purpose.[50] The wealthy could buy plague literature: not only the medical tracts drawn on above, but also the works of writers such as Thomas Dekker who told humorous stories about infectious disease and death, defending their writings on the respectable medical ground that 'mirth is both physical and wholesome against the plague'.[51] They could employ doctors, who were notorious for fleeing from infected towns with their richer patients. Dr John Symcotts' account of his visit to a plague case in the mid-seventeenth century shows how little he could do for the victims; and surgeons' administrations, when they included bleeding and lancing plague buboes, can have done little to ease their pain.[52] But a professional presence was no doubt some reassurance to the relatives of the sick.

In the absence of professional assistance, more prosperous Englishmen could use the medicines and perfumes which they copied into their commonplace books and collections of household recipes. The evidence we have from these sources, as well as from doctors' casebooks, suggests that self-medication and professional treatment alike borrowed the simpler remedies to be found in the printed literature. Until the very end of plague in England, drinks and potions compounded from rue, rosemary, onions, wormwood, mithridatium and treacle were used by those who could afford them. The two latter remained in the *Pharmacopoeia* of the London College of Physicians throughout the seventeenth century, and all of them turn up in the household books of the period, whether their sources were said to be printed tracts, the recommendation of friends, or personal experience.[53] At a more exalted level, Charles I's physician, Dr Theodore de Mayerne, recommended a treacle water and mithridatium, as well as newer medicines such as 'snake root' and crabs from the Isle of Wight, as defences against plague. Oliver Cromwell was as conservative in this as the king: he took mithridatium to protect himself from plague, and found as a bonus that it cured his pimples. In 1638 a Dutch family in Sandwich used treacle when they were infected.[54] The prescriptions in the popular medical literature of the sixteenth century were those recommended to their patients by an Oxfordshire doctor in the 1590s, a London apothecary in 1625, an Essex apothecary in 1644, and a Devonshire cleric in the 1660s.[55] Small variations and embellishments were introduced from time to time, advertised by foreign correspondents, by gossip and personal letter, and even by one town council to another. One slight variant of a common nostrum became famous in 1665 because it had been used by four men who robbed infected houses, murdered their inmates, and lived to enjoy the spoils.[56] But the occasional fashionable novelty was always very strictly limited by the conservatism of medical practice and by the authority of tradition.

Outside the ranks of the literate classes, however, people had less professional advice and less practical choice available to them; and they have left little evidence from which to judge how far they interpreted plague, and tried to treat it, in the same ways as their superiors. William Perkins' reference to the superstitions of the common sort suggests that popular attitudes embodied less articulate rationalisation, and more simple acceptance of magical explanations and remedies, than did the views of the elite which are reflected in printed literature. This may well have been so. There is no sign in the printed tracts of the sixteenth century of those overtly magical talismans and antidotes which occur in some fifteenth-century manuscripts: the suggestion, for example, that the Pater Noster, Ave Maria and Creed should be said while making a cross over each eye, armpit and thigh – near the points where buboes might appear.[57] But charms of one kind or another may well have continued to be part of the stock in trade of popular practitioners: of the 'wizard' who lived in the plague-ridden parish of St Peter Parmentergate in Norwich in 1666, for example;

or of the cunning woman a century earlier in Seacoal Lane, London, another notorious area of infection, who, according to one critic, had 'more skill in her coal basket than judgment in urine or knowledge in physic or surgery'.[58] Popular responses to plague probably combined crude magic with the cheaper natural remedies such as vinegar and rue. Yet this sort of ambivalent combination was not confined to the very poor. In the early seventeenth century, the respected astrological practitioner Richard Napier both recommended mithridatium to his patients and also invented a talisman to be hung on doors to protect households against plague. Conversely, poor Londoners who sought advice from another astrologer, William Lilly, during the plague of 1665, brought samples of their urine to be inspected just as if they were gentry consulting their physician; and they were sent away with the usual cordials.[59] It would be a mistake to assume that there was any real social or cultural divide in medical treatments or medical attitudes.

Rather, the many facets of contemporary assumptions about plague allowed a plurality of approaches and permitted people of different social class, education and temperament to make their own selection without necessarily rejecting the whole framework. There was undoubtedly increasing scepticism among the elite about the cruder forms of magic in the later sixteenth and seventeenth centuries, and that was associated with some of the newer attitudes towards plague which will be discussed later. Yet even in 1665 plague still seemed so extraordinary a phenomenon that it was an obvious invitation to people of all social backgrounds who believed or half-believed in occult forces, charms, omens and portents. One writer asserted that it was the 'vulgar menialty' who found any far-fetched story of 'fabulous divination' credible, and who accepted, for example, that the appearance of a heron on the top of a church was a harbinger of plague. But it was not only the vulgar who gossiped in 1665 about whether ravens and rooks were especially numerous immediately before an epidemic.[60] A similar common superstition supposed that when 'young children flocked themselves together' and played at funerals in the street 'in a mournful sort', an epidemic was about to occur. By the seventeenth century that belief was being transformed into the less occult suggestion that children playing in the streets spread contagion.[61] But for much of our period faith in such omens was a natural corollary to be drawn from the more sophisticated proposition that manifold disorders in the microcosm and in the macrocosm were interconnected. The many writers on plague in the sixteenth and early seventeenth centuries who described meteorological disturbances and natural wonders as harbingers of plague would not have been surprised by a popular ballad in 1662, telling of an earthquake which had resulted in the birth of three children prophesying famine and great mortality.[62] Neither the illiterate nor the educated viewed plague as a distinct entity to be studied in isolation. They interpreted it as part of the natural order, or more accurately as part of the unnatural disorder, of things.

It will be evident that these wide-ranging and various assumptions about plague had serious limitations. Most obviously, there was no appreciation of the role of rats and fleas in its transmission.[63] Some of the recommendations based on the concepts of contagion and miasma may have had an indirect effect. Airing or burning the bedding and clothing of the infected, and burning fumigants, especially those with an arsenic or sulphur content, [64] could do something to cut down the risks from plague fleas, for example. Medicines with an opium base may have eased the pain of the patient, just as strong drink, and later tobacco, which were popularly thought to be cures, perhaps brought some temporary relief.[65] No one could argue, however, that the appeal of contemporary medical knowledge lay in its instrumental success.

Yet failure was not a serious setback. For it too could be explained in terms of the multifaceted but coherent explanation of plague which has been described. The eclecticism of the medical collections was justified by the view that a disease as changeable and complex in its origins as bubonic plague could not be attacked by one antidote. A single medicine was not enough, one writer explained, 'considering that one disease may come of sundry causes'. Failure in any particular case could be explained easily by faulty diagnosis or neglect of some part of the necessary prophylaxis. Most writers urged their readers to consult a physician about the exact treatment to be adopted. Few gave precise directions for the measurement of the ingredients in each compound. If treacle seemed less effective than it had been in Galen's time, it was because some of the secrets of its manufacture had been lost.[66] Furthermore, all medicines worked only by the grace of God. Duchesne asserted that physicians had few effective medicines against plague because 'when God will punish he taketh away the virtue from remedies'; and Bullein thought that only a miracle could help a man who caught the plague and remained untreated for twenty-four hours.

Another writer warned his readers and excused himself: 'You shall understand that all cannot be helped, for that God Almighty hath made us to die, and when that time cometh medicines will do no good'.[67] The chain of explanation and interpretation was circular and self-confirming.

(ii) The probability of controversy

Resilient and flexible as contemporary interpretations of plague were, they nevertheless contained within them the seeds of doubt and conflict. If particular emphasis were given to any part of this system of thought, inconsistencies might easily appear and controversy result. We have seen that there could be debate about the role of the stars or the utility of charms and amulets: and there were to be more important disputes in the early eighteenth century about the relationship between miasma and contagion, as some writers came to see them as mutually exclusive hypotheses.[68] The strains which could be introduced into the framework of inherited assumptions can best be illustrated, however, by a conflict over two issues which were referred to, if often only obliquely, in much of the literature of the sixteenth century, and which had implications for the whole history of the battle against plague in England.

The first issue was the question of the relationship between first and second causes, between God's will and the natural machinery of the universe. Could divine providence work independently of the natural order? Secondly, there was the problem of reconciling private and public interests. Was an individual justified in shunning infected people and places if in so doing he neglected the care of the sick and his duty to his friends and neighbours? Should the steps apparently necessary for self-preservation be allowed to override social and moral obligations, whose breach might be one of the sins provoking the divine punishment of plague in the first place? The first issue might seem to be a narrowly intellectual one, the second a matter of individual conscience. But both disturbed contemporaries because they had obvious implications for behaviour; and they both arose in the context of the sixteenth-century debate over flight from plague. Controversy centred on two practical questions: who might legitimately flee from infected towns, and could those who remained behind count on the special providence of God to protect them?

These interlocking problems became especially controversial when the supernatural causes of plague, the workings of divine providence, were singled out for special stress, as they often were in the mid- and later sixteenth century. One reason for this was a general growth of lay spirituality, a spread of religious interest and commitment, which was both a cause and an effect of the Protestant evangelism which nourished and fortified the English Reformation. The Reformation had, it is true, removed some of the religious defences against plague which remained popular in Catholic countries. Those processions of the sacraments which demonstrated a community's repentance and its spiritual health during an epidemic came to an end. In 1636 the vicar of Ross-on-Wye may have led his parishioners through the High Street, bare-headed in humiliation, repeating the Litany: but by then such practices were certainly eccentric. As early as the 1530s the procession of a candle round a churchyard in Windsor, and its preservation as protection against plague, were officially censured as superstitious.[69] There had been public processions against epidemic disease in London in 1528, but the City aldermen asked the bishop for such a ritual act of collective contrition for the last time in 1543.[70]

Yet in 1563 the corporation of London suggested that householders should attend church daily during an epidemic; in 1569 people in infected households were urged to pray regularly; and there were special prayer-books printed for both purposes.[71] Attendance at extraordinary exercises and fasts 'for the plague' continued to be officially encouraged and popularly practised until the last appearance of the disease in England, and private prayers were equally common, at least among the educated. John Prideaux, Rector of Exeter College, Oxford, in the 1630s, remembered that his father had recommended to him a collect for use in time of plague, probably during an epidemic in Devon in 1590. In 1597 a Puritan diarist in Cambridge lamented his negligence in not praying for his Durham countrymen 'who now were grieved with the plague: O Lord, grant from thence it be not dispersed into the south parts.'[72] If religious responses to plague were driven off the streets by the Reformation, they continued in churches and in homes. To an extent they were internalised, but they were not destroyed. On the contrary, they were invigorated by the increasing volume of religious literature concerning plague published in the later sixteenth century.

That literature powerfully underlined providential and supernatural interpretations. It did not overtly deny natural causes or attack natural

remedies. There was never an absolute dichotomy between medical
and devotional works, partly because many divines were also medical
practitioners. Both sets of publications combined natural and supernatural explanations. God works 'for the most part . . . by ordinary
means', noted the divine, Thomas Brasbridge. 'All the cause of a
plague is not to be attributed to . . . near and inferior causes or
beginnings', responded the French physician Paré.[73] The titles of
many sermons and devotional tracts on plague show that they were
intended to stand side by side with their medical counterparts: *An
Approved Medicine* (1593), *Medicines for the Plague* (1604) and *The King's
Medicine . . . prescribed by the whole Colledge of the spirituall physitians*
(1604).[74] One manuscript collection of physical medicines could therefore include the following prescription against plague without incon-
sistency, though perhaps with some conscious irony:

> Take a quart of the repentance of Nineveh and put thereto both
> your handfuls of fervent [faith] in Christ's blood, with as much
> hope and charity of the purest you can get in God's shop, and
> put it into the vessel.[75]

Nevertheless, the very existence of two genres of publications on
plague, with their separate emphases, encouraged exaggeration of one
or other side. In many medical tracts reference to divine providence
was a final caveat or an introductory formality in an otherwise secular
account of the origins of epidemic disease.[76] Devotional works, on the
other hand, naturally insisted on the role of providence and on the
possibility of its action outside the normal course of nature.

Extraneous intellectual developments worked in the same direction.
The Paracelsian attack on Galenic medicine, in so far as it was
reflected in English writings, stressed the spiritual causes of disease.[77]
Calvinist theories of predestination gave even stronger support to this
trend. But its roots lay deeper than that. Since the later Middle Ages
there had been a succession of religious manuals on the proper way
to approach death, on the 'craft' of dying well. Fundamental to that
art was simple acceptance of the fact that the time of man's death was
unpredictable and wholly in the hands of God. Patient submission to
God's will was therefore the only rational attitude in the face of
sickness.[78] Of course, natural medicines were a divinely ordained gift
and should not be neglected. That would be to tempt God presump-
tuously, and it might amount to suicide since a man's allotted span of
life could 'easily be shortened'. But one should not place too much

trust in physicians. Sin was the chief cause of untimely death, and flight from sin should be the primary concern.[79] While many writers attacked those who condemned natural medicines as useless, and none ever openly adopted such a view themselves, their rhetoric very often betrayed a contrary stance.

One devotional manual, for example, argued that a sick man should not 'seek out skilful physicians' if God called him. When that final call came, physic could not 'infringe the ordinance of God, nor once save us from his anger, nor any iota turn away from us the effects and execution of his divine will'.[80] The writer would no doubt have admitted that in most sicknesses it was difficult to know when death was predestined. Yet plague was not like most sicknesses: it seemed to bear all the marks of a divine and inescapable summons. Had not many victims felt a 'sensible blow' as the infection struck them?[81] It was true that it sometimes killed the just with the wicked, although at least one preacher was alleged to have disputed this fact.[82] But if the just died, it was their good fortune to be brought early to heavenly bliss; and if the wicked survived, they had to suffer the continuing pains of this life. In fact, it was the haphazard incidence of plague which more than anything else proved its divine origin. The way in which it hit one house and not another, one town and not another, could be explained only by the hand of God.

It was easy to show too that the alleged natural causes of plague did not always function. Epidemics sometimes declined in the winter, but they did not invariably do so. Neither did they always occur at regular intervals, or in the hovels of the poor. Several writers condemned those 'carnal' men, 'naturians' or 'deists' who had an absurd faith in secondary causes, and who held that epidemics occurred as a 'matter of course' when the infection in the elements reached a peak.[83] Richard Leake, preaching in 1598, shortly after an outbreak of plague in Westmorland, confidently stated that

> it was not infection of the air, distemperature in [men's] bodies, much less the malicious and devilish practices of witches, or yet blind fortune, or any other such like imagined causes, which were the breeders of these evils, but the mass and multitude of our sins.

Thomas Dekker summed up the burden of much religious commentary on plague in the later sixteenth century:

Only this Antidote apply,
Cease vexing heaven, and cease to die.[84]

The role of providence had more than theological argument and
homiletic assertion to recommend it. It also offered the only effective
consolation for people afflicted or threatened by plague. They had
little choice but 'with all humble patience to submit' to God's 'divine
power'. A Manchester woman, for example, who found herself sitting
near an infected person at church in 1645, 'being satisfied she was
in her way of duty . . . confidently cast herself upon God's protection,
and was accordingly preserved'. Otwell Johnson's apprentice died of
plague in 1545 because 'his time was come, and so shall all ours at
the Lord's pleasure'; the master could only trust in God, who 'is
mightiful to deliver or preserve his elect in the midst of all tribu-
lations'.[85] Predestination alone explained why plague was apparently
irresistible, and why some people nevertheless escaped.

Yet predestination might also be taken to imply that plague should
not be resisted. Carried to its logical fatalistic conclusion, it removed
the necessity for any action against disease. Why should men avoid
those who were infected, for example, if it was God who determined
who should live and who should die? The growing stress on providence in the later sixteenth century thus had practical implications. It
was the question of how to act during an epidemic, and how to advise
or compel others to act, which most often forced writers to grapple
with the latent inconsistencies in their assumptions about the origins
of plague.

There was no dispute about how the sick themselves should behave.
They were a danger to others, through contagion, and 'should willingly
keep their own houses, or places of abode, without being conversant
with those that are whole'. If they did not, they could be accounted
murderers.[86] The problem arose with the behaviour of the healthy. It
was not so easy to advise them to shun the infected, and thus neglect
their charitable obligations to visit, comfort and relieve the sick. 'Let
it not grieve you to visit the sick, for thereby shall ye be strengthened
in the faith', asserted one writer.[87] People who deliberately took in
plague victims from other towns, villages or parishes, and nursed them
in return for cash, could be criticised. As the authorities of one
London parish complained in the later fifteenth century, they were
using the pretext of a 'work of mercy or pity' to justify 'a singular
profit' which 'hurteth and harmeth a common weal'.[88] But mercy and

the interests of the commonwealth alike seemed to dictate that the sick of one's own community, one's own relations, friends or neighbours, should be cared for. Many writers castigated friends and kinsfolk who deserted the infected when they had most need of help; and most condemned the wholesale flight from London at each rumour of plague. They were naturally tempted to use arguments from providence to support their criticisms. 'Let not gentlemen and rich citizens by flying . . . think to escape scotfree', warned Francis Herring. 'The Lord will find them out.'[89]

Perhaps the most effective literary presentation of these issues was William Bullein's *Dialogue against the Fever Pestilence*, first published in 1564. In this work, in which characters representing various professions and social groups discussed their obligations in time of plague, the author showed his contempt for the behaviour of many doctors, lawyers and priests, who neglected their duties, and his sympathy for the poor whom they abandoned. But his most moving passages were reserved for the dilemmas of his central figure, *Civis*. The citizen had sent his children away from London early in the epidemic. Later, under pressure from his wife, he consented to flee from the city himself. He did so reluctantly, however, and only after he had justified his action by rehearsing approved biblical examples of retreat from danger of death. Even so, *Mors*, God's angel of punishment and pestilence, struck him down in the end. Despite the medical information which he gave earlier in the book and the sensible precautions taken by his protagonists, Bullein demonstrated the independent role of divine providence at the close.[90]

It is understandable, therefore, that the problem of flight should dominate much of the devotional literature on plague in the sixteenth century. Indeed, it was an issue which continued to perplex until plague disappeared, and one whose discussion was not confined to England. At the height of the last epidemic, in 1665, a London bookseller, Richard Smyth, translated three Latin works on the question of who might and who might not flee from plague. The earliest was Gabriel Biel's *De fugienda peste*, a fifteenth-century sermon which shows that the terms and the tone of later discussion had been established well before 1500.[91] But the problem was naturally of particular interest for the Reformers of the sixteenth century, with their concern about faith and grace. In 1527 Luther composed an influential tract, 'Whether one may flee from a deadly plague'. Calvin attacked the same problem in a letter of 1560.[92] Osiander's sermon on the question was twice translated into English, by Coverdale and, probably, by Thomas Cartwright. Finally, Theodore Beza reached conclusions in a work, published in 1579 and translated in 1580, which influenced all later English writings.[93]

There were never two clear sides on the question; there was no sharp antithesis between advocates of flight and its opponents. But there were evident differences of emphasis, as one might expect from what has been said already about the influence of providential theories. All writers acknowledged that God had given men medicines to use, and that flight was a sensible precaution. Although Calvin argued that if death was predestined, medical precautions were useless, he also admitted that to deny contagion and miasma and willingly court infection was to act against the evidence of the senses.[94] All writers quoted Scripture to show that practical remedies might be adopted, and agreed that flight from plague was as sensible as flight from fire or war.[95] All equally accepted that some people could not flee: their obligations as magistrates, clergy, husbands, fathers and neighbours might prevent them. The differences arose over how long the list of people thus obligated was; and how enthusiastically their remaining in infected places should be encouraged.

Luther set the tone at one extreme. Pastors and magistrates could not flee. Servants should care for their masters and masters for their servants. Neighbours should not desert neighbours unless there were others to take their place. Furthermore, he refused to censure those who stayed simply because they were 'strong in faith' and willing to accept God's punishment. Indeed, he clearly admired them.[96] This had also been the implication of Biel's sermon; and it was repeated by Osiander and his English translators. Admiration was reserved for those who stayed and censure for those who left: 'The farther we depart from the love of our neighbour, the more we load sin upon us, and deserve this plague but the more.' Another German tract translated by Coverdale concluded on the same note:

> Whoso will help himself from the pestilence with flying away,
> leaving his own wife, friends and neighbours: he declareth
> unperfectness of faith, and standeth not with Christian charity.[97]

English writers could therefore draw on respectable authorities when they denied that flight was possible for any who were bound by the obligations of 'their country, their calling and Christian charity' – evidently a large segment of the population. They were also quick to point out that, since some could not flee, God had not intended flight as an essential and infallible preservative. 'This cannot be a sufficient remedy', argued Bishop Hooper, 'for there be certain persons that cannot flee although they would: as the poorer sort of people that have no friends nor place to flee unto, more than the poor house they dwell in.' Faith and providence, it was implied, would protect those who stayed out of necessity or who responded to the call of duty and conscience. In these cases, Francis Herring noted, 'we may confidently expect a protection from Heaven'.[98]

On the other side, however, were writers who stressed the need for caution in the use of such arguments, and the necessity to avoid infected persons and places as far as possible. This was the burden of Beza's tract. Although he agreed that the 'common bond of human society' imposed obligations, these should not be allowed to encourage reckless neglect of this 'most contagious' disease, whose natural causes he described. He sought a 'golden mean' on the question of flight, and thus implicitly rejected the conclusions of less circumspect writers. Beza's translator, John Stockwood, was inspired by a similar desire to answer those who neglected sensible precautions, 'under a pretence of Christian charity, but indeed of a blind zeal without knowledge'. A preacher at St Paul's Cross in 1577 agreed that there was 'a desperate kind of tarrying with preposterous words, which I utterly mislike'.[99] Such advocates of prudent self-preservation thought that flight was the sensible course for the many, including physicians, who were not 'public persons'. Even magistrates and ministers could leave if they found substitutes, for these 'profitable members of Church or Commonwealth' should take every possible precaution to preserve themselves.[100]

According to some of these prudential commentators, the extreme providential interpretation which they attacked had led to the common opinion that plague was not infectious at all, 'as though God could not be God and the plague infectious'. There were, however, remarkably few overt statements in the printed literature to this effect, and none at all before 1603.[101] To that extent the balance between natural and supernatural accounts of plague described at the beginning of this chapter held together. It is no doubt true also that in practice behaviour was governed more by common sense than by the exhortations of writers and preachers; their arguments were simply used as rationalisations after the event. But rationalisations, justifications or excuses for behaviour were needed. When a minister in Leicester urged his uncles, Nicholas and William Herrick, to flee from the plague in London in 1593, he had to deal with the arguments we have just examined:

> I grant that in London there walketh a contrary opinion . . .
> Tarrying (even wilfully and without necessity) is counted a virtue and the part of a resolute man. But sure, as it is evident to be no point of wisdom so to do, so do not I see how it can be allowed in divinity. For our bodies are not our own, to dispose, use or hazard at our own pleasure: but they are God's, only committed unto us to keep carefully.[102]

If the Herricks could have their flight justified on the grounds of divinity, no doubt those who did not flee – the poor and some of their pastors and governors – also found support in their predicament from the same source.

Intellectual debates thus had immediate practical relevance. An unbalanced stress on divine providence might encourage a fatalism which was reassuring to some but which many found unacceptable. On the other hand, prudential actions grounded on physical explanations might appear callous and unchristian infringements of traditional norms of neighbourly and charitable behaviour. This was the basic antithesis in contemporary attitudes towards plague in the sixteenth century. It was more often expressed by implication and innuendo than by direct argument; but it remained a continuing source of controversy. We shall see in a later chapter that it became especially divisive when the arguments from divine providence and Christian obligation, which had been used to oppose flight, were also employed to oppose the new methods adopted by governments to control epidemic disease.[103] It is to this other side of the coin that we must now briefly turn: the practical proposals for measures to safeguard public health which might be drawn from assumptions about the natural causes of plague.

(iii) The possibility of action

If some published tracts emphasised God's hand in the origins and incidence of epidemics, others stressed their natural and predictable features and deduced that action could be taken against them. Individuals could act effectively by keeping their houses clean, avoiding sources of infection, burning the bedding and clothing of the sick and so on. The dangers of miasma and contagion could also be attacked, and potentially more successfully, by governments. Against miasma, fires might be lit in the streets, and health hazards like butchers' shambles, refuse in the streets and open and shallow graves could be more strictly controlled. Against infection, it should be possible to prevent contact with infected places, to isolate the sick, and to try to restrict the movement of domestic animals – cats, dogs and pigs – who might transmit disease from house to house. A whole programme of administrative activity and regulation could be built upon commonplace assumptions about plague.

The role which might be adopted by public authorities was first described to English audiences in translations of foreign works. In 1583 John Stockwood translated a German tract on the duties of a 'faithful and wise magistrate in the time of the plague', and Thomas Lodge's treatise of 1603, based on a French original, included a chapter on the same subject.[104] From the epidemic of 1593 onwards, English writers themselves began to refer to the obligations of magistrates during epidemics.[105] They should keep their cities clean to prevent infectious miasmas, and above all they should guard against the transmission of infection from person to person. They could prevent the movement into their towns of strangers, and especially of vagrants, from infected localities. If plague arrived, those who were infected should be kept in isolation in their houses. They might be quarantined for forty days, or for some shorter or longer period. Ideally there should be special hospitals, pesthouses, built for them, just as there were for lepers, because the disease was equally contagious. Their contacts should carry distinguishing marks, badges on their clothes or sticks in their hands, if they went out into the streets. So should the special officers who would be needed to care for, guard or bury the sick.

These recommendations followed the administrative practices of Continental cities, some of them dating back to the fourteenth or fifteenth centuries. Pistoia and other Italian towns had appointed officials specially to deal with plague at the first appearance of the Black Death, in 1348. At the end of the fourteenth century the first commissions of health appeared, in Milan, and permanent boards of health followed in Florence and Venice in the fifteenth century. By 1400 there were sophisticated codes of health regulations in Italian towns for these magistrates and their officers to enforce. The movement of merchandise and men from infected towns was monitored and controlled. The victims of plague were quarantined, sometimes in their own houses, sometimes in hospitals built for the purpose. By the end of the fifteenth century French and Spanish towns were copying these Italian examples. At the same time urban authorities in southern Europe were also beginning to insist that ships should carry bills of health testifying to the freedom from infection of their ports of origin. Local governments were endeavouring to prevent the transmission of disease from person to person, from town to town, and from country to country.[106]

This remarkable achievement, the development of a strategy for an active war against plague, has yet to be given the historical attention it deserves. One of its extraordinary features is the fact that it owed more to practical experience than to medical theory. It rested on observation of the ways in which plague moved, not on inherited concepts of miasma; and although it involved some appeal to notions of 'contagion', these were scarcely defined, let alone understood. With the hindsight provided by modern medical knowledge, we can see that the strategy was scientifically limited: it took little account of the immediate vectors of the disease, rats and fleas. That is not to say that it could not have an instrumental effect, however. Without taking action against rats, it might be difficult to prevent the movement of plague from one house to another in a crowded urban neighbourhood. But plague must often have been transmitted from town to town, and even from one part of a town to another, by fleas carried in the clothes or baggage of men.[107] Control of human movement might sometimes prevent that. Similarly, efforts to check the movement of ships from infected harbours may sometimes have successfully protected ports or even whole countries from sea-borne plague. Such measures were plainly fallible. They were expensive. They depended on uncorrupt and rigorous administration. They required implementation by governments over wide areas. No contemporary could argue with complete confidence – or prove from experience – that they always worked. But the historical evidence suggests that on occasion they were locally effective in protecting towns against plague: in Barcelona and northern Italy in the later sixteenth century, for example.[108] We shall see that it can even be argued that they were responsible for the complete disappearance of plague from western Europe at the end of the seventeenth century.[109] They were certainly the one part of the armoury inherited by Europeans in the sixteenth century which might have some real effect against plague.

Compared with other countries, however, England was late in adopting these weapons and especially in adopting the most promising of them. By the end of the fifteenth century some Scottish towns already had ordinances designed to prevent the import of infection, and their councils were soon trying to force some measure of segregation on the sick and their contacts. But the first English attempts at regulation occurred only in 1518, and the isolation of the infected was not official policy throughout the kingdom until 1578.[110] Pesthouses, plague doctors and special officials for the management of the sick were similarly late developments, and the most effective weapon of all – rigorous control of shipping – was achieved only in the mid-seventeenth century. The story of the English adoption and modification of Continental practices will be told in the second half of this book.

For the moment it is sufficient to note that the potential for these developments existed in England by the beginning of the sixteenth century. As early as 1349, according to one chronicler, the council of Gloucester had closed the town gates to people coming from the infected city of Bristol. In the fifteenth century some towns banned dogs from the streets because they might carry infection, although exceptions were made for the pets of the gentry. In 1476 the authorities of a London parish tried to stop infected people moving into the neighbourhood.[111] The transmission of plague across space could easily be observed. As in the rest of Europe, too, the treatment of lepers provided a precedent and biblical sanction for the isolation of people suffering from infectious diseases.[112] In 1500 theories of miasma still had a greater impact in practice than ideas of contagion, directing attention to the environment which nurtured rather than to the people who carried infectious disease, and producing by-laws and statutes against public nuisances, for example.[113] But contemporary assumptions about plague permitted new departures in policy, and foreign models showed what could be done. It needed only a central government responsive to foreign examples and determined to demonstrate its power, its paternalism and its civilised attributes for the English battle against plague to begin.

The set of explanatory ideas about plague outlined at the beginning of this chapter could thus be developed and modified in one of two ways. Its supernatural elements could be isolated and used to construct a providential interpretation which stressed the unpredictable but orderly hand of God. Alternatively, its natural elements could be combined with experience to show that plague had physical causes and predictable courses, and that it could be resisted. We shall see that both tendencies, the religious and the secular, had great appeal in sixteenth- and seventeenth-century England: the one nourished by Calvinist Protestantism, the other by close observation of epidemics themselves and by the ambitions of local and central governments. We shall see also that the two occasionally came into conflict in England as elsewhere.[114] Religious arguments were employed against such practices as the quarantine and isolation of the sick, just as they were used by Italian clerics and popes in the seventeenth century against restrictions imposed on religious processions in the interests of public health.[115] But religious scruples did not prevent, though they might delay, the gradual acceptance and implementation of a code of administrative practice against plague; and that achievement brought with it a far more secular approach to epidemic disease than most Englishmen in 1500 would have found acceptable.

To present these alternative views and imply that the secular won a victory over the religious is, however, to oversimplify. So tidy a dichotomy does violence to the historical facts and injustice to the exponents of providential views. As has been suggested earlier, most people imbibed some part of each standpoint and continued to think them compatible, for understandable reasons. Divine providence was not excluded from the theories of even the most determined advocates of quarantine measures at the end of the seventeenth century. For there remained features of plague which appeared inexplicable in secular terms, and secular controls might themselves be thought to depend upon divine blessing for their success. Similarly, the providential view could go hand in hand with pronounced activism: it inspired some Puritan ministers and magistrates, for example, who renounced the idea of flight but battled with extraordinary vigour in their own communities to isolate as well as care for the sick.[116] In short, attitudes towards plague remained eclectic: the set of ideas and assumptions available at the beginning of the sixteenth century was never discarded, despite its logical inconsistencies and controversial potentialities. The balance between its various elements certainly changed with time, as new meanings were given to old forms. There was gradual reinterpretation and adjustment. But no part of the old explanatory system wholly disappeared.

There is one further consideration which would lead us to empha-
sise the resilience and coherence rather than the tensions and inconsistencies to be found in contemporary perceptions of plague in early
modern England. The most striking contrast between different
approaches to the disease is not that between religious and secular
views in Christian Europe, but between the attitudes of Christian
Europe as a whole and those of the Muslim world. The Ottoman
Empire was notorious for its 'Turkish fatalism' when confronted by
plague. No effort was made to take precautions, to isolate the victims
or prevent the transport of infection. Indeed, the very idea of contagion
was vehemently denied. The teachings of the Prophet held sway and
they dictated three principles: plague was a mercy and a martyrdom
sent by God; no Muslim should flee from a plague-stricken land;
plague could not be contagious, because disease came directly from
God. Flight occurred, of course, though it was never officially sanc-
tioned; but the other principles prevented any public efforts to control
infection until the nineteenth century.[117]

It might appear that these Islamic tenets were close to the providential views which were expounded by some English writers.[118] The only
difference, it might be argued, was that Islamic towns were ruled by
a coherent religious and administrative elite, able and determined to
put its religious tenets into practice. But there was in fact a profound
difference between the two. While the Muslim saw plague as a reward
and a mercy, which should simply be accepted, the Christian saw it
as a punishment for sin which ought to have been unnecessary.[119]
This might lead the Christian to stress the role of providence, but it
also led him to seek out the causes which provoked God's intervention:
to try to identify particular sins, often therefore to find scapegoats,
and in general to reform the disorders of society. In short, the Christian view predisposed men to action, and to the hope that action might
prevent epidemic disease. Moreover, action against sin was not totally
separated from, or opposed to, action against some of the natural
causes of plague: unruly public assemblies, dirty vagrants, disorderly
alehouses. As we have seen, 'corruption' and 'disorder' were at one
and the same time spiritual and physical dangers, and those who
battled against them were unwilling to give up either the religious or
the secular justification for doing so.[120] The contrast with Turkish
fatalism shows that natural and supernatural interpretations of plague
in early modern Europe sprang from and remained part of one intellec-

tual tradition, a tradition which encouraged preventive action without sacrificing the reassurance of appeals to divine aid.

The ways in which attitudes assisted, and sometimes impeded, actions against plague in England will be considered in a later chapter. We shall see too how the structure of politics, the nature of popular reactions and the quality of urban government influenced the English development of those administrative measures and secular ambitions which other countries had adopted before 1500. But there is another side to the subject which demands prior consideration. Attitudes and actions were not only shaped by each other and by extraneous features of the social and political system; they were also governed by the nature of plague itself, by its frequency and by the social groups and localities it hit. We might expect fatalistic resignation to greet short-term disasters affecting a whole society, for example, and precautions and organised relief to be a more likely response to those crises whose impact was more prolonged and more partial.[121] We must look at the chronology and incidence of plague in Tudor and Stuart England before we can understand why attitudes and actions were gradually transformed and why those transformations occurred when they did.

Part II

The dimensions of the problem

Chapter 3

The chronology of epidemics 1485–1665

... from plague, pestilence and famine ... Good Lord, deliver us.
Cranmer's Litany, 1549

Although the population of the country was at last increasing after the long stagnation of the later Middle Ages, the demographic landscape of sixteenth- and seventeenth-century England was in many respects bleak. In the background there were still high death rates and unremitting sickness; and in the foreground, dominating and obscuring all else, were the frequent crisis years in which epidemic disease swept through large proportions of the population and mortality rates rose rapidly, often doubling or trebling. There are few historical records to tell us about the incidence of sickness and pain themselves in these years; the immediate effects of disease remain essentially immeasurable. We shall never know how many people in all felt the direct and personal impact of plague and other infections. But parish registers and other sources allow us to count the number of those – generally a minority – for whom disease had fatal consequences. It is the expectation of death which will largely concern us in the following pages.

As Cranmer's Litany reminds us, plague was only one out of several causes of exceptionally high mortality and short-term crisis in pre-industrial England. It was indeed commonplace for contemporary writers to compare the three great scourges of famine, pestilence and war, and to discuss their relative horrors.[1] On more than one occasion all three seemed to threaten the country at the same time, as in 1563, between 1587 and 1592 and for most of the 1620s,[2] and it was a matter for congratulation when Englishmen were delivered from them. In 1594, for instance, William Lambarde could thank God that Elizabethan England had not recently 'been touched with any extreme mortality, either by sword or sickness'.[3] It was usual also for contemporaries to compare one outbreak of plague with another, and to identify 'the great' plague until its place was usurped by a later visitation. In sixteenth-century Norwich, Yarmouth and Lynn, memorials were displayed listing the 'great pestilences that hath been in those towns'. In London the epidemics of 1563, 1603 and 1665 were successively known as 'the great' or 'greatest' plague.[4]

If we are to measure the dimensions of plague as a problem we must follow the practice of contemporaries. We need to know something about the ferocity of plague itself – as measured by the frequency with which epidemics occurred, their severity in particular places, and the geographical area and range of localities which they affected. In addition, if we are to identify the characteristics which marked it out from other diseases, we must compare plague with other determinants of high mortality. We must ask whether plague was in fact the unique and capricious phenomenon which contemporary reactions to it seem to imply.

Some of these questions can be considered most satisfactorily by means of local case studies of the kind attempted in later chapters. They will describe the impact of plague in two different counties, Devon and Essex, in three major provincial towns, Exeter, Bristol and Norwich, and in the much larger city of London. The aim of this preliminary chapter is to survey the national scene more generally, to investigate the frequency of years of high mortality and the relative importance of plague and other diseases in causing them. It will try briefly to set plague in its context.

(i) Crisis years

The student of crisis mortality in early modern England has two important sets of sources at his disposal. For the period after 1538, when parochial registration of baptisms, weddings and burials began, he can examine the lists of burials entered in parish registers and note the years or months when they were most numerous. For the period before 1538 he must rely on the less direct evidence of probate records, observing changes in the number of wills proved from year to year and assuming that an unusually large number of probates indicates an unusually high level of mortality. Much of the following chapters will be based on these invaluable sources. Neither of them is perfect, however, and their limitations should be emphasised at the outset.

Parish registers were drawn up by fallible parochial officials. Few of them can have had any interest in the vital events in the lives of the migrant and mobile sections of the population, and some of them made entries in their registers only fitfully. In many cases registration broke down altogether at times of political uncertainty – at the end of Mary's reign and during the Civil War, for example. The most obviously deficient registers can, of course, be easily identified and excluded from calculations. But even the apparently best-kept registers are unlikely to give a complete record of mortality. They list, after all, burials in the churchyard, not deaths in the parish, and they are particularly liable to understate the extent of mortality during the crisis caused by an epidemic. There are numerous examples of the reluctance of parishes to contaminate their churchyards with plague corpses, of unregistered burials of plague victims in gardens and fields, and of parochial registration ceasing altogether at the height of an epidemic.[5] Although a reasonably coherent account of periods of crisis mortality can in fact be derived from these sources, it is important to stress that the numbers of burials and deaths given in the following pages are necessarily minima. The figures in tables and on graphs should not be taken to imply a certainty and accuracy which the original records do not possess.

Our second source is also far from perfect. The only readily available evidence for years of high mortality in different parts of England before 1538 is that provided by testamentary sources: the registers of wills proved in ecclesiastical courts. The number of wills proved from year to year ought in theory to reflect changes in mortality in the diocese or archdeaconry under the jurisdiction of a particular court.[6] Not everyone made a will, however, and deductions cannot readily be drawn about mortality trends in the population as a whole from the experience of a small and unrepresentative social group – those adults, most of them males, who had property to bequeath. This is a particularly serious limitation when one is studying a disease like plague which hit the poor, and probably also the young, disproportionately hard, as we shall see.[7] Fluctuations in the annual totals of wills may therefore understate changes in mortality in a whole population, and even fail altogether to reveal years which were critical for that section of it which did not make wills. Nevertheless, we must make the best of what evidence we have. These sources furnish our only pointers to annual fluctuations in the number of deaths before 1538 and the only evidence available for large stretches of the country before 1560, when parish registers become relatively plentiful. They have therefore been used to indicate years of crisis mortality in the first part of the Tudor period for comparison with information drawn from parish registers about later decades.

The numbers of wills proved in ecclesiastical courts covering eight different areas of the country have been counted, and the notable peak years before 1560 are shown in Table 3.1.[8] Some peaks were more pronounced than others. In every case except that of London the later 1550s were wholly exceptional, with the number of wills rising to well over twice the annual average for two or more years in succession. The increases in earlier years were generally rather less violent, though still suggesting mortality rates in the will-making class approximately 100 per cent above the norm. Where the number of wills did not quite reach twice the annual average for the previous decade, the dates have been given in brackets. While making every allowance for the quality of the data, it would seem that mortality crises hit many parts of the country in the 1520s and 1540s and were of unusual severity in the later 1550s. They may also have been common between 1487 and 1518.[9] Only the 1530s appear as a decade of relative stability in mortality.

When this analysis of probate records is extended beyond 1560, it appears that mortality among that section of the population which made wills never rose as dramatically in the later sixteenth and early seventeenth centuries as it had in the later 1550s and in some years before that. Years in which the number of wills doubled are extremely rare, although there continued to be marked, if smaller, changes in the total numbers of wills proved. It would seem that, while mortality crises continued, they were of lesser severity than they had once been – at least for the more prosperous sections of society.

This conclusion receives some support, and considerable amplification, from the evidence provided by parish registers for the period after 1538. Drawing on a sample of 404 registers of parishes scattered across the whole of England, E.A. Wrigley and R.S. Schofield have identified and measured the most critical years for mortality between the sixteenth and the early nineteenth century. Their findings for the period 1540–1666 are summarised in Table 3.2, which shows all the crises which they classify as 'two-star' or 'three-star' – that is, those

Table 3.1 Years of high mortality 1485–1560 (from probate records)

Area	P?	P?	P+	P	P	P+
London: Commissary Court (1475–)	1497–1500	1504	1513+ (1518)	1540		(1558)
Essex (1479–)		1504	1518	1540	1545	(1550) 1557–8
Berkshire (1508–)			1521 1529	1540–1	1545	(1550) 1557–9
Worcester diocese (1509–)			1527–9	1538		1557–9
Leicestershire (1510–)			1517 (1526)		(1543)	1557–8
Lichfield diocese (1516–)			1521 1524	(1540)	(1546)	(1551) 1557–9
Exeter diocese (1532–)			1527		1546	1551 1557–8
East Sussex (1540–)			1530		1545	1551 1557–8

P = presumed plague P+ = plague and other diseases
Source: See n. 8, p. 358.

which raised the death rate 20 per cent or more above the trend.[10] We should note that the statistics in Table 3.2 are rather more comprehensive for the later part of the period than the earlier. The results for 1665–6 are based on all 404 parish registers, and those after 1596–7 on at least 300; but only 56 registers have provided information for 1544–5 and only 58 for 1545–6. This may explain why the rise in mortality in the latter year suggested by the registers is smaller than that suggested by probate statistics. Nevertheless, the conclusions drawn from the parish registers broadly confirm what the wills tell us about crisis years between 1540 and 1560, and they are supported by other studies of groups of parish registers in particular localities covering the whole period.[11]

Table 3.2 *Years of high mortality 1540–1666*
(from parish registers)

Year (1 July– 30 June)	National death rate (% above trend)	% of parishes affected	
1544–5	23.3	19.6	P
1545–6	26.6	15.5	P
1557–8	60.5	32.5	
1558–9	124.2	39.1	
1587–8	29.5	16.1	
1592–3	29.8	9.1	P
1596–7	20.9	17.6	
1597–8	25.6	18.7	
1603–4	21.0	14.8	P
1624–5	26.6	13.0	
1625–6	43.0	14.6	P
1638–9	35.1	17.9	P+
1643–4	29.3	14.0	P+
1657–8	42.9	16.8	
1658–9	25.1	11.5	
1665–6	31.7	9.7	P

P = presumed plague
P+ = plague and other diseases
Source: E. A. Wrigley and R. S. Schofield, *The Population History of England 1541–1871: A Reconstruction* (1981), Table A10.2, p. 653.

Taking Tables 3.1 and 3.2 together we can conclude that there were at least seventeen periods of crisis mortality – whether single years or sequences of years – in England between 1500 and 1670. They occurred, therefore, once every decade on average, although there were long intervals of comparative stability like the 1530s and, more remarkably, the decades after 1559, when population growth could occur without the check of a major crisis. The parish registers also confirm what one might suspect from the probate evidence: that there was no crisis after 1558–9 which caused the death rate over large stretches of the country to double. In the words of Wrigley and Schofield, the violent upsurges in mortality of the 1540s and 1550s 'look as if they may have been the last throes of a late medieval regime of widespread epidemic mortality'. Nevertheless, severe crises continued until at least 1665, after which the same authors detect a further decline in the frequency and violence of upswings in mortality.[12] In other words, the disappearance of plague brought further stabilisation in mortality. The causes of the seventeen crises will be discussed shortly, and not all of them were the result of outbreaks of bubonic plague. But the identifications indicated in Tables 3.1 and 3.2 suggest that at least half of them were the consequence of plague epidemics, and that plague was one, but not the only, disease involved in others.

The evidence adduced thus far, however, has its weaknesses as an indicator of the frequency and severity of mortality crises. By aggregating information from different places, whether over a whole diocese, as in the case of wills, or over the whole country, as with the sample of parish registers, it fails to reflect the real experience of any single community. Table 3.2 shows that only a minority, and often a small minority, of parishes were affected by the crises identified there. Most places escaped them, but those which did not were large enough and suffered severely enough to affect the aggregate. In 1592–3 and 1665–6, for example, when less than 10 per cent of parishes were affected, it was clearly the ravages of plague in London which created major crises. The statistics for death rate understate the effects of plague in London in these years but exaggerate its impact elsewhere. At the same time these figures may fail altogether to identify purely local but nonetheless serious mortalities. We shall see, for example, that an outbreak of plague in Devon in 1546–7 was probably the worst crisis in that county of the whole period.[13] Yet it finds no place in Table 3.2, although the effects of plague elsewhere in the two preceding years are indicated. This example also illustrates a further point. Aggregate statistics for single years, whether beginning on 1 January or 1 July (as in the case of the Wrigley and Schofield figures) will not fully reflect the impact of a disease like plague which spread slowly from one place to another, in waves often extending over more than twelve months.

We can cast further light on the chronology, frequency and severity of mortality crises, therefore, if we turn from aggregate statistics to look at the experience of single communities. Tables 3.3 and 3.4 show the years in which there was increased mortality and presumably also epidemic disease in fourteen English towns spread across the country from London to Newcastle and from Norwich to Exeter.[14] Any year in which the number of burials in a large proportion of parishes in the town rose to more than twice the average of the previous decade has been included. So have years in which only a small part of the town was seriously affected, and years in which an epidemic disease afflicted most of the town without raising mortality by 100 per cent; but in both these cases the dates are given in brackets. Where parish registers are not available, for all towns before 1538 and for some even later, identifications are more tentative and have been based on literary references in local records to plague, pestilence or high mortality. However, where the evidence is slight the dates have again been enclosed in brackets. And the major epidemics, those in which the level of mortality in one year appears to have been three times the normal, are printed in italics. In London one can find evidence of epidemic disease in almost any year: here the well-known severe outbreaks of plague have been italicized and other epidemic years indicated only when there is evidence of an exceptional number of burials in other towns at the same time.

There is a reassuring correspondence between the epidemic years in these towns and those indicated in Tables 3.1 and 3.2. The early years of the sixteenth century, the mid-1540s, the 1550s, the later 1590s and the first decade of the seventeenth century appear again to have been particularly unhealthy; and the middle years of Elizabeth's reign look to be relatively, though not entirely, free from crises. There are, however, some interesting discrepancies. The epidemics, probably of plague, which affected several towns between 1535 and 1540 had no impact on probate evidence, either because they were confined to the poorer sections of the population, or because they did not spread beyond the major towns to rural areas. On the other hand,

Table 3.3 Epidemic years in fourteen English towns 1485–1580

	P?	P+	P	P	P	P	P	P	P	P	P	P
London	(1485)	1498–1500 +1504	1513+ 1518	1521	(1535–6)	1543	(1548)	1558	1563	(1569–70)	(1574–5)	1578–9
Reading					1537							
Salisbury						1543–4 1546		1558	1564	(1570–1)		1579–80
Bristol					1535	1544–5	1551–2	1557–8	1563–4			
Exeter		1503–4		1528	1537	1546–7	1553 (1551)	1557–8	1565 (1563–5)		1575	
Worcester		1502			1536–7	1545	(1551)	1558		1570		
Shrewsbury									(1563–4)		1575–6 1574	
Chester		1506	1518					1558				
Norwich	(1485)	1500+ 1503–4	1513–14 1520			1544–5	1554–5	1557–9				1579–80
Leicester								1559	(1564)			
Lincoln						1546	(1550–1)	(1557–8)				
Hull					1537						1575–6	
York	(1485–6) +1493	1501+ 1505–6		(1521)	1538–41		1550–2	1558–9				
Newcastle						1544–5				1570–1	1576	1579

P = presumed plague
P+ = plague and other diseases
Source: See n. 14, p. 358.

Table 3.4 Epidemic years in fourteen English towns 1581–1666

	P	P	P	P	P	P	P	P	P	P+	P	P
London	1582	1592–3	(1597)	1603+ (1606–10)		(1623–4)	1625	(1630)	1636	1641+ (1646–7) 1645	(1661)	1665–6
Reading			1596–7	1606–8								(1665)
Salisbury			1596–7	1604			(1625) 1626–7		1638–40	1646–7	(1661)	1666
Bristol			1597	1603					(1637–8)	1643+ 1645	(1650–1)	(1666)
Exeter	(1586–7)	1590–1	1596–7	(1603–5)			1625					
Worcester	1587	1593–4	1597–9	1609–10		1624			1637	1643		
Shrewsbury	1587		1597	1604–5		1624		1631		1644	1650	
Chester			1597	1603–5+ 1608	(1613–4)	(1623)				1647–8	(1654)	
Norwich	1584–5	1589–92	(1597–9)	1603–4	(1618)	(1622–4)	1625–6	(1631)	1636–8			1665–6
Leicester		1593–4		1610–11	1615	(1623)	1625–6		1638–9			
Lincoln	1586–7	1590–1	(1597)	1610–11				1631		(1642)		
Hull	1582		(1597–8)	1602–3					1637–8	1643–5 (1645)	(1660)	
York				1604				1631	1636		1651	
Newcastle		1588–9	1596–7	1604–10			1625		1636	1642+ 1644–7		(1665)

P = presumed plague
P+ = plague and other diseases
Source: n. 14, p. 358.

the fevers, apparently involving virus infections,[15] which had a clear impact on the national sample of parish registers between 1657 and 1659, were not particularly fatal in any of the fourteen towns. In the first case we may have an example of epidemics which severely affected individual communities but were not dispersed widely enough to raise aggregate mortality significantly; in the second case, disease was probably spread over a large area and range of different communities but it was not unusually severe in any single community – or at least not in the particular towns cited in Tables 3.3 and 3.4.

This distinction between local severity and geographical spread has wider implications. Although the aggregate statistics suggest some stabilisation in mortality after the mid-sixteenth century, it is clear that this was not the experience of the main English towns. Crises which raised the death rate by 100 or even 200 per cent in towns continued into the seventeenth century. Moreover, the crises which find a place in Table 3.2 because they affected many places simultaneously were not always the worst in any individual town. In Exeter, for example, the greatest mortalities during Elizabeth's reign occurred in 1570 and 1590, and in Norwich in 1579, 1584 and 1589, not – as one might have expected from Table 3.2 – in 1558–9, 1587–8, 1592–3 or 1597–8. There could be serious epidemics in single places which did not affect national mortality trends because they did not spread far enough fast enough; their impact was diffused over space and time.

These urban crises were almost always caused by bubonic plague; and the distinction between local crises of exceptional severity and more widespread increases in mortality is largely a distinction between epidemics of plague and epidemics of other diseases. Of course, plague often did affect the aggregate totals, as Table 3.2 makes clear. But sometimes it spread so slowly, or to so few places, that its immediate effects on the national picture were limited, as after the epidemics in London in 1563 and 1578. Even the epidemic wave beginning in 1603 has its impact understated by the annual figures in Table 3.2. For, as Table 3.4 makes clear, it continued to cause major increases in mortality in one town or another for the rest of the decade. Consequently, plague was more often responsible for the crises in our fourteen towns than it was for the broader crises in Tables 3.1 and 3.2. Two-thirds of the urban mortalities in Tables 3.3 and 3.4 were caused by it. Looking only at the period after 1538, for which we have more than literary evidence, we can see that plague crises occurred on average one year in every sixteen in these fourteen towns, and that a mortality crisis of one sort or another occurred one year in every eleven.

Mortality crises caused by plague were less common in villages than in towns, with their large rodent populations. To that extent the sparse distribution of crises in Table 3.1 and the small proportion of parishes affected by them in Table 3.2 probably give a fairer picture of rural experience than does the crowding of epidemic years in Tables 3.3 and 3.4. Yet we shall see in the next chapter that when plague did strike a village, it often raised mortality by well over 100 per cent. 'Plague comes seldom, but then very sore' was the saying in rural England.[16] The contrast between the individual and the aggregate, between the local and the extensive mortality crisis remains; and since it was largely a consequence of the difference between plague and other diseases, we must look more closely at each of these in turn in the remainder of this chapter.

(ii) Plague

Although it must be admitted that there can rarely be absolute certainty about the causes of mortality crises in this period, outbreaks of plague can be identified more easily than others. There are, to begin with, many more contemporary references to it than to any other disease. Few burial registers provide regular information about the cause of death. Some of them, in one or two years or individual cases, may refer to smallpox or the sweating sickness, to 'flux' or 'fever'. Much more common, however, are the terms 'plague', 'pl.' or 'pest.' inscribed against the burials in a year of heavy mortality; and 'plague' and 'pestilence' are the words applied by our sources to the majority of the crisis years in Tables 3.3 and 3.4.

It would clearly be hazardous always to rely on such descriptions as clinical diagnoses. 'Plague' might still occasionally be employed to mean any stroke of ill fortune, and 'pestilence' to refer to almost any epidemic disease. In 1562, for example, Sandwich was said to be suffering from 'a threefold plague – pestilence, want of money, dearth of victuals'.[17] By the later sixteenth century, however, both terms were being more often used, usually with the definite article, to describe a specific disease, and to try to distinguish it from others. Thus in Shropshire in the 1580s a disease might be described as 'much like the plague but ... not the plague', while in Surrey in 1626 high mortality was attributed, not to 'the plague' but to 'a disease somewhat akin to it'.[18] As these instances suggest, even when separate diseases were recognised, diagnosis was not always easy. Bubonic plague normally produced clear symptoms, buboes and black, blue or purple spots, readily recognised by contemporaries. But there were cases of septicaemic plague without the usual symptoms, and the spots of plague, 'God's tokens', could sometimes be confused with those of the 'spotted fever', typhus. Nevertheless, by the early seventeenth century the authorities of towns such as London and Norwich were themselves aware of the need to try to discriminate between the two diseases, and there was some slight progress towards a more precise definition of disease entities in the course of the period.[19] 'Plague' increasingly referred to a special and usually identifiable disease.

Moreover, contemporary descriptions can be supplemented by the information about the chronological distribution of burials in severe epidemics which parish registers supply. For outbreaks of bubonic plague have a characteristic seasonal incidence, dictated by the climatic conditions favouring the development of the fleas which carry the disease. All over western Europe these epidemics were marked by a rapid rise in the number of deaths in the summer; burials normally reached their peak in the months between July and September, and then fell more gently with the onset of colder weather between October and January.[20] This is not to say that any abnormal concentration of burials in the third quarter of the year must necessarily be due to bubonic plague; and even when we know that there was plague in a locality other diseases might also contribute to high mortality in the summer or autumn. There was 'fever' and smallpox as well as plague in parts of Norfolk and Essex in 1665–6, for example.[21] But where there is supporting evidence in the shape of contemporary description or assertion as well as a major rise in mortality in the late summer, the presence of bubonic plague can reasonably be assumed. The absence of burial registers precludes such an investigation into epidemic mortality in the little-known decades before 1538. We cannot confirm the strong literary evidence that there was plague in many parts of the country between 1498 and 1504 and between 1535 and 1538.[22] It is probable, however, that the majority of the years of high mortality between 1538 and 1665 noted in the tables above were caused by bubonic plague. These years are marked in the tables by the letter 'P'.

In other respects besides their seasonal incidence several of these epidemics conform to the patterns suggested by modern studies of the epidemiology of plague. They began in ports and major towns; they spread along main routes of communication to other urban centres and from there to smaller communities and to some of the less isolated villages. The local movement of plague within two counties will be described in the next chapter. But Table 3.3 alone suggests that the plague of 1563 in London moved to Reading in the following year and on to Bristol in 1565. Similarly, the plague of 1543 in the capital reached Reading in the same year, Bristol in the following one and Worcester in the year after that. In this slow movement, in which infected individuals, or rats and fleas in their baggage, carried the disease by river and road, epidemics of bubonic plague differed from the diseases, whatever their identity, which struck many towns virtually simultaneously in 1558 and 1597.

The tables also suggest, however, that the epidemiology of English plagues, like that of modern Asian ones, was not always as straightforward as this. Although London was often the first major town infected, a virulent strain of the bacillus might enter the country by other routes. The outbreak of 1592 in London had been preceded by the introduction of plague into Devon from Portugal in 1589.[23] In the first decade of the seventeenth century both Hull and Great Yarmouth were infected in 1602, before the major outbreak in London, while in 1624 there appears to have been plague in Scarborough, in 1635 in North Shields, and in 1664 in Yarmouth, again one year before London suffered severely. In these cases the Low Countries were probably the source of the disease. In the early 1650s, on the other hand, plague appears to have spread into parts of Wales and some towns of western England from Ireland.[24] A large town like Norwich or ports such as Hull, Chester and Newcastle might thus be open to infection from several directions and it is often difficult to identify the origin of any particular outbreak.

It is equally difficult to account for variations in the severity of the disease in different places and at different times. If one wished to define a typical epidemic of plague, it would not be inaccurate to describe it as one which killed 10 or 12 per cent of the inhabitants of an infected community. Such losses very often occurred. But no outbreak of plague was in fact typical. Some swept away as many as a third of the inhabitants of a town. Others were much less serious. In 1579, for example, there were major outbreaks only in Salisbury,

Norwich and Newcastle of the thirteen provincial towns in Table 3.3. But the disease had been present in one household in Leicester and in another in Reading in 1578. In the latter 'John Johnson and his wife and four of his children were buried of the plague'.[25] No epidemic occurred in either town, however, perhaps because these cases were not followed by an epizootic among the town's rats which would have guaranteed the spread of infection. The heaviest mortality of all occurred in the shortest epidemics, when plague entered a town in the spring, reached its height in August or September and disappeared before the end of December. But when plague arrived in a town late in the year it might smoulder among the rat population and cause a recrudescence of human plague whenever climatic changes favoured the development of the fleas which transmitted the disease to men.[26]

In some towns, therefore, we find plague burials spread over several months and occurring at different times in different parishes. The outbreak of 1606–8 in Reading provides a good example. There were a few registered cases of plague in 1603 and 1604 but no major epidemic. In the spring of 1606, however, the number of deaths attributed to plague rose rapidly in St Giles's parish, where the London road entered the town. At the end of the following year there were many burials in the two other parishes of Reading, and cases of plague were registered in St Giles's again in August 1608. Similarly, plague smouldered for several years in Leicester before the major outbreak of 1610. In London itself there were frequent cases of plague between 1606 and 1610, although the truly epidemic stage of the disease was never reached.[27] A similarly haphazard distribution of cases over a long period has been noted in some modern outbreaks of bubonic plague, and on such occasions, as one seventeenth-century writer remarked, plague 'was not so dangerous for the greatness of the infection, as for the strange dispersing of it'.[28]

The slow movement of plague from place to place, together with these prolonged bouts of infection in single towns, meant that the disease was rarely absent from England between 1485 and 1665. It would not be difficult to trace a succession of outbreaks year after year for a decade or more, as, for example, between 1584 and 1597. In 1587 and 1597 it is clear, as we shall see, that diseases other than plague were responsible for high mortality in most parts of the country. But in 1587 there was certainly plague in Chesterfield, and perhaps also in Bury St Edmunds, while in 1597 the disease was said to be in Cranbrook and Sandwich in Kent. These instances may have been the result of the local persistence of infection after the major outbreaks elsewhere in 1584–5 and 1589–93, for there was plague in Ipswich in 1585–6 and in Chatham and Maidstone in 1595.[29] In fact plague appeared in different parts of the country every year from 1584 to 1597, and by infecting the rodents of various localities in succession it may temporarily have become endemic in England.[30] Local research could well extend this sequence of plague years and it would certainly reveal others. The only periods of any length when the country was free from epidemics of the disease appear to have been between 1612 and 1624 and between 1654 and 1664.[31]

This is not to say, however, that epidemics of plague in England can be treated in isolation, divorced from the history of plague in Europe. On the contrary, despite the long-term persistence of the disease in the British Isles, the importation of a more virulent strain of the plague bacillus from outside appears to have been necessary for a major epidemic. Plague was certainly endemic for long periods in major towns, in Norwich as well as in London,[32] but it is striking that serious epidemics in London followed those in Antwerp or Amsterdam, and devastating epidemics in Norwich followed those in the metropolis or in the Low Countries. Epidemic waves might take several years to sweep across England, as long as a decade after 1602; and they seem often to have overlapped with one another. But all the evidence suggests that they had their origins abroad. They were in fact the end result of broad tides of infection moving from the eastern Mediterranean across the whole of Europe. The contemporary who described the plague of the first decade of the seventeenth century as the 'Egyptian plague' was not very far from the truth.[33]

The foreign origins of plague explain some of the features of its geographical incidence which are indicated in Tables 3.3 and 3.4. It is clear that ports were more at risk than inland towns, and towns close to the east or south coasts were more often visited than those furthest from the Continent. The south-eastern half of the country was in fact much more prone to plague than the north-west.[34] York, with no plague at all between 1552 and 1603, was therefore in a fortunate position; Norwich, with several outbreaks, was particularly vulnerable. The tables also show, however, that some waves of plague spread further than others. The most general outbreaks, all coinciding with years of plague in Germany and the Low Countries,[35] seem to have begun in 1498, 1535, 1543, 1563, 1589, 1603, 1625 and 1636. The visitation beginning in 1603 appears to have been particularly widely diffused. 'Then were all the shires in England grievously visited', commented a contemporary. 'Note the work of God.'[36] By contrast, the final outbreak, beginning in 1665, seems to have been one of the most restricted in its impact. As we shall see, it had no less violent an effect on mortality in the towns it hit than previous outbreaks. There was no decline in the disease's virulence as it disappeared. But both Table 3.4, and the example of Essex discussed in the next chapter, suggest that in 1665 it was much more restricted spatially than it had sometimes been in the past, a feature which has also been noted in the last outbreak of plague in Switzerland.[37]

It should not be concluded from this, however, that plague was changing its character on the eve of its departure. There had, after all, been restricted outbreaks in the sixteenth century, like that beginning in 1578. So far as anyone could tell, there might equally well have been another generalised visitation like that of 1603 after 1665. The tables above provide no firm ground for suggesting that plague was gradually withdrawing in the seventeenth century, and contemporaries could certainly never feel secure. In 1665 itself the menace of plague was felt all over the country, and the danger did not quickly disappear. According to the London bills of mortality, cases of plague continued to occur in the capital until 1679,[38] and even after that its reimportation into the country was felt to be a constant threat – a threat which reached its climax in the 1720s with the fears aroused by the plague in Marseilles.

Those scares, and the several possible reasons why they proved unfounded, will occupy our attention in the final chapter. For the moment it is sufficient to note the frequency and the variability of plague's visitations between 1485 and 1665 which justified them. Epidemics might spread far and wide or be closely confined; they might cause large or small increases in mortality; but they were common and the threat of disaster was always there. The most important conclusion to be drawn from the tables above is that bubonic plague was the commonest cause of mortality crises throughout the sixteenth and for most of the seventeenth century.

(iii) Other diseases

Plague was not the only disease causing widespread sickness and heavy mortality in English towns and villages between 1485 and 1665.

Other diseases were responsible for some of the epidemic years noted
in the tables above, and also for epidemics which, while having less
serious effects on mortality, left a mark on contemporary literature.
In 1615 there was a 'burning fever' in Leicester about which we know
little, though it coincided with a 'contagious sickness' and fevers
elsewhere in England and Europe. There were fevers again in many
parts of England in 1638 and in 1660 and 1661. We hear of outbreaks
of smallpox all over the country in the early seventeenth century, most
notably in 1634–5, and of several epidemics of 'gaol fever', in Oxford
in 1577 and York in 1581, as well as in Exeter in 1586, Lincoln in
1590 and Hereford in 1636. There was always malaria in the marshes
of East Anglia and the Fens, and there were often epidemics, probably
of virus infections, which spread rapidly over the whole country and
incapacitated large numbers of people, as in 1657–9.[39]

These diseases brought sickness and an increase in mortality to
many towns and villages. But they rarely pushed the total number of
burials in any community to double or treble the average, as bubonic
plague regularly did. The only epidemic diseases which rivalled plague
in their pronounced local effect on mortality between 1485 and 1665
fall into four categories: the 'sweating sickness', the influenza epidemic
of 1557–9, epidemics (probably of typhus) directly associated with
troop movements during the civil wars of the 1640s, and finally those
diseases which coincided with or followed immediately after harvest
failure, especially in 1587, 1597 and 1623.

The sweating sickness may be considered first, because its
successive outbreaks, in 1485, 1507–8, 1517 and 1551, may have
been responsible for some of the early years of high mortality in the
tables above. The exact nature of the disease remains mysterious,
though it may have been an arbovirus infection of some kind.[40] But
an element of myth as well as mystery has surrounded the sweat, and
has perhaps attracted to it more historical attention than it warrants.
It impressed contemporaries because it was spectacular. It killed within
twenty-four hours. It attacked a community suddenly and then was
gone. In particular, unlike bubonic plague, it struck the prosperous:
aldermen and mayors in London and other towns, the sons of the
duke of Suffolk in 1551, the king's Latin secretary and even Cardinal
Wolsey himself in 1517. Yet when we have some precise evidence of
its demographic effects, in the last outbreak of July and August 1551,
it is not impressive. The disease swept through a parish in the space
of a very few days, a fortnight at most, and only in the smallest villages

did this short-term increase in mortality amount to a serious loss of population.[41]

It is possible, but by no means certain, that previous outbreaks were more serious. Their coincidence with some of the years of high mortality in Tables 3.1 and 3.3 seems persuasive until one finds that these were also reported to be years of plague. It is likely that there was bubonic plague as well as the sweat in York and Norwich in 1485–6, and in 1517 the former disease was again present in various parts of the country. Certainly in 1551 and 1552, it was bubonic plague not the sweat which was largely responsible for high death rates in York and Bristol, as it may have been in Lincoln too.[42] It seems probable that the sweating sickness caused high morbidity, especially noticeable among the social elite, that it was a serious scourge in some scattered rural parishes, but that it had only a minor effect on mortality in larger communities.

Yet the 'sweat' had become part of contemporary medical vocabulary, and the word was applied to later outbreaks of what were probably virus diseases. In the middle of Elizabeth's reign, for example, an astrologer's prediction of the sweat's return was thought to have been fulfilled because there had recently been 'many strange and grievous sicknesses', including a wave of influenza which had affected much of England in 1579–80.[43] The term was particularly revived, however, to describe the epidemics of 1557–9 whose importance is evident from the tables above. Unlike the sweating sickness itself, these infections were responsible for a major disaster: the greatest mortality crisis to hit England between 1485 and 1665. The population of England probably fell by at least 6 per cent between 1556 and 1560.[44]

It is unlikely that the complex epidemic picture of 1556–9 can ever be precisely reconstructed, but its severity was partly due to the fact that it was a 'composite' or 'mixed' crisis, with at least two components. At the beginning, in 1556 and 1557, there were 'burning fevers' and 'spotted fevers' over much of the country, probably including outbreaks of typhus, the classic famine disease, following disastrous harvests in 1555 and 1556. The crisis was extended and considerably aggravated, however, by a 'new ague' or 'new disease', as contemporaries described it, probably a form of influenza, which caused even greater mortality in 1558 and 1559. It was this second wave of disease which transformed what had earlier been localised distress into the worst demographic disaster in the country's history in the whole period covered by parish registers.

Whatever the exact combination of diseases involved, however, the pattern of mortality in the later 1550s differed in several respects from that common in outbreaks of plague. In its later stages, for example, the crisis seems to have affected the prosperous classes at least as much as the poor, as the will statistics suggest; and like the sweating sickness these epidemics removed several members of the governing class in towns.[45] They also had a less restricted geographical incidence than plague: they hit rural as well as urban communities over wide areas of the country simultaneously. As a result they unquestionably had a more serious demographic impact than any epidemic of bubonic plague in the period. Yet in the short term, and in individual communities, plague was often much more devastating, raising mortality rates not to two but to three, four or five times their normal level within a year. The greatest outbreaks of plague caused heavier mortality than the epidemics of the later 1550s in all the towns in Table 3.3, with the solitary exception of Worcester.[46]

The terms 'new disease' and 'sweating sickness', used or revived to describe the fevers of the 1550s, were employed again in the 1640s, another decade of regular and widespread mortality crises in English towns and villages. Table 3.4 above and the parish registers of Devon, discussed in the next chapter, reflect the high death rates common in these years, and once again more than one epidemic disease was involved. This time bubonic plague had a part to play. It was responsible for the greatest mortalities, as in Bristol in 1645. But there were also numerous outbreaks of typhus, the occupational disease of armies and the inevitable concomitant of the English Civil War. In Bristol in 1643, in Exeter in the same year, and in many rural parishes, including much of Devon throughout the war, typhus caused an exceptional number of deaths. It seems probable that this was the 'new disease' whose ravages in the Royalist forces can be followed in the papers of Sir Samuel Luke, and it was quickly communicated to civilian populations whenever towns were placed under siege or troops billeted on villages.[47]

The association of soldiers with the spread of typhus, plague and other epidemic diseases was nothing new. It had been a threat at the time of the Elizabethan rebellion of the northern earls, and an actuality in some western counties on the return of Buckingham's expedition from the Ile de Ré in the 1620s. During the Civil War it became commonplace. Lady Fanshawe, writing in the middle of the siege of Oxford, noted 'at the windows the sad spectacle of war, sometimes

plague, sometimes sicknesses of other kind, by reason of so many
people being packed together'; and the spectacle was repeated in many
other towns and villages.[48] Though less prolonged than in the Thirty
Years' War in Germany, a savage resurgence of epidemic disease was
not the least important consequence of the English Civil War.

Englishmen were fortunate that the third great scourge, famine, did
not coincide with war and pestilence between 1642 and 1646. There
were temporary, often severe, shortages of food in towns under siege,
like Bristol and Plymouth in 1645. But it was only in parts of Lancashire during the campaigns of the Second Civil War in 1648 that a
general dearth accompanied disease. According to a petition from
Wigan in 1649, 'In this county hath the plague of pestilence been
raging these three years and upwards, occasioned chiefly by the wars.
There is a very great scarcity and dearth of all provisions, especially
of all sorts of grain.'[49] For most parts of the country, however, the
bad harvests of the later 1640s followed two or three years after
serious epidemics; it was war, not dearth, which aggravated the impact
of disease in that decade.

Although diseases connected with harvest failure, our final category
of epidemics, were not of major importance in the 1640s, there is
considerable evidence to suggest that they were significant in several
crisis years before then. The first indication is a simple matter of
chronology. Between 1500 and the 1630s – when agricultural
productivity at last began to catch up with demographic growth – bad
harvests were very often followed by an increase in mortality. The
bad or disastrous harvests of 1501–2, 1520–1, 1527–8, 1545, 1550–1,
1555–6, 1562, 1586, 1594–7, 1622 and 1630, all coincided with or
were succeeded by years of crisis mortality, as the tables above make
clear.[50] There was, of course, no long-term correlation between food
prices and mortality: the diseases and infections which have already
been considered often raised mortality when prices were low and so
prevented any systematic statistical association.[51] But the fact that
virtually every bad harvest up to 1630 was followed by a period of
high mortality suggests that those other infections simply overlay,
and hence obscured, an underlying connection between nutrition and
disease. It certainly justified the contemporary assertion that 'experience teacheth us that after a great dearth cometh a great death'.[52]

There is stronger evidence than mere chronological coincidence
for the connection between dearth and disease in some of the crisis
years noted above, particularly in 1596–8, but also in 1586–7 and

1622–3. Simple starvation was reported from parts of northern England, where these crises were worst, and where their effects have been most thoroughly examined.[53] There were also epidemic fevers over much of the country, which appear to have included typhus, and there is evidence of pulmonary ailments such as tuberculosis and of outbreaks of dysentery, which may well have been aggravated by malnutrition. In 1587, as in 1556, there was said to be 'a strange sickness named the burning ague ... all England over'; there are similar descriptions of fevers and also of dysentery in the notebook of an Oxfordshire doctor in 1597; while in the early 1620s there was 'a general sickness and disease ... mortal to many and infectious to more', which in parts of England was described, like typhus, as 'spotted fever'.[54] The seasonal distribution of burials also suggests that these epidemics were worst when the shortage of food was most acute: they were concentrated in the winter or spring, not in the late summer.[55]

In a few cases bubonic plague may have played a part in these mortalities, as in Chesterfield in 1587 and Cranbrook in 1597. There was also plague in Scotland in 1597, and it spread to the northern English towns of Newcastle, Carlisle and Penrith in this and the following year.[56] It is certain, however, that plague played only a minor role in these years. It was not involved in most parts of England where mortality was high, in Devon, for example; and although some cases of plague were reported in London and Norwich in the later 1590s, it was not the predominant scourge there.[57] There can be little doubt that in many areas of England – in rural villages and hamlets particularly in the North and the West, and in the poorest parts of the larger towns – 1587, 1597 and 1623 were years in which food crises, diseases other than plague, and high mortality were inextricably associated. In the terminology used by French historians, these were genuine 'crises of subsistence'.

Similar circumstances may have been responsible for some of the other years of crisis mortality which coincided with dearth. But we can be less certain that on these occasions high mortality was always the result of infections commonly associated with famine, like typhus, or of diseases like dysentery and tuberculosis, resistance to which is seriously reduced by malnutrition. Rather, these may have been 'mixed' crises, when autonomous epidemics were at least as important as a shortage of food in causing high mortality. In the 1550s, for example, it is unlikely that malnutrition reduced resistance to the virus infections which hit the will-making class so hard in 1558–9, although it may have helped to increase mortality in 1556 and 1557. In other years, in 1563 and 1630, for example, bubonic plague was certainly the major culprit, and vulnerability to the plague bacillus is not known to be increased by lack of food.[58] The parish registers also suggest that it was plague and not typhus which followed the disastrous harvest in Devon in 1545, and it was the same disease which, according to the corporation, hit Lincoln after the 'great famishing . . . of the whole people of this city' in the winter of 1550–1.[59] Although the evidence is necessarily less secure, there may have been comparable mixed crises, combining plague and dearth, in the crisis years before parish registers began in 1538. It is not unlikely that in 1501 and 1502, in 1520 and 1521, and in 1527 and 1528 crisis mortalities were the product both of plague, to which there are references in some parts of the country, and of harvest failure. Such a combination probably accounts for the demographic disaster in Coventry in the early 1520s, which left a quarter of the town's houses empty.[60]

The significance of subsistence crises pure and simple in English demographic history must not be overstated therefore. It was common for infectious diseases not aggravated by malnutrition, such as plague, to follow dearth, and make the major contribution to mortality. When this happened, there may well have been important indirect connections between harvest failure and epidemic infections. The large-scale shipment of grain from country to country or locality to locality in years of famine might aid the movement of rodents carrying disease; equally the migration of individuals, of vagrants and beggars in search of food and charity, which commonly increased when harvests failed, might serve to disseminate an epidemic. In these ways the economic and social circumstances consequent upon bad harvests could facilitate exposure to infection and accelerate the spread of disease.[61] Even so, in the final analysis it was disease rather than dearth which in these instances played the greater role in mortality and which must be accorded the greater importance.[62]

The crises of 1587, 1597 and 1623 seem thus to have been exceptional in the relatively isolated role which malnutrition played in them, and this accounts for some features of their incidence. They had a more extensive effect on rural areas than outbreaks of plague, but it was largely confined to pastoral and highland regions: areas which produced little corn even when harvests were good, and where large sections of the population were dependent on industrial by-employments which were badly hit when high food prices cut consumer demand for textiles. In the South and East of England their impact was greatest in declining industrial centres such as Reading and Salisbury and in the poorest suburbs of other towns, but even in the latter death rates rarely rose as far and as fast as they did in outbreaks of plague.[63]

These three subsistence crises would certainly have been much worse if plague had happened to coincide with them, as it had done in the past. That it did not was probably fortuitous, a consequence of the slow and haphazard movement of plague across the Continent. For the virulent wave of plague which followed harvest failure in parts of France and northern Spain and in Scotland in 1596–8 did not reach most of England until 1603, after two years of good harvests; while the plague in northern France in 1586, which reached northern Spain when grain prices there were still high, arrived in Devon in 1589 again after two good harvests.[64] In the 1620s also plague came in 1625 not in 1623, although the gap between dearth and plague was filled on this occasion by the spread of fever in much of southern England in 1624.[65] Compared with some areas of the Continent, England was fortunate in the timing of its plague epidemics in the later sixteenth and early seventeenth centuries.

As a result of these chance chronological factors bubonic plague was more clearly divorced from other causes of high mortality in England after 1563 than it had been before. In the first decade of the sixteenth century and in the 1520s it had followed shortly after bad harvests. It had hit Devon in 1546 and Bristol and Lincoln in 1551 as food prices there reached their peak. In 1551 plague also coincided in some towns with outbreaks of the sweating sickness, as it had done in 1517 and perhaps in 1485. Again, in 1563, plague hit London immediately after a bad harvest, and there was at least one recorded death from 'famine', in St Margaret's Westminster at the end of July 1563, just as the toll of plague deaths was rising to a crescendo.[66] Small wonder that one contemporary referred to 'that vehemence of plague, which naturally followeth the dint of hunger'.[67] When the epidemic beginning in 1563 reached other parts of the country, in 1564 and 1565, however, harvests were good and prices low; and for a century after that coincidences of plague and dearth were rare. It was only in 1630 that plague could again be seen with some justification as 'the ordinary effect' of famine; and in that year the cumulative impact of the two was slight because both plague and dearth were less serious than they had been in the past.[68]

For more than a century after 1563, therefore, plague was separated from other causes of high mortality. This may be one reason for the apparent decline in the severity of mortality crises after the mid-sixteenth century, which was noted earlier in this chapter. Different diseases were now set apart in time and had no simultaneous cumulative impact. The chronological distinction between plague and other diseases may also have affected contemporary perceptions of it. It may have encouraged people to compare and contrast it with famine and to regard it as an individual entity. It certainly showed them that plague alone – not associated with other diseases or afflictions – was, as it had always been, the major cause of sudden and devastating upsurges in mortality.

This brief account of years of high mortality, based on the information summarised in Tables 3.1–4, has tried to set bubonic plague in its context among other causes of demographic crisis in England between 1485 and 1665. The picture is not a simple one. It contains a multitude of variables, it is drawn from evidence which is partial and often puzzling, and it includes subjects like the diagnosis of epidemic disease and its relationship with malnutrition which remain uncertain and controversial. Nevertheless the dominant themes are obvious and eloquent: the frequency with which death rates in a community could double or treble in one year, the extent to which early modern Englishmen were subjected to epidemics, and the common but not invariable connection of pestilence with the other scourges of war and famine.

It is clear also that plague can be distinguished from other causes of death and demographic disaster in early modern England, and its peculiar features help to explain its unique social impact. In the first place, plague epidemics were the commonest and most threatening causes of serious mortality. They did not produce a single spectacular crisis, which was never repeated, like the epidemics of 1557–9. They were more regular occurrences, and they therefore stimulated the carefully articulated and developing response which will be considered in Part III of this book. In other respects, however, epidemics of plague were anything but regular. They were not visibly dependent on conditions of civil war or of food shortage for their ravages, and they did not cease when war stopped or harvests improved. They were not readily predictable phenomena as famine fevers were, but strokes of fortune, to be explained satisfactorily only as acts of God. In this sense plague was an autonomous cause of high mortality, unrelated to the major fluctuations in the economic and social·life of pre-industrial England.[69] We shall see in later chapters that the local incidence of epidemics of plague was in fact closely connected with other features of the environment – with bad hygiene and over-crowding, for example, and hence with social class and population density; but their timing and their severity could never be foreseen.

These were some of the reasons why specific administrative measures were taken against plague, and why it provoked panic and terror when other epidemic diseases did not. At a time when 'new' fevers were raging in the Civil War, for example, one writer might yet reassure his readers that 'it is not the *Plague* (as the relations and hopes of our enemies, and the fears of others have suggested)'.[70] The unique impact of the disease lay largely in the fact that it was at the same time a common occurrence and an unpredictable one. The local studies in the following chapters are intended to show both its recurrent and its random features.

Chapter 4

The local context

Raffe Dawson . . . came from London about 25th day of July last past, and being sick of the plague, died in his father's house and so infected the said house and was buried, as it is reported, near unto his father's house . . .
Richard Dawson [Raffe's uncle] being sick of the plague, and perceiving he must die at that time, arose out of his bed, and made his grave, and caused his nephew, John Dawson, to cast straw into the grave, which was not far from the house, and went and laid him down in the said grave, and caused clothes to be laid upon, and so departed out of this world. This he did, because he was a strong man, and heavier than his said nephew and another wench were able to bury . . .
John Dawson . . . having laid him down in a ditch, died in it the 29th day of August 1625 in the night.
Rose Smyth, servant . . . and the last of that household, died of plague, and was buried . . . the 5th day of September, 1625, near unto the said house.

Parish register of Malpas, Cheshire[1]

Unfortunately, few parish registers are as informative as this about the origins of an epidemic and its local impact. Few parish clerks, perhaps, had so memorable a story to tell. If we wish to investigate the local incidence of plague in any detail, therefore, we need to look beyond such exceptional records, evocative as they are. We must take into account those registers which simply listed an increasing number of burials in plague-time, and also the negative evidence of registers which recorded no increase in mortality at all. In fact, in order to see which kinds of community were most affected by plague in the course of our period, we need to obtain as complete a coverage of parishes over as wide an area as possible. One way of attempting this is through an examination of two counties in different parts of England, whose experience of the disease might be expected to be dissimilar.

The counties of Devon and Essex have been chosen for this purpose. This is partly because a large proportion of their parish registers are available for study: it has been possible to see the original or transcribed burial registers of 138 Devon parishes, about a third of the total in the county, and of 150 parishes in Essex, slightly more than a third of the whole.[2] These counties also provide a valuable geographical contrast: the first a western county, most of it part of the pastoral highland region of England; the second in the South-East, part of the lowland zone of mixed husbandry and close to the commonest source of plague in England – London. There were some similarities between them. They were among the more populous of English counties in the sixteenth century, with Devon slightly in the lead. Parts of eastern Essex and much of southern Devon were indeed, to judge by the early Tudor subsidy returns, some of the most densely populated as well as the most prosperous areas of the country.[3] Their experience may not be unrepresentative of that of much of central and southern England. At the same time, however, the upland areas of northern and central Devon were in many respects similar to the thinly populated and impoverished North of England. Between them these two counties encompass much of the economic diversity which existed in England as a whole, and there is no reason to suppose that they were in any significant way exceptional in their history in the Tudor and Stuart period.

Before discussing the effect of plague upon them, a methodological comment is necessary. The conclusions about the impact of plague in this and the following chapters are based upon comparisons between the severity of epidemics in different parishes. It is the great virtue of parish registers that they refer to small geographical units which can be compared with one another, often single village communities, or, in the case of towns with several parishes, subdivisions of a larger settlement. In order to make these comparisons it is necessary to measure in some way the degree to which mortality rose during an epidemic in each village, town or part of a town. Since there are no adequate sources giving the total populations of local communities in this period, we cannot calculate annual mortality rates and then compare them. Neither, in most cases, can we isolate deaths caused by plague from those which had other causes in an epidemic year, and thus compute 'excess' mortality. Instead we have to rely on what the registers tell us about fluctuations in the number of burials from year to year, and hence about the relative severity of an epidemic year compared with more 'normal' periods in any parish.

When in one year the number of burials jumped to twice the average annual level of preceding years, for example, there is some probability that mortality rates in that parish roughly doubled. If burials in other parishes in the same year rose to three or four times their usual level, and if we have evidence that plague was present in the area, we can begin to compare its impact in different places. In the following pages, therefore, the severity of an epidemic in a particular parish will be measured by dividing the number of burials in the twelve months during which mortality was at its height by the average annual number of burials for the same parish taken, wherever possible, from the previous decade. This ratio of epidemic to normal burials provides a simple index of mortality which may be used for comparing one parish with another, and one epidemic with another. For the sake of brevity, we shall refer to it as the 'Crisis Mortality Ratio'.[4]

No attempt will be made in this chapter to draw firm conclusions about real mortality rates from the calculated ratios. A Crisis Mortality Ratio of 3.0, that is a threefold rise in the number of burials, will simply be taken *prima facie* as a sign of an exceptional crisis. If mortality rates were normally close to twenty-six per thousand in this period, which is a reasonable assumption,[5] such an increase would imply a loss of approaching 8 per cent of the population of a parish. But normal mortality rates varied considerably from place to place and from period to period. For the purposes of this chapter it is sufficient to note a trebling of the normal number of burials in one year as a mark of a serious and exceptional loss of population. In fact, as will be seen, the increase in the number of burials was often even greater than this in epidemics of bubonic plague.

This method of analysis has limitations which ought to be mentioned. First, it cannot easily be adapted to deal with epidemics of more than twelve months' duration. It tends, for example, to underestimate the extent of mortality in the late 1550s and later 1590s, when epidemic diseases other than bubonic plague caused an increase in the number of burials over two or even three years. But since our concern here is primarily with the sudden crises caused by epidemics of plague, which usually ran their course in less than twelve months, this is not as grave a limitation as it would be in a more general study of mortality. Secondly, it is a method difficult to apply to the smallest parishes normally producing three or four burials a year, where the accident of a shipwreck or a fire might easily double their number. It should be noted that this applies to several of the Essex parishes considered later; in Devon the parishes with registers available for study were generally larger. Even in Essex, however, when there was an unusually large number of burials in several of the smallest parishes at the same time as in larger communities, it is probable that some epidemic disease was at work.

Thirdly, there is the problem of identifying which mortality crises were caused by bubonic plague and which were not. The task is easiest in the towns considered in Chapter 5, where there are always literary references to 'plague' in urban records as well as the characteristic signs of the disease in parish registers: a concentration of burials both in particular families and in the late-summer months, often with a recrudescence in mortality in the following spring. Plague epidemics in large cities, and also in some of the market towns of Devon and Essex, can hardly be missed, and it is easy to exclude doubtful cases. With small rural parishes, like many of those considered in this chapter, the task is more difficult. The possible number of misidentifications has been reduced, however, by excluding surges in mortality obviously associated with harvest crises or with the known fevers of 1551 and 1556–9; and by identifying as plague only those rises in mortality which occurred at a time when there was, first, a specific reference to 'plague' somewhere in the county (or, in the case of Essex, in London), and, second, a late-summer concentration of burials in more than one other parish. A single crisis in a single parish without supporting evidence of plague elsewhere has not been counted. It is likely that one or two of the mortalities attributed to plague in the pages and tables which follow were in fact caused by other diseases which coincided with waves of plague infection. This may be the case, for example, in Essex in the years 1637–40, when there were 'fevers' as well as 'plague' in England. But it seems reasonable to suppose that the number of errors of this kind is small.[6]

A final limitation in our methodology is provided by the deficiencies in the parish registers themselves, to which we have already referred. Not all of our sample of nearly 300 registers are equally reliable. Modern copies of many Devonshire registers have been consulted, and there is the possibility of error by the transcribers. More seriously, the earliest registers which survive are frequently parchment transcripts made in 1598 or 1599 from earlier paper records. Few can have been so carefully checked with the original by the churchwardens and their 'honest neighbours' as that of Ardleigh, Essex; more contain comments by the clerk on the lacunae in the original itself. Others are still more remote from the vital events they purport to record. When the parish register of High Laver, Essex, was stolen in 1618, for example, the memory of parishioners was relied upon for the recording of earlier events in a new volume.[7] Those registers which are most obviously unreliable have been ignored in the following pages, but since the purpose of this chapter is to study epidemics over a wide area it has been impossible to restrict attention only to the most perfect of them. Even with apparently reliable registers, we must admit the probability of under-registration, and we cannot be sure that the level of under-registration was constant from year to year, although the absolute accuracy of our ratios depends on this.[8] Our method of analysis is therefore necessarily a crude one, applied to imperfect sources.

It is reassuring to find, however, that it does produce a relatively consistent picture of the incidence of plague epidemics in the counties and towns discussed in the following pages. The ratios are not the precise measures of mortality which their numerical form might seem to imply; but they are useful and suggestive indicators of changes in the level of recorded burials. Our method also has the great virtue, unlike some of the more sophisticated techniques applied to parish registers, that it does not depart very far from the original records: the simple and eloquent lists of burials in parish after parish from year to year. As far as possible these should be allowed to speak for themselves.

(i) Devon

Demographic crises of one kind or another were familiar events in sixteenth- and seventeenth-century Devon.[9] Although only a small proportion of the surviving registers date from the 1540s, and they do not become numerous until the end of the sixteenth century, they show that crises afflicted some part of the county on average once in every decade between 1540 and 1650. Not all of them were caused by bubonic plague. Some of the earliest to be observed in local registers were the result of the virus infections mentioned in the previous chapter. The sweating sickness of 1551 caused an unusual number of deaths in August of that year in nine of the thirty-five parishes with extant registers; and at the end of the same decade there are signs of the fevers which afflicted many parts of the country, the number of burials being especially large in eastern Devon, in the parishes of Colyton and Broadhembury.[10] Sequences of bad harvests also had a serious impact. There were increases in mortality in several parishes in the later 1580s, in 1622–3 and especially in the later 1590s. But outbreaks of bubonic plague were more common than other epidemics, regularly striking villages and towns scattered across the county in a manner which appeared to be utterly capricious.

There were several successive waves of infection, some limited to particular parts of the county, others engulfing almost all of it. Although there are references to plague in Exeter and other parts of the county in 1503, and again in 1537,[11] the first epidemic which we can study in any detail is the plague of 1546–7. This was probably the most serious outbreak of the whole period. It began at a time of unprecedentedly high food prices, following the disastrous harvest of 1545, and the spread of plague across the county may initially have been assisted by the movement of vagabonds and grain supplies, both of which were notable phenomena in years of dearth.[12] The number of burials began to increase in the late spring and early summer of 1546 in several parishes: in St Petrock's parish in Exeter, in Colyton in the east, Stoke-in-Teignhead and Stoke Fleming in the south and Barnstaple in the north. It is clear that the epidemic was not wholly dependent on dearth for its effects, however, since the disease continued to cause havoc in the county even after the better harvest of 1546. It now moved inland from coastal parishes and towns to villages like Plymtree, Kenn, Bovey Tracey, Braunton and Buckland Monachorum, where burials rose in the spring and summer of 1547. Of the thirty-five parish registers with entries for these two years, only seven – all of them from villages in the north or north-east of the county – supply no evidence of increased mortality. Elsewhere we have all the signs of bubonic plague: summer peaks in the number of burials where the disease was worst, a large number of deaths occurring in a few families in each parish, and the apparent slow movement of disease from place to place, burials rising in one village a fortnight or a month after they had done so in another a few miles away.

No later outbreak of plague covered so much of the county, and some were extremely localised in their incidence. In 1563 there was an epidemic confined almost entirely to the coastal parishes of the south. Plague had devastated London during the summer of that year, and by December it was in the ports of Plymouth and Dartmouth,[13] spreading from there into neighbouring parishes including St Budeaux, Stoke Gabriel and Paignton. In the summer of 1568 burials rose again in Paignton, to be followed by high mortality in nearby Newton Abbot in 1569 and 1570, and by undoubted outbreaks of plague in Exeter and Plymouth in 1570[14] and in some villages around them in 1570 and 1571. At the end of the decade there was another localised outbreak, this time in the heart of the county, in Hatherleigh in 1577 and in South Tawton and Spreyton in 1579.

The next epidemic, beginning ten years later, was on a much larger scale, affecting most parts of the county, and on this occasion we can specify its origins precisely. Plague was brought into Devon, probably with other diseases, by the fleet which returned from Portugal to Plymouth on 1 July 1589.[15] Immediately, the number of burials rose in Plymouth, and then after a few days' interval in Dartmouth. Between 1589 and 1591 the infection spread to several towns and villages in the south and centre of the county, including Exeter. 'The diseases which the soldiers brought home with them', noted Richard Carew, 'did grow more grievous as they carried the same farther into the land' and proved in the end to be 'the very pestilence'.[16] In 1592 and 1593 plague attacked again, this time from the east and no doubt originally from London, causing epidemics in eastern parishes like Sidmouth and Colyton. In all, between 1589 and 1593, there is evidence of the disease in fifty-three of the eighty-nine parishes with surviving burial registers.

For the next fifty years its impact was again more localised, as it had been after 1547. Plague may have been responsible for high mortality in Dartmouth and Plymouth in 1602, one year before the great epidemic in London. It was almost certainly the culprit in Otterton and Axminster in 1611–12.[17] In 1625 it was present in some of the southern ports, in the towns of Exeter and Honiton, and later in some inland villages; and one or two parishes were visited in 1636 and 1637. But it was during the Civil War between 1642 and 1646 that demographic crises comparable to those of 1546–7 and 1589–93 again afflicted most of Devon. Once more there was a significant rise in the number of burials in the majority of the villages and towns for which registers survive. Although bubonic plague was not the only disease at work in these years, as we shall see, it probably caused the worst crises, especially in 1645 and 1646. These were the last epidemics of plague in Devon. There were fears that the disease would return in 1665, as it did to London and parts of eastern England; but for once this western county escaped.[18] The epidemics of 1645–6 brought to a close a century during which plague had been a constant threat and a recurrent fact for villages and towns up and down the county.

Plague was all the more threatening in that its movement was so haphazard. We can see some patterns in it. The disease most often began in ports, introduced by fleas from the rats, men or merchandise on infected ships; and it moved from there up estuaries and along navigable rivers like the Coly, Teign, Exe and Dart. In 1546–7, for example, there seem to have been distinct areas of infection, around Colyton, Exeter, Plymouth and Barnstaple, and in the South Hams around Dartmouth and Stoke-in-Teignhead. Many of the later epidemics began in Plymouth, Paignton, Exeter or Dartmouth. In 1636 plague was brought into the latter port by a ship from London, and in 1646 it was said to have entered Bideford in a cargo of wool from Spain.[19]

Land transport was rather less important in the long-distance movement of the disease, probably because the volume of merchandise carried on most highways was less than that on river and sea routes. Roads played a crucial role in the transmission of plague over short distances, of course. The fleas which brought plague to the village of Kenn in 1546 must have come in the goods or on the backs of men travelling along the main road from Exeter. It is likely too that the plague of 1579 reached central Devon by road from Cornwall, where in April 1578 the musters had been postponed because of infection.[20] But it was only the main western highway through Honiton which was regularly a channel for the movement of plague into the county. Villages away from this road and distant from the navigable waterways of Devon were much less vulnerable than closer ones.

Sometimes the unfortunate carriers of the disease to a village or a town can be identified from the registers. Thus in 1590 the first victim of plague in Totnes was 'Marjorie, the daughter of Mr Wyke of Dartmouth',[21] while in Dean Prior it may well have been 'Richard Budmere of Exon, found dead in the way'. When plague returned to Crediton in 1591, after an interval of six months, the first burials included a landlord who 'took the infection by lodging one of Torrington' and another Torrington man 'who died in the highway'. In the middle of the 1620s, soldiers gathering for, and then straggling back from the Cadiz expedition, carried disease across the county with them. They were among those buried in probable outbreaks of plague in such parishes as Buckfastleigh, Wolborough, Staverton and Plympton St Mary.[22] On occasion the movement of disease could be more deliberate than this. In September 1625 William Rowland brought a man 'infected with some dangerous and infectious disease' from Crediton to Okehampton, and then left him 'upon the ground without the door'.[23] Villagers' suspicions of strangers in plague-time were founded on hard experience.

Although some of the links in the chain of infection were often visible after the event, however, its shape was never predictable in detail. Much of the pattern described by any epidemic seemed wholly random. Plague did not gain a hold on every community in its passage along a river or road, but often left several villages free. In our first great epidemic, in 1546–7, for example, there is no indication of a rise in mortality in the north Devon parishes of Northam and Charles, although the neighbouring parishes of Braunton and North Molton were both heavily affected. In the same years the disease was carried south from Exeter to Kenn, but it does not seem to have moved up-river to Shobrooke. Many similar instances could be cited from later epidemics. Dependent as it was on the successful migration of infected fleas from rats or individuals to other vulnerable hosts, the spread of plague owed a good deal to chance.

Contemporaries thus had every reason to think that the local incidence of an epidemic was not solely determined by human action: it must be the result of some divine, if mysterious, providence. A report which reached Exeter about the introduction of plague into one south Devon village in 1589 nicely conveys the assumption of supernatural agency, and points only incidentally to the role of river transport. In Newton Ferrers plague began with

a vision of a corpse or a dead body carried to the parish there to be buried, and a great troop or company following the same. Sundry of that parish, seeing afar off such a company, and knowing none to be sick in the parish nor any bell to be rung, they also followed after. But when they came to the church they found nothing but only a hole newly made in the churchyard. Immediately the same vision went thence unto a ferry fast by, where the ferryman sat in his boat awaiting for passengers: and at the sight of the vision some of that company in the boat fell sick and some one of them fell half amazed and went to his own home and died. The sickness brought out of Portingal [Portugal] so reigned in that parish and all that sea coasts in South Hams that it continued long after.[24]

It was not only the geographical distribution of plague which was unpredictable. Epidemic mortality rates also fluctuated widely from parish to parish. In some places the number of burials scarcely doubled; in others it multiplied five or six times. The Crisis Mortality Ratios calculated for different parishes thus cover a wide range. The divergences which might occur in one epidemic are illustrated in Table 4.1, which shows the impact of the plague of 1546–7 only in those parishes worst affected, where the ratios were 3.0 or more.

Table 4.1 *Plague in Devon 1546–7*

Parish[1]	Plague year[2]	Burials in plague year a	Average annual burials[3] b	Crisis Mortality Ratio a/b
North Devon:				
Barnstaple	June–May '46–7	192	40.0	4.8
East Devon:				
Colyton	1546	37	12.0	3.1
Plymtree	July–June '46–7	14	4.4	3.2
Central Devon:				
Bovey Tracey	Oct.–Sept. '46–7	89	13.4	6.6
Bridford	1547	26	4.7	5.5
Exeter: St Petrock	1546	21	4.6	4.6
Kenn	1546	60	9.9	6.1
South Devon:				
Bere Ferrers	1547	31	6.3	4.9
Buckland Monachorum	Aug.–July '46–7	61	15.1	4.0
St Budeaux	1547	15	4.7	3.2
Stoke Fleming	1546	26	6.9	3.8
Stoke-in-Teignhead	May–Apr. '46–7	103	6.7	15.4
Ugborough	May–Apr. '46–7	104	19.6	5.3

Notes
[1] In this and later tables market towns are printed in italics.
[2] In this and later tables, the year is Jan.–Dec. unless otherwise stated. The twelve consecutive months of heaviest mortality have been taken.
[3] Usually for 1539–45, but 1548–56 in the cases of Bridford, Kenn and Ugborough.

At this early date in the life of parish registers it is more than usually hazardous to accept the ratio of epidemic to normal burials as a true index of mortality. Certainly, the severity of the plague in Barnstaple is understated due to a break in burial registration in the middle of the epidemic; and it is probably overestimated in Stoke-in-Teignhead, where burials seem to have been under-registered in the years before the plague. Nevertheless, the variations in mortality even among the most unfortunate parishes are clear, and they appear to bear no relation to the size of the community involved. The epidemic was as bad in the small parish of Bridford, south-west of Exeter, consisting mainly of scattered farms, as it was in the large village of Ugborough, north of Modbury in the South Hams; and it was less serious in the market town of Colyton in east Devon than in either of these. Similar apparently random differences are evident in Table 4.2, which includes the parishes worst affected by later epidemics of plague between 1568 and 1626. Again the greatest Crisis Mortality Ratios did not always occur in the largest settlements.[25] The variations would have been even more striking if it had been practicable to include all parishes in which there was evidence for the presence of bubonic plague.

The severity of plague in different communities in the same epidemic depended on a host of variables, few of which can be reconstructed from the historical evidence. It was no doubt related to the degree to which the community's rodent population was infected; it must have been associated with the extent of overcrowding in houses and farms; it was also influenced by changes in climate, villages infected in the summer often suffering more than those where plague arrived in autumn. The precise reasons for the differences in the ratios in Tables 4.1 and 4.2 cannot be specified at this distance in time. The tables do, however, point to two broad patterns in the geographical incidence of plague, besides its association with transport facilities which we noted earlier. First, it was concentrated in the southern half of the county, along the coast between Exeter and Plymouth and between Dartmoor and the sea; and secondly, it frequently occurred in towns.

The concentration of plague in the lowlands of south Devon was a feature of the disease which may well have been evident during the Black Death of the fourteenth century.[26] By the sixteenth century it was certainly marked. Two-thirds of the parishes in the tables were in this area of the county, which included the fertile area of mixed

Table 4.2 *Plague in Devon 1568–1626*

Parish		Plague year	Burials in plague year a	Average annual burials[1] b	Crisis Mortality Ratio a/b
North Devon:					
Coldridge		1591	36	6.6	5.5
Georgeham		1571	27	8.0	3.4
Hatherleigh		1577	49	14.0	3.5
Holsworthy		Aug.–July 1590–1	60	13.1	4.6
Littleham		1591	11	2.2	5.0
Molland		1590	19	6.1	3.1
Shirwell		1607	23	6.2	3.7
East Devon:					
Feniton		1591	10	3.3	3.0
Offwell		1591	18	3.4	5.3
Ottery St Mary		1604	138	38.4	3.6
Tiverton		1591	550	94.3	5.8
Widworthy		1591	43	4.3	10.0
Yarcombe		1625	35	10.1	3.5
Central Devon:					
Bovey Tracey		Apr.–Mar. 1592–3	90	23.9	3.8
Bridford	1	1570	22	4.5	4.9
	2	1591	26	5.1	5.1
Crediton[2]	1	1571	543	51.3	10.6
	2	Aug.–July 1591–2	419+	57.0	7.4
Dunchideock		1591	14	2.7	5.2
Exeter: St Mary	1	1570	171	21.5	8.0
Major[3]	2	Aug.–July 1590–1	142	31.5	4.5
	3	1625	214	34.1	6.3
Ideford		1627	15	3.6	4.2
Shillingford		1591	5	1.6	3.1
South Tawton		1579	73	17.8	4.1
Spreyton		1579	22	4.3	5.1
Whitestone		1625	32	6.6	4.8
South Devon:					
Ashburton		Aug.–July 1625–6	388	47.0	8.3
Bere Ferrers		1589	46	11.5	4.0
Brixham		July–June 1580–1	101	12.7	8.0
Dean Prior		1590	56	6.0	9.3
Denbury		June–May 1589–90	21	4.6	4.6
Ilsington		1626	43	13.6	3.2
Paignton		1568	156	31.5	5.0
Plymouth	1	July–June 1589–90	473	149.0	3.2
	2	1626	1,488	260.5	5.7
Plympton St Mary		Oct.–Sept. 1625–6	150	33.1	4.5
Plymstock	1	1591	89	18.8	4.7
	2	1626	266	32.4	8.2
St Budeaux		1589	20	5.6	3.6
Stoke-in-Teignhead		June–May 1590–1	104	13.7	7.6
Totnes		June–May 1590–1	285	52.7	5.4
Ugborough		July–June 1589–90	97	19.7	4.9
Widecombe-in-the-Moor		June–May 1590–1	68	17.8	3.8

Notes

[1] As far as possible these annual averages and those employed in later tables are for the decade preceding the epidemic; where gaps or other epidemics make this calculation impracticable, other neighbouring years have been used.

[2] There are gaps in the Crediton register for 1591, and the ratio is therefore an underestimate.

[3] One Exeter parish only has been taken for illustration; for others, see Chapter 5 below.

farming along the edge of Torbay and in the South Hams, as well as clothing towns like Totnes. Totnes itself, the port of Plymouth, the small market town of Bovey Tracey on the Teign, and the hamlet of Dean Prior on the southern edge of Dartmoor were some of the varied range of parishes worst affected by bubonic plague.

That this spatial pattern is not simply an optical illusion, caused by a bias in our sample of parish registers, is shown by the very different incidence of the demographic crisis of the later 1590s. This harvest crisis proved more serious than those which afflicted some Devon parishes in 1586–7 and 1622–3, although mortality rates rarely jumped to the high levels common during epidemics of plague. Crisis Mortality Ratios of at least 3.0 were registered in seventeen parishes in at least one year between 1596 and 1599; but in only one parish, Oakford, did the ratio reach 5.0.[27] The greatest contrast between these subsistence crises and plague, however, was one of geography. Almost all the parishes affected in 1596–9 were in the northern half of the county, especially in upland areas: Rose Ash, Witheridge, Oakford and Clayhanger in the foothills of Exmoor, Ilsington and South Tawton on the edge of Dartmoor, and a group of parishes stretching across the Culm Measures from Holsworthy to Crediton. The contrast between the two areas can be seen clearly in Figure 4.1, which shows parishes where the number of burials doubled, either in the later 1590s or during the plague epidemic of 1589–93.

There were several differences between the two areas of Devon which help to explain their separate experience of epidemics. Climate was one factor. The warmth of the coastal belt between Exeter and Plymouth favoured the breeding of fleas and therefore plague, while the heavier rainfall in the rest of the county probably made any harvest failure worse in the north.[28] There was also more corn grown in the area south-west of Exeter and in the South Hams than elsewhere, and hence more corn stored for use in years of scarcity. Transport facilities were equally important. Easy communication by water with other parts of the country and with London and the Continent brought grain supplies as well as plague quickly to the south; highland areas were more isolated from both.

Finally, there were important social differences between the two parts of the county. The early Tudor subsidies show that the south was richer than the north, which helps to account for the distribution of subsistence crises; but it was also more densely populated, which has implications for the contrasting distribution of plague. If we

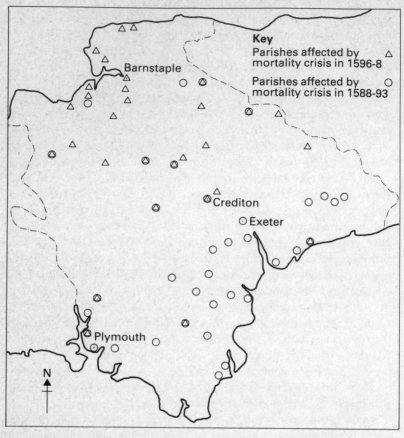

Figure 4.1 Mortality crises in Devon 1588–93 and 1596–8

measure wealth by the amount of tax paid per square mile, the region between Exeter and the Teign valley emerges as the most prosperous part of the county, 'the fruitfullest part of all Devonshire', as Leland said; while the pastoral highlands and northern Devon were as impoverished as the upland areas of northern England, which also suffered severely from harvest crises.[29] Rural poverty and dearth were plainly associated; rural poverty and plague apparently were not. 'Poverty' needs careful definition here, however, and the amount of tax paid per square mile may not be the most illuminating way of measuring it. We shall see that the poor suffered more from plague than the rich in the towns considered in the next chapters. It is highly unlikely that this was not also the case in smaller communities. There must have been large populations of relatively poor labourers and artisans in the villages and market towns of southern Devon, alongside the farmers, clothiers and merchants whose names swell the subsidy rolls. Until we know more about the social structure of individual Devonshire villages it would be dangerous to generalise about correlations between poverty and disease over a whole county. What we can say is that rural communities with the resources of a large and prosperous tax-paying class were less likely than others to suffer the more extreme consequences of bad harvests.

They were not less likely to find plague in their midst, however; rather, in Devon they were unusually vulnerable to it. The reason for this was not their wealth, but the density of their populations, both human and (in consequence) rodent. The Tudor subsidies suggest that the mixed-farming region of southern Devon was much more populous than other parts of the county;[30] and bubonic plague depended more on crowds than did a disease such as dysentery which was aggravated by malnutrition. Once again it is necessary to enter a qualification. Population density and plague epidemics are not invariably or necessarily related: the disease can spread in thinly populated settlements. But in its main centres of infection and in major epidemics it feeds on concentrations of rodents and men. It seems likely therefore that the geographical concentration of plague was determined by a combination of factors, climate, communications and population density being the most important.

Communications and density of population obviously shaped the second regularity to be observed in Tables 4.1 and 4.2: the frequency with which plague affected towns and market towns (shown in italics in the tables).[31] Of the thirty-eight parishes in Table 4.2, only five are represented by more than one epidemic. Three of them were populous urban parishes, Crediton, Plymouth and part of Exeter, while Plymstock was close enough to Plymouth to share its fate. Bridford is the odd man out, a thinly populated hill parish of scattered farmsteads, which was decimated in 1570 and 1591 as well as in 1546–7. But this parish was only nine miles south-west of Exeter, within a day's journey, and on each occasion it may have been a refuge for Exeter citizens fleeing from the plague.[32] In general it was only in the largest centres, where contact with potential sources of infection was greatest, that a devastating epidemic of plague, removing as much as 10 per cent of the total population, was likely to occur more than once in sixty years. These 'thoroughfare' towns, as one contemporary remarked, were 'more subject to be infected than other places'.[33]

Table 4.3 *Devonshire parishes most often affected by mortality crises 1540–1640*

Parish	Year register begins	Crisis years		
Barnstaple	1538	1546–7,	1597,	1622–3
Bridford	1538	1546–7,	1570,	1591
Crediton	1559	1571,	1591–2,	1596–7
Colyton	1538	1546–7,	1558,	1622–3
Exeter: St Mary Major	1561	1570,	1590–1,	1625
Plymouth	1580	1589–90,	1602,	1626
St Budeaux	1538	1546–7,	1586,	1589
Stoke Fleming	1538	1546–7,	1557,	1565

If we extend our view to include all mortality crises, not simply those caused by plague, this impression of urban vulnerability to demographic disaster is strengthened. Table 4.3 lists the parishes with Crisis Mortality Ratios of at least 3.0 on more than two occasions in the century after 1540. Five of the eight were towns or market towns, and the others were geographically close to them. The example of Bridford again reminds us that there are exceptions to all epidemiological generalisations. Plague could cause extreme mortality in a parish like this without a compact village settlement, as it did again in Dean Prior in 1590. It could also sweep through upland parishes like Spreyton and South Tawton. Moreover, once plague was brought to a small village, as it was to Widworthy in 1591, it might have as serious an effect on mortality as in a town like Crediton. Nevertheless we can see that the incidence of these epidemics agrees broadly with the generalisation that 'the probability that infection will reach a community increases with its size . . . and with its proximity to lines of transit'.[34]

It is in the towns of Devon, therefore, that we can best observe the successive blows which epidemic disease might deliver to individual communities. Exeter, the county town, will be examined in the next chapter, but it is worth looking briefly here at three smaller towns, in different parts of the county. The major crises in Barnstaple, Crediton and Plymouth appear clearly in Figure 4.2, which shows annual fluctuations in burials and baptisms where they can be obtained from sometimes imperfect registers.[35]

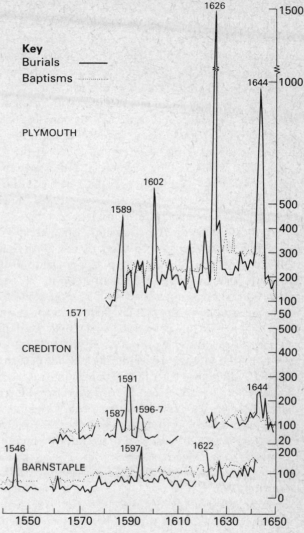

Figure 4.2 Burials and baptisms in three Devon towns 1540–1650

As we might expect from its situation, the northern port of
Barnstaple stands in sharp contrast to the other two towns. There
were subsistence crises in 1597 and 1622–3, but only one serious
outbreak of plague before the Civil War, in 1546. Plague seems to

have entered the port on several occasions after that, despite the fact that the corporation regularly 'took great pains and travail to preserve the town from infection' by cutting off contact with other infected places. Concentrations of burials in the register suggest that there were probably cases in 1563, 1580, 1604–5 and 1628. But these did not spark off major epidemics. As one observer succinctly reported in November 1604, 'the plague entered into this town; few died'.[36] For most of the period there was consequently little to stop the population from growing naturally, and there were 2,500 more baptisms than burials between 1539 and 1642. The rising level of baptisms suggests indeed that the population grew from around 2,000 in the 1540s to roughly 4,000 in the 1630s.[37] The plague of 1546–7 may thus have removed more than 10 per cent of the inhabitants,[38] and the harvest crises of 1597 and 1622–3 rather less.

The inhabitants of Crediton were much less fortunate. A textile and market town midway between the two contrasting areas of Devon, it was vulnerable both to the harvest crises of the north and to the plagues of the south. It was growing in size, its population rising from about 2,000 in the 1560s to slightly less than 4,000 in the 1630s, but this expansion was a consequence of immigration not of natural growth. There were rather more burials than baptisms in the years when both were recorded between 1564 and 1649, and epidemics were particularly severe. The plagues of 1571 and 1591–2 were two of the worst in any Devonshire parish in the period, perhaps killing nearly a quarter and about a fifth of the population respectively. In the subsistence crises of 1587–8 and 1596–7 there were increases in mortality which appear minor only by comparison. Crediton suffered four serious mortalities in a generation, and there may have been others in the years when burials were only fitfully entered in the register. Crediton's experience was summed up, not by the confident municipal action of Barnstaple, but by the parish's regular purchase of shrouds for the poor.[39]

Unlike Crediton, Plymouth did not feel the full weight of harvest crises, as Figure 4.2 shows, since it could be well provisioned by sea. 'The life of the city is navigation', noted Cosimo de Medici on his visit in 1669, 'and hence . . . the town is exceedingly well supplied.' The port was 'sufficiently relieved' in the dearth of 1586, and in 1597 corn was imported from Danzig.[40] Epidemic diseases also followed one another in quick succession into the harbour, however. Although the population appears to have doubled in half a century, rising to about 9,000 in the 1630s, the number of burials greatly exceeded the number of baptisms between 1582 and 1650. Even more than Crediton, Plymouth depended on immigration for its rapid growth, thanks to a series of epidemics which gave the port its reputation as the most unhealthy spot in the county.

Two of them occurred shortly before the parish register begins, in 1570 and 1581.[41] In 1588 and 1589 there were two more: the first may have been caused by some form of food poisoning beginning in the fleet gathering against the Armada; the second, which killed roughly 10 per cent of the population, was probably bubonic plague brought by the ships returning from Portugal.[42] In 1602 an infection again started in the fleet, on the *Warspite*, the *Garlande* and the *Mary Rose*, and then spread to the town, where 10 per cent of the population died; it may not have been bubonic plague, since burials were numerous throughout the year, February and July being the worst months. Burials rose again in the summers of 1616 and 1622, and in the latter year three of those buried came from foreign ships. The greatest crisis of all occurred between 1625 and 1627. There were several waves of infection and probably more than one disease. The first began in September 1625, when there were Londoners among the casualties who may have brought bubonic plague. In the following December and January mortality rates received a further boost thanks to the arrival of a fleet full of sick soldiers returning from Cadiz. After a lull in February the number of burials rose once more, to reach its height in the summer of 1626 when bubonic plague was reported to be in the town. Finally, there was another epidemic at the end of 1627 on the return of English forces from the Ile de Ré.[43] In 1626 alone, 1,488 people were buried in Plymouth, perhaps one-sixth of the total population. Small wonder that the corporation, when considering the problems caused by rapid population increase, should think that in Plymouth 'the air is often infected, men's bodies corrupted, divers dangerous and infectious diseases bred, and the lives and welfare of a multitude of his Majesty's subjects . . . endangered'.[44]

The epidemic history of different towns as of different villages might thus vary considerably in the century before 1640. We may note that in each of them it was plague which caused the worst of the many short-term crises: in Barnstaple in 1546–7, in Crediton in 1571 and in Plymouth in 1626. But Plymouth was wholly exceptional because its role as a naval base attracted epidemic disease, while Barnstaple was unusually fortunate. In the 1640s, however, earlier distinctions between different communities were obscured by the last great mortality crises in Devon's history. In 1643 and 1644 no fewer than 514 people were buried in Crediton, perhaps one-eighth of the population; in Barnstaple, although burials were not registered, there was a savage epidemic at the same time;[45] while in Plymouth as many as 2,658 people were buried in the three years 1643–5, at least a quarter of the inhabitants. Nor were towns the only communities to suffer in these years. Villages in every corner of Devon, from Braunton in the north to Ugborough in the south and Widworthy in the east, were badly affected at some time between 1641 and 1646.[46] The high mortalities of the 1640s erased the geographical patterns established in earlier epidemics.

They did so because epidemic disease was no longer dependent on the normal movement of traffic by river and road for its dispersal, as in previous outbreaks of plague, or on the nature of the local economy, as with harvest crises; it marched across the county with the armies of the Civil War. No less than on the Continent, military activity aggravated disease, raised death rates and brought crisis to many parts of England in the 1640s.[47] The great siege of Plymouth was simply the most spectacular case, creating famine conditions and exceptional mortality in the town itself and filling the burial registers of neighbouring parishes with the names of soldiers and civilians.[48] More than one disease was carried on the coat-tails of Royalist or Parliamentarian troops. In South Molton there were 'many contagious sicknesses and diseases'. In Culmstock a widow who was buried as a precaution 'in her own garden not in the churchyard' died of 'contagion or plague'. In Barnstaple the epidemic was described noncommittally as 'the contagion' and in Hemyock as the 'infectious disease'.[49] The classic diseases of armies and sieges, typhus and dysentery, were undoubtedly at work in 1642 and 1643, as in Exeter during the siege of the latter year. Bubonic plague also made its contribution, perhaps in a few parishes such as Ashburton in 1643, more certainly in many of the larger concentrations of population in the county in 1646, when it produced some of the worst mortalities. In Colyton and Bideford in that year, for example, Crisis Mortality Ratios of more than 6.0 were recorded.[50] Although it is often impossible to diagnose the causes of these multiple crises, they included the last visitations of plague in Devon, and they served to obscure the patterns of incidence evident in earlier epidemics. They confirmed for contemporaries the universality of the threat posed by pestilence.

That threat had taken various forms in Devon in the century between the 1540s and the 1640s, all of them associated with one of 'God's Three Arrows: Plague, Famine, Sword'.[51] We must now ask which of these series of crises was the most serious. The gradual increase in the number of registers surviving over time gives the impression that the later epidemics affected a larger area than the earlier, but it is possible partially to correct this distortion by looking only at the thirty-three registers which cover the whole period from the 1540s onwards.[52]

Although these registers are not a random sample, they suggest that the most serious epidemic after 1538 was the first outbreak of plague in 1546–7. It caused a three-fold increase in burials in twelve of the thirty-three parishes; no later epidemic was so devastating. The plague beginning in 1589 was its closest competitor, having a similar effect in nine of these parishes, while the various epidemics of the early 1640s were as severe as this in seven of them. If we lower our threshold and consider the parishes where burials doubled in epidemic years, the demographic crises associated with harvest failure and the Civil War appear more significant; but the plague of the 1540s still outdistances them all. There were seventeen out of the thirty-three thus affected in the 1640s, twelve between 1596 and 1599, thirteen in the plague beginning in 1589, but twenty in the epidemic of 1546–7. The earliest visitation of plague which we can examine in detail had a heavier impact over a wider area of Devon than any later epidemic.

Bubonic plague seems thus to have had a diminishing hold on the county over the period. There was a major wave of infection between 1589 and 1593, but in general after 1547 plague was a recurrent phenomenon only in the larger centres of population and in villages close to them. Before drawing any firm conclusions, however, we should examine another county to see whether similar patterns can be observed there.

(ii) Essex

It turns out that there are contrasts as well as points of similarity between epidemics in Devon and Essex. Plague was no less common in Essex than in the West, but its outbreaks were rather less severe and their timing was different. There was no great series of crises in the 1640s, because Essex was much less of a Civil War battlefield than Devon. On the other hand, Essex did not escape the last visitation of plague in 1665–6, and the plague epidemics of the early seventeenth century were worse than those of the later sixteenth. The imprint left by plague on different counties, as well as on different towns, was never identical.

There was a greater correspondence in the timing of other epidemic diseases in the two counties. The effects of the sweating sickness are apparent in seven of the thirty-two Essex parishes with register entries for July 1551, while the fevers of 1557–9 hit many parts of the county and proved to be more fatal than in Devon. In thirteen parishes the number of burials reached at least three times the average in twelve months, and this was undoubtedly the greatest demographic crisis in the county during our period. Harvest crises, however, were less serious than in the West, though they occurred at the same time. Mortality rose in a handful of parishes after the harvest of 1586, and again in several parishes across the county, from Stanford Rivers to Colchester in the early 1620s; but it was only in the years immediately after 1596 that Crisis Mortality Ratios of 3.0 were common. Burials reached this height in at least one year between 1596 and 1599 in seven parishes in the north and west. They included some of the county's poorest villages, which had been described in 1595 as 'pasture towns and little or no tilling used by them, the occasion whereof at this present dearth of grain hath caused a great and lamentable cry of the poor'.[53]

For the inhabitants of all parts of Essex, however, outbreaks of plague were more frequent causes of suffering. The probate evidence indicates that there may have been severe epidemics in 1504 and 1518, when there was plague in London.[54] The early parish registers suggest that there was plague in at least four parishes in 1539–40. Between 1543 and 1546 plague again spread into the county from London and although not so serious as the slightly later epidemic in Devon, it caused four times the usual number of burials in one Colchester parish. There were minor epidemics of plague in 1563 in several villages and towns, including Epping, Chelmsford, Maldon[55] and Romford, where the first victims included two orphans from London who were being nursed in the town. And in the century after 1565 the disease was rarely absent from the county for more than a decade. There were epidemics presenting all the signs of bubonic plague in one or more Essex villages in 1570–1, 1577–80, 1582–5,

1593–4, 1603–10, 1625, 1631 and 1637–40, as well as in the final outbreak of 1665–6.[56]

The geographical diffusion of plague was no more uniform than in Devon. The village of Terling, for example, suffered three serious epidemics during the period, while the neighbouring parishes of Faulkesbourne and Fairsted had none. But the chief routes of infection can be reconstructed. Several visited parishes lay near the coast from Clacton to Maldon and may have received plague from London or the Continent by sea. Others in the north were probably infected from Cambridgeshire and Suffolk. There was an epidemic in Great Chesterford in 1631, soon after the inhabitants complained of the arrival of refugees from the plague in Cambridge.[57] Above all, plague was often carried from London to villages which lay close to the main Essex highway from the metropolis to Colchester and Harwich.

Contemporaries were well aware of the dangers of contact with London. When a Colchester man took lodgings in an inn in Westminster in 1603, for example, 'for fear of the sickness he durst not go to any bed but sat up by the fireside ... all night all alone without any company'.[58] Such individual self-help could not protect the whole county, however. The burgesses of Maldon cited 'daily experience' to show that carters trading with the capital brought plague. In 1574 the disease was taken to Chipping Ongar by a London surgeon, and four years later the queen's royal progress probably took it to Colchester and then to Norwich.[59] Lesser culprits were also identified. 'A notable harlot' brought plague to Great Coggeshall in 1578. In 1626 'a wretched fellow' from Colchester lodged an infected family in 'a little base cottage' he owned in the Suffolk village of Polstead, 'whereby it pleased God that the infection did spread itself'. In 1638 a labourer allegedly spread plague from one village to another while moving to harvest work, and was then driven from parish to parish by terrified villagers. Three years later a vagrant who had been employed to cart the dead in an infected parish caused a similar scare.[60]

As in Devon, contacts like these help to explain the apparently random selection of parishes attacked by plague. Those which suffered the worst mortalities (ratios of 3.0 or more) are shown in Table 4.4 for the period between 1570 and 1610 and in Table 4.5 for the epidemics of 1625–6 and 1637–40. Many more places were infected than appear in the tables, of course. The number of parishes would more than double if those with Crisis Mortality Ratios of 2.0 were included. Chelmsford, for example, suffered two such epidemics of plague, in 1578–9 and 1603–4, and there were two in Romford, in 1571 and 1603. Plague could also have striking effects without raising the number of deaths as much as that. In Heydon the churchwardens spent large sums on the care of the sick in 1603, although there were hardly more burials than usual.[61] Selective as they are, however, the tables suggest that the epidemics of the early seventeenth century spread further than those of the later sixteenth; and an examination of all the extant registers confirms this. The plagues beginning in 1603, 1625 and 1637, which had their origins in London, affected parishes over most of the county. That of 1625–6 moved with great rapidity through the heart of Essex; the epidemic of 1637–40 moved more slowly and was particularly widespread. Parishes recording Crisis Mortality Ratios of 2.0 or more in the outbreaks of the 1620s and 1630s are shown in Figure 4.3.

We can see the increasing diffusion of plague clearly if we look

Table 4.4 *Plague in Essex 1570–1610*

Parish	Plague year		Burials in plague year	Crisis Mortality Ratio
Bradwell-on-Sea	1) July–June 1584–5		45	3.0
		2) July–June 1605–6	47	3.3
Colchester:				
St Botolph		1603	77	3.0
		1604	82	3.2
St Nicholas		1603	73	3.5
Cold Norton	1594		15	3.0
Dunton		1603	14	5.4
Epping		May–Apr. 1603–4	56	4.5
Gt Chesterford	1592		32	3.9
Gt Clacton	July–June 1570–1		42	3.0
Gt Coggeshall	1578		94	3.8
Gt Easton	1571		20	3.4
Helion Bumpstead	1571		13	3.3
Maldon[1]		Sept.–Aug. 1603–4	170	3.3
N. Fambridge		1606	14	3.0
N. Weald Bassett	1577		23	3.8
Purleigh		1606	43	4.1
Terling	1) Sept.–Aug. 1584–5		25	3.0
		2) June–May 1603–4	43	3.6
Tillingham	1) Aug.–July 1592–3		43	3.2
		2) 1606	60	3.7

Note
[1] Aggregate for all three parishes.

Table 4.5 *Plague in Essex 1625–6 and 1638–9*

Parish	Plague year		Burials in plague year	Crisis Mortality Ratio
	1625–6	1638–9		
Blackmore		1638	20	4.0
Boreham		Aug.–July 1638–9	44	3.0
Chelmsford	June–May 1625–6		199	3.0
Childerditch	1625		16	3.8
Colchester:				
St Botolph	1625		101	3.0
	1626		156	4.7
St Runwald	1626		18	4.6
St Peter	1626		75	5.2
Dunton	1626		12	4.0
E. Hanningfield		1639	22	3.7
Gestingthorpe		1639	16	5.2
Gosfield		1638	22	3.2
Gt Sampford		1639	25	3.1
Lamarsh	1) 1625	2) 1639	13	3.3
Lt Chesterford	1625		18	6.4
Marks Tey		Apr.–May 1638–9	15	4.5
Pentlow		1638	13	3.5
Terling	1625		59	3.4
Thaxted		1638	71	3.0

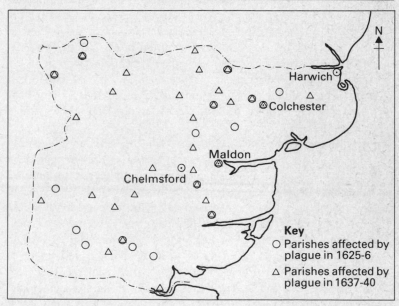

Figure 4.3 Plague epidemics in Essex 1625–6 and 1637–40

only at those parishes whose registers are complete for the whole period from 1565 to 1640. There were eighty-two of these, and many more of them were affected by the later epidemics of the period than by the earlier. Mortality Ratios reached 2.0 or more in twenty-seven parishes in the plague beginning in 1637, in nineteen in that of 1625–6 and in sixteen in the epidemic of 1603–10. No earlier outbreak had the same effect in more than eight parishes. In Essex therefore, unlike Devon, the plagues of the early seventeenth century were more virulent than those of the later sixteenth.

This was not the only divergence between the two counties. Tables 4.4 and 4.5 support our earlier observation that the level of mortality bore little relation to the size of the community involved; but they do not convey as great an impression of urban vulnerability as the equivalent data from Devon. This is probably a result simply of the level of mortality taken as a qualification for inclusion in the tables, however. If places where the number of burials doubled had been added, market towns and ports like Romford, Harwich and Burnham-on-Crouch would have entered the tables, and epidemics in Maldon and Chelmsford have been listed more often. The major contrast between the two counties, which creates this distortion, is the fact that epidemics of plague were less severe in Essex than they were in Devon. Very few Crisis Mortality Ratios of 4.0 or more have been discovered in the eastern county; they were more common in the South-West. At the same time, major epidemics of plague appear to have affected a larger proportion of parishes in the West than in the East: two-thirds of the parishes with surviving registers in Devon in 1546–7 and two-fifths in 1589–93; only a third in Essex in the later 1630s and a quarter in 1625–6.

These contrasts raise more questions than they answer. We cannot even be sure that they were as great in reality as they appear from the available evidence, although there seems no reason to suppose that the surviving Essex registers come from parishes less prone to plague than those without registers, or that the reverse was the case in Devon. As far as the overall difference in severity is concerned, climate may help to account for that: the greater humidity of Devon, as compared with Essex, may have encouraged the development of the plague flea and exacerbated epidemics there.[62] The divergence in the development of plague over time is more difficult to elucidate, partly because we know so little about the pre-parish-register era. It may be that the epidemics of the very early sixteenth century in Essex

– those which had such a marked effect on probate records in 1504 and 1518 – were much worse than any which followed; and that there was then a decline in the impact of plague, just as there was in Devon slightly later, after 1547. The fact remains, however, that in Essex the epidemics of Elizabeth's reign were milder than those of the early Stuart period, while the reverse was true in Devon.

Social and economic developments may have had something to do with the increasing severity of plague in Essex after 1600. The growth of London and the consequent increase in road traffic opened up more and more of the county to metropolitan influence. The growth of the textile industry, and especially of the new draperies, may have been equally important.[63] Besides increasing contact with London, and perhaps facilitating the movement of plague-infected fleas in bales of wool and cloth,[64] it produced relatively densely populated villages and towns where plague, once introduced, might quickly take root. It is notable also that plague epidemics grew worse at a time when there was depression in the woollen industry of the county and a related increase in poverty in its towns. In 1625 'many of the parishes' of Essex were 'extraordinarily taxed for the relief of the poor . . . as well of such as are infected with the plague as of such as want means of work'.[65] Again, between 1637 and 1639, there was unemployment in Bocking, Coggeshall and Colchester, and 'poor folks' in Chelmsford complained about 'the extreme hardness of these times'. In some of the clothing towns plague lingered on into the early 1640s, as in Witham where 140 families were said to be 'in great want and likely to perish' in 1641.[66] Industrial occupations, poverty and disease seemed often to go hand in hand.

Often, but not always. The example of Terling is there, like that of Bridford in Devon, to remind us that there was no invariable connection between plague and urban or industrial centres.[67] Neither can a divergent economic history explain the contrast between our two counties, since there was industrial growth and early Stuart depression in Devon without epidemic consequences as grave as those in Essex.[68] Nevertheless, dense communities of poor industrial workers provided an unusually favourable environment for plague, wherever they occurred. Their importance in Essex was clearly demonstrated in the last visitation of plague in 1665–6.

The final plague epidemic to strike Essex was in some ways unlike those which had preceded it. It did not have the wide geographical spread of epidemics earlier in the century; it was much more heavily concentrated in towns and affected few villages seriously; and yet in some towns the casualties were far more numerous than in any previous outbreak. The burial registers of more than 100 Essex parishes with entries for the years 1665–6 have been examined, and only eight of them reveal epidemics in which the number of burials was twice the average.[69] That compares with twenty-seven in 1637–40 and eighteen in 1625–6. Even if we add the towns where we know mortality was severe but where there are gaps in the parish registers – Braintree, Colchester, Harwich and possibly Coggeshall – we reach a total of only twelve communities seriously affected in 1665–6. Mortality was certainly low in rural Essex, only three parishes producing Crisis Mortality Ratios of more that 3.0: Great Oakley near Harwich, Widford near Chelmsford, and East Tilbury on the Thames. Yet high mortality is not the whole story. There are references to plague or the infection in at least nineteen other parishes, where the number of burials did not reach twice the norm, and in some of them the disease seems to have been widespread. In Hornchurch, for example, more than £60 was spent on the visited poor in 1665–6, although the number of burials increased by only 30 per cent. Elsewhere too, as in Chelmsford and Horndon, the parish registers record no major increase in the numbers dying, although the quarter sessions records show that many were sick and needed public support.[70] High morbidity seems to have been more common than high mortality, and it is unfortunate that it is only in the last epidemic of the period that there are ample references to it. On that occasion, as perhaps earlier, it was sickness rather than death which marked the progress of plague in much of rural Essex.

In some of the larger towns, however, the plague of 1665–6 was far more deadly. Although burials were only fitfully recorded in the register, its 'sad' impact in Coggeshall was noted by Ralph Josselin, parson of Earls Colne, in his diary. So also was news of plague casualties in Harwich, where fragmentary notes in the register suggest that a quarter of the population may have perished.[71] A similar mortality rate is likely in Bocking, where 423 people died of plague in the year beginning April 1666. As early as May one inhabitant reported the town 'so wholly infected that we know not who are clear'.[72] The death rate was even greater in neighbouring Braintree. A memorial list commemorating those visited in 1665 and 1666 recorded 665 deaths, more than a third and perhaps as much as 40 per cent of the whole population. According to this source there were only 284 households in the town and 221 of them were infected, a massive proportion even allowing for omissions.[73] The great city of Colchester suffered most of all. Several different records of weekly mortality make it clear that more than 5,000 people died in the sixteen months between August 1665 and December 1666, all but 500 of the casualties being ascribed to plague. The population of the town is unlikely to have been over 12,000 and may have been as low as 10,000 before the epidemic. This disaster may have killed half of the inhabitants, and it certainly killed more than 40 per cent of them – the highest death rate so far discovered in any major urban centre in the period.[74] It was for these towns and not for the county as a whole that the epidemic of 1665–6 was, in Josselin's words, 'the greatest plague in England since that in Edward the Third's time' – since the Black Death.[75]

The wholly exceptional mortalities in Braintree and Colchester, contrasted as they were with the much milder impact of the disease elsewhere in the county (and indeed in the country as a whole in these years), can be given no precise or adequate explanation. They were not simply a function of the size of the community involved: Chelmsford and Saffron Walden, where there were a few cases of plague but apparently no major epidemic, had populations larger than those of Braintree and Bocking. There may, however, have been significant differences in the demographic and social structures of these towns, about which we as yet know all too little. The growing textile towns of northern Essex, which included Colchester, Braintree and Bocking, may have had relatively young populations living in overcrowded and insanitary conditions; they certainly had large numbers of poor workers, spinning and weaving, whose standard of living could only deteriorate when plague disrupted employment. By 1670 these towns had some of the highest proportions of poor people in the kingdom. In Colchester 52.8 per cent of all householders were exempted from the hearth tax of that year, in Braintree 66.4 per cent, in Bocking no less than 80.9 per cent.[76] Once the disease arrived in these communities, it is perhaps not surprising that its effects were so spectacular.

The epidemic of 1665–6 thus underlined what was sometimes evident earlier in Essex, and often in Devon: the position of towns as foci of infection from which disease threatened the countryside. The consequence for villagers was not a confident appreciation of their favourable position, but rather mounting anxiety when urban mortality

rose, suspicion of all strangers, and a heightening of established antagonisms between town and country. Several parishes appointed
watchmen, and one or two issued them with powder and shot, the
better to keep outsiders away.[77] In Earls Colne the rising tension is
reflected month after month in Josselin's diary, as the villagers waited
for plague to come marching in from Colchester. 'Now Colchester is
infected, and when will Colne lay it to heart?' Josselin asked on 13
August 1665. A week later he was disturbed to see that Colchester
men were flying into 'the country for dwellings', and on 27 August
he noted that a boy recently come from the city had died. By 22
October three people had plague sores at one end of the village, and
there was fever and a possibility of plague in several families over the
next six months. Only five deaths were attributed to plague in the
parish register and it is certain that no serious epidemic developed.
But Josselin was amazed that 'Colne, sinful Colne' was spared. In
December 1666 the additional threat of invasion from France led him
to summarise his and the county's recent experience: 'One wave after
another is this life's portion.'[78]

The case studies in this chapter will have served their purpose if they
have made Josselin's perplexity and insecurity intelligible. For the
historian, as for contemporaries, the predominant impression left by
the local impact of plague is one of often inexplicable randomness.
The number of variables involved in the incidence of an epidemic
over a whole county was so large that we cannot in the end point to
one factor – climate or communications, distribution of wealth or
population or industry – and say that that explains why one place
suffered more than another, or why one epidemic was more or less
serious than the last. We have seen some blurred patterns but also
observed that there are exceptions to all of them. Nevertheless, despite
the diversity within and between them, two modest conclusions can
be drawn from the epidemic histories of Devon and Essex.

First, it is clear that within any single parish bubonic plague could
cause greater mortality in a shorter space of time than any other
epidemic disease. The epidemics of 1597 might strike more parishes
than some of the minor outbreaks of plague, but their effect on the
number of burials was comparatively uniform. The Crisis Mortality
Ratios were rarely greater than 4.0 in Devon or 3.5 in Essex. Only
the influenza epidemic of 1557–9 approached in some Essex parishes

the violence of the worst epidemics of plague, and that was a single unique occurrence.

Secondly, plague was sufficiently common for most communities, villages as well as towns, to expect one epidemic in the course of a century and count themselves fortunate if they had no more. Table 4.6 summarises the experience of those parishes whose registers cover the greater part of the century from 1565 to 1666.[79] If we had been able to extend our analysis back to 1545 for all the seventy-five parishes in Devon, the number with more than one serious outbreak of plague would certainly have been much larger. It is also unfortunate that the Devon registers, unlike those of Essex, rarely provide evidence in the form of references to 'the plague', 'the sickness' or 'the infection', which would help us to identify more minor outbreaks. Nevertheless, it is evident that there was at least one serious epidemic of plague in half the parishes, and there were two or more in nearly a quarter; while less than one in eight of them had no experience of plague or some other killing epidemic disease between 1565 and 1666.[80] Ralph Josselin's apprehension about the threat to Earls Colne in 1666, though unrealised in the event, was a faithful reflection of rural experience over the previous century.

Table 4.6 *Plague in Essex and Devon parishes 1565–1666*

Number of parishes in which:	Devon	Essex
Burials doubled in one plague	33	29
Burials doubled in more than one plague	10	33
Other evidence for the presence of plague[1]	7	30
No evidence of plague, but at least one other serious mortality crisis[2]	15	6
No evidence of plague or mortality crisis	10	14
Total parishes	75	112

Notes

[1] References to 'pl' etc. in the register, or ratios rather less than 2.0 when there was plague elsewhere.

[2] Crisis Mortality Ratio of 2.0 or more in a non-plague year.

The risks were greater and more real, however, in the towns. Although the tables in this chapter suggest that there was no correlation between the size of the community affected and the severity of an epidemic of plague within it, the likelihood of infection was much greater in the larger centres of population. The parishes in Table 4.6 include twenty-nine of the seventy-two market towns in Devon and

Essex: only six of them witnessed no major epidemic of plague in the century, and to judge by the parish registers there were cases of plague in all of them on more than one occasion. Plague was thus an inevitable hazard in urban centres, even in Essex, whose towns, with the exception of Colchester, were smaller than those of Devon. Maldon and Harwich, tiny ports by comparison with Plymouth, were each visited four times between 1588 and 1640. Epidemics were as frequent, though not as severe, in Chelmsford as in Crediton, and they were as common in Colchester as in Exeter. There were minor outbreaks of plague too in Saffron Walden, though this was the exceptional town in Essex as Barnstaple was in Devon, since the only serious mortalities occurred in 1559 and 1597. The urban incidence of bubonic plague was the most predictable of its features.

It was also in the largest centres of population that the impact of plague was most spectacular and most disruptive, if only because the gross number of deaths was so much larger. We rarely hear of the effects of high mortality on village and manorial life;[81] it is from the clothing towns and ports of Essex and Devon that complaints of loss of trade and the burden of the sick on the poor rate come. And if epidemic disease was a serious problem in Chelmsford and Crediton, it was a vastly greater one in the largest provincial towns, as the examples of Plymouth and Colchester show. Having examined the phenomenon which caused panic in the countryside, we must investigate its repeated incursions into three of the largest English towns.

Chapter 5

The urban impact

1544–5. This year there was a great plague in this city which endured
for a year.
1551–2. This year was the greatest mortality by pestilence in Bristol that
any man knew . . . whereof many people died.
1565.   This year there was a great plague in Bristol. The number that
died . . . was 2,070.
1575.   This year began the plague to be very hot about St James's tide,
and . . . there died about 2,000 persons.
1603.   In this year . . . began the greatest plague that ever was in Bristol,
. . . and died the number of 3,000 and more.

Civic annals of Bristol[1]

After the contrasts between different counties noted in the previous
chapter, it is something of a relief to find great similarities in the
history of plague in the three provincial cities which have been chosen
for detailed consideration here: Exeter, Bristol and Norwich. There
were differences in the timing and in the severity of the epidemics
which they suffered – Norwich was attacked more often and more
savagely than Bristol or Exeter – but in outline the impact of plague
on these great towns of provincial England was identical. In each of
them there was more than one serious epidemic between 1535 and
1555, at a time when urban populations generally were stagnant or
falling, and when urban economies were in decay. Plague did not
disappear with the end of the mid-Tudor depression, however.
Between 1565 and 1626 each town suffered another three major
outbreaks of the disease, killing 15 per cent or more of the inhabitants,
shattering every semblance of civic stability, and temporarily impeding
the processes of economic recovery. Finally, in each town plague
epidemics were closely bound up with the economic and social fabric
of the urban community. Plague appears less as an autonomous factor,

a *deus ex machina* occasionally imposing its will on towns from outside, than as an integral and in the end familiar part of urban life.

The normal course of commerce explains the frequent visitations of plague in these great provincial capitals. Exeter and Bristol were major ports; Norwich had as great a long-distance trade, conducted through Great Yarmouth; and all three towns were centres of provincial marketing. The regular introduction of epidemic disease from London or the Continent was therefore inevitable. From the middle of the sixteenth century onwards, mayors and aldermen did what they could to prevent it, cancelling or postponing fairs and markets, and imposing imperfect *cordons sanitaires*. Sometimes their efforts may even have succeeded. Watchmen at the gates of Exeter may have stopped plague from advancing beyond the extramural suburbs, and thus have averted major epidemics in 1563–4 and 1603–4.[2] More often, however, such measures conspicuously failed. Negligent watchmen allowed infected goods into Exeter in 1625, with disastrous results; and they did so again, though without such serious consequences, in 1645.[3] Similar precautions proved as fallible in Bristol. The first, somewhat hysterical record of a plague-death in one parish register in 1603 illustrates just how easy it was for infection to enter a busy port:

> A sailor being of Hamburg . . . died without the gate; . . . and being dead he was carried in the night and laid in the street; he was of a ship called *The Plague* [*sic*] which then lay at the quay.[4]

Once plague arrived in these populous cities, the quality of the urban environment played a major part in determining its incidence. Mortality was heaviest where housing conditions were worst, where poverty and overcrowding together provided ideal conditions for the transmission of disease. Exeter, Bristol and Norwich were three of the biggest towns in the kingdom outside London, with populations of more than 7,000 in 1520 and more than 11,000 in 1660. Since they were industrial as well as commercial centres, employing large numbers of unskilled and semi-skilled labourers, each of them contained residential areas dominated by the labouring poor. Although not rigidly segregated from middle-class neighbourhoods, these poor districts were common on the periphery of towns, and they were growing in size, and perhaps also in squalor, from the 1560s onwards. By the seventeenth century, as we shall see, the most conspicuous feature of urban epidemics of plague was their exceptional impact precisely here, in parishes on the edges of towns.

Plague remained a threat to the whole urban community, however, even if an unequal one; and like other general disasters it elicited that mobilisation of communal resources which was possible only in large towns with developed political structures. In 1626, for example, the rulers of Bristol saw their town menaced by 'pestilence, famine and the sword' all at once. They took what precautions they could and prepared for the worst. Cornish rye was imported for the town's granary; the trained bands were mobilised against a possible Spanish invasion; goods and men from infected towns were turned back at the gates; watchmen were ready to quarantine any infected citizens; and the Dean preached a sermon on the need for repentance and prayer. In the event none of these crises materialised. But the succession of epidemics recorded in the annals quoted at the beginning of this chapter made plague at least seem inescapable, and preparations to deal with its effects simple common sense. As one preacher reiterated for years afterwards, Bristol's deliverance from pestilence in 1626 was 'miraculous'.[5]

The increasingly active response of civic authorities to plague, which will be described in detail in a later chapter, has left valuable records for the historian. The most remarkable of them are the weekly reports of the number of burials in Norwich between 1579 and 1646, which allowed the Mayor's Court to monitor the advent and progress of epidemics there. This unique series of vital statistics, paralleled only by London's bills of mortality, makes it possible to circumvent one of the difficulties in measuring gross mortality in large English towns: the uneven survival of registers for the many parishes which they contained. A similar developing awareness of the need to quantify epidemic mortality can be found in the figures included in descriptions of plague in Bristol's civic annals. They similarly help to fill gaps in the surviving registers. We shall begin, however, with the other great western town, Exeter, where the evidence for the ravages of plague, though incomplete, is no less telling.

(i) Exeter

The rich manuscript records of Exeter refer to only two epidemics between 1485 and 1540. Both described as 'plague', they were noted in the commonplace book of John Hooker, Recorder of the town, because two mayors and two stewards, as well as 'many people', died in the first in 1503–4, and another mayor and Hooker's own father in the second in 1537. They may have been exceptionally severe, since the city was faced with a problem of vacant tenements and declining rent rolls in 1504 and 1538; but we know nothing further about them.[6]

There is scarcely more evidence for the epidemics of the middle of the sixteenth century. Of the twenty parishes in the town (shown in Figure 5.1), fourteen have registers beginning before 1625, but only two date from the 1540s.[7] They suggest, however, that the plague which ravaged Devon in 1546–7 may well have been equally serious in the county town, where a mayoral proclamation in September 1546

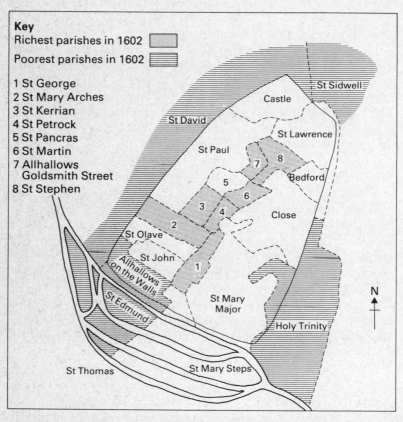

Figure 5.1 The parishes of Exeter

referred to 'the plague of pestilence now reigning'.[8] In St Petrock's parish the number of burials in 1546 was nearly five times the annual average for the next decade, while in the neighbouring parish of St Mary Arches the rise in mortality was larger still.[9] Even the influenza epidemic of 1558 did not cause as great a crisis as that, although relatively high mortality among the richer citizens prompted the corporation to display a table of recent charitable bequests in the Guildhall as an encouragement to potential benefactors.[10] Five years later, in 1563–4, plague returned, but on this occasion the number of burials rose only slightly and only in some suburban parishes, in St David's and Holy Trinity, for example; the central parishes of St Petrock and St Mary Arches were not affected. The epidemic of 1546, coming at the end of a year of dearth in the city,[11] was clearly the major crisis of the middle years of the sixteenth century.

In the century after 1565 there were three disastrous, and better-documented, outbreaks of plague. None occurred in 1665–6, although the corporation feverishly prepared itself for such an emergency. Neither was there a serious outbreak at the time of the plague in London in 1603–4, although mortality was unusually high in two parishes on the edge of town, St Sidwell's and St Thomas's. It was in 1570, 1590–1 and finally in 1625 that plague spread across the whole city, with devastating effect. The surviving registers allow us to plot its progress. In 1570 and 1590 both the suburban parish of St Sidwell and the central parish of St Mary Major were among the first to record an increase in the number of burials. Infection may have come by the London road which entered the first or up the river Exe to the second. On the second occasion, however, it did not arrive until the late summer, and it revived again in the spring of 1591. In 1625 plague spread more clearly from the northern suburbs through the heart of the town. It was perhaps brought from the capital by a 'youth who came from London', buried in St David's in July. In the same month the number of burials began to increase in St Sidwell's, in August in central parishes like St·Mary Major, and then in November in St Thomas's on the far side of the river, where the disease had its worst effects in the early summer of 1626. By then the whole town was desolate. Ships no longer visited the port; tradesmen had moved out to keep shop elsewhere in the county and refused to return; and those citizens who were not victims of plague were impoverished, close to famine, and rioting in the streets.[12]

Table 5.1 *Epidemic mortality in Exeter 1570–1643*

Parish[1]	Crisis Mortality Ratios[2]			
	1570	*1590–1*	*1625*	*1643*
Close	–	–	3.5	2.4
St Petrock	1.8	4.7	2.8	3.3
St Martin	–	2.9	5.6	4.1
Allhallows Goldsmith Street	3.8	9.3	2.5	3.8
St Mary Arches	–	0.6	7.4	2.5
St Kerrian	4.7	1.0	1.7	–
St Olave	–	–	3.4	2.3
St Mary Major	8.0	4.5	6.3	3.3
St Paul	6.2	–	7.1	3.4
Holy Trinity	9.4	9.2	–	3.5
St Edmund	–	6.9	6.2	2.0
St Sidwell	5.2	7.0	12.6	2.4
St David	8.3	6.3	7.0	–
St Thomas	4.1	4.9	6.2	–

Notes
[1] In approx. descending order of wealth. See n. 14, p. 368.
[2] See n. 13, p. 368.

Despite its rapid dispersal across the city, however, the severity of plague varied from area to area in each of these epidemics, and on each occasion mortality rates were exceptionally high in the poorer quarters, in the suburbs. This important conclusion can be demonstrated by comparing the level of epidemic mortality in the different parishes with what we know about their relative social status. Table 5.1 gives the Crisis Mortality Ratios in each parish with surviving registers,[13] and data from various taxation records have been used to list the parishes in roughly descending order of wealth. While not agreeing in every detail, the subsidy assessments of 1544 and 1602, the poll tax of 1641 and the hearth tax of 1671 all show that the richer citizens of Exeter congregated in the central parishes, particularly in St Petrock's and St Martin's, while the fringe parishes of Holy Trinity, St David and St Sidwell were among the poorest in the town;[14] and St Thomas's, across the river, must have been equally impoverished.[15] It is significant, therefore, that Crisis Mortality Ratios in plague years were often twice as high in the latter parishes as in the former. Moreover, in each of the three epidemics of 1570, 1590–1 and 1625, the highest ratios tend to cluster in the bottom half of the table and the lowest ratios in the top half. It appears that plague rarely had as firm a grip in the centre of town as on the periphery.

There are some exceptions to this pattern. There was occasional heavy mortality in some of the richer parishes: in Allhallows, Goldsmith Street, in 1590–1 and in St Mary Arches and St Martin's in 1625. The situation may also have been different before 1570, given the uniformly high mortality in 1546 in two of the richest parishes, St Petrock's and St Mary Arches, although we have no means of knowing whether the death rate was even higher elsewhere. From 1570 onwards, however, plague took its greatest toll outside the main gates, or in the populous parishes of St Mary Major and St Paul close to them, where people lived crowded together in ill-ventilated tenements or narrowly confined courtyards, and where open drains and garbage in the streets attracted vermin. By 1600 St Sidwell's was indeed the notorious slum area of Exeter, famous for its destitution and disorder as well as for its disease.[16]

The last three epidemics of plague in Exeter thus had two main characteristics. Their impact was felt across the whole town, mortality levels rising in virtually every parish by at least 100 per cent; and yet they also discriminated heavily against impoverished neighbourhoods. This ambivalent combination distinguished plague from other epidemics in Exeter in this period, which were either much more selective or much more uniform in their incidence. In 1587 and 1597, for example, there were mortality crises associated with bad harvests, and probably caused, at least in part, by typhus; and they were wholly confined to the poorest parishes. An outbreak of gaol fever at Exeter Assizes in 1586 was followed by 'sickness and scarcity of grain and victuals' among the poor. In 1587 the number of burials in some of the suburban parishes rose by 50 per cent, while there was no increase at all in the centre of the town. Ten years later mortality was much worse. There were twice as many deaths as usual in the five parishes of St David, St Thomas, St Sidwell, St Mary Major and Holy Trinity, and at the same time the aggregate number of conceptions in these parishes fell by 40 per cent: another indication of a crisis of subsistence. Yet once again the more prosperous neighbourhoods of the town entirely escaped. On these occasions poverty was evidently the prime regulator of mortality.[17]

On the other hand, there was one epidemic, the last of the period, which appears to have had a remarkably consistent effect on the different parts of Exeter. During the Civil War, in 1643, a Royalist force laid siege to the town, the citizens were 'kept from taking the air without their own walls, and from being supplied from the country markets', and they fell victim to 'contagious sickness'.[18] It was probably typhus again; but now siege conditions brought want and defending soldiers brought disease to every parish, with relatively homogeneous effects. As Table 5.1 shows, Crisis Mortality Ratios ranged between 2.0 and 4.1 in all parishes for which records survive. Just as military operations spread disease all over Devon in the 1640s, in spite of the usual difference between north and south, so the contagion of 1643 temporarily erased the normal topographical distinctions in the distribution of epidemic mortality in Exeter.

Whether they were more restricted or more uniform in their impact than outbreaks of bubonic plague, however, none of these other epidemics had such serious demographic effects, either in individual parishes or over the town as a whole. The total number of deaths in each of the last three epidemics of plague can be roughly estimated if we multiply the number of burials in parishes with surviving registers by a ratio calculated from the distribution of taxpayers in a thorough assessment of 1641.[19] The results suggest that 16 per cent of the population died in 1570, 15 per cent between August 1590 and July 1591, and over 18 per cent in 1625. In 1643, by contrast, mortality was probably less than 9 per cent. Death rates were higher still, of course, in those parishes which were worst hit by plague. If the Mortality Ratios can be trusted, the 206 people who died in Holy Trinity in 1590–1 may well have been a quarter of the population of the parish. In St Sidwell's parish in 1625, when 550 people were buried, the proportion killed was closer to one-third.[20]

Successive mortalities of this magnitude did not prevent demographic growth. The population of Exeter rose from less than 8,000 in 1570 to between 10,000 and 12,000 in 1640.[21] It is even possible that there was some natural increase, for there were many more baptisms than burials in the town over that period. The aggregate picture again conceals important differences on the ground, however. In the four poorest parishes of St Sidwell, St David, St Edmund and Holy Trinity, the number of burials far exceeded the number of baptisms between 1571 and 1640. Because of plague there were more deaths than births in the peripheral parishes of Exeter, while there were many more births than deaths in the centre. If we exclude the plague years 1590–1 and 1625–6 from the calculations, there was still a distinct disparity between different parts of the town. The four poorest parishes produced 120 baptisms for every 100 burials; the four parishes of St Petrock, St Mary Arches, St Martin and Allhallows, Goldsmith Street, had 160. But plague added a heavy weight to the biological scales, decisively depressing what were already low levels of public health in the poorer sections of urban society.[22]

This social and topographical imbalance had far-reaching consequences. Despite heavy mortality, the rising level of baptisms in St Sidwell's, St David's and Holy Trinity parishes shows that their population was increasing rapidly between 1570 and 1640, more rapidly indeed than the population in the centre of the town. Growth was made possible only by immigration, partly perhaps from other Exeter parishes, certainly from the country around. Like many a corporation in the later sixteenth and early seventeenth centuries, the council of Exeter regularly complained of the influx of 'many poor, idle and lascivious persons with their wives and children' who set up home on the fringes of the town and became fodder for the next serious epidemic.[23] High mortality rates and heavy immigration in tandem thus dictated a much swifter turnover of population in these parishes than in others, and magnified the problems of poverty, disease and crime which were commonly associated with suburbs and migrants. In so far as bubonic plague was one cause of this suburban instability, it had an even greater and more lasting impact on social conditions than the burial registers alone would suggest. Plague did not stop suburban growth; but it did help to determine the means by which growth took place, and in so doing it exerted a powerful influence on the social life of urban communities.

(ii) Bristol

The only major difference between epidemics in Bristol and Exeter lay in their chronology. Once again there were visitations of plague in the second third of the sixteenth century, but in Bristol they occurred in 1535, 1544–5 and 1551–2.[24] Although the evidence relating to them is slight, the few surviving registers – all of them from parishes in the centre of the city – show unusually heavy mortality in the two later outbreaks.[25] In two parishes, St Ewen's and Christ Church, the Crisis Mortality Ratios were 7.7 and 5.9 for the year between August 1544 and July 1545; and in the calendar year 1552 they reached 5.8 and 5.9 in St Nicholas's and Christ Church respectively. Combined as they were with bad harvests and high food prices in 1550 and 1551,[26] these epidemics must have brought a crisis of major proportions to the central parishes of Bristol.

The level of mortality can be calculated more accurately for three later outbreaks of plague, in 1565, 1575, and 1603–4, which were comparable to those of 1570, 1590 and 1625 in Exeter. According to civic annals, 2,070 people died in 1565 and 2,000 in 1575, and another chronicler cited full authority for his figure for 1603–4: the number dying between July 1603 and February 1605 'according to the Church books and printed tickets' was '2,956, whereof of the plague 2,600'.[27] Unfortunately, these printed bills of mortality do not survive, but it is possible to check the accuracy of the annalists' totals by comparing them with surviving parish registers. The burials in half of the eighteen parishes of Bristol can be inflated to provide rough totals for the town by means of a multiplier derived from the parish distribution of communicants in 1547.[28] These calculations suggest that 1,800 people were buried in Bristol in each of the calendar years 1565 and 1575, and 2,200 in the year from August 1603 to July 1604, when plague was at its height. Despite historians' suspicions of contemporary numeracy, the figures given in the annals do not seem to have been grossly exaggerated. Since the total population of Bristol rose little above 11,000 between 1547 and 1603,[29] the mortality rate in each of these three epidemics may well have been between 16 and 18 per cent: serious blows for a town which was clearly failing to attract immigrants in large numbers.

After 1603, however, the population expanded relatively rapidly, reaching almost 20,000 in 1700,[30] and at the same time serious epidemics became much rarer. Plague appeared in the town on several occasions but not in explosive form. A few deaths were attributed to it in 1609 and 1611; houses were quarantined in two parishes in 1626; and there were rather more casualties, requiring a pesthouse and payments to the sick in 1637–9. There were to be further preventive measures and a few cases of plague again between 1651 and 1653, and then finally in 1666.[31] But it was only during the Civil War that epidemic disease again decimated the population and it did so on two occasions. One epidemic was an outbreak of plague, the other, as in Exeter, an outbreak of typhus.

At the end of 1641 there was already 'sickness' among the soldiers in Bristol castle, and by the summer of 1642, as the town prepared for war, it had spread into several parishes around. In the following year, when the king's forces besieged Bristol, the death rate rose all over the city. There can be little doubt that this was typhus, since a Parliamentary tract complained that the soldiers who took the town in July infested their beds 'with lice, so that the houses where they quartered are like gaols for nastiness'.[32] Two years later, during a second siege, there was an even more serious epidemic when bubonic plague returned, in order, as one contemporary put it, to complete the 'great misery' of the citizens.[33] In all, in the two years 1643 and 1645, nearly 2,800 people were buried in ten parishes, whose total population cannot have been more than 10,000.[34] In Bristol civil war meant total war.

Even in the special circumstances of siege and war, however, plague followed topographical patterns which were similar to those in Exeter and which had been evident in earlier visitations. We can again use subsidy assessments to rank the parishes of the town in order of wealth, and compare the level of mortality in each of them. Table 5.2 shows the effects of major epidemics after 1560 in the parishes with surviving registers, ranging from the richest, All Saints and St Nicholas's, to the poorest, St Mary Redcliffe, St James's and Temple.[35]

No parish wholly escaped the impact of these epidemics of plague, save perhaps St Werburgh's in 1645. There were no completely

Table 5.2 *Epidemic mortality in Bristol 1565–1645*

Parish[1]	Crisis Mortality Ratios				
	1565	1575	1603–4[2]	1643	1645
All Saints	8.4	4.2	3.8	2.9	1.7
St Nicholas	5.2	6.7	4.9	2.9	2.3
St Ewen	–	3.8	–	2.4	5.5
St Werburgh	6.2	2.9	5.5	3.2	1.0
St Stephen	7.2	8.6	5.6	2.8	4.8
Christ Church	7.4	7.9	2.4	2.9	–
St John	8.5	5.6	10.2	3.5	4.2
St Augustine	–	–	7.3	2.4	5.4
SS. Philip and Jacob	–	–	8.6	1.4	–
St Mary Redcliffe	8.7	9.0	8.0	3.1	7.8
St James	8.2	7.7	10.2	3.1	8.1
Temple	9.9	10.8	8.5	5.2	8.1

Notes
[1] In approx. descending order of wealth. For sources, see n. 35, p. 370.
[2] Aug.–July. In other cases the years are Jan.–Dec.

exempt areas, as there were when diseases associated with dearth raised mortality only in four of the poorer parishes in 1597.[36] At the same time, it is evident from the table that plague did not hit parishes with the even hand exhibited by the typhus epidemic of 1643. Plague was usually most violent on the urban periphery, especially in the parishes of St Mary Redcliffe, Temple and St James. The two former, together with St Thomas's, comprised the poorest ward in the town, on the southern banks of the Avon where industrial suburbs had grown up in the later Middle Ages; while St James's was in the second poorest ward on the opposite side of the city.[37] (See Figure 5.2) Conversely, the central parishes of All Saints, St Nicholas and St Werburgh were normally those least seriously affected. We should

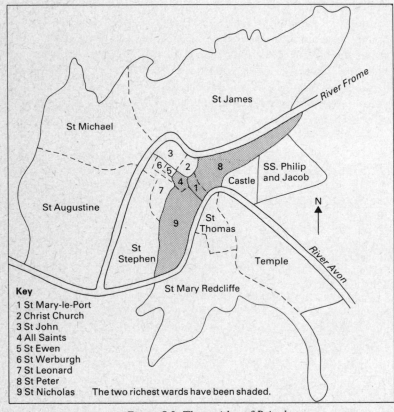

Key
1 St Mary-le-Port
2 Christ Church
3 St John
4 All Saints
5 St Ewen
6 St Werburgh
7 St Leonard
8 St Peter
9 St Nicholas   The two richest wards have been shaded.

Figure 5.2 The parishes of Bristol

note that this pattern was much less obvious in 1565 than in later epidemics. Not only was All Saints then hit hard, but the Mortality Ratios in all parishes were much closer to one another than they were to be in 1575, 1603 or 1645. Together with the high burial rates in the central quarters in 1544 and 1552, this suggests that the topographical concentration of plague grew more pronounced as time went on. But the pattern was established by 1603 and unshakable in 1645.

Its persistence in 1645 is particularly striking. In 1643 siege conditions and military occupation had dispersed typhus, a disease normally associated with poverty, evenly over the whole city. Yet similar circumstances two years later did not alter what had by then become the characteristic incidence of bubonic plague. The difference presumably lies in plague's dependence upon infected colonies of rats. The level of human mortality was dictated not only, as in the case of typhus, by the movement of human parasites from person to person, but also by standards of housing and public hygiene which either separated or brought together men and rodents.[38] The central parishes of Bristol were certainly its most fashionable and salubrious areas. By the end of the sixteenth century St Werburgh's even contained a street of stone houses, which may have been relatively rat-proof. Although St Mary Redcliffe also had some large merchants' houses, there were many more tightly packed tenements for labourers.[39] The condition of the streets varied as much as that of the houses. Visitors often praised the cleanliness of Bristol, with its paved roads and underground drains, a town 'where nothing is wanting . . . either for neatness or health'. But such comments applied only to the central parishes. It is abundantly clear that by the early seventeenth century the streets south of the Avon in Redcliffe ward were littered with decaying animal and vegetable matter. Conditions were so bad in St Thomas's, for example, that 'people will hardly come to church by reason of the stench'.[40] In such an environment plague flourished.

All this confirms what might have been predicted from the example of Exeter. In the case of Bristol, however, we can go further and show the influence of the urban environment on plague mortality, not only in different parishes, but in different parts of the same parish. We can show, in fact, that when it did strike the centre of a city plague picked out the narrowest alleys and poorest houses and hit them hard. The churchwardens of Christ Church parish in the middle of Bristol kept 'Easter Books' listing every year the names of all the communicants, street by street and household by household. It is thus possible to discover the approximate location of the houses from which most of the people buried in the plagues of 1575 and 1603 came.[41] The households visited are shown in Figure 5.3 and the total number of deaths in each street is given in Table 5.3.

Table 5.3 *Christ Church parish, Bristol: communicants and burials*

	Communicants listed at Easter					Burials[1]	
Streets	1575	1576	1579	1601	1604	1575	1603
Broad Street	81	63	78	100	78	13	2
Wine Street	211	179	207	208	134	30	8
Tower Lane	46	36	32	27	27	4	1
Pithay	71	60	68	79	67	26	24
Total	409	338	385	414	306	73	35
				Unidentified burials		19	7

Note
[1] For the months June–Dec.

Wine Street and Broad Street were two of the main highways of the town, meeting at its centre, and they contained several large households, complete with servants and apprentices. The Pithay, on the other hand, was an overcrowded alley of poor tenements leading to a workhouse in one of the towers in the city walls. It is clear, to begin with, that burials during the plague epidemics were scattered over a wide area, and that the disease moved haphazardly, sometimes missing out two or three households in its progress along a street. It is also clear, however, that the Pithay lost a higher proportion of its inhabitants in both epidemics than any other part of the neighbourhood. This was especially so in the milder outbreak of 1603, but even in 1575 the death rate was apparently twice as high in the Pithay as in Wine Street. Bubonic plague was concentrated in the back street of this otherwise prosperous parish.

The Easter Books of Christ Church also illustrate the demographic effects of plague on different social groups. The books of 1575 and 1576 suggest that there was a radical fall in the number of communicants in the space of one year. But not all of this decline was due to epidemic mortality, and there were significant differences from street to street. The fall in numbers in Wine Street and Broad Street was largely a consequence of the flight of the most prosperous householders, for several names occur in both the listings of 1575 and 1579 which were not present at Easter 1576. In the Pithay, by contrast,

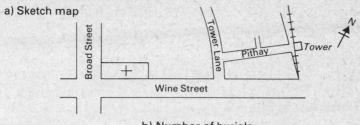

a) Sketch map

b) Number of burials
in separate households 1575 and 1603 (June-December)

Broad Street	1575	[ ][ ][2][ ][ ][ ][2][ ][5][2][ ][ ][1][1][ ]
East Side	1603	[ ][ ][2][ ][ ][ ][ ][ ][ ][ ][ ][ ][ ][ ][ ][ ][ ][ ][ ][ ][ ][ ]
Wine Street	1575	[ ][2][ ][ ][1][ ][ ][1][ ][ ][1][1][1][6][ ][ ][4][1][ ][ ]
North Side	1603	[ ][ ][ ][ ][ ][1][ ][ ][ ][ ][ ][ ][ ][ ][ ][ ][ ][ ][ ][ ][ ][3]
Wine Street	1575	[1][ ][1][ ][ ][2][3][ ][ ][1][ ][ ][1][2][ ][1][ ]
South Side	1603	[ ][4][ ][ ][ ][ ][ ][ ][ ][ ][ ][ ][ ][ ][ ][ ]
Tower Lane	1575	[ ][1][ ][1][ ][1][ ][ ][1][ ][ ][ ][ ]
	1603	[ ][ ][ ][ ][ ][ ][ ][ ][1][ ][ ]
Pithay	1575	[2][ ][1][ ][1][ ][ ][1][1][3][ ][ ][3][2][ ][1][3][1][1]
? South Side	1603	[ ][ ][1][ ][ ][3][1][ ][ ][1][3][ ][ ][5][4][ ][ ][1][ ]
Pithay	1575	[1][ ][ ][3][ ][2][ ]
? North Side	1603	[ ][ ][ ][2][ ][3][ ]

Each square represents one household unit. Where the same household
was afflicted in both 1575 and 1603 the squares have been joined.

Figure 5.3 Christ Church parish, Bristol

most of the absentees were victims of plague, and by Easter 1576 a
few poor families had already migrated into the street to fill their
vacant tenements. Others followed them in the years before 1579.
The Easter Book of 1604, when compared with the burial register
and the book of 1601, suggests that the next plague had an even more
disparate effect on different streets. Nearly one-third of the adults in
the two main streets appear to have fled, while newcomers rapidly
moved in to fill empty spaces in the alley behind them. Although the
total number of communicants in the parish changed little between

1575 and 1604, the turnover of population, and especially of heads of households, was much greater in the Pithay than elsewhere.

The social inequalities in urban communities and the ways in which plague reinforced them can thus be seen in microcosm in Christ Church parish; and their consequences are shown most vividly by the contrasting fate of individual parishioners. Among the more fortunate was William Yeomans. Throughout the period from 1575 to 1604 he lived with his wife at the end of Wine Street, in what was clearly a large house. He had five or six apprentices and servants, and no doubt two or three children not listed in the Easter Books. The identity of his servants changed regularly, as they came to the end of their term, but this very fact made the death of one of them during the plague of 1575 of little consequence. Scarcely touched by demographic crises, Yeomans' household continued to be a stable pillar of the parish.

There was no such continuity a few yards away in the Pithay, where plague destroyed and dispersed whole families. Thomas Walker lived there with his wife and children in 1575; they were probably poor – at any rate they had no servants. Thomas and two of his children died in the plague of that year, and his widow disappeared from the parish. Near neighbours of his, John Baker and his wife, also lost two children during the plague and apparently left their house: after a succession of different families, their place was taken in 1601 by William Oliver and his wife, and they in turn lost two of their children in the plague of 1603.

These are extreme cases. Even in Wine Street heads of household sometimes died of plague. But it did not happen very often, and when it did family resources were often sufficient to maintain continuity. William Slack, for example, died during the plague of 1575; but his widow, Elizabeth, took his place at the head of a large household which now contained another married couple, probably her daughter and son-in-law. It would be foolish to pretend that plague was not a threat to the Slacks of Bristol and their neighbours; but it was a far greater menace, with immeasurably more destructive consequences, for the labouring poor of the back streets, the Walkers and the Bakers.

(iii) Norwich

In turning to Norwich we must lay aside the microscope and move back from individuals to examine the broader impact of plague on a town. We can do this more thoroughly than in the cases of Exeter and Bristol, however, partly because the records are fuller, and partly because epidemics were more numerous. Norwich was larger than the two western towns: with a population of around 12,000 in 1520, 15,000 in 1600 and 30,000 in 1700, it was England's biggest provincial town.[42] It had more parishes than Exeter or Bristol, thirty-four in all, and the registers of twenty-eight of them can be used to plot both the distribution of high mortality and, more particularly, the way in which it changed down to the last great outbreak of plague in 1665–6.[43]

Norwich is also of special interest because it was in some respects cosmopolitan. It had close ties with the Low Countries, and in the later sixteenth century it attracted a large immigrant population of Dutch and Walloon refugees from the wars in the Netherlands. These 'Strangers', as they were called, provided a stimulus to economic and intellectual innovation such as few other towns enjoyed. They help to account for Norwich's position as a centre of Puritanism, of new advances in social welfare, and of medical expertise from the 1570s onwards;[44] and all this no doubt encouraged the deliberate interest in plague which is evident in the corporation records of the period. But the Strangers, like later immigrant communities, were also unusually vulnerable to infectious disease. They suffered far more than native citizens in a series of outbreaks of plague which began in 1579. Like the inhabitants of the Pithay in Bristol, they illustrate the social determinants of plague mortality.

There was no lack of serious mortality crises in Norwich in the century before 1579, but it is impossible to say with any confidence how many of them were caused by plague. Fluctuations in the number of wills proved by Norwich citizens show the effects of the great plague of 1479, which is mentioned in other records of the town, and of the virus infections of 1557–9.[45] They suggest also that there was lesser, but still high, mortality in 1485–6, 1500, 1503–4, 1520 and 1523, when there were sicknesses of various kinds in other parts of the country. Because of their bias towards higher age- and social groups, however, probate records provide an inadequate index of mortality in the whole urban community; and the early parish registers of Norwich suggest that they may be seriously misleading. For the registers reveal epidemics in 1544–5 and 1554–5 which were at least as serious as the fevers of 1557–9, and which nevertheless had a much slighter effect on the number of wills proved. The chronological distribution of burials indicates that both were outbreaks of plague, and on each occasion the number of people buried in the ten parishes for which registers survive was three times greater than usual.[46]

In these early visitations, plague appears to have been relatively evenly distributed across the town. Although most of the ten parishes were in the centre, it may be significant that two of the wealthiest of them – SS. Simon and Jude and St Martin at Palace – suffered no less than the rest in each epidemic. By contrast, in the later outbreaks of plague which will be considered shortly these parishes were always comparatively fortunate. Within each parish, however, it is likely that plague fell hardest on the poor. The failure of testamentary evidence adequately to record the level of mortality in each outbreak must be due to plague hitting those who were not rich enough to make wills, or those who were too young to do so; and the normal class- and age-incidence of the disease makes it probable that both played a part.[47] In 1557–9, on the other hand, neither wealth nor maturity protected the will-making class from infection. Influenza redressed the balance of mortality in no uncertain terms. The probate evidence indicates a bigger jump in the number of deaths than that shown in the surviving burial registers, and there was undoubtedly heavy mortality among the political elite. At least ten aldermen died in 1558–9, and in the same year the Recorder and twelve of the sixty common councillors disappear suddenly from the records.[48] Plague never had anything like that effect on the governing class.

With their different incidence, the three epidemics of the 1540s and 1550s can only have further weakened a local economy whose staple cloth industry was already in decline. It is not surprising that there were complaints of depopulation and of merchants leaving the town, and that the population remained around 12,000 between the 1520s and the 1560s.[49] Recovery began only after 1565, with the influx of Dutch and Walloon immigrants. In 1571 there were already 4,000 Strangers looking for 'peace and riches . . . here at Norwich', and bringing new skills with them.[50] They brought no improvement in public health, however: rather the reverse. In 1579 there occurred the worst outbreak of plague of the period and the first of a series of major epidemics. One chronicle recorded that in the mayoral year 1579–80 (beginning in June) 'there deceased within this city of all diseases 4,841 persons', of whom 4,193 died of plague. More than 2,000 of the victims were 'foreigners'.[51]

The annalist was able to give an exact figure because, from 26 June 1579 onwards, the number of burials in the town was reported every week to the Mayor's Court. Designed in the first instance to provide reliable information on the progress of epidemic disease, this practice continued with some modifications and few interruptions until 1646. Victims of plague were distinguished from other burials after 1590; reports of the number of baptisms were added in 1582; and the burials of Strangers were separately recorded from November 1579, and their baptisms after 1604. All the information came initially from parish clerks, and the fact that it was gathered centrally makes it no more complete and no more accurate than the entries in the parish registers. Nevertheless, the figures entered weekly in the Court Books of Norwich provide the fullest series of vital statistics for any town in the country in this period; and the annual number of burials, shown in Figure 5.4, reveals the successive outbreaks of plague from 1579 to 1625 with great clarity.[52]

The first epidemic of 1579 was easily the most serious. In only six months, between the end of June and the end of December 1579, eight times as many people were buried as in any normal period of twelve months. The plague had in fact begun weeks before the first reports of burials to the Court. One contemporary thought it came in the 'trains of her Majesty's carriage, being many of them infected', during a royal progress in August 1578, and there is some evidence of an epidemic disease in one parish in the autumn of that year. In February 1579 there were rumours that the common well in St Andrew's parish was poisonous, 'to the great peril and danger of infection', and at the end of March the aldermen admitted that plague was present in another two parishes.[53] By June it was raging fiercely, and we can follow its progress from then on in the weekly reports. (See Figure 5.5.) The weekly death toll mounted from 56 at the end of June to 167 by the end of July, and to a massive peak of 352 in the middle of August. It did not fall to below 200 until the end of October. The worst was over by December, although the numbers dying fell back to relatively normal levels only in June 1580.[54]

This was probably the greatest mortality crisis in the town's history after the Black Death. No exact computation of its dimensions is possible. Not all deaths were recorded in the surviving registers from twenty-four parishes which must be used as a source for the early months of the crisis, nor indeed in the later reports which equally depended on the diligence of overworked parish officials. But the two sources together make it clear that more than 5,000 people died in the calendar year 1579. Since it is likely that the total population was

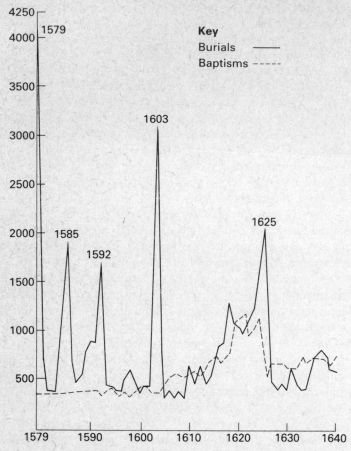

Figure 5.4 Burials and baptisms in Norwich 1579–1640

rather less than 17,000, at least 30 per cent of it was swept away. The proportion may even have been as high as a third.[55] In the short term, the tragedy was still more acute than this implies: in only three months, from August to October, more than 3,000 people, nearly one in five of the citizens, perished.

The survivors scarcely had time to draw breath after this disaster before plague returned. Further epidemics in 1584–5 and 1589–92 decimated the population. There were 1,827 burials in 1585 and 1,646 in 1592, while the number rarely rose to 500 in non-epidemic

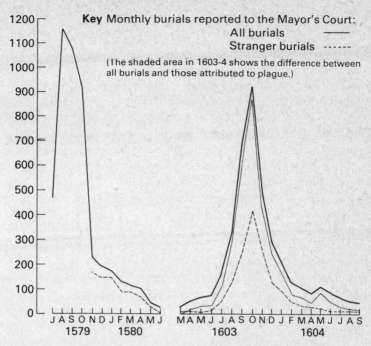

Figure 5.5 The plagues of 1579 and 1603 in Norwich

years. After another short interval, cases of plague were reported again between 1597 and 1599, although they were responsible for only a small part of the increase in mortality in these years of dearth: as in other towns, this was largely a food crisis.[56] Then came an outbreak of plague which approached that of 1579 in severity. Eight burials were attributed to plague in the summer of 1602, when the disease was in Great Yarmouth,[57] and the epidemic proper began in the spring of 1603, as Figure 5.5 shows. The peak occurred rather later than in 1579, in the middle of September, when 218 people died in a week; and there was a modest recrudescence of infection in the spring of 1604 before its final decline, the last plague casualty being returned in January 1605. In the twelve months between August 1603 and July 1604, 3,481 people were buried; almost 3,000 of them died of plague. Assuming that the population was no greater than 15,000, which is what the level of baptisms suggests, nearly a quarter of the inhabitants died in one year. A few further cases of plague, notified in 1609 and 1610, ended a remarkable series of visitations. The disease had been present in Norwich in one form or another in half the years between 1579 and 1610.

An intermission of longer duration than usual preceded the next great epidemic in 1625–6, when more than 3,000 people were buried in two years. As Figure 5.4 indicates, however, there was a rising trend in both burials and baptisms in the interval which makes it difficult to estimate the city's population and hence to calculate the death rate in 1625–6 even approximately. Neither is it possible to account for the fluctuations on the graph between 1612 and 1624 with any conviction. The population may have risen to a sudden but temporary peak, or birth and death rates may for a time have been exceptionally high, or both may have occurred. There were certainly agues and fevers in the town between 1618 and 1624, although it is hard to believe that these can explain the whole of the rise in registered mortality before the onset of plague in 1625.[58] As for the high level of baptisms, that perhaps reflected the high birth rate of recent immigrants to the town.

For what we can say with some confidence is that the enormous mortalities of the generation after 1579 produced heavy flows of migration into Norwich, and these may not have dried up when epidemics became less frequent after 1603. Even excluding the plague of 1579, there were almost twice as many burials as baptisms between 1582 and 1606, a deficit far greater than that encountered in any other provincial town. Yet the population appears not to have declined seriously, for the level of baptisms remained stable throughout the period before 1610 and increased rapidly thereafter. Although we have little evidence of it, there must have been a quite exceptional amount of immigration to account for this. Certainly by 1640, when the number of baptisms had settled at an annual average of 710, the population of Norwich had increased considerably and probably reached at least 20,000.

For twenty years after 1626 plague was a constant but never a critical problem. Several cases were reported between 1630 and 1633, and between 1637 and 1639; and there were probably others in 1646 and 1647. In each of these minor outbreaks, the disease was confined to particular localities. In 1631, for example, the number of burials rose more than threefold in two parishes,w6.5[59] but elsewhere it scarcely rose at all. Although the corporation records are full of references to plague in the 1630s, no general epidemic developed and the aldermen's concern was aroused, not so much by high mortality itself, as by the coincidence of disease with economic depression and bad harvests.[60] Perhaps as a result, the Mayor's Court apparently felt no need for weekly information on mortality after 1646.

If so, the aldermen relaxed too soon. When plague returned for the last time in 1665, printed bills of mortality were hurriedly compiled, and they recorded an outbreak more serious than that of 1625–6. Casualties were most numerous in the summer of 1666, with 200 people dying weekly at the end of August. In the year from 3 October 1665 to 3 October 1666, for which we have complete records, 3,012 people were buried, 15 per cent of the estimated population, and 2,251 of them were said to have died of plague.[61] Plague left Norwich with a final reminder of its devastating potential.

Such a rapid sequence of visitations – four great epidemics and six or seven lesser outbreaks in the ninety years after 1578 – suggests two conclusions. In the first place, there must have been well-established chains of infection, bringing virulent strains of the plague bacillus into the city. The regular flow of migrants from the Netherlands created one of them, especially in the pestilential years from 1579 to 1610. It is no accident that there were epidemics in Yarmouth, their port of arrival, in 1588 and 1602, one year before the disease attacked Norwich. Traffic with the Low Countries was as dangerous as traffic with London in plague years, as the aldermen quickly appreciated.[62] At the same time, however, it seems that when plague arrived it could linger in the city for several years, as it did between 1589 and 1592 and between 1630 and 1633, remaining active in the rat population but emerging only sporadically in epidemic form, in different parts of the town at different times. The result was that alternation of short sharp eruptions of plague and more prolonged, less acute tremors which is evident between 1579 and 1666.

A third feature of epidemics in Norwich can be observed if we examine the distribution of plague mortality across the town during the same period. Although we only have information about the number of burials in all parishes in 1665–6, sufficient registers survive from 1579 onwards to show that the disease was gradually strengthening its hold on the outer fringes of the town and leaving the central parishes progressively more free from infection. The divergence between centre and periphery was always greatest in minor outbreaks. The epidemics beginning in 1584 and 1589, for example, swept round the outskirts of the town, scarcely affecting the parishes of St Andrew, St Michael at Plea, SS. Simon and Jude or St George Tombland, in the fashionable area between the castle, the river and the cathedral. No quarter of the town escaped as lightly as that in more serious outbreaks. A definite change can, however, be observed in the incidence of the major epidemics. We have seen that epidemic mortality was probably relatively evenly spread in the 1540s and 1550s. It was so again in the great epidemic of 1579. In the plagues of 1603–4, 1625–6 and 1665–6, on the other hand, there was a topographical bias as clear as that in the later epidemics in Exeter and Bristol, and it had the same social implications.

Table 5.4 shows the Crisis Mortality Ratios in the epidemics of 1579, 1603–4 and 1625–6 in each of the parishes whose registers have been examined. The parishes are listed in declining order of wealth, determined not in this case by the subsidies (though these assessments give similar results) but by the proportion of the English population of the parish listed as 'poor' in a comprehensive census of the poor taken in 1570.[63] For ease of reference, they have been divided into three groups and the ratios of the aggregate burials in each group have also been given. Finally, Crisis Mortality Ratios have been calculated for the total number of registered burials in all parishes in order to provide an average against which the experience of any single parish can be judged.

In none of these epidemics was there a consistent and neat fall in mortality in step with the decline in wealth. It would be unrealistic to expect that. Some parishes in the middle group were always hit comparatively severely, especially St Margaret's and St Lawrence's.[64] As we shall see, this was in part the result of the substantial number of Strangers, many of them poor, who were resident in these two parishes and who were not counted in the 1570 census. It is notable, however, that the difference between the worst-affected and the least-affected parishes was much greater in 1603–4 and in 1625–6 than in 1579, and that in the two later outbreaks parishes with high and low mortality tended also to be parishes of high and low poverty. In 1603–4 the eight poorest parishes had a combined Mortality Ratio well above the ratio for all burials, and in 1625–6 the eight richest parishes had a ratio well below the overall figure.[65]

The same developing contrast can be seen if we plot on a map the areas of the city which had more than average mortality in each of the three epidemics. Figure 5.6 shows those parishes whose Mortality Ratios were higher than the ratio for all burials in 1579, 1603–4, and 1625–6. Of the thirteen unmarked parishes, eight are blank because

Table 5.4 *Plague mortality in Norwich 1579–1626*

| Parish | Crisis Mortality Ratios | | | % poor in |
	1579	1603–4[1]	1625–6[2]	1570[3]
St Andrew	9.6	3.1	1.9	3.8
St Edmund	9.0	7.6	2.0	7.7
SS. Simon and Jude	4.6	1.7	2.6	8.3
St Michael at Plea	6.3	9.8	2.0	12.1
St Peter Mancroft	13.3	6.8	1.4	14.6
St Saviour	9.0	2.2	1.1	17.2
St Michael Coslany	9.6	3.1	5.0	17.5
St Martin at Palace	8.8	4.1	2.9	18.2
8 rich parishes	10.1	5.3	2.3	
St Margaret	17.6	8.2	8.4	22.6
St Lawrence	13.7	8.6	7.7	27.6
St Gregory	17.1	6.7	2.7	27.7
St George Colegate	15.6	3.8	3.9	28.2
St Stephen	15.5	6.7	2.4	29.8
St John Maddermarket	19.6	5.1	2.5	29.9
St Clement	3.6	5.0	2.2	30.5
St James	16.4	7.1	6.6	31.6
8 medium parishes	15.0	6.6	4.4	
St Mary Coslany	14.8	10.8	4.5	32.1
St Julian	–	8.4	2.9	35.3
St John Timberhill	13.7	6.6	2.6	41.3
St Peter Southgate	12.3	–	–	41.9
St Giles	13.1	15.1	4.8	43.0
St Benedict	7.6	5.5	6.3	45.2
St Peter Parmentergate	10.9	8.0	4.9	49.0
St Augustine	11.1	5.1	–	53.9
St Paul	–	–	4.2	57.4
All Saints	13.1	13.8	5.2	58.8
8 poor parishes	11.9	8.8	4.4	
24 parishes	12.3	6.9	3.8	

Notes
[1] Aug.–July.
[2] Year of worst mortality, normally Aug.–July.
[3] See n. 63, p. 372.

no parish register with continuous registration survives;[66] nothing can be known about these cases. However, of the remaining five parishes, all of which had less than average mortality in each epidemic, four were among the eight richest parishes in town, and three were in the

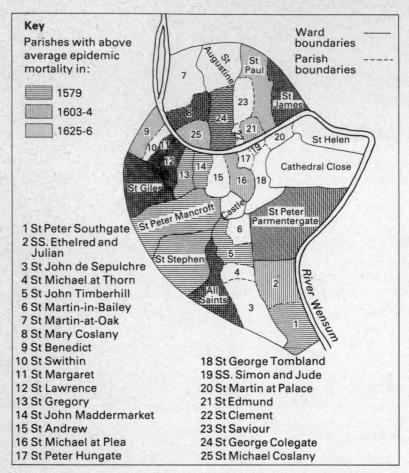

Figure 5.6 *The parishes of Norwich: the plagues of 1579, 1603 and 1625*

neighbourhood of the cathedral: St Andrew, SS. Simon and Jude, and St Martin at Palace.[67] More striking still on the map is the disappearance of unusually heavy epidemic mortality from other central parishes after 1579, and its persistence and consolidation on the fringes. The parishes of St Peter Mancroft, St Gregory and St John Maddermarket were added to the more fortunate ones after 1579. On the other hand, All Saints, St Giles's and St James's remained heavy plague areas, and they were joined in 1603 by St

Peter Parmentergate and in 1625 by St Benedict's, where (as in St James's) there was a growing suburb just outside the city walls.

The polarised fortunes of different parishes were clearer still in 1665–6. On this occasion we can measure local variations in mortality with unusual, though not complete, precision. We know the number of burials in every parish from 3 October 1665 to 3 October 1666. A census of 1693 gives the number of inhabitants in each parish, and if these figures are scaled down by 30 per cent they provide rough estimates of population in the 1660s.[68] That permits the calculation of approximate mortality rates for all parishes in 1665–6.[69] Finally, we can use the hearth tax returns of 1671 to rank the parishes in social order.[70] The calculated mortality rates are given in Table 5.5, and the extremes shown on Figure 5.7.

These illustrations speak for themselves. In the last visitation of plague in Norwich mortality was heaviest at the geographical and social margin. One-quarter of the deaths in fact occurred in three parishes in the south, on low-lying land close to the river, which together contained less than one-tenth of the population: St Peter Parmentergate, St Peter Southgate, and SS. Ethelred and Julian. Here, in the wards of North and South Conesford, in what was now by far the poorest area of town,[71] nearly two in every five of the inhabitants died in one year. The physical distance separating these slums from the rest of Norwich should not be exaggerated. As the map shows, the northernmost part of this neighbourhood, in St Peter Parmentergate parish, was only a step away from the prosperous and healthy households near the cathedral close, in the parish of St George Tombland. Yet there was a deep and significant demographic gulf along this parish boundary. It was in fact St Peter's, not St George's, which was part of the real 'Tombland' of Norwich.

The conditions which created such clear discrepancies over short spaces must have been similar to those in Exeter and Bristol: poor hygiene, bad housing, overcrowding, and a rapid turnover of population. None of these variables is easily quantified. The degree of congestion was almost certainly increasing over time, since demographic growth took place without any considerable new building in Norwich before the 1660s; but topographical variations cannot easily be measured. The number of people per acre was in fact much lower in the poorer parishes than in the rich, since the former were larger and contained more open spaces. The number of people per room would be a better indicator of overcrowding in the neighbourhood of

Table 5.5 *Plague mortality in Norwich 1665–6*

Parish	No. of burials (3 Oct.–3 Oct.)	Mortality % of estimated population
St John Maddermarket	54	11.7
St Clement	37	8.9
St Andrew	37	5.6
St Peter Mancroft	153	11.2
St Michael at Plea	17	5.1
SS. Simon and Jude	20	7.9
St Peter Hungate	16	8.6
St George Tombland	25	5.0
St George Colegate	70	8.7
St Saviour	21	4.3
St Edmund	18	6.9
11 rich parishes	468	8.2
St Martin at Palace	53	9.2
St Helen	18	7.6
St Giles	74	11.6
St Lawrence	76	16.2
St Gregory	34	6.3
St Stephen	185	14.9
St John Timberhill	72	15.4
St Michael Coslany	93	13.0
St Swithin	39	11.2
St Martin at Oak	132	15.2
St Mary Coslany	73	11.0
11 medium parishes	849	12.6
St Augustine	88	14.8
St Paul	68	9.9
St John de Sepulchre	88	16.1
St Margaret	94	20.2
All Saints	71	23.8
St Michael at Thorn	233	38.4
St Benedict	29	6.4
SS. Julian and Ethelred	254	45.0
St Peter Southgate	94	28.6
St James	75	25.8
St Peter Parmentergate	367	38.1
11 poor parishes	1461	25.2
33 parishes	2778	14.7

Source: See text and n. 68, p. 373.

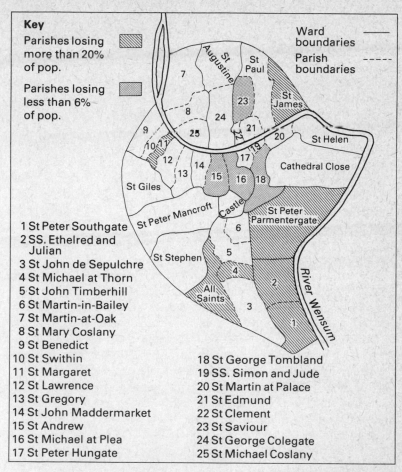

Key

Parishes losing more than 20% of pop.

Parishes losing less than 6% of pop.

Ward boundaries ———

Parish boundaries - - - - -

St Augustine
St Paul
7
St James
23
8 24
21
St Helen
9 25 20
10 11
12 19 22
13 14 15 16 18 17
St Giles Cathedral Close
St Peter Mancroft Castle St Peter Parmentergate
6
St Stephen 5
4
All Saints 2
3
1
River Wensum

1 St Peter Southgate
2 SS. Ethelred and Julian
3 St John de Sepulchre
4 St Michael at Thorn
5 St John Timberhill
6 St Martin-in-Bailey
7 St Martin-at-Oak
8 St Mary Coslany
9 St Benedict
10 St Swithin
11 St Margaret
12 St Lawrence
13 St Gregory
14 St John Maddermarket
15 St Andrew
16 St Michael at Plea
17 St Peter Hungate
18 St George Tombland
19 SS. Simon and Jude
20 St Martin at Palace
21 St Edmund
22 St Clement
23 St Saviour
24 St George Colegate
25 St Michael Coslany

Figure 5.7 The parishes of Norwich: the plague of 1665–6

rats, and that was probably higher in the poor parishes, as the figures of hearths per household in the hearth tax returns perhaps suggest. Much of North and South Conesford, for example, was not built up until the nineteenth century, and most of the population lived in a dense jumble of houses and yards along King Street.[72] The importance of all these circumstances in the spread of plague can be inferred, however, from one final noteworthy aspect of the disease in Norwich: its heavy incidence among the two Stranger communities of Dutch and Walloon refugees.

Until the 1620s, when their numbers began to decline, it was the foreign immigrants even more than the English poor who provided the fodder for epidemic disease in Norwich. Their susceptibility cannot be attributed to a lack of prior experience of plague, and hence to a failure to develop some natural immunity. Flemish towns were as well acquainted with the disease as Norwich itself. Rather, their vulnerability lay partly in the fact that they must often have brought the disease across the Channel with them, and partly in the environment which they created on their arrival. Few of them were men of wealth, merchants or entrepreneurs; most of them were artisans and labourers, working with cloth and wool (always a ready source of fleas), packed into dilapidated and rat-infested houses. Their presence was welcomed in 1575 precisely because 'by their means our city is well inhabited, and decayed houses re-edified and repaired that were in ruin, ... and now good rents paid for the same'. No less revealing was the complaint in 1579 that the aliens encouraged plague by 'the corrupt keeping of their houses'.[73]

The consequences were tragic. When the plague of 1579 began, Strangers probably comprised no more than one-third of the total population; there may have been about 5,000 of them. Yet in the last months of the epidemic, when they were first distinguished from the English in reports to the Mayor's Court, they accounted for 71 per cent of all burials in the town. It is not impossible that half the Strangers died in that year. By 1583 new arrivals had boosted their population to 4,679,[74] more than in 1571, but plague continued to hit them hard and further substantial migration was necessary to maintain their numbers. Although alien burials made up only 33 per cent of the total in the relatively healthy years 1586–8, the proportion rose to 51 per cent in the plague of 1585 and to 45 per cent in that of 1592. The percentage declined slightly in 1603; but the Strangers nevertheless suffered a death rate twice as high as that of the English citizens. While the number of English burials in 1603 was less than six times the average of the previous decade, the number of alien burials was twelve times the average. The Dutch and Walloons may well have lost one-third of their population in that single epidemic.

Like most immigrant communities, the Norwich Strangers congregated in tight clusters in particular parts of the town. In 1571 their largest concentrations were in the small wards of Middle and West Wymer, in the parishes stretching from St Michael at Plea to St Benedict's; and the subsidy returns of 1581 show that the poorest of them lived in West Wymer, particularly in the parishes of St Margaret and St Lawrence.[75] It was in the burial registers of these two parishes that substantial numbers of alien names were listed in all epidemics before 1665, and this helps to explain their prominence in Figure 5.6. The Strangers cannot account for the other variations in plague mortality between parishes which have been noted above, however, for it is probable that, outside these two parishes, the vast majority of Stranger burials were not entered in the parish registers at all. In every epidemic year between 1579 and 1625 less than half the number of deaths reported to the Mayor's Court were recorded in the burial registers of twenty-four of the thirty-four parishes, despite the fact that these parishes contained at least two-thirds of the population; and in each case the discrepancy was approximately the same as the number of alien burials returned. It would seem, therefore, that the Strangers not only had their own churches (one each for the Dutch and Walloon congregations), but also their own burial grounds or at least their own registers of alien burials in the parish churchyards.[76] If it were not for the weekly reports of burials to the Court, we should know little about the most dramatic of all aspects of plague epidemics in Elizabethan Norwich.

In the early seventeenth century the Stranger population declined. The level of alien baptisms suggests that their numbers hovered around 3,000 for a decade after 1603, but there was a steep fall after 1616. The truce in the Netherlands in 1609 must have deterred further migration, and at the same time resident Strangers were being assimilated into the English population. By 1620 the two congregations were complaining bitterly of desertions, and ceasing to be representatives of a large and identifiable foreign community in the city.[77] In the forty years before 1620, however, it had been plague and not assimilation which enabled Norwich to absorb, or more accurately to consume, an alien population much larger than that attracted to any other provincial town. The selective incidence of bubonic plague was as conspicuous in Norwich as in Bristol or Exeter, but for part of our period its target was more precisely defined.

Norwich stands out as the exception among the towns in this chapter. Certainly after 1560, and perhaps before, epidemics of plague were more common there than in Exeter or Bristol, and the worst of them were more violent. There appears to be no simple explanation for this. The close proximity of Norwich to the Low Countries must have

played a part, but we cannot attribute everything to it, since plague
proved to be less serious in Essex, which was similarly situated, than
in Devon. Norwich was the largest of the three towns, and the disease
may more easily have become enzootic there, as it did in London. Yet
Bristol and Exeter were much closer in size to Norwich than Norwich
was to London.

Differences in social structure may well have been more important
than differences in situation or size. The large number of foreign
immigrants in Norwich, its most obvious distinguishing feature, was
probably connected with the severity of disease. Other English towns
with alien populations, Southampton and Colchester, for example,
also suffered badly from plague.[78] In addition, it is possible that in the
later part of the period Norwich had a more impoverished labouring
population than either of the western towns. The subsidy assessments
of 1524–5 suggest that their social structures were not significantly
different in the early sixteenth century: 40 per cent of taxpayers were
assessed at less than £2 in Norwich, compared with 48 per cent in
Exeter and 36 per cent in Bristol.[79] By the time of the hearth taxes
of the 1660s and 1670s, however, the social pyramid in Norwich
apparently had an unusually broad base: 62 per cent of the households
there were exempted from the tax on the grounds of poverty, while
40 per cent were exempted in Exeter and only 21 per cent in Bristol.[80]
Although the comparative study of urban social structures has scarcely
begun, and we need to know more, for example, about the criteria
for exemption from the hearth tax, these figures are suggestive.
Between the great census of the poor in 1570 and the last outbreak
of plague in 1665, Norwich may have been exceptional in the number
of poor as well as in the number of foreigners it contained.

When all the differences have been noted, however, the similarities
between the three towns remain the more striking. Plague was a
regular visitor to all of them, and regular often in a literal sense. Five-
or ten- or twenty-year intervals, which may be a result of demographic
cycles among rodents, can be observed between several epidemics:
1544, 1554, 1579, 1584, and 1589 in Norwich, 1565 and 1575 in
Bristol, 1570 and 1590 in Exeter.[81] Of more immediate import for
the towns themselves was the fact that plague often arrived at critical
moments: during civil war in Bristol in the 1640s, at times of high
prices and food scarcity in Exeter in 1546 and Bristol in 1550–1,
shortly before the peasant revolts and sieges of 1549 in Exeter and

Norwich. It is easy to see why the 1540s were a troubled decade in the history of English towns.

But for our purposes it is the regularities in the social impact of plague which are of prime importance, since they determined some of the social responses to it which will concern us in the second half of this book. By the early seventeenth century plague was concentrated in clearly distinguishable areas of each town, in the fringe parishes which were chiefly, though not wholly, inhabited by the labouring poor. It may not always have been so. There is some evidence of a growing disparity between centre and periphery in the course of the sixteenth century, for reasons which will be considered when we have looked at comparable developments in London. In the seventeenth century, however, the disparity was evident; and its meaning for contemporaries was succinctly summarised in two remarks made during the epidemic of 1665–6 in Norwich. People at the bottom of the social scale were complaining about the environment which threatened them with disease: 'They will live in better houses than now they do.' People at the top, like the Town Clerk, were concerned much more about its secondary consequences: 'We are in greater fear of the poor than the plague.'[82]

Chapter 6

Metropolitan crises

Death (like a Spanish Leaguer or rather like stalking Tamberlane) hath
pitched his tents (being nothing but a heap of winding sheets tacked
together) in the sinfully polluted suburbs: the Plague is muster-master
and marshal of the field: burning fevers, boils, blains and carbuncles, the
leaders, lieutenants, sergeants and corporals: the main army consisting
(like Dunkirk) of a mingle mangle, *viz.* dumpish mourners, merry sextons,
hungry coffin-sellers, scrubbing bearers, and nasty grave-makers: . . . fear
and trembling (the two catch-poles of death) arrest everyone. No parley
will be granted, no composition stood upon. But the alarum is struck up,
the toxin rings out for life, and no voice heard but *Tue! Tue! Kill! Kill!*
                          Thomas Dekker, *1603. The Wonderfull Yeare* (1603)[1]

The writings of Samuel Pepys and Daniel Defoe have made the
'Great Plague' of London of 1665 so much a part of the common
currency of historical knowledge that it has obscured earlier epidemics.
That outbreak was simply the last of a series of metropolitan crises
which shaped the consciousness of the literate and governing classes
with regard to plague. For more than a century epidemics in London
had prompted medical and religious tracts, been the subject of
macabre stories by writers such as Thomas Dekker, and finally, in
1662, produced the first serious work on English demography, by
John Graunt.[2] They also forced the government to develop those
policies for public health which will be considered in later chapters.
As in other spheres of English life, events in the capital played a large
part in determining national attitudes and actions.
  The definitive account of plague in London has still to be written,
and it cannot be attempted in the space available here. The effects of
epidemics in the more than 100 parishes which made up the city and
liberties, and in the outlying suburbs, could easily occupy a whole
volume, and much has already been written about them without

exhausting the subject.[3]   This chapter will concentrate on two themes which furnish comparisons with the towns already considered: first, the frequency and severity of plague outbreaks, and second, the changing geographical distribution of epidemic mortality within the metropolis. In neither respect was London fundamentally different from Norwich. The epidemic history of provincial towns was simply replicated on a larger scale.

(i) Chronology and severity

In the early sixteenth century London was already notorious for its ill-health. This 'stinking city', 'the filthiest of the world', as Philip Hoby described it, was also, the French ambassador complained, one of the most subject to plague.[4] It has indeed become a truism that there was scarcely a year in the sixteenth and the early seventeenth century when the disease was absent from the capital. It is a truism which requires some qualification. There were intermissions between outbreaks, each of them ending when another virulent strain of the bacillus reached the city. But the intermissions rarely lasted for as long as a decade and were often much shorter. For a large part of the period, plague was present in one of two guises. Either it persisted in moderate form for years at a time, raising normal mortality levels sometimes by 10 per cent, sometimes much less; or it caused major mortality in a single summer and died away in the following year.

The persistence and variability of plague's hold on London is clearest in the seventeenth century, thanks to the continuous record of all burials and of plague burials which the bills of mortality provide. The annual totals, shown in Figure 6.1, reveal a consistent pattern.[5] There were great surges of infection, in 1603, 1625, 1636 and 1665; there were two long periods between 1606 and 1610 and between 1640 and 1647 (with a slight remission in 1643) when plague was responsible for more than 10 per cent of recorded burials every year; and between them there were plague-free intervals. The length of the intervals is uncertain. It was shorter than appears in the figure, since the number of cases of plague reported was often too small to show there. Between three and seventy plague deaths were recorded every year from 1612 to 1624, in 1627 and 1628, in 1632 and 1634, and again from 1649 to 1664. The number was also very low from 1667 to 1669 and from 1671 until 1679, when the last two cases of bubonic

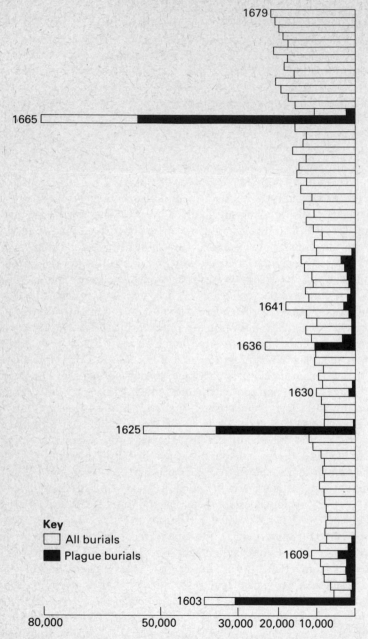

Figure 6.1 Burials in London 1603–79 from the bills of mortality (Source: See n. 5, p.

plague in England were notified. It is unlikely, however, that all these were in fact deaths from plague: it would be wrong to assume that the disease was in London in years when only one or two fallible searchers of the dead thought they saw it. Yet even if we ignore years in which less than 100 casualties were notified, plague was present in twenty-eight of the sixty-four years between 1603 and 1666. It was therefore endemic in London for much, perhaps most, of the early seventeenth century, and a constant drain on the population. At least a fifth of all deaths from 1603 to 1665 can be attributed to it.

There is no reason to suppose that the picture in the sixteenth century was any different, although the sources are less complete. Figures taken from bills which no longer survive show the extent of mortality in the two major epidemics of Elizabeth's reign, in 1563 and 1593.[6] There was also a long period of less heavy plague mortality between 1577 and 1583, with a peak in 1578; and some of the parish registers reveal another, rather less serious, between 1568 and 1571.[7] Before 1563, however, the evidence is more sparse. We have only parish registers, and before 1538 only wills.

Figure 6.2 shows the number of wills proved each year in the Commissary Court of London between 1478 and 1565.[8] With one

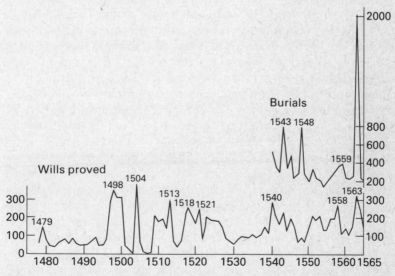

Figure 6.2 Mortality in London 1478–1565 (Sources: See nn. 8, 10, pp. 374–5)

exception, in 1558, the successive peaks all occurred in years when there were contemporary references to plague in London;[9] and the frequency of such crises between 1498 and 1521 is particularly notable. There may well have been even more outbreaks of plague than those indicated here, however. As in Norwich, the burials recorded in the earliest parish registers show that probate evidence relating to adults and the prosperous gives only a partial picture of total mortality. Annual burials in eighteen city parishes, also shown in Figure 6.2,[10] reveal two severe epidemics in 1543 and 1548 whose very existence might not have been suspected from the probate statistics; and both of them seeem to have been caused by plague. There were doubtless others before 1540, as in 1535–6 when the literary evidence for a severe outbreak is particularly strong.[11] Plague was probably more common in the early sixteenth century than in the early seventeenth.

The inadequacies of the probate evidence prohibit any attempt to measure the severity as well as the frequency of epidemics before 1540. It is evident from comparison with the registered burials in Figure 6.2 that variations in the number of probates may either understate the rise in gross mortality, as they clearly do in the case of the plague of 1563, or overstate it, as they appear to do in the case of the influenza epidemic of 1558–9. The parish registers provide somewhat firmer ground after 1540 and suggest that plague was at least as serious in London as in our other major towns in the mid-sixteenth century. In 1543 and 1548 the aggregate number of burials in the eighteen parishes was three times the average level for the decade 1549 to 1558, indicating mortality approaching 8 per cent; and in 1563 it rose nearly eight-fold, implying that as many as 20 per cent of the population may have died. From 1563 onwards, however, we can rely on a much more comprehensive record of the impact of plague in London: the bills of mortality.

At first the weekly collection of vital statistics from the clerks of each parish was intermittent. It probably began in 1519, when Cardinal Wolsey wanted the Court to have advance warning of disease in the capital; and the mayor and aldermen soon appreciated the utility of information not only about plague but also about gross totals of burials and christenings. By 1563 there were occasional annual bills summarising the weekly totals: they were the source for figures of the death toll in the plague of that year which circulated widely. In 1593 and in later epidemic years the bills were printed as broadsheets, and this was the regular practice from 1629 onwards when causes of death other than plague were also always given.[12] As a result, the general public had regular bulletins about the health of the capital, and they used them. As early as 1610 the authorities feared that the circulation of the bills abroad as well as at home damaged London's trade 'to the public hurt'. It could not be stopped. By the middle of the seventeenth century, the bills had become

> a text to talk upon in the next company, and withal in the plague-time [to see] how the sickness increased, or decreased, that so the rich might judge of the necessity of their removal [from London], and tradesmen might conjecture what doings they were like to have in their respective dealings.[13]

Informative as they were and are, the bills are not, of course, a wholly reliable source. Their statements about the cause of death depended on the opinion of those 'ancient matrons', the 'ignorant and careless searchers', and hence they greatly understate the proportion of plague casualties in major epidemics, as John Graunt showed.[14] When the bills are compared with parish registers, there is a remarkable degree of agreement on total mortality, at least after 1603: small discrepancies between one source and the other in individual parishes tend to cancel one another out.[15] But the parish registers were themselves incomplete records of burials and even more of deaths. The licensing of new graveyards for some city parishes in the seventeenth century and the establishment of a Quaker burial ground after 1660 make it likely that under-registration gradually increased;[16] and there was always the problem that the number of casualties in a major epidemic was simply too large for either churchyards or parish clerks to cope with.

At the height of the epidemic of 1665 more than fifty people were being buried and their names entered in the register every day in several of the larger parishes, and many churchyards must have been like that of St Stephen's Coleman Street which 'began to smell and annoy the inhabitants'. Much earlier, in 1563, the parish clerk of St Botolph's Bishopsgate was reduced to noting the burial of 'two corpses' or 'three corpses' without further identification. His colleague in St Saviour's Southwark in 1625 sometimes found 'twenty or thirty corpses left at the place of burial' and he 'knew not who brought them thither'.[17] In the circumstances it is remarkable that registration never broke down altogether.

A further problem involved in the use of the bills of mortality arises from a more general difficulty in the study of early modern London. The built-up area of the metropolis was growing, and as it did so the area covered by the bills was also extended. The earliest bills list the ninety-six (later ninety-seven) parishes within the walls of the city, and annual bills for the major crises also included sixteen parishes, partly within the liberties of the city but outside the walls. This was the area of the 'city and liberties'. From 1603 onwards, however, a third group of nine 'outparishes', including St Giles-in-the-Fields and St James Clerkenwell, was added; and from 1636 there was another permanent addition of seven 'distant' parishes, including St Margaret's Westminster, St Mary Islington, Lambeth, Stepney, St Mary Newington and Hackney. The growth of the capital makes it impossible to use a constant area for the study of plague in 'London'.

Nevertheless, when all reservations have been made, the bills remain an indispensable source. Provided we remember that they understate mortality to an unknown, but perhaps increasing degree, we can use them to estimate the dimensions of the great plagues which hit London between 1563 and 1665. The relevant statistics are summarised in Table 6.1, which is based on Dr I. Sutherland's sophisticated and exhaustive analysis of all the surviving bills.[18] The first columns give the total number of burials and the number attributed to plague in each major plague year: for the city and liberties up to 1625, and for the city, liberties and outparishes in the epidemics of 1636 and 1665. Then there are indices of relative mortality. These have been calculated by Dr Sutherland rather differently from our earlier Crisis Mortality Ratios, but they are comparable in their implications since they measure the ratio between burials in the epidemic year and 'normal' mortality.[19] Finally, the table shows Dr Sutherland's estimated total population of the area of London covered by the bills, and the percentage gross mortality rate which can be derived from it.[20]

It appears that the epidemic of 1665 was the 'Great Plague' in one sense only: in terms of the gross number of deaths. In terms of mortality relative to population or relative to normally expected death-rates, it was less serious than the plagues of 1563 and 1603, and perhaps less serious than that of 1625. Too much should not be made of the precise indices and percentage mortality rates in Table 6.1. They are extremely sensitive to the assumptions about 'normal' rates and population on which they are based. Different indices, constructed

Table 6.1 *Major epidemics in London 1563–1665*

Year	All Burials	Plague burials	Index of relative mortality	Est. total population	Mortality %
City and liberties					
1563	20,372	17,404	7.70	85,000	24.0
1578	7,830	3,568	2.29	101,000	7.8
1593	17,893	10,675	4.25	125,000	14.3
1603	31,861	25,045	6.74	141,000	22.6
1625	41,312	26,350	6.18	206,000	20.1
City, liberties and outparishes					
1636	23,359	10,400	2.25	313,000	7.5
1665	80,696	55,797	5.41	459,000	17.6

Source: See nn. 18–20, pp. 375–6.

like Crisis Mortality Ratios from epidemic and average burials in the bills of mortality or in parish registers, yield slightly different results, while still suggesting that 1665 was a less serious outbreak than those of 1563 and 1603.[21] But all the calculations amply confirm William Petty's dictum that plagues in London 'do commonly kill one fifth part of the inhabitants'.[22]

That was roughly the proportion in 1603 and 1625; it was almost reached in 1665; and it had been exceeded in 1563, when scarcely less than a quarter of the population died. Besides these crises there was another epidemic in 1593 as severe as the worst in Exeter and Bristol, and in 1578 and 1636, as in 1543 and 1548, there were epidemics during which normal mortality rates more than doubled. In all, then, there were nine serious epidemics of plague in the metropolis between 1540 and 1666, one every fourteen years on average. The disease was not only endemic for years at a time; it also regularly reached epidemic proportions.

(ii) The distribution of mortality

The bills of mortality and parish registers of the city show the gradual movement of disease across the metropolis in each of these great epidemics. Many parishes escaped for a month or two after plague had reached London, but few remained unaffected once it had a hold in mobile human and rodent populations. As one might expect, the parishes first infected were sometimes in the east, near the river and the docks. In the last and best-documented outbreak, in 1665, however, plague reached epidemic proportions first in St Giles-in-the-Fields to the north-west of the city, moving from there round the edge of the built-up area and finally invading the city proper across the walls.[23] Parish officers tried in vain to stem the tide. Time and again churchwardens paid out sixpence or a shilling to men 'to carry away a sick man for fear he should die in the streets within this parish' or to carry off a woman who 'fell down in the night'.[24] The city hospitals sometimes picked up the debris. In the plague of 1563 Christ's Hospital took in a youth 'turned out in the plague-time' by his master, a fifteen-year-old boy 'taken up in the street all comfortless', and a baby girl, fourteen days old, whose mother had died after she 'did comfort . . . one Moore . . . who with his wife and a child . . . died of the plague'. Hospital governors soon learned the folly of such charity, but even when they turned away suspected cases, they saw plague relentlessly invading the houses and parishes around them.[25]

Ineluctable as its progress might seem, the incidence of disease was in fact no more uniform in London than in other towns in the period. There was no lack of parallels to the Pithay in Bristol. Exceptional plague mortality can be plotted in the alleys of the parishes of St Bartholomew Exchange and St Margaret Lothbury; and plague casualties were numerous also in the back streets of St Michael Cornhill, St Dunstan in the West and St Saviour's Southwark.[26] Some contemporaries attributed this to the filth and refuse indoors and out, which brought with it 'an unavoidable danger to breed contagious and infectious diseases'. Others found the root of plague in inadequate housing: its victims commonly lived in cellars or sheds where 'if one die infected, it is more dangerous than in any house'.[27] Above all, however, pestilence seemed to be generated by overcrowding in tenements and subdivided houses. The Recorder of London noted that in 1603 there were 800 cases of plague in a single building, formerly one of four large mansions which now together housed 8,000 people. Such instances inspired the vigorous campaign against subdivision and new building which the government waged, to no avail, between 1580 and the Civil War. Infection in 'small and straight rooms and habitations' was 'one of the chiefest occasions of the great plague and mortality'.[28]

In the mid-sixteenth century these problems were evident in some parts of the inner city, wherever there was still room for in-filling.

But by the early seventeenth century they were most striking in the suburbs where urban growth was rapid: just outside the walls east of the Tower, outside Cripplegate and Bishopsgate in the north and north-east, and north of the Strand between the city and Westminster.[29] Here, it was recognised, plague mortality was always heaviest. In 1603 it was 'especially in the suburbs on every side, and in the outplaces' that plague flourished. In 1630, when there was a minor epidemic, it was almost entirely confined to the liberties and outparishes, beginning in St Giles in the west and in Whitechapel and Shoreditch in the east. As Dekker vividly put it, 'the cannon of the Pestilence' did not fire on the city, but 'the small shot' rained 'night and day upon the suburbs'. Even when the cannon exploded, in 1665, it did so with uneven effect. As *The Newes* reported in July, plague was worst in the suburbs because of 'the misery of a close and smothering confinement' with its 'poverty and sluttishness', and the few victims within the walls similarly lived 'in close and blind alleys'.[30]

It is a remarkable feature of plague in London, however, that the topographical bias in the distribution of mortality was much less obvious in the mid-sixteenth century than in the seventeenth. In the earlier period, in fact, it was not obvious at all. The gradual emergence of a distinct urban topography of plague, of which there are signs in provincial towns, can be seen clearly in London. We can observe this important change if we look, as in the case of Norwich, at different groups of parishes and at the Crisis Mortality Ratios of epidemic to normal burials in them.

From the annual bills of mortality we can calculate ratios for each London parish in the great epidemics from 1625 onwards.[31] Before 1603, we have no long series of bills to give us the normal average number of burials in individual parishes. For the major epidemics of 1563, 1593 and 1603, therefore, the ratios have to be derived from the data in the surviving parish registers. In all, fifty-six registers relating to the metropolitan area from 1563 onwards have been examined. Nine of them come from outparishes, distant parishes and Westminster;[32] five from the liberties outside the walls of the city;[33] and forty-two from the ninety-seven parishes within the walls.[34] Altogether, registers of rather less than half the parishes in the city and liberties have been seen, but since they include some large parishes, they cover more than half of the built-up area of London in the later sixteenth century.

It would be impractical to present all the data from these parishes here, and we must deal in summary terms. It is convenient first to look at the parts of the city and liberties which were most seriously and least seriously affected by plague. Using the Crisis Mortality Ratios we can pick out in each great epidemic the ten parishes in which the rise in mortality was greatest and the ten in which it was smallest. These two groups of parishes are shown for each of the four worst epidemics of the period, those of 1563, 1603, 1625 and 1665 in Figures 6.3–6.6.

In the epidemics of the seventeenth century the pattern was reasonably consistent. The parishes least affected were in the centre of the city. The worst affected were on its fringes: in the north-east, in St Botolph's without Aldgate and St Botolph's without Bishopsgate outside the walls, and in Allhallows London Wall, just inside them; in the north, in St Giles Cripplegate, or again just within the walls in St Stephen's Coleman Street in 1625; to the west and north-west in Bridewell precinct and St Bartholomew the Great in 1625; or in places along the riverside, as in 1603. Although it is not shown on a map, the pattern in the epidemic of 1593 was much the same. In 1563, however, this pattern was almost exactly reversed. The suburbs

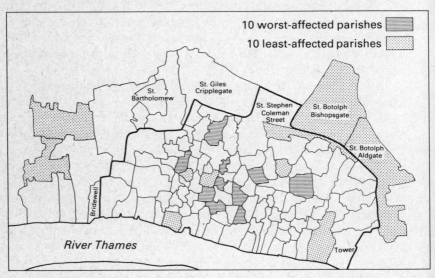

Figure 6.3 London parishes in the plague of 1563. The heavy line indicates the limits of the city within the walls. (Based on the map in London Inhabitants Within the Walls 1695, *p. xxii.)*

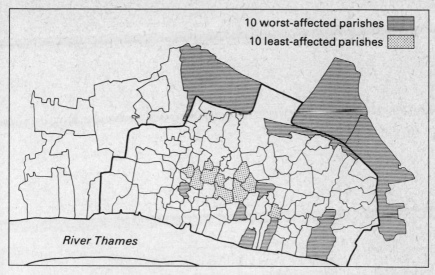

Figure 6.4 London parishes in the plague of 1603

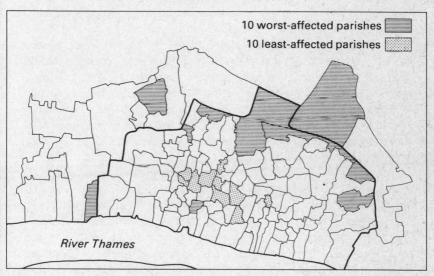

Figure 6.5 London parishes in the plague of 1625

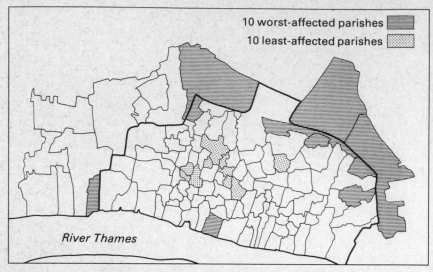

10 worst-affected parishes

10 least-affected parishes

River Thames

Figure 6.6 London parishes in the plague of 1665

and riverside parishes were less seriously affected than parishes in the heart of the city.[35]

Unfortunately, we cannot push this analysis back beyond 1563, because the registers of the fringe parishes do not begin early enough. But there is no reason to suppose that the epidemic of 1563 differed in its distribution from those earlier in the century, and some evidence to suggest the contrary. The eighteen parishes whose aggregate burials are shown in Figure 6.2 include one, St Stephen's Coleman Street, near the edge of the city. There the rise in mortality in the plagues of 1543 and 1548 was smaller than in more central parishes. Some of the latter, on the other hand, like St Lawrence Jewry, suffered a rise in mortality in 1543 and 1548 which was greater than in any later epidemic save that of 1563.[36] The surviving registers suggest that the distribution of plague mortality changed markedly in the later sixteenth century, and specifically between 1563 and 1593.[37]

This development cannot be explained by any equally radical alteration in the location of prosperous and impoverished areas in the city. They did not change places. The social geography of London in the later seventeenth century, which has been established by historians working on the poor relief records of the 1650s and on the tax returns of the 1690s, was in broad terms the same as it had been in the sixteenth century.[38] The richest parishes were always in the centre of town and the poorest on the periphery. Using evidence drawn from the subsidy returns of 1522–3 and 1572, from a survey of rental values in the city in 1638 and from the tax assessments of 1695, we can pick out a group of fourteen parishes which were among the poorest throughout the period and a group of thirteen which were among the richest.[39] Our information is incomplete for the western fringes of the city before the 1690s and hence many parishes there cannot be classified. But the two sets of parishes shown in Figure 6.7 reveal a typical urban pattern of poverty and lower-class housing close to the walls and along the riverside, with wealth concentrated in the centre.

If the social geography of London did not in fact change in any fundamental way in the later sixteenth century, and if the distribution of plague did change in the way we have suggested, it would follow that the mortality experience of central rich parishes in epidemics markedly improved, while that of the poorer parishes deteriorated enormously. That is indeed what we find when we examine mortality in successive epidemics in parishes at the two social extremes. Seven of the fourteen poor parishes and nine of the thirteen rich ones have registers dating from 1560. Their burials have been aggregated, and Crisis Mortality Ratios for each group during epidemics have been

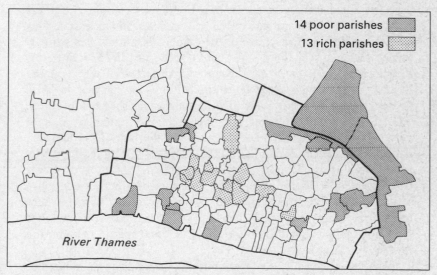

14 poor parishes
13 rich parishes

River Thames

Figure 6.7 Rich and poor parishes in London

calculated. They are shown in Table 6.2, together with the ratios for
all burials in the forty-seven parishes in the city and liberties whose
registers are available.[40]

Table 6.2 *Plague mortality in London by status of parish*
(CMR = Crisis Mortality Ratio)

Date of plague		City and liberties (47 parishes)		9 rich parishes		7 poor parishes	
1563	Burials	7,718		624		1,793	
	CMR		6.1		6.6		5.8
1593	Burials	8,716		361		3,274	
	CMR		4.7		3.2		5.8
1603	Burials	13,436		557		4,526	
	CMR		7.3		5.0		8.0
1625	Burials	17,587		577		6,222	
	CMR		5.8		3.8		6.5
1636	Burials	7,737		182		3,152	
	CMR		2.5		1.2		3.3
1665	Burials	27,268		621		9,955	
	CMR		5.9		3.4		6.8

Source: See n. 40, p. 378. All burials from Jan. to Dec. have been counted.

In the major epidemics after 1563 mortality in the poor parishes
was always higher than the average for London as a whole, and it was
always lower than the average in the rich parishes. In the least serious
of these epidemics, that of 1636, the number of burials was scarcely
higher than in normal times in the centre of the city. In 1563, however,
the situation appears to have been very different. There is some
difficulty in calculating accurate Mortality Ratios for that year, because
of the absence of registration in many of the parishes before 1560.
The 'normal' annual averages, from which the ratios are derived, have
necessarily been taken in several cases from the years 1564 to 1573,
and since that decade included minor outbreaks of plague, the calculated ratios are probably too low. This explains why they are lower
than the ratio given in Table 6.1.[41] Nevertheless, whether one looks
at the groups shown in Table 6.2 or at individual parishes where
burials were registered before 1563, it is clear that the richer parishes
were not healthier than the poorer in 1563, and that if anything the
reverse was the case.

It should not be concluded from this that plague in 1563 and earlier
hit rich and poor people (as distinct from parishes) equally. The fact

that the number of registered burials rose more dramatically than the number of proved wills in that year strongly suggests that the normal social incidence of plague was as evident in that epidemic as it was later. (See Fig. 6.2.) In the central parishes of the city the disease was probably concentrated in alleys and poor tenements. There is also some evidence to suggest that there were significant differences between parishes within the central area of the city which can be explained by relative poverty. Some of the parishes worst affected, shown in Figure 6.1, were not the richest parishes shown in Figure 6.5, although they were geographically close to them. St Mary Aldermary, St Mary Bothaw, St Peter Cornhill and St Thomas's all recorded ratios of 8.0 or more, and none was among the very richest parishes in the city. It was in a group of central parishes of moderate wealth that the highest mortality was recorded in 1563.

If economic and social status was a significant variable in 1563 as later, why did the poorest parishes not suffer more in that year? The answer probably lies in their low population density at that time. A dense population was not a sufficient cause of major plague mortality, as the relative good fortune of crowded central parishes in London and Norwich in the seventeenth century shows. But it probably was a necessary condition for serious epidemics. Heavy mortality from a disease carried by rats and fleas depended upon more than the presence in dilapidated houses of people with few or no changes of clothing. It required a large number of such people in close proximity to one another, to dirt and to rats. It is likely that the parishes in our poor sample had not yet reached the necessary density threshold in 1563, and that they did not do so until after 1580, when demographic growth at last became intense and the demand for housing in London could not be satisfied closer to the centre.[42] Most of the poor parishes were large: together they covered an area more than four times bigger than the group of rich parishes. But the average recorded burials would suggest that in the 1560s their aggregate population was no more than three times as great. By 1600, however, the population in the poor parishes was probably five times that in the rich, and by 1660 it may have been eight times greater. As population grew along the riverside and above all in parishes just outside the walls in the last decades of the sixteenth century, so there occurred that deterioration in the quality of the environment which bred disease.

It was no accident that these parts of the city had contained monastic houses before the dissolution. Their destruction left empty spaces to tempt speculative builders and attract the immigrant poor. It also left liberties, technically in the king's hands and out of the direct control of the city, where vagrants and rogues soon began to congregate. It was prophetic for the future social status of these quarters that they were the site of some of the hospitals founded or refounded in the later 1540s, Bedlam outside Bishopsgate and St Bartholomew's in the north-west. A similar area of rapid housing development at the end of the century was in Bridewell precinct, just outside the western wall of the city, by the river. Once a royal palace, Bridewell itself was finally abandoned by Henry VIII in 1529 after an outbreak of plague. It became the city workhouse and the heart of one of the areas worst hit by the epidemics of 1625 and 1665. Close to it was the disputed liberty of Blackfriars, just inside the walls. By 1600 these two precincts together formed one end of a semi-circle of slums, which stretched around the walls back to the river and ended with the very similar territory of the Minories and St Katherine's by the Tower in the east.[43]

Some of the recent developments on the outskirts of the city attracted the attention of John Stow surveying London at the very end of the sixteenth century. There were new tenements on the riverside, in Queenhithe and Billingsgate wards, for example, and filthy cottages east of the Tower and in Farringdon Without ward in the north-west; while to the north along Bishopsgate Street many houses had 'been built with alleys backward, of late time too much pestered with people (a great cause of infection)'.[44] The fuel for epidemic disease gradually accumulated here, and so did the carriers of plague. Rats were attracted by the granaries and major markets of the city, some of which were by the river or just outside the walls: at Queenhithe and Billingsgate, Bridewell and Smithfield.[45] Here too foreign refugees from the Netherlands congregated in and after the 1560s. They settled first along the river, in Blackfriars, Billingsgate ward, the parishes of St Dunstan in the East and St Katherine by the Tower, and across London Bridge in Southwark. By 1593, however, they were especially numerous in the north-west – in Aldgate, Portsoken and Bishopsgate wards on either side of the walls; and, as in Norwich, there were complaints that they were 'pestered together' in small houses.[46] Given all this, it is not surprising to find that by 1600 infant and child mortality rates in non-epidemic years were relatively high in precisely these quarters, along the river and near the walls.[47] Plague simply exaggerated an established feature of metropolitan life.

The number of foreign immigrants declined in the early seventeenth century, but there was no fall in English immigration into the liberties, which were almost overwhelmed by poverty. In 1638 there were said to be between 700 and 800 families of 'miserable poor' in St Bride's, just north of Bridewell. Moving further round the walls, there was 'a multitude of poor people' in St Giles Cripplegate and heavy expenditure on the poor in Allhallows London Wall. Further to the east, the more respectable parishioners who attended the church of St Botolph without Bishopsgate during the plague of 1636 had the churchyard fenced off 'to keep the poor from us'. In St Botolph's without Aldgate, the beginning of the East End, which was becoming known for its industrial pollution and for its plague, the minister complained of his and the parish's poverty in 1638: the major part of his income, he said, came from burial fees, and 'if people do not die, I cannot live'.[48] He need scarcely have worried.

The most important change in the development of plague in London was thus its increasing hold in outer parishes with growing populations. There, as in the suburbs of provincial towns, plague was both a symptom of suburban instability and an independent variable which aggravated it, raising death rates which were already abnormally high and accelerating a turnover of population which was already rapid. In London, however, the process occurred on a much larger scale than elsewhere, and it was not confined to the extramural parishes, precincts and liberties we have so far considered. For growth burst out of these bounds in the later sixteenth and even more in the seventeenth century. It occurred in Southwark across the river, always a haven for vagrants and no doubt for rats, since it contained the city's main granary at the Bridgehouse by the Thames; in the hamlets of Stepney beyond St Botolph's Aldgate, which gradually became part of the East End; in Clerkenwell beyond Cripplegate, which had once been an exclusive upper-class neighbourhood, but which now began to decline in status as its population grew; in the parishes to the west along and to the north of the Strand; and finally in Westminster, where the mansions of nobles and courtiers rubbed shoulders with blind alleys, sheds and penthouses, springing up around, behind and against them.[49] As growth occurred on the periphery of the metropolis, so the ravages of plague grew heavier there, both in terms of absolute numbers and relative to the central area of the city, as Table 6.3 makes clear.[50]

Once again a full analysis of the distribution of mortality is imposs-

Table 6.3 The spatial distribution of plague mortality in Metropolitan London (CMR = Crisis Mortality Ratio)

Plague year		(1) City centre	(2) West	(3) North	(4) North-East	(5) East End	(6) South
1563	Burials	1,595	1,641	1,167	1,057	–	688
	CMR	6.9	4.1	6.2	4.8	–	3.1
1593	Burials	971	1,683	1,770	2,453	1,862	1,160
	CMR	3.6	3.4	5.5	6.0	4.5	3.8
1603	Burials	1,406	2,776	2,878	3,486	4,120	2,323
	CMR	5.2	5.6	9.0	8.5	7.9	7.6
1625	Burials	1,379	5,317	3,988	4,907	7,725	2,746
	CMR	4.1	3.7	6.3	6.6	5.8	6.7
1636	Burials	410	2,533	2,374	2,740	3,661	1,269
	CMR	1.2	1.8	3.7	3.7	2.7	3.1
1665	Burials	1,318	11,786	8,069	8,390	13,364	4,235
	CMR	3.0	4.9	7.3	7.0	6.5	7.9

Notes
1 21 central parishes: Allhallows Bread Street, Allhallows Honey Lane, SS. Antholin, Benet Fink, Christopher le Stocks, Lawrence Jewry, Martin Ironmonger, Mary Aldermary, Mary Bow, Mary Magd. Milk Street, Mary Woolchurch, Mary Woolnoth, Matthew Friday Street, Michael Cornhill, Mildred Poultry, Nicholas Acon, Olave Old Jewry, Pancras Soper Lane, Peter Cornhill, Stephen Walbrook, Vedast.
2 SS. Margaret Westminster, Martin-in-the-Fields, Clement Danes, Mary le Strand.
3 St Giles without Cripplegate.
4 SS. Botolph Aldgate and Botolph Bishopsgate.
5 SS. Dunstan Stepney and Mary Whitechapel.
6 St Saviour Southwark.

ible because of the absence of many parish registers, and because few of those which do survive have entries before 1563. The Crisis Mortality Ratios for 1563 are perhaps again too low, having been calculated from average burials after 1563. Nevertheless, the changing distribution of mortality between one area of the metropolis and another is evident from the table. It reinforces the point that in 1563 mortality was heaviest in the centre of the city. In 1593, however, it was greatest just outside the walls, outside Cripplegate, Aldgate and Bishopsgate. By 1603 Southwark and the East End had almost caught up and the former was the area worst affected in 1625. Westminster and the West End throughout suffered less than the other edges of the metropolis, because of their generally higher social status. Yet the number of poor tenements was growing, particularly in St Margaret's Westminster, and population density was increasing to dangerous levels, so that by 1665 mortality here was notably higher than in the city centre.

It was not only the relative level of mortality which made the impact of plague so much greater in the suburbs. The absolute number of the dead imposed on their parochial authorities a burden such as central parishes of the city never had to bear. Even in Westminster, the victims of plague were as numerous in a single parish as in a medium-sized provincial town. In the minor epidemic of 1636 in St Martin-in-the-Fields, for example, 324 houses containing 1,328 people had to be quarantined, and in some of them all the inmates were soon dead.[51] In the East End the situation was far worse. There were more deaths in Stepney and Whitechapel in 1665 than in the whole of the city within the walls. At the height of the epidemic more than 600 people were dying each week in Stepney, where 30 was the normal total, and on one day, 11 September, no less than 154 people were buried.[52] One can only wonder at the physical feat involved in burying so many, and speculate about its effect on the parish. On the same day many parish officers in the more fortunate heart of the city had less than a dozen corpses to dispose of.

This is not to say, of course, that plague had ceased to be important in the central parishes. As Table 6.3 shows, they suffered mortality levels three times higher than usual. That could not be shrugged off. When compared with their toll of death in 1563 and with that of other areas of the city in 1665, however, it could perhaps be tolerated with relative equanimity. Between 1563 and 1665 plague became a less serious problem for the City of London proper, and a much greater one for the metropolitan suburbs, first the liberties and then the more distant parishes which were wholly outside the jurisdiction of the corporation.

(iii) Topographical and social divergence

In the towns we have considered, in London and in the provinces, there is thus some evidence of a significant change in the incidence of plague after the middle of the sixteenth century. It became what it had not been before, a conspicuously suburban phenomenon. It is unfortunate that the origins of this transformation are obscured by the lack of parish register evidence for the 1540s, especially from the poorer parishes. But the extent of the change in London after 1563 is clear, and it supports the slighter indications that something similar happened in Bristol and Norwich, and even perhaps in Exeter.[53] So important a development demands some general consideration.

There is no reason to suppose that it was caused by a sudden or radical change in the social incidence of disease. The discrepancy between the evidence of wills and parish registers, which we have noted both in London and in Norwich in the mid-sixteenth century, does not prove that mortality rates among the poor must have been considerably higher than among the rich even then. The heavy concentration of plague mortality among young people under twenty complicates the picture, and helps to explain why those who made wills suffered less than the population at large.[54] But the possibility that social distinctions were also an important cause of that divergence cannot, to say the least, be ruled out. Moreover, there is no sign that plague ever hit the governing class of town or country as hard as the influenza epidemic of 1557 to 1559 did. Deaths of mayors and aldermen from plague were exceptional, accidents, one might say, arising from the proximity of the houses of the governing class to poorer tenements in the cities.[55] What needs to be explained is not a change in the social incidence of plague but the fact that that incidence became more visible on the ground. The evident distinctions were now not only between one house or one street and another, but also between different parishes, between whole areas of a town.

The difference between urban quarters was always most obvious in minor epidemics, when rich parishes could hope to escape relatively unscathed, as in Norwich and London in the 1630s. The concen-

tration of mortality in the Pithay in Bristol was similarly greater in
1603 than in the more serious outbreak of 1575. The relative decline
in the severity of plague in London after 1563 and in Norwich after
1579 may thus have had some influence on the distribution of
mortality there. We should not generalise from these two cases,
however. The serious epidemics in Exeter in 1625 and in Bristol in
1645, and the increasing severity of plague in Essex, will not permit
a conclusion that the disease was declining in virulence generally from
the 1560s and 1570s onwards.

A much more plausible explanation for the changing distribution
of plague is a change in the social geography of towns. As we have
seen in the case of London, it did not alter in any fundamental way.
The social mix on the fringes of a pre-industrial town was always
different from that in the mercantile quarter in its centre. Equally, it
should be stressed that in any urban parish there were always well-
to-do households and some poor families living side by side. Trade
and occupation often helped to determine the character of a neighbourhood as much as wealth or status; and the very poorest parishes
– St Mary Redcliffe in Bristol, St Botolph Aldgate in London – had
large houses for a few members of the social elite who wanted to take
advantage of the open spaces still available there. The 'poor' and 'rich'
parishes to which we have so often referred were never homogeneous
in their social make-up.[56] None the less, it is probable that in the later
sixteenth and seventeenth centuries the suburbs of the larger English
towns became increasingly populous, impoverished, dirty and therefore unhealthy; and it is possible that the central parishes became
more salubrious, more respectable and more exclusively middle-class
quarters. It may be argued, in fact, that there was a growing polarity
between the two areas both in the social composition of their populations and in the quality of their environment.

In the case of London, we have seen how population growth after
1580 led to a deterioration in the environment in the outer parishes,
and there are signs of some reciprocal improvement in the centre of
the city even before the fire of 1666.[57] The social geography of other
towns shifted more slowly, if only because urban growth was less rapid
in the provinces than in London. The suburban parishes of several
towns still had many open spaces at the end of the sixteenth century
when they were already badly affected by plague.[58] Even so, poor
parishes probably grew poorer. In Norwich the poor wards of Conesford and Ber Street in the south of the city contained 23 per cent of

those receiving poor relief in 1576–7, but 34 per cent in 1633–4.[59] The difference was not enormous, but it suggests the continuing concentration of poverty on the outskirts of the town. A similar development can be identified in Exeter, where the proportion of the city's poor in the suburban parishes of St Sidwell and Holy Trinity rose from 23 per cent in 1565 to 35 per cent in 1691.[60]

At the same time, it is likely that there was a real improvement in standards of hygiene in the centre of towns, as their residents acquired more changes of clothing and rebuilt or more often refurbished their houses, and as corporations began to develop more efficient machinery for cleaning the streets.[61] This process was encouraged by the development of the larger provincial cities as social centres for the county gentry. As early as 1563 there were complaints in Norwich that 'gentlemen came to the city to buy up the houses and to pull down poor folk's houses, to the intent that they would not have poor people to dwell near unto them'; and in the following decades there was considerable renovation of houses, some of them no doubt the residences of the urban elite, who appear to have been increasingly congregating in the central parishes.[62] The evidence is admittedly fragmentary, and no one would pretend that there was any rigid social zoning in towns, even at the end of our period. But it may well be that a gradual decline in the social heterogeneity of certain residential areas and an increase in the contrasts between them had a major effect on the urban distribution of plague mortality.

There is one further determinant of the incidence of plague whose importance we have neglected until now, and whose role may have changed in ways which help to account for changes in parochial fortunes: flight. Thus far we have stressed the importance of the urban environment and of socially determined variations within it; but divergent patterns of behaviour in different social groups may have been quite as formative. The rush to escape from infected towns removed substantial numbers of potential victims, and most of them were people who had houses of their own in the country or the means to pay for lodging there. Flight undoubtedly helped to shape social differentials in plague mortality, therefore. The difficulty is to know the extent to which it did so.

Since the Crisis Mortality Ratios are calculated from average burials before each epidemic, they necessarily underestimate real mortality rates in parishes from which large numbers of people fled. For a true index of mortality we should need to know how many people remained to be at risk in a parish, and we do not. Clearly, the greater the exodus, the higher the mortality among those actually at risk. It would even be possible to argue that flight explains the whole of the measured differences between one parish and another. That, however, seems an extreme and unjustified case. Although none of the evidence is conclusive, there are several indications that both behaviour and environment must be allowed a role in social differentials in mortality.

The evidence of Christ Church parish Bristol perhaps tells us something. The Easter Book of 1604 shows that a third of the adults in the two main streets were absent at the end of an epidemic; but more than three-quarters of the inhabitants would have needed to be absent to raise the death rate there to the level it reached in the Pithay.[63] The persistence of social differences in plague mortality in siege conditions in Bristol in 1645 similarly suggests that flight cannot explain the whole of the difference between one parish or one street and another; so does the fact that very few of the members of the governing elite who stayed behind to maintain civic administration died in the later epidemics of the period. We can point also to the ample contemporary comment that plague flourished in poor alleys and tenements.[64] But since we cannot measure flight at all precisely, we cannot measure the relative importance of environment and behaviour in determining the topographical incidence of plague.

For the same reason it is difficult to know whether the habit of escaping from an infected town was becoming more common in the later sixteenth century, and whether it was therefore in part responsible for the declining vulnerability of the rich parishes to plague. Literary evidence suggests that this may have been the case. The controversy about the efficacy of flight, which occupied some writers of the mid-sixteenth century, could be interpreted as a reaction to a practice which, while not novel, was increasingly popular.[65] Escape to the country was doubtless the obvious precaution at all periods in the history of plague. There are references to it from 1485, when friends urged one another to get out of London, until 1665, when Simon Patrick found that in Covent Garden there were only 'the ordinary sort of people ... all the gentry and better sort being gone'.[66] But evidence for the flight of crowds rather than just individuals becomes plentiful from the end of the sixteenth century onwards. Flight emptied many of the larger houses of Colchester in 1666 just as it did those of Christ Church, Bristol, in 1603–4. It prevented adequate provision for the poor in Plymouth in 1626, when nearly half the householders rated in one ward were out of town, and in Norwich in 1666, when collections at church on fast-days slumped by two-thirds.[67] By the seventeenth century the reaction was plainly well established. One London observer thought that the exodus in 1665 was much greater than 'in the great sickness time', that is in 1625; but in 1625 itself most of the 'chief inhabitants' of the central parishes had fled.[68] Yet references such as these can only illustrate patterns of behaviour. They do not prove that behaviour changed.

The best quantitative measure of the propensity of the richer classes to flee is perhaps to be found in the baptism registers of the central parishes of towns. If the number of baptisms fell dramatically at the height of an epidemic in parishes where mortality was relatively low, this would be presumptive evidence of flight. A fall in the number of marriages would provide less certain evidence, for marriages might well be postponed during an epidemic crisis. But the increased risk of death ought to have made baptism in the parish church soon after birth more desirable than ever – provided that parents and children were still resident in the parish.

Unfortunately, the testimony of registered baptisms does not all point in the same direction. In St Peter Mancroft parish, Norwich, for example, the number of baptisms fell in 1544 and 1579, but it rose above the average in 1554 and in 1603. In the richer parishes of Bristol there was no noticeable change at all during epidemics of plague, while in Exeter there was a slight fall in baptisms in some central parishes in 1625 but not in all. In London, however, the evidence is more definite. The baptisms in seven of the sample of rich parishes have been examined, and the total number registered between July and October in each epidemic year has been compared with the average for the same months in the five years preceding the epidemic.[69] We find that the number of baptisms fell by 50 per cent in 1665, by 70 per cent in 1625 and by 40 per cent in 1603; but by only 1 per cent in 1563, despite the high mortality in these parishes in that year. Here, at any rate, there is evidence that flight was not as common in 1563 as it became later.

It is possible therefore that an increasing tendency to flee from infected towns helps to explain the observed incidence of plague. Certainly, as its advocates suggested and as its clerical critics denied, flight worked. Although their relative importance remains uncertain, both social action and the changing environment of towns materially affected the distribution of mortality. The two were, of course, interrelated. If the social geography of towns was becoming more polarised, as has been suggested, then the proportion of the population who could afford to follow fashion and take to their heels was increasing in some parishes while it declined in others. Moreover, social zoning was itself the product of human decisions and a response to fashion: it sprang in part from the desire of the well-to-do to avoid the health risks in some urban quarters and to move to others where the danger of epidemic disease, while never negligible, was less. We still know all too little about social change in early modern English towns, but there can be no doubt that the social context did much to shape the urban impact of plague.

Appendix to Chapter 6

Rich and poor parishes in the city and liberties of London

The rich and poor parishes shown in Figure 6.7 are identified in Table 6.4 below, and those with parish registers which have been used in the samples in Table 6.2 are given in italics. The indices of wealth in Table 6.4 have been calculated for the four different dates as follows:

(1) 1522: the average assessment in pounds of the people named for each parish in the 'loan book' of that year.[70] The source includes no one thought to be worth less than £5 in goods. The coverage of some parishes appears to have been incomplete, and in these cases the averages are given in brackets.

(2) 1572: the average assessment in pounds of those included in the subsidy of that year.[71]

(3) 1638: the average 'moderate rent' value per house in pounds, calculated from a survey of that year.[72] The survey was the product of an attempt to settle tithes in London. It does not always distinguish individual tenements, which were especially numerous in the poorer parishes. Some of the averages are hence shown as approximations, where they include numbers of tenements estimated from their known rental value elsewhere. Individual shops have been included, but not whole blocks of them.

(4) 1695: the percentage of 'substantial households' in the parish, from the assessment of the tax on marriages, burials and births of that year.[73]

The indices thus measure wealth in slightly different ways: in terms of the relative wealth of the richest inhabitants in 1522 and 1572, in terms of property values in 1638, and according to the wealth of all householders in 1695. As might be expected, the relative position of the parishes varies according to which index is employed. There were many changes in the ranking of individual parishes, and over the whole period there seems to have been a tendency for wealth to shift westwards in the inner city, with some eastern parishes within the walls declining relative to the rest. Nevertheless, the variations are not usually large and at each date the parishes listed in Table 6.4 were at one or other extreme of the range. Thus, all the poor parishes were among the lowest twenty-one in the city and liberties in at least three of the four sources; and on none of the four occasions were more than two of them outside the bottom twenty-seven parishes. Similarly,

Table 6.4 *Rich and poor parishes in the city and liberties*

Parish	Indices of wealth			
	1522	1572	1638	1695
Rich				
Allhallows Bread Street	83.7	102.9	24.4	60.0
Allhallows Honey Lane	(162.0)	136.0	27.0	42.3
St Antholin	255.3	112.0	c. 16.7	49.3
St Benet Gracechurch	(87.8)	105.5	21.1	46.2
St Benet Sherehog	(274.2)	105.7	21.1	44.1
St John Evangelist	258.9	136.0	28.0	60.9
St Mary le Bow	211.0	81.4	20.7	53.8
St Mary Woolnoth	209.7	92.3	22.6	31.8
St Matthew Friday Street	169.7	77.7	21.9	69.6
St Michael Bassishaw	173.5	76.7	12.7	44.4
St Mildred Poultry	253.8	134.8	19.6	46.7
St Peter Westcheap	190.3	110.3	19.9	–
St Stephen Walbrook	163.5	100.0	25.0	–
Poor				
Allhallows London Wall	33.1	58.7	8.1	9.7
Allhallows Staining	20.8	68.2	8.1	16.1
St Andrew Hubbard	17.5	39.3	c. 10.5	17.1
St Andrew by the Wardrobe	30.4	56.4	8.3	6.6
St Anne Aldersgate	(13.1)	30.0	11.4	9.7
St Botolph without Aldgate	44.4	47.3	3.6	7.5
St Botolph without Bishopsgate	30.5	36.2	c. 3.3	5.8
St Ethelburga	23.2	50.0	c. 9.2	20.3
St Katherine Coleman	(8.3)	30.0	c. 7.3	21.1
St Martin Vintry	44.9	47.5	7.9	15.2
St Mary Magdalen Old Fish Street	48.5	48.3	c. 8.8	14.4
St Mary Mounthaw	(31.1)	–	6.8	12.8
St Mary Somerset	14.4	–	9.1	6.0
St Mary Staining	(5.8)	53.3	9.4	7.3

all the rich parishes were in the top twenty-five in three out of the four sources, with the sole exception of St Michael Bassishaw (which appeared lower in 1572 and 1638); and on no occasion were more than two of them below the top twenty-five. There can be little doubt that these were among the poorest and richest parishes of London throughout the period.

Chapter 7

Counting the costs

In August how dreadful is the increase! ... Now people fall as thick as the leaves in autumn, when they are shaken by a mighty wind. ... Now shops are shut in, people rare and very few that walk about, in so much that the grass begins to spring up in some places, and a deep silence almost in every place; ... no prancing horses, no rattling coaches, no calling in customers nor offering wares. ... Now in some places, where the people generally did stay, not one house in an hundred but what is infected; and in many houses half the family is swept away; in some the whole from the eldest to the youngest; few escape but with the death of one or two. Never did so many husbands and wives die together; never did so many parents carry their children with them to the grave.

Thomas Vincent, *God's Terrible Voice in the City* (1667)[1]

The frequency and severity of plague epidemics in London and in some of the larger provincial towns have now been described, and we have seen the lesser but by no means remote chance of their occurring in smaller places in Devon and Essex. In order to complete our survey of the problems posed by plague, we must now turn away from the standpoint of particular localities, and view the phenomenon from two different perspectives: one more general, the other still more specific. We must consider the impact of epidemic disease more broadly on the population and economy of pre-industrial England. We should also try to see its effects on the household and the family, on the individual cells which made up the country's economic and demographic structures.

(i) The number of victims

Some impression of the gross damage done by plague can be gained from the simple totals of casualties to which we have already referred.

Taking the towns and villages discussed earlier, we can add up the extra deaths caused by plague in the period from 1570 to 1670, when the records are most complete. According to the bills of mortality, there were at least 225,000 plague deaths in London and its spreading suburban parishes in that century. The Norwich returns of deaths and the excess burials in Exeter and Bristol in plague epidemics would suggest that there were at least 25,000 victims in those three major towns. In Essex and Devon (excluding Exeter) there were 15,000 probable plague casualties in the villages and towns whose records have been examined.[2] There is evidence in these few areas, therefore, of 265,000 victims of plague in a century. That is double the known number of deaths caused by cholera in the whole of England and Wales in the nineteenth century, when the total population at risk was, of course, very much larger.[3]

If we go further and try to estimate the number of deaths attributable to plague in England as a whole between 1570 and 1670, we enter the realm of conjecture. Artificial as it obviously is, however, the exercise is perhaps worth attempting. We have a total for London. We can arrive at a minimum number of plague victims for the whole of Devon and Essex if we add the total for Exeter to the 15,000 already mentioned, and if we assume that plague deaths in those parishes whose records have not been examined (two-thirds of the whole) were at least as numerous in aggregate as in the non-urban parishes whose registers have been seen.[4] That would give us a total of 26,000 for the two counties. By the middle of the seventeenth century, Devon and Essex probably contained around 6 per cent of the country's population outside London.[5] If plague-mortality rates in other counties were the same as in these two (and it is perhaps an unwarranted assumption) the total number of casualties in England excluding London can be estimated at 433,000. Adding London gives a gross figure of 658,000. It can be suggested, therefore, that two-thirds of a million people died of plague in England between 1570 and 1670.

This is no more than an indication of the probable magnitude of the mortality caused by plague, but the calculation does reveal in striking fashion the very large part of it which was borne by London and by other towns. Exeter, Plymouth and Colchester provide no less than 10,000 of the 26,000 estimated deaths in the whole of Devon and Essex. Applying that proportion to the rest of the country, we might infer not only that one-third of all plague deaths between 1570 and 1670 occurred in London, but that a further quarter took place in the fifty or sixty country towns and ports of provincial England. In the century before 1570 this urban concentration may well have been less marked: towns were smaller, London was very much smaller, and plague may have spread more widely, at least in Devon. On the other hand, the population of the country as a whole was also smaller, and consequently the death toll from plague was probably far less in the century before 1570 than in the century after, despite the fact that epidemics may have been more frequent. If the total for 1470–1570 was only a quarter of that calculated for 1570–1670, however, it would mean that 822,000 people died of plague in England in two centuries, and that at least half of them died in towns. Plague may well have killed more than three-quarters of a million people in the course of our period.

Speculative as this conclusion is, it is unlikely to be an overestimate. It is certainly an underestimate of the number of people who suffered from the disease. We have concentrated on mortality in earlier chapters, because burial registers are normally the only sources available to us; but there were, of course, many who caught plague and recovered. The difficulty is to know precisely how many. In Yorkshire 'the better half' of those who had plague in 1631 were said to have escaped death, while in Hitchin, Hertfordshire, twenty-two people died of plague in 1637 but twenty 'recovered of plague sores'.[6] There can be no doubt, however, that the case-mortality rate of bubonic plague varied widely in past epidemics. Where calculations have been possible, for some epidemics in Europe and for more in Asia, rates as low as 40 per cent and as high as 80 per cent have been found.[7] In general it is probable that the case-mortality rate was higher at the beginning than at the end of an epidemic,[8] and, more important, that it was higher in severe outbreaks than in minor ones.

A low mortality rate during an epidemic might therefore conceal a high morbidity rate: there could be very many cases of plague even when there were very few deaths. Only 149 people died in Carlisle in 1597–8, for example, but three-quarters of the town's households, 242 out of 323, were infected.[9] Perhaps the best evidence for the vast extent of sickness comes from Salisbury in 1604. Every week during the epidemic the corporation compiled a list of visited households which had to be supported from municipal funds, and occasionally the number of inmates in them was also noted. Over the whole year 411 different households received help, and the average number of people per household, where this was recorded, was slightly over three.[10] This suggests that at least 1,315 people were supported during the plague, nearly one-fifth of the population of the town. The parish registers show that 605 members of these households were buried during the epidemic, a mortality rate of 46 per cent. That is not equivalent to a case-mortality rate for the whole town. Some members of these families may never have caught plague; and more than 400 deaths during the epidemic occurred in families whose size is unknown because they were not included in the weekly lists. None the less, the figure does illustrate that the morbidity rate was potentially double the mortality rate: that up to twice as many people may have been infected by bubonic plague as died of it. In Salisbury that would mean that a third of the inhabitants suffered in 1604.

The burden of sickness must therefore be placed alongside the burden of death in drawing up an account of the social and economic costs of plague. The burden of sickness might indeed be the greater, because it was more prolonged. Death sometimes came within a day or two of the first symptoms. When Simon Forman caught plague and recovered in 1592, however, he was ill for twenty-two weeks.[11] Some households were completely and very quickly wiped out by plague, while others suffered long and hard. In Salisbury the family of John Silvester, a joiner, was given help early in November 1604. By 28 November four of his children, his wife and John himself had been buried; and payments to the household ceased, presumably because there was no one left alive. Disaster came equally suddenly to William Hyde's family. One of his apprentices died of plague in June. After a fortnight's interval, during which infected fleas perhaps engendered an epizootic among the rats in the house,[12] a second apprentice also died. In the next three weeks, Hyde himself, his wife, two sons, two daughters and another servant were buried; and that was the end. By contrast, other Salisbury families were supported for three or four months at a stretch, suffering at most one or two deaths, but seeing their income disappear and their savings drain away. Households were sometimes subjected to these stresses for even longer periods. One family in Sandwich was compulsorily isolated for nine months in 1638, as plague spread from one member to another.[13]

Tudor and Stuart Englishmen thus had to contend not just with the death by plague of more than three-quarters of a million people, but with the illness of perhaps as many more who subsequently recovered. The nature of the sources will make it necessary once again to consider mortality alone when examining the effect of plague on the family; but we must recall the costs of morbidity when we come to look at its economic consequences.

(ii) Household and family

The most terrifying aspect of the incidence of plague was the clustering of deaths in family groups. Only a small minority of households was completely eliminated: John Silvester and William Hyde and their relations were exceptions. But it was usual for two or three members of a family to die in quick succession. Once plague reached a household, no one could feel safe. To an extent, of course, this is a characteristic of all infectious diseases; but in epidemics of plague the family grouping of deaths was quite exceptional. During the different epidemics caused by influenza in the later 1550s and by dearth in the later 1590s, it seems to have been rare for more than a quarter of all deaths to occur in households where three or more people died.[14] In epidemics of plague, however, these clusters of three or more deaths were much more common. They comprised at least 40 per cent and sometimes more than 60 per cent of all burials, as Table 7.1 shows.

In the first three instances in Table 7.1, in the parishes of Norwich, Bristol and Salisbury, the number of plague deaths in households with

Table 7.1 *The household distribution of plague deaths*

Place and date	No. of households with				5 or more burials	Proportion of all burials in households with 3 or more
	1	2	3	4		
St Peter Mancroft, Norwich, 1579	87	28	10	10	6	42%
SS. Philip and Jacob, Bristol, 1603–4	91	36	19	17	17	57%
Salisbury: 1604						
– all burials	380	124	49	40	28	42%
– burials from isolated households	92	73	36	35	22	61%
Colyton, 1645–6	80	32	19	15	7	51%
Eyam, 1666	25	22	20	10	12	72%
Braintree, 1666	80	58	42	21	22	63%

Source: See n. 15, p. 381.

only one may be overstated. Since the information is taken from registered burials in the months when plague was at its height, the figures include some deaths which were not caused by plague, and also perhaps some burials of apprentices and servants in large households who have not been identified as such. The four later instances are more reliable indicators of the clustering of plague deaths. In the second Salisbury case, the information comes from burials which have been matched with the households which were officially recognised to be infected, and whose members were 'kept in' and supported by the city. For Braintree, Essex, the statistics are similarly taken from a contemporary list of infected families in the town, and in this case the record also gives the number of deaths in each household. The figures for Colyton, Devon, and Eyam, Derbyshire, are based on recent reconstitutions of the families in those parishes.[15]

The variations which appear between one place and another in the table are therefore in part a consequence of different kinds of sources. They also reflect differences in the level of mortality and, no doubt, differences in the size of households in the communities concerned. For pronounced clustering of this kind was to some degree a function of two things: of exceptionally high death rates, and of the large proportion of the population of Tudor and Stuart England living in large households. It was not only that, however. In the Colyton case, Dr Schofield has shown that the deaths were not randomly distributed between families: they did not fall as they would have been expected to fall, given the level of mortality and the size of households.[16] Thanks to its dependence on domestic rodents and fleas as carriers, plague had an independent clustering effect; and this was one of its most conspicuous distinguishing features in early modern England.[17]

Like its urban incidence, the household incidence of plague was ambiguous in its repercussions. On the one hand it magnified the horrors of pestilence by concentrating them: as the table shows, a person dying of plague was much more likely to see one or two of his relations or servants succumb than to suffer alone. On the other hand, these clusters of casualties were socially beneficial, since many families were wholly or largely unscathed. Thus in Colyton in 1645–6 and in Eyam in 1666 more than 60 per cent of the families suffered no deaths at all during the epidemic, although some of them may have been infected.[18] Even after the worst outbreaks, there were many complete families left to provide continuity in the local community and the foundation for demographic recovery.

At the same time, however, other families were severely damaged. The extent to which that damage was irreparable depended in part on the sex- and age-incidence of plague. If women suffered more than men or vice versa, the chances of remarriage for widowers or widows would be severely reduced. If young adults were hit more heavily than young children, they could not immediately be replaced through an increase in the birth rate; indeed, their deaths might well depress the number of subsequent births. Unfortunately, these are subjects about which few generalisations can be made with any confidence. In modern outbreaks of plague both sex- and age-incidence appear to vary according to the exposure of different groups to infection. The former varies more than the latter, however; and the same seems to have been true in past European epidemics.[19]

In parts of Europe women were said to be more susceptible to plague than men, and there is some evidence to support this observation.[20] In England, on the other hand, men were thought to be hit particularly hard. Francis Herring called 1603 'the women's year', and a thorough study of St Botolph's Bishopsgate parish in London has amply confirmed that male deaths vastly outnumbered female deaths in that epidemic.[21] It has even been suggested that this selective incidence of plague gave England a large surplus of women in the seventeenth century.[22] One parish is flimsy support for so sweeping a conclusion, however, especially when other evidence suggests that it was eccentric. The studies of plague in Eyam and Colyton have shown that men were not affected to a greater degree than women there.[23] Moreover, an analysis of other London parishes in 1593, 1603 and 1625 has revealed surprising differences between parishes and between epidemics. Overall, more males than females did die in plagues in London before 1665, but this was because there was a surplus of men in the population: it was only in 1603 that death rates were relatively higher for men than for women.[24]

In provincial towns there were similar puzzling variations. Figure 7.1 shows the sex ratio of people buried in plague epidemics in various towns, alongside the normal ratio of burials there immediately before the plague.[25] The parishes of Exeter, Bristol and Plymouth reveal movements like those in St Botolph's Bishopsgate. Although the difference from the norm was substantial only in Exeter, men were apparently hit harder by plague than women in these towns. In Barnstaple, Chelmsford and Stratford-on-Avon, on the other hand, the sex ratios fell decisively during epidemics. Here females outnum-

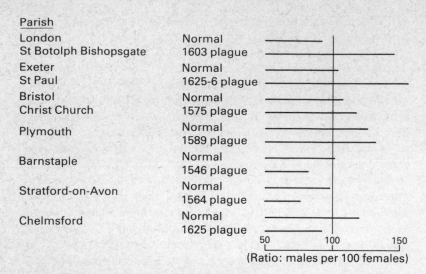

Figure 7.1 *Sex ratios of burials during plague epidemics (Source: See n. 25, p. 382)*

bered males among plague victims. These contrasts might have been the consequence of differences in occupations or social habits. Men who worked on the wharves of Plymouth or in cramped workshops in Exeter were clearly more vulnerable than men engaged in agricultural occupations in some of the smaller market towns. It is difficult to be more precise than this. The evidence of the smaller provincial towns does not, however, support the hypothesis that women escaped plague because they were less likely to come into contact with infected persons or infected rats.[26] Rather the contrary. It suggests that women may have been more susceptible in some communities because they spent more time in rat-infested houses and because they nursed the sick.[27]

Investigation of these possibilities is impeded, however, by our lack of accurate information about the distribution of the sexes in the population (as opposed to the burials) of provincial towns. We cannot be sure in any instance whether there were more men or women *at risk* on the eve of an epidemic. If the age-distribution of burials in epidemics was different from that in normal years (and we shall see in a moment that it was), and if at the relevant ages there was an imbalance in the sexes (as there well might be), then the sex ratio at death during an epidemic may do no more than reflect the actual sex ratio of that part of the population which was most vulnerable to plague. The balance of the sexes at the ages between fifteen and twenty-five is crucial here. This was one of the age-groups most seriously affected by plague; it was poorly represented among burials in non-plague years; and it might well have an unbalanced sex ratio, depending on the number of apprentices and male labourers, or of maidservants, in the population. In that case, unusual sex ratios during epidemics would not indicate differential plague-mortality rates between the sexes but rather a disproportionate number of young men or young women in the parish concerned.

Some support for this suggestion may be found in the fact that the contrasts mentioned earlier appear to be related to the size of the towns involved. The larger towns had an abnormal excess of male over female burials; in smaller communities the reverse was the case. If places like Barnstaple, Stratford and Chelmsford contained large numbers of maid servants, then the excess of females among plague burials would be easily explained. It is striking that sixteen of the twenty-three 'servants' buried in Barnstaple during the plague of 1546 were women.[28] A larger proportion of apprentices and young labourers in bigger conglomerations like Exeter and Plymouth might similarly explain the figures there.[29] In Christ Church parish, Bristol, we know from the Easter Books that the communicant population in 1575 had a sex ratio of 118, largely because of the number of male servants and apprentices; and this was almost exactly the sex ratio of burials (117) in the plague of that year.[30] In short, although mysterious cases like St Botolph's Bishopsgate and other London parishes in 1603 remain,[31] it would be premature to suggest that plague hit either of the sexes disproportionately. If more women or men died in a particular outbreak, it may well have been simply because there were more women or men around.

Similar problems arise in analysing plague mortality by age. We can begin by comparing the age-distribution of burials in epidemic years with that in non-epidemic years, using those few parish registers which give age at burial and drawing on the findings of recent family-reconstruction studies. In every case we find abnormalities in plague years greater than those relating to sex; and this time the changes are consistent. The age-group from five to nineteen seems to have been everywhere the one which contributed far more than its normal share to mortality during epidemics of plague. Figure 7.2 shows the proportions of people buried who came from that age-range, both in epidemic years and in normal years, in three London parishes and in

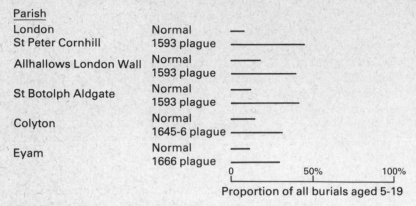

Figure 7.2 Proportion of plague victims aged 5–19 (Source: See n. 32, p. 383)

Colyton and Eyam.[32] In each instance the percentage in plague years was at least twice the norm, and no other age-group appears to have suffered so disproportionately. In general those under five and over fifty, the very young and the old, made a smaller percentage contribution to mortality in plague years than in normal years, while the proportion for adults up to fifty was about the same. All this is consistent with the findings of modern epidemiologists that the age-groups from roughly ten to thirty-five provide the largest number of plague-deaths.[33] Older children, adolescents and young adults filled the pages of burial registers in plague years.

This is to consider only *numbers* of deaths at certain ages, however. Their distribution says nothing about comparative mortality *rates* at different ages. Once again we need to know the characteristics of the population at risk, and in this case its age- rather than its sex-structure. Where this has been investigated, by applying models of stable populations, it appears that death rates during epidemics may well have declined with age. Although mortality rates were much higher than normal for all age-groups, both the gross rate and its excess above the norm gradually fell from infancy onwards.[34] The number of infants and very young children dying in plague years was therefore small only because their overall numbers were small: as a general rule, though with exceptions,[35] their death rate was higher than that of older children and adolescents. This is not to say that all of them died of plague. Many must have been secondary casualties, victims of the many hardships, including the death of nursing mothers, which plague caused. Infants suffered most because they were most vulnerable in the total crisis brought by an epidemic.

Contemporaries would have found nothing remarkable in that, however, given that infant mortality was always high in pre-industrial England. Indeed, for them numbers may well have been more important than rates. An increase in infant mortality must have seemed less striking than the numerous deaths of children and adolescents who had apparently survived their most vulnerable years. It was the latter which made plague mortality abnormal, and which distinguished plague from other epidemic diseases which either hit the very young alone, or were most serious among adults.[36] The obvious fact was that those who died of plague were for the most part 'children and young folks'. Hence the common superstition that children's games in the streets were an omen of plague to come, and the view that children spread contagion from house to house. 'We see few ancient people die in comparison of children, and the younger sort,' James Balmford noted in 1603.[37]

Unnatural as plague's destruction of the young must have seemed, it was in some respects demographically propitious. The damage done to families was more easily repaired than it would have been if mortality had fallen more heavily at slightly later ages, between twenty and forty. To begin with, since the age at marriage was normally late in England, the crucial nucleus of the family – the married couple – was seldom destroyed altogether by plague. The fullest information on this subject comes from the family-reconstitution studies of Eyam and Colyton at the time of the epidemics of 1666 and 1645.[38] Each of these settlements was small and each had outlying hamlets less affected by plague than a central township. They may thus have been more fortunate than some of the major towns. However, the death rates for the whole parishes – 20 per cent in Colyton, 30 per cent in Eyam – were high enough to suggest that they are not totally unrepresentative of other communities during serious epidemics. In Eyam less than 15 per cent of all families lost both husband and wife in the plague; in Colyton the proportion was only 6 per cent. As a result, few complete replacement families were required after the crisis, and many of them could be provided by marriages of children from resident households little affected by plague. In Eyam only thirteen out of seventy new families appearing in the registers after the epidemic were wholly new to the parish.

Many more families lost either husband or wife, of course, and then the consequences could be long-lasting. The possibility of remarriage was open to the survivor, but it was more often a possibility than an actuality, both in Eyam and still more in Colyton. The chances of widows and widowers in the marriage market depended on their property, and few survivors of plague can have had very much. Families broken and impoverished by disease very often remained so, as the number of widows with young children in contemporary listings of the poor amply demonstrates.[39] Nevertheless, the death of one parent was socially less destructive than the death of both, and more likely to leave opportunity for family reconstruction.

Secondly, a considerable number of the victims of plague could be replaced by the normal processes of migration. In so far as the disease hit adolescents and young adults, it also hit apprentices and servants; and these age-groups and occupations were the most mobile in the population.[40] Since they were migrants, the techniques of family reconstitution throw little light upon them. But it is evident that they existed in large numbers in urban societies, that they were often victims of plague, and that they could easily be replaced by an increase in the flow of recruits from the countryside, provided that plague retained its heavy urban incidence. Similar recruitment through migration filled some of the gaps left by those few young married couples and the more numerous husbands or wives who died during a plague; and this avenue of recovery may well have been more important for large towns than for Eyam and Colyton. We have seen that couples new to the parish were common in the Pithay in Bristol after a plague, for example. Their arrival meant a greater disruption of the local community than the influx of single apprentices or servants. Yet here too immigration was simply an acceleration of a phenomemon which already existed. Plague did not demand or create any new pattern of mobility.[41]

Thirdly, children and infants who died of plague could be replaced by new births, whether to couples already established in the community or to new immigrants in their twenties. Again, the smoothness of the recovery should not be overstated. The missing children left a palpable gap, which must often have been visible in the age-structure of a population long after the crisis. In Lichfield, for example, the figures collected by Gregory King in 1695 clearly show a depleted cohort between the ages of fifty and fifty-five. That may well be attributable to the deaths of children under five in a plague epidemic in 1645.[42] It was probably influenced also by a drop in the number of births in 1645–6, for plague often reduced fertility as well as increasing mortality. It is not easy to judge the extent of the reduction. It seems usually to have been smaller in England than in France,[43] and it was certainly smaller than the falls in the number of baptisms during epidemics might suggest, since the flight of mothers and priests might simply delay the ceremony. When the number of baptisms fell by 20 per cent in Plymouth in 1626, for example, postponement may have played a greater part than the deaths of pregnant women or the abortion of foetuses, which some observers noted as a common corollary of plague.[44] In some cases, however, the number of baptisms fell immediately after the epidemic, and this is more certain evidence that the death or illness of potential mothers depressed fertility. In Salisbury the number of children conceived during the plague year of 1604 (and baptised between October 1604 and September 1605) was 127, compared with an annual average of 157 before the crisis: a fall of nearly 20 per cent. Yet in both towns the same source, the baptism register, records rapid recovery. In Salisbury conceptions were back to their average level in 1605. The number of baptisms in Plymouth actually exceeded the average in 1627, and while some of them were ceremonies deferred from 1626, others must have been the product of conceptions which had occurred in the last months of the epidemic.[45] Given the extent of mortality in both towns, the maintenance or rapid restoration of pre-epidemic levels of fertility is remarkable.

There were thus two ways by which a population could recover from plague: through remarriages, new marriages and new births in that section of the population which was not severely affected; and through migration from outside. Both mechanisms need further study, but their relative contribution probably varied from place to place. The former seems to have been most important in Eyam, and no doubt also in other small villages and towns where plague was a rare occurrence. In larger towns, immigration must have played a far greater role, as we have seen in the case of Norwich and as all students from Graunt onwards have appreciated in the case of London.[46] There was some capacity for natural growth, and hence for some endogenous contribution to recovery from plague, in major towns. In Exeter, as in some smaller places, the number of baptisms could exceed the number of burials for long periods at a time between epidemics, and in London the inhabitants of a few of the more prosperous parishes may well have been able to more than replace themselves in this period.[47] They may thus have contributed something to the demographic recovery of the poorer parishes. But their contribution was slight when compared to that of urban immigrants. Even in Eyam it would have taken at least thirty years for natural increase alone to restore the population to its pre-plague level. Where plague occurred more than once in a generation, as in the larger towns, such self-sufficient growth was impossible.

Whatever the precise balance of factors involved in demographic recovery, however, the speed with which households and families were reconstructed or replaced is evident from most urban records. It is perhaps clearest, not in the recovery of baptisms immediately after an epidemic, but in the surge of marriages which often began while plague was still present. In Plymouth, for example, there were normally between 110 and 120 weddings in the early 1620s; but the number jumped to 198 in the epidemic year, 1626, 88 of them being celebrated between October and December, as soon as the worst of the mortality was over. Similarly, the number of marriages in Salisbury in 1604 was 57 per cent higher than usual, and a large proportion of them took place in the last quarter of the year, as mortality declined. Whether those who rushed to the altar were newcomers, or established residents no longer compelled to postpone marriage by a shortage of houses and employment, their behaviour testifies to the resilience and adaptability of demographic and social structures in the crises caused by plague.[48]

That resilience did not make the crises any less painful in the short term. Lady Grenville scarcely exaggerated the dangers for individual families inherent in the common incidence of plague when she explained her flight from Exeter in 1625: 'The sickness increases here . . . and when it comes it goes through the house and ends all. I am determined to leave tomorrow on account of the children.'[49] But the concentration of plague deaths in certain neighbourhoods, households and age-groups, which made it so tragic in the short run, also permitted recovery in the longer term, and lessened the potential impact of plague on the country's population and economy as a whole.

(iii) Population and economy

The fact that the population of England doubled in the course of the sixteenth and seventeenth centuries is a sufficient demonstration that epidemics of plague had no irreparable demographic effects. Substantial growth was possible in social groups and localities which were not affected by them. We cannot even argue that demographic growth would have been more rapid in the absence of plague epidemics. Not only have recent studies shown that changes in fertility were at least as important as changes in mortality in determining long-term demographic trends; it is also clear that fluctuations in mortality and fertility were often related to one another, increases in the former producing increases in the latter.[50] Without plague, fertility might have been lower and the population have grown at the same rate.

In the shorter term, epidemics could reduce the country's population by a small proportion and for a time. It required a rapid succession of them to postpone recovery for more than a year or two, however, and in the period after 1540 plague seems never to have accomplished this alone. The population appears to have fallen between 1544 and 1546, largely no doubt as a result of plague. But the fall was much greater in the later 1550s, thanks to the fevers of 1557 to 1559 which had a more even social, geographical and age-incidence.[51] From 1592 onwards London was large enough for serious epidemics there to have a marked effect on the gross national death rate, but even then it was a gradual rise in 'background' mortality rather than a sequence of plagues which contributed to the deceleration of population growth in the country as a whole.[52] We cannot attribute a more than temporary effect to high epidemic mortality, therefore. In the fourteenth century plague had been a major demographic regulator; it may have continued to be so in the fifteenth. In the sixteenth and seventeenth centuries it no longer filled that role.

What plague did do was exaggerate features of the demographic scene which would not without it have been so obvious. It emphasised distinctions in health and mortality between different sorts of settlement and different social groups. Most obviously, it was plague which gave towns their reputation as consumers of men. It is probable that death rates were always higher in urban than rural communities, but epidemics made that difference vastly greater. The demographic gulf between town and country can be oversimplified. The fact that there was often a surplus of burials over baptisms in the former, and usually a surplus of baptisms over burials in the latter, presents a distorted picture, since the line between town and country was blurred by migration. By definition, migrants to towns do not enter urban baptism totals though they add in large number to urban burials. Consequently, the calculation of vital rates for pre-industrial towns is a hazardous business.[53] Yet the crowded burial registers of urban parishes do demonstrate one simple fact: that whatever the levels of fertility achieved by their permanent and temporary residents, towns were above all places where people died. Contemporaries were well aware that plague was to a large degree responsible for that.

Plague similarly contributed to the contrasts between different localities and different social groups within a town, widening the gap between the two extremes of urban society. On the one hand there was a relatively stable, healthy patrician class, able to achieve respectable levels of demographic growth. On the other, there was a transient group of servants and labourers, always moving into and out of towns, but made all the more transient by high mortality. Many citizens, perhaps the majority, fell uneasily between the two stools. The freemen of a town, master craftsmen, shopkeepers, heads of large households like John Silvester and William Hyde in Salisbury, no doubt regarded themselves as part of the stable centre of the community, until plague destroyed their security. The distinction between top and bottom was obvious, however, and epidemics simply pushed men in the middle towards one or other pole. They either shared the view of aldermen and councillors that vagrants, squatters, inmates, lodgers, and strangers were a cause of plague; or they shared the fate of those marginal groups whose high death rates contributed still further to the stream of poor migrants rushing to towns in search of houses and jobs.

Plague's impact on the economy was similar to its impact on the demography of England. In the short term, it spelled havoc for normal patterns of behaviour. In the longer term it merely confirmed existing trends and accentuated existing weaknesses. The immediate economic effects of plague were more far-reaching than its demographic results, because towns were more crucial to the nation's economic than to its demographic well-being. When urban marketing and business collapsed during epidemics, large hinterlands were disturbed. Plague in Newcastle disrupted the coal and salt trades down the whole east coast, while the rural economy of Herefordshire was depressed by the epidemic in Bristol in 1603. Common experience led Sir Thomas Wentworth to predict that if plague infected Leeds and Halifax in 1631, 'it would mightily distress and impoverish' the whole of the West Riding of Yorkshire.[54]

Deliberate government action contributed something to these

circumstances, as merchants complained when fairs were cancelled
or postponed in an effort to prevent the spread of contagion. At root,
however, lay an instinctive dread of infection which was popular and
pervasive. People needed no encouragement to stay away from shops
and stalls in infected towns, and corporate revenues from markets as
well as fairs slumped in epidemic years.[55] Alderman Cockayne was
informed that no one wanted to buy anything in London in 1625.
Even if they had, a shortage of cash and credit would have prevented
large-scale transactions, since gentlemen stopped leaving their money
in the hands of scriveners and goldsmiths, and merchants refused to
lend when plague threatened.[56]

The consequences of mounting anxiety and declining confidence
could be seen in small matters and in large. Fear of plague kept
people away from alehouses and inns anywhere near a main road or
major town during an epidemic, or so collectors of the excise tax in
every part of England alleged in 1665–6. They had good reason to
exaggerate, but the government showed little reluctance to accept their
claims.[57] The overseas trade of the kingdom suffered as much as
internal trade when plague hit its major outlet, the port of London.
In 1603 the number of shortcloths exported from London sank by a
third, and in 1625 the trade of Exeter was hit as hard as that of the
capital. These depressions did not last for more than a few months,
unless they were prolonged by war, as in 1625. But they temporarily
turned the balance of payments against England, diminishing the
money supply still further and leaving clothiers with unsold textiles
on their hands and country weavers and spinners with no work and
no wages.[58]

All this meant economic disaster, not simply depression, for infected
towns themselves. Even when work was available, there were few able
hands if mortality or morbidity was high. Labourers' wages had to be
raised in Cambridge in 1666 in order to get enough men together to
bring the harvest in. Whatever the level of mortality, however, there
was usually little food and no work because country farmers stayed
away from markets and urban employers fled to the countryside. In
1636 one London parish was forced to support extra pensioners and
paupers who were, 'through the hardness of the times, brought to
great necessity although free from the infection'.[59] It was not only in
Norwich that poverty appeared a greater threat than plague during an
epidemic, and in several towns starvation seemed the inevitable
corollary of both. The poor of Winchester in 1625, like those of

London in 1665, were 'like to famish for want of work and relief'. In Salisbury 2,000 people were said to be 'sick of the famine' in 1627, and 'many of them begin to look as green and pale as death'. Southampton, Nantwich and Poole were similarly 'threatened with famine as well as pestilence' in plague years.[60] No less common was the statement that 'grass grew in the streets' of a once bustling, but now infected and dead town.[61] These were well-worn clichés, but there was harsh repetitive reality behind such images of urban desolation.

Like urban populations, urban economies appear nevertheless to have recovered very quickly once the crisis was over. The output of textiles in Colchester may have fallen by two-thirds in the plague of 1666, but it was back to its pre-plague level by 1668. In Norwich, Dutch and Walloon production of cloth reached its peak shortly after the plague of 1579, although successive epidemics naturally produced temporary depressions.[62] Despite the death of skilled hands and the expenditure of scarce capital resources on the support of the sick, urban industries were somehow rebuilt. Increasing numbers of admissions to the freedom after plagues, as in Norwich after 1603 and York after 1550, suggest that young men with skills and capital were available to fill vacant places: some of them had certainly been apprentices, no doubt in households little affected by plague, but the background of others is unknown.[63] At the same time, migration brought in journeymen and labourers, some of whom had had experience of rural textile industries, and that must have eased their assimilation into urban industries and urban life. Even so, the process of recuperation remains mysterious and deserves further investigation. Much would depend on the relative importance in any industry of self-employed artisans, who needed working capital, and of journeymen, who required few resources apart from their labour. The latter were more easily replaced and may well have been hit harder by plague. The most we can say with confidence, however, is that recovery was very often rapid.

There were some towns which did not recover, but the many contrary examples show that plague was never the sole cause of decline, despite the claims of some contemporaries. The population and economy of Salisbury ceased to grow after the plague of 1604 because the textile industry was contracting: the town consequently failed to attract immigrants.[64] There were similarly more fundamental reasons to account for the decay of smaller places such as Stafford and Ashby de la Zouche after mortality crises in the 1640s. John

Aubrey thought that the small market town of Highworth in Wiltshire was ruined by plague in the 1630s, but competition from Swindon, which he also mentioned, was probably a more important factor.w6.5[65] In the light of these examples, it is difficult to believe that the drastic changes which appear to have occurred in Colyton after 1645 can be attributed solely to the epidemic of that year: if ages at marriage rose · and fertility fell there must have been some change in real economic circumstances or in contemporary perception of them.[66] When other factors pointed in the same direction, plague no doubt accelerated decline, for it always aggravated the underlying fragility of urban economies. It retarded capital accumulation and the concentration and development of new skills. It imposed a series of new beginnings on an urban labour force. But epidemic disease did not itself dictate that some towns should fail to meet the challenge of discontinuity.

The economic stresses brought by plague were more likely to be fatal for individual households than for whole communities. Epidemics confirmed the status of those already in poverty and reduced others to the same level. It might seem in the very short term that they had the reverse effect. Many paupers died. In Salisbury, for example, twenty-seven people listed in a survey of the poor in 1625 were buried in the plague of 1627. But disease pulled many people into the top of the class of the dependent poor, while it took others out of the bottom. Sometimes downward social mobility followed the death of a wage-earner: further listings of the poor in Salisbury in 1635 show eight families which had lost a parent in the epidemic of 1627.[67] Sometimes the expense of prolonged sickness had the same effect, as journeymen and artisans spent their savings, pawned their clothes and furniture and then had to seek parish relief. When two tradesmen in Hitchin were isolated with their families in the plague of 1636, they were forced to shut up shop and spend all they had on food; afterwards they asked the justices for some help in providing stock so that they could work again.[68] Two years after the plague of 1631 the corporation of Lincoln similarly noted that 'divers tradesmen ... which were heretofore able to maintain themselves and their families by their trades were by the late visitation ... impoverished by spending their poor estates and getting nothing'. Plague was only one of several 'calamities' which had led a Lambeth man by 1667 to consume 'that little estate which I and my wife have long laboured to get together'; but it was probably the worst.[69] The revolving loan stocks which many philanthropists founded in this period were intended precisely for cases such as these. They sprang from a society in which saving was difficult in normal times and impossible in the crises caused by fire, dearth, economic depression or disease.

Urban corporations fully appreciated the vulnerability of large numbers of normally self-sufficient households. In New Romney in 1597 several families were 'likely upon the least visitation to be chargeable to the parish'. One hundred and sixty Sheffield householders in 1616 were 'such (though they beg not) as are not able to abide the storm of one fortnight's sickness but would be thereby driven to beggary'. One-half of the population of Salisbury in 1626 would need to 'be relieved by the city if they happen to be sick but one week'.[70] For the less fortunate of these people, in their precarious situation at the bottom end of respectable society, an epidemic spelled the end of aspirations to comfort and the beginning of dependence, if not of destitution. They were victims of the vicious circle in which plague encouraged some of those features of the economic and demographic environment which enabled it to flourish: poverty, population mobility and their combined consequences in some quarters of English towns.

(iv) Plague as a social problem

The manifold problems posed by plague which have been described in preceding pages fall essentially into two categories. First, there were those which demonstrated the immediate, destructive and superficially indiscriminate incidence of the disease. In some places mortality rates were high, in others low. Some houses and villages were decimated while their neighbours escaped. Over the period as a whole epidemics declined in intensity in Devon, while they apparently grew more severe in Essex. Populations and economies were subjected to abnormal stresses of unpredictable dimensions. Secondly, however, there were regularities in the geographical and social incidence of the disease which shaped its longer-term impact, moulding it to fit established features of early modern English society. It was both a catastrophe which attacked society from outside, and one which in detail blended into it, emphasising its pre-existing divisions and highlighting its fundamental weaknesses.

This peculiar combination, of unpredictable and predictable features, of terrifying and tolerable effects, helped to determine the diverse social reactions to plague which will be described in subsequent chapters. For the balance between the two aspects of the phenomenon was not stable; neither were contemporary perceptions of it unchanging. Religious attitudes or secular ambitions might lead men to stress one aspect at the expense of the other; and at the same time the phenomenon itself came gradually to appear more regular and hence more comprehensible.

Plague was never wholly predictable, of course. The stress laid in earlier chapters on distinctions between town and country and between rich and poor parishes should not obscure the artificial rigidity of those dividing lines and the frequency with which epidemic disease crossed them in reality. The council-house in Winchester and substantial residences next to the best inn in Oxford were infected, along with the overcrowded tenements of those towns, thus justifying moralists who continued to assert, even in 1665, that plague hit rich and poor alike.[71] In gross, plague mortality exhibited a clear social bias; but the social elite could draw little reassurance from statistical probabilities of infection if some of their friends and neighbours were attacked. They no doubt saw the poor beggars dying in the streets whose burials were entered in the parish registers of London, Salisbury and other towns. They must have noticed the frequent deaths during epidemics of those who were in closest contact with the sick or the dead: nurses and buriers of the dead,[72] sextons and churchwardens,[73] parish priests and parish clerks,[74] and the odd surgeon and apothecary.[75] But precautions based on these observations were plainly fallible. Although plague more often killed mayors of towns in the early sixteenth century than later,[76] its victims in the seventeenth century included two or three aldermen of London, the mayor of Lymington, a Sussex justice of the peace, leading lawyers and perhaps one or two Members of Parliament (in 1641).[77] It was not a large toll, but it was sufficient to stimulate flight, even in a mild epidemic. As John Davenant, bishop of Salisbury, explained from the safety of his country retreat in 1627: 'The number of those who die weekly is not great, but the danger is that ever and anon some new house is infected.'[78]

Dread of creeping infection propelled the social elite towards the efforts to control plague which will be described shortly. That endeavour could have had no rationale and no strategy, however, if those in authority had been unable to distance themselves from the phenomenon and to observe its fundamental characteristics. In part, they were driven to take a more objective view by intellectual and political changes, as we shall see. But new approaches were also encouraged by those shifts in the chronology and impact of plague which we have detected or suggested.

First, there was the accidental fact that epidemics of plague coincided much less often with dearth and high prices after 1563 than they had in the early sixteenth century. Only in 1630–1 did serious epidemics follow shortly after a bad harvest, and then only in a few towns.[79] Hence it became easier to view them as discrete events with their own definable patterns of behaviour. People did not wholly abandon the view that plague and famine were associated, and that plague was connected with other diseases; but they did begin to try to distinguish its symptoms from those of typhus, and to regard it as a normally distinct entity.[80]

If it was in this respect increasingly differentiated from other causes of crisis, plague was also increasingly associated with particular places, notably with towns. We have seen that the epidemic of 1546–7 apparently spread more widely in rural Devon than any later outbreak until the exceptional circumstances of civil war made disease universal in the 1640s. Although the same trend cannot be detected in Essex, it may well be that the epidemic of 1546–7 in the South-West was a late example of those medieval outbreaks which had an extensive geographical impact. Certainly, when compared with the fourteenth century, the epidemics of the later sixteenth and seventeenth centuries were narrowly urban in focus.[81] Moreover, plague had conspicuously taken root in towns, as the recurrent minor and major outbreaks recorded in the mortality statistics of London and Norwich showed. It had an evident urban source and that encouraged the view that it might be confined and treated there.

Most important of all, within the larger towns plague became ever more obviously a suburban phenomenon; and hence it became easier to recognise that it was, as it had always been, the product of particular social conditions.[82] It is true that the social roots of epidemic disease were not as visible in every town as they were by the seventeenth century in the cities of London, Norwich, Exeter and Bristol. Some smaller centres had a quarter or parish more poverty-stricken than the rest. In Reading, for example, the river Kennet separated the poor of St Giles's parish from the more prosperous areas of town, and plague mortality was higher in St Giles's than in the other two parishes in 1607–8.[83] More commonly, however, parish boundaries had no social significance in small towns. Salisbury was not small, but it was perhaps more representative of lesser towns than Reading in this respect; and it was an observer in Salisbury in 1666 who commented that when plague 'comes to rage in these little towns, it is more dangerous than in London itself, because less means of avoiding it'.[84] Yet this implies that in London plague might in fact be avoided; and it was observation of London, not of Salisbury or Reading, which moulded the governing elite's perception of plague.

Furthermore, stimulated perhaps by the example of London, contemporaries increasingly noticed the concentration of plague in a particular environment even in smaller towns: 'in the suburbs and dispersed places' of Carlisle in 1597; 'in back lanes and remote places and not in the heart' of Leicester in 1626; in Frogs Lane and Pricks Lane in Worcester in 1637; in 'four inconsiderable cottages upon the skirts' of Lichfield in 1665.[85] Contemporaries saw too that these topographical distinctions had an obvious social base. Plague was spread by beggars, migrants and strangers, and most of the casualties were 'in the families of poor people'. By 1631 these assumptions were so prevalent that when the disease entered a noble household in Yorkshire it went unrecognised because 'no man could suspect a lady to die of the plague'.[86] It was becoming possible to view plague not as a catastrophe of immeasurable proportions, but as the particular problem of certain social groups and localities. From there it might spread and threaten respectable society; but it had identifiable origins which must be attacked if epidemics were to be controlled.

The social and geographical concentration of plague thus provided a necessary condition for new perceptions and for consequent action. Governors and moulders of opinion could begin to distance themselves from the phenomenon as they saw how distant it was in reality, both socially and spatially. They could see it in fact as a social problem. It was a problem potentially greater and personally more threatening than the problems of poverty, vagrancy and suburban disorder; but it was a problem linked with those other social diseases and similar in kind to them. It is scarcely surprising that it was treated in a very similar way.

Part III

The social response

Chapter 8

Public authority and a policy for control

... to frame a perfect and absolute order and model, which may be useful as well for future as these present times, we must particularly determine what is to be observed and done, both before, during the sickness and after it, leaving it entire to the Right Honourable the Lords of His Majesty's Privy Council ... to take and put in execution ... so much as they shall find ... necessary.

Sir Theodore de Mayerne to Charles I, 1631[1]

Social reactions to bubonic plague in the sixteenth and seventeenth centuries produced a variety of defence mechanisms promising safety, comfort and help against infectious disease. They were set in motion at four different levels. Most prominent was the administrative code of plague regulations developed by the central government, which was designed to prevent contagion and deal with its consequences. Secondly, there was the response of intellectuals, of doctors and divines, who discussed the causes of plague and its meaning, and thus brought new policies for public health into harmony with traditional modes of thought. Thirdly, there was the activity of local governors, particularly in towns, who had to enforce centrally designed policies in the intractable realities of crisis circumstances. And finally there were the reactions of ordinary men and women, who bore the brunt of plague and who were the victims of the methods invented to control it. Each of these four aspects of the subject will be considered in this and succeeding chapters.

Since the strategy of the battle against plague was laid down by the government in London, we must begin there. New devices for the protection of public health grew out of the government's general pursuit of novel social policies which might benefit the common weal, improve public order, or win international acclaim. They thus had many similarities with the Tudor poor law, with which their development was closely connected. Unlike the poor law, howeyer, plague policy did not originate in provincial experiments, which were then adopted by parliament and the Privy Council.[2] The movement was decisively in the opposite direction, from centre to periphery. Plague orders were one part of the administrative burden deliberately laid on justices of the peace by Tudor and Stuart governments. Once the basic principles of isolating the sick and supporting them from public funds had been defined at the centre and accepted in the provinces, they became permanent elements in local government. This had been accomplished in most of the larger towns by 1610 and in most counties by 1625. As a result, magistrates increasingly assumed that the consequences of epidemics of plague must be dealt with, and that their progress might in some respects be controlled.

Several distinct stages in this process of invention and elaboration can be discerned. It began in 1518; it was given fresh impetus and new direction in 1578; and it was adapted and promulgated with new force again in 1630. We shall see that there were various features common to each of these occasions. Most obviously, none of them coincided with major epidemics of plague, either in London or in the country as a whole.[3] In the immediate crisis caused by a great epidemic like that of 1563 or 1603, there was little opportunity to develop new policies. Rather, innovation occurred when relatively minor outbreaks of plague seemed to aggravate other pressing social problems, especially in London. It depended also on the drive of politicians determined to display the reality of royal paternalism: Cardinal Wolsey in 1518, William Cecil in 1578, and the councillors of Charles I in 1630, all found the possibilities of social engineering attractive. One further ingredient on each occasion came from abroad: foreign models helped to inspire the actions of the English government. Policies for public health cannot be interpreted simply as an obvious response to a social need, therefore. They arose out of the political arena, and they reflected its weaknesses as well as its strengths. They were shaped as much by the competing forces of English political life as by the phenomenon of plague itself.

(i) The beginnings 1518–77

We saw in an earlier chapter that England was unlike many other European countries in having no public precautions against plague at all before 1518.[4] By comparison with Italy or France, it was in this respect a benighted, backward country, as anxious foreign visitors often remarked. Cardinal Campeggio's crossing to England in 1517 could be stopped by the mere hint of plague in London, since 'Italians are afraid of coming into a place where there is danger of death'.[5] In the following year, however, the government intervened. A royal proclamation of 13 January 1518 set out to control those 'contagious infections' which were 'likely to continue if remedy by the sufferance of Almighty God' was not provided. The remedy was the public identification of sources of contagion, so that they might easily be avoided. Infected houses in London should be marked by bundles of straw hung from their windows for forty days, and their inmates must carry a white stick when they went into the streets. These orders were 'devised' by Cardinal Wolsey for London; they were taken to Oxford by Thomas More and enforced there in April 1518; and they marked the beginning of an English policy for public health.[6]

The role played by Wolsey and More suggests some of the political and intellectual origins of the policy. It was part of Wolsey's ambition – shared perhaps by Henry VIII and certainly by humanists such as More – to put England on a par with other Renaissance states, in social policy as in everything else. That design was manifested in various ways at this time. In 1517 there was the cardinal's famous commission of inquiry into enclosures, a new attempt to enforce sumptuary regulations, and a centrally directed campaign against vagrants and beggars in London and perhaps in other towns.[7] In 1518 Wolsey founded the College of Physicians in order to improve English standards of medical care, along the lines suggested by humanist physicians like Thomas Linacre, who published his first translation of a Galenic text in that year, and John Clement, a friend of More.[8] The author of *Utopia* himself clearly shared their view that the duties of a magistrate included the safeguarding of public health. As under-sheriff of London he must have been familiar with the problem of epidemic disease there; and he had joined Henry VIII's Council in 1517, having finally resolved that some part of the humanist programme could be realised through political action.[9]

The epidemic and social circumstances of these years were also important. The sweating sickness hit London and infected some members of the Court, including Wolsey himself, in 1517. Plague followed at the end of the year, and both diseases coincided with popular unrest in the capital.[10] Epidemic disease must have seemed less a temporary threat, easily avoided by refuge in the country, than a permanent irritant of other social problems which had to be attacked. The fact that Henry VIII was rebuilding Bridewell Palace as his chief residence in the city no doubt made the need for action against disorder and disease all the more immediate.[11] The situation demanded a response from a government which was disposed to provide it; and there were foreign models on which it could draw. Bundles of straw and white wands were used to distinguish infected houses and their inmates in Paris in 1510; and at least two French towns had issued new lists of plague orders as recently as 1516 and 1517.[12]

The steps taken in 1518 were admittedly slight and tentative, as well as late. It is perhaps surprising that England had no similar policies, just as London had no professionally organised medical elite, earlier than 1518. English urban corporations were obviously less sophisticated than their Continental counterparts. England did, however, have an unusually centralised political structure, and consequently, once begun, administrative innovations acquired their own momentum. The Council recommended regulations like those of 1518 to the aldermen of London in every succeeding epidemic of plague before the great outbreak of 1563. The aldermen never responded with alacrity. In the epidemic of 1535–6, for example, they postponed action for several weeks, still 'trusting to God that the sickness shall cease'.[13] Nevertheless, on each occasion they did something in the end, marking houses, cooperating in the collection of vital statistics, which ultimately produced the bills of mortality,[14] and even adding new regulations of their own from time to time.

The city fathers were particularly concerned about supposed sources of infectious miasmas, and some of their by-laws would in fact have been promising weapons against rats and fleas, if they could have been effectively enforced. They made new orders for cleaning the streets in time of sickness, forbade the use of clothes and bedding from infected houses for three months after the disappearance of plague there, and arranged for rushes and straw from the same dwellings to be burnt. The Council, however, was much more worried about infection between persons; and it was the contagionist rather than the miasmatic theory of epidemic causation which it regularly stressed in its letters to the City. It always insisted on the marking of infected houses, ultimately arriving at the practice of putting ·a cross and the words 'Lord Have Mercy Upon Us' above the doors.[15] More than that, it soon began to urge that the inmates of infected houses should be forcibly prevented from leaving them: they should be allowed out only when they had to fetch provisions.

In 1543 the Council pinned the responsibility for infection firmly on the disorders of the infected, and gave a reasoned justification for its recommendation of stricter segregation. Any passive deductions drawn from concepts of miasma were censured, since plague increased 'rather by the negligence, disorder and want of charity in such as have been ... infected ... than by corruption of the air'. Men, not the elements, were responsible for disease and they should be carefully controlled. The government also revealed some of its own motivation when it invited the aldermen to add to their prestige by aping the more civilised practices of Continental towns. It encouraged

such of you as have travelled in outward parts to set forth such devices to be put in execution ... as you have seen there observed and kept; so as we may be seen to have learned that point of civility, and to have among us as charitable a mind for preservation of our neighbours, as they have.[16]

Civility came slowly. The city fathers still did little to impose the necessary police controls. But by the middle of the sixteenth century they were at least beginning to recognise their responsibilities in time of plague.

Things moved no more quickly in the provinces. For two decades after More's journey to Oxford, we have only infrequent references to the problems caused by sick paupers, plague corpses and infected migrants.[17] Between 1537 and 1545, however, several provincial municipalities tried to limit the danger of contagion, and they adopted a slightly different policy from that in London. Since the number of the infected was generally smaller than in the capital, they were able to follow the practice of many European cities and to isolate them, like medieval lepers, in houses or sheds outside the walls of the town. This happened in Shrewsbury and York in 1537 and 1538, no doubt at the instigation of the Councils in the Marches and in the North, and then in Windsor in 1540 and in the military base of Berwick in 1545, two other towns about whose health the government had good

reason to be concerned.[18] The same policy was implemented in
Nottingham in 1537, Durham in 1538, and Newcastle in 1545. A by-
law of 1540 in Liverpool similarly ordered that those visited with
pestilence there should 'depart out of their houses and make their
cabins on the heath' in summer; in winter they should stay at home
and 'keep their doors and windows shut'.[19]

The principle of segregating plague victims, whether in their own
houses or in special pesthouses, was thus widely proclaimed by 1550.
Its financial and administrative implications were more reluctantly
recognised, however. Few towns met the need for salaried watchmen
or subsidised those who were isolated before the 1570s. York was
probably the first to try. The prolonged stresses caused by epidemics
of plague and the sweat between 1549 and 1552, and heavy pressure
from the Council in the North to stem the apparently irresistible flow
of contagion, forced the aldermen into new administrative habits.
Unlike the magistrates in Bristol and Norwich, they did not stop when
they had banned pigs and other animal carriers of infection from the
streets.[20] They isolated some of the sick outside the walls, and shut
up others in their houses. They stationed watchmen on Ouse Bridge
to prevent the movement of infected people across the town, and
appointed special officers to bury the dead and clean infected houses.
More remarkably still, in February 1550 the town council imposed a
fixed weekly rate on each parish for the support of the infected and
the poor; and churchwardens were to levy the money by distraint if
necessary.[21] Although there had been an attempt at a compulsory
assessment for the infected in York in 1538, this was the first
successful compulsory plague rate, and one of the first compulsory
poor rates, in the land. It was copied in Lincoln in 1550, and in
Cambridge in 1556.[22]

It is no accident that administrative practice was precocious in York,
where epidemics were unusually common in the first half of the
century, and in ports such as Liverpool and Newcastle, where the
introduction of infection from abroad was a constant threat. Educated
opinion in the universities may have helped to encourage new measures in Oxford and Cambridge, and intervention by the Privy Council
or its provincial agents was important in some other towns. Most
urban corporations were still reluctant to invest in expensive novelties,
however. There were some exceptions in the 1560s. While the usual
crosses were being fixed above doors in Winchester in 1563, the
council of Canterbury was taking a detailed survey of the city, tracing

such health risks as beggars and dogs and listing householders who
might need to be supported if plague spread. When the queen moved
to Windsor in the same year, savage penalties were announced against
any threats to health there.[23] In 1564 victims of plague were kept off
the streets of Leicester and Exeter. The fourth example of a compulsory rate for the sick also comes from Exeter, in 1570; and in 1571
infected households were being segregated and supported in the
neighbouring town of Crediton as well.[24] Yet half a century after the
first plague orders, few town councils went so far. Many of them were
ready to exclude visitors from other towns and postpone fairs in an
effort to ward off the danger of plague; but they rarely controlled the
movement of the infected poor or supported them in isolation. The
problem was evaded in Dartmouth in 1563 by expelling the sick poor
from the town altogether.[25]

Even in London progress towards a coherent code of administrative
practice during epidemics was slow. In 1563 the aldermen adopted
no firm policy until the crisis was almost over – understandably,
perhaps, in view of the level of mortality in the centre of town. Crosses
were being attached to the doors of infected houses in June, dogs
were massacred as potential carriers of infection, and there were fires
in the streets to dispel the infectious miasma. There was no special
financial provision, however, apart from a few small payments from
City funds to the parishes worst affected and aldermanic support for
the usual charitable collections for the poor. In July parsons and
curates were at last instructed to tell parishioners to stay in their
houses for a month after infection; but some of them had to be allowed
out to collect food. It was only in February 1564, when the Privy
Council signified its displeasure at 'the great negligence and remiss
slackness of the citizens', that complete segregation of infected households was insisted on and that special officers were appointed to
supply and guard them.[26]

As a result, much depended on the initiative of those closest to the
problem, the authorities of the parishes; and they seem to have been
as overwhelmed by the crisis as the aldermen. The surviving parish
records show that churchwardens had to make special arrangements
for the burial of the dead, by employing more grave-diggers, for
example. Several of them bought the special forms of prayer against
plague which had recently been published. But there is no evidence
of any unusual expenditure on the poor or the sick.[27] In humiliating
contrast, the congregation of the Dutch Church in London was

debating as early as July whether or not plague was contagious, and appointing surgeons and making provision for the care as well as the segregation of infected members of its refugee community.[28] Here was an example of foreign civility close to home.

The corporation responded more actively to the minor outbreaks of plague in the decade after 1563 than it had in 1563 itself. Infected houses were shut up in 1568, 1569, 1570 and 1572. There were orders for searchers of the dead and surveys of the poor. Yet the corporation still had no consistent policy. The period of isolation recommended varied from only twelve days to forty. In 1568 aldermen and constables were to provide food for infected households; in 1570 inmates were to be allowed out if they carried wands.[29] And the major problem of finance remained. Despite – or perhaps because of – the wealth of its citizens and the sophistication of its charitable institutions, there was still no compulsory taxation for the sick in the capital. As in years of dearth, the aldermen preferred to deal with a crisis by exploiting the philanthropy of the governing class and the generosity of the livery companies, rather than to strain still further a complex system of collections for the poor and the hospitals which was already proving cumbersome and controversial.[30] Paradoxically, the early development of a corporate reaction to plague was prevented in London by too elaborate a political and administrative structure – rather than by one too primitive, as in provincial towns.

Between 1574 and 1585, however, ambitious lists of plague precautions appeared, at least on paper, in towns all over the country. Some of them were places we have already mentioned, where earlier precedents could be followed: much closer attention than before was paid to the isolation of the infected in Cambridge, Shrewsbury and Newcastle in 1574, 1575 and 1576. Other towns – Chester, Hull and Maidstone – issued plague regulations for the first time in these years.[31] In London itself revised orders were printed and set up on posts around the city in 1574, although they were not widely enforced or supported by special rates; and several parishes at last began to appoint searchers and keepers of the sick.[32] After 1577, this trickle of examples became a flood. Collections or rates for the sick, pest-houses, or padlocks on infected houses, watchmen and bearers of the dead are to be found for the first time in many towns. Some of these instruments were adopted in Colchester and Northampton in 1578, and in Norwich, Ipswich, Leicester and Rye in 1579. Doncaster, Winchester, Yarmouth and even such small towns as Wisbech and

Bishop's Stortford followed their example between 1580 and 1585.[33] Only in Norwich was there a really devastating outbreak of plague: a royal proclamation in 1580 rightly pointed out that the health of England was 'in better estate universally than hath been in man's memory'.[34] All this activity was a response, not to unusually severe epidemics, but to a new initiative by the central government.

(ii) The plague orders 1578–1625

In 1578, sixty years after the first plague regulations, conditions were once again ripe for decisive intervention by the Council. The Elizabethan regime was now firmly established, having survived the crisis of the rising in the North in 1569. Partly as a result of that emergency, however, there was quickening public anxiety about social problems of all kinds. It had produced the poor laws of 1572 and 1576, and it was shared by the queen's chief minister, William Cecil, Lord Burghley. Since the 1540s Cecil had been as great a friend of projects and projectors as Wolsey. In the 1570s, when London's population began its rapid growth, he was particularly worried about poverty and vagrancy in the capital. He discussed the problems with the City's Recorder, William Fleetwood, and in 1580 he may have initiated the Privy Council's campaign against new building and the subdivision of houses which attacked the related questions of overcrowding, disease, poverty and public order in the metropolis.[35]

Attention was directed towards public health in particular by smouldering and persistent infection. Although plague was more virulent in the provinces in the 1570s, we know from statistics collected by Cecil himself that it pushed up mortality in London every summer between 1578 and 1583. At the same time, another epidemic disease attacked members of the political elite, just as the sweat of 1517 had done: gaol fever killed two judges and several gentlemen after the Summer Assizes at Oxford in 1577.[36] Foreign influences were also important again. After the epidemic of 1563 an Italian physician and graduate of Padua, Cesare Adelmare, sent Cecil a project suggesting ways of 'providing against plague and other calamities which aggravate poverty in London'. He identified the faults in current practice: the lack of an effective bureaucracy to manage the health and welfare of the city, and the need for special financial provision for it. He recommended imitation of the best of the plague orders enforced in other countries.[37]

Although Adelmare did not specify which models he had in mind, they must have been Italian ones. Powerful boards of health, able to regulate movement and isolate the infected during epidemics, had been common there for decades. So familiar were they by the 1570s, that in Venice there could be a sophisticated debate about their efficacy, about whether the segregation of plague contacts in their own homes served any purpose, and whether miasma was more important than contagion.[38] Fundamental issues like these were not raised in England until later. At this stage the English government copied without question the more rudimentary regulations common in northern Europe. In France, the Netherlands, north Germany and even Russia town governments imposed isolation on the sick by every possible means, and in practice that usually meant at home; and they played down miasmatic theories and stressed contagion in order to justify doing so.[39] Accordingly, when announcing its new programme in 1578, the Privy Council asserted that plague was not 'of the air, as in other times it hath been seen, but only carried and increased from place to place through want of good order and severing the sick from the whole'. Magistrates had so far shown 'great slackness' in their efforts; the aim now was to minimise infection 'so far forth as by human policy the same may be prevented'.[40]

If the government's ambitions were borrowed from abroad, the means adopted to implement them were native ones. Uniformity was to be imposed on the nation through justices of the peace and the printing press. Circular letters to local magistrates had already proved an effective means of publicising Tudor grain policy in years of dearth, and printed proclamations had helped to familiarise local authorities with some of the new concepts of public health. A proclamation of 1563, for example, prescribed the isolation of diseased soldiers returning from Le Havre in 'some remote places'.[41] When plague reached London in 1563 the press was put to other uses. There were special forms of prayer against plague, and printed instructions from the bishop to be read in churches, exhorting the sick to separate themselves from the healthy. In March 1564 Cecil took the process a stage further. He had a set of orders printed for Westminster, where he was High Steward, providing that infected houses should be shut up for forty days and that no one was to leave them.[42] By 1577 the problem of managing infection in his town of Stamford, in Cambridge and in Oxfordshire had persuaded him that this experiment must be extended.[43]

Towards the end of 1577 or in the early months of 1578 a draft list of 'orders to be put in execution throughout the realm' was drawn up.[44] It was not immediately enforced, perhaps because the winter seemed to have killed off infection. At the end of 1578, however, after another summer of scattered outbreaks of plague, the Privy Council returned to the task and revised its draft. In November it wrote to the College of Physicians declaring its intent to provide 'some general order through the realm' by means of printed directions, and asking the College's specialist advice. In December a circular letter went out to fifteen counties, recommending action 'for staying of the infection of the plague'.[45] It probably had the new printed directions with it, for the first book of plague orders was certainly in print by the end of March 1579. It was bought by the churchwardens of Lambeth before then, recommended to the bishop of Norwich in July, and purchased by other local authorites soon afterwards.[46] Its title was *Orders thought meet by her Majesty and her Privy Council to be executed throughout the Counties of this Realm in such . . . places as are . . . infected with the plague*; and it had appended to it *An Advice set down . . . by the best learned in Physic within this Realm, containing sundry good rules and easy medicines*.[47]

The medical prescriptions at the end, drawn up by the College of Physicians, were trite and conservative. Perfumes were recommended to counteract poisonous air; clothes and bedding should be changed frequently; the old stand-bys, mithridatium, rue, valerian, wormwood and vinegar, were all included in suggested remedies. This *Advice* had to be rewritten in 1630, as we shall see. The *Orders* which preceded it, however, were innovative, far-reaching and permanent. They were reprinted with no more than minor alterations of style in 1592, 1593, 1603 and 1625; they were included without serious emendation in collections of statutes and orders on social policy in 1609, 1630, 166 and 1646; and they were radically revised only in May 1666.[48] Until almost the last breath of the disease in England, the *Orders* of 1578 dictated policy from one end of the kingdom to the other. They had no statutory support until 1604; they did not even have a royal proclamation to legitimise them. Like the slightly later and more famous series of dearth orders, for which they formed a model, they derived their authority from the royal prerogative unrestrained and undiluted.[49] Yet they turned the attention of local governors in new directions, orchestrated previously haphazard local endeavours, and permanently shaped administrative habits in the English provinces.

There were seventeen orders in all, each of them putting new burdens on justices of the peace, either in towns or in their developing county divisions. They were to meet once every three weeks during epidemics, to receive reports on the progress of infection from 'viewers' or searchers of the dead in each parish, and to 'devise and make a general taxation' for the relief of the sick, extending it where necessary to villages and towns around the afflicted community. The clothes and bedding of plague victims should be burnt, and funerals take place at dusk to reduce the number of participants. Above all, infected houses in towns should be completely shut-up for at least six weeks, with all members of the family, whether sick or healthy, still inside them. Watchmen were to be appointed to enforce this order, and other officers should provide the inmates with food. Only in small villages, where one house was distant from another, could men be allowed out to tend their crops or cattle, and they must distinguish themselves by some mark on their clothing or by carrying a white stick in their hands. The *Orders* ended on a prophetically defensive note. Punishment was threatened against anyone who criticised these rules as uncharitable: they were 'manifestly' designed to give 'succour and relief' to the victims of plague.

Charitable or not, the *Orders* were similar to those enforced in Continental towns. Certification of deaths, appointment of searchers, control of times of burial and the fundamental policy of household segregation were all part of precautions widely adopted in Europe against epidemic disease. The English regulations had two peculiarities, however. The first was the insistence on taxation to meet the cost of supporting the sick – a provision borrowed from the poor law of 1572. There were special taxes during epidemics in many parts of the Continent, but they were not regular and they did not become habitual across a whole country.[50] That was the unique achievement of English centralisation and of the English poor law.

Secondly, the isolation of the infected in English towns was, in theory, unusually strict. Other countries sometimes mitigated the rigours of household quarantine. In the Netherlands, for example, visits to the sick were not only permitted, but to an extent encouraged, for purposes of religious consolation and medical help; and inmates of infected houses might be allowed out to 'refresh themselves' as long as they carried distinguishing marks.[51] There was no similar laxity in English towns. The incarceration of whole families in infected houses characterised English policy between 1578 and 1665, and we shall see that it was this which stimulated most controversy.

These two features were highlighted when the *Orders* were given the support of statute in 1604. A measure on plague was included along with a bill on granaries and corn provision in a programme prepared for the parliament of that year, possibly in government circles; it was probably seen as part of the whole corpus of legislation on poor relief passed in the years after 1597.[52] The Plague Act accordingly provided for local rates for the sick, and for their extension beyond infected places, first to parishes within a radius of five miles and then, if necessary, to whole hundreds or counties. But the statute also had a deliberately punitive purpose. In 1603 Robert Cecil had been warned that the infected in Westminster were unruly and needed some 'sharp punishment' to control them; and the new king, James I, may have noticed that the Scots had harsher medicines for plague victims than the English.[53] The Act of 1604 closed the gap by providing the first penal sanctions behind the policy of isolation. Watchmen now had legal authority to use 'violence' to keep people shut up. Anyone with a plague sore found wandering outside in the company of others was guilty of felony and might be hanged; anyone else going out could be whipped as a vagrant rogue. As its title said, the statute had two aims: 'the charitable relief and ordering of persons infected with the Plague'.

Like much social legislation, this measure had to be renewed from parliament to parliament, until it was made perpetual in 1641. Strictly speaking, it was not in force between 1626 and 1628, and as late as the 1660s it was possible to question its validity, perhaps because the continuation of 1641 had been tacked unobtrusively at the end of a subsidy bill.[54] Yet in practice the statute was accepted as permanent from the beginning. It was enforced between 1626 and 1628 no less than before and after. Its provisions were included in handbooks for justices soon after 1604, and copied into the manuscript notebooks of individual magistrates until at least the 1660s. All agreed that the statute was rational and desirable: as Edward Coke said, it was 'grounded upon the law of God'.[55]

Its impact was less than it might have been, and it was accepted so readily, because the *Orders* of 1578 had already done much of its work for it. Despite the lack of statutory sanctions, plague rates had been levied before 1604 under the authority of the 1572 poor law, and offences against the *Orders* had been punished as breaches of the peace. By 1603 the new regulations were being enforced in almost all the larger English towns, and plague rates and household quarantine were becoming a reflex action in periods of epidemic disease. Besides the towns mentioned earlier, they are to be found in Sandwich, Gloucester and Worcester in the 1590s, and in Salisbury, Bristol, Southampton and Maldon by 1604.[56]

The statute had a rather greater effect on commissions of the peace in the counties, some of whom seem to have regarded the *Orders* as intended primarily for the towns. A few had responded to the publication of 1578. There was an order for a county levy for Chesterfield in Derbyshire in 1587, and assessments for those visited with plague in parts of Gloucestershire in 1592, in the West Riding of Yorkshire in 1598, and in Kent, Devon, Cheshire and Hampshire in 1603 or the early months of 1604.[57] Other instances may be hidden by the lack of evidence for the activity of justices out of sessions. But the rush of plague rates between 1604 and 1612 in at least eight other counties,[58] and the evidence of houses being shut up in small villages in Kent, Lincolnshire, Staffordshire, Hampshire and Nottinghamshire at the same time, are eloquent.[59] The statute of 1604 made all the difference in rural England. A justice shutting up a house in Cheshire in 1603 had been abused for doing 'more than he can stand to'. 'What hath he to do here?' asked a prominent parishioner. In 1605, by contrast, the Cheshire bench was able to cite both the 'King's Book' and the laws of the realm to justify its actions.[60]

In short, like the books of orders, the statute was effective propaganda for the government's policy. By 1625 all provincial magistrates had been persuaded that it should be implemented. There were practical obstacles, as we shall see in a later chapter. There was also continuing popular opposition, and that also deserves separate treatment.[61] When people escaped from infected houses, they were sometimes whipped as the law required, or alternatively fined or stocked. As far as we know, none of them were charged or punished as felons. Like similar offenders, a Westminster widow, Ellen Fauster, was merely put in the stocks with a certificate tied to her head, 'for going abroad ... having a rising which was adjudged to be the plague'.[62] As so often at this time, the death penalty was a deterrent rather than a reality. But it was a deterrent signifying a consensus among the governing elite about what was dangerous behaviour in time of plague, and about how it should be prevented. 'Politic government' as well as 'the omnipotent blessing, favour and government of God' could therefore preserve Shrewsbury from plague in 1593. In Waltham, Essex, the justices made the infected 'keep good order and tarry in their houses' in 1603. In Portsmouth in 1625, 'by the goodness of God, the orders for the securing the infected hath in many places taken good effect and succeeded well for the stay and preservation of many'.[63]

At the level of policy-making, therefore, the major problems did not lie in the provinces, where inferior magistrates were readily persuaded to play the government's tune. They lay in London, where the practical difficulties loomed so large that they could not be ignored and where the city fathers had their own view on how they should be met. From the start, the Privy Council accepted that a separate book of orders was needed for the metropolis, and it pushed for one more rigorous and more elaborate than that imposed on the kingdom as a whole. In 1577 it showed its displeasure with previous efforts. It sent the City a printed questionnaire, inquiring with obvious irony 'what orders have been put in execution for the restraining of the infected of the plague', and implying that houses had not been shut up, or if they had, that they had been only those of 'the poorer sort'. Late in 1578 the Privy Council returned vigorously to the attack. It summoned representatives of the City to a conference on the subject, and threatened that if they did not act voluntarily it now had 'means and ordinances in readiness more chargeable and heavy'.[64] To prove its point, the Council gave the mayor a draft set of regulations which survive with the City's comments, and after much argument and revision, these provided the foundation for a printed book of plague orders, published in May 1583.[65]

The debates which took place over this prolonged period of gestation illustrate the standpoints of the two sides: the ambitions of councillors, which the City thought hopelessly unrealistic; and the reservations of the City, which the Council thought the product of self-interested parochialism. There was much common ground in the final orders of 1583. The bedding and clothing of the sick should be aired, funerals carefully controlled, streets cleaned and vagrants expelled. There was general agreement now and later that all plays and interludes should be banned in plague-time because of the danger of infection. But there was no consensus on how the sick should be treated, or how their care and control should be paid for.

To begin with, the Council advocated a large corps of officials who would make the policy of household segregation enforceable in practice. In every parish there should be visitors and keepers of the sick, 'purveyors' of provisions with which to supply them, and overseers and treasurers, with their clerks, to arrange finance. The City replied that it could not afford so large a complement. The Council also hoped for a team of physicians, apothecaries and surgeons. Here the City's difficulties stemmed from its equivocal relations with the College of Physicians, a separate chartered corporation, which often consulted with the aldermen about medical aid but produced the necessary volunteers only slowly.[66] The orders of 1583 held out the hope of medical personnel, and while omitting treasurers and their clerks, provided for two overseers, two viewers of the sick, two searchers and purveyors of necessities in each parish. These were plainly only pious aspirations, however, and few of them were realised before 1625.[67]

The Council wanted new institutions as well as personnel. There should be a special hospital, a pesthouse, in which some of the infected might be isolated. With its usual combination of flattery and complaint, the Council noted in 1583 that pesthouses existed in other 'cities of less antiquity, fame, wealth, circuit and reputation' than London. Again, however, the City found itself unable to respond quickly. It was short of funds and suitable property, it argued. A small pesthouse was finally begun in St Giles Cripplegate in 1594, financed partly by a levy on city companies which had made a windfall profit from the seizure of a Spanish treasure ship. But it remained wholly inadequate.[68]

Finally, and at the root of all else, there was the problem of finance. The first article in the Council's draft of 1578 proposed that there should be a 'general taxation' to cover the costs of quarantine, officials and pesthouses. This the corporation vehemently resisted. Church collections and charitable bequests would suffice, it argued. New impositions could only undermine the existing, overstretched system of rates for the hospitals and parish poor relief. The City remained implacable, and no mention was made of special plague rates in the orders of 1583. Perhaps in consequence, these orders also failed to insist on the strictest household segregation. Infected houses should be shut up for four weeks, but one inmate might be licensed to go out for food.

The London orders were thus less demanding than those for the nation as a whole on the two central points of taxation and segregation, and they remained so when they were reprinted in 1592 and 1603. In view of the statute of 1604, it is not surprising that the government returned to these themes in 1608 and 1609 when, again in a period of mild but persistent infection, the London orders were radically revised.[69] In 1608 there was to be a weekly tax in infected parishes, and the clause allowing one member of each household to be at liberty was omitted. The orders at last conformed to the national programme of 1578 and after. In 1609 there was a further revision, providing for the appointment of six surgeons who were to divide the city between them and supervise medical aid. We shall see that these new requirements had no immediate practical result. But the London orders were now as standardised and as permanent as those for the kingdom. They were reprinted without major alteration in 1630, 1636, 1646 and 1665.[70]

The differences between the Council and the City had two general implications which deserve comment here. The first, which lay behind the disagreements over finance, was the whole question of authority in the metropolis. The aldermen were inhibited by the number of institutions which they had to supervise and whose interests they had to respect and reconcile. Not only did they find it difficult to put pressure on the College of Physicians, and, as they complained, on the bishop if they wished to use the city clergy to promulgate their orders and overawe their critics. They also had to manage the representatives of their own citizens in wards and parishes which were both far more numerous than in any other English town and far more independent and politically active.[71] Moreover, the growth of London and the spread of plague with it placed an increasing proportion of the burden outside the unfettered jurisdiction of the city corporation: in liberties, in Westminster, or in the counties of Surrey, Middlesex and Essex, where there were governors whom the City could only consult or influence, not browbeat or command. The mayor often excused himself to the Council with the plea that he lacked full authority: there was too great a multitude 'who are to be governed' and who 'will hardly conceive what is for their good provided'.[72]

The arguments about the precise degree of household segregation raised a second fundamental issue: the efficacy of this particular method of preventing contagion. The City was quick to seize on this point when seeking to justify its failure to quarantine houses successfully. 'To shut up the sound and infected together', it argued in 1583, 'seemeth by experience rather to increase than decrease the

infection.' When people were 'pestered together' in their houses, 'for
want of room and shift of beds and bedding ... very few of them
escape the infection'. Self-serving though the City's advocacy of it
was, there was plainly a good deal of force in this argument.[73] The
difficulty lay in finding an alternative which was financially and admin-
istratively viable. Large pesthouses for the infected would be much
the best thing, the aldermen thought; they did not, of course, provide
them. All that could be suggested in the printed orders of 1609 was
that the sick should be separated from the healthy in separate rooms
within each isolated house.

Although the City had finally accepted the necessity of household
isolation, the doubts it expressed about its ability to enforce it and the
wisdom of doing so were to reverberate over the next half-century.
The two problems of authority and policy dominated the subsequent
history of the strategy devised in 1578.

(iii) Authority and policy 1625–66

It is remarkable that the first move was made, not by the Council, but
by parliament, acting for once in an executive capacity. Parliament
rarely met during epidemics, for obvious reasons. In 1625, however,
the king's need for supply kept the Houses in session, first at
Westminster and then, as infection mounted, in Oxford; and members
were much exercised by the evidence of God's judgment on the
nation, by the misery of London, and by their own peril.[74] In August,
the Lords appointed a committee to consider the relief of the city.
No less a figure than the duke of Buckingham was responsible for
this move, and the two orders of the Lords which resulted were no
doubt prompted by the government.[75] First, the poor rate in the whole
metropolitan area was to be doubled for the benefit of the infected.
This had little effect in the face of the City's passive resistance.
Secondly, however, there was to be a general collection throughout
the kingdom for London and Westminster. It was raised under a
charitable brief, like those issued earlier by the Lord Keeper for towns
suffering from fire; and it was the model for later briefs for plague-
infected towns in the 1630s.[76]

The City was happy with that, and it advanced loans to the parishes
until the collections came in. But there was a *quid pro quo*. Like
parliament, the country was paying for protection and expecting effec-

tive isolation measures in the city. In 1626 the Lords inquired anxiously what steps had been taken for 'regulating of visited persons'. In the Commons, Dudley Carleton was equally worried. He had observed public-health procedures on the Continent and he proposed a select committee to draw up a bill containing regulations like those enforced in Paris, Venice and other great cities.[77] No statute emerged, and plague declined. When it reappeared in 1630, parliament had been dissolved, not to reassemble for a decade. It was the Council's turn to resume the battle for order and control.

As in 1518 and 1578, a combination of factors inspired government intervention in 1630. Once again it was far from being a period of critical epidemic disease. Plague was mild in London in 1630–1, though serious in Cambridge and parts of the North. The danger of infection in London was of some concern to Charles I, because the queen was pregnant and she wished to remain either at St James's Palace or at her new house in Greenwich. But more was at stake than the health of Henrietta Maria and of the future Charles II. There was an even greater determination than in 1518 and 1578 to tackle many interrelated social problems. The years 1630 and 1631 saw a new book of dearth orders, the famous Caroline 'Book of Orders' controlling many aspects of local government, and a new drive to cleanse the metropolis of public nuisances and make it a capital fit for an absolute king.[78]

No single councillor, no Wolsey or Burghley, was reponsible for this programme. Wentworth and Laud supported it later, but its initiation owed more to experienced councillors like the earl of Manchester and Dudley Carleton, to men on the fringes of government such as Inigo Jones and the king's physicians, and probably to the king himself – all of them aware of European developments and all of them concerned about disorders in London. It was a concerted effort, and the policies promulgated at the beginning of Charles I's personal rule have all the hallmarks of a new regime parading impeccable credentials and flexing its political muscles. The protection of public health was an integral part of the exercise, and if it proved in the end as fragile and temporary as the rest, it began with considerable energy.

As soon as plague was known to be in the capital at the beginning of 1630, the Council wrote to the justices of the City and Middlesex advising a change of policy. It recommended the isolation of the sick in pesthouses or hospitals as a 'better and more effectual course' than their incarceration in their own homes, and it wished to see new pesthouses set up around London from Westminster to Greenwich. As a model for the city to copy, it also sent a memorandum describing the Hôpital Saint Louis, which had been founded by Henry IV in 1607 for the infected in Paris.[79] At the same time, the Council called on the College of Physicians urgently to revise the *Advice* which was attached to the book of plague orders. The College's reply, published in April 1630, no longer confined itself simply to the prescription of medicines: it described the conditions of overcrowding and poverty which endangered public health in London; and it implied that the sick should be separated from their healthy relatives in order 'to preserve the whole, as well as to cure the infected'. It referred for support to the admirable practices used in 'Paris, Venice, Padua and many other cities'.[80]

The inspiration for all this did not come from the College, sympathetic though Fellows like William Harvey must have been. It came from the most fashionable doctor of the day, the king's Hugenot physician, Sir Theodore de Mayerne. He had been Court physician in Paris at the beginning of the century, when Henrietta Maria's father, Henry IV, had been trying to improve public health there; and in March 1631 he presented to Charles I a long report on the precautions necessary to prevent epidemics of plague in London. His treatise expounded the rationale and purpose of the whole campaign.[81]

It began with a general description of the environmental and social disorders, from poverty and drunkenness to unregulated new building and vagrancy, which were major hazards to health. That was conventional enough, although the ramifications of what Mayerne called 'the public health of all' had never been stated so comprehensively before. Familiar too, by then, at least on paper, was the recommendation of a salaried corps of doctors, surgeons and apothecaries to look after victims of plague. Mayerne's condemnation of household quarantine was more novel in the English though not in the European context. Everything must be done to prevent contagion, and that meant separating the sick from the healthy. There should be four or five pesthouses for the sick, one to be called King Charles's *Maison de Dieu* or the King's Hospital of Health. Contacts and relatives of the infected should also be isolated for forty days, if possible in separate accommodation, but if necessary at home. As the Council noted, these were practices 'used in other countries and found to be the safer course' – a judgment which modern medical science would very probably echo.[82] Only if contacts were isolated at home, still close to infected rats, would the procedure have been dubious; and it is remarkable that Mayerne, alone among his contemporaries, pointed to 'rats, mice, weasels and such vermin' as some of the carriers of plague.

Mayerne went further and attacked the problem of authority, taking up a point made sixty years earlier by Cesare Adelmare. What was needed above all in London was some magistrate with 'absolute power' to control both city and suburbs in times of crisis. This was to be achieved by a board of health on Italian models. There should be a 'chamber, court or office of health' in London, including the mayor and selected aldermen, but also two Privy Councillors and two bishops, one of them the bishop of London. It was to be permanent, so that it could deal both with epidemics and with the conditions which produced them – vagrancy, overcrowding, bad hygiene and inadequate food supplies. It must have power to 'repress all opposition'; and it should rule over (and presumably overrule) all authorities in the metropolis from Richmond to Greenwich. Mayerne had identified the crux of the problem. When the Council wrote again to the College of Physicians for advice in March 1631, it significantly asked for 'political' as well as 'natural' remedies. The College now knew what the Council wanted to hear. It suggested a 'commission or office of health' covering the whole metropolis with authority to punish delinquents. Such a body had been 'found useful in Spain, Italy and other places'.[83]

Had it been created, the metropolitan board of health would have been a splendid plank in Charles I's claims to enlightened absolutism. But it was not. It was never more than a paper project. The government had other, more immediate concerns, and when no epidemic developed in 1631 the idea was abandoned. There was no great new hospital to commemorate Charles I either, and hence household quarantine could not be jettisoned. It was indeed enforced more rigorously than before in London in 1630 and 1636, thanks to the activity of the Council. Councillors faced facts, accepted that household isolation was better than no isolation at all, and themselves coordinated government in the metropolis to that end, transmitting orders to the parishes of Surrey and Middlesex, the burgesses of Westminster and the aldermen of the City.[84] That was no substitute for a separate authority, however. The abortive attempt to incorporate the suburbs, which caused so much controversy in 1636 and 1637, bore witness to the continuing problem of metropolitan government and to the continuing failure to arrive at any solution.[85]

For a time, the impetus of 1630 spilled over into the provinces, first to Cambridge and then to York. Intervention in Cambridge was provoked by a serious outbreak of plague in 1630, and by the failure of county, town and gown to co-operate in managing it. Through Lord Coventry, the University's High Steward, the Council encouraged regular joint meetings of University and town authorities, supported rates and watches, and advocated the new concepts of isolation.[86] Forty 'booths' were built outside the town as pesthouses; and although many of the sick and their relatives had to be quarantined in their houses, a printed list of *Orders* issued by the Vice-Chancellor and the mayor recommended that they should be 'sequestered in the same house, if it be possible, one from another, and so continue with one person to attend the sick . . . for six weeks at the least'.[87] It was unlikely that many infected households had space to comply, of course. The government's main interest was plainly to prevent contagion as quickly as possible and by whatever means possible.

This was even clearer in York, where Thomas Wentworth, President of the Council in the North, took firm control. As plague approached in 1631, he prohibited the entry of goods and people from infected places. When it was detected in the suburb of Walmgate and in the villages of Huntington and Heslington close by, he imposed watches at the gates, forced the justices around York to co-operate, approved the erection of pesthouses, and ordered the levying of 'liberal assessments' for the relief of the sick and payment of watchmen. There were only a few cases of plague within the walls, but their contacts were traced and all were quarantined. Much of this would have been done in York anyway, even without Wentworth. But he brought unusual vigour to the exercise. The words 'order', 'guard' and 'strong watch' occur again and again in the records of this visitation, and justices and aldermen had to suffer the Lord President's censure along with their inferiors. 'The greatest pity' that could be shown in a plague, Wentworth thought, was to take 'severe and strict courses' from the start.[88]

For the rest of the 1630s, however, Wentworth and his colleagues had other problems to occupy them; and in 1640 the Long Parliament began to dismantle that single, relatively unquestioned central authority on which both new policies and severe and strict enforcement of them depended. It was therefore to parliament, not the Council, that the next project on plague was sent, in 1641. Louis Du Moulin, another Huguenot physician and acquaintance of Mayerne, lamented that the infected were allowed to die in their houses 'in a most unchristian manner, without any succour, relief and comfort of any physical help'. His suggestion that visitors and medical aid should be provided for them evoked no response. Parliamentary committees discussed the obvious necessity for greater control of the sick, and reached no new conclusion.[89] Earlier books of plague orders were reprinted by parliament with little alteration in 1641 and 1646, and there were ordinances for national collections for infected towns like the earlier charitable briefs.[90] For his part, the king issued orders for Oxford and Oxfordshire between 1644 and 1646, based again on past publications.[91] Unadventurous continuity was the keynote of this aspect of government in the localities too. Although the ravages of civil war prevented the collection of plague rates and left many of them in arrears for years, justices of the peace in the 1640s followed the policies of isolation and taxation established in the 1620s and 1630s.[92]

Whether the Councils of State of the English Republic would have done more if plague had attacked London we cannot say. There was no such crisis to test them between 1646 and 1650. The Interregnum did, however, see a modest advance in one aspect of plague policy which we have so far neglected: the protection of England from ship-borne infection from abroad. Unlike other states, England had no regular mechanism for controlling communication with infected foreign ports before the seventeenth century. The government simply acted *ad hoc*, when an obvious threat was brought to its notice. In 1580, for example, ships from Lisbon were stopped in the Thames until their merchandise had been aired, and in 1585 a ban was placed on imports from Bordeaux because of plague there. In 1602 provincial ports as well as the port of London were told to watch for ships from infected harbours in the Low Countries, and to impose forty days' quarantine on passengers and goods coming ashore.[93] But the first efforts to enforce a uniform policy through use of customs officials seem to have been made only in 1629 and 1635. When there was plague in the Netherlands again, in 1655, similar measures were taken, and they were followed up more effectively. The Dutch ambassador was consulted; a twenty-day quarantine on ships from the Netherlands was imposed in the place of irregular periods of isolation earlier; and steps were taken to prevent abuses. The orders were to be enforced in every port and extended where necessary to other infected countries.[94]

Despite the damage to trade, the Protectorate Council built on the precedent set by that of Charles I.

Yet all this had apparently been forgotten by the 1660s. In 1663, when plague threatened once more from the Low Countries, the Privy Council asked the corporation of London what precautions had been taken against it in the past, and a search of the city records could provide no answer. The Council established a sub-committee to advise it, and considered a project for a lazaretto outside London where ships could be held and examined. The author, Thomas Chiffinch, appealed to the example of 'most other well governed kingdoms and Republics professing Christianity', and implied that hitherto nothing had been done in England. The Council was already acting, however, imposing first a 'trientane' of thirty days on ships from infected ports, and then, in May 1664, a full quarantine of forty days. The protests of the Dutch ambassador were ignored, ships were halted at the mouth of the Thames, and the government tried as best it could to impose similar controls in provincial ports.[95]

The failure of these precautions and the great epidemic of 1665–6 in London faced the Council with all the problems of authority and policy of the past. The old solutions were toyed with and the old failures recorded. Another conciliar committee, starting in May 1665, reviewed all previous regulations. It had the *Advice* of the College of Physicians reprinted, but without the prefatory national *Orders* of 1578.[96] It seemed as if the latter were at last to be radically revised. From the beginning the committee also had before it a 'short proposal of some few expedients for the prevention of the plague', probably written by Hugh Chamberlen. It repeated the points which Adelmare, Mayerne and Du Moulin had made long before. There had so far been a 'total neglect of the prevention' of plague, a task which 'belongs to the magistrate'. The isolation of whole households had spread contagion, not reduced it, and led 'the infected to conceal their infection'. Proper medical care for the sick was the first essential. Special commissioners would be needed to superintend the work, and ample funds to pay for it. A second missive from Chamberlen in 1666 supported his earlier project, suggested a regular tax to pay for necessary precautions in the future, and repeated that political as well as medical provision was needed against plague.[97]

There could be no cool pondering of that familiar refrain at the height of the crisis of 1665, however. The Council had to act, and act quickly. It supervised the building of new pesthouses around the city, and suggested that 'if possible' the sick should be removed to them. They could contain only a fraction of the infected, and the shutting up of whole households was undertaken again, under authority of the plague orders for London, which were now republished.[98] On the financial issue, there was no time to debate new taxes. There were national collections once more, money being sent to the bishop of London for parishes in the city and Westminster.[99] Neither was there any new board of health, although metropolitan government was supervised more closely than ever before. Some members of the Council's plague committee fled from London with the Court and king in July 1665. But George Monck stayed in Westminster, in overall charge, and the earl of Craven, the mayor and two or three justices did what they could to impose order, directing the constables and searchers, the quarantining of the sick and burial of the dead in the city and suburbs. Craven in particular brought to the task an independent mind and power of decision. As a Fellow of the Royal Society, courtier and son of a former Lord Mayor, he was uniquely qualified to be a supreme magistrate in an epidemic which was almost unmanageable.[100]

He was also well qualified, when the crisis was over, to reflect on its lessons. Early in 1666 he concluded that household quarantine had been difficult to enforce, and even when effected, it had not prevented further contagion. Hindsight showed that the only reliable procedure would have been 'the timely removing of infected persons' from their houses 'in the beginning'.[101] The Council responded and at last remodelled the national plague orders of 1578. In May 1666 *Rules and Orders* was published as a replacement. The sick were now to be moved to 'pesthouses, sheds or huts, for the preservation of the rest of the family'. Every town was to build a pesthouse ready for the purpose. Healthy members of plague-infected households were to be shut up at home for forty days.[102] It was Mayerne's policy of 1631 revived, and it came too late for London.

The Privy Council of 1665–6 was not quite the Council of 1630–1, however. Not only did it have a major disaster on its hands; it also lacked the confidence of its predecessor. It could not ignore parliament, and that assembly was itself reconsidering plague policy in the course of this last epidemic. When the Council failed to reissue the national orders in 1665, and when it hesitated for so long before revising them, it may well have been because – as one contemporary asserted – it wished to proceed 'legally'.[103] It was waiting for statutory backing. In October 1665, as in August 1625, parliament was forced to meet at Oxford to consider the king's need for war finance. It also considered the battle against plague, and decided that it was failing, in part 'through the defect of the law'. Both Houses embarked on revision of the 1604 Act, and a new bill passed the Commons, only to fail in 1665 and again in 1666 because of differences between the two Houses.[104]

Although the bill itself does not survive, its contents can be reconstructed from the proceedings surrounding it. To begin with, it made it clear that the Act of 1604 was still in force and should continue: there had been some doubt on this point. It provided for new burial grounds for the infected and gave authority for action against inmates and lodgers, where there had again been uncertainty about the powers of justices. On the vexed issue of isolation, it adopted a sensible compromise. It apparently provided for the erection of pesthouses in every parish, although it may not have insisted on them. More realistically, it also gave magistrates authority to shut up whole households for forty days. The latter had been implied but not explicitly stated in the 1604 statute; and Craven, who was a member of the Lords committee on the bill, wanted some clear 'legal power' for the purpose.[105] In short, the bill would have brought the law more closely into line with current practice and encouraged investment in various methods of isolation.

Its failure was not due to any dispute on matters of principle. It arose from the narrow but passionate self-interest of the Lords. The Upper House insisted that peers should be exempted from having their houses shut up, and that no pesthouse or graveyard for the infected should be close to 'any considerable mansion house of any gentleman'. The Commons eloquently retorted that 'no dignity can exempt from infection; and therefore none to be freed from what is for the safety of the people ... Death equals all'.[106] It was to no avail. The bill fell, and the issues – along with the social prejudices they aroused – had to be taken up again, as we shall see, in the 1720s.[107]

Parliament had proved itself incapable of providing solutions to outstanding problems. The Council had done more, but only slowly. In the provinces, however, local authorities eagerly followed past practice, whatever doubts some of them may have had about their legal authority. From the spring of 1665 onwards, there were strict watches on roads and at the gates of towns all over the country. Boats from the capital were quarantined outside Whitby. In York, the king's brother,

James, ordered all innkeepers to report newcomers to the town to the mayor. Elsewhere suspect wanderers were traced and where necessary confined to their houses. Such regulations were justified in Oxford as consistent with 'the laws of God, of Nature and this Realm'.[108] When the Council's new *Rules and Orders* appeared in 1666, town councils and county benches took note of them. Household isolation was still practised: we find it in Southampton, King's Lynn, Bristol and Norwich, for example.[109] But there was also a remarkable investment in pesthouses, not only in infected towns but in several others. We know that they were set up in Bedford, Exeter, Yarmouth, Oxford, Dorchester, Salisbury, Bristol, Cambridge, Beverley and Norwich.[110] There was in fact a genuine national alert in 1665–6, more extensive than in any previous epidemic year.

There was also pride in the results. Local authorities were quick to congratulate themselves, even when their optimism was premature. In Beverley, for example, the 'effectual care' of the justices in 'separating the infected from the free' was thought at first to have prevented a major epidemic; and the London newspapers were full of reassuring tributes to the care and vigilance of provincial magistrates at the first sign of infection.[111] We shall see in the final chapter that this confidence may on occasion have been justified. Whether justified or not, however, there could be no better testimony to the profound effect on local government of the repeated orders against plague since 1578.

The government had thus had some considerable success in imposing the strategy for public health first announced in 1518. There had also been two failures. The problem of authority was never satisfactorily solved. There was no supreme magistrate and no sovereign board of health for London or anywhere else. Although Privy Councillors themselves occasionally filled that role, the royal prerogative was not in the end an effective foundation for social policies, and parliament failed to provide an alternative. Their efforts had shown the limitations as well as the creative potentialities of the English body politic. Informed criticism of household segregation, evident as early as 1583 in London, also failed to make a decisive impact before 1666. Other forms of isolation proved to be even more expensive and impractical, and they were no less dependent on a strong directing hand. The keynote of plague policy in England remained the shutting-up of houses, and although that could never be wholly enforced either, its widespread adoption was the major achievement of the government between 1578 and 1665.

This chapter has concentrated on politics and in particular on the role of the Council in that achievement. From this perspective it has no doubt appeared to be a piece of old-fashioned Whig history. From small beginnings, moderately enlightened policies gradually became commonplace and were imposed on the nation. It was by no means as simple as that, of course. We have concentrated on the centre because it was there that the new policies began. Before they could be widely accepted, however, they had to meet the challenge of principled opposition and to overcome many practical obstacles. Some established attitudes towards plague had to be adjusted, and the ambitions and activities of local government had to be stretched. In order to understand these developments, we must turn our attention away from politics and the centre, first to attitudes and intellectuals, and then to the localities and their rulers.

Chapter 9

Controversy and compromise

What a madness and cruel foolishness is this, that in the time of any great plague, such as are infected, you shut up in houses, set marks upon them, keep them in prison, strangle them with cares and solitariness, and kill them for hunger . . . . Do you in this sort love your neighbour as yourself . . . when as at no time . . . there is greater need of fellowship, company, comfort and help than in the time of plague?

Paracelsus, *A hundred and fourteene Experiments and Cures* (1596)

If we make a mock of all preservatives of Art: if we neglect all evil and infectious savours and refuse the benefit of the purer air: if we run desperately and disorderly into all places and amongst all persons and pretend our faith and trust in God's providence, saying: 'If he will save me, he will save me, and if I die, I die' – this is not faith in God but a gross, ignorant and foolhardy . . . presumption.

Certaine Prayers . . . to be vsed in the present Visitation (1603)[1]

It was inevitable that controversy would be provoked by the administrative procedures whose development has just been described. As we saw in Chapter 2, commonplace assumptions about plague could be used to justify that kind of government intervention; but they also embraced a stress on divine providence which might inhibit any sort of human action – apart from repentance and prayer. Contemporaries were not unaware of this ambiguity in their intellectual inheritance. It was brought out into the open during the epidemic of 1603, and it was only after that that an uneasy but generally acceptable compromise was arrived at. It was a compromise which relegated the Almighty to a subordinate role and permitted the growth of secular interpretations based on observation of the phenomenon. Controversy was renewed in 1665, but it took a different, less religiously oriented form, and it showed by comparison with 1603 how much had changed in the interim.

(i) Controversy 1563–1604

The most striking aspect of the English debate about plague policy was its lack of intellectual rigour, and hence of clarity. Just as differences over the vexed question of flight were implied by subtle distinctions of emphasis rather than overtly stated,[2] so too most writers for and against the government's programme held back from extreme positions. Its opponents were inhibited from attacking all precautions: they concentrated their fire on those with the most damaging social effects – in particular rigid household quarantine. On the other hand, the supporters of the programme never denied that divine providence played a part in its success or that religious as well as secular remedies were essential. Nevertheless, the defensive tone adopted by many of the early advocates of the plague orders betrayed their own uncertainties and their appreciation of the powerful case that could be made against them. They knew they were on dangerous intellectual ground.

One reason for the paucity of open controversy was the fact that the leaders of the established church were firmly on the side of the government. In part this was because many of the clergy were as worried about the danger of infection as anyone else, though they often pretended otherwise. The Prayer Book of 1552 assumed that priests would visit the sick 'in the time of plague, sweat or such other like contagious times'. In 1578, however, Bishop Aylmer of London told his clergy that they should select a few volunteers for the duty and that the rest could avoid such dangers; and in 1604 the new Canons stressed the obligation to visit only 'if the disease be not known or probably suspected to be infectious'. Some clerics opposed Aylmer, 'thinking it a part of their duties to suffer with their flock, and to submit to God's will'.[3] Others must have been relieved.

The Church was also bound to the State by personal ties and a common interest in maintaining obedience to authority. Nothing illustrates this better than the history of the special forms of prayer against plague, in which religious and secular points of view were inextricably intertwined. The first of them was planned by Archbishop Parker of Canterbury, Bishop Grindal of London and William Cecil in 1563. Parker wanted simply to adapt the short order of prayer which had been used in 1560 against unseasonable weather and the threat of war; but Cecil encouraged Grindal to produce something more novel and more demanding.[4] Borrowing extensively from Genevan practice, Grindal constructed a printed form of prayer which was to be used in all churches on Wednesdays and Fridays and combined with a public fast. Meditation and abstinence at home were to be accompanied by church services lasting through the greater part of the day, with seven sermons read in succession from the authorised volume of homilies, and one further sermon on 'the justice of God in punishing impenitent sinners', specially written for the occasion by Alexander Nowell.[5] Grindal was also responsible for special prayers of thanksgiving printed for use after the end of plague; and both pamphlets became models for later publications in epidemic years.[6]

There could apparently be no clearer manifestation of the religious interpretation of plague. Although Grindal disapproved of Popish processions, he had replaced them with a demonstration of national repentance and an invocation of supernatural forces only slightly less public. Archbishop Parker and others indeed had doubts about Grindal's form, thinking that it departed too far from the Prayer Book, gave too much freedom for Puritan exercises and excesses, and kept congregations together too long at a time of infection.[7] When the form was revised by Aylmer in 1593, it provided for only one homily besides Nowell's, and that not more than an hour long, in order to discourage both religious 'faction' and pestilential 'contagion' in 'thick and close assemblies of the multitudes'.[8]

Yet Grindal himself had been well aware of the second danger, if not of the first, and had been anxious to prevent it as far as possible. He advised against 'general assemblies' of several congregations, like those which had taken place in 1560. Instead he ordered services in every parish church, where 'prudent' care should be taken 'to keep the sick from the whole'. He published a special manual of plague prayers for private use by householders, including those who were shut up because of infection, and recommended that the houses should be 'perfumed . . . with frankincense or some other wholesome thing' before the prayers were said.[9] In an admonition read in the churches of London early in 1564, Grindal even went out of his way to support the Lord Mayor's regulations, and he did so in terms which showed his appreciation of their controversial potential. The sick should 'forbear to company with the whole' and the healthy should 'not resort to places infected, whereunto by their duty and vocation they are not bound to resort, lest by rash and wilful entering into companies or places of danger, they tempt God'. This was consistent with divine law, as references to leprosy in Scripture showed, and with the obligations of charity:

> Even by the rule of charity all men are bound in conscience not to do anything that by common judgement and experience may bring a manifest peril and danger to their brethren or neighbours.[10]

The same support for the secular arm was articulated more clearly and more stridently in 1603, when the plague prayers were issued for a third time. A long 'Exhortation' on the natural causes of plague now replaced Nowell's homily. Nowell had stressed the need for religious submission: men should commit themselves 'wholly to the holy will of our most merciful Father'. The Exhortation had a completely different tone. The role of contagion was elevated above that of miasma, and in words very close to those in the government's plague orders of 1578 a blistering attack was launched against those who argued 'that the disease of the plague was not contagious and infectious'. Experience, the judgment of learned men, the practices of other countries, and biblical examples all showed their folly and perversity. People who thought they were 'not bound in conscience to shun and avoid the persons and places that are infected' tempted God with their presumption, and brought about 'a public and manifest detriment to the state'.[11]

The power of the pulpit was thus brought into play behind the government's programme, and it echoed the government's paranoia. Much the same fear of providential interpretations and attacks on contagion can be found in the orders of 1578 and in one or two sermons and pamphlets published at the same time.[12] The authorities clearly thought that their precautions against plague, and particularly the isolation of the sick, were vulnerable to two arguments, each of them familiar from the contemporary debate on flight which was described in Chapter 2. First, it could be claimed that government policies, and the notion of contagion on which they rested, were a denial of God's pre-eminent role in the incidence of an epidemic. Secondly, it could be argued that they were a denial of the obligations of charity and neighbourliness. Unfortunately for the historian who wishes to measure its strength, the opposition case was never put quite as succinctly or as forcefully as that; its appeal has to be reconstructed from fragmentary evidence.

Most of the criticism of public-health measures came from people who were either on the fringes of authority or subject to it. Clerics, like those who opposed Bishop Aylmer in 1578, were particularly prominent; and they appear to have been men who were already both theologically disposed towards a predestinarian stance and politically out of sympathy with the ecclesiastical establishment. They were Puritans, in fact. In the epidemic of 1563 Grindal heard of preachers who 'persuaded the people to break the orders set forth' against plague, apparently on providential grounds: one of them, who criticised the bonfires lit in the streets to dispel miasma, had himself 'been sick ever since of the plague . . . so that God hath sufficiently corrected him'.[13] The mayor of Norwich was rumoured in 1580 to have said that plague regulations were of no importance, 'seeing God hath appointed and limited unto every man a certain tenure of life'. Although the allegation may have been prompted by the malice of Bishop Freke, who was then embroiled in disputes with his Puritan cathedral city, Norwich undoubtedly sheltered ministers who stressed providential interpretations of plague; and it is notable that in 1603 the city fathers wanted general assemblies for fasting and prayer in three or four places in the town, rather than in every parish church.[14]

In the years around 1600 there may have been many Puritan preachers whose sermons implicitly or explicitly denied the efficacy of natural remedies. One observer thought so. A Spanish visitor to London in 1609 reported current views of plague:

> The Puritans say that it should not be avoided, that it is good
> fortune to die of the plague, and that although they are close to
> it, it will not attack any but those already singled out by God, let
> them take what measures they may. That this is infallible and
> that it is false madness to try to guard against it. But with all that,
> I think a great many of them leave London.[15]

That final jibe was indeed a damaging one, and it should make us hesitate before we conclude that English Puritans were wholeheartedly, let alone unanimously, opposed to natural precautions against infection. One Norwich Puritan, Nicholas Bownd, certainly supported the isolation of the infected in 1604, and the alderman of the city were no more consistent. They were actively quarantining the sick from at least 1585 onwards.[16] Common though they were, occasional expressions of piety or disquiet did not make Puritan ministers and magistrates the leaders of a principled attack on the government's health policy.

The government's greatest fear, however, was that even the most qualified criticism of its policy encouraged popular resistance to it. The opposition case seemed to be a rationalisation of popular prejudices and a potent justification for disobedience. Several writers asserted that fatalistic attitudes towards plague were held by 'the rude multitude' and 'the ignorant sort', those who suffered most from the disease and against whom public-health measures were primarily directed.[17] The 'common sort' were also seen to be capable of taking a stand on moral principle. According to the Vice-Chancellor, some of the common people in Cambridge in 1574 said that 'a Christian ought not to avoid the company of another that is infected', while the poor of London in 1637 were reported to 'hold it a matter of conscience to visit their neighbours in any sickness, yea though they know it to be the infection'. And recognition of these moral imperatives might well provoke, or excuse, resistance to quarantine measures. It was to be a proverb among ordinary Londoners in 1636 that 'the plague would not decrease till the infected had their liberty'.[18]

Popular reactions were nothing like as uniform or as articulate as these perceptions of them suggest, of course. We shall see in a later chapter that ordinary men and women were often as anxious to flee from plague and avoid infection as their rulers. But they had fewer opportunities to do so; and when they were infected and then cruelly isolated, their only psychological defence was a fatalism which could be articulated as reliance on divine providence. Doubts about contagion were inevitable too. As one writer pointed out, many people thought plague infectious until they or their relatives caught the disease and they suffered the consequences.[19] They might then begin to doubt whether the sacrifices imposed on them had any rational or moral justification. Divisions of opinion owed a good deal to different experiences of plague and to the social distinctions which plague often respected. The governing classes wished to justify precautions such as flight and quarantine which protected them. The victims of plague could not be expected to share their view.

From this perspective, it is easy to see why the attacks of secular and ecclesiastical authorities on fatalistic opinions were so vehement, and why these opinions rarely got past the censors, and the caution of authors, into print.[20] There were, however, a few who ventured to publish their doubts, especially about the practice of household isolation. Even so prominent a defender of new policies as Thomas Lodge was forced to admit that some moderation might be necessary, because of the 'fright and fear' the sick 'conceive when they see themselves void of all succour'.[21] Other writers, arguing from a less secular standpoint, were able to force the same point home more starkly. One was the advocate of Paracelsian notions of the spiritual origins of disease, whose defence of neighbourly charity in 1596 is quoted at the beginning of this chapter. In 1603 a diatribe against the sins which brought plague on London similarly poured abuse on governors and their practices:

> You atheistical politicians! Shut up your doors, keep narrow watch and ward, use your gifts of nature, try your wits, practise your physicians, lavish with your purses! Matchavill [Machiavelli] himself will not serve, no not so much as to add one potion of comfort to the distressed.[22]

The most dangerous assault on the establishment position came from a divine, Henoch Clapham. Although he was clearly a Calvinist, it is difficult to know quite where to place Clapham in the ecclesiastical spectrum. He had fallen foul of church authorities in England and then been involved in sectarian squabbles among the English exiles in Amsterdam in 1597 and 1598. Back in England, he wrote works against Catholicism and the Popish inclinations of some Anglican divines 'on the left hand', and against the excesses of Presbyterians, Separatists and Brownists 'on the right'.[23] Not surprisingly, he antagonised and was distrusted by English clerics of every hue from Bancroft downwards. He was cantankerous, inconsistent, opinionated, an undoubted maverick. Only such a man, perhaps, could have brought the tensions inherent in contemporary attitudes towards plague so unapologetically into the light of day.

Clapham's short *Epistle Discoursing upon the present Pestilence*, published in 1603, dismissed all natural explanations for plague and attributed everything to divine providence. Those who accounted plague a 'natural disease' were 'atheists, mere naturians and other ignorant persons'. Galen was no more than a 'Greek heathen physician'. All sensible doctors admitted that plague exceeded 'the compass and reach of all their natural reason'. Scripture pointed unambiguously to the conclusion that pestilence was God's handiwork, and so too did experience. Clapham alleged that many stricken with plague had 'felt and heard the noise of a blow; and some of them have upon such a blow found the plain print of a blue hand left behind upon the flesh'.[24] Moreover, it was evident that many people took no medicines, came into close contact with the sick, and yet were preserved. Trust in God's providence protected them, as it would others who scorned flight and similar precautions. If any true believer died of the pestilence, it was because of his lack of faith, not because he neglected natural remedies.

Clapham's conclusions were implicit, but obvious. He had not actually stated that plague was not infectious, but that was what he meant and he was alleged to have said so in his sermons. His targets were equally plain: the plague orders of 1603, those who defended and enforced them, and public officers who deserted their posts and neglected the care of the sick, especially in London. Clapham had even been found encouraging 'the meaner sort of people' to flock in crowds to funerals, despite the Lord Mayor's order limiting the number attending to six.[25] That was more than enough. Bancroft had him imprisoned in November 1603 for criticising the published orders of Church and State. He was interrogated by an unsympathetic Court of High Commission and by an irate Lancelot Andrewes, who had himself fled from his Deanery, Westminster, and his parish, St Giles, at the height of the epidemic.[26] Clapham stayed in gaol for eighteen months, despite publishing a second edition of his *Epistle* in 1603 with important modifications and a further treatise in 1604 in which he retracted some of his views. Even that was not the end. He appealed to the king and the Prince of Wales for support, published another tract in 1605 shifting back towards a more providential position, and then – as a final irony – found himself hauled before the College of Physicians after his release for advertising cures in the streets of London.[27]

Clapham was eccentric, if not unbalanced, but he was clearly not negligible. He had simply put into print what many Puritan preachers were said to be hinting in their sermons, and his challenge had to be rebutted. Francis Herring was one author who volunteered. He reasserted what he considered to be the lessons of other epidemic diseases: 'Shall the itch, scab, measles, smallpox &c be acknowledged catching and infectious, by the experience of every silly woman; and shall the plague be esteemed . . . an harmless and innocent creature?' He also thought it necessary to reaffirm the proven efficacy of flight, except in cases where people carried the 'seminaries' of the sickness with them.[28]

James Balmford also defended the plague orders, this time on Clapham's own ground of Scripture. The rules for lepers in Leviticus justified the isolation of the infected, and the Sermon on the Mount could be interpreted as requiring only 'charitable ministering to the necessities of the sick', not actual contact with them. 'Extraordinary providences' might occur, but they were visible only after the event and were not to be depended on.[29] Balmford was himself answered point by point by 'W.T.', whose anonymity allowed him to express Clapham's position in more extreme form. Both biblical example and present experience showed that 'the infection is not general, but unto those whom [God] will have it touch'. The poor should therefore be permitted to visit their sick neighbours and to attend funerals, and ministers and magistrates should not confine the infected but care for them.[30] While Balmford defended the view of the establishment, W.T. voiced popular grievances.

The pamphlet controversy of 1603 illustrates very well the complex interaction between theological considerations, experience of plague, government policy and popular behaviour. Before new policies could be generally accepted and popular behaviour altered, the uncertainties arising from theology and experience had either to be resolved or pushed out of sight once more, if necessary by force of authority. Since resolution proved impossible, the issues raised by infection and providence had, in effect, to be fudged. When Lancelot Andrewes drew up a recantation for Clapham to sign, he did more than justify his own flight: he defined the sort of blurred compromise which those in authority hoped to impose:

That howsoever there is no mortality, but by and from a supernatural cause, so yet it is not without concurrence of natural causes also, for the most part . . . . And I clearly and expressly hold the plague to be infectious and that it is most expedient for the parties infected to be severed and shut up (they having things necessary and convenient provided for them) . . . . That a faithful Christian man, whether magistrate or minister, may in such times hide or withdraw himself, as well corporeally as spiritually, and use local flight to a more healthful place (taking sufficient order for the discharge of his function).[31]

(ii) Compromise 1604–65

Henoch Clapham would not have been the man he was if he had accepted Andrewes' form of words. He refused, partly because he wished to give priority to points which Andrewes touched on only in parentheses.[32] He did, however, find a way of accommodating himself to orthodoxy, and it was a route which other divines followed after him. Some earlier writers had suggested that there might be two different kinds of plague, one wholly natural, the other wholly supernatural.[33] Clapham seized on the idea in his retraction of 1604. The disease might be purely supernatural, 'the absolute mortality of the Angel's stroke', and that was not infectious; but it might also be natural, propagated by corruption in the air and by infection between persons. The vital point was that both forms of plague could occur simultaneously and they could not easily be distinguished one from another. God's tokens, the purple and blue spots of plague, still suggested the stroke of an angel, Clapham argued; but these symptoms had seldom been seen recently, 'as if the Lord would give us no sign by reason of past abuse of signs'. On every occasion, therefore, both spiritual and natural remedies should be applied.[34] This deliberately equivocal approach was adopted by many later writers.[35] It was a crucial concession, and it guaranteed that arguments from divine providence would never again be used with conviction to deny the efficacy of every precaution against plague.

It did not resolve all the controversial issues, however. The problem of flight was still a vexed one, for example. Granted that escape from infection was now generally acceptable, except for those with public or private obligations, there remained the question of who the exceptions were and whether God would protect them. Robert Abbot, brother of the Archbishop of Canterbury, continued to hold that those doing God's work might hope for an 'extraordinary providence' and he only grudgingly admitted the prevailing view that plague 'noisomely infecteth (I think)'.[36] A more instinctive revulsion against the wholesale flight of Londoners also continued to inform much of the popular literature on plague, which rarely avoided a providential final note. 'Where can they run', asks Death in one of these publications, 'but I am still behind them?'[37]

Observations of the sufferings of the poor led equally to criticism of the cruelty of household quarantine. Humanitarian arguments against it were as common after 1603 as those medical and practical reservations which we observed in government circles in the last chapter. The policy might be sensible to begin with, George Wither thought, but

> When our sickness and our poverty
> Had greater wants than we could well supply
> Strict orders did but more enrage our grief
> And hinder in accomplishing relief.

It is significant that Wither took care to tone down the distrust of natural remedies evident in his manuscript before he published it;[38] and no one now argued from supernatural interpretations that the government's precautions were useless. But there were some who hinted that the plague of 1625 only began to decrease when the policy of isolating households was abandoned.[39] The moral and practical objections to shutting up the infected were to be developed at greater length in 1665.

Some of the old controversial themes were also revived by a dispute over plague fasts which began in 1625. Charles I and his Council were as worried as Bishop Aylmer had been in 1593 about the opportunities which long services on these occasions gave for Puritan enthusiasm and, so they claimed, for the spread of infection. In August 1625 the Wednesday fasts against plague in London were banned; and in the next epidemic, in 166, they were to be shortened by the omission of sermons in all plague-stricken towns.[40] Those who thought prayer 'to God in extraordinary manner and humiliation' essential naturally objected to these orders as Arminian or Laudian innovations.[41] Attitudes were polarised both on the religious issue and on its medical consequences. Some argued that plague had been declining in 1625 before the ban: public fasts had worked. Others showed that it only declined afterwards: private fasting at home worked equally well.[42] A few writers held that Arminian novelties were themselves among the sins causing plague in 1636, while more conservative clerics attacked what they alleged to be the fatalistic views of sectaries and Anabaptists.[43] The question of pastoral duties was resurrected too. Archbishop Laud was quick to act against a preacher in Oxford in 1630 who discussed the obligation of ministers to visit the infected with too much stress on divine intervention.[44] Laud's client, Thomas Swadling, put the contrary view: 'No priest is bound to go to a man sick of the plague, not bound by any law of man or God.'[45]

These squabbles were no more than a temporary by-product of the debates aroused by Arminianism, however. There could be no great divide between Puritan advocates of fasts on the one hand and Arminian supporters of flight on the other because by 1630 virtually all writers and preachers supported both in moderation. There were differences of emphasis but there was no new Henoch Clapham to break the overall consensus. While defending practical precautions, Thomas Swadling also dwelt at length on the need for repentance and prayer, including fasting.[46] From the other side, the famous Puritan divine William Gouge allowed that 'special providences' might sometimes protect against infection, but he strongly denied that plague was the immediate stroke of God: experience showed that it was 'no more immediate than many other diseases' and hence 'means of escaping it' should be used.[47] It was a significant statement which showed how much has changed since 1603. Not all Puritans moved as far towards natural explanations as Gouge. Robert Jenison of Newcastle, for example, carefully avoided such treacherous theoretical ground; but he found it difficult to maintain a wholly religious approach to plague when he had to defend his own flight to his parishioners. Like some other authors, Jenison also conceded more than he knew when he described the sufferings of the poor in quarantine, deprived of friends and neighbours, as an inevitable part of that divinely ordained punishment which plague, in his view, represented.[48] The essence of the government's health policy had been accepted as a *fait accompli* by the vast majority of commentators on the subject.

Something more than mere acquiescence was encouraged by other developments in the early seventeenth century. Close observation of the regularities in plague epidemics led some authors towards a positively secular view of their causation. Despite continuing reliance on authority, and a heavy dependence on traditional medicines,[49] there was a marked increase in the amount of contemporary comment and personal reflection in the plague literature. Doctors began to refer to their own experience and other writers to seek comparisons with epidemics in the recent past as well as in the ancient world.[50] The means by which plague was carried from one place to another were often noted. It had reached Oxford more than once in clothes from London, for example, and the rag trade was soon, and rightly, identified as a potential source of infection.[51] A popular broadside of 1625 even applied contemporary lessons to the past, asserting that the Black Death had spread from the East 'by reason of passengers from one province to another'.[52] Only Mayerne noted that rats and other vermin 'running from house to house and creeping over stuff may receive and carry the infection'; but the more common view that 'abundance of mice and rats' was a portent of plague may have pointed attention in the same direction.[53] At least one man in 1665 told his servant to 'take all course you can against the rats', although he also continued the old precaution of killing cats as well.[54]

The circulation of printed bills of mortality did most to stimulate discussion and analysis of plague. When the London bill-for 1603 reached Lady Margaret Hoby in Yorkshire, she naturally compared the extent of infection in the two localities.[55] After 1603 such comparisons became easier, as provincial towns inaugurated their own bills. Precise totals of deaths in plague years were available, though not always in print, in Norwich, Bristol, Chester, York, Newcastle and Oxford; and provincial statistics were printed in some of the earliest London newspapers.[56] The incidence of plague, in households and among children and foreigners, was quickly appreciated;[57] and the distinctions which searchers of the dead had to make between plague and other diseases stimulated attempts to distinguish different infections.[58] In London people could compare mortality in successive visitations, judge which had been the 'great plague', and ask whether the latest visitation was really as serious a calamity as it seemed.[59] They also noted the regular seasonal periodicity of plague and acted accordingly. In 1641 a London citizen could suggest that a proposed day of humiliation against plague was unnecessary, because 'winter was coming on, and then the plague would be stayed'.[60]

Most obvious from the London bills was the concentration of plague in suburban parishes and hence among the poor. The correlation between poverty and plague was already a cliché in 1603; but from then on it could be given statistical support against the diminishing number of preachers who still asserted that God's punishment was socially indiscriminate. By the middle of the seventeenth century there were even some who welcomed plague as 'a broom in the hands of the Almighty with which he sweepeth the most nasty and uncomely corners of the universe'. It might be a necessary, almost a Malthusian, check when 'fruits of wombs pass fruits of earth'. William Gouge thought God had designed 'the poorer and meaner sort' to be the chief victims of plague 'because they are not of such use' and 'may better be spared'. According to Robert Harris, others saw plague as a blessing, because those who died were 'of the baser and poorer sort, such whose lives were burdensome, whose deaths are beneficial' to society.[61]

This may have been an extreme, minority reaction, but it illustrates the extent to which plague had become widely identified as a limited social problem rather than a universal and divinely ordained threat. By making plague familiar and measurable, the bills of mortality undermined those supernatural interpretations which are reserved in most societies for unusual afflictions and sudden calamities. As early as 1583 the translator of a foreign work on plague described the standpoint of the rulers of London in terms which applied to many other educated people by 1640: plague had become

> a disease so usual . . . that albeit it were somewhat feared at the first, yet use hath now at length made it unto many so familiar, that there is little more regard had of it than of any other common and light malady.[62]

We must not carry this line of argument too far. Plague was never wholly assimilated among the 'common and light maladies'. If observation showed some of its regularities, it also brought its haphazard features fully into the limelight – features which could only be explained by chance, or, as contemporaries preferred, by providence. The bills of mortality could be employed by preachers to demonstrate God's mercy to one town rather than another or in one epidemic rather than another, as mortality varied.[63] Appeals to divine aid would never be pointless, and there continued to be a large body of religious literature for those threatened by infection. In 1636–7, as in 1625–7, more than half of all the works published on the subject of plague were sermons or devotional tracts providing religious consolation.[64] That is why we referred earlier to a compromise between secular and religious interpretations, not to the triumph of one over the other.

It was undoubtedly a compromise in which the balance was weighted heavily in the secular direction, however. For in a sense the divines protested and published too much. When, like Robert Jenison, they printed full mortality statistics, they demonstrated how much men could learn as well as how much remained a divine mystery. Thomas Brewer's deductions from fluctuations in mortality were scarcely convincing: 'one bill rising, another falling; the increase bidding fly from sin, the decrease not to fly from the city'.[65] It could as easily be said that increasing mortality dictated flight and that its fall showed the irrelevance of sin. When preachers attacked those 'deists' and 'naturians' who interpreted plague in terms of the weather, or the humours, or physical circumstances in the suburbs, or some other 'causes in nature', they showed how much they were on the defensive.[66] In 1603 that beleaguered aggressive tone had belonged to the advocates of plague regulations fighting their critics. By 1640 the roles were clearly reversed. Robert Harris said people should not think plague could have been prevented, 'had such a place been scoured, such traffic stayed, such means used . . . Hereafter, I'll be wiser.'[67] As he must have known, this was exactly what most of the social and political elite did think.

Their perception of the compromise can sometimes be glimpsed in their correspondence. The Reverend Joseph Mead, for example, wrote at length about the London plague of 1625 to one of his friends. He speculated about whether the decline of plague after the seventh plague fast in the city could be compared to the fall of the walls of Jericho after seven trumpet calls. He also repeated one of the stories of men who fled from London and were struck down by plague soon afterwards, and pointed the moral. But he remained sceptical: 'You may judge of this, or suspend, as you shall see cause', he told his correspondent. He gave a careful analysis of the bills, perceptively pointed to some of the discrepancies in them which suggested that plague deaths had been undercounted, and praised God's mercy only when he saw a decline 'in a week that gave no reason to expect it'.[68]

The Almighty was even more firmly relegated to second place, and often to parentheses, in the self-congratulatory orders passed by town councils against infection. As early as 1595 the Common Council of Sandwich merely added the proviso that they would work '(as far forth as it shall please God)'. The justices in Westminster in 1625 promised that their precautions would prevent miasma and contagion '(if the Almighty God say Amen)'. When confidence in quarantine led to its use against smallpox in New Romney in 1615, '(If it may please God)' was inserted, literally between the lines of the order, as an obvious afterthought.[69] It is usually impossible to tell when appeals to supernatural agencies were merely the formal lip-service paid to outdated assumptions; but this stage had clearly been reached by the governing classes of some English towns well before 1640.

Whether quite the same mixture of attitudes obtained lower down the social scale, it is difficult to say. The ingredients were the same, but their relative weights may well have been different. There was no doubt less intellectual consistency and coherence than among the elite, and probably less movement away from the confused eclecticism of traditional views which was described in Chapter 2.[70] One thing is certain, however. Popular attitudes were not dominated either by religious faith or by gullible superstition. The literate had ready access to information and exhortation, not only in the bills of mortality, but also in works of what would now be called 'faction': accounts of alleged incidents during epidemics in London which were designed to be entertaining and morally instructive rather than accurate. The genre had been poineered by William Bullein's *Dialogue* of 1564, and the last example was arguably Defoe's *Journal of the Plague Year*; but it reached its apogee in the early seventeenth century in the work of Thomas Dekker and his contemporaries.[71]

Their pamphlets had pathos, often a macabre humour, as preachers complained,[72] and a moral point. They were cautionary tales, usually warning against too much faith in natural means, but occasionally also against too much faith in providence. Alongside the stories of Londoners stricken as they fled from the city, there was that of the parish officer who died after lying on a plague corpse to show that providence would protect him.[73] Readers were encouraged to denounce the flight of aldermen but also the cruelty of countrymen who shunned refugees from the city. They were expected to laugh at absurd precautions, like the avoidance of letters and even spotted fish; but they were not taught to run needless risks. This literature offered ridicule of extremes of behaviour, a defence of charity, and a necessary hard realism which enabled people to come to terms with plague.[74]

The range of intellectual options open at the popular level was perhaps most clearly revealed in the cheapest publications concerning plague, the single-sheet broadsides, often headed 'Lord Have Mercy Upon Us'.[75] Several of them had striking borders occupied by skeletons, death's heads, corpses in winding sheets. There was sometimes an illustration showing Londoners fleeing from the city and God's angel of death triumphant over it. There were often cheap medicines for the poor and prayers of repentance. Taking up much of the space on most of them, however, were statistics from the bills of mortality, showing how the present visitation compared with those in the past and how the weekly totals of burials had fluctuated in earlier epidemics. Ordinary Londoners, as well as their governors, were thus able to anticipate a rise or fall in mortality, and to turn to medicines or prayers as circumstances and inclination dictated. Even if the more intellectual problems which were hinted at in London sermons swept over them unheard, they had the materials to formulate their own compound out of discordant elements. Finally, they saw around them every day the most eloquent manifestation of the compromise between public provision for health and appeals to divine providence: the shut-up doors of infected houses with the words 'Lord Have Mercy' written above them.[76]

The great surge of Puritan enthusiasm and millenarian expectations which came with revolution and civil war in the 1640s produced a temporary revival of providential interpretations of calamities, including plague. One early symptom was the special form of prayer for plague published in 1640, in which the Exhortation on natural causes was replaced by a 'Homily of Repentance'.[77] National and local fasts against epidemic infections were common up to 1658.[78] So too were accusations that one party or another in the divided political nation was responsible for plague, and anxiety when disease hit the godly rather than their enemies. Henry Ireton ordered public humiliation and weekly fasts against plague in Ireland in 1650, and wondered why the 'destroying Angel . . . seems to come near to us . . . those whom [God] hath so wonderfully preserved and provided for . . . and owned'. Had the army's Irish campaign been too savage, or not savage enough?[79] The Barnstaple plague of 1644 was attributed by some townsfolk to the heresy of the local Independent congregation, and by the Independents to the perversity of their critics.[80] Royalist divines adopted a similar tone. Lionel Gatford attacked the sins of covetousness and extravagance, especially in female fashions, which had brought epidemic disease to Oxford in 1644; and he criticised those who absented themselves from church in time of infection: 'Very few, if any, of those who have been infected with the plague . . . could say, and say truly, and upon certainty, that they caught the infection . . . by frequenting the house of God.' There is tragic irony in the fact that Gatford died of plague in 1665, having contracted it in the course of his ministry in Yarmouth.[81]

The search for providences during the Interregnum did not reverse the trend towards a greater understanding of epidemic disease which we have been considering, however. On the contrary, as recent scholars have shown, millenarian enthusiasm contributed positively to medical inquiry, and stimulated projects for practical medical reform, including better provision for public health.[82] A revival of interest in 'new diseases' and their aetiology was also encouraged by the epidemics of the 1640s and by the strange virus infections of 1657–8 and 1661.

The foundations were laid in this period for major advances in medical observation, by Thomas Willis and Thomas Sydenham,[83] and in medical and political arithmetic, by William Petty and John Graunt. Both lines of inquiry continued to flourish when religious enthusiasm became disreputable again in 1660. Petty and Graunt were particularly interested in the impact of plague, and Graunt's *Observations on the Bills of Mortality* of 1662 pushed contemporary understanding of that disease and of public health in general onto a completely new plane. Among the topics Graunt considered were the chronology and variable severity of plague, its distinction from other diseases, and its effects on and relationship with demographic growth. None of them had been analysed in such depth before. Graunt made only one tentative reference to divine providence, and that was employed in order to dismiss old 'superstitions' about the timing of epidemics.[84]

By 1665 therefore the ground had been prepared for a more confident and objective approach to plague than had been common in 1603. The revised Book of Common Prayer of 1662 revealed something of the change when it substituted 'the contagious sickness' for 'the noisome pestilence' in one of the collects. In 1665 the new form of prayer for plague not only restored the Exhortation of 1603; it also replaced weekly fasts with monthly ones. There was no outcry like that of 1625. Most educated men would now have agreed with Hugh Chamberlen's cool assessment: natural remedies against plague promised 'as much reason, certainty and success as most other sublunary undertakings'.[85] There was controversy about plague in 1665, but it did not have the relationship between sublunary and supernatural agencies at its centre.

(iii) Controversy renewed 1665–6

The plague epidemic of 1665, the first serious visitation in London for nearly thirty years, generated responses which were partly familiar, partly novel. Much of the novelty lay in the amount of information about the epidemic which was made available to contemporaries. At least forty-six publications concerned with plague appeared in 1665 and 1666, rather more than in 1625–6, and a much larger proportion of them – nearly two-thirds as opposed to one-third – dealt directly with the natural causes of plague, with natural remedies or with the incidence of disease. There were analyses of past and present bills of mortality, borrowing heavily from Graunt, which allowed people to plan their movements in and out of the city with care.[86] There was a bewildering array of preservatives and remedies on offer, down to new amulets and 'celestial waters' advertised in broadsheets. George Monck, the Council's lieutenant in the metropolis, had a broadsheet summarising old Galenic medicines, including treacle, distributed in bulk to all churchwardens, so that it might be given to any householder on request.[87]

In addition, there were now newspapers, They began to give weekly totals of burials in London somewhat belatedly, at the beginning of July, but once the practice had begun, the government's press agents quickly realised the superiority of suitably presented statistics over ill-founded rumour and the panic it might cause. The bills were cited to show that mortality within the walls was quite small, as opposed to the suburbs: people in the provinces need not, therefore, shun every parcel and passenger from the city.[88] On the basis of past experience, the papers accurately predicted a decline in mortality at the end of September 1665, and accounted for an unusual increase in December by 'that unseasonable weather which it pleased God to send forth about a fortnight since'. In August they had attributed the high death rate to 'the wilfulness and disorders of the patients themselves', who neglected or misused medicines and escaped from houses which were shut up.[89] They reported news about plague in the provinces, in Gosport, Yarmouth, Cambridge, Bristol and Norwich, as an antidote to panic and a practical aid to merchants and travellers.[90] All this may have done something to increase confidence in the face of calamity.

The newspapers also printed advertisements, some of them for recent publications, others for specific remedies. Readers were told where they could buy the medicines recommended in the official publication by the College of Physicians, the rival antidotes of 'chemical' practitioners, and the potions of empirics and quacks. 'That admirable preservative against the plague, wherewith Hippocrates preserved the whole land of Greece' could not fail; neither could a powder which recently preserved houses from infection in St Giles-in-the-Fields. The Privy Council itself backed a fumigant invented by a Frenchman who alleged that it had stopped the infection at Lyons, Paris and elsewhere. When burnt, this concoction of brimstone, saltpetre and amber was supposed to dispel miasma; it may well have driven rats out of houses if the stench could be tolerated by the inmates for long enough.[91]

There was not only more medical advice available than ever before in 1665; there were more medical men. Many practitioners fled with their patients as in the past. But some apothecaries stayed to take advantage of the market, like William Boghurst, who advertised his wares and his crowd of patients – fifty or sixty daily – in *The Intelligencer*.[92] Several physicians also remained, members of the College as well as adherents of the chemical school, like George Thomson, who prided themselves on doing so. For the first time the College of Physicians took its own recommendation that five or six doctors were needed during epidemics seriously. In 1625 only two volunteers had come forward. In 1665 a team of ten or eleven physicians, headed by Nathaniel Hodges, was employed by the City, some of them having responsibility for particular wards.[93] Boghurst, Thomson and Hodges wrote tracts on plague, drawing on their experiences. Thomson was even responsible with others for the famous dissection of a plague corpse, which was thought, probably wrongly, to have led to the death of some of the participants. Several physicians did die in 1665, however, probably of plague.[94] Medical provision was clearly ineffective; and it was small in relation to the need. The number of qualified physicians in the city at the height of an epidemic in which there were 60,000 plague deaths is unlikely to have exceeded thirty, although there were many more apothecaries, surgeons and empirics. But by previous standards this was a major achievement.

The clergy also provided examples both of prudent flight and of courageous, and sometimes fatal, devotion to duty. Archbishop Sheldon was praised for remaining at Lambeth, while the Dean of St Paul's, William Sancroft, was criticised for his flight.[95] Sancroft was probably the more typical. Attacks on clerical deserters were as common as in earlier epidemics, especially from Dissenting ministers who wooed the congregations of absent incumbents just as chemical physicians tried to take over the patients of absent Fellows of the College.[96] Neither Anglicans nor Dissenters had a monopoly of heroism or caution, however, and both sides contributed to the flow of sermons and devotional tracts on plague which were almost as numerous now as in 1625–6, although they formed a smaller proportion of total publications. The conformist Simon Patrick, who stayed in his parish of St Paul's Covent Garden during the epidemic, published devotional instructions for the infected who were shut up; so did the Nonconformist Richard Baxter, who was absent from London throughout.[97] Other writers condemned national sins which had brought plague: swearing, covetousness, women's dress and make-up, and the prophanity of the Restoration Court.[98] As in the past, the epidemic was also used as a stick to beat political or religious opponents. It was a punishment for the Great Rebellion and execution of Charles I, or for sectaries and schismatics, or for the persecutors of the godly, the friends of Popery and Antichrist, and the perpetrators of the Clarendon Code. Even Baxter, who was inclined to doubt such vulgar conclusions, hoped that the incidence of plague in corporations would lead the authorities to reflect on the wisdom of the recent Corporation Act.[99]

Yet despite the obvious temptation to point to the role of providence, most writers, even divines, were more cautious in their conclusions than they had been in the past. Richard Kephale was one of the few who still argued that some kinds of plague were wholly supernatural, and that some people might depend on 'God's special providence' to protect them; Baxter was more typical when he mocked 'the religiouser sort' who at first escaped plague and 'began to be puffed up and boast of the great difference which God did make'. 'Quickly after', they all 'fell alike', he noted.[100] Although Baxter could not resist adding that two of the godly ministers he remembered had died while fleeing from London, he stressed the evident fact that plague hit the righteous as well as the wicked.[101] That was not new, but the conclusions other preachers drew from it were. Thomas Vincent, whose ministry in London during the epidemic had been much admired by Baxter, concluded that 'peculiar providences' were not common nowadays, though they might happen on occasion. Biblical pestilences had been different. Then 'there was such an immediate hand of God in the disease, I suppose he did make a greater discrimination between the righteous and the wicked'. Now plagues came more gradually and by contagion, and 'whatever extraordinary hand of Providence do send them as a punishment for sin' they had 'not that ministration of Angels in the inflicting of them, more than other diseases'.[102]

This was a far cry from Henoch Clapham, for whom angels had been an immediate reality in 1603; and it was very close to the view of many medical scientists in the later seventeenth century. Sydenham acknowledged plague to be 'the scourge for the enormity of our sins', but he concentrated on understanding its relationship with the weather and on searching for treatments for it, rather than delving into its remoter causes. Thomas Willis accepted that one of the duties of the magistrate was to see divine worship observed in churches during epidemics; but he thought God did not interfere with the secondary causes of plague in any 'miraculous' fashion.[103] Robert Boyle reached a similar view. Although his distrust of neo-Platonic idealisations of nature led him to give greater weight to the role of divine providence in calamities than many natural philosophers, he thought supernatural interpretations as unhelpful as astrological ones when analysing the 'particular symptoms and phenomena' of plague. Yet this unanimity did not mean that there was any consensus among educated men about what should be put in the place of heaven or the stars in order to explain what Boyle called the 'wonderful diversity' exhibited by the disease when it occurred.[104] Opinions were varied and divided. God's hand having been relegated to the background, it was on the subject of the natural causes of plague and its treatment that fresh controversy erupted in 1665.

In its origins, much of the controversy had little to do with plague, and a good deal to do with the conflict between Galenic and chemical medicine which was one strand in the complex intellectual ferment of the years between 1640 and 1660. The Paracelsian challenge to Galen had first reached England only in diluted form: in the shape of chemical medicines which were quickly added to the traditional pharmacopoeia. Chemical prescriptions were included in the remedies for plague published by the College of Physicians in 1665.[105] During the Interregnum, however, Paracelsianism had become a controversial and aggressive creed. Strengthened and invigorated by the writings of J.B. van Helmont, it was used as a weapon by those who wished to challenge the monopoly rights of the College; and it appealed to men searching for new keys to knowledge and to some more radical groups who found in it possibilities which Boyle and others considered dangerously anti-religious. The plague of 1665 prolonged these conflicts. Helmont's work, *The Tomb of the Plague*, had been opportunely translated into English in 1662, and in 1665 his adherents founded a short-lived Society of Chemical Physicians in open rivalry to the College.[106] The iatrochemists rushed to demonstrate their superior knowledge and treatment of plague, and they contributed to the unprecedented quantity of medical literature occasioned by the epidemic of 1665.

They contributed little to a clearer understanding of the origins of plague, however. For Helmont, the key to disease lay in the 'Archeus': his term for the vital spirits of man. A man was infected when the Archeus conceived the 'image' of plague; or, as Helmont's chief

English follower, George Thomson, put it, no one ever had plague 'but the Soul formed a character or idea thereof in the Archeus'. The power of the imagination alone might achieve this, when people were afraid, angry or otherwise disturbed. Paracelsus had drawn much the same conclusion, but so had more traditional writers when they assumed that fear of plague was in itself dangerous.[107] Moreover, Helmontians did not deny that changes in the Archeus could also be imposed from outside by natural forces, by the poisonous gases which arose from 'fermentation' either in the earth or in other infected bodies. Thus the notions of miasma and infection between persons were also retained. Chemical physicians might replace Galenic humours with the Archeus, and refer to 'fermentation' rather than 'putrefaction', but it was the terminology – the metaphors, as Henry Stubbe rightly called them – rather than the basic understanding of disease which had changed.[108]

Much the same might be said about other new concepts introduced into the plague literature in 1665: the corpuscular theory of infection and the idea of *contagium animatum* which some writers borrowed from Gassendi and Kircher respectively. Whether the agents transmitting plague were conceived to be 'atoms', 'worms', 'venomous gases' or the old contagious 'miasmes', they were used to explain not to challenge the traditional view that the disease was both in the air and could be carried invisibly from an infected person to others.[109]

By rejecting earlier Paracelsian speculation about the metaphysical connection between macrocosm and microcosm and between sin and disease, the more rigorous Helmontians may have helped to encourage that investigation into the natural manifestations of epidemics which we have seen developing for other reasons too; but their examination scarcely took them very far. They claimed, with some justice, that their attack on Galen permitted a realistic view of plague as a distinct entity and not simply as an imbalance in the humours. It was, said Marchamont Needham, a 'real substantial thing'. Yet the chemical theorists also thought that it was closely connected with scurvy and syphilis, whose recent severity explained the 1665 plague.[110] The iatrochemists' prescriptions for treatment had rather more to recommend them. They sensibly criticised the practice of phlebotomy in cases of plague, since bleeding weakened the vital spirits, although the same point had also been made by a non-Helmontian authority, Diemerbroeck. They also advocated the use of sulphur in fumigants for houses, and this may have had some effect against fleas.[111] As a whole, however, the Helmontian system was no more, if no less, convincing when applied to plague than the hypotheses it sought to replace. As one of Needham's critics said, novel theories added little to the practice, as distinct from the ornaments, of physic.[112]

None the less, the ornaments were of some importance. From our point of view, the chemical debate shows that approaches to plague, which for more than a century had been largely traditional and empirical, were at last being given a revitalising injection of new concepts. The iatrochemical challenge was also connected with the second controversy of 1665 which we must consider. This was the older issue of the wisdom of the English policy of strict household segregation. In effect there was not so much a debate about it as a unanimous campaign against it, and it was materially assisted by the Helmontian stress on the importance of the imagination. Helmont himself was not antagonistic to quarantine, since 'forty days shutting up' could dispel the 'pestilent poison' from infected bodies 'as it perisheth of its own accord'. While agreeing that contagion was a real danger, however, George Thomson urged some mitigation of English practices in order not to destroy that confidence which helped to fortify the human Archeus against infection. Hence he concluded that 'those nations are highly to be commended, that forbear to mure up in too severe, solitary and doleful manner those that are infected'. Even the Muslims were to be admired for encouraging visits to the sick – a decisive break with the general criticism of Turkish fatalism.[113] A more popular and less exclusively Helmontian tract borrowed the same idea: shutting up houses was 'a great cause of the increase of the contagion; for by how much the more men are abridged their customary liberty, by so much the more are they subject to fear'.[114]

Earlier objections to the policy, which we have seen in a Paracelsian tract of 1596, in W.T.'s pamphlet of 1603 and in Mayerne's treatise of 1631, were also revived. The campaign drew heavily on arguments from the obligations of charity and neighbourly duty. Thomson, for example, stressed the need to observe 'the bond of charity towards my neighbour', and another writer criticised the cruel terrors imposed by authority on one disadvantaged section of the population: 'Those who stand upon their sword to execute this violent advice upon the poor so generally, would not be willing to ... have their wives and children so dealt with in their calamity'.[115] The government's own lack of conviction, its known wish to revise the national plague orders of 1578, opened the floodgates to criticism. So establishment a figure as Nathaniel Hodges, Fellow of the College and medical adviser to the City, anticipated the new *Rules and Orders* of 1666 and recommended the removal of the sick and the sound from infected houses to separate pesthouses. He even agreed with Thomson that the 'dismal apprehension' of those who were shut up made people easier prey to plague.[116] William Boghurst, the apothecary, concurred. Quarantining whole families had been 'oft enough tried and always found ineffectual', and his own experience had been decisive: 'One friend growing melancholy for another was one main cause of [plague] going through a family, especially when they were shut up, which bred a sad apprehension and consternation on their spirits, especially being shut up in dark cellars.'[117]

All the arguments were summed up in a frontal assault by the anonymous author of *The Shutting Up Infected Houses as it is practised in England Soberly Debated* (1665). There were the arguments from charity, 'from the communion of Saints and the practice of the primitive Christians', and from 'experience of former times when plague did not cease' until there were so many victims that isolation was abandoned. There was 'the condition of those houses and the inhabitants thereof' which built up infection and broke down the physical and psychological resistance of the inmates. Each isolated household became a furnace of infection from which the disease was spread by dogs and cats whose movement could not be controlled. The policy had damaging side-effects. It prevented doctors from observing and therefore understanding the disease. It caused fear outside as well as inside houses, disrupting markets and reducing employment. The poor had nothing left to do but 'to commit those sins, which certainly deserve, and infallibly bring the plague upon them'. The author did not deny the reality of infection and the need to regulate contacts with the sick, but he thought that could be done in more gentle and charitable ways. 'Infection may have killed its thousands, but shutting up hath killed its ten thousands', he concluded.[118]

These criticisms did not undermine the whole of the government's achievement over the previous century. Although there was general agreement that, in Graunt's words, 'the troublesome seclusions in the plague-time are not a remedy to be purchased at vast inconveniences', there was also agreement that public action was necessary and could be effective. Many critics were in fact asking for more government activity rather than less, more specially appointed visitors and physicians for the sick, more pesthouses and places of isolation for the infected and their contacts, better quarantine against the introduction of plague from overseas.[119] Some authors placed more stress on infection than others, Hodges more than Boghurst, for example; and some continued to fear that anti-contagionist views were common among the poor.[120] But only one writer ventured to hint that plague was not infectious at all, and that all human efforts against it were superfluous. The astrologer John Gadbury sought to make the most of his successful prediction that there would be an epidemic in 1665 by publishing an account of it when it happened. He elevated the stars above other secondary causes, castigated the 'tyrannous' custom of isolation, and attacked those blasphemers who denied the role of the Almighty: 'the plague carrieth not in it so much of infection, as it doth of affliction'.[121]

Gadbury's was a lone voice in the publications of 1665. The intellectual battle for an activist policy against plague had plainly been won. Yet the controversies of 1665 indicate how insecure its intellectual foundations were. The isolation of infected households was, after all, the central plank in the government's programme. If it could be shown to have failed in practice, if it might even have been counterproductive, there was little to justify the confidence which magistrates regularly expressed in it. More generally, there was no agreed conceptual framework which would explain what plague was, what its causes were, and how precisely it spread. It is not surprising, therefore, that the private papers and correspondence of the educated elite in 1665 reveal as mixed a set of attitudes and approaches as in the past, alongside a straightforward pragmatic assumption that plague was contagious and that its victims must be isolated and avoided.

Samuel Pepys' diary perhaps illustrates best how much people rich enough to take precautions could learn from past experience of plague and from current information about its incidence. Every week Pepys examined the bills of mortality in order to see when infection moved from the suburbs towards his house in the inner city, and he discussed them with his friends. He was well aware of the risks to himself, especially when business, his curiosity, or his pleasures took him into infected areas. He carefully set all his affairs in order in case he was suddenly struck down. He had read or been told that melancholy was dangerous and he tried to avoid it; he was greatly fortified by a dream that he had the king's mistress in his arms.[122] But he was also able to minimise the hazards more deliberately. He kept away from infected houses and from corpses in the streets, until he could not avoid them and became hardened by familiarity. He moved his wife to Woolwich early in July, as soon as plague entered his own neighbourhood. He stayed behind for the moment because the disease was still largely confined to beggars and vagrants, servants and the poor. When his own servant complained of a headache, he tried immediately to move him out of the house, however; and after his doctor died of plague in late August, he quickly joined his wife.[123]

Pepys clearly had every reason to support government policies. The victims of plague he saw or heard about were mostly 'plain people', shopkeepers, alehouse-keepers, watermen, labourers and the servants of his acquaintances. Hence, although he pitied their condition and was dismayed by the cruelty practised on those who were shut up, he never doubted that household isolation was necessary. He was very worried in September when the practice broke down. In Woolwich and then later, when he moved to Greenwich, he naturally co-operated with local magistrates in their efforts to prevent the movement of infection out of the metropolis.[124] He had much less use for religious than for secular protection; Pepys is not renowned for his piety. It was the making of his will which brought a 'much better state' to his soul, and he seems to have paid little heed to the monthly public fasts. Like the references to divine mercy in the orders of town councils, his acknowledgments of God's hand and blessings were generally little more than a way of keeping his fingers crossed. Only occasionally, when his danger seemed particularly acute, did Pepys appeal more urgently to the Almighty.[125]

People living in the midst of plague, in the poorer parishes and the suburbs, may have turned to religious comforts and defences more often, without rejecting others. The letters written from Southwark in 1665 by John Allin, an excluded minister with a lively interest in alchemy and medicine, demonstrate an extraordinarily broad range of responses. He took note of astrological omens and favoured some protective amulets, but criticised those who had too much confidence in chemical medicines. He carefully stayed away from his brother-in-law when the latter caught plague, and he used the bills of mortality to deduce the probable course of infection; but he also referred to the old idea that some plagues were the 'immediate stroke of the destroying Angel'. In one sentence he could worry about the 'indiscretion used in not shutting up but rather making great funerals', and at the same time suggest that plague would not end until 'sin be left and suppressed more than it is'.[126]

Henry Oldenburg, the Secretary of the Royal Society, who also remained in London during the epidemic, exhibited a predictable interest in more sophisticated speculations, but he reached no more consistent conclusions. He corresponded with Robert Boyle about the virtues of medicines containing treacle and mithridatium, and with others about the ways in which plague reached the Mediterranean and thence Amsterdam. He was sceptical about Gadbury's conclusion that plague was not infectious. Yet, he admitted, 'there are very odd instances alleged by the broachers of this opinion, which I know not well how to answer, otherwise than ascribing it to the immediate preservation of Almighty God'.[127] Like Allin, Oldenburg had something of that eclectic curiosity which led later seventeenth-century virtuosi to substitute the indiscriminate collection of information for real scientific enquiry. In the case of attitudes to plague, however, more was involved than intellectual fashion. Personal hazards and medical ignorance alike dictated a trust in God and the keeping of every sort of powder dry. It was as obvious to Oldenburg as to Pepys that plague generally missed the prosperous, those who lived 'orderly and comfortably', but he still took every care to preserve himself: 'I strive to banish both fear and overconfidence, leading a regular life and avoiding infected places as much as I can, leaving the rest to God.' Plague, he concluded, 'is a mysterious disease, and, I am afraid, will remain so, for all the observations and discourses made of it'.[128]

Despite the scientific and religious controversies which for a century had often touched upon plague, the mystery surrounding it had not been dispelled in 1665. Simple observation of infection, and of the conditions in which it occurred, had helped to demolish extravagant claims that supernatural intervention alone explained the phenomenon. But it had not removed the necessity to seek religious protection and consolation against its continuing hazards. Neither had it finally identified the real carriers of plague, despite some near misses; and advances towards the germ theory of disease and the concept of disease entities were no substitutes for that. Experience and observation had not even given lasting support to the heart of the government's policy: household isolation. On the contrary, in the end they called it into doubt. Over the years intellectual assumptions about plague had been adjusted to remove potential obstacles to new policies of public health. They had not been remodelled so as to put those policies beyond the range of scientific or empirical dispute.

Chapter 10

Towns under stress

As for you, upon whom the charge of government doth lie, whether you be the chief magistrate or such as are assistants unto him: the Lord hath tied you to residence. Your Christian charity to relieve the distressed, your provident care to prevent danger, your godly wisdom to set down good orders, your pains and industry to see the same observed, and your authority to punish the disobedient, was never more needful than at this time. And if any of you depart, be sure the hand of the Lord can follow you, whithersoever you go.

Thomas Pullein, *Ieremiah's Teares* (1608)

Thomas Pullein, vicar of Pontefract, told the aldermen of York what their duties were during the plague of 1604.[1] In doing so he demonstrated that the attitudes described in the last chapter did not determine action in any simple linear way. The rulers of towns must not seek refuge in flight. To that extent they had to ignore the fact that plague was infectious, and to assume that God willed their presence and might protect them. On the other hand, they must not be passively fatalistic. They must act, both to relieve the sick and to prevent further contagion. It was the need to encourage this nice balance of selfless dedication and prudence which led the Privy Council so often to attribute the growth of epidemics to negligence on the part of magistrates, rather than to an infected atmosphere which might lead to wholesale magisterial flight.[2] As one might expect, however, the psychological balance was more easily stated on paper than achieved in practice.

It was also easier to list the actions incumbent on resident magistrates than to put them into effect. The protection of public health by means of quarantine and all that that implied could only be achieved through an unprecedentedly precise, expensive and time-consuming

255

regulation of local affairs. Such strict supervision by aldermen and councillors was bound to arouse opposition, from vested interests and rival sources of authority as well as from the infected and their relatives. Like plague itself, therefore, plague regulations strained and tested the fabric of urban life: in this case its political and administrative structure.

(i) The responsibilities of magistrates

The initial reaction of all urban magistrates to outbreaks of plague was to pretend that they did not exist. When medical writers warned against the very thought of the disease, town councillors took their advice to heart. The minutes of the Common Council of Bristol referred to plague only on 19 July 1603, more than a month after burials in the parish registers had begun to reflect rising mortality. The Assembly of Norwich reluctantly admitted in March 1579 that 'certain places of the city are infected with sickness'; but it was only in July that the existence of a major epidemic, evident three months earlier, was fully acknowledged.[3] By 1665, bills of mortality, newsletters and newspapers had undermined these attempts at secrecy. Like other local authorities, the aldermen of Norwich then had to try to restrict the local circulation of bills and to manipulate the news of them which appeared in the London papers.[4]

This was not merely wishful thinking. Covering up the existence of plague was a matter of policy, dictated by the interests and reputation of a town. Thomas Lodge advised magistrates that

> If by chance, or by the will of God, the city becometh infected, it
> ought not incontinently to be made known: but those that have
> the care and charge of such as are attainted ought in the beginning
> to keep it close, and wisely conceal the same from the common
> sort.[5]

The aim was partly to prevent panic, and partly to avert the damage which the merest hint of plague did to urban economies, from the greatest ports to the smallest markets. In 1610 the leading men of Ruthin demanded certain knowledge of the health of Chester before they would allow their citizens to attend the next fair there: 'Notwithstanding that rumours commonly are false and uncertain, yet [as] in previous cases they are to be harkened unto.' We can see why the leet jury of Nottingham once charged a local man with 'slandering our town with the sickness, which will be to our decay', and why an Ipswich surgeon with a grudge against the corporation falsely reported two plague deaths in 1665.[6]

Consequently, all town councils tried to prevent the introduction of plague in the first place, even if that itself meant temporary economic disruption. In the seventeenth century, ships coming from infected Hull to York and from plague-stricken Yarmouth to Norwich were stopped outside the town and their merchandise left in the open to dispel any infection that might be in it.[7] Men and goods from London were kept outside the gates of Bristol for airing for twenty days or more; and the Londoners were only to enter the city in a change of clothes. In 1625 as many as twenty watchmen were appointed to enforce the orders.[8] Such precautions were obviously sensible, but they were always unpopular, they could rarely be sustained for as long as three months, and they could only be justified by experience of the consequences which followed when they failed. Then the burdens on urban magistrates were immense – if they stayed to shoulder them.

Some urban patricians were no doubt persuaded against flight by a sense of duty. An alderman of Hull sent his family out of town in the plague of 1637 and decided to stay himself, though not without misgivings: 'Had not persuasions of eminent persons both of church and commonwealth wrought upon me, and considering my place and ward so sore visited, I should never have done it.'[9] Many other magistrates took to their heels along with their friends and neighbours. They sometimes had country houses ready and waiting for them,[10] they often had the excuse of pressing matters of business to take them away, and they had families to protect. As a result, councils and courts ceased to meet for weeks at a time and the whole structure of urban government was put at risk. In 1546 the councillors of Exeter threatened to disfranchise freemen who did not attend the election of the mayor 'for fear of the plague'; but many of them were absent themselves in later epidemics. Exeter's town council, the 'Chamber', met only three times between 2 August and 5 December 1570, when more than ten meetings would normally have occurred. In 1590, when the epidemic began rather later in the year, there was only one meeting between 28 September and the following January. In Bristol in 1603 and in Salisbury in 1604 the council met only once in the second half of the year, on both occasions for the vital business of electing the mayor.[11] The mayor himself could not be relied upon: Pullein's 'chief

magistrate' fled from Hull in 1575, from Bideford in 1646 and from
Southampton and Colchester in 1666.[12]

The worst of these corporate abdications of authority occurred
during epidemics in Exeter and Salisbury in the 1620s. The mayor-
elect of Exeter, Thomas Walker, refused to serve in 1625, claiming
that he was no longer an inhabitant of the town. In fact he had moved
out with other aldermen. In his absence, a former mayor, Ignatius
Jorden, acted as his 'lieutenant'. The few recorded meetings of
Chamber and quarter sessions show that he was almost alone; and
the mayor's example was not lost on lesser citizens. One man said he
would only pay his rate for the infected 'when Mr Mayor had done
what he could'.[13] When Walker was finally persuaded to return by the
Privy Council in December, he reported on the chaos in the town:

> There hath happened many dangerous tumults in so much that
> the poorer sort assembling in bodies of 2 or 300 have resisted
> the officers and threatened by violence to relieve themselves; and
> the number of poor being 4000 or thereabouts and many of them
> infinite needy.

In May 1626 there were still 'outrageous disorders' in the town, and
even in October 1627 plague rates were unpaid and the councillors
feared the 'disordered people' who had 'set strange projects awork
threatening to burn the city'.[14]

By this time a similar crisis had occurred in Salisbury. The mayor,
John Ivie, was one of the few aldermen to stay during the epidemic
of 1627. In a pamphlet written long after, in 1661, he graphically
described his experiences. 'There was none left to . . . comfort the
poor in so great a misery, neither Recorder, justice, churchwarden or
overseers in all the city, . . . but only two of the petty constables that
had no friend to receive them in the country.' Rioting broke out when
local farmers stopped bringing corn to market and poor relief began
to break down: 'the rude people were out of order weekly, and gave
out they were two hundred strong, and would have better allowance'.
These might be dismissed as the exaggerated reminiscences of old
age, were they not confirmed by letters written in 1627 from Ivie to
the Recorder of Salisbury, Henry Sherfield, who was safely ensconced
in his chambers in Lincoln's Inn. Although the epidemic was not of
major severity, almost all marketing in the city had stopped. A third
of the citizens were sick from famine. Justices, constables, overseers
and even buriers of the dead could not be found: 'I am enforced to

do all myself.' As in Exeter, 'our rebellious people' rioted in the streets, resisting attempts to control their movements and demanding charity.[15]

It would be easy to take these occasions as symptoms of the precarious state of urban government in early modern England, and to conclude that plague could easily bring it toppling to the ground. What is remarkable, however, is how few such incidents there were and how, even in the midst of them, some fragment of magisterial authority remained. Ivie in Salisbury and Jorden in Exeter continued to parade in their gowns in the streets, symbols of a resilient magistracy, however diminished in numbers. Often by sheer force of personality, they dragooned the citizens who remained into raising money for the poor and helping to provide for them.[16] Their importance can be seen if we look at what happened in a town which did not have aldermen or councillors at all. Manchester was still an unincorporated township, governed by lords of the manor, leading townsmen in a court leet, and parish officers, all of them often at odds. When plague struck in 1605, and again in 1645, all internal government collapsed, and order had to be restored by county justices in the first instance and by parliamentary soldiers in the second.[17] Manchester is the exception which proves the rule. Incorporated towns did not fall into anarchy, and most of them did not get as close to it as Salisbury and Exeter.

More typical examples of what was a common urban experience are the English cities which suffered most from plague, Norwich and London. In both towns there was a distinction between two bodies of governors, a large Common Council, called the Assembly in Norwich, and a small Court of Aldermen, which in practice supervised civic administration.[18] In each case, the aldermen continued to hold the reins of government during epidemics while their juniors in the larger councils dispersed. As late as the epidemic of 1665, the Common Council of London held no meeting at all between 4 July and the end of the year. The aldermen, however, met sixteen times in the same six months. Although there would normally have been around fifty aldermanic meetings, and attendance fell from a customary eighteen or nineteen to only seven at its lowest point, there was, as Charles II's Privy Council had wished, 'a competent number of them to make a Court and give despatch to the public affairs of the city'.[19] The same had been true in earlier epidemics. In the great crisis of 1563, the Court met nine times between the beginning of August and the

end of November, and the number of aldermen present only once fell
below eight.

In Norwich there was a similar substantial rump of aldermen who
remained even when most councillors had disappeared. The Assembly
met only once during the epidemic of 1579 and not at all at the height
of the plague of 1666, but the Court of Aldermen was always more
assiduous, even when attendances dropped by half. In 1579 and 1603
the Court met almost as regularly as in normal years. In the next
major epidemic, in 1625–6, it met precisely as usual, twice a week.
Although the number present fell from an average of fifteen to seven,
the inner caucus of aldermen stayed behind. They also recognised
the existence of plague more readily than in the past. In 1603–4 no
orders for the quarantine of infected houses were formally recorded
until January 1604, as plague declined. In 1625, on the other hand,
the Court was shutting up houses from July onwards, even before the
weekly reports of burials had begun to refer to plague.[20]

It is necessary to ask, therefore, what it was that differentiated one
urban patriciate from another, or one alderman from another. Why
did crises of government occur in some towns and not in others, and
one alderman stay behind when his colleagues did not? It was not
simply the blandishments of the Privy Council which impelled devotion to duty, for these were common. Neither can it have been only
a man's concern for his local reputation, or the hope of achieving
fame in the annals of a town or even, in 1665, in the newspapers.
Although that was no doubt often a motive, and dedicated patricians
were applauded and rewarded once the crisis was over,[21] there were
always impulses propelling them in the other direction. Resident
aldermen were shunned by their acquaintances, as John Ivie was by
Bishop Davenant of Salisbury. They had to dip into their own pockets
to help the poor, and might already be in deep financial trouble, like
Sir Thomas Lodge, father of the plague pamphleteer, in London in
1563. They might occasionally find themselves shut up because of
the suspicion of infection, as Alderman Lawne's family was in York
on two occasions in the 1630s.[22] In such circumstances it needed
more than a letter from the Privy Council or the plaudits of their
citizens to make them stay.

One influential factor was undoubtedly the nature of the epidemics
themselves. Just as the corporation of London had done more to
control plague in the sporadic outbreaks of the later 1560s than in
the great disaster of 1563, so the aldermen of Norwich were more

active in the plagues of 1584–5 and 1589–92 than in the more serious epidemic of 1603. In 1585 watchmen were appointed for the first time to see that the sick stayed in their houses, and in 1590 there is the first evidence of the punishment of offenders against the regulations. In 1603 neither occurred until the plague had declined.[23] It was also in milder epidemics that the concentration of plague in the poorest quarters of towns was most obvious, and that aldermen could trust with some confidence in their own safety. Similarly, it was easier to stay cool and in command when epidemics occurred in mild form relatively frequently, than when they came after an interval of twenty years, as in Exeter and Salisbury in the 1620s. Yet this cannot be the whole story. The fact that the epidemic of 1627 in Salisbury was much milder than that of 1604 did not prevent flight;[24] there was an epidemic in the same town in 1665–6, again after twenty years' freedom from the disease, and yet there was no wholesale desertion of duty; and even in the crises of the 1620s in Salisbury and Exeter, some aldermen stayed behind.

In the case of the latter, the religious convictions of the rulers were of major importance, although they did not work quite in the direction which the authors of the plague orders of 1578 and the form of prayer of 1603 would have predicted. We saw in the last chapter how the Puritan emphasis on predestination was thought to have prompted opposition to plague regulations from some preachers, and even from a mayor of Norwich in 1580. We also saw that it had not been a united campaign, and that any threat which it may have represented to the government's programme had certainly withered away by 1630.[25] When we look at Exeter and Salisbury in the 1620s, however, the striking fact is that Puritan magistrates were not simply accepting the need for direct action against plague; they were taking the lead in providing it.

Ignatius Jorden of Exeter was a notorious 'Arch-Puritan'. In the parliaments of the 1620s he was a famous advocate of the death penalty for adultery; and his views on plague were superficially similar to those which had been attributed to the mayor of Norwich in 1580. According to his biographer, he stressed the determinist position. When punishing 'uncleanness' (presumably adultery) at quarter sessions in the town hall before the epidemic began, he was reported to have said that the watch at the gates should be removed, 'for the plague was in the Guildhall of the city'. When disease arrived, his faith in divine providence gave him the confidence to stay while his colleagues fled. He distributed alms to the infected in 1625 and declared that he was not afraid of 'God's visitation: let us fear rather the plague sore of our own heart'. Yet he certainly did not neglect natural precautions against infection. He must have supported the appointment of the watchmen who were paid to guard infected houses, and when the poor flocked round him for relief, 'he would not causelessly expose himself to danger; yet being in the discharge of his duty he feared not the plague'.[26]

This same consciously aggressive Puritanism impelled John Ivie in Salisbury. Like his friend and ally, Henry Sherfield, he was noted for his religious radicalism. For both of them the duty of a magistrate was 'to advance God's glory', and Sherfield pressed Ivie to become a justice of the peace because 'God's time is come'. Ivie regarded the plague of 1627 as in all respects God's handiwork. But he also saw himself as God's agent, ordained to stay in the city, to relieve the poor, and to stamp out contagion as well as sin. When plague killed the owners of an unlicensed alehouse who resisted his campaign against those sources of prophanity and disease, Ivie commented: 'It pleased God to give me power to suppress all, saving that one house; then the God of power did suppress that house in his own judgment.' There was a similar judgment on six tailors who disobeyed Ivie's ban on company feasts, another cause of infection: five of them died of plague. When Ivie forcibly shut up an infected family in their own home and then moved them to a pesthouse, and all survived, it was God again who had 'so ordered for them through his mercy'.[27]

For Puritan aldermen, epidemics were in fact occasions for the exercise of godly rule; and that embraced the plague regulations which were by now a familiar part of local government. In Salisbury Ivie and his allies went further and saw the plague literally as a heaven-sent opportunity for complete social reform. For three years before 1627 they had been trying to force a radical and expensive scheme for poor relief through a reluctant town council. Now, according to the Reverend Peter Thatcher, 'God's providence' in the plague had put the opposition to flight, and the proposed reforms could be implemented.[28] A new workhouse, a new storehouse and tight control of the drink trade would purge Salisbury of poverty, sin and disease. A similar vision inspired Henry Sherfield in a remarkable speech to the first quarter sessions after the plague. God's hand had been evident at every stage in the recent epidemic, and it had shown the need for a new discipline, a new cleanliness, a new godliness. There must be 'a reformation, a true and real reformation of this city'. Sherfield summed up that Puritan activism which had motivated Ivie and Jorden:

> I well know that no good thing can be effected without the hand and blessing of God and it is he that worketh both the will and the deed. Yet I do also know that we must use all the good ways and means which God shall discover unto us to bring to pass even what God hath determined to do.[29]

The interest of the Salisbury case lies not only in its unusually rich documentation, but in its demonstration of how religious ideology influenced behaviour in ways far less simple than those envisaged by bishops and Privy Councillors. It provides a practical example of that association between sin and plague, and between the campaigns against both kinds of infection, which we have noted in the sermon literature and to which we will return in the next chapter.[30] But it must be admitted that the events in Salisbury and Exeter were exceptional. The motives of Ivie and Jorden may well have inspired some other Puritan aldermen in the early seventeenth century. The mayor of Haverfordwest in the plague of 1652 said that a woman appointed to visit the sick was guided by 'providence', and assured his deputy that although 'thousands fall at your left hand and ten thousand at your right, He hath said it shall not come near you'.[31] Yet not all aldermen who stayed in infected towns were Puritans; neither were the devout among them all impelled by religious zeal. The aldermen of Norwich, who had been famous for their Puritan sympathies in the later sixteenth century, were most of them wary of religious enthusiasm by 1625; and it was not that which persuaded known conservatives like Alexander Anguish to work with Puritans like Thomas Shipdam in controlling infection in the 1630s.[32]

By the 1660s certainly, there was scarcely room for those godly alliances of magistrates and ministers which had sought to remodel towns such as Salisbury earlier in the century. Some Puritan zeal may have survived. Perhaps it flickered still in the old men who had ruled Norwich in the Interregnum, and who, along with a mayor of Dissenting sympathies, were the most regular attenders in council during the epidemic of 1666.[33] But it cannot have burned very brightly, and it might even be turned in quietist rather than activist directions by Restoration circumstances. Owen Stockton had been lecturer at Colchester before 1660. When his offer to help the magistrates in the epidemic of 1665–6 was turned down, he found justification for flight from the city in Isaiah: 'Hide thyself for a little moment, until the indignation be overpast.'[34]

The importance of religious motivation thus varied over time and from one town to another. A more common and persistent inspiration for those patricians who remained was hard political self-interest: the need to maintain the coherence and authority of the ruling clique. It was to the group interest of 'magistrates' threatened by disorderly commons that mayors of York more than once appealed when urging their colleagues to remain in the city;[35] and it was when the magistracy was divided in other towns that chaos followed. Only the division of the Salisbury council into what Ivie called 'factions' can explain the exceptional exodus of the elite in the minor epidemic of 1627.[36] The parliamentary election disputes in Exeter in 1626 and 1628, in which Jorden was the candidate of the freemen opposed by most of the magisterial bench, suggest a similar split there.[37] The Puritan commitment which engaged a few magistrates in dangerous work alienated others. It was not needed in London or Norwich, where the aldermen were more united and the political crisis which accompanied epidemics consequently less grave.

As a result the aldermen who regularly attended meetings in the heat of a plague in London were not eccentrics or enthusiasts. They were venerable men of affairs, patricians sometimes in their sixties or seventies, who had ruled for a decade or more and who could not tolerate the notion of relinquishing the reins of power.[38] They always included the mayor, generally a somewhat younger man, whose entry into the charmed circle of elder statesmen depended on his assiduity in that burdensome office. But he was surrounded by four or five of his seniors, aldermen who were governors of the city hospitals and leading figures in their livery and trading companies. The most remarkable of them in the later sixteenth century was Rowland Heyward, a man involved in every aspect of civic business, a member of a committee on plague policy in 1570, and a mainstay of the Court of Aldermen throughout the epidemics of 1563 and 1593, when he was in his seventies.[39] In 1603 three of the four most regular attenders besides the mayor were all on the committee of the East India Company; and the fourth, Thomas Bennett, was active again in 1625. In the next epidemic, in 1636, three of the most energetic aldermen were likewise East India magnates, as were three of the five who bore the chief burden in 1665. Other things divided the men of 1636 and

1665. James Campbell and Christopher Clitherow tended to opposing sides on religious issues in the 1630s. In 1665 John Frederick and William Turner had different political stances, the former being removed from office after the Exclusion Crisis along with the mayor of 1665, John Lawrence.[40] But business interests, the government of the hospitals, and city affairs in general bound them together.

The dedication of these London aldermen, and of their counterparts in towns such as York and Norwich, was not the inertia of a secure governing class, however. Although the term 'oligarchy' best describes the small group which ran most English towns in this period, it was rarely as stable or as closed as that word suggests. New men were always pushing their way to the top, and rivals and critics threatening the elite from below. Not the least concern of the more established members of the oligarchy during an epidemic, therefore, was a positive one: to protect and if possible to consolidate the hold of the inner ring. The aldermen of Norwich were attacked by demagogic leaders of the 'commons' in the early 1620s, and isolated by their general lack of Puritan sympathies in the 1630s.[41] They naturally took every step to increase their corporate solidarity during the epidemics of the period. When the Privy Council tried to stop the mayor's feast in time of plague, they claimed that it was an essential meeting for the discussion of town business; and they succeeded in retaining this expression of their corporate unity while they banned the similar feasts of guilds and companies.[42]

The milder epidemics of plague even gave the aldermen opportunities to increase their authority. In 1629 the Norwich Assembly had authorised the Court of Aldermen to 'proceed in every necessary business concerning the good of the city which shall upon any sudden occasion or in private manner be thought fit to be done'. By their very nature epidemics were just such occasions. In the 1630s plague orders were among the subjects discussed, not only in the Court, but at informal 'group meetings' of the mayor and aldermen, where individual houses were ordered to be closed or opened up as the progress of the epidemic dictated.[43] The day-to-day administration demanded by plague regulations encouraged the concentration of power in the hands of a few, and the few welcomed the opportunity.

In towns where there were separate assemblies for aldermen and common councillors, like London and Norwich, the more numerous meetings of the former than the latter in plague-time had the same effect. In towns where the governing council was a more representative gathering, the fact that justices and aldermen turned up more often than councillors worked to the same end. There were small committees of mayor and aldermen in Bristol, Lincoln and Chester dealing with plague.[44] In York in the epidemic of 1631 the town council, which comprised both the aldermen and the 'Twenty-Four' ordinary councillors, voted to meet three times a week during the emergency. It did so, and while the number of the 'Twenty-Four' attending fell from an average of sixteen to six, the aldermanic presence – usually of six or seven – remained steady.[45] Such experiences had a lasting effect in some towns. After the plague of 1630, and in response to the constitutional weakness the epidemic had revealed, Cambridge was granted a new charter which concentrated power in the hands of a 'private council' of twelve aldermen plus the mayor. John Ivie hoped for an equivalent charter for Salisbury after the epidemic of 1627, again creating an inner council of twelve.[46] Ivie's wish was not granted, but his drive for select, rather than for 'godly', rule echoed the feelings of his peers in every other English town.

There is no sign in England, therefore, of that increase in popular representation in urban government which was occasionally the result of epidemics in Continental towns.[47] Quite the reverse. Far from uniting the community, disease widened political gulfs which already existed. Sometimes these divisions occurred within the urban patriciate, as in Salisbury; but more often they were external to it: defensive trenches which sustained rather than fractured its unity. While the middle classes fled, perhaps in increasing numbers, the leading governors generally had good reason to stay. They needed all the corporate solidarity they could muster for the tasks which then lay before them.

(ii) Rival authorities

In order to rule effectively, even in normal times, the governing elite of a town needed the assistance of other authorities both inside and outside its jurisdiction. External relations were the most delicate because a town council had to make concessions in return for outside support, and to recognise what it would often wish to deny – its dependent status.

We have seen already how the Privy Council regularly imposed new burdens on urban rulers and chastised them for their negligence. It could also be helpful. Its orders were cited when unpopular regulations

were promulgated, and it was an essential court of appeal when fairs
had to be stopped, when Londoners objected to restrictions on their
movement in the provinces, or when other local authorities refused
to co-operate by levying rates.[48] The relationship of towns with the
counties around them was similarly ambivalent. Towns with county
jurisdictions of their own were in an especially vulnerable position,
since rural justices were happy to recognise those proud cities as
independent entities for whom they had no responsibility. Bristol and
Norwich never benefited from county rates, and in Exeter only the
suburban parishes of Heavitree and St Thomas's ever received help
from other parts of Devon.[49] The Privy Council had to order Cheshire
to contribute to the relief of Chester in 1605; and in 1637 the large
sums raised all over Yorkshire for Hull were obtained in the face of
opposition from the Ridings and through the intervention of the
Council in the North.[50] Lesser towns were more fortunate. But in
their case financial support usually came late and always had formi-
dable strings attached.

The Wiltshire justices levied county rates for Salisbury in 1604 and
1627. In 1627 they amounted to £50 a week by the end of the
epidemic. Food supplies were also arranged: provisions were to be
brought to the suburb of Fisherton and sold to townsmen there. In
each instance, however, all aid was to stop if people wandered freely
out of town.[51] It was no idle threat. In 1627 Salisbury had to appeal
to the Lord Chief Justice because the county bench refused to extend
its rate-support, on the grounds that the mayor allowed the citizens
to leave 'in great companies and to wander abroad into the country
unto the great damage, annoyance and danger of the inhabitants'.
Mayor Ivie himself was presented before quarter sessions for housing
infected people in tenements within the county's jurisdiction at Fisherton, and for resisting the local watchmen who tried to remove
them.[52] In effect, the county paid to have the town isolated as if it
were a single infected household.

It is easy to understand the suspicion and hostility of county magistrates when they were faced with a multitude of appeals for assistance
under the terms of the statute of 1604. A wave of infection spreading
from one village to another might require a succession of five-mile
rates. In Cheshire, for example, there were seven separate plague
rates, some of them extended to the whole county, between 1603 and
1606; and complaints to the Assize judges about unfair assessments
naturally followed.[53] The gradual dispersal of plague through southern

Devon between 1625 and 1628 necessitated rates for no less than sixteen different towns and villages; and in theory they should all have fallen on the same part of the county. In the end the principle of local rates had to be abandoned. When Plymouth required relief in July 1626 the hundreds of Braunton and Exminster, far away in the extreme north and east of the county, were assessed. Other parts of Devon, the justices declared, should 'have a feeling of [the] miseries of the southern parishes'. As a result only two hundreds of the county escaped plague rates altogether in these years. When a rash of similar impositions came at the end of the Civil War, including the unprecedented sum of £100 a week for the benefit of Tiverton, the justices feared that they might 'debar the country from paying the weekly assessment imposed by ordinance of parliament', and troops had to be used to collect them. Ratepayers were entitled to expect guarantees of security in return. In 1646 the Devon bench agreed that watchmen might shoot any of the 'riotous and disorderly . . . poorer sort' who wandered from infected towns.[54]

Infected communities thus had to cut themselves off entirely from the counties around them if they were to receive financial help. They had to acquiesce in what amounted to a local *cordon sanitaire*. Marketing and movement were strictly controlled by the Kent justices around Sandwich in 1610 and 1644 and by the Dorset and Somerset justices on two occasions round Sherborne. 'The danger and damnification of the whole county if timely prevention be not applied' motivated magistrates who acted similarly in Rutland, as it did their colleagues in Cheshire and Nottinghamshire.[55] When the justices of Herefordshire and Radnorshire provided money and food for Presteigne in the plague of 1636, Sir Robert Harley agreed that 'if the inhabitants . . . do wander abroad as heretofore they have done in troops', the delivery of bread should be stopped. One man refused to contribute to the rate because the inhabitants 'came with the plague abroad upon them; therefore I will give nothing'.[56]

It was this pressure from outside as much as any altruistic desire to prevent the further spread of infection which created the famous tragedy at Eyam in Derbyshire in 1666. The rector, William Mompesson, and his Interregnum predecessor, Thomas Stanley, persuaded the parishioners to stay in the village, despite raging infection. In the end four out of every ten of the inhabitants died. Mompesson and Stanley have been given credit for courageous self-sacrifice, saving neighbouring settlements at the expense of their own; and a pious dedication to the common good is certainly evident in Mompesson's letters. But so also is a hard-headed appreciation that this was the only way of guaranteeing some sort of assistance from other parts of the county.[57] The clergy and inhabitants of Eyam were not by any means making a free decision. It does not lessen the tragedy to admit that they were compelled to act as they did.

The price paid by isolated communities for the protection of the rest extended beyond increased risks of infection for those who could not escape. The number of burials did not reach twice the average in Chelmsford in 1637, but the town had to petition the Essex quarter sessions for aid, since the poor were not 'suffered for the preservation of others to seek abroad for their relief as in former times'. Similar complaints came to the Cheshire justices from Nantwich in 1604 and from Stockport in 1606. When Preston was cut off from the rest of Lancashire in 1631, it was reported that 756 out of the 887 people in the town needed relief – not because of plague, but through the secondary consequences of their isolation: 'Their miseries are enough by the plague; it were pity famine should also destroy them.'[58]

Such circumstances naturally exacerbated tension between town and country. When justices of the peace around London ordered constables to drive citizens away, and when carriers and carts taking provisions to the city were stopped in Essex and Surrey, that cruelty of the 'Country' against the 'City' of which London pamphleteers so often complained was manifest.[59] In 1665 the London newspapers reported a horror story which might have come straight from the pages of Dekker. A Londoner coming to Dorchester was confined to a shed in a field: when he died after four days' illness 'a pit was digged and both hovel and corpse were buried together'.[60] Small incidents like this also generated resentment in the provinces. A servant girl who left her master in Leicester at the end of her term in 1626 was ignominiously sent back by the vicar and constables of her own parish, who alleged that she had come from an infected house. They appealed to the statute of 1604 and insolently advised the Leicester council on its duties: 'All good magistrates' should take 'good orders and courses for the safety of themselves and the country. Fail not to do your best office at your peril!'[61]

The same sort of disputes and impediments to corporate action occurred within towns, as sectional interests found new fuel to rekindle old antagonisms during epidemics. In cathedral cities the enduring rivalry of ecclesiastical and secular authorities led to controversy. At the instigation of the House of Lords, the plague statute of 1604 included a proviso exempting cathedrals from the jurisdiction of local justices and mayors.[62] Accordingly, deans and chapters vigorously asserted their independence. In Salisbury, Exeter and Norwich residents of the cathedral close resisted efforts to include them in plague rates and watches.[63] One Salisbury annalist acidly recorded that in 1627 'the great Robins of the close' were 'so affrighted that they shut up their gates not suffering any to come in'. When the townspeople nevertheless penetrated the precincts one Sunday morning, the porters ran and shut the cathedral doors against them. The canons of Norwich and Windsor acted similarly in 1637.[64] Cathedral clergy often fled, leaving small gifts of alms for the infected, and their congregations in the charge of lecturers, one of whom was said to have died of plague in Bristol in 1575. On their return to Exeter in 1626, the canons there had the nerve to complain that in their absence ministers, perhaps Puritans, had 'preached turbulently and erroneously'.[65]

Bishops were rather more useful than cathedral chapters, especially in the organisation of charitable collections for the sick; but their local political authority was declining as towns increasingly gained independence of episcopal control. Bishop Freke had been the intermediary passing plague orders from the Privy Council to Norwich in 1579, and the Bishop of Salisbury, as justice of the peace, was one of those issuing plague regulations there in 1603.[66] Their successors played no similar role. In Salisbury, for example, the new charter of 1612 separating the government of town and close gave Bishop Davenant an obvious excuse to absent himself in 1627. Some of the secular institutions of a town were similarly neither a hindrance nor much of a help during an epidemic. Trade guilds and companies might complain when their feasts were banned, but most of their leading members had already dispersed, after reluctantly agreeing to make some financial contribution to the relief of the infected.[67] The only subordinate authorities on whose aid councillors and aldermen could regularly call, and on whose co-operation they must necessarily rely, were the lowest organs of civil and ecclesiastical government, the parishes.

Churchwardens and overseers of the poor, parish clerks and even incumbents, sextons and constables, had to do the dirty work of identifying, confining, supplying and burying the infected; or they had to employ someone to do it for them. They often had little help. The clergy of Colchester were required to supervise the searching of the dead in 1578, and parish clerks and sextons had to write 'Lord Have Mercy' above doors in Norwich in 1580.[68] Payments to infected households were often made by churchwardens and entered in their accounts. But in large towns, and especially in the bigger suburban parishes, extra manpower was required. In St Mary Redcliffe parish, Bristol, there was a parochial nurse and a burier of the dead, and each of them was provided with a black buckram uniform, probably copied from Continental models.[69] The plague orders for London of 1583 brought more numerous additions to the staff of city parishes. The vestry of St Andrew's Holborn puzzled over instructions apparently telling them to appoint 'viewers, searchers, keepers, watchers, surveyors, collectors, providers, deliverers, and such like officers . . . to be attendant about the sick shut up of the plague'. The parish in the end had four viewers, two keepers, and two overseers to supervise them.[70] Other London parishes similarly began to appoint some of the more essential of these officers. Perhaps significantly, only one case has been found of 'providers', in 1593; but 'surveyors' of plague orders and searchers of the dead were common from 1579 onwards, and there were watchers and nurses for the sick in some of the richer parishes by 1608.[71]

None of this machinery was as efficient as it looks on paper, of course. Neither were parishes easily persuaded to erect it. Churchwardens and overseers fled, had to be bribed or cajoled into acting, and occasionally pocketed funds at their disposal.[72] They were always more concerned to transport plague suspects across parish boundaries than to acknowledge their responsibilities towards them.[73] Relations between parishes were often as unneighbourly as those between towns and villages. Similarly, relations between city magistrates and parish elites could be as tense as those between county justices and infected villages. Parishes sometimes objected to the new demands made on them.[74] Yet they were ready enough to ask councillors for loans and rates in aid when infection struck. In return they were expected to enforce the orders, and they necessarily complied. In London, where parishes were relatively independent, many, perhaps most, vestries were supporting infected households in the prescribed manner by 1603.[75] In towns where the administration of social welfare was more centralised by 1600, greater uniformity could be imposed. There are detailed accounts listing visited families and the money paid to them week by week in Salisbury in 1604, and impressive records of householders and what they contributed to the same purpose in Reading in

1607. Like similar documents from other places later in the century, they testify to the continuity of local government even at the street level.[76] Like town government, parish government did not break down under the weight of an epidemic.

The efforts of urban parishes were put into the shade, however, by the activities of the last subordinate institutions we must consider: the foreign congregations of Dutch and Walloon refugees who had gathered in five or six English towns by 1580. From the point of view of town councillors the great virtue of the Strangers was the fact that they paid all rates raised for the native inhabitants of a town, and at the same time separately supported their own poor and sick.[77] Thus in Norwich, where aliens constituted more than a third of all plague casualties between 1579 and 1604, a large part of the burden of dealing with the infected could be left to the Dutch and Walloon congregations. The Mayor's Court imposed health regulations on them in March 1579, three months before similar rules were made for the native population; and in 1584 it again made plague orders more palatable to the English by imposing them on the aliens first.[78]

The Strangers scarcely needed instruction in their duties, however. They brought from the Low Countries methods of dealing with plague which combined prudence and charity more successfully than their English equivalents. During the epidemic of 1563 in London, for example, the Dutch agreed that it would be reckless for their preachers to visit the sick; but they appointed other people to undertake that duty, and they even permitted healthy members of infected households to attend church, so long as they sat on separate benches. The Lord Mayor's order that only one person should be allowed out of an isolated house was first entered in the congregation minutes and then, significantly, struck out. The Dutch also had regular collections for the sick; they appointed keepers to 'tend' them; and they discussed their procedures with the French congregation.[79] In Norwich the Walloon Church similarly provided for regular visits to its sick members in the later sixteenth century, while at the same time advising the corporation on the need to control the sale of goods from infected houses.[80] As refugees, the alien communities were no doubt predisposed to treat their infected compatriots as 'brethren'; but it is nevertheless striking that their orders spoke in terms of 'care', 'comfort' and 'consolation' far more often than those drawn up by English magistrates.

The English learned less from this confrontation than they might have done. They gradually imposed their own habits on the Strangers, forcing them to appoint watchmen outside infected houses in Norwich and Canterbury, and criticising uncontrolled visits to the sick. The mayor and jurats of Sandwich borrowed the titles of 'pestmaster' and 'tender' of the infected from their Dutch congregation in 1638; but they applied them to officers who shut up houses and watched them.[81] Yet the alien congregations were too valuable to be dispensed with altogether. The Strangers therefore remained a distinct social group, obviously susceptible to plague and easily identified as scapegoats for it. In Norwich they were thought to have poisoned the river by washing their cloth in it in 1579, and in 1580 there were 'divers complaints and riots against them' when they continued to do so. In the next epidemic, in 1585, a few foreigners were assaulted in the streets, and some of the aliens retaliated in 1589. In 1632, when their numbers and hence their plague casualties had declined, the Walloons nicely turned the tables by objecting to paying poor rates for 'the pestiferous English'.[82] Roles were reversed but communal tension remained.

The relations between foreigners and English, alien congregations and city corporations, were the most conspicuous example of those flexible associations of often competing authorities and social groups on which the everyday stability of a town depended. All of them had been subjected to unusual strain in the crises caused by epidemic disease.

(iii) The charge of government

Whether supervised by magistrates, churchwardens or Dutch elders, government during an epidemic depended in the end, not on corporate authorities, but on the efforts of individuals, usually small fry. At a rudimentary level, there had to be strong bearers of the dead. If more sophisticated policies were to be implemented, there must be knowledgeable searchers, sympathetic nurses and diligent watchmen. These tasks also required and inculcated other qualities. They demanded an insensitivity to suffering and danger, and a readiness to share the stigma of plague along with its victims. Courage, a certain brutality, a modicum of skill and care were all needed. It was an unlikely combination.

The bearers of the dead employed in Salisbury, for example, had to swear to 'carefully shun and avoid . . . coming into company not infected with the plague', and to carry a red staff in their hands at all times. In Colchester plague officers had to stay away from their own families and carry a white wand so that 'people may know you and shun and avoid you'. People did precisely that. Jane Jacquet, perhaps an alien refugee, was paid by one Kentish parish to nurse the rest of her family during an epidemic. Afterwards, 'she was shunned and abhorred' by her neighbours: women chased her from parish to parish until she became 'a mere idle vagrant person, leading a very loose life, making her habitation under hedges and in the woods in the summer time'.[83]

It was naturally difficult to find volunteers to face such consequences, and those who came forward were usually unreliable. Sometimes parish pensioners were compelled to act on pain of expulsion from an almshouse or removal of the dole if they refused: they were often old and infirm.[84] In Salisbury the bearers of the dead went on strike for higher wages in 1627. In Norwich one of them stole goods from an infected house and fled to Yarmouth and then to Colchester with a 'lewd woman'. Searchers could be bribed to conceal deaths from plague, and watchmen to allow people out of isolated houses. Bearers extorted high fees from the relatives of the dead before they would carry corpses to the grave.[85]

In these circumstances, rumours that searchers and keepers of the sick strangled their patients or buried them alive in order to plunder their houses spread like wildfire. As with doctors and body-snatchers in the eighteenth century, there was considerable popular suspicion of anyone who apparently profited from the misfortunes of others; and suspicions sometimes had foundation in fact, since it cannot have been easy to determine the precise moment of death from plague. One wonders, for example, what lay behind the notice which Samuel Pepys' physician inserted in the papers in 1665, testifying that his servant had died of plague and had not – as some alleged – been murdered by his master, the doctor.[86] In the better-documented case of Ursula Barrett of Salisbury we can see very well how rumour and reality fed off one another in a plague-stricken neighbourhood.

Barrett was one of the women called on as a specialist searcher of the dead in 1604, in 1625 and again in 1636. She must have been experienced, tough, and an object of dread – a harbinger of disaster. In 1625, however, she made herself unpopular with her betters in Salisbury by reporting that a gentleman had died of plague, and by insulting his friends. This row encouraged others to come forward and accuse her of trying to bury people alive in 1604. A servant, Elizabeth Taylor, said that she had been 'stripped and laid out for dead' by Barrett, but had somehow escaped. A neighbour alleged that Barrett carried a little girl of eight, perhaps Elizabeth, out of a house next-door to his; and he 'heard the child cry'. When he intervened, Barrett shouted: 'Hold thy peace and say nothing: I may do as much for thee.' Anne Denneade, another neighbour, said the child had cried out in horror at the sight of her winding sheet: 'You shall not put me into a bag as you did my sister.'[87]

Much of this was gossip, no doubt embroidered twenty years after the event, and it was partial. Anne Denneade complained that Barrett had hung infected clothes out to dry in the garden, and so spread the infection next-door, where Denneade's husband, children and servants had all died of plague. She was hardly an unprejudiced witness. But the whole incident, carefully recorded in depositions taken by Henry Sherfield, accurately reflects the atmosphere of anxiety and terror to which plague officers contributed and in which they had to work. Whether Barrett was innocent or not, one would like to know how the citizens of Salisbury reacted to her employment again in the same job in 1636.

From the point of view of urban rulers like Sherfield, however, such horrors were less worrying than the evident inadequacies of searchers as diagnosticians. Their prime function was to identify cases of plague so that magistrates might plot the spread of infection and try to control it. No doubt women like Ursula Barrett soon learned to recognise the buboes and blue or purple 'tokens' which marked obvious cases: two Norwich searchers reported in 1630 that a child did not die of plague because 'there is nothing to be seen, neither spot nor rising'.[88] On the other hand, cases of septicaemic plague which did not produce these symptoms must often have been missed; and other spotted diseases, such as typhus, might easily be confused with plague. In Norwich again, the chancellor of the diocese recommended the employment of an elderly Swiss doctor rather than those 'old blind women, whose judgements is as dim as their eyes, and will censure it to be the plague, if a body dies spotted, either with the pox or spotted fever'. Although the idea was not taken up, the Norwich authorities were beginning to appreciate the difficulties of diagnosis, and their doubts seem to have percolated down to the odd searcher. In 1636 one of them reported that a corpse was covered with 'spots black and blue. . . . But she saith she dare not say upon her oath that it is not of the plague nor that it is of the plague.'[89]

Town councils were more concerned about diagnosis than they were about treatment. Medical care for the sick was never a high priority, even when specialists could be found who were willing to give it. Several towns were employing physicians, surgeons or apothecaries to treat the diseases of the poor from the later sixteenth century onwards.[90] They did not rush to do the same in cases of plague, perhaps because they thought them incurable. In the early seventeenth century, a few corporations recognised the need for professional assistance. The York councillors sent to Newcastle to get advice on how infected houses should be fumigated. Their colleagues in Leicester inquired in Oxford and Lincolnshire for a skilled plague doctor. The corporation of Shrewsbury employed William Boraston, author of a plague tract, in the epidemic of 1630.[91] But these doctors were a tiny proportion of the total number of medical practitioners in towns; they often served only for a short time; and they were expensive. The man who worked in King's Lynn in the 1630s had to appeal to the Privy Council to get the fee of £100 which matched what his private patients had offered him as an inducement to stay with them in the country.[92]

Little more was achieved in London. Some parishes occasionally employed surgeons to search the sick or dead, and the corporation had three of them at the pesthouse in 1609.[93] But efforts to get help from the College of Physicians bore little fruit until 1625, when two doctors were certainly engaged by the City. Only then were large sums, amounting to £300 in all, paid for the expenses of members of the various branches of the medical profession.[94] English towns did not catch up with their Continental neighbours in the use of professional assistance until the 1660s, when most infected towns seem to have employed at least one physician or surgeon. The corporation of Norwich negotiated with London apothecaries and surgeons, including William Boghurst, and got two men to serve. London, as we have seen, had a medical team of a dozen.[95] It was scarcely enough.

Not many of the infected can have had the dubious benefits of professional treatment – bleeding and the lancing of buboes – therefore. They and their relatives were left to treat themselves as best they could, and the prime aim of authority was to prevent anyone coming into close contact with them. For some, that meant isolation in a pesthouse. Like doctors, however, pesthouses were expensive, and hence always inadequate. They were modelled on the lazarhouses, once used for lepers, which still existed outside the walls of towns and now generally housed cases of syphilis. But unlike leperhouses they were seldom permanent structures since they were not in regular use. Often they were no more than temporary wooden shacks, quickly thrown up and as quickly burnt down. Someone set fire to the Salisbury pesthouse in 1627, and the eighty-seven inmates were left 'sitting in the field upon the bare earth in a miserable condition, many of them almost naked'. In major epidemics these cabins – or 'hovels' as they were more accurately termed in Bristol – could house only a minority of the sick and their contacts.[96] In Worcester in a great epidemic in 1637, a quarter of the deaths – 405 in all – occurred at the pesthouse; and that was exceptional. The proportion in Norwich in 1665–6, less than 10 per cent, was more usual.[97]

Pesthouses were more permanent, but no more adequate given the greater need, in London. Despite the campaign for plague hospitals which the Privy Council waged from 1580 through to 1665, the first pesthouse, built in the 1590s, probably housed no more than fifty people in 1603 and fewer than 250 even in 1665. Conciliar pressure in 1630 produced at least two new pesthouses, but the one in Westminster had fewer than 100 people in it in 1636. By 1665, when there were five of these institutions in the whole metropolis, it is unlikely that they together contained as many as 600 patients.[98] Quite apart from the expense of erecting and maintaining them, they can have had few attractions for anyone, least of all for the inmates. The cost of lodging and basic medicines had to be met by the patients or by their parishes if they were poor; and whole families might find themselves carted off for incarceration, in spite of the Privy Council's declared objective to separate the sick from the healthy.[99] In short, the fashionable schemes of 1630 and 1665 never had any chance of success. All concerned had good reason to prefer the alternative of household isolation, and to fall back on it with some relief.

That did not make household quarantine welcome, of course, especially when it might last for months on end. The plague orders were inconsistent in their prescription of the time limit: six weeks in the national orders of 1578, four weeks in those for London in 1592, forty days – a genuine quarantine – more commonly in the seventeenth century and in the new orders of 1666.[100] In all cases, however, the period was to begin only after the recovery or death of the last plague case. When the disease spread slowly through a family, houses were shut up for four or five months, and the inmates had to bear the cost of food and nursing throughout.[101] If they could not afford it, the burden again fell on the parish and the local poor rate.

In either case, the condition of the inmates must have been pitiable by the end. In some towns there were padlocks on the doors as well as watchmen outside them to prevent exit or entry. Boards were nailed over the doors and windows in Norwich and York for the same purpose: one wonders how food was passed in.[102] When the bearers of the dead broke into one such house in Salisbury in 1627, 'the smell of the house, with the heat of the infection, was so grievous they were not able to endure it. . . . It was a close house and but one little door to the street and a little window.' In the parish of St Martin-in-the-Fields, Westminster, large subdivided mansions were shut up in the 1630s, with three or four families and ten or more people in them; sometimes all were found dead when the house was opened up.[103]

Isolation was obviously imposed only too efficiently in some cases; and it was supported by public opinion, at least in the early stages of an epidemic. When the London astrologer Simon Forman tried to move a sick maidservant to a house in Lambeth in 1603, she was returned by local people and the whole household was shut up. Forman was 'much abused' by the Lambeth men: 'They could say to me that it was better that I and my household should starve and die than any of them should be put in danger.'[104] Yet there was a limit to the number of houses which could be quarantined in this way. In large towns, it is only in minor outbreaks of plague that we have repeated evidence of infected houses being identified, shut up and then after a period opened again: in some central parishes in London, and in Norwich and York, in 1630–1 and 1636–8.[105] Stupendous efforts were sometimes made in serious epidemics. We know from the surviving accounts that 411 infected households received some support in the Salisbury plague of 1604, at least a quarter of all those in the city; and that at its height in September, 132 households were somehow 'kept in'. In 1665 the parish of St Margaret's Westminster tried to relieve and control more than 1,500 people in infected households, besides the 40 who had been removed to the pesthouse.[106] They cannot all have been guarded night and day, however, and simply providing money for them was a major achievement.

Assistance from the parish no doubt helped to persuade some of the infected to stay in. In 1630 one of the Westminster justices assured the Privy Council, somewhat optimistically, that the poorer sort never 'went out to seek relief; for that most of them care not how they be shut up so they may have that relief the parishes allow them'. But parish relief itself broke down in the greatest crises, as the London aldermen admitted when they allowed one member of every infected household to go out for provisions in 1625.[107] Even this was wishful thinking when applied to the poorest parishes of London. By the middle of August 1625, and at about the same time in 1665, all attempts at household segregation seem to have been abandoned. As early as July 1625 one observer reported that 'it is not certain who is clean or foul at London, and they have given over the closing up of houses'.[108] Similar experience in the provinces led to rumours like that which Margaret Hoby recorded in 1603: 'I heard the plague was so great at Whitby that those which were clear shut themselves up, and the infected that escaped did go abroad.'[109]

The enforcement of household quarantine thus depended both on the extent of infection and on the amount of money available to pay for it; and the greater the infection, the more money was needed. The financial costs of an epidemic made unparalleled demands on urban resources. In the later sixteenth century there was little established machinery for mobilising urban wealth, and hence only minimal provision for the sick. Like the Crown, town corporations were still expected to 'live of their own', and poor rates were a recent invention. As a result, councils had to raise money from loans and gifts, especially from their own members, and to borrow from endowed funds for the poor.[110] Even when additional poor rates were raised for the sick, income was tiny because so many of those assessed had fled. In Bristol more money could be raised and spent on the sick in 1609 than in 1603, when there was a major epidemic.[111]

Statutory provision for the levying of plague rates outside infected communities in 1604 did something to change this picture. There were initial problems in deciding how the rates should be assessed. Should they be based on parliamentary subsidies, on existing rates for gaols, or, as was ultimately most common, on rates for the poor?[112] What sorts of wealth should be taxed and what should be done about non-resident property-owners? There was often argument about how far the five miles in a five-mile rate extended; and payments were always in arrears.[113] For small towns which had few other resources, however, the proceeds were indispensable. In 1604 £176 was spent on watches, buriers, 'overseers' of the infected and the sick themselves in Nantwich, Cheshire, and five-sixths of it came from a county rate.[114]

Another source of revenue which was increasingly exploited by infected towns in the seventeenth century was charity. It was not philanthropy in the form of permanent endowments, like those for schools and poor relief; they were obviously inappropriate. It took the form of once-for-all gifts from individuals and corporate bodies, a more casual and more traditional kind of almsgiving whose continuing importance has been grossly neglected by historians. Sometimes it was essentially conscience-money, extorted from those who fled, as with the alms somewhat grudgingly left in London by Alderman Cockayne in 1625 and by Dean Sancroft in 1665.[115] But it was often generous. Of the £400 spent on the maintenance of 114 infected houses in Sandwich in 1644, for example, only one-third could be raised from the county; another third was contributed by assessments within the town; but the rest came from individual gifts. These ranged from fourpence given by 'three poor sailors and a woman' to £41 sent by the city of Canterbury.[116] An even larger proportion of the £1,115 spent in Plymouth during the great epidemic of 1626 came from similar sources. An extra poor rate brought in only £130. The county rate raised £292. More than £600 came from benevolences: from merchants, from local gentry and especially from other corporations. The council of Exeter alone gave £92: a return for the donation of £50 which Plymouth had sent when there was plague in Exeter in 1625.[117]

These reciprocal gifts from one town to another, which were common throughout the seventeenth century, are conspicuous reminders of the power of charitable impulses in pre-industrial England. The same sources were tapped more systematically by charitable briefs for infected towns, once the example had been set by the national collections for London ordered by the House of Lords in 1625. In the last outbreak of plague in England the charity of the nation was mobilised still more effectively. Collections were taken at monthly fasts throughout the kingdom, and the money distributed by the bishop of London, initially for the relief of the infected in the capital and then, in 1666, for the victims of plague in provincial towns. There were delays and disputes, some of which had to be settled by statute; and there were small returns from some of the poorer dioceses. Bangor proved particularly stony ground, perhaps, one observer thought, because 'those that are born and bred amongst the rocks . . . participate too much of the nature of the soil'. But the newspapers publicised the collections at length, and in general the response was good.[118] The corporation of Colchester spent £2,800 on the sick in

1666: £1,165 came from a county rate but no less than £1,449 was money collected in churches in London and Essex.[119]

The sums of money which have been mentioned show what was possible, and what was necessary, during epidemics in early modern towns. In every case total expenditure was more than double the normal annual income of the corporation concerned, and sometimes five or six times as much. These were unprecedented sums for early modern communities to raise. Yet that is not to say that they were sufficient. Colchester in 1666 and Plymouth in 1626 were probably best provided for. The cost of maintaining the sick and the poor in Norwich in 1666 was put at £250 a week;[120] if that was an accurate estimate, then the money raised in Colchester, where twice as many people died, might have sufficed for six to eight weeks. It would have served for the period of heaviest mortality, but not for the six or seven months that the epidemic lasted. If we compare the number of burials in Plymouth in 1626 with the known cost of housing and guarding infected people elsewhere,[121] we can calculate that the corporation could afford to keep each fatal plague case for a fortnight. That would have been impossible in the sixteenth century, but it still left little room for manoeuvre.

Moreover, the fact was that corporations cut their coat according to their cloth; and the cloth was sometimes very short indeed: before 1665, in towns which could not benefit from county rates as Colchester and Plymouth did, and in heavily burdened parishes. Norwich had no help from the county until 1666, when the Norfolk justices arranged for a house-to-house collection and when there were also contributions from London.[122] Until then the city was largely dependent on its own limited resources. It raised plague rates in every epidemic after 1579, but they sufficed only in the mildest outbreaks. An assessment of 1603 would have brought in less than £300 if fully collected; more than that was raised in the two plagues of the 1630s. In 1637 and 1638 expenditure on a relatively small number of infected people amounted to £510, as much as the Crown was demanding from the city in Ship Money in one year.[123] In 1666, on the other hand, despite an assessment equal to twenty-four months' poor rate, the corporation quickly found itself short of cash and heavily in debt, while it waited for alms from the county to come in.[124]

As ever, London provided the crucial test. There adequate public provision was long impeded by the assumption that private benevolence and existing parochial endowments could cope. Until 1625 most parishes relied on their charitable funds and on casual gifts to finance household relief; we know of only three vestries which imposed a special rate for the sick before then.[125] The mayor and aldermen did little to help beyond ordering charitable collections, persuading companies to contribute, and paying small sums to the parishes which were hardest hit, like St Saviour's Southwark in 1603.[126] As a result some parts of the city were much better off than others. Benevolences cannot have sufficed in St Botolph's Bishopsgate, for example, where expenditure on the poor in 1593 and 1603 only rose by the same proportion, around 50 per cent, as in some of the rich central parishes, despite enormously heavier mortality.[127] Even in 1625, the Lords' order for an extra poor rate had only patchy and belated results at the parish level, although the City paid out £1,000 to the worst affected areas.[128] Not until 1636 did the aldermen themselves order an additional rate for the infected.[129]

Fresh national collections made things easier in 1665. On the strength of them, the City Chamberlain distributed £600 to infected parishes every week throughout the summer, an unprecedented amount; and the aldermen ordered two extra years' poor rates as additional relief.[130] Although no complete accounts of the money spent in 1665 survive, it seems clear that the central parishes of the city were relatively well provided for. They were able to identify households as soon as they were infected, to transport some of the sick to pesthouses and isolate many others in their houses, and even occasionally to provide nurses for them.[131] The insoluble problems lay, of course, in the suburbs. Westminster was relatively well off. The flight of its richer inhabitants vitiated any attempt to levy rates successfully, but the runaways had left lavish gifts behind them. Out of £1,652 received in St Margaret's for expenditure on the infected, £1,117 came from 'honourable persons'. But other fringe parishes were wholly unable to cope. In St Giles Cripplegate – ironically the site of the City pesthouse – it was reported in August 1665 that 'all have liberty lest the sick poor should be famished within doors, the parish not being able to relieve their necessity'.[132]

Plague had thus tested the financial and administrative capabilities of towns as well as the determination of their rulers. It had elicited new corporate responses but also exacerbated old sectional divisions, arising from differences within communities and between them. The deliberate mobilisation of traditional charitable impulses and of novel forms of taxation produced an ambitious machinery of control and relief which would scarcely have been conceivable before 1603. But it was never sufficient for a major epidemic. All infected households could not be rigidly isolated, still less could all the inmates be moved to pesthouses, in the heavily afflicted parts of Norwich or London or Colchester in 1665 and 1666. For this reason, the government's isolation policies were never put to the ultimate test to see if they worked. As we shall see in the last chapter, it is as difficult now as it was then to know whether or not they reduced mortality. The costs were always more obvious than the benefits.

It was as clear to contemporaries as it is to the historian, however, that the first charge on the resources of corporations was not the control of infection but the imposition of public order. Norwich had a prison in one of the towers in the town walls in 1625 where 'the unruly infected' were 'manacled and kept carefully'. The justices in York similarly needed to deal with 'those that are rebellious and will not be ruled' in 1631; and their colleagues in London exerted themselves in 1665 so that 'the people may be better governed'. Pesthouses and guards were themselves a means of 'disposing of' the troublesome sick, as the council of Bristol revealingly put it.[133] Of all the interlocking relationships on which the stability of a town depended, that most basic of ties between the rulers and the ruled was subjected to most strain during an epidemic.

Chapter 11

Police and people

The ignorant vulgar are stupid, and know not what use to make of anything they feel.

Richard Baxter, 1665[1]

But now alas, the common people say,
'Tis we must bear the burden of the day.

E.N., *London's Plague-Sore Discovered* (1665)

The reactions of the common people to plague are the most difficult of all to reconstruct. When their words were recorded, it was usually in the context of court proceedings arising from their crimes and misdemeanours. Observers who described their behaviour similarly concentrated on manifestations of riot and disturbance. Only rarely do we hear of popular humanity, patience, courage or charity. William Lilly, the astrologer, noted that the poor who came to consult him in the plague of 1665 'were so civil ... they would stand purposely at a distance'; and Thomas Vincent visited one boy in the same epidemic who 'boldly enquired whether the tokens did yet appear, saying that he was ready for them'.[2] But Richard Baxter's blanket dismissal of the ignorant rabble was much more common. As so often, the weight of the historical evidence can easily give the impression that the lives of the poor were brutish as well as short.

There was unquestionably a good deal of disorder, as we shall see. Popular disorder posed the greatest threat to the government's policy for public health; and popular disorder helped to determine the nature of that policy. If we wish to understand the reasons for disturbance and resistance by the vulgar, however, we must first try to illustrate the wide range of actions and attitudes which was open to ordinary people in the face of plague.

284

(i) Popular reactions

A short period of exceptionally high mortality naturally created insecurity. When each serious illness was marked by the tolling of a passing bell and each funeral by the ringing of a knell in the parish church, the fact of an epidemic was proclaimed loud and long. Since knells might last for an hour or more, depending on the social status of the deceased, it is not surprising that the bells of St Martin's Church, Salisbury, suffered such wear and tear that they had to be repaired after the plague of 1627. 'The doleful and almost universal and continual ringing and tolling of bells' marked out an infected town, and inclined listeners, if not to prayer, as was the intention, at least to reflection on and preparation for imminent death.[3]

'Hearing divers passing bells go' in 1579, a Norwich woman said men 'had need remember God and make their wills while they be in health, for now they have but small time to make them if they be once taken sick'. One of her neighbours began to collect money owing to him, 'doubting of his life being then in the sickness time'; and another Norwich man took the opportunity to press his stepfather to make his will. He claimed that he did not like to see the old man unprepared for his end, 'left alone . . . desolate and distressed among the snares of death, and expecting every day the stroke of death that sends so many to their graves'.[4] Wills were indeed made in infected houses where one member of the family died after another. A widow in Gateshead in 1570 was able to say that 'being visited with the plague, I thank God of the same', before directing that she and her children should be buried in the churchyard. Another Gateshead citizen honestly admitted that he had drawn up his will after his house was visited 'and my wife departed to the mercy of God', and 'being myself partly crazed'.[5] We know from administrators' accounts in probate records that many testators had watched husbands, wives or children die, before they succumbed themselves.[6]

It may be that Englishmen were to some degree inured to high mortality in the seventeenth century, especially to high infant mortality. It was common, as in more normal times, to give new babies the names of children who had died during epidemics.[7] But that does not mean that they were effectively replaced or that there had been no suffering when they died. Among the sad sights watched by Thomas Vincent in the plague of 1665 was 'a woman coming alone, and weeping by the door where I lived . . . with a little coffin under her arm, carrying it to the new church-yard'. And nothing could accustom people to the emotional demands made by several deaths in a family. In 1665 again, a schoolmaster visited 'a poor woman, who had buried some children of the plague'; he found 'the room so little, that it scarce held any more than the bed whereon she lay, and an open coffin wherein she saw her husband lie dead of the same disease'. It is not difficult to appreciate the feelings of the woman in an infected hovel in Salisbury who told John Ivie that 'my husband and two of my children cannot speak to me' and that she hoped for better days. Neither is it difficult to understand why a Londoner buried in 1593 'died of grief being now shut up in his house this sickness time'.[8]

Plague brought grief, shock and a pervasive sense of impotence. It also weakened those formal and informal defences which might have protected people against them. It was the church's business to console the bereaved and fortify the dying; but it is doubtful whether its ministrations were any more effective during epidemics than at other times. That many priests fled with their respectable parishioners is evident from the applause given to, or claimed by, those who stayed.[9] The bishop of London was unable to persuade sufficient pastors to stay in London in 1665, and parishes sometimes had to make special payments to ministers who 'prayed with the visited'.[10] Where there were services, there is some evidence that attendances were large. Although church collections declined dramatically in such infected towns as Norwich and Bocking in 1665 and 1666, because of the flight of the rich, observers elsewhere reported larger congregations than usual, including many who did not normally come to church. One minister in Shrewsbury actually complained in 1632 about the resort of the poor to church in 'a greater number than formerly', to his own 'great danger, the infection breaking as it doth sometimes in places which are never suspected'. The danger was real. William Lilly remembered a great communion in St Clement Danes, London, in the plague of 1625, which required three priests, two of whom soon after fell sick of the plague.[11]

The potential may well have existed for a temporary increase in religious commitment such as occurred in Marseilles in 1720, or even for the sort of religious revival which was sometimes associated with epidemics of typhus in the eighteenth century.[12] Some of those who broke out of infected houses were later found in church, no doubt seeking spiritual consolation; and justices in Kent were alarmed by the hundreds who left infected Sandwich in 1644 in order to find religious services in neighbouring villages.[13] Those outside the established church who showed more dedication than Anglican divines found a ready response. Thomas Vincent reported 'vast concourses' of people at services given by excluded ministers in London in 1665. The Catholic priest Henry Morse made converts among the poor whom he visited in London in 1636. Thirty years later the separatists noted an increase in their numbers when plague threatened Bristol: 'There appeared, seemingly, a spirit of life entering into the people not of [our] church, more unanimously resolved for meetings separate from the worship of the world.'[14] Yet all this perhaps reflects a short supply of religious consolation rather than increased demand for it. If plague did provide fertile ground for religious enthusiasm, there were few ministers and preachers present and willing to sow the seed.

Moreover, plague also gave rise to impulses which were contrary to religious practices. One was the common-sense desire to avoid contagion which, according to some divines, kept congregations down. Recusants certainly used plague in their neighbourhood as an excuse for non-attendance, and many people must have considered it a powerful deterrent. If we listen to the preachers who congratulated themselves on their large congregations, we should also notice those who complained that flight to sin, whoredom and drunkenness was more common in a plague than flight to religion.[15] Formal religion normally had only a marginal impact on many people's lives, and popular habits of mind could not be altered quickly and were seldom permanently transformed. Ralph Josselin was pleased to see attendances at prayers and fasts in Earls Colne increasing when plague threatened in August 1665; but there was a decline in winter as the threat declined, and when plague seemed about to strike again in July 1666 some people complained about the fast because it took men away from hay-making.[16] In short, the diverse religious behaviour of early modern Englishmen seems not to have been radically affected by outbreaks of plague. They reinforced the godliness of some, and perhaps brought a few new converts, but they did not obliterate the indifference of the many.

For most people the ties of neighbourhood and friendship were more important defences against suffering than religion. Yet they too were often found wanting during an epidemic. It was difficult to maintain neighbourly ideals when disease invaded one or two houses in a street, and posed a threat to all around. Deliberate neglect by their 'friends and neighbours' forced many testators to make their final wishes known orally, to warders and keepers or even to strangers through a window, when their houses were shut up.[17] It is important to recognise that popular pressure very often forced people to smuggle plague corpses out of back doors, to bury them in gardens or at night, and to avoid needless company if they were sick.[18] When houses in Marygate, just outside the walls of York, were infected in 1604, the inhabitants 'were very disorderous and would not be kept in by the watchmen'. They marched up towards Bootham Bar to beg food. The householders of Bootham, however, supported one of the watchmen who fired a gun at them and drove them back.[19] Then, as now, the residents of Bootham were probably socially superior to those of Marygate: plague once again revealed social distinctions. But in this instance it created a real divide where there had been only subtle social gradations, and put a barrier between neighbours who were physically only a few yards apart.

The divisive impact of plague on social ties also extended into the household. Relations between masters and servants were always brittle: they could rarely survive when maids, apprentices or journeymen brought plague into a prosperous home. In his absence during an epidemic, a Calne weaver advised his wife to 'let your spinners and weavers come in at the lower entry, and so up into the wool loft; and let them come into no other part of your house'. When the nanny employed by a gentleman in Greenwich caught plague, she was boarded up in a separate part of the house and a stranger was paid to look after her.[20] Often, however, sick servants were simply thrown into the streets. A clothier in St Katherine's Fenchurch Street, London, found a maidservant 'sick of the plague and full of tokens' and moved her out. She went home 'to her mother's house at Whitechapel and died the next morning'. Other servants, far from home, died in the streets or in temporary lodgings.[21] Such savagery was not universal. Two gentlemen gave money to the constables for their father's servants in Nantwich; more remarkably, a maidservant and a foreman in Plymouth gave small amounts of cash towards the relief of infected members of their master's family in 1626.[22] But the bond of employer and employee was seldom strong enough to withstand the stresses of plague.

When employers or their families caught plague themselves, the balance of advantage shifted. Then masters needed help, and some servants responded, nursed the sick and were left legacies if they survived.[23] If the servants were already dead, nurses had to be found from outside, and that was expensive and difficult. The woman who looked after a Dutch family in Sandwich in 1638 received 8 shillings a week. A nurse who was given clothes in part-payment in Hungerford claimed that they constituted a promise of marriage by her employer.[24] In 1665 Widow Foster of Danbury in Essex was persuaded to act as nurse to a family suffering, so the householder claimed, from 'nothing but a common ague and a fever'. It proved to be plague, and when she caught it herself she was left by her master lying dead 'almost three days in the yard at the mercy of hogs and dogs, most shamefully and unchristianly as the like was never heard'. It is not surprising that John Potter of Bristol could not find a paid nurse for his pregnant wife when she caught plague in 1645 and her 'neighbours were fearful to go to visit her'. His wife delivered her own stillborn child, and was later found 'in a very sad and distracted condition . . . as though she had been dead'.[25]

When the persuasions of neighbourhood and money failed, people were thrown back onto the bonds of family and kinship. Marital kin, especially women, seem to have recognised their obligations much more readily than neighbours. The neighbours of a Wiltshire man tried to persuade his sister-in-law to stay, like them, 'no nearer to the house wherein he lay sick than about the distance of the breadth of an acre and a half'; but she said she would go to him, 'live or die'. A gentleman in Bury St Edmunds similarly relied on his wife's relations when he 'could get nobody to help me, and . . . all my household fled from me and left me both comfortless and helpless'. [26] Old women took in their orphaned grandchildren when parents died of plague, and servants and apprentices sometimes went home to care for their infected relations.[27]

There were stresses and problems even here, however. Kin often did not live near one another in the mobile society of early modern England, and when they did they were not always willing to help. 'Feeling himself at the beginning of his sickness, weak and faint', one Londoner went across the city to his aunt's house in 1593 and begged her aid:

> Good aunt, stick to me now for I am very sick and my wife also
> is more sick and I know and am persuaded myself that not any
> of my friends or kindred or of hers will venture to come and visit
> us this time of infection; wherefore I do request you to take the

pains to come to my house and look unto us in this time of our
visitation.

He promised her a legacy, and she went. But she might not have
done, since people often had to choose between obligations to their
kinsfolk and loyalty to their immediate family. They might have to be
cruel to the former in order to be kind to the latter. Philip Pine of
Salisbury 'put forth of my house my own sister in the disease, by
which means, thanks be to God, I saved her and the rest of my family'.
The decision had contributed to his being 'overwhelmed with grief
and perplexed on every side, with miserable comforters, which hath
brought me low in all degrees'. But the choice had to be made.[28]
When it came to the point, all friendships and all ties were not alike.
As Beza had perceived, in an epidemic 'that which is not so near must
give place to the nearer'.[29]

In the last resort the nuclear family alone could be relied upon
absolutely. Husbands nursed their wives, just as William Mompesson
of Eyam did; and parents nursed their children. In London some poor
householders ran what amounted to private hospitals and continued
to find customers, no doubt for higher fees, during epidemics. The
patients may have been orphan children or solitary adults, but if they
were not, their relatives no doubt thought they were doing their best
for them.[30] Only two certain cases of parents deserting their infected
children have been discovered.[31] The closest ties of blood and affec-
tion remained strong in a plague, though scarcely adequate for the
burdens imposed on them. Just as the disease had a marked household
incidence, so people's reactions to it isolated the individual family and
left it to its own resources. The official form of prayer for plague of
1603 put the lesson very neatly: 'Now the chief remedy to be expected
from man is that everyone would be a magistrate unto himself and
his whole family.'[32]

Many of the instances cited above come from the social milieu of
the 'middling sort', those who made wills, had property to be adminis-
tered after their death, wrote letters, journals or autobiographies. They
are not direct evidence for the behaviour or attitudes of the poor.
There is no reason to suppose that the reactions of the 'poorer sort'
were completely different, however. They probably went to church
less often. They had no servants to help them, no money to employ
nurses, and probably few kin whose whereabouts they knew. That
simply meant that they were all the sooner reduced to dependence on

those nearest to them, on their immediate family. The poor had some psychological defences which were perhaps denied to their social superiors. Once plague had taken hold in poor alleys and tenements, a common suffering might create a desperate sense of community. Some of the cases of disorder which we shall shortly examine show that stress could be channelled into aggression against authority, and that it drew common people together while simultaneously separating them from everyone else.

Tension could also find an outlet in a black humour, which reduced the emotional temperature during an epidemic by making light of it. Jokes were not confined to the pamphlets of Dekker and his successors. A Yorkshireman appointed a blind woman to watch for infected vagrants; and there was real wit in the 'knave' who wrote above a house where brass farthings were minted: 'Lord Have Mercy upon us, for this house is full of tokens.' More caustic was the York man who told an inquiring constable in 1632 that all in his house 'were in health but his cat was sick'. The magistrates of York were as incensed by this as they were by a man 'dancing and fiddling' among the infected houses outside Walmgate Bar. The bearers of the dead in Salisbury similarly vented their feelings, and similarly offended authority, when they were found in the churchyard in 1627, with pots of ale on their backs, 'dancing amongst the graves, singing "Hie for more shoulder-work" in a fearful manner'.[33]

Popular reactions were not wholly unthinking, however. Ordinary men and women were no less in need of a convincing reason for plague than the social elite were; and they adapted religious and secular explanations to fit the facts as they perceived them. Just as the educated thought plague was caused by the sins of the poor, so some of the poorer sort must have been tempted to think it the consequence of the uncharitable behaviour of the rich. There was an obvious appeal in sermons and pamphlets condemning the flight of ministers and magistrates, and the point could be extended to the monarch himself. 'Where is your King now, that grand Papish?' one Yorkshireman asked another in 1665. 'He flieth from the plague, but it will follow him, I'll warrant.' As it happens, Charles II made himself popular in Salisbury by inquiring after the health of people in an infected inn in 1665; but the northerners did not know that. Another Yorkshireman took speculation about the first cause of plague to the point of sedition:

The King is the only causer of the plague and pestilence, and

hath provoked God to send this judgement upon us by taxing
and assessing the poor. If this King had been hanged when the
other was beheaded, we should have had none of these taxes;
but I think we must all rise.[34]

Yet there was in fact remarkably little overt class prejudice in
popular reactions to plague in England. Plague might be used as a
threat and a potent curse against social superiors, magistrates or
gentry. After the suppression of the 1549 rebellion, prophecies were
spread around Norwich that pestilence would devastate the city as it
had done in 1545, and this time kill the enemies of Robert Kett and
the commons. In 1666 a persecuted Quaker similarly expected a
'worse plague' to follow that of 1665 and the subsequent fire.[35] But
when plague occurred the poor did not in general rush to blame the
rich for it. They looked for scapegoats, but they wanted substantiating
evidence before they identified them. People knew from their own
experience, and they were often told, that contagion was a cause of
epidemics; and a disease which obviously came in from outside was
easily blamed on strangers. We have seen the suspicion towards foreigners in Norwich in 1579. Fear of plague may also have been a reason
for the attacks on aliens which took place in London in 1593 and
1636: xenophobia can only have been encouraged by the city's view
that the 'filthy keeping' of foreigners' houses was 'one of the greatest
occasions of the plague'.[36] In Liverpool in 1558 there was 'great
murmur and noise that the plague should be brought in . . . by an
Irish man . . . coming sickly from Manchester . . . which after could
not be found true'.[37]

Because of the social incidence of the disease, however, popular
antagonism was rarely directed towards targets higher up the social
scale. The complaint made to the Hampshire sessions against a vicar
who had not shut up his house when there was plague in it, but
behaved 'in a very unneighbourly, malicious and abusive manner', was
necessarily unusual. The scapegoat was normally on the lower margins
of society. There was Widow Smith, whose arrival in Salisbury from
an infected house in 1641 caused great 'clamour', and 'Dumb John',
a beggar selling secondhand (and potentially infected) clothes and
wandering from house to house in York in 1551: he was attacked by
a crowd and had to be defended and given lodging by one of the
aldermen.[38]

The search for those responsible for the introduction or dispersal of plague could thus unite sections of a community against outsiders of one kind or another. It did not always do so, however. In the early stages of an epidemic it might be the members of a well-established household, rather than marginal beggars, who were shunned by people around. Plague could inflame old resentments and be used as a weapon to pay off old scores between neighbours. They refused to bury one another's dead, and accused one another of bringing infection into a street. To allege that someone was infected was as powerful a local slander as the accusation that a man's wife was a whore. Plague could also be a weapon in domestic squabbles, as with the Worcestershire husbandman in 1637 who threatened to go to Presteigne and 'fetch the plague' back to his wife and children.[39]

Sometimes the hysterical outbursts which punctuated epidemics were simple cries of pain, as in the case of the Norwich mother who screamed that she would 'hang or kill her two children' if she was shut up. But expressions of fury and desperation could be dangerously indiscriminate. A woman was whipped in York in 1631 for saying that 'if the sickness would come in fast enough, she would run among the thickest' crowds in town, and another woman was found in Salisbury in 1608 'affirming herself to have the plague' and running 'into divers houses to the great terror of many people'.[40] Some victims of plague may well have turned threats into action and tried to make others share their suffering. In Worcestershire in 1617 a plague suspect thrust himself 'into other men's seats' at church; and a writer in 1721 remembered his mother's story that she caught plague in Worcester in the Civil War when an infected soldier deliberately breathed on her. Pepys similarly heard reports in 1666 of sick people isolated in Westminster leaning out of windows and breathing 'in the faces . . . of well people going by'. 'Poor infected people' in Somerset in 1646 and Portsmouth in 1666 were said to throw rags from plague sores indiscriminately through windows. This is all hearsay and rumour, of course. The only established case of a deliberate attempt to cause plague is the abusive letter containing an infected rag which John Pym opened in the Commons in 1641 – much to the consternation of the House; and that was clearly exceptional.[41] But rumours and threats are sufficient in themselves to show the divisive impact of plague on social relationships at every level.

Since responses to plague were so various it is impossible to depict popular reactions in uniform tones. Instances of neighbourly charity and neighbourly antagonism could both be listed at length, without

our arriving at any reliable balance-sheet. The latter would be more
numerous than the former simply because the sources concentrate on
examples of cruelty and barbarous neglect. Like modern newspapers,
they tell us little about the ordinary acts of kindness which kept life
going in critical times. It should be emphasised also that, even in the
most serious epidemics in England, there were none of those great
panics and scares which seem sometimes to have ravaged Continental
cities. As far as we can tell, there was no hysterical hunt for scapegoats,
no terror of plague sowers, no rumour that plague had been deliberately caused by witches or other agents of the devil.[42] There was not
even any great explosion of prejudice against the social elite, who by
the seventeenth century demonstrably escaped the sufferings of the
poor. There were social and sectional discontents in abundance, as
we have seen; but they never reached the point of mass neurosis. By
comparison with some European societies, the social fabric in England
appears to have been stable and resilient.[43]

This is a relative picture, however. If we must not exaggerate the
social breakdowns caused by plague, neither must we paint idealised
portraits of harmonious English communities. We only need to
compare London or Norwich in the middle of an epidemic with
London or Norwich at other times to see the social strains brought
by plague. Where divisions existed already, as between rich and poor,
magistrates and citizens, masters and servants, the ruptures caused by
plague were quickest and deepest. Where neighbours were already at
odds, disease might be a further cause for conflict. But the need to
preserve oneself against infection could also conflict with the maintenance of previously harmonious relationships between neighbours and
friends, if one participant was infected and the other was not. In that
situation, people had hard choices to make.

It is in this social context that the reactions of the government must
be viewed. When people had to choose between self-preservation and
charitable obligations, the attitudes of those in authority could be
crucial. In 1665 Henry Newcome's cousin fled from London to stay
with him in Lancashire. Newcome decided to turn him away:

> I was sadly put to it, because they proclaimed that none should
> receive either person or goods without the consent of the
> constables . . . I sent to him therefore to stay at his inn for that
> night, till I could speak with the constable; and he weakly took
> it ill, and after would not come to me.[44]

Whether Newcome's behaviour would have been any different without the intervention of the constables, we cannot say. But in this case the voice of authority made it absolutely certain that plague would disrupt family relations. We shall see other examples, in a moment, of government policy exacerbating the social damage done by disease; and it is popular opposition to that policy which demonstrates most clearly that the common people appreciated the need for social solidarity during epidemics and wished to resist some of the pressures which threatened it.

(ii) Protest and disorder

Opportunites for mutual support and consolation were severely curtailed by the restrictions which local and central governments tried to impose on popular behaviour and popular assemblies during epidemics. We have already noticed the deliberate contraction of religious ceremonies, for example. General processions and large assemblies demonstrating repentance stopped after the Reformation. In the early seventeenth century fasts and sermons were shortened and gradually reduced in number. Puritans in Northampton might complain of attempts to 'starve their souls', and town councillors in Hull free Andrew Marvell the elder, who had been shut up, so that he could 'bestow his pains in preaching' in the plague of 1638; but they were fighting a losing battle.[45] By 1665, when one London parish deliberately cut down the number of services, it was not only the infected who had to say their prayers at home.[46]

Not everyone wanted to attend church, as we have seen, but secular assemblies were also banned by authority. The feasts of companies were stopped. So were feasts after mayoral elections, which often extended beyond the oligarchy and were intended, as it was admitted in Winchester, 'for the maintaining and preserving of love and unity among the citizens and rejoicing one with another'.[47] The postponement of the Lord Mayor's Show and the celebration of James I's coronation in 1603 must have caused resentment in London.[48] Prohibition of popular games and efforts to close down alehouses, which frequently occurred during a plague, were still more provocative, removing as they did the commonest convivial occasions which might have preserved some semblance of normal social intercourse.

There was strong resistance. In Nottinghamshire men gathered 'unlawfully' to play football in the middle of an epidemic. In Winchester crowds assembled for 'their habitual bullbaiting and other unlawful exercises' in 1593. Restrictions on normal meetings in Norwich inevitably led to 'unlawful assemblies' in the fields close to the town.[49] There was an obvious incompatibility here between policy and social reality, just as there was when town councils closed down schools but tried at the same time to prevent children playing in the streets.[50] There was also a bland refusal to comprehend popular mentality. Aldermen and councillors could not understand the men in York who met to drink at night 'in these heavisome times of the infection'; they fined them.[51]

The interference of government was most deeply resented when it disturbed the customs surrounding death itself. Searching the bodies of the dead was offensive enough, but it was made doubly so when searchers were instructed to view the corpse alone and 'not suffer any to be then in the chamber with them because they should not be corrupted by any bribe'. In at least one case, the friends of the victim understandably refused to leave the room.[52] The enormous number of deaths during an epidemic produced orders which sought to alter established habits. Lack of room in the churchyard led one London vestry to forbid burials in coffins in 1593, although other local authorities insisted on this practice in order to avoid contagion.[53] When graveyards were filled literally to overflowing, and the 'noisome stench' from them seemed an obvious cause of miasma, burials there could be stopped altogether. New burial grounds were hurriedly licensed in London, especially in 1665, sometimes without consecration.[54] In the provinces, churchyards were sometimes guarded from contamination even more jealously: the churchwardens of Chelmsford stationed armed watchmen on the bridge to prevent corpses being brought from the suburb of Moulsham to their normal place of burial by the parish church.[55] From the 1540s plague corpses had been refused entry to churches and carried straight to the grave; and the logical conclusion was reached in 1666, when the government's new plague orders forbade the burial of plague victims in ordinary churchyards altogether: they were to be treated like excommunicates in death, as they had been in their sickness.[56]

Above all, the government imposed stringent restrictions on attendance at funerals. The national orders of 1578 prescribed the burial of the dead only at dusk, and suggested that ministers officiating should 'be distant from the danger of infection of the person dead, or of the company that shall bring the corpse to the grave'. By 1665 there were regulations in several towns shortening the knells which summoned people to funeral services, and limiting the number who might be present at funerals and burial dinners to the immediate family and a dozen or even fewer 'next neighbours'.[57] There were similar controls on attendance at weddings, christenings and child-births, but crowds at funerals were clearly thought to present the greatest public danger. In 1603 the city marshal of London, an official normally charged with the apprehension of vagrants, was told to keep the number of people present at plague burials down to six. He found it an impossible task. 'The meaner sort' continued to accompany the dead, and attacked the officers who tried to stop them. They were encouraged by ministers 'preaching at funeral sermons and accompanying the corpses', and especially by 'one Mr. Clapham'.[58]

For once Henoch Clapham, the eccentric pamphleteer, had majority opinion firmly on his side. Funeral ceremonies fulfilled important social functions and indispensable psychological ones. The elaborate-ness of a knell, the numbers present at a burial, and the lavishness of a funeral dinner, all marked the social status of the deceased and reconciled his friends and relations to his death. Attendance at funerals was also a public demonstration of communal defiance against plague. One London preacher complained that 'the poorer sort, yea women with young children, will flock to burials, and (which is worse) stand (of purpose) over open graves, where sundry are buried together, that (forsooth) all the world may see that they fear not the plague'. The Lord Mayor himself once recognised the therapeutic value of such an occasion. In 1625 he arranged a public funeral for a captain of the trained bands, with 244 troops in procession, watched by a crowd of thousands. Its purpose was to confute rumours in the country that the city was in total disarray in the face of plague.[59] The Privy Council can scarcely have been pleased; but many citizens must have welcomed this indication that, for a moment, the city fathers felt as they did.

After that, however, the government's campaign against large public funerals was resumed. In 1630 poor mourners were driven away by force: they returned and ignored the risk of infection. Eleven trum-peters were thrown into Newgate in 1636 for marching behind a colleague dead of the plague, 'with trumpets sounded and swords drawn'.[60] In 1665 the Privy Council was still doing everything in its power to stop neighbours and friends following coffins to burial,

including having prohibitions read in every church. The comments of
Pepys and others about the 'madness of people of the town, who . . .
come in crowds along with the dead corpses', show that the effort
again failed utterly.[61] On this point the new public-health policies had
come into conflict with ingrained social habits and deeply respected
moral obligations, and they had been defeated.

In other areas there was the the same conflict and consequently
similar popular resistance; but there was no popular victory because
public opinion was divided. We have seen that plague itself led some
people to shun their neighbours and break moral conventions. While
many would have been appalled by its social implications, others must
have welcomed the order of the aldermen of Hull in 1575 that no
inhabitant should 'approach or go nigh to the doors or windows of
any house infected or suspected to be infected with the . . . sickness,
there to talk with them that be within'.[62] Pesthouses and household
isolation similarly elicited no unanimous opposition. There was resistance nevertheless; and although it naturally came most often from the
victims of these new devices, it was not wholly self-regarding. Its
strength lay in its defiance of perils which many people shared and
its defence of principles which everyone claimed to uphold.

There was sometimes an appealing heroism in it. In 1665 the
mother of a girl isolated in an infected house in Southampton hired
two sailors to rescue her; they succeeded, but one of them was caught
with the girl and they were then shut up afresh.[63] The opposition was
usually less premeditated, however, and almost always immediate. In
Norwich in 1584 'one Watson whose house is visited with the plague
said that if either constable or alderman should come to visit his
house, he would scald them out'. Fifty years later a woman swore 'by
God's blood, that she would break Taylor's head' when he tried to
nail up her house; he took the point and was afterwards dismissed
from his post as watchman for neglecting his duties.[64] In Exeter and
Bristol, in Beverley and in Essex villages, and above all in London,
people refused to be shut up, or broke out of their houses when they
were, hurling abuse at constables and aldermen as they did so.[65]

In some cases people put part of their feelings into their words,
attacking the authorities for breaking the simple rules of charity and
humanity. Robert House of Norwich asked those nailing up his house
in 1631: 'What, will Mr Mayor make my house a pesthouse, or will
he starve me?' A woman whose family was taken to the Salisbury
pesthouse asked Mayor Ivie 'whether [he] came of a woman or a beast

that [he] should do so bloody an act upon poor people in their condition'.[66] Behaviour could also be expressive, even if its meaning was only dimly perceived by the actors. When watchmen in London joined with the inmates of infected houses in 'knocking off padlocks off the doors' and obliterating the red crosses above them, they were seeking to wipe out something of the reality which lay behind the symbols – the cruelty of isolation and the horror of plague.[67] The London constable whose house was infected in 1603, and who assaulted the city marshal and then marched off to see the Lord Mayor, must have had a great deal he wanted to say to him. The men who tried to shut up the Lord Mayor's house in 1665 clearly wanted to give him a taste of his own medicine.[68]

Popular behaviour could carry several meanings at once. The inmates of pesthouses in Worcester and Aylesbury who ripped up fences and gates and used them as fuel, simply needed something to keep them warm;[69] but the women who burned down the pesthouse itself in Salisbury in 1627 and in Colchester in 1631 were engaged in a demonstration at once as direct and as complex as that of the rioters who demolished hedges in the sixteenth century and Dissenting meeting-houses in the eighteenth. The Salisbury arsonist had been incarcerated in the pesthouse herself; in part she expressed the feelings of the inmates. She had other supporters too, however. The erection of the house had been opposed by a crowd of local residents, led by their landlord, Alderman Matthew Bee, who feared that infection would spread to them.[70] Motives in the Colchester case were equally mixed. The pesthouse was burned down, before any epidemic had begun, by a woman who lived next-door; she was no doubt afraid of contagion when there were rumours that plague cases were to be sent there. But she had also been told that she would herself be shut up if the pesthouse was used, and she and her relatives and neighbours protested against the injustice of this.[71] In short, pesthouses were hated as symbols of plague as well as of plague-controls: to attack them was to attack infection and isolation at one and the same time.

This confused but powerful perception of oppression and menace animated the crowds who appeared in the streets of plague-stricken towns. It was not just pesthouses but the whole paraphernalia of public-health regulations which aroused popular antagonism. Every new form of government interference was opposed because it seemed allied to, and as threatening as, the disease itself. Just as Londoners forced their way past an Essex watchman who asked them for certificates of health in 1665, so Dutch sailors rioted in Plymouth and Yarmouth in 1635 when attempts were made to quarantine their ships. In Colchester in the plague of 1626, a crowd gathered in St John's Fields and one man said 'before the next fair there would be another course taken for watchmen'.[72] He might have wished for another course for infection too, but his anger was transferred to a more manageable and better-defined target.

In many respects popular disturbances during epidemics were like crowd behaviour in other circumstances, like food riots in the eighteenth century, for example. They had similar motives, similar participants, and similar claims to legitimacy. They often sought, or were accorded, the approval of people in authority. Aldermen and councillors sometimes opposed plague regulations as individuals;[73] and on occasion, like Alderman Bee in Salisbury, they led popular opposition. An alderman of Norwich, Robert Gibson, was the chief defender of popular celebration of the coronation in 1603, attacking the mayor who tried to control it with 'many reproachful scornful contemptuous and foul speeches'.[74] Gibson was already at odds with his colleagues and unlikely to succeed; but popular pressure could sometimes manipulate political divisions more effectively. Some of the poor in Exeter threatened to appeal to the bishop against his rival, the town council, unless the latter stopped 'cozening' them of their normal poor relief in 1625; the council responded. When ninety householders from Chesterfield planned in 1587 to march to the earl of Shrewsbury, he quickly ordered the local justices to raise an assessment for their relief, lest they 'do some unlawful act'.[75]

In the absence of help or encouragement from the top, respectable artisans and junior officials, those caught in the vital middle ground between magistrates and citizens, took the lead in disturbances. We have seen watchmen and constables helping to undermine the regulations they were supposed to enforce. A barber, a tailor and a shoemaker emerge from the mass whom aldermen and councillors castigated as the 'disorderly poor'. Disorder was accurately attributed to 'a dozen of the middle sort of men' during an epidemic in Manchester in 1645.[76] The rank and file, however, were very often women. A 'troop' of women supported Matthew Bee in Salisbury; the arsonists there and in Colchester were widows; and women were conspicuous in the crowds at London funerals. In 1630 the wives of two tailors in St Martin's Lane, Westminster, abused the justices and encouraged others to break out of their houses; two widows supported them. Two women – both of them dressed as men – led an unlawful assembly one night in Exeter in 1625.[77]

Wives and widows were, of course, more deeply involved with the care of the sick and the support of their neighbours than men; and they may therefore have clung more tenaciously to those social habits and ideals which plague regulations threatened. For, as with food riots in which women also took a leading part, one element in plague disturbances was the defence of traditional social norms and traditional neighbourly obligations, however inarticulately perceived.[78] The five York men who were reported to the town council twice in a fortnight for visiting their sick friends showed their views by their actions.[79] It was left to outside observers to put them into words: the poor thought it a 'matter of conscience' and a 'Christian' duty to visit their neighbours when they were infected. We have seen that these opinions were taken as evidence that common people shared some of Clapham's attitudes; and they certainly had good reason to be fatalistic about their chances during a plague.[80] But they were also reasserting standards of behaviour which might be positive defences against the social consequences of epidemics.

This is not to say that all the common sort held these opinions, still less that they consistently put them into practice. Men refused to pay extra poor rates for the sick and abused those who tried to levy them;[81] sometimes they were the same people who demanded poor relief when they caught plague themselves. If watchmen encouraged the infected to break out, searchers and nurses occasionally ransacked houses and stole the cash, furniture and even bedding of their patients. Householders abused and attacked these officials in order to protect their property as well as their liberty.[82] People broke into houses to loot them, as well as to visit the sick.[83] Disorder could clearly get out of hand, as it did in Exeter and Salisbury in the 1620s and in Manchester in 1605 and 1645. Yet some of the actions of the crowd implied that an alternative to disorder could be found in neighbourly and mutually supportive action. If they did not always practise it, that did not reduce its appeal. When 'Dumb John' was suspected of selling infected clothes in York in 1551, it was Alderman Beane who gave him lodging and the crowd which attacked him. 'Rather than you should be thus disquieted with him', Beane told the crowd, 'let him remain still under mine nose.' It was an eloquent and persuasive gesture, and it was designed to be so. The crowd responded: 'Well worth you, good Mr Beane', they cried.[84]

Magistrates were expected to set this sort of example, not least because their own rhetoric encouraged the assumption that they would reinforce the harmony of the common weal, not disrupt it. As the newspapers said when appealing for charity in 1665, the social elite would surely be sensible of, and respond to, 'a common calamity'.[85] When the policies of government seemed to demonstrate the opposite, they could reasonably be thought to contribute to disorder and be criticised on the government's own ground. Some such allegation seems to have been behind the assertion of a householder shut up in 1631, again in York, who said that 'he could govern as well as any' of the aldermen, 'and that he could have done wiselier' himself.[86]

Equally understandably, governors normally saw things differently. Alderman Beane of York was the exception; his successors in 1631 were typical. They viewed popular disturbances as sedition, and their alternative to disorder was the imposition of stricter, and still more divisive, controls. Right at the start, in 1518, Wolsey was told about popular opposition to the first plague orders: many in London had 'murmured and grudged and also have had seditious words whereby a commotion or rebellion might arise'.[87] At the end, in 1666, the gentry assumed that those who broke out of their houses in Portsmouth were engaged in a 'mutiny': the crowd had opened up the gaol, and it had to be dispersed by the trained bands, who killed one man and wounded three more.[88] Fears of rebellion in fact reached fever pitch in 1665 and 1666. When failure in war and plague at home destroyed the government's credit, it was thought that popular discontent might be whipped up by sectaries and Dissenters who welcomed disease as a punishment for their enemies. 'Now is the time, if we will stir', one Yorkshireman said, echoing this view; 'for the Anabaptists and Quakers are not afraid of the plague.' Yet in general the government's informers found that Dissenters wished only to pray together for the removal of pestilence, and objected when their meetings were broken up.[89] Two different perceptions of how best to maintain public confidence and prevent disorder in the face of plague clashed.

Little change can be discerned on the popular side as these confrontations were rehearsed over the period. Behaviour and attitudes remained much the same. It would be absurd to suggest that government policies destroyed either the practices or the ideal of a neighbourly society. The practices had never existed in urban reality, least of all during epidemics; and popular attachment to the ideal seems to have been as strong in the seventeenth century as it had been in the sixteenth. It had to be voiced more often, however, because the government tightened the screw. The government's responses did develop. Far from deterring further regulation, successive disorders encouraged it; and so the vicious spiral in which public disturbances and efforts at control chased one another grew ever narrower.

(iii) Social control

Central and local governors were preoccupied during epidemics with concepts, not of neighbourliness, but of 'order'. The word was constantly reiterated in documents concerning plague, in contexts which show that it carried two meanings: command and direction, on the one hand; tidiness, peace and quiet, on the other. The same word covered both because they were inseparable: one followed from the other. Thus the classic text of authority, the national plague *Orders* of 1578 and after, ended with a resounding condemnation of the fact that the queen's subjects had previously been left in 'very disorder ... for lack of direction'. The London regulations of 1583 were endorsed: 'Orders to be set down of the Lord Mayor for repressing of disorders.' Thomas Lodge's treatise of 1603 expanded on the 'order and policy that ought to be held in a city during the plague time', while a proclamation of the same year asserted that plague had spread throughout the realm 'through lack of order' – in both senses.[90]

The word sometimes retained overtones which did not quite leave it as naked as the government intended. It might imply harmony between individuals and social groups, each with reciprocal rights and duties. Governors could be urged to stay in infected localities in terms which implied the maintenance of that sort of balanced social order. Charles I would not allow the bishop of Carlisle to leave his diocese in 1636, because 'he thought it unreasonable that a main pillar of the country should be absent in such needful times'; and Wentworth said that the people of York 'took much comfort' from his presence in 1631: 'They conceive they are much the better for my stay amongst them.' Wentworth's intent was plain from his elaboration of this ambiguous remark, however: 'I think they are much more orderly than they would be under the government of the mayor alone.' The intention was even clearer by 1665, though still occasionally expressed with some hesitation, as in a newspaper report of plague precautions in Newark: 'We keep strict watches here and hereabouts to all purposes,

although in some cases perchance not in any respect more necessary
than to uphold the custom and habit of good discipline.'[91]

'Rule' was a similar term, echoing in the context of epidemics with
mixed but consistent associations. The mayor of York made no bones
about appealing to his colleagues' magisterial rather than charitable
aspirations when he asked them to remain in 1604:

> The infection doth so greatly increase in this city that unless we
> the magistrates have great care and do take pains in the governing
> and ruling of this city, and in taking order for the relieving of
> them, the poorer sort will not be ruled.[92]

In 1631 the justices in Huntington, just outside the same city, reported
to Wentworth that they found the infected 'very unruly; yet we so
prevailed what by threats and other persuasions to submit themselves
to the will of God'. 'The unruliness of infected persons and want of
government' drove people out of Manchester in 1605.[93] *Rules and
Orders* – the evocative title of the final plague regulations of 1666 –
had behind it the ambition to regulate and direct much more than
plague itself.

It is not mere playing with words either if we return to a point
made in Chapter 2: disorder and unruliness of all kinds were
commonly conceived to be both physical and moral sources of disease.
In Cranbrook in 1597 plague could be seen in a house 'out of which
much thievery was committed', in the home of 'a pot companion and
his wife noted much for incontinency', and in inns and alehouses,
'places then of great misorder: so that God did seem to punish that
himself which officers did neglect'. It was carried by 'lewd women' into
York and Hitchin, and spread in a 'lawless alehouse' in Hampshire
and Somerset.[94] Preachers' association of plague with the 'sin of the
suburbs' and of the poor, and their attacks on idle vagrants, drunkards,
alehouses, plays and popular games, therefore supported magistrates
whose public-health regulations included control of precisely the same
people and assemblies.[95] That was one reason why religious interpretations of plague were welcomed even by authorities who were anxious
about their fatalistic implications. The quest for godly discipline could
give powerful support to the administrative battle against plague. It is
important to recognise also that the relationship worked the other
way: the need to control plague could justify a whole programme of
social and moral reform. The two imperatives were never separated.

Public-health policies were part and parcel of a general drive towards greater social control.[96]

The connection was closest in the minds of Puritan magistrates, for whom even attempts to limit funeral knells and funeral crowds during epidemics had a moral and theological purpose.[97] The 'reformation' which Sherfield and Ivie wished to push through in Salisbury after the plague of 1627 was paralleled elsewhere. The mayor of Plymouth wrote to his counterpart in Exeter in the same year, after both cities had been devastated by plague, expressing the hope that they might 'by reformation of ourselves and as far as in us lies of the people in both places, provide that the like or greater judgement may be prevented'. Robert Jenison similarly wanted to make Newcastle and other towns 'Cities of God' in order to avert his 'overflowing scourge of plague'.[98] Less godly magistrates would not have used the same language. Yet they would have agreed with many of the practical implications of reformation. In London, for example, the threat of plague was used to justify the repression of brothels, taverns and poor tenements which 'pestered' the suburbs with 'disorder and uncleanness'. Mayerne's treatise on plague presented to Charles I in 1631 began with the premise that 'order is the life and soul of all things'; and it made it clear that plague was a threat brought by 'unprofitable and wasteful' vagrants, by 'idle and naughty' assemblies and alehouses, in short by the 'unruly, base sort of people'. John Ivie was not the only magistrate to feel himself threatened during an epidemic by 'all the drunkards, whoremasters, and lewd fellows'; or to conclude that his first priority must be to control the 'great unjust rude rabble'.[99]

These reactions were not confined to magistrates: they were the property of many of the polite and respectable who felt themselves threatened by infection. If the poor did not derive an aggressive consciousness of social divisions from the differential incidence of plague, the rich certainly did. It was from them that outbursts of what might reasonably be described as class prejudice came. Some of the citizens of Oxford complained in 1603 that the increase of plague was due to 'the most lewd and dissolute behaviour of some base and unruly inhabitants'. Twenty householders in Chester had thought the same thirty years earlier.[100] A tavern and a bowling alley were sources of infection offensive to 'many better minded neighbours' in Westminster; so were 'divers poor nasty people' who should be moved 'out of their hovels to the sheds, there to air their bedding as also themselves'.[101] By 1665 it was axiomatic that the poor should be blamed for a disease which was demonstrably not socially random. If it spread beyond them it was due to the 'carelessness of the common sort of people' and 'the incorrigible licence of multitudes'. People in Kent knew very well that the poor of St Giles-in-the-Fields, London, were responsible for the threat to the rest of the country in 1665.[102]

Justices of the peace could not have ignored this combination of empirical observation and social prejudice, even if they had wanted to. Like the aldermen of Norwich in 1603, they had to listen when the 'better sort of people' were 'much grieved and offended that the under sort would not be stayed nor by the magistrates restrained'.[103] Their response was the public-health programme described in this book; and it is clear that it was designed with the poor in mind. We have seen that it marched forward in step with the poor law. Its recipes – pesthouses and household support – were akin to the workhouses and outdoor relief prescribed for the idle and impotent. The Act of 1604 treated the disorderly sick as vagrants, and one of the first charges on municipal finances during an epidemic was often a whipping post.[104] Pesthouses and sheds in the fields were for the 'meaner sort' not for their betters.[105] When regulations did impinge on polite society, they had to be handled carefully. Plague in Cambridge unfortunately compelled the council of Beverley to order that local boys in college there should be shut up if they came back home: the execution of this potentially offensive order was left to the tact and discretion of the mayor.[106] Tact was not necessary very often.

This view of plague as part of the broader problems of poverty and disorder unquestionably strengthened the resolve of governors in the pursuit of novel policies. It helps to explain why they persisted with the isolation of households despite intellectual uncertainties, despite the financial and administrative costs it imposed, and despite the fact that in the end its critics alleged that the policy was ineffective, even perhaps counterproductive. It appealed because it was consistent with other endeavours which brought greater government interference in everyday life and sought control through order and rule. By the beginning of the seventeenth century plague was recognised as one element in that generalised threat which the rough 'poorer sort' presented to the respectable sections of English society; and the measures taken against it were primarily intended to defuse the danger. In a real sense, therefore, the effort to control infection was secondary. In adopting plague orders local magistrates were motivated by a less precisely focused but unshakable conviction that social problems as a whole demanded firm treatment. This might account for what is otherwise puzzling in our story: the growth in this area of a practical and optimistic attitude towards the possibilities of human action and a decline in the appeal of supernatural interpretations, even before there were reliable technical solutions to the problem of epidemic disease.[107]

As presented so far, however, the argument threatens to push the phenomenon of plague too far into the background. It may not have been clearly separated from other social dangers; but it did have a singular force of its own. We can, indeed, turn the argument around, and assert that it was precisely because the 'base sort of people' were seen as carriers of contagion that they were so much feared in the sixteenth and seventeenth centuries. Infectious disease was itself an important stimulus to new methods for the regulation and relief of the poor.[108] If we want to go to the root of the matter, therefore, if we wish to dissect this complex mixture of motives (which contemporaries never did), and to identify the essential reason for policies of isolation, it is not to an objective scientific search for instruments against infection that we should turn. Neither, however, should we stop when we have demonstrated that contemporaries wished to deal with the general problems of poverty and disorder by segregation and discipline. More basic still was a primitive revulsion from plague and its victims.

The power of that impulse becomes evident once we compare plague policies with other social policies and note the differences. For despite connections and similarities, there were also important contrasts. Government reactions to plague were not akin to government reactions to harvest crises, for example. The accepted programme for the latter, as enshrined in the books of dearth orders published between 1586 and 1630, was consistent with popular aspirations. Prices were to be kept low and food provided for the poor; social harmony was maintained. Far from being in conflict with the morality of the crowd, the dearth orders became a bible for it.[109] Even the poor laws insisted to an extent on the obligations of the rich towards the poor. There were strict punishments for vagrants, but vagrants were in practice marginal men and women who could reasonably be defined as outside the boundaries of the common weal;[110] and there were doles for the impoverished who were safely within them.

In the case of plague, on the other hand, there can be no doubt where the stress of public policy lay: on isolation, on the forcible exclusion of large numbers of people from most of the consolations and many of the material benefits of social support. Quarantine enforced an almost ritual purification of the social order, and defined social roles more rigidly than the institutions of the poor law ever did. The 'great confinement' of the early modern period, which some historians have found in the definition and treatment of insanity or idleness, in fact lay here: in the effort to banish from public view the victims of plague. In England at least, madhouses and workhouses were arguably never large enough to affect or even reflect the attitudes of a whole society: lunatics and layabouts were often tolerated and treated with some humanity.[111] For as long as plague lasted, the segregation imposed on the infected impinged much more on contemporary consciousness and testified to the instinctive desire of the healthy to shut the menace away. Contagious disease made all the difference to the response to social need.

Not all contagious diseases evoked the same response as plague, however, and comparison with other epidemics shows the importance of the various characteristics of the disease discussed in the second part of this book. Typhus provoked no similar reactions, partly because mortality was not so concentrated in time. Neither did smallpox, for the same reason. Although households were often isolated before the introduction of inoculation, the practice being borrowed from plague policy, there were never so many of them.[112] Cholera seems superficially more comparable. Measures adopted to deal with it in the nineteenth century proved as controversial as those used against plague in the seventeenth. Yet in England the authorities were careful not to invoke the strictest measures of quarantine, because of the popular opposition they would arouse.[113] They may have learned something from seventeenth-century experience; but it is also the case that cholera was not the great killer that plague was. There were only 53,000 deaths in the whole of England and Wales in its worst outbreak, fewer than the number of deaths from plague in London alone in 1665.[114] Moreover, like typhus, cholera very rarely spread beyond the poor to the social elite. When it came to the point the threat was not great enough to persuade the government that savage policies were worth the opposition they provoked.

Yet high mortality and the rapid spread of infection are not in themselves enough to account for reactions to plague. The great influenza epidemic of 1557 to 1559 manifested both to an extreme degree. It affected all classes of society, but there was no attempt to control its spread. In only two towns have efforts to isolate the sick in 1558 been discovered, in Liverpool and Lincoln; and in each case the disease was thought to be 'plague'.[115] In part, of course, plague was uniquely horrible because of its symptoms. But that was not all. For what was special about plague was the fact that it combined high mortality and unpredictable incidence with a particular, and increasingly obvious, association with poverty. The first two features caused shock, anxiety and insecurity. The third gave these emotions an outlet: it provided an external target against which they could be directed, and moreover a target which was already being attacked for other reasons.

At the level of the social elite, therefore, fatalism and impotence were unlikely consequences of the disasters brought by plague, though they might be a response to the very different catastrophe of 1557–9. Positive action was possible: the destruction, or incarceration, of everything which had been in contact with the disease – clothes, bedding, houses and the victims themselves. None of this could have been undertaken with enthusiasm if the impact of plague had been, or had appeared to be, totally random: hence, perhaps, the inertia of the London aldermen in 1563.[116] But it was increasingly easy as the incidence of infection in certain disorderly neighbourhoods became obvious, without being invariable. Plague became a pressing social problem and a powerful influence on perceptions of the social gulf between rich and poor – all the more pressing and powerful because it did not always stay within its socially determined limits.

The unique tragedy of plague lay in this complex interaction of disease and society. The results were divisive in every possible way, combining all the cruelties which one man might inflict on another. Thomas Swadling rightly thought that plague was worse than leprosy, with which it was often compared, because it brought the two greatest punishments in common and civil law on its victims: outlawry and excommunication.[117] Other contemporaries were equally aware that the social consequences were profoundly destructive. 'A commonwealth is a body, and one member methinks should nourish another', argued Benjamin Spenser in a protest against the way Londoners were treated in time of plague. Henry Holland, a London clergyman, urged his readers not to ignore the 'duties of humanity' in their households and neighbourhood during epidemics: 'For if we break these bonds, I see not how human societies may continue.'[118] They spoke in vain. The plain fact was that the crises brought by plague did not permit responses which increased social solidarity; they forcefully encouraged those which undermined it.

Chapter 12

The end of plague 1665–1722

> We may keep our shipping to strict quarantine, we may form lines, and cut off all communication with the infected, we may barricado up our cities and our towns, and shut ourselves up in our houses, Death will come up into our windows, and enter into our palaces, and cut off our children from without, and the young men from the streets.
>
> William Hendley, *Loimologia Sacra* (1721)[1]

As it turned out, William Hendley was wrong. Death in the form of plague never returned to England once the epidemic beginning in 1665 in London had run its course. There were recurrent scares that it would, the greatest of them at the time Hendley was writing, between 1720 and 1722 when there was plague in Marseilles. But the fears proved unfounded. England had been delivered from pestilence. No contemporary knew why that had happened, or could be sure that deliverance was permanent, and historians have similarly been unable to agree on the reasons for it. The end of plague remains the greatest of the mysteries surrounding the disease.

No final solution to the mystery can be advanced here. The problem, and therefore its answer, extends beyond England to embrace the whole of western Europe, if not the world.[2] Plague disappeared from most of Europe in the years between 1656 and 1721, and it may even have withdrawn from parts of Asia at the same time. English evidence may throw light on that development but it can only be partial. The issue cannot be avoided altogether, however. We must seek a tentative hypothesis to explain the end of plague if we are to make any final judgment on the measures which were taken against it. If quarantine and the isolation of the sick helped to eliminate the disease after 1665, they may also have helped to control it earlier: contemporaries would have stumbled on viable solutions. In short, the problem of the disappearance of plague is associated with that vital question which we have so far left largely unanswered: whether the new anti-plague devices adopted by the English government in the sixteenth and seventeenth centuries could have had any instrumental effect. Were they potentially effective mechanisms, vitiated only by the enormous obstacles to their implentation? Or were they no more than empty rituals, which many people rightly resisted?

There can be no unqualified answer to these questions. Uncertainty is dictated both by our ignorance of the reasons for global changes in disease patterns, and by the fact that what we do know shows complexity not simplicity. An epidemic of plague, like an epidemic of any other disease, depended on a multitude of variables: climate, the density of human, flea and rodent populations and contacts between them, proximity to sources of infection, and so on. The presence or absence of an epidemic could be determined by changes in any one or more than one of these. It would therefore be as simplistic to search for a single explanation for changes in the distribution of plague as for a single explanation for a political or an industrial revolution. It will be argued that the actions of government sometimes played a decisive role in stopping the spread of infection. But they did not invariably do so, any more than heavy taxation and centralised bureaucracies invariably produce political crises in history, or Calvinist ethics the growth of capitalism. It is not just our present ignorance of the epidemiology of disease in the past which dictates caution when discussing changes in the incidence of plague, therefore; it is the nature of historical circumstance.

Uncertainty and complexity are understandably annoying to the historian. But they are also salutary and particularly in this case. They help us to understand the perplexed reactions of contemporaries. If the measures taken against plague worked in some circumstances and not in others, if they prevented epidemics when other conditions were favourable and not when they were not, we can see why Englishmen in the past disagreed so violently about them. For contemporaries were no less tempted than some historians have been to pick out single variables to account for the whole phenomenon of plague; and they were equally inclined to underestimate the number of contingent factors involved in it. This search for simple answers is most evident in the great plague scare of 1720 to 1722, which will be considered at the end of this chapter. Then reactions were determined by the same complex of interests and attitudes which had shaped responses to plague over the previous two centuries.

(i) Good fortune or good management?

Most of the measures taken by governments to control the spread of the disease were obviously directed towards human agents.[3] It was the transmission of infection by men or their goods which was attacked by quarantine and isolation. Some effort was made to stop domestic animals, dogs and cats, moving from house to house and carrying plague with them, but this did nothing to stop rodents; rather the reverse. In order to judge the potential of contemporary policies for the control of plague, therefore, we need to determine the relative importance of men and rats in the origin of epidemics. If men played the major role, those policies may have had an effect. If rats played the major part, it was unlikely to have been good management and more likely to have been good fortune which protected households, towns or countries from plague.

Unfortunately, as we saw in the first chapter, there is still considerable uncertainty about several aspects of the aetiology and epidemiology of plague which are relevant here. In particular there is the problem of whether the disease could be carried by the human flea, *Pulex irritans*, from man to man, as well as by the rat flea, *Xenopsylla cheopis*, normally moving from rat to man and only occasionally from one man to another.[4] Some of the controversial points can perhaps be circumvented for our purposes, however, if we consider the normal course of an epidemic in early modern England, using the evidence provided in earlier chapters. Four separate stages can be distinguished: the introduction of plague into England; its movement from town to town; its spread within a single town or village; and finally, its transmission between one member of a household and another. Men and rats played a part in all of these, but their relative significance varied from stage to stage.

Human agency was vital at the first stage. Plague was always imported into Britain. We have seen the role of ports – Hull, Yarmouth and Plymouth as well as London – at the beginning of each epidemic wave. The disease might linger for several years afterwards, as it spread from one town to another; but in the end it disappeared and had to be reintroduced from outside.[5] The origins of English plagues are therefore to be found in ships from infected ports overseas, often in the Low Countries: they brought infective fleas, either in their merchandise or on infected rats or, conceivably, in the clothing of infected passengers and crew, into English harbours.

It is probable that men were also important at the second stage, in the long-distance movement of plague from ports to other towns, though there can be less certainty here. There may have been cases, like those documented in modern outbreaks, in which wild rodents carried the disease from field to field in haphazard fashion across the countryside. Against this, however, we have noted that infected villages tended to lie along main routes of human transport, on rivers and roads; that plague often spread very quickly from one town to another, much more quickly than one would expect if wild rodents had been the carriers; and that there is ample contemporary reference to particular individuals or bundles of merchandise being responsible for initiating a local outbreak. The black rat itself is known to be reluctant to move far from its nest, and the balance of the evidence suggests that fleas on the backs of men, in bales of cloth or trunks of clothes in their carts, boats and baggage, formed the usual link between one rat population and another.[6]

Rats were much more important at the third and fourth stages, in sustaining a major epidemic and in spreading plague within a household. This is emphatically not to say that they were solely responsible. The human flea, *Pulex irritans*, can transmit infection directly from one man to another, provided that it is present in sufficient numbers and provided that the first human host has sufficient plague bacilli in his blood-stream.[7] Both conditions must often have been satisfied in Tudor and Stuart England. The movement of fleas from man to man was easy in a society in which the poor were short of beds and bedding as well as of clothes, and in which even the rich often slept together in crowded inns. In these circumstances, indeed, *X. cheopis* might also readily spread plague directly between one man and another. There is no reason to doubt contemporary observations that people caught plague when they stayed in inns and found themselves sharing beds with unsuspected plague victims.[8]

Nevertheless, there is persuasive indirect evidence that major epidemics in towns had an epizootic foundation. The persistent and heavy incidence of plague in suburbs and back alleys suggests that urban epidemics had their roots in the close proximity of rodents and humans in the poor tenements of these neighbourhoods. The plague of 1645 in Bristol may be particularly instructive in this regard. Although it occurred in siege conditions, when flight was impossible, it was not equally serious over the whole city. By contrast, in 1643 an epidemic of typhus did spread evenly over the town. Lice apparently dispersed typhus through the whole population in 1643. Since fleas did not transmit plague in a similar way two years later, they are unlikely to have been the most important vectors of the disease. A similar conclusion might be drawn from the way in which plague often missed out odd houses in its progress along a street: close contact between neighbours did not guarantee infection. Even at the fourth stage, within a household it seems likely that rats played an important role, since it has been noted that there was no correlation between the level of mortality and household size. The number of people present in a house does not seem to have determined the extent of infection. The number of rats, and the opportunities available for their fleas to find human hosts, probably did.[9]

Both inter-human and rat–human transmission should therefore be granted a role in English epidemics. When there were only a few sporadic cases of plague in one or two households, as in Leicester and Reading in 1578, rodents may well not have been involved.[10] Fleas had not moved from men to rats, or if they had, they had not sparked off an epizootic. The transmission of infection then depended on close contact between men; and once the presence of plague was recognised, that was more easily avoided than contact with the unseen and unsuspected danger of dead and dying rodents. In major epidemics in large towns like London, Norwich or Bristol, on the other hand, when there were clearly separate foci of infection in different, widely spaced parishes, there can be little doubt that the human disease had a rodent base. It might be communicated directly between members of a family and perhaps between neighbours, but plague was also moving irregularly from house to house with rats searching for food; and the epidemic could not end until the rat population had been largely destroyed by it.[11]

This is a tentative, not a definitive picture of the origins of plague epidemics, and it may be amended by future study of particular outbreaks. Speculative as in parts it is, however, it suggests two firm conclusions which are supported by all the available evidence, and which are indeed applicable to some degree to all epidemic diseases. First, it was much easier to prevent the introduction of plague in the first place than to control its spread once it had gained hold in epizootic or epidemic form. If ships from infected ports overseas or passengers and goods leaving infected English towns could be stopped, those epidemic waves which swept across Europe and then across England might be cut short. In other words, quarantine of shipping, which the English government developed late, and watches at town gates, which it took for granted, were potentially more effective weapons than household isolation, to which so much of the government's public-health campaign was directed.

There is a second point, which makes it difficult to test this hypothesis, however. When infection did arrive, an epidemic of plague depended on the conjunction of a whole set of circumstances, and therefore to an extent on chance. It required initial transmission by infective fleas – and not all infected fleas are infective – not just to one man or one rat's nest, but to several. It needed an environment where rats and men were crowded together and where fleas were common and taken for granted. There must be the warm climate necessary for the survival and reproduction of the fleas themselves. And all these conditions would need to be met in each successive town visited by plague if there was to be a series of major epidemics.

This explains some of the haphazard features which we have observed in the incidence of plague in the sixteenth and seventeenth centuries: variations in mortality rates, for example, and the way in which in every epidemic wave some towns and parishes escaped entirely. Low mortality might sometimes occur because rodent populations had not had time to re-establish themselves after an earlier epizootic, as perhaps in the cases of London and Norwich in 1630 and 1631, five years after major epidemics.[12] Towns might also escape simply because infective fleas happened not to arrive, or having arrived not to find new human or animal hosts; or because plague invaded so late in the year that cold weather snuffed it out before more than a handful of cases had developed. Even without government intervention, there was a large range of possible outcomes once the plague bacillus had been introduced into an English town.

As a result, the historian can never be certain whether it was good management or good fortune which prevented a serious outbreak of plague in any particular instance. He cannot reconstruct a convincing controlled experiment, comparing the epidemic experience of towns where public controls were imposed and those where they were not. The variables involved are too many; and even when administrative action was taken, we can never judge how efficiently the regulations were enforced. They were certainly often evaded, as we have seen. People slipped past the watches or bribed them, and goods from London were smuggled into other towns.[13] What we can do, however, is examine probabilities, on the assumption that some kinds of human action could raise the threshold which plague had to surmount, and so reduce the limits within which mere chance operated. While never wholly effective, efforts to prevent the movement of people and goods from infected places restricted mobility to some degree. Watch and ward at a town's gates cut down the number of infective fleas arriving and thus reduced the risk that one of them would spread plague to native rodent and human populations. It was not infallible, but it could be decisive; and the more rigorous the measures taken, the more likely they were to succeed.

We can see examples both of obvious failure and of apparent success in 1665 and 1666. In Exeter the normal precautions of cancelling fairs and arranging watches against men and merchandise coming from London appear to have succeeded: there was no plague in the city.[14] In Norwich, however, they conspicuously failed. A ban on imports and immigrants from infected towns was first imposed in July 1665. It was lifted in November, in spite of a few cases of plague outside and inside St Benedict's Gate, because no major epidemic had developed. When mortality increased once more, early in 1666, the watch was tightened up again; but by then it was too late. Plague had probably already taken hold of the rat population, and from June to September it ravaged all the poorer parishes of the city.[15] There were several reasons for Norwich's misfortune. It was threatened from more directions than Exeter: there had to be orders against travellers from Yarmouth and then from Colchester, as well as from London. The corporation records suggest that the watchmen were more negligent than those in Devon. Most important of all, perhaps, the city was physically less easy to defend than Exeter against an invasion by disease, just as it had been less easy to defend against peasant revolt in 1549. Its walls did not extend round the whole perimeter, and guards at the gates could be circumvented without much difficulty.[16]

Even well-walled cities often had problems in preventing the introduction of plague, since their extra-mural suburbs remained vulnerable. Exeter's suburban parish of St Sidwell had proved its Achilles heel in earlier epidemics;[17] and it was perhaps good fortune rather than the watch which protected it in 1665 and 1666. Walls still remained a useful barrier, however, hindering the passage of domestic rats across them, and presenting opportunities for the control of human movement too. The case of Bristol suggests that energetic action could sometimes confine plague to extra-mural suburbs and shield the inner city.

The council there imposed a strict watch against Londoners in June 1665, both at the gates and on main roads at the outer limits of the built-up area. It failed. By the end of 1665 there were cases of plague in Pile Street and St Philip's parish, both outside the walls, and the outer watch was abandoned in February 1666, leaving only guards at the gates. In the spring there were more plague cases, and the council had to isolate and support their families. Yet there was no epidemic disaster like that in Norwich. Less than 100 people appear to have died of plague, and the vast majority of them lived outside the walls, in St Philip's and St James's parishes. There was only a handful of cases in the inner city: five suspected plague-deaths in St Nicholas's and St Stephen's parishes and two or three more certain victims in Tucker Street in St Thomas's.[18] The fate of Bristol was probably balanced on a knife-edge in the spring of 1666: if fleas had spread plague from men to many of the rats in St Thomas's and St Nicholas's there would no doubt have been a serious epidemic. But continuous watches at the walls and the isolation of the few infected households within them had reduced the number of occasions on which that might happen.

A still better-documented example of plague being held at bay is provided by York in 1631, where we have seen Sir Thomas Wentworth taking firm control. As in Norwich in 1665, plague could be observed approaching from more than one direction, from Lancashire as well as from Lincolnshire; and once again it could not be prevented from infecting outlying villages like Huntington and then the suburb of Walmgate. But it was kept outside the walls by prompt magisterial intervention, Wentworth insisting that an epidemic might 'be the easier prevented in the beginnings than hereafter'. Goods coming from infected parts of London were traced and burnt. Suburban houses were shut up when infected, and so were the houses of people who had been in contact with them. When cases of plague were suspected within the walls, their houses were also shut up and in some instances, though not in all, the suspects were quickly removed to extra-mural pesthouses. We do not know how many victims there were altogether, but there cannot have been many in the centre of town, since the parish registers show no sign of an abnormal increase in mortality.[19] The evidence suggests that plague had not reached the rats of the inner city.

York was in many respects exceptional, and not only because of Wentworth's foresight and drive. Throughout the sixteenth and seventeenth centuries its council was unusually, possibly uniquely, active against the threat of infection. As early as 1536 it insisted on having a certificate of health before it would admit a stranger from Maldon, where plague was suspected, a practice not common in other towns for another hundred years. Similarly, the careful tracing of contacts which was undertaken in 1631, and again in 1637–8, cannot be paralleled anywhere else in England at this date.[20] It was helped too by its still intact walls and by its geographical position, further removed from London and the Continent than many towns. All these factors worked together to ensure that the city had fewer serious epidemics than any other town of comparable size in Tudor and Stuart England.

Even so, York's case does suggest that contemporary mechanisms for the control of plague were not without empirical justification. They could work in England, just as they seem often to have worked on the Continent in the seventeenth and early eighteenth centuries.[21] They could keep plague from penetrating a town's defences, and their widespread use in the national alert of 1665 and 1666 may well explain why many English towns and villages escaped serious epidemics then, although they had not done so in earlier waves of infection beginning in 1603 and 1625.[22] Furthermore, we can see that the isolation of the infected could also be useful in the early stages of an epidemic. It was clearly better to move the sick and their contacts away from their homes, to locations outside the walls, than to shut them all up together with domestic rats; the government's increasing preference in the seventeenth century for pesthouses over household isolation was eminently sensible. But even the more common practice of shutting up houses would be likely to reduce the risk of further infection to some degree, when there were only a few cases. It limited the number of human and rodent hosts available to infective fleas. Plague might be confined to one or two households or even, though this could not be guaranteed, to one or two rats' nests.

If these measures failed, however, as they very often did, there could be little point in persevering with them. Once plague had spread to several streets and gained a hold among rats in different parts of a city, household segregation could not hold it back, even if it could have been enforced. There were too many opportunities for rat–flea–rat and then rat–flea–man transmission. The only recipe for self-preservation then, as contemporaries well understood, was flight. The question to be asked in the circumstances of established infection was not whether household quarantine was useful, but whether it was positively detrimental, whether it increased mortality.

It is probable that it did, although it is impossible to prove the assertion. A comparison of mortality rates in places where isolation was practised and where it was not would tell us little, since there might be many other reasons for local variations. Differences in the degree to which deaths were concentrated in household or family groups may tell us more, however. It is notable that the household incidence of plague was sometimes unusually high when people were forcibly restrained from escaping from infection. We have seen that between 40 per cent and 70 per cent of all burials during an epidemic of plague occurred in families which had three or more deaths; and the proportions were highest in cases where it appears that some form of quarantine was attempted. In Salisbury, those families which were 'kept in' and relieved by the city in the epidemic of 1604 probably did stay more or less isolated: they would not have been given financial support if they had not. It is notable, therefore, that while 42 per cent of all burials in the town occurred in family groups of three or more, 61 per cent of the deaths in the isolated households were similarly concentrated. Even more strikingly, the figure was as high as 72 per cent in Eyam when the whole village was isolated in 1666.[23] It is hard to believe that the proportions would have been as great if people had been able to move themselves or their wives and children away.

In the Eyam instance, the slaughter of whole families would have been defended by contemporaries with the argument that it helped to preserve neighbouring villages. There was justification for that view: increased suffering in Eyam was arguably the price that had to be paid to prevent the medium- and long-distance transmission of plague from there. There was much less foundation, however, for the argument that household isolation in the poorer parts of cities protected the more prosperous quarters. Once an epidemic had begun, the rich had more potent defences than that: their relative freedom from fleas and their distancing from rats in large houses. At the height of an epidemic, the strict confinement of the healthy with the sick did more harm than good. On balance, therefore, it seems clear that resources were misdirected. Some of the effort invested in household quarantine would have been better spent tightening up watches in advance, and establishing *cordons sanitaires* round whole towns rather than round single houses. Controls on movement from infected communities were developing rapidly in the seventeenth century; but even in 1665 they were not as complete and therefore not as successful as they were in Italy.[24] Wentworth was right: early prevention was easier than later cure.

Yet it is anachronistic to judge contemporary reactions with all the benefits of hindsight. Contemporaries did not distinguish between watches outside gates and watches outside houses: both were directed against infection, and they were generally accepted or rejected together. We can now see that the proponents and the opponents of public policies each had cases which were intelligible and defensible. In the early stages of an epidemic, household segregation, like watch and ward, sometimes paid off; and that supported the hypothesis that 'infection' between men explained plague. At the same time, along with watch and ward, isolation often failed; and then the alternative explanation that the roots of an epidemic lay in 'miasma', in the polluted air of certain localities, seemed justified. As long as the role of the rat was unacknowledged, people could scarcely be expected to distinguish clearly between the circumstances which favoured success and those which did not: between the importance of human trans- mission in the introduction of plague in the first place, and the equally vital and far more intractable part played by rats and a congested and unhygienic urban environment in sustaining a major epidemic.

This distinction between, as it were, first cause and necessary conditions is also useful when we come to consider the part played by public policies in the final disappearance of plague from England. Most of the explanations which have been put forward to account for that event can be divided into two groups: those which seek to show why plague never reached England (or western Europe) in the first place; and those which purport to show why, if it did reach England (or western Europe), no serious epidemic developed. The first concern human actions, and especially the use of quarantine against infected ships. The second relate to improvements in the urban environment which reduced the likelihood that men would be infected by fleas from rats. There is also a third category of explanation: the hypothesis that the disease itself changed its nature in the later seventeenth century, as the relationship between the micro-organism and its animal, insect or human hosts evolved.[25]

Although none of these explanations can be rejected out of hand, those in the second and third categories – relating to the environment and the development of the micro-organism – worked, if at all, only in the long term. Moreover, they do not explain the precise chrono-

logical and geographical patterns described by plague as it disappeared
from western Europe. Although it is known that many diseases change
their nature over time, there can obviously be no direct historical
evidence of mutations in the plague bacillus. It is evident, however,
that plague could still produce major mortalities in those parts of
Europe where it occurred after 1670 – in some of the Baltic ports in
the second decade of the eighteenth century, in Marseilles in 1720
and in Moscow as late as 1771.[26] There is thus no sign of any decline
in the disease's infectivity or virulence in the later seventeenth century.
There are similar objections to the argument that a build-up of human
or rodent resistance to the disease explains its withdrawal. If that were
so, one would expect plague to disappear first from those towns which
it had most often visited, where there were few susceptible humans
or rodents left. But the reverse was the case. In England, it was not
London which escaped serious mortality in 1665–6 but ports like
Hull, Newcastle and Bristol, and towns like Exeter and York, which
had been much less often infected in the past.

There is more to be said for the importance of improvements in
the environment. More frequent changes of linen as standards of
living rose in the later seventeenth and early eighteenth centuries no
doubt freed many early modern Englishmen from the hosts of fleas
which were a necessary condition for major urban epidemics. Equally,
houses built of brick separated rats from men, and in the end, in the
eighteenth century, removed favourable ecological conditions for the
black rat and encouraged the growth of brown rat populations. As
early as 1652 the London bricklayers themselves pointed out that the
substitution of brick for timber would reduce the risk of plague: they
thought this benefit would come from the disappearance of houses
with overhanging stories 'stifling' the streets, though they also noted
that brick would be a better protection against infestation by vermin.[27]

These changes worked gradually, however. We have seen evidence
of their impact before 1665, in the withdrawal of plague from the
residential areas of the social elite in towns; and their effects can
sometimes be demonstrated quite precisely. In one London alley,
several of the houses were rebuilt in the mid-seventeenth century and
plague mortality was noticeably lower in 1665 than it had been in
1625.[28] But this process had not ended by 1665, as the great mortality
on the fringes of the capital shows. By the end of the eighteenth
century environmental improvements had no doubt made serious
epidemics of plague in the more prosperous parts of Europe unlikely;

but they do not explain their complete disappearance as early as the 1660s.

For a more plausible explanation for the disappearance of plague from western Europe after 1665 we must turn to the first category of hypotheses, those relating to the introduction of the disease. If the tinder was still there for a major epidemic in the later seventeenth and early eighteenth centuries, it is probably that it was the initial spark which was missing. It is not stretching the evidence to argue that the widespread adoption of quarantine against ships from infected ports gradually reduced the risk of plague reaching western Europe, until in the end the risk was negligible.

Quarantine was not, of course infallible, any more than the watch and ward erected around towns like York and Bristol. Some ships would always penetrate even the most imposing defences, and merchandise be smuggled ashore from those which were caught. As with watch and ward, however, the more often and the more widely the machinery was employed, the more likely it was to prove effective. Moreover, just as it was easier to protect a town like Exeter or Norwich if plague threatened only from a single distant source, so it was easier to protect the whole of England if the threat of infection came only from a port in southern Europe, North Africa or the Levant.[29] Here England was fortunate. The sophisticated quarantine procedures adopted in Italy and southern France in the seventeenth century increasingly restricted plague to a few distant harbours.[30]

The protection of England against plague thus depended both on action taken elsewhere and on the English government's own defences against ship-borne infection. We have seen that the latter were rudimentary before 1620, and they failed at least twice after that. In 1635 and 1664 the disease reached England from the Low Countries, with disastrous consequences for London immediately afterwards. It did not arrive in 1655, and quarantine, along with the commercial disruptions caused by the Dutch and Spanish wars, may help to account for that.[31] There may also have been local successes. The measures taken in Hull against ships from the Netherlands and London between 1663 and 1665 helped to prevent an epidemic in that vulnerable east coast port.[32] Similarly, between 1667 and 1669, precautions against shipping from northern France and the isolation of Frenchmen suspected of suffering from plague in Dover and Yarmouth may have stopped the introduction of a new and more virulent strain of the bacillus.[33] As a general rule, however, once plague had reached north-western Europe from the Mediterranean, and particularly when it had reached Amsterdam, whose trade with English ports was so continuous, it was difficult to keep it out of Britain.

After 1670 that dangerous proximity never recurred. Precautions taken in other countries kept plague at a safer distance, usually in the eastern Mediterranean. The voyage from Smyrna to England, for example, was long enough for many infected fleas in cloth or cotton to have died on the way,[34] and certainly long enough for the government to be warned of the danger in time to take appropriate action. Orders were issued against shipping from Malaga in 1680, from the Baltic ports between 1709 and 1713, from Marseilles and the Levant between 1720 and 1722, and from various Mediterranean harbours in the 1730s and 1740s. Quarantine was even enforced against ships from the West Indies when, as in 1692, infectious disease seemed to threaten from there.[35] With each fresh emergency, the government sought advice on how the policy had worked in the past and how it was enforced in foreign countries, including the Netherlands.[36] Administrative practice was given the support of statute law in 1710, and a ship was forfeited to the Crown in 1713 for failing to comply with it. Further statutes, in 1721, 1722, 1728 and 1753 added the death penalty for those refusing or escaping quarantine, and confirmed the erection of a quarantine station at Standgate Creek, at the mouth of the Medway, for ships intending to enter the Thames.[37]

The most public test of this machinery came in 1720–2, when there was plague in Marseilles and southern France. Customs officials in the provinces urgently asked for troops or frigates in order to enforce quarantine properly; they could be provided only in the neighbourhood of Portsmouth, at Milford Haven, and off Standgate Creek.[38] In the event, however, that proved to be enough, since the few suspect vessels from infected ports could now be closely monitored. The government was rightly told that there was no need for precautions against ships from Italy, thanks to the model regulations enforced there. On the other hand, it was quickly informed by the British consul in Venice that two ships were approaching London from Cyprus, where there was plague; that one of them had been turned away from Messina and Leghorn because it was suspect; and that they carried cotton, which experience had shown could often harbour infection (and, modern epidemiologists would note, fleas). The ships were isolated when they arrived and finally burnt by order of the king in Council under authority of the statute of 1721, parliament voting £24,000 as compensation to the owners.[39]

Public awareness of the danger of imported infection was also productive. Forewarned by newspaper reports of plague in foreign towns, local officials in Channel ports turned away vessels coming from the Mediterranean. When goods were smuggled into Canterbury from the two ships which were soon to be burned, the Council was told immediately.[40] People rushed to report suspected cases of plague in the Isle of Man, in Portsmouth and Hartlepool, and the government responded with advice on how to isolate them if the cases were confirmed.[41] They were not. A combination of public awareness, relatively rapid government action and quarantine in other countries seemed to have worked.

Chance played a part in the success of such endeavours, of course. Public vigilance could falter, and the fallible administration of quarantine might have led to an outbreak of plague in London after 1665 as it did in Marseilles in 1720.[42] In the end, indeed, both vigilance and quarantine were deliberately relaxed. By 1824 parliamentary inquiries into the functioning of the quarantine laws were eliciting complaints that they needlessly harmed trade; and in 1825 the penalties for infringement of the regulations were reduced, as a prelude to later modification of the laws themselves.[43] At the very beginning of the twentieth century, when steam transport by-passed the quarantine defences of the Mediterranean and eastern Europe, plague reached Britain again. Then it was improvements in hygiene and the urban environment, associated with the disappearance of the black rat, which dictated that its effects on men – in Liverpool, Glasgow and Suffolk – would be small and sporadic.[44] In the century and a half before 1825, however, there is no evidence that plague ever arrived. Over that long period, we may conclude, quarantine had succeeded. It made the risk of initial infection remote; and as a result, the much more difficult problem of controlling an epidemic once it had begun could be shelved – and shelved, as it turned out, for good. Management had largely replaced fortune as the determinant of the European incidence of plague.

So sanguine a conclusion could not be established beyond dispute at the time. Neither could the reasons for it be understood until the epidemiology of plague had been fully worked out, at the end of the nineteenth century. Until then the relative importance of human transmission and local environmental conditions, and the relative merits of 'infection' and 'miasma' as explanatory hypotheses, could not be precisely determined. Hence it was easy for eighteenth-century writers to reject the argument which has been presented here and to suggest alternatives. From the 1720s until the 1820s, defenders of free trade often denied the efficacy of the quarantine laws, arguing that Britain's overseas trade was simply too voluminous to be monitored effectively. Some writers, like some historians, attributed the absence of plague to social improvement. They pointed out that in the seventeenth century the disease had largely been confined to 'the squalid classes', and they concluded that 'improved habits of life' in the eighteenth century had produced a 'continued diminution of susceptibility' to it. Others could find no satisfactory explanation for the end of plague apart from divine providence.[45]

Edward Gibbon was an exception. Less insular in his historial perspective than most of his contemporaries, armed with all the secular self-assurance of the Enlightenment, he could refer coolly and confidently to 'those salutary precautions to which Europe is indebted for her safety' from plague.[46] Gibbon was right; but most Englishmen before him could not be so certain. Least of all could they feel confident in 1720, when London seemed about to become another Marseilles.

(ii) Recapitulation: The scare of 1720–2

Apprehensions about plague were often revived in the half-century after 1665. Its approach via the Mediterranean or the Baltic was anxiously watched in the newspapers; the Royal Society heard learned papers about its effects in eastern and northern Europe; and preachers warned of its coming as a deserved punishment for the nation's sins. Some towns kept their pesthouses in repair, just in case, and housewives continued to copy the old prescriptions for plague medicines into their recipe books.[47] Between 1720 and 1722, however, an unprecedented panic occurred. It began in the autumn of 1719 when, according to one of Defoe's newspaper columns, sickness in London and plague in Hungary led to 'a sad outcry . . . especially by ancient females, of a plague, pestilence and what not'. Within a year Defoe was himself describing the havoc caused by the great plague at Marseilles. As it spread to other parts of southern France in 1721, newspaper comment and the precautions taken by the government to keep

3p

The government's reaction to the threat from Marseilles was commendably quick and unusually comprehensive. In 1720 there were proclamations imposing quarantine on ships from infected ports and ordering a day of national fasting and prayer, for which a special form of service was issued. A new Quarantine Act, replacing that of 1710, was rushed through parliament in the winter of 1720–1, and we have seen that it was rigorously enforced against suspect shipping. Besides introducing stiffer penalties for those who evaded quarantine, however, the statute had new provisions with major domestic implications: it permitted the government to copy the practices adopted in France if plague reached London. 'Lines' of armed guards – a military *cordon sanitaire* – could be set up round any infected town in England to prevent the dispersal of infection; magistrates could compel members of infected households to move to plague hospitals or other places of isolation; and resistance might incur the death penalty.[49]

The government had taken advice before drawing up the statute. It had obtained a report on up-to-date precautions from Richard Mead, one of the foremost physicians of the day. Although he had not seen cases of plague himself, Mead had access to previous advice given to the Council, including Mayerne's report of 1631; he had read the available literature on English and European epidemics; and he had even spoken to the son of the rector of Eyam, William Mompesson, about the outbreak of plague there in 1666. All this left him in no doubt about the danger of contagion. As we have done, he distinguished between the methods to be taken against the introduction of plague and those necessary when it arrived. As to the first, plague had always come from the East, and quarantine and lazarettos were essential against ships, men and goods from infected places. As to the second, he repeated all the earlier criticisms of household isolation: it had done nothing to prevent the spread of plague; it might even have prolonged it by concentrating infection and engendering infectious miasmas in the air; and it had 'always had the appearance of a severe discipline and even punishment, rather than of a compassionate care'. Instead, infected families should be removed from their houses and the sick isolated in different places from the sound. To prevent the spread of plague from one place to another, there should be lines around infected towns which men could pass only after twenty days' quarantine.[50]

Given the limited medical knowledge of the time, Mead's recommendations were remarkably enlightened, and it is difficult to find fault with the government's acceptance of them. Although he made no mention of rats and fleas, all his precautions against the carriage of infection would have been useful, and they owed a good deal to Italian practices which had proved their worth in the past. Mead suggested, for example, that the infected and their contacts should be stripped of all their clothes and washed and shaved when they were isolated: a Venetian policy which might well have been instrumental against flea-borne infection. He was clearly aware of the part played by men, clothes and bedding in the short- and long-distance transmission of plague.

The virtues of Mead's tract and of the Quarantine Act were not so apparent to the general public, however. They occasioned a controversy which arose partly out of memories of the past and partly out of the circumstances of the present. Publications describing events in Marseilles, the flight of the rich, the suffering and disorder of the poor, and the commercial damage done by plague precautions, heightened the emotional temperature and raised the old issues of private and public behaviour during epidemics.[51] Some of the pamphlets of 1665, including the London plague orders, were reprinted and had the same effect.[52] And contemporary views of the social and political order moulded public reactions. No more than in the past could plague be approached simply as a known hazard against which there were obvious defences.

Preachers had the first opportunity to reflect on, and make propaganda out of, the subject. The national fast on 16 December 1720 produced sermons on the sins of the time, some of which were rushed into print early in 1721. The approach of plague was a clear call to the nation to repent, and to reverse the decline in religious commitment which had come with the new prosperity and tolerance of early eighteenth-century England. Avarice in society, faction in politics and latitude in religion all made divine punishment inevitable – unless a complete 'Reformation of Manners' was embarked upon.[53] It was a short step from this to scarcely veiled attacks on the government itself. The South Sea Bubble, for example, was easily interpreted as a sign of that corruption in high places which had brought the threat of plague on the kingdom.

At the second public fast, on 8 December 1721, preaching before the Lord Mayor and aldermen in St Paul's, Edmund Massey skilfully employed this and similar accusations in what amounted to an indictment of the whole Hanoverian establishment in Church and State.[54] No one now ventured to borrow from Henoch Clapham and oppose medical precautions altogether: in 1722 Massey was to attack inoculation against smallpox on providential grounds, but he refrained from such extremities in 1721. Like several others, however, he castigated the Deism and heresy which he saw rampant in the Church, and 'the national crimes of avarice and ambition, which spread themselves almost over every order and degree of men among us'. He insisted that plague should not be seen as a chance, secular phenomenon: 'It is unnatural to say it cometh of itself . . . These things are not casual or spontaneous.'[55] Such appeals to providence against the sins of the Venetian oligarchy, which Walpole and his allies were erecting in 1721, did not encourage confidence in the government's anti-plague measures – borrowed from Venice as in part they ironically were.

That confidence was undermined still more by tracts criticising Mead's standpoint on secular grounds. As in the past, much of the medical literature on plague published between 1720 and 1722 was uncontroversial and traditional. It summarised old ideas and old remedies. It referred to the authorities of the later seventeenth century, to Diemerbroeck, Kircher, Sydenham, Willis and Boyle, and did not advance beyond them. If it discussed quarantine, it did so only in the most general terms.[56] But five tracts attacked Mead directly, and in doing so denied that plague could be passed from person to person. Four of them were anonymous, three of them probably by the same author, but the fifth, by a younger and far less eminent physician than Mead, George Pye, clearly delineated the medical issues involved and set the tone for the rest.[57]

Pye emphasised the role of miasma as against contagion; and where Mead saw plague as a single disease spreading across the Continent, Pye viewed it as an affliction which arose from and varied with local circumstances. John Graunt had shown that plague fluctuated with the seasons, and Pye concluded that it depended more on the disposition of the air than on 'effluvia from the bodies of men'. Everyone agreed that shutting up houses had been of no use: if isolation failed there, how could it be justified in the form of lines and trenches around whole towns? England's trade with the Levant had increased vastly since 1665, but plague had not come with it. Other critics of Mead agreed. Plague plainly had local origins, and hence, one of them argued, its absence from England after 1666 was to be explained

by improvements in the urban environment, in housing, in popular
industriousness and in personal cleanliness.[58]

In the hands of these writers that tension between contagion and
miasma, between emphasis on the external and the local origins of
plague, which had been implicit in medical writing from the beginning
of our period, came out into the open. For the first time in England
the concept of contagion was criticised, not because it conflicted with
God's will, but because it seemed incompatible with observation and
past experience.[59] There were several reasons for this novel polarisation. In part it was a consequence of the absence of censorship and
the new intellectual tolerance of the early eighteenth century. In the
seventeenth century people had often observed that those closest to
the sick did not always catch plague from them; but they had seldom
dared to go further and openly question the contagionist assumptions
on which the government's activity was avowedly based. That they
were still afraid of the consequences in 1721 is shown by the fact that
only Pye dispensed with the cloak of anonymity.

Anti-contagionist views were also encouraged by recent intellectual
developments. There was the new understanding of the local determinants of disease patterns which had come into English medical writing
with Sydenham and his successors. There was contemporary dispute
about whether even smallpox was contagious.[60] There were publications by physicians in Marseilles, some of them taking an anti-
contagionist line.[61] Not least important, however, was the fact that
English writers had no direct acquaintance with plague themselves,
despite their appeals to experience. They were therefore very easily
tempted to see contagion and miasma as mutually exclusive hypotheses, and to suppose that because plague was not in all conditions
transmitted from one person to another, it could never be so. To an
extent, of course, they were right. The disease was not communicated
by touch or breath, but by fleas. Yet their rigorously simplistic
approach and their refusal to consider the possibility of contingent
contagion would have led them to deny the importance of insect as
well as human vectors. They could argue, for example, that the
flourishing trade with Turkey showed by 'millions of experiments' that
plague was not carried in bales of cotton.[62]

The heaviest weapons in the armoury of Mead's critics did not
come from logical analysis or epidemiological observation, however,
but from a description of the economic and social consequences of
quarantine and isolation. Pye started from the assumption that 'the

good and happiness of mankind' necessitated the demolition of Mead's argument; and he concluded that 'the all-wise and prescient Author of Nature' had obviously designed plague so as to avoid the 'dreadful inconveniences' which would follow if it were contagious. Foremost among these inconveniences was the impact of quarantine on a trading nation. 'Deficient customs, loss of public and private credit, poverty, starving and destruction' could prove worse than the disease itself. Secondly, lines, guards and compulsory isolation in hospitals were examples of those 'most inhuman restraints and confinements' which contagion had justified in the past, which had increased the terrors which made men vulnerable to plague, and which had prevented friends and neighbours from helping one another. So much was familiar ground. But Pye and his allies added a new political and patriotic note. Lines of guards and savage isolation were the marks of an 'arbitrary' power in France; they were intolerable to people under a 'free government' in England.[63]

These arguments gave the anti-contagionist views espoused by only an insignificant minority of medical writers wide public support. Something of the strength of their appeal can be seen in the preface which Mead added to later editions of his work, significantly qualifying his original conclusions. He now disclaimed responsibility for the Quarantine Act: it was for politicians not for him to judge what precautions were expedient. Moreover, the powers taken by the government should at all times be limited, 'that they may never endanger the rights and liberties of a people'. He had never intended that lines around London should be rigid, or that all infected households should be compulsorily removed to lazarettos. People could be allowed out of London after a period of quarantine; and the infected should be forced out of their homes only at the beginning of an epidemic, when the disease largely affected the poor: the interests of the latter, he assumed, could be ignored. Mead further admitted that it was sometimes necessary to amend 'even the best laws that can be made' when they aroused 'popular prejudices and clamours'.[64] Mead was in fact responding less to Pye than to a general public outcry against the Quarantine Act and the government's plans for further precautionary measures. It was a clamour to which Sir Robert Walpole no less than Richard Mead had to attend.

The Quarantine Act which had passed so smoothly through parliament in January 1721 was radically amended by a new statute which received the royal assent one year later, in February 1722. Although quarantine on ships remained, the clauses empowering the government to act if infection reached England were repealed: there were to be no lines around infected cities defended by troops, no powers to remove people from their houses and no death penalties to support them.[65] It was a striking and rapid government retreat, and it is largely to be explained by the political circumstances of 1721. During that year Walpole was trying to establish himself as chief minister. Threatened by Jacobite plots, by 'Country' opposition, and by the aftermath of the Bubble Crisis, he had also to deal with the menace of plague without giving his opponents an issue around which they could coalesce. It proved an impossible task; and in a piece of political trimming as brisk as that which he showed later in the Excise Crisis, Walpole made the necessary concessions.

He began with no thought of defeat, however. In the summer and autumn of 1721 he introduced bills to tighten quarantine by enabling the government to impose a ban on all commerce with infected countries and deal more effectively with smuggling. There was immediate opposition from mercantile interests, especially the Levant Company, and heated parliamentary debate; and it was partly in order to get these measures through that Walpole compromised on the domestic clauses of the original Quarantine Act.[66] At the same time, the City of London was resisting government pressure to build pesthouses and the inhabitants of Westminster were opposing proposed legislation forcing them to improve public hygiene.[67] The opportunity given to Walpole's parliamentary opponents was too good to miss. At the end of 1721 they seized it, orchestrating these sectional complaints into a concerted 'Country' attack on a ministry which was enamoured of standing armies, corrupt absolutism, and other foreign monstrosities.

The biggest guns fired in the Lords. Disaffected Whigs like Lord Cowper and Tories led by Bishop Atterbury joined forces to attack those parts of the Quarantine Act which borrowed lines, guards and compulsory isolation from the example of Marseilles. These were practices 'utterly unknown to our Constitution, and repugnant . . . to the lenity of our mild and free government'. The plague statute of 1604, they somewhat speciously argued, had shown a more 'tender regard' to the liberties of the subject by confining people to their own homes. It had not introduced measures copied from France, a government 'conducted by arbitrary power and supported by standing armies'.[68] The newspapers joined in. In November 1721 the opposition paper, *Applebee's Original Weekly Journal*, advertised schemes for dealing with plague 'without terrifying the people, or giving room for a new usurpation on our liberties, which is strongly suspected'. Defoe, writing in the same journal, tried to tone down the more hysterical opposition by noting the empirical sense of the precautions taken in France; but he admitted that they could not be practised in England 'unless many of our laws are repealed, and standing forces raised for the purpose, which, I hope, we shall not see done'.[69]

Surprised no doubt by the sudden opposition to a measure which had passed without demur twelve months before, Walpole employed his Whig henchman, Edmund Gibson, bishop of London, to answer his critics. In a pamphlet distributed freely throughout the country, Gibson accused political factions of making capital out of a perfectly innocuous piece of legislation and of inflaming popular fears without justification. He attacked those writers whose denial of infection or insistence on the hand of providence undermined the government's endeavours; and he made the perfectly sound point that 'where the disease is desperate, the remedy must be so too'. There was no sense in dwelling 'upon rights and liberties, and the ease and convenience of mankind' when there was 'plague hanging over our heads'.[70] Gibson failed to stem the tide, however; for the fact was that the danger of plague was now receding. It had not arrived in the summer of 1720 or in that of 1721, and there was nothing to stop a confident opposition sweeping all before it in the winter of 1721–2. Walpole backed down and consented to the repeal of the offending clauses.

There was rather more to this wrangle than persuasive rhetoric and political opportunism. There was some justification for public alarm. As in the past, any attempt to deal with plague raised real issues of political authority. It required some unusual concentration of power in the hands of government; and the Whig ministry, like the early Stuart Privy Council, was planning to exercise it, if necessary. In October 1721 the government began to make plans for action, should plague hit London. It sought advice from the appropriate medical authorities, from Mead and from his colleagues in the Royal College, John Arbuthnot and Sir Hans Sloane, the President. Their replies were ambitious. The inner city should be divided into six health districts, with searchers of the dead – euphemistically termed 'visitors' – for each of them; and there should be a further team of nearly fifty searchers in the suburban parishes. Any householder concealing plague and any physician who refused to examine the sick would be fined. All the infected must be housed in 'barracks', of which there

should be six, on Blackheath, Clapham Common and other open
spaces round the city; and, some distance away from them, there
should also be separate quarters for their healthy contacts, who were
expected to be four or five times as numerous.[71] The debt to
Mayerne's report of 1631 and to the Council's deliberations of 1665
and 1666 was clear. The aim was to avoid household isolation, and
thus the confinement of sick and healthy together in an infected
atmosphere, by compulsory removal to pesthouses.

The government's response also looked back to 1631. It began to
consider Sloane's recommendation of a public-health commission to
implement these proposals. The law officers of the Crown were asked
to look into the constitutional position. They reported that the royal
prerogative as it now stood at common law was defective: it could not
impose pains and penalties. A royal commission might investigate the
working of the Quarantine Act, but it could not enforce it. Nevertheless, a commission was drafted and its members were to include the
Lord Mayor and four aldermen; five bishops including Gibson of
London; representatives of the customs and excise; justices of the
counties around London; and Sloane, Arbuthnot and Mead.[72] Here
was Mayerne's board of health again, albeit without legal powers. It
may be that Walpole was contemplating legislation to give it teeth. In
the event, however, any plans he might have had were overtaken by
developments in parliament. Talk of 'barracks', fines and commissions
only added to the opposition to lines and guards in the Quarantine
Act, and all fell together in February 1722. What had first been
conceived as a component of prerogative rule in 1631 could not be
realised by a parliamentary ministry ninety years later.

It was not only the problem of central authority which was raised
again in 1721. The spectres of public disorder and popular licence,
which might be both cause and consequence of plague, haunted some
writers still. Sir John Colbatch, another physician who advised the
government, made it clear that he thought barracks necessary only for
the 'miserable and indigent', the dangerous classes. He proposed that
there should be twelve armed militia men in each health district to
prevent disturbances, and troops quartered near the city in case the
poor proved ungovernable. In order to make the danger clear, he
reminded his readers of how people had deliberately spread plague
in the past. Another projector bracketed together the war against
plague and the war against sin. Close investigation into causes of
death, and strict penalties against offenders against health regulations,

should be combined with a Reformation of Manners which would eradicate the fundamental roots of disease.[73] If the point needed illustration, newspaper reports of disturbances in southern France provided it in ample measure.

Daniel Defoe was one of those who publicised the social horrors which might be at hand. His articles for *Applebee's Journal* told of starving crowds of the infected attempting to break out of the lines at Toulon, and of the similar confusion which would follow if plague reached England. His initial purpose was probably to show that strict quarantine against foreign ships was essential in order to avoid such consequences on this side of the Channel. Although he opposed anything that smacked of French despotism, he was no less vehement in his attack on London merchants who resisted restrictions on foreign trade, thus venturing 'the welfare of the whole kingdom . . . for the wretched gain of a private man'. Defoe supported the quarantine provisions of the Quarantine Act while opposing its domestic clauses; and this has been taken to be one symptom of his ambivalent position as a secret supporter of the government among the ranks of opposition journalists.[74]

Yet there was also an independent drive and commitment in Defoe's writings on the subject of plague. His acuteness as a social observer and his ability to see all sides of any question led him beyond mere sensationalism and political propaganda. They brought him face to face with the real dilemmas posed by plague to governments and subjects alike; and they stimulated his interest in the epidemic of 1665. In his journalism, in *Due Preparations for the Plague* which appeared in February 1722, and in *A Journal of the Plague Year* which followed a month later, he addressed problems which we have seen to be perennial in the history of plague. He was not always consistent about them. He wrote too quickly to develop a coherent argument, and saw too much. He knew as well as Dekker the popular appeal of short dialogues and imagined incidents, not all of which had obvious relevance. But his eagerness to describe the issues in human terms gave his writing flashes of insight which none of his contemporaries or predecessors could match.

Many of the subjects which interested him were commonplace in plague pamphlets: the economic effects of epidemics; the question of whether secrecy was worse than public knowledge of an outbreak, which might harm trade and create panic; the problem of flight; the difference between proper religious piety in the face of infection and passive 'Turkish predestinarianism'.[75] But he was particularly intrigued by the problem of how far the interests of public safety should be allowed to override those of private individuals. In *Due Preparations* he concluded that lines around towns locked up so many sound people with the sick that this was 'really shedding innocent blood, which is a kind of evil not to be done that good may come'. The old practice of shutting up houses could be justified more easily, since members of a family 'have some obligations upon them to take the risk one with another'.[76] In the *Journal*, however, he turned to the policy of household isolation again, and gave it more considered treatment.

He saw it now as a focal point where the well-meaning ambitions of authority and the equally justifiable sentiments of ordinary people clashed. Throughout the work Defoe was concerned to understand both sides and not to condemn either. He doubted whether the poor often spread plague deliberately, whether nurses often murdered their patients, and whether popular violence was common or unjustified.[77] People did not deserve the treatment they received. They were not vicious. They were victims. At the same time, however, Defoe showed that there was some reason behind the policies adopted by the City in 1665. Plague was contagious, and 'it was a public good that justified the private mischief' of shutting up infected households. Something had to be done to stop the sick from being 'both very troublesome and very dangerous in their running about the streets with the distemper upon them'; and some sort of provision had to be made for 'the dangerous people ... the begging, starving, labouring poor'. Local officers had on the whole been as charitable as they could be, given the orders they had to enforce.[78]

Defoe had no doubt that household quarantine proved to be 'of little or no service on the whole'. It was resisted by its victims, who disguised the fact of plague for fear of the consequences, and who were driven to escape to get food, see their friends and seek diversion and entertainment. Where it was enforced, it increased mortality within households: it would have been much better to have removed the sound into quarantine elsewhere, and to have left only the sick to be cared for in their houses. But Defoe was not primarily concerned to advocate alternative policies whose practical difficulties he could see well enough; his interest lay in the social repercussions of what had necessarily been done in the past. Just as his journalism showed that the strict measures taken in France in 1720 had contributed to disorder there, so in the *Journal* he demonstrated that 'the severity of those confinements' and not natural depravity made people desperate and disorderly in London in 1665.[79]

There have been various opinions as to the historical accuracy of *A Journal of the Plague Year*. No one would now use it as primary evidence for what happened in 1665, although there is more to be said in its favour in this respect than against it, granted the limitations of Defoe's sources: the printed literature of 1665 and 1721, contemporary recollections and the known topography of London.[80] Much criticism of Defoe has missed the point, and underestimated him, however, by assessing the *Journal* as if it were a chronicle. Its value lies in its striving for genuine historical understanding. Though confused in its focus and often repetitive, it was an original and profound inquiry into the social consequences of plague and of the measures adopted against it. In fact it marks a watershed. It came at the end of the period in which plague was a tangible threat to England, and it was the first serious attempt to come to grips with the social reality of the disease in the past. It showed why public-health measures were adopted and also why they were resisted.

These have been the twin themes of the second half of this book, and Defoe's balanced view brings us appropriately towards a conclusion. For Defoe pictured people and governors as equally victims of circumstance, at the mercy of ignorance and the brutal impulses of self-preservation: 'There was no remedy; self-preservation obliged the people to those severities which they would not otherwise have been concerned in.'[81]

Conclusion

Dr Rieux resolved to compile this chronicle, so that he should . . . bear witness in favour of those plague-stricken people; so that some memorial of the injustice and outrage done them might endure; and to state quite simply what we learn in a time of pestilence: that there are more things to admire in men than to despise.

Nonetheless, he knew that the tale he had to tell could not be one of a final victory. It could be only the record of what had had to be done, and what assuredly would have to be done again in the never-ending fight against terror and its relentless onslaughts . . . by all who, while unable to be saints but refusing to bow down to pestilences, strive their utmost to be healers.

Albert Camus, *The Plague* (1947)[1]

Reactions to plague, like reactions to other disasters, provide rich material for imaginative writers – for Camus as for Defoe and Dekker – because they encapsulate in a single incident the whole range of human strengths and weaknesses. They illustrate the resilience and the perversity of humanity. For the historian their interest is more prosaic and more precise. They reveal the connections between immediate problems and a society's response to them, and they show how that response was shaped by, and in turn helped to mould, broader historical developments.

The social response to plague, in all its diversity and confusion, was clearly related to the equally diverse and confusing dimensions of the problem. Plague as catastrophe, the cause of sudden and widespread sickness and death, naturally encouraged the view that society must unite against it. The community as a whole must seek divine deliverance from a common scourge which was evidently a punishment for common sins. At the same time, however, the unpredictable movement of infection from place to place proved divisive, bringing the need for self-preservation into conflict with other, deeply felt but less immediate obligations. And finally, the social incidence of the disease, which became increasingly obvious, provided a target against which the fears engendered by catastrophe and infection could be directed. Tension could be relieved by attacks on the poor, vagrants, inmates – the victims of plague.

It would be crudely deterministic to stress the connection between the nature of a social problem and its perception to the exclusion of all else, however. We have seen the many other features of early modern English society which determined reactions to epidemic disease. Plague emphasised and exaggerated many of them; but it did not create them. In principle, there were two possible approaches to the crises caused by epidemics, based on different but equally broad concepts of 'public health'. The notion that the health of the body politic depended on harmony between its parts, on the reciprocal recognition of responsibilities, supported those who sought to counter the divisive effects of plague by encouraging generosity in the performance of religious, charitable and public duties. On the other hand, the deep-seated assumption that disease was the product of disorder led to a very different view of public health and its imperatives. Plague could be conquered only by cleansing society from the physical and moral ills associated with it – poverty, popular disturbance, drunkenness, filth of all kinds.

The interventionist and regulatory policies implicit in the latter view inevitably triumphed because they had intellectual, political and social authority behind them. Religious beliefs about the role of divine providence sometimes encouraged fatalistic resignation; but they more often impelled action because they connected plague with intolerable sins which it was the duty of magistrate and minister to eradicate. Ecclesiastical authority gave full support to a policy for public health because those who opposed it were disruptive, subversive elements in the church. Secular authority similarly welcomed and developed the policy because it was wholly consistent with the ambitions of central and local governors to extend their control over their subjects. Measures such as household quarantine also appealed to weighty social prejudices: the insecurities and anxieties not only of the ruling elite, but also of the middling sort, who saw their lives menaced during epidemics by those popular disorders which posed a mounting threat to their status and peace of mind at other times. The later sixteenth and seventeenth centuries have been seen with some justice as a period of social and political polarisation.[2] The gap between rich and poor and between the rulers and the ruled grew wider. Plague emphasised the first dichotomy and the response of government to it accentuated the second.

If public-health policies were in part instruments of social control, however, they were not only that. They could be justified on the grounds of medical efficacy. Observation of plague showed quite clearly the importance of the environment in which it flourished and the importance of some of the means by which infection was transmitted. We have seen that there were no great scientific discoveries which furthered understanding of plague in this period. The role of rats and fleas was as little understood in 1720 as in 1520. But experience produced an *ad hoc* strategy which, despite its brutality and its social costs, had sound empirical foundations: restrictions on movement and public assembly, and the isolation of households, made sense in the context of contemporary knowledge. Moreover, it can be persuasively argued that parts of that strategy, when employed over Europe as whole, freed whole countries from plague. It would be unduly condescending to suggest that the actions of government were based simply on self-interest and prejudice, and that they could not be defended with some force because they were likely to work.

It would be equally condescending, however, to see the history of the battle against plague simply as a success story, in which secular enlightenment banished the forces of ignorance and superstition; and to argue that consequently its good sense and its potentiality for social advance should have been evident from the beginning. We have seen how often the battle failed, and how widely its tactics could be criticised, even on medical grounds, in 1665 and 1720. At the end of our period there could be no assurance of final victory; there could be still less in the sixteenth and early seventeenth centuries. Men were groping in the dark towards solutions which were bound to be controversial to a problem which they only dimly understood. We may admire the extent of their success; but we should not understate the difficulties in their way or denigrate those who resisted new solutions because their immediate costs were far more obvious than their long-term benefits.

This is to say no more than that Englishmen faced with plague in the sixteenth and seventeenth centuries were confronted by the predicament which social problems pose at all times. The need for some answer was evident, but the answer could never be objective, clean, unsullied by extraneous considerations. Presuppositions founded on prejudice or principle determined men's perception of the problem and their preferred solutions to it. The problems of our own society, from nuclear armaments to environmental pollution provide obvious parallels. Although they have not yet visited us with the horrors and destruction of bubonic plague, simple agreed solutions have been no easier to find. The modern observer can no doubt regard plague more objectively than he does threats to social health in his own day. Yet even now it would be difficult to pass final judgment on the early experiment in public health which has been described above, and to say, without qualification, that its advocates or its victims deserve the greater sympathy.[3] The historian can only describe their predicament, and seek to understand their different views of it.

That endeavour may throw light on many aspects of a past society, as we have seen. Perhaps it also gives the historian a modest place in the company of those novelists and pamphleteers from the sixteenth century to the twentieth who turned to stories of plague for some understanding of the human condition. An observer of an epidemic in Lincoln in 1590 was one of the first to argue that histories such as this had a more than descriptive function:

> Recounting griefs and dolours long-time done,
> Or blazing forth the danger none can shun,
> Might seem a study altogether vain:
> Yet outward words oft easeth inward pain.[4]

Abbreviations

Agric. Hist. Rev.	*Agricultural History Review*
Annales ESC	*Annales: Économies, Sociétés, Civilisations*
AO	Archives Office
BAO	Bristol Archives Office
BL	British Library
Bodl.	Bodleian Library, Oxford
Bull. Hist. Med.	*Bulletin of the History of Medicine*
Bull. Inst. Hist. Res.	*Bulletin of the Institute of Historical Research*
Cal. SP Dom.	*Calendar of State Papers, Domestic Series*
DNB	*Dictionary of National Biography*
DRO	Devon Record Office
ECA	Devon Record Office, Exeter City Archives
Ec. HR	*Economic History Review*
Eng. Hist. Rev.	*English Historical Review*
ERO	Essex Record Office
GL	Guildhall Library, London
GLCRO	Greater London Council Record Office
HMC	Historical Manuscripts Commission, Reports
LCRO	Corporation of London Record Office
NNRO	Norfolk and Norwich Record Office
NS	New Series
OS	Old Series
P&P	*Past and Present*
Privy Council Acts	*Acts of the Privy Council*
PRO	Public Record Office
QS	Quarter Sessions
RO	Record Office
SCA	Salisbury Corporation Archives
Slack, thesis	P.A. Slack, 'Some Aspects of Epidemics in England 1485–1640' (Oxford Univ. D.Phil. thesis, 1972)
STC	*A Short-Title Catalogue of Books Printed in England . . . 1475–1640*, by A.W. Pollard and G.R. Redgrave (Oxford, 1926), revised by W.A. Jackson and others (1976 and forthcoming).

Trans. Roy. Hist. Soc.	*Transactions of the Royal Historical Society*
VCH	*Victoria County Histories*
WHO	World Health Organization

Notes

Place of publication of books referred to is London unless otherwise stated.

Chapter 1 Disease and society

1 Bodl., MS. Gough Eccl. Top 7, f. 1.
2 See, for example, G.W. Baker and D.W. Chapman (eds), *Man and Society in Disaster* (New York, 1962); A.H. Barton, *Social Organization under Stress: A Sociological Review of Disaster Studies* (Disaster Study no. 17, Washington DC, 1963); G.H. Grossler, H. Wechsler and M. Greenblatt (eds), *The Threat of Impending Disaster: Contributions to the Psychology of Stress* (Cambridge, Mass., 1964).
3 M. Wolfenstein, *Disaster: A Psychological Essay* (1957), p. 13; Baker and Chapman, *Man and Society in Disaster*, pp. 13, 188, 237–8; Barton, *Social Organization under Stress*, p. 88.
4 Grossler *et al.*, *Threat of Impending Disaster*, p. 67; M. Barkun, *Disaster and the Millennium* (New Haven, 1974), pp. 6, 55; Wolfenstein, *Disaster*, p. 61; Barton, *Social Organization under Stress*, pp. 46–8, 140–1.
5 T.D. Kendrick, *The Lisbon Earthquake* (1956). Cf. G.S. Rousseau, 'The London Earthquakes of 1750', *Cahiers d'hist. mondiale*, 11 (1968–9), 436–47.
6 A. Briggs, 'Cholera and Society in the Nineteenth Century', *P&P*, 19 (1961), 76–96; L. Chevalier (ed.), *Le Choléra* (La Roche-sur-Yon, 1958); R.J. Morris, *Cholera 1832* (1976); M. Durey, *The Return of the Plague: British Society and the Cholera 1831–2* (Dublin, 1979). For reactions to an outbreak of cholera in China in 1942, see F.L.K. Hsu, *Religion, Science and Human Crises* (1952).
7 For stimulating modern studies of Continental reactions to plague, see E. Carpentier, *Une Ville devant la peste: Orvieto et la peste noire de 1348* (Paris, 1962): B. Bennassar, *Recherches sur les grandes épidémies dans le nord de l'Espagne à la fin du XVIᶜ siècle* (Paris, 1969); C.M. Cipolla, *Cristofano and the Plague* (1973); J.T. Alexander, *Bubonic Plague in Early Modern Russia: Public Health and Urban Disaster* (Baltimore, 1980); and the general survey

in J.-N. Biraben, *Les Hommes et la peste en France et dans les pays européens et méditerranéens* (Paris, 1975–6), vol. II.

8 Cf. Barton, *Social Organization under Stress*, pp. 14–15, 134–5, 141.

9 Anthropological and sociological approaches to this subject are illustrated in D. Apple (ed.), *Sociological Studies of Health and Sickness* (New York, 1960); R. and E. Blum, *Health and Healing in Rural Greece* (Stanford, 1965); V.W. Turner, *Lunda Medicine and the Treatment of Disease* (Rhodes-Livingstone Museum, Occ. Paper, no. 15, 1963); E.H. Ackerknecht, *Medicine and Ethnology: Selected Essays* (Baltimore, 1971); J.B. Loudon (ed.), *Social Anthropology and Medicine* (ASA Monograph 13, 1976). An excellent historical analysis of popular attitudes to disease is contained in Keith Thomas, *Religion and the Decline of Magic* (1971).

10 For European interpretations of leprosy along these lines, which deeply influenced attitudes towards plague, see S.N. Brody, *The Disease of the Soul: Leprosy in Medieval Literature* (Ithaca, 1974).

11 A stimulating approach to disease in this larger historical context is W.H. McNeill, *Plagues and Peoples* (Oxford, 1977).

12 L. Chevalier, *Labouring Classes and Dangerous Classes* (1973), p.20; Chevalier, *Le Choléra*, p.13.

13 For brief summaries of modern views on plague, see Biraben, *Les Hommes et la peste*, I. ch. I, and L. Bradley, 'Some Medical Aspects of Plague', in *The Plague Reconsidered* (Local Population Studies Supplement, 1977), pp. 11–23, to which I am much indebted. The latter symposium also contains a translation of Biraben's chapter. Fuller accounts are in the two standard works in English: R. Pollitzer, *Plague* (WHO, Geneva, 1954) and L.F. Hirst, *The Conquest of Plague* (Oxford, 1953).

14 Sir D'Arcy Power, 'The Rev. John Ward and Medicine', *Trans. Med. Soc. London*, XLIII (1920), 259; C. Severn (ed.), *Diary of the Rev. John Ward* (1839), p. 241. Cf. Pollitzer, *Plague*, pp. 411–12, 420, 435–6.

15 Biraben, *Les Hommes et la peste*, I. 86; P. Ziegler, *The Black Death* (1969), p. 19; Carpentier, *Une Ville devant la peste*, pp. 113–14; M.W. Dols, *The Black Death in the Middle East* (Princeton, 1977), pp. 79–82; R.S. Gottfried, *Epidemic Disease in Fifteenth Century England* (Leicester, 1978), pp. 50–1.

16 A.B. Appleby, 'The Disappearance of Plague: A Continuing Puzzle', *Ec. HR*, 2nd ser., XXXIII (1980), 163.

17 Hirst, *Conquest of Plague*, pp. 238–46; Pollitzer, *Plague*, pp. 378–81. Cf. E. Le Roy Ladurie, 'Un Concept: l'unification microbienne du monde (XIVe–XVIIe siècles)', *Revue Suisse d'Histoire*, 23 (1973), 632.

18 E.g. R.S. Roberts, 'The Use of Literary and Documentary Evidence in the History of Medicine', in E. Clarke (ed.), *Modern Methods in the History of Medicine* (1971), p. 42; E. Rodenwaldt, *Pest in Venedig 1575–1577: Ein Beitrag zur Frage der Infektkette bei den Pestepidemien West-Europas* (Sitzungsberichte der Heidelberger Akademie der Wissenschaften, Mathematisch-Naturwissenschaftliche Klasse, Heidelberg, 1953), pp. 218–59.

19 This has been admitted even by the foremost French historian of plague and advocate of the role of the human flea, J.-N. Biraben: *Les Hommes et la peste*, I. 355 and n. Cf. Appleby, 'Disappearance of Plague', p. 164; J.

Norris, 'East or West? The Geographical Origin of the Black Death', *Bull. Hist. Med.*, 51 (1977), 16–17, and 52 (1978), 117–19.

20 R. Schofield, 'An Anatomy of an Epidemic: Colyton, November 1645 to November 1646', in *The Plague Reconsidered*, pp. 104–8. For instances of the household incidence of plague, see below, pp. 177–8.

21 The intervals between successive deaths in single households tend to cluster between zero and three days and between nine and thirteen days: *The Plague Reconsidered*, pp. 94, 108; Slack, thesis, p. 205. Short intervals may be due to rapid transmission by human fleas but equally to infection from a single rat source followed by variable incubation and illness periods; the longer intervals are certainly consistent with the hypothesis that fleas from the first human case deserted their human host for rats which were then infected, and that the rodents' fleas later attacked other humans and caused plague in them. Cf. *The Plague Reconsidered*, pp. 79, 84 n. 18, 109.

22 Cf. Hirst, *Conquest of Plague*, p. 246; Pollitzer, *Plague*, p. 380.

23 Kent AO, QM/SB 926 (Peter Clark kindly drew this document to my attention). For similar examples, see *Cal. SP Dom. 1664–5*, p. 548; HMC, *Bath IV: Seymour Papers 1532–1686*, p. 255; Sheffield City Library, Strafford Correspondence, 12/236.

24 BL, Lansdowne MS. 7, f. 64; ERO, Chelmsford parish register, December 1624. For the few contemporary references to rats in the context of plague, see below, pp. 238–9.

25 Below, pp. 86–7; Hirst, *Conquest of Plague*, pp. 310–28. L. Bradley, 'The Most Famous of All English Plagues: A Detailed Analysis of the Plague at Eyam 1665–6', in *The Plague Reconsidered*, pp. 68–9, doubts the traditional explanation of the origins of this outbreak, but it seems to me more persuasive than any alternative so far suggested.

26 M. Baltazard, 'Epidemiology of Plague', *WHO Chronicle*, 14 (1960), 419–26.

27 Cf. *The Plague Reconsidered*, pp. 127–32; below, pp. 84–7.

28 Pollitzer, *Plague*, p. 498; Biraben, *Les Hommes et la peste*, I. 118–29. Cf. below, pp. 313–14.

29 Below, pp. 67–8.

30 Biraben, *Les Hommes et la peste*, I. 336; McNeill, *Plagues and Peoples*, pp. 159–60. There is now evidence that black rats were present in Europe long before the fourteenth century: J. Rackham, '*Rattus rattus*: The Introduction of the Black Rat into Britain', *Antiquity*, LIII (1979), 112–20.

31 Below, pp. 321–6.

32 A.M. Campbell, *The Black Death and Men of Learning* (New York, 1931); C.M. Cipolla, *Public Health and the Medical Profession in the Renaissance* (Cambridge, 1976), pp. 11–15; Biraben, *Les Hommes et la peste*, II. ch. VIB.

33 Biraben, *Les Hommes et la peste*, I, 55–71.

34 M. Meiss, *Painting in Florence and Siena after the Black Death* (Princeton, 1951); R. Crawfurd, *Plague and Pestilence in Literature and Art* (Oxford, 1914); T.S.R. Boase, *Death in the Middle Ages* (1972), pp. 97–126; M.C. O'Connor, *The Art of Dying Well: The Development of the Ars Moriendi* (New York, 1942); Carpentier, *Une Ville devant la peste*, pp. 220–1. Cf.

also the classic account in J. Huizinga, *The Waning of the Middle Ages* (1952), ch. xi.

35 John Hatcher, *Plague, Population and the English Economy 1348–1530* (1977), pp. 21–5; C. Dyer, *Lords and Peasants in a Changing Society: The Estates of the Bishopric of Worcester 680–1540* (Cambridge, 1980), p. 225; Z. Razi, *Life, Marriage and Death in a Medieval Parish: Economy, Society and Demography in Halesowen 1270–1400* (Cambridge, 1980), pp. 99–113. The arguments of J.F.D. Shrewsbury in *A History of Bubonic Plague in the British Isles* (Cambridge, 1970), pp. 122–5, for a much lower mortality from plague in 1348–9 than that suggested here are contradicted by the historical evidence and can be disputed even on epidemiological grounds. Cf. Christopher Morris, 'Plague in Britain', in *The Plague Reconsidered*, pp. 37–47, and Gottfried, *Epidemic Disease*, pp. 238–40. Not all the points made by Morris and Gottfried seem to me wholly persuasive, but unlike Shrewsbury they recognise the importance of historical evidence and the complexity and variability of plague itself.

36 Gottfried, *Epidemic Disease, passim*, and on pneumonic plague, pp. 50–1. Cf. T.H. Hollingsworth, *Historical Demography* (1969), Appendix 3. It should be said that the local evidence for the chronology of plague in England suggests high mortality in summer and autumn even during the Black Death, and therefore the predominance of bubonic and not pneumonic plague in this visitation: e.g. Razi, *Life, Marriage and Death*, p. 102. There is thus room for debate on the precise relationship between the two forms of the disease in the fourteenth century. But there is no doubt that pneumonic plague had ceased to play an important role by 1500, if it had indeed ever done so. Cf. the works cited in n. 15 above.

37 R.S. Gottfried, 'Population, Plague and the Sweating Sickness: Demographic Movements in Late Fifteenth-Century England', *J. British Studies*, 17 (1978), 12–37. Cf. P. Slack, 'Mortality Crises and Epidemic Disease in England 1485–1610', in C. Webster (ed.), *Health, Medicine and Mortality in the Sixteenth Century* (Cambridge, 1979), pp. 52–5; below, pp. 99, 104–6.

38 Gottfried, 'Population, Plague and the Sweating Sickness', pp. 12–13, 36.

39 Below, pp. 107, 130; R. Howell, *Newcastle upon Tyne and the Puritan Revolution* (Oxford, 1967), pp. 2, 7–8.

40 GL, MSS. 4887, p. 278; 2968/1, f. 112v; 2968/3, f. 519r; 1176/1, 1637 acct; 6836, f. 146r; J.M.S. Brooke and A.W.C. Challen (eds), *The Transcripts of the Registers of S. Mary Woolnoth and S. Mary Woolchurch Haw 1538–1760* (1886), pp. 371, 372.

41 The title of a poem of 1609 on plague by John Davies.

42 BL, Harl. MS. 3785, f. 35v.

43 C.D. Chandaman, *The English Public Revenue 1660–1688* (Oxford, 1975), pp. 23, 57, 91.

44 Cf. William Muggins, *Londons Mourning Garment or Funerall Teares* (1603), sigs C4v, D1r.

45 DRO, ECA, D2/141, f. 127r. For the increased activity of London's Orphans' Court after the plagues of 1563 and 1593, see C. Carlton, *The Court of Orphans* (Leicester, 1974), p. 25.

46 H. Ellis, (ed.), *The Obituary of Richard Smyth* (Camden Soc., OS, XLIV, 1849), pp. 59–70.

47 Cf. J.S. Cockburn, *A History of English Assizes 1558–1714* (Cambridge, 1972), p. 25; ERO, Q/SBa 2/104; GL, MS. 9680, f. 150r.

48 Edward, earl of Clarendon, *History of the Rebellion and Civil Wars in England*, ed. W.D. Macray (Oxford, 1888), I, 381–2; M.F. Keeler, *The Long Parliament 1640–1: A Biographical Study of Its Members* (Philadelphia, 1954), pp. 6, 107, 156, 184, 321, 323–4, 368, 398n.

49 C. Russell, *Parliaments and English Politics 1621–9* (Oxford, 1979), pp. 214, 229, 235; S.R. Gardiner (ed.), *Debates in the House of Commons in 1625* (Camden Soc., NS, VI, 1873), p. 151; below, p. 216.

50 J.F. Larkin and P.L. Hughes (eds), *Stuart Royal Proclamations I: 1603–25* (Oxford, 1973), nos 19, 23; ERO, D/DP L36/16, letter about the coronation of Charles I; P.L. Hughes and J.F. Larkin (eds), *Tudor Royal Proclamations* (New Haven, 1964–9), nos 160, 237 *et al.*

51 For examples, see 'A Calendar of Dramatic Records in the Books of the Livery Companies of London 1485–1640', *Malone Soc. Collections*, III (1954), xxxiv, 61; C.M. Clode, *Memorials of the Guild of Merchant Taylors* (1875), pp. 130–1.

52 A. Clark (ed.), *The Life and Times of Anthony Wood I: 1632–63* (Oxford Hist. Soc., XIX, 1891), pp. 185–6; *Cal. SP Dom. 1591–4*, p. 474. See also pp. 291–2.

53 J. Bowle, *John Evelyn and his World* (1981), p. 9.

54 E.B. Jupp, 'Richard Wyatt and his Almshouses', *Surrey Arch. Coll.*, III (1865), 286; ERO, Quarter Sessions Rolls, 414 (Mich. 1667), doc. 63.

55 E. Calamy, *A Continuation of the Account of the Ministers . . . who were Ejected* (1727), p. 864; ERO, Q/SBa 2/34. doc. 10; HMC, *Various*, VII. 58; W.E.A. Axon, 'The Plague in Cheshire', in *Bygone Cheshire* (Chester, 1895), p. 127.

56 A.M. Oakley (ed.), *Actes du Consistoire de l'Église Française de Threadneedle Street, Londres, II: 1571–7* (Hug. Soc. of London, XLVIII, 1969), p. 205; Exeter College, Oxford, MS. 47 A. 6, sermons of Edward Harrison, pp. 168–9.

57 William Lilly, *History of his Life and Times* (1822), pp. 46–7.

58 *A Brief Account of the Life of the Reverend Mr. John Rawlet* (1728); J.M. Osborn (ed.), *The Autobiography of Thomas Whythorne* (Oxford, 1961), pp. xli, 145, 151, 158. For a similar reaction to the threat of plague in 1665, see D.G. Greene (ed.), *The Meditations of Lady Elizabeth Delaval* (Surtees Soc., CXC, 1978), pp. 85–6. Thomas Nashe turned his literary activity in a more sombre direction than usual during the plague of 1593, perhaps not wholly out of a desire to take advantage of the market: Thomas Nashe, *The Unfortunate Traveller and Other Works*, ed. J.B. Steane (Harmondsworth, 1972), pp. 34–7, 484–5.

59 G.R. Batho, 'The Plague of Eyam: A Tercentenary Re-evaluation', *J. Derbyshire Arch. and Nat. Hist. Soc.*, LXXXIV (1964), plate xvii. Cf. below, pp. 268–9.

60 R.F. Hunnisett (ed.), *Calendar of Nottinghamshire Coroners' Inquests 1485–1558* (Thoroton Soc., Rec. Ser., XXV, 1969), p. 115.

61 Bodl., Ashm. MSS. 229, f. 140r; 216, f. 47v. Cf. Ashm. MS. 228, f. 134r. (I owe these references to the kindness of Dr M. MacDonald.)

Chapter 2 Attitudes and actions

1 Nicholas Bownd, *Medicines for the Plague* (1604), p. 67; William Laud, *Works* (Oxford, 1847–60), VII. 308.

2 P. Slack, 'Mirrors of Health and Treasures of Poor Men: The Uses of the Vernacular Medical Literature of Tudor England', in C. Webster (ed.), *Health, Medicine and Mortality in the Sixteenth Century* (Cambridge, 1979), pp. 237–73. Much the most illuminating account of popular attitudes towards disease is to be found in K. Thomas, *Religion and the Decline of Magic* (1971), chs 7 and 8, to which I am indebted.

3 [Canutus], *Here begynneth a litil boke the whiche traytied and reherced many gode thinges necessaries for the Pestilence* [*c.* 1486].

4 Slack, 'Mirrors of Health', pp. 238–9, 243; calculations for 1603–4 and 1625–7 from A.W. Pollard and G.R. Redgrave, *A Short-Title Catalogue of Books Printed in England . . . 1475–1640* (Oxford, 1926), and the revised edition by W.A. Jackson and others, of which vol. II has appeared (London, 1976).

5 E. Cuvelier, '"A treatise of the plague" de Thomas Lodge (1603)', *Études Anglaises*, XXI (1968), 395–403.

6 BL, Sloane MS. 3866, f. 91r.

7 See A.M. Campbell, *The Black Death and Men of Learning* (New York, 1931); D.W. Singer, 'Some Plague Tractates (Fourteenth and Fifteenth Centuries)', *Proc. Royal Society of Medicine* (History of Medicine Section), IX (1916), 159–212. Cf. R.S. Gottfried, *Epidemic Disease in Fifteenth Century England* (Leicester, 1978), pp. 63–71.

8 [Alessio], *The secretes of Alexis of Piemont* (1558), sig. +ivr; W. Bullein, *A Newe Boke entituled the gouernement of healthe* (1558), f. cxxi; J. Jones, *A Diall for all Agues* (1566), sigs Aiv, Bir; A.T., *A Rich Storehouse or Treasury for the Diseased* (1596), title page; William Clever, *The flower of phisicke* (1590), 'To the Reader'.

9 H. Holland, *Spirituall Preseruatiues against the pestilence* (1603), p. 77; J. Ewich, *Of the duetie of a faithfull and wise Magistrate . . . in the time of the Plague*, trans. J. Stockwood (1583), sig. xx2r; PRO, SP 16/533, f. 35v (the king's physicians' advice on plague, 1631).

10 Cf. L.G. Stevenson, 'New Diseases in the Seventeenth Century', *Bull. Hist. Med.*, XXXIX (1965), 1–21; O. Temkin, 'The Scientific Approach to Disease: Specific Entity and Individual Sickness', in A. Crombie (ed.), *Scientific Change* (1963), pp. 629–47; below, pp. 64–5, 275–6.

11 Bodl., MS. Gough Eccl. Top 7, f. 1; S. Kellwaye, *A Defensative against the Plague* (1593), f. lr.

12 J. Hall, *A Sermon of Publike Thanksgiving* (1626), pp. 48–9; A. Borde, *The Breuiary of Helthe* (1547), f. cxxvii; T. Cogan, *The Hauen of Health* (1584), pp. 279, 282; S. Bradwell, *Physick for the Sicknesse commonly called*

the plague (1636), p. 49: J. Goeurot, *The Regiment of Life* [1543?], 'Treatise of the pestilence', f. xxviiir.

13 Bodl., Ashmole MS. 208, ff. 110–34; A. Paré, *A Treatise of the Plague* (1630), p. 2.

14 Kellwaye, *Defensative*, ff. 15, 16r, 35r; Bradwell, *Physick for the Sicknesse*, p. 2. Cf. Goeurot, *Regiment*, 'Treatise', f. xxv; T. Brasbridge, *The Poore Mans Iewel* (1578), sigs Civ–v; S.H., *A New Treatise of the Pestilence* (1603), sigs A3v–4r; T. Thayre, *A Treatise of the Pestilence* (1603), p. 33.

15 T. Pullein, *Ieremiahs Teares* (1608), sig. E3v; Goeurot, *Regiment*, 'Treatise', f.vi^v.

16 Satan was only rarely referred to in English tracts as a cause of disease, except as an intermediate agent of God's will: cf. W. Boraston, *A Necessarie and Briefe Treatise of the Contagious disease of the pestilence* (1630), p. 2; Holland, *Spirituall Preseruatiues*, pp. 72–4, 181–3. For a more direct emphasis on the devil, possibly influenced by Luther's writings, see J. Hooper, *An Homelye to be read in the tyme of pestylence* (Worcester, 1553), sigs Diiv–iiir; and also Simon Forman in Bodl., Ashmole MS. 208, f. 114.

17 *The Seconde Tome of Homelyes* (1563), sig. Bbir; R.B. McKerrow and F.P. Wilson (eds), *The Works of Thomas Nashe* (Oxford, 1958), II. 136–8, 163; M. Maclure, *The Paul's Cross Sermons 1534–1642* (Toronto, 1958), pp. 210, 218; HMC, *Franciscan MSS*, p. 80; G.R. Elton, *Policy and Police* (Cambridge, 1972), p. 181; J.E. Cox (ed.), *Miscellaneous Writings and Letters of Thomas Cranmer* (Parker Soc., 1846), p. 14; John Williams [*pseud.*], *Punition de Dieu arrivée à Londres* (Saint-Omer, 1626), *passim*; *Cal. SP Dom. 1636–7*, p. 514; below, pp. 237, 243, 247.

18 R. Fenton, *A Perfume against the noysome Pestilence* (1603), sig. A9v; J. Godskall, *The Kings Medicine for this present yeere* (1604), sigs D4v–5r, E7r.

19 W. Cupper, *Certaine Sermons concerning Gods late visitation* (1592) p. 209; G. Wither, *The History of the Pestilence*, ed. J. Milton French (Cambridge, Mass., 1932), p. 54; R. Milton, *Londoners their Entertainment in the Countrie* (1604), sig. A4v: Bownd, *Medicines for the Plague*, p. 82.

20 Paré, *Treatise*, p. 3.

21 BL, Add. MS. 27582, f. 70v; T. Moulton, *This is the myrour or glasse of helthe* (1546 edn), cap. i.

22 T.T., *A view of certain wonderful effects . . . of the comete* (1578), sig. A4; T. Forestier, *Tractatus contra pestilentiam* (Rouen, 1490), sig. Aiir; Goeurot, *Regiment*, 'Treatise', f. xi^v; R. Harvey, *An Astrological Discourse* (1583), p. 15; T. Paynel, *A moche profitable treatise against the pestilence* [? 1534], sig. Biiir.

23 *The Dr. Farmer Chetham MS.*, part 2, ed. A.B. Grosart (Chetham Soc., OS, XC, 1873), p. 129; T.R., *A Confutation of the tenne great plagues* (1587), sig. A4; Brasbridge, *Poore Mans Iewel*, sigs Bvi–viii; T. Lodge, *A Treatise of the Plague* (1603), sigs B4r–Clr; W. Fulke, *Antiprognosticon* (1560), sig. Dviir.

24 B. Capp, *Astrology and the Popular Press* (1979), p. 224; D. Parker, *Familiar to All: William Lilly and Astrology in the Seventeenth Century* (1975), pp.

223, 227. The role of astrology in medicine is explored in Thomas, *Religion and the Decline of Magic*, esp. pp. 328, 354–5.
25 T. Elyot, *The Castel of Helth* (1539), f. 12r. Cf. Thayre, *Treatise*, p. 5. On graveyards, see G.E. Corrie (ed.), *Sermons and Remains of Hugh Latimer* (Parker Soc., 1845), p. 67, and cf. below, p. 296.
26 PRO, SP 16/533, f. 39r; J. Jones, *A Diall for all Agues* (1566), sig. Fviii; J.F. Larkin and P.L. Hughes, *Stuart Royal Proclamations*, I (Oxford, 1973), pp. 164, 238, 251.
27 *Litil boke,* f 3v; Cogan, *Hauen of Health*. p. 265; Kellwaye, *Defensative*, f. lv.
28 Bradwell, *Physick*, pp. 6–7. For comparable descriptions, see Lodge, *Treatise*, sig. B2v; F. Herring, *A modest Defence of the Caveat given to the wearers of Amulets* (1604), sig. A3.
29 Cf. J.-N. Biraben, *Les Hommes et la peste* (Paris, 1975–6), II. 18–24, 182–3; Campbell, *The Black Death and Men of Learning*, pp. 56–62; L.F. Hirst, *The Conquest of Plague* (Oxford, 1953), ch. III: W.P.D. Wightman, *Science and the Renaissance* (Aberdeen, 1962), pp. 268–9: below, pp. 329–30.
30 Elyot, *Castel*, f. 84v; Moulton, *Myrour*, cap. i; W. Clever, *The Flower of Phisicke* (1590), p. 11; Jones, *Diall*, sig. Gir; *Litil boke*, f. 3r.
31 Bradwell, *Physick*, p. 37; *Litil boke*, f. 7r.
32 Goeurot, *Regiment*, 'Treatise', f. xii; *A Compendium of the rationall secretes of L. Phioravante*, trans. J. Hester (1582), Book I, pp. 1–2.
33 Cupper, *Certaine Sermons*, p. 33; Hooper, *Homelye*, sig. Biiir.
34 F. Herring, *Certaine Rules* (1625), sig. A4v; Brasbridge, *Poore Mans Iewel*, sig. Bivr. The attack on theatres at times of epidemic disease is described in F.P. Wilson, *The Plague in Shakespeare's London* (Oxford, 1963), pp. 51–5, 110–13, 170–2.
35 ERO, D/P 36/1/1, parish register of Great Coggeshall, 10 August 1578. See also pp. 304–5.
36 Paynel, *Treatise*, sig. Avr.
37 A.H. Pearson, *The Sarum Missal* (1884), pp. 586–9; C. Wordsworth, *Ceremonies and Processions of the Cathedral Church of Salisbury* (Cambridge, 1901), p. 280; W.G. Henderson (ed.), *Missale ad usum Insignis Ecclesiae Eboracensis*, II (Surtees Soc., 60, 1874), 171–2, 233; Cambridge Univ. Library, MS. LL. i. 18, f. 3r; BL, Lansdowne MS. 332, f. 135r; HMC, *Salisbury*, XV. 387.
38 See below, pp. 228–30. There were public prayers against the sweat in 1551: *Cal. SP Dom 1547–80*, p. 33; C. Nevison (ed.), *Later Writings of John Hooper* (Parker Soc., 1852), p. 139. The first plague fast was prescribed in *A fourme to be vsed in Common prayer twyse aweke . . . duryng this tyme of mortalitie* (1563). C.F. Mullett, *The Bubonic Plague and England* (Lexington, Kentucky, 1956), p. 57, refers to a prayer book for the plague of 1519, but I have been unable to trace this.
39 W. Clay (ed.), *Private Prayers put forth by Authority during Queen Elizabeth's Reign* (Parker Soc., 1851), p. 535; J. Sanford, *Gods Arrowe of the Pestilence* (Oxford, 1604), p. 48; below, p. 237.

40 E.g. A.T., *Rich Storehouse*, f. 65v; Goeurot, *Regiment*, 'Treatise', f.xiv^v; Borde, *Breuiary*, f. liiii^v.

41 Lodge, *Treatise*, sig. E4r; L. Fuchs, *A most worthie practise of L. Fuchsius* [1562?], sig. Biiiv. Although fleas were not connected directly with plague, medical compendia sometimes suggested ointments against them: Borde, *Breuiary*, f. Cxiv^v; *The Treasure of pore men* [1560?], f. lxxviii^v.

42 E.g. Paré, *Treatise*, p. 50.

43 *London Tryacle, Being the enemie to all infectious diseases* (1612), pp. 3, 9; *A Discourse of the Medicine called Mithridatium* (1585), sigs A8, B6, D4. Cf. G. Watson, *Theriac and Mithridatium* (1966); *A History of the Worshipful Society of Apothecaries*, ed. C. Wall, H.C. Cameron and E.A. Underwood (1963), pp. 33–4.

44 Paynel, *Treatise*, sig. Avi; Thayre, *Treatise*, p. 32; P. Levens, *The Pathway to health* (1587), f. 82.

45 T.C., *An Hospitall for the Diseased* (1579), pp. 1–6.

46 Goeurot, *Regiment*, 'Treatise', f. xiv; Thayre, *Treatise*, pp. 50–1; Kellwaye, *Defensative*, sig. 17r; Paré, *Treatise*, p. 81; F. Herring, *Certaine Rules Directions or Advertisements for this time of Pestilential Contagion* (1625), sig. C2. Cf. *The secretes of Alexis of Piemont*, f. 39r.

47 Brasbridge, *Poore Mans Iewel*, sigs Cv–Div; S.H., *A New Treatise* (1603), sig. B2r; T.C., *Hospitall*, pp. 4, 73; *Discourse of . . . Mithridatium*, sig. Dl.

48 A. Bertholdus, *The wonderfull and strange effect of a new terra sigillata found in Germania* (1587), sig. A3, pp. 1, 15. For other Paracelsian remedies, see J. Duchesne, *The Practise of Chymicall and Hermeticall Physicke* (trans. T. Tymme, 1605), sigs N1, U4, Aal; Paracelsus, *A hundred and foureteene Experiments and Cures* (trans. J. Hester, 1596), p. 14. On the reception of chemical medicines in England, see A.G. Debus, *The English Paracelsians* (1965), ch. II.

49 Herring, *Certaine Rules*, sigs B2–4; P. Turner, *The Opinion of Peter Turner concerning Amulets* (1603), p. 2; Lodge, *Treatise*, sig. A4; Kellwaye, *Defensative*, f. 5v; W. Perkins, *A Salue for a Sicke Man* (Cambridge, 1597), p. 31.

50 H. Colvin, *A Biographical Dictionary of British Architects 1600–1840* (1978), p. 256; information from Prof. C. Russell. On Oxbridge Colleges, see, for example: C.W. Boase, *Register of Exeter College* (Oxford Hist. Soc., XXVII, 1894), pp. lxxxvii–lxxxviii; W.H. Stevenson and H.E. Salter, *The Early History of St. John's College Oxford* (*ibid.*, NS, I, 1939), p. 179; BL, Add. MS. 4376, ff. 77–8.

51 T. Dekker, *The Wonderfull Yeare* (1603), in F.P. Wilson (ed.), *The Plague Pamphlets of Thomas Dekker* (Oxford, 1925), p. 3. Cf. W. Bullein, *A Dialogue against the Fever Pestilence*, ed. M.W. and A.H. Bullen (Early English Text Soc., extra ser., LII, 1888), p. 71; below, p. 242.

52 F.N.L. Poynter and W.J. Bishop (eds), *A Seventeenth-Century Doctor and His Patients: John Symcotts, 1592?–1662* (Bedfordshire Rec. Soc., XXXI, 1951), pp. 62–4. For another case of a doctor visiting a wealthy infected household, see HMC, *Salisbury*, V. 201. Payments for physic and surgery are sometimes noted in probate accounts of expenses in infected households: e.g. Kent AO, PRC 2/17, ff. 210, 292.

53 *Pharmacopoeia Londinensis Collegarum* (1668), pp. 192–3, 196–9. For examples from household books, see (in chronological order) BL, Sloane MS. 4, f. 27; Add. MS. 16166, f. 187v; Sloane MS. 118, ff. 1–4; Add. MS. 6704, f. lv; Add. MS 28327, ff. 9–14; Sloane MS. 785, f. 8v; Bodl., Tanner MS. 397, f. 112.

54 Theodore de Mayerne, *Medicinal Councils and Advices* (1677), pp. 104–6; Bodl., Rawl. MS. C516, ff. 31 *et seq.*; BL, Sloane MS. 2059, ff. 164v–168v; Sloane MS. 2078, ff. 119v–120v; Sloane MS. 1989, f. 191v (I owe these references to Mayerne's notes in Sloane MSS. to the kindness of H.R. Trevor-Roper); Poynter and Bishop, *Symcotts*, pp. xxiii, 76; Kent AO, PRC 2/34, acct no. 269.

55 Bodl., Rawl. MS. A369, f. 108; Cambridge Univ. Library, MS. Add. 3071, f. 27v; BL, Sloane MS. 1529, ff. 164, 144; BL, Loan MS. 9 (at rear).

56 BL, Add. MS. 4376, f. 80. For examples of other recommended variants, see BL, Sloane MS. 223, f. 1; F.P. and M.M. Verney, *Memoirs of the Verney Family* (1892–9), IV. 118; *Cal. SP Dom. 1666–7*, p. 55; J. Crossley (ed.), *The Diary and Correspondence of Dr. John Worthington*, II (Chetham Soc., OS, XXXVI, 1855), 182–3; Bodl., Ashmole MS. 1477, vii. 43. Cf. O. Temkin, *Galenism: Rise and Decline of a Medical Philosophy* (Ithaca, 1973), p. 115, on the continuity of Galenic practice in medicine despite the fall of Galenic science.

57 BL, Add. MS. 6716, f. 98r. For another example, see BL, Add. MS. 39638, f. 14. Cf. Slack, 'Mirrors of Health', p. 266. Talismans against plague were said to be commonly sold by friars before the Reformation: P.M. Zall (ed.), *A Hundred Merry Tales* (Lincoln, Nebraska, 1963), pp. 270–1.

58 NNRO, Norwich Mayor's Court Book 23, f. 276v; W. Clowes, *A prooued practise for all young chirurgians* (1588), sig. A3; Jones, *Diall*, sig. Fviiiᵛ.

59 Bodl., Ashm. MS. 1473, pp. 680, 703, 461; BL, Sloane MS. 1087, ff. 8r, 10v, 76v (I owe these references to Dr M. MacDonald); William Lilly, *History of his Life and Times* (1822), p. 214.

60 R.B. McKerrow and F.P. Wilson (eds), *The Works of Thomas Nashe* (Oxford, 1958), II. 172–3; W.G. Bell, *The Great Plague in London in 1665* (2nd edn, 1951), p. 246; *Cal SP Dom. 1665–6*, pp. 51, 538. For other examples of bird omens, see J. Toy, *Worcester's Elegie and Evlogie* (1638), p. 3; J. Aubrey, *The Natural History of Wiltshire* (1847), p. 64; and for their origin in Thucydides, T. Sprat, *The Plague of Athens* (1659), sig. A3v.

61 Kellwaye, *Defensative*, f. 2v; W. Boghurst, *Loimographia. An Account of the Great Plague of London*, ed. J.F. Payne (1894), p. 20 and n. William Lilly noted crowds of children playing before the plague of 1625 (Lilly, *Life and Times*, p. 45), and some urban corporations tried to stop them during epidemics: Hull Corporation Records, Bench Book 5, f. 232v; W.B. Willcox, *Gloucestershire: A Study in Local Government 1590–1640* (New Haven, 1940), p. 225, n. 64.

62 *Newes from Hereford, or A Wonderful and terrible Earthquake* [1662?]. For other portents and prophecies of plague, see BL, Add. MS. 35331, f.

65v; Bodl., Ashm. MS. 384, f. 175v. Cf. K. Park and L.J. Daston, 'Unnatural Conceptions: The Study of Monsters in France and England', *P&P*, 92 (1981), 40–3.

63 See also below, pp. 238–9.

64 J.-N. Biraben, 'La Peste en 1720 à Marseille à propos d'un livre récent', *Revue historique*, 247 (1972), 416.

65 Ewich, *Duetie of a . . . Magistrate*, f. 19r; Bodl., Ashm. MS. 1436, f. 127v; Biraben, *Les Hommes et la peste*, II. 181; I. Diemerbroeck, *Several Choice Histories of the Medicines Manner and Method used in the Cure of the Plague* (1666), pp. 33–4; T. Willis, *A Plain and Easie Method for Preserving . . . from the Infection of the Plague* (1691), p. 21.

66 P. Moore, *The Hope of Health* (1565), sig. Fviii; Cogan, *Hauen of Health*, p. 277; T. Bright, *A treatise wherein is declared the sufficiencie of English Medicines* (1580), p. 14. Cf. A.T., *Rich Storehouse*, sig. Bl.

67 Duchesne, *Practise*, sig. N4; *Secretes of Phioravante*, Book I, p. 24; W. Bullein, *A Newe Boke entituled the gouernement of healthe* (1558), f. xxvᵛ. Cf. Jones, *Diall*, sig. Iiv; Thomas, *Religion and the Decline of Magic*, p. 641.

68 See pp. 329–31.

69 A.W. Langford, 'Plague in Herefordshire', *Trans. Woolhope Nat. Field Club*, XXXV (1957), 151–2; Elton, *Policy and Police*, p. 92. For examples of processions in Catholic countries, see J. Charlier, *La Peste à Bruxelles de 1667 à 1669* (Brussels, 1969), p. 151; C.M. Cipolla, *Faith, Reason and the Plague in Seventeenth-Century Tuscany* (Ithaca, 1979), chap. IV; BL, Add. MS. 36448, f. 100 (Malaga, 1637); and for the use of candles, see Biraben, *Les Hommes et la peste*, II. 71–2.

70 *Letters and Papers of Henry VIII*, IV (ii), pp. 1956, 1963; LCRO, Rep. x, f. 347r.

71 LCRO, Journal xviii, f. 140v; Journal xix, f. 188r; below, pp. 228–9.

72 John Prideaux, *The Doctrine of Prayer* (Oxford, 1841), pp. 214–15; M.M. Knappen (ed.), *Two Elizabethan Puritan Diaries* (Chicago, 1933), p. 116. Cf. BL, Lans. MS. 1197, f. 146.

73 Brasbridge, *Poore Mans Iewel*, sig. Ci; Paré, *Treatise*, p. 4.

74 By Anthony Anderson, Nicholas Bownd, and James Godskall, respectively.

75 BL, Lans. MS. 777, no. 10, f. 279v.

76 E.g. John Caius, 'Counseill against . . . the sweate' in *Works*, ed. E.S. Roberts (Cambridge, 1912), p. 36; Elyot, *Castel of Helth*, f. 86r. Cf. P.H. Kocher, *Science and Religion in Elizabethan England* (New York, 1953), chs 12, 13, *passim*.

77 E.g. R. Bostocke, *The Difference between the auncient . . . and the latter Phisicke* (1585), sigs Av, Dii; Duchesne, *Practise*, sig. L3. There was, however, no full description of the Paracelsian theory of the origins of plague in England before 1640. Cf. W. Pagel, *Paracelsus* (New York, 1958), pp. 172–89; P.M. Rattansi, 'The Helmontian-Galenist Controversy in Restoration England', *Ambix*, XII (1964), 18–21, below, pp. 248–9.

78 E.g. T. Becon, *The Sicke Mans Salue* (1572 edn), p. 304; *Two Liturgies*

... *of King Edward VI* (Parker Soc., 1844), p. 474; Richard Sibbes, *Works*, ed. A.B. Grosart (Edinburgh, 1862), I. 67; T. Swadling, *A Manuall of Devotion Suiting each Day* (1643), pp. 419–21, 449. Cf. N.L. Beaty, *The Craft of Dying: A Study in the Literary Tradition of the Ars Moriendi in England* (New Haven, 1970).

79 W. Tyndale, *An Answer to Sir Thomas More's Dialogue* (Parker Soc., 1850), p. 119; Hooper, *Homelye*, sig. Ciir; John Woolton, *The Christian Manuell* (Parker Soc., 1851), p. 93; H. Latimer, *Sermons* (Parker Soc., 1844), pp. 540–1; Nashe, *Works*, II. 165–6; Perkins, *Salue*, p. 32.

80 *The sicke-mans comfort* (1590), p. 4. Cf. *Secretes of Alexis*, sig. +iiii.

81 Nashe, *Works*, II. 171–2, V. 247n.

82 T.F. Barton (ed.), *The Registrum Vagum of Anthony Harison*, part I (Norfolk Rec. Soc., 32, 1963), p. 163. Cf. Capp, *Astrology*, p. 135.

83 R. Jenison, *Newcastles Call to her Neighbour and Sister Townes* (1637), p. 61; S. Price, *Londons Remembrancer* (1626), p. 20; Holland, *Spirituall Preseruatiues*, pp. 36–7; R. Fenton, *A Perfume against the noysome Pestilence* (1603), sigs A6v, A9v; Cupper, *Certaine Sermons*, pp. 95–6, 145; B. Spenser, *Vox Civitatis* (1625), p. 17.

84 E.M. Wilson, 'Richard Leake's Plague Sermons 1599', *Trans. Cumb. and Westm. Antiq. and Arch. Soc.*, NS, LXXV (1975), 155; Dekker, 'Newes from Gravesende', in *Plague Pamphlets*, p. 102.

85 J. Rutherford (ed.), *The Miscellaneous Papers of Captain Thomas Stockwell* (Southampton Rec. Soc., 1932–3), I. 24; R. Parkinson (ed.), *The Life of Adam Martindale* (Chetham Soc., OS, IV, 1845), pp. 54–5; B. Winchester, *Tudor Family Portrait* (1955), p. 55.

86 A.T., *Rich Storehouse*, f. 65v; Cupper, *Certaine Sermons*, p. 363; J. Manning, *I am for you all, Complexions Castle* (Cambridge, 1604), p. 2.

87 *A myrrour or glasse for them that be syke* [1536?], sigs Bvʳ, Biⱽ. Cf. C. Hueber, *A riche storehouse, or treasurie, for the sicke* (1578), f. 7.

88 E. Freshfield (ed.), *Some Remarks upon the Book of Records ... of St. Stephen Coleman Street* (1887), p. 34.

89 Herring, *Certaine Rules*, sig. A3. Cf. below, pp. 236, 242.

90 Bullein, *Dialogue*, *passim* (see n. 51, above).

91 BL, Sloane MSS. 790, 791 (for date see 791, f. 21v). Cf. G. Biel, *Sermones* (Hagenaw, 1519). Biel died in 1495. He was probably drawing on earlier discussions of the same theme: see Mullett, *Bubonic Plague and England*, p. 53 n. 10; and for Ottoman discussion of the same subject in the sixteenth century, M.W. Dols, *The Black Death in the Middle East* (Princeton, 1977), p. 299.

92 J. Pelikan and H.T. Lehmann (eds), *Luther's Works* (Philadelphia, 1968), vol. 43, pp. 119–38; W. Baum, E. Cunitz, and E. Reuss (eds), *Ioannis Calvini Opera Quae Supersunt Omnia* (Brunswick, 1878), XVIII. 105, letter 3212.

93 A. Osiander, *How and whither a Christen man ought to flye the horrible Plage* (trans. M. Coverdale, 1537); T.C., *A Godly and learned sermon upon the 91 Psalme* (1603); T. Beza, *De Peste Quaestiones Duae Explicatae* (Geneva, 1579); *idem*, *A shorte learned and pithie Treatize of the Plague* (trans. J. Stockwood, 1580). Cf. A. Peel and L.H. Carlson (eds),

Cartwrightiana (1951), p. 12; P.-F. Geisendorf, *Théodore de Bèze* (Geneva, 1949), pp. 333, 356.

94 Calvin, *Institutes*, I. xvii. 3, cited in Thomas, *Religion and the Decline of Magic*, p. 85; *Ioannis Calvini Opera*, XVIII. 105.

95 The biblical texts most frequently cited in plague tracts were: (in favour of prudential action) Genesis 12.10, 27.42–3; Proverbs 22.3; II Samuel 24; Ephesians 5.29; (stressing the role of providence) Ezekiel 9; II Kings 20; II Chron. 16.12; Psalm 91.

96 *Luther's Works*, vol. 43, pp. 120–3, 130–1.

97 Osiander, *How . . . a Christen man ought to flye*, sig. Avir; O. Werdmueller, *A most frutefull . . . treatyse, How a christen man ought to behaue*, trans. M. Coverdale [*c*. 1553], p. 66.

98 J. Godskall, *The Arke of Noah* (1603), sig. C3r; Hooper, *Homelye*, sig. Ciir; Herring, *A Modest Defence*, sig. B2.

99 Beza, *Treatize*, sigs A1, A3r, D1v; Ewich, *Duetie of a . . . Magistrate* (also translated by Stockwood), sig. xx4r; T. White, *A Sermo[n] Preached at Pawles Crosse . . . in the time of the Plague* (1578), pp. 78–9.

100 J. Balmford, *A Short Dialogue concerning the Plagues Infection* (1603), pp. 26, 72.

101 White, *Sermon*, pp. 78–9; Ewich, *Duetie*, dedication by translator; below, pp. 233–5. For other comments on the issue, see Kellwaye, *Defensative*, f. 2v; Cogan, *Hauen of Health*, pp. 266–7; Jones, *Diall*, sigs Giiiv–ivr; Fuchs, *Worthie practise*, sig. Aviii; Sanford, *Gods Arrowe*, pp. 50–1.

102 Bodl., MS. Eng. hist. c. 475, f. 145.

103 See pp. 230–5, 250–1, 301.

104 Ewich, *Duetie of a . . . Magistrate*; Lodge, *Treatise*, ch. viii.

105 E.g. Kellwaye, *Defensative*, f. 13v; Bownd, *Medicines*, p. 90; Herring, *Certaine Rules*, sigs A4, C1.

106 Biraben, *Les Hommes et la peste*, II. 86–9, 102–5, 139–41, 174; C.M. Cipolla, *Public Health and the Medical Profession in the Renaissance* (Cambridge, 1976), pp. 11–15; Campbell, *Black Death*, p. 115; S. D'Irsay, 'Defense Reactions during the Black Death 1348–9', *Annals of Medic. Hist.*, X (1927), 170, 176. R.J. Palmer, 'The Control of Plague in Venice and Northern Italy' (unpublished PhD thesis, Kent Univ., 1978), discusses the origins of plague control in Italy in detail.

107 Cf. M.W. Flinn, 'Plague in Europe and the Mediterranean Countries', *J. Eur. Ec. Hist.*, VIII (1979), 146–7; R. Pollitzer, *Plague* (Geneva, 1954), pp. 300–1, 386–7; Hirst, *Conquest of Plague*, 303–9; above, pp. 11–12.

108 Biraben, *Les Hommes et la peste*, I. 198, 205–6.

109 See below, pp. 321–5.

110 C.F. Mullett, 'Plague Policy in Scotland, 16th–17th Centuries', *Osiris*, 9 (1950), 436–8; below, Chapter 8.

111 J.F.D. Shrewsbury, *A History of Bubonic Plague in the British Isles* (Cambridge, 1970) p. 39; LCRO, Rep. i, f. 228v; J. Vowell, *The Description of the Citie of Excester* (Devon and Cornwall Rec. Soc., 1919–47), p. 898; Wilson, *Plague in Shakespeare's London*, p. 56.

112 For an example of the compulsory isolation of a leper, in 1419, because of 'contagion', see G.O. Sayles (ed.), *Select Cases in the Court of King's*

Bench, VII (Selden Soc., LXXXVIII, 1971), 247–8. The biblical source is Leviticus 13.45–6.

113 E.g. A. Raine (ed.), *York Civic Records*, I (Yorks. Arch. Soc. Rec. Series, XCVIII, 1939), 142; LCRO, Journal xi, ff. 195v–196r, Rep. ii, f. 166v; *Statutes of the Realm*, 4 Henry VII, c. 3; NNRO, Assembly Book 1491–1553, ff. 101v, 202r; F.B. Bickley (ed.), *The Little Red Book of Bristol* (Bristol, 1900), II. 31–2.

114 See below, Chapter 9.

115 Cipolla, *Public Health*, pp. 36–7. Cf. A.D. Wright, 'The People of Catholic Europe and the People of Anglican England', *Hist. J.*, XVIII (1975), 465–6.

116 See below, pp. 261–3.

117 Dols, *Black Death in the Middle East*, pp. 23, 109; Biraben, *Les Hommes et la peste*, II. 8; D. Panzac, 'La Peste à Smyrne au XVIIIe siècle', *Annales: Économies, Sociétés, Civilisations*, 28 (1973), 1086.

118 The comparison was in fact made by some English critics of providential views: e.g. W. Kemp, *A Brief Treatise of the Nature, Causes, Signes . . . and Cure of the Pestilence* (1665), pp. 15–16.

119 For an illuminating discussion of this difference, see Dols, *Black Death in the Middle East*, pp. 285–98.

120 For examples, see below, pp. 304–6.

121 Cf. A.H. Barton, *Social Organization under Stress* (Washington, DC, 1963), *passim*.

Chapter 3 The chronology of epidemics 1485–1665

1 E.g. Thomas Dekker, 'A Dialogue betweene Warre, Famine and the Pestilence', in *The Meeting of Gallants at an Ordinarie* (1604).

2 Cf. T. Wright, *Queen Elizabeth and her Times* (1838), I. 134; H. Holland, *Spirituall Preseruatiues* (1593), f. 21r; E. Cardwell, *Documentary Annals* (Oxford, 1839), II. 163.

3 C. Read (ed.), *William Lambarde and Local Government* (Ithaca, 1962), p. 182. Lambarde seems to have ignored the great London plague of 1593.

4 J. Leland, *Itinerary*, ed. L.T. Smith (1906–8), IV. 122; GL, MS. 4249, p. 154; G. Roberts (ed.), *The Diary of Walter Yonge* (Camden Soc., OS, XLI, 1848), p. 1; A.F.W. Papillon, *Memoirs of Thomas Papillon* (Reading, 1887), p. 279. Cf. C.J. Palmer (ed.), *A Booke of the Foundacion and Antiquity of the Towne of Greate Yarmouthe* (Yarmouth, 1847), p. 27.

5 E.g. H.H.E. Craster, *A History of Northumberland*, IX (1909), 23; E. Lloyd, 'Weybridge Parish Registers', *Surrey Arch. Coll.*, XVII (1902), 45. Cf. *VCH Sussex*, VII. 16. On the origins and deficiencies of parish registers, see J.C. Cox, *The Parish Registers of England* (1910), chs I and II; E.A. Wrigley and R.S. Schofield, *The Population History of England 1541–1871* (1981), ch. I.

6 Cf. T.H. Hollingsworth, *Historical Demography* (1969), pp. 237–40, on the use of this method.

7 See below, pp. 127, 148. I have discussed some of the problems involved

in using wills in 'Mortality Crises and Epidemic Disease in England 1485–1610', in C. Webster (ed.), *Health, Medicine and Mortality in the Sixteenth Century* (Cambridge, 1979), pp. 12–14.

8 The information in Table 3.1 has been drawn from calculations based on the calendars of wills published by the British Record Society, Index Library, vols 7, 8, 24, 27, 31, 39, 46, 78, 79, 82, 86 (1892–1974). The Exeter series used is that of the consistory court, because this provides the longest continuous series. The date after each area is that when an apparently reliable series of registrations for this period begins.

9 1502–3, 1508–9, and 1527–8 seem also to have been years of high mortality in Herefordshire: M.A. Faraday, 'Mortality in the Diocese of Hereford 1442–1541', *Trans. Woolhope Nat. Field Club*, XLII (1977), 163–74. On Worcestershire, see also C. Dyer, *Lords and Peasants in a Changing Society* (Cambridge, 1980), pp. 221–3.

10 Wrigley and Schofield, *Population History*, pp. 334, 653. See also *ibid.*, Appendix 10, for an extensive and illuminating discussion of local mortality crises.

1 Cf. below, Chs 4–6; Thomas Short, *New Observations on City, Town and Country Bills of Mortality* (1750), pp. 85–7; M. Drake, 'An Elementary Exercise in Parish Register Demography', *Ec. HR*, 2nd ser., XIV (1962), 427–45; A.B. Appleby, 'Disease of Famine? Mortality in Cumberland and Westmorland 1580–1640', *EcHR*, 2nd ser., XXVI (1973), 403–32; D. Palliser, 'Dearth and Disease in Staffordshire 1540–1670', in C.W. Chalklin and M.A. Havinden (eds), *Rural Change and Urban Growth 1500–1800: Essays in Honour of W.G. Hoskins* (1974), pp. 54–75.

12 Wrigley and Schofield, *Population History*, pp. 178–9, 316–18, 335.

13 *Ibid.*, p. 654; below, p. 99.

14 Tables 3.3 and 3.4 are based on detailed research in the parochial and corporation records of the towns of London, Norwich, Bristol and Exeter (on which see below) and of Lincoln, Reading and Salisbury; information on other towns has been drawn from C. Creighton, *A History of Epidemics in Britain* (Cambridge, 1891–4); J.F.D. Shrewsbury, *A History of Bubonic Plague in the British Isles* (Cambridge, 1970); A.D. Dyer, *The City of Worcester in the Sixteenth Century* (Leicester, 1973); *The Register of St Chad's Shrewsbury*, ed. W.G.D. Fletcher (Shropshire Parish Register Soc., Lichfield diocese, XVI, 1913), and *The Parish Register of Shrewsbury St Mary*, ed. G.W.S. Sparrow (*ibid.*, XII, 1911); J.E.O. Wilshere, 'Plague in Leicester 1558–1665', *Trans. Leics. Arch. and Hist. Soc.*, XLIV (1968–9), 45–69, and parish registers in Leicester Corporation Archives; *VCH Yorks: East Riding*, I. 154–7 (Hull); D.M. Palliser, 'Epidemics in Tudor York', *Northern History*, VIII (1973), 45–63; R.H. Morris, *Chester in the Plantagenet and Tudor Reigns* (Chester, 1893), pp. 78–9, and *The Parish Register of the Holy and Undivided Trinity, Chester*, ed. L.M. Farrall (Chester, 1914); G.B. Richardson, *Plague and Pestilence in the North of England* (Newcastle, 1852).

15 Creighton, *History of Epidemics*, I. 568–76; *Cal. SP Dom. 1658–9*, p. 82.

16 *Letters and Papers of Henry VIII*, XIII (i), 1538, p. 14.

17 Kent AO, Sa/ZB6 Sandwich Annals, under 1562. On the problems of

diagnosis in the past, see the remarks in *Problèmes de mortalité*, ed. P. Harsin and E. Helin (Congrès et Colloques de l'Université de Liège, XXXIII, 1965), p. 460; J.-P. Peter, 'Malades et maladies', in J.-P. Desaive *et al.*, *Médecins, climat et épidémies à la fin du XVIIIᵉ siècle* (Paris, 1972), pp. 146–7.

18 Shrewsbury, *Bubonic Plague*, p. 236; T. Milbourn, 'Notes on the Parish and Church of Carshalton', *Surrey Arch. Coll.*, VII (1880), 146.

19 Cf. above, pp. 8, 25; below, p. 275; *Cal. SP Dom. 1637–8*, p. 395.

20 Cf. above, pp. 7–8; and for examples from Norwich, fig. 5.5 below, p. 131. The more general relationship between weather and epidemics of plague is discussed in: D.J. Schove, 'Chronology and Historical Geography of Famine, Plague and other Pandemics', *Proc. XXIII Congress of History of Medicine* (1972), p. 1271; A.B. Appleby, 'Epidemics and Famine in the Little Ice Age', *J. Interdisc. Hist.*, X (1980), 647–9.

21 *Cal. SP Dom. 1666–7*, p. 41; M. Verney (ed.), *Memoirs of the Verney Family* (1892–9), IV. 124.

22 Cf. Creighton, *History of Epidemics*, I. 283–4, 287–8, 297–302.

23 See below, p. 85.

24 *VCH Yorks: East Riding*, I (1969), p. 155; NNRO, microfilm 24*, register of Great Yarmouth; Hull Corporation Records, Bench Book 5, f. 62; R. Welford, *History of Newcastle and Gateshead* (1883–7), III. 337; *Cal. SP Dom 1664–5*, pp. 78, 90, 92, 95, 196; Shrewsbury, *Bubonic Plague*, pp. 435–45; J.A. Picton (ed.), *City of Liverpool: Selections from the Municipal Archives* (Liverpool, 1883), p. 194. For precautions taken in Kent in 1602 against plague in Amsterdam, see Staffs. RO, D593/S/4/52/9.

25 M. Bateson *et al.* (eds), *Records of the Borough of Leicester* (Cambridge, 1899–1905), III. 179; Berkshire RO, parish register of St Giles's, Reading.

26 Hollingsworth, *Historical Demography*, pp. 365, 373–4; R. Pollitzer, *Plague* (Geneva, 1954), pp. 486–7, 494–5; J. Brownlee, 'Certain Aspects of the Theory of Epidemiology in Special Relation to Plague', *Proc. Roy. Soc. Med.*, XI, pts 1–2 (1918), 103.

27 Shrewsbury, *Bubonic Plague*, pp. 294–5. For the sources for Reading and Leicester, see above n. 14.

28 E. Burghall, *Providence Improved* (Lancs. and Cheshire Record Soc., XIX, 1889), p. 3. Cf. Pollitzer, *Plague*, p. 495; L.F. Hirst, *The Conquest of Plague* (Oxford, 1953), p. 267.

29 W.E. Godfrey, 'The Plague of Chesterfield 1586–7', *J. Derbyshire Arch. and Nat. Hist. Soc.*, LXXIV (1954), 32–42; *Register of St James' Parish, Bury St Edmunds* (Suffolk Green Books, XVII, 1916); Kent AO, transcript of Cranbrook parish register; Sa/AC 6, f. 240r; J. Webb (ed.), *Poor Relief in Elizabethan Ipswich* (Suffolk Records Soc., IX, 1966), pp. 114–15; Staffs. RO, D593/S/4/37/14; *Records of Maidstone* (Maidstone, 1926), p. 209. Plague probably continued in Kent into 1598: *ibid.*, p. 210; Kent AO, PRC 2/10, ff. 294r, 305v, 340r, 398v.

30 Cf. above, pp. 12–14.

31 Isolated cases of plague were in fact reported in the London bills of mortality in these intervals, but they may have been mistaken diagnoses:

see below, pp. 145–7. There were certainly no serious epidemics in these periods.

32 See below, Chs 5, 6.

33 A.W. Langford, 'The Plague in Herefordshire', *Trans. Woolhope Nat. Field Club*, XXXV (1957), 150. Cf. J.-N. Biraben, *Les Hommes et la peste* (Paris, 1975–6), I. esp. p. 122; above, pp. 000–00/

34 Wrigley and Schofield, *Population History*, p. 14.

35 Cf. *Problèmes de mortalité*, pp. 173–84, 192, 369–77, 461; E. Woehlkens, *Pest und Ruhr im 16. und 17. Jahrhundert* (Hanover, 1954), pp. 150–1; L. Porquet, *La Peste en Normandie du XIVe au XVIIe siècle* (Vire, 1898), p. 128.

36 MS. note in a seventeenth-century hand in Bodl., Gough London 154.

37 See below, pp. 105–7; E.A. Eckert, 'Boundary Formation and Diffusion of Plague: Swiss Epidemics from 1562 to 1669', *Annales de Démog. Hist.*, 1978, p. 75. The maps in Wrigley and Schofield, *Population History*, pp. 674–5, suggest no difference in diffusion between the epidemics of 1603–4 and 1665–6, but by confining themselves to single years, and to only a small number of urban parishes, they probably understate the spread of plague in the first visitation. On the other hand Biraben's manipulation of the printed evidence (*Les Hommes et la peste*, I. 115) gives a false impression of the increasing severity of epidemics in the seventeenth century, simply because the later the epidemic, the more voluminous the evidence.

38 C.H. Hull (ed.), *The Economic Writings of Sir William Petty* (Cambridge, 1899), II. 458. Shrewsbury, *Bubonic Plague*, p. 537, is mistaken in his statement that there was plague in Cornwall in 1671: the 'Redriff' of his source is the London district of Rotherhithe, not Redruth.

39 Slack, thesis, pp. 21–2; Creighton, *History of Epidemics*, I. 465, 536–7, 541–3, 568–76; Wellcome Historical Medical Library, London, MS. 3921, under 1616; *Cal. SP Dom. 1658–9*, p. 82. On malaria, see M. Dobson, '"Marsh Fever" – the Geography of Malaria in England', *J. Hist. Geog.*, VI (1980), 357–89.

40 J.A.H. Wylie and L.H. Collier, 'The English Sweating Sickness (Sudor Anglicus): A Reappraisal', *J. Hist. Med.*, 36 (1981), 425–45. See also A. Patrick and R.S. Roberts, 'A Consideration of the Nature of the English Sweating Sickness', *Medical History*, IX (1965), 272–9, 385–9.

41 Slack, 'Mortality Crises', pp. 25–7. Cf. Wrigley and Schofield, *Population History*, p. 337.

42 Palliser, 'Epidemics in Tudor York', pp. 46, 49–51; Creighton, *History of Epidemics*, I. 290–1; John More, *A table from the beginning of the world to this day* (Cambridge, 1593), p. 209; F.F. Fox (ed.), *Adams' Chronicle of Bristol* (Bristol, 1910), p. 100; BAO, register of St Nicholas's.

43 Thomas Cogan, *The Hauen of Health* (1584), p. 281. There is an excellent description of influenza in Berwick in 1580 in J. Stevenson (ed.), *The Correspondence of Robert Bowes* (Surtees Soc., XIV, 1842), pp. 84–5.

44 For discussion of this crisis, see Slack, 'Mortality Crises', pp. 27–32; Wrigley and Schofield, *Population History*, pp. 234, 311, 663–6.

45 E.g. Kent AO, Sa/AC4, ff. 115r, 129v; below, p. 128.

46 Dyer, *Worcester in the Sixteenth Century*, pp. 21, 44–5.

47 I.G. Philip (ed.), *Journal of Sir Samuel Luke* (Oxfords. Rec. Soc., XXIX–XXXIII, 1950–3), II. 102, 114, 133, 140, 152, III. 217; below, pp. 118, 121. Cf. W.O. Hassall, 'Typhus in Oxfordshire Billets 1643–4', *J. Roy. Army Medic. Corps*, 101 (1955), 244–5; H.P. Kendall, 'The Plague in Halifax Parish', *Trans. Halifax Antiq. Soc.* (1931), pp. 16–17. For a reference to the sweating sickness in 1644, see W. Harding, *The History of Tiverton* (Tiverton, 1845), I. 60.

48 *An Homilie agaynst Disobedience and wylful Rebellion* [?1571], pt iii, sig. Eiii; T.G. Barnes, *Somerset 1625–1640* (1961), pp. 254–5; W.J. Hardy (ed.), *Hertford County Records* (Hertford, 1905–39), I. 76; C.W. Boase, *Oxford* (1890), p. 156.

49 G. Ormerod (ed.), *Tracts Relating to Military Proceedings in Lancashire during the Great Civil War* (Chetham Soc., OS, II, 1844), pp. 277–8. Cf. W.A. Shaw (ed.), *Minutes of the Manchester Presbyterian Classis 1646–60*, pt. 2 (Chetham Soc., NS, XXII, 1891), p. 114.

50 W.G. Hoskins, 'Harvest Fluctuations and English Economic History, 1480–1619', *Agric. Hist. Rev.*, XII (1964), 44–6; idem, 'Harvest Fluctuations and English Economic History, 1620–1759', *ibid.*, XVI (1968), 28. Professor Hoskins' analysis is based on the price of wheat. A review of other grain prices affects the assessment of some years, though not of the major harvest failures: C.J. Harrison, 'Grain Price Analysis and Harvest Qualities, 1465–1634', *ibid.*, XIX (1971), 135–55.

51 Cf. Wrigley and Schofield, *Population History*, pp. 325–9, 350, 399.

52 John Cheke, *The hurt of sedicion* (1549), sig. Dvⁱᵛ. Only three out of fifteen periods of bad or disastrous harvests (according to Hoskins' definition) between 1485 and 1630 were not obviously followed by crisis mortality: those of 1565, 1573 and 1608.

53 By A.B. Appleby in 'Disease or Famine?', *passim*, and *Famine in Tudor and Stuart England* (Liverpool, 1978), chs 7 and 8. For evidence of these crises in other localities, see Slack, 'Mortality Crises', pp. 33–9; Drake, 'An Elementary Exercise', *passim*; Palliser, 'Dearth and Disease in Staffordshire', *passim*; and for a possible local crisis of a similar kind in 1613–19, see V. Skipp, *Crisis and Development* (Cambridge, 1978), ch. 4.

54 Shrewsbury, *Bubonic Plague*, pp. 237, 315–16; D. and S. Lysons, *Magna Britannia*, II, pt ii (1810), 702; Bodl., Rawlinson MS. A 369, f. 35; J.F. Larkin and P.L. Hughes (eds), *Stuart Royal Proclamations* I (Oxford, 1973), p. 606; T.R. Forbes, *Chronicle from Aldgate* (New Haven, 1971), p. 105. Cf. E.M. Wilson, 'Richard Leake's Plague Sermons 1599', *Trans. Cumb. and Westm. Antiq. and Arch. Soc.*, NS, LXXV (1975), 157; Benjamin Spenser, *Vox Civitatis* (1625), p. 13; Slack, 'Mortality Crises', p. 39.

55 Slack, 'Mortality Crises', p. 37; Slack, thesis, p. 28.

56 Shrewsbury, *Bubonic Plague*, pp. 261–2; Welford, *Newcastle and Gateshead*, III. 116–17; Appleby, 'Disease or Famine?', p. 419; T. Hughes, 'The Plague in Carlisle 1597/8', *Trans. Cumb. and Westm. Antiq. and Arch. Soc.*, NS, LXXI (1971), 52–63.

57 Slack, 'Mortality Crises', pp. 35–9; Forbes, *Chronicle*, p. 127; *Economic Writings of Petty*, II. 433; NNRO, reports of burials in Norwich Court Books 1595–1603.

58 On the complex and controversial relationship between disease and malnutrition, see N.S. Scrimshaw, C.E. Taylor and J.E. Gordon, *Interactions of Nutrition and Infection* (Geneva, 1968), esp. pp. 70, 177–82; A.B. Appleby, 'Nutrition and Disease: The Case of London 1550–1750', *J. Interdisc. Hist.*, VI (1975), 1–22; J.D. Post, 'Famine, Mortality and Epidemic Disease in the Process of Modernization', *Ec. HR*, 2nd ser., XXIX (1976), 14–37; and, in general, I. Gantzea, *Nutrition and Anti-Infectious Defence* (Basel, 1974). On plague, see Biraben, *Les Hommes et la peste*, I. 147.

59 Below, p. 84; Lincolnshire RO, Lincoln Entries of Common Council 1541–64, ff. 79, 89v. Cf. the corn shortage in Bristol in December 1550, shortly before a plague epidemic: BL, Lansdowne MS. 2, f. 91.

60 Shrewsbury, *Bubonic Plague*, pp. 159, 163, 167; Creighton, *History of Epidemics*, I. 287–8, 292; C. Phythian-Adams, *Desolation of a City* (Cambridge, 1979), pp. 52–7, 65, 196–7. For evidence of sickness in Beverley in 1521, see Beverley Corporation Records, Keepers' Account Rolls, 1520–1, 1522–3.

61 Cf. Post, 'Famine, Mortality and Epidemic Disease', pp. 31–4.

62 For a reassessment of crises in France, stressing the role of disease rather than dearth even there, see F. Lebrun, 'Les Crises démographiques en France au XVIIᵉ et XVIIIᵉ siècles', *Annales ESC*, 35 (1980), 205–34. Cf. the discussion of types of famine in D.J. Oddy, 'Urban Famine in Nineteenth-Century Britain', *Ec. HR*, 2nd ser., XXXVI (1983), 70–2.

63 Slack, 'Mortality Crises', pp. 33–40; Wrigley and Schofield, *Population History*, pp. 670–2, 675–7.

64 D.V. Glass and D.E.C. Eversley (eds), *Population in History* (1965), p. 465; P. Deyon, *Amiens, capitale provinciale* (Paris, 1967), pp. 17–18; J. Nadal and E. Giralt, *La Population catalane* (Paris, 1960), pp. 39–40; B. Bennassar, *Recherches sur les grandes épidémies dans le Nord de l'Espagne à la fin du XVIᵉ siècle* (Paris, 1969), pp. 60–6; M. Flinn et al., *Scottish Population History from the 17th Century to the 1930s* (Cambridge, 1977), p. 109.

65 Wrigley and Schofield, *Population History*, pp. 340, 675–7.

66 On 1546 and 1551 see n. 59 above, and on 1563, Appleby, 'Nutrition and Disease', p. 8; Slack, 'Mortality Crises', pp. 53–4.

67 Cheke, *Hurt of sedicion*, sig. Eiᵛ–iiʳ.

68 *Privy Council Acts 1630–1*, p. 113; P. Slack, 'Books of Orders: The Making of English Social Policy 1577–1631', *Trans. Roy. Hist. Soc.*, 5th ser., 30 (1980), 5–6. Plague was most severe in northern England: R. Sharpe France, 'A History of Plague in Lancashire', *Trans. Lancs. and Cheshire Hist. Soc.*, XC (1939), 59–70; and in Cheshire at least it was accompanied by 'fevers and other sore diseases': E. Burghall, *Providence Improved* (Lancs. and Cheshire Rec. Soc., XIX, 1889), 4.

69 Cf. J.D. Chambers, *Population, Economy and Society in Pre-Industrial England* (Oxford, 1972), ch. 4.

70 E. Greaves, *Morbus Epidemius Anni 1643, or The New Disease* (Oxford, 1643), sig. A2r.

Chapter 4 The local context

1 Quoted in D. and S. Lysons, *Magna Britannia*, II, pt ii, *Cheshire* (1810), 845–6.
2 All these registers have entries beginning before 1640. Most of those from Devon are transcripts in the library of the Devon and Cornwall Record Society, Exeter; most of the Essex registers are the originals in ERO. They are listed in Slack, thesis, pp. 400–5. The Devon total excludes the registers of Exeter, considered in the next chapter. There is an excellent description of the Essex registers in F.G. Emmison, *Catalogue of Essex Parish Records 1240–1894* (Chelmsford, 2nd edn, 1966), and of those of Devon in H. Peskett, *Guide to the Parish . . . Registers of Devon and Cornwall* (Devon and Cornwall Rec. Soc., Extra Ser., II, 1979).
3 W.G. Hoskins, *Devon* (1954), p. 170; E.E. Rich, 'The Population of Elizabethan England', *Ec. HR*, 2nd ser., II (1950), 254; J. Sheail, 'The Distribution of Taxable Population and Wealth in England During the Early Sixteenth Century', *Trans. Inst. Brit. Geographers*, 55 (1972), 117, 118, 120; R.S. Schofield, 'The Geographical Distribution of Wealth in England 1334–1649', *Ec. HR*, 2nd ser., XVIII (1965), 506.
4 This is a very crude way of calculating changes in the level of mortality, and it is open to criticism, particularly in its assumptions about 'normal' mortality. In each case the annual average with which the epidemic year is compared has been computed from years when there were no mortality peaks, since the purpose of the calculation is to permit comparison of crisis levels in different epidemics and different places. If the epidemic was in 1591, for example, the average has normally been taken for the years 1581–90; but if there was another epidemic in the parish in 1587, the average has been calculated for the years 1580–6 and 1588–90. As a result, the 'normal' average is in fact abnormally low. It would have been impossible in the time available, however, to apply more exhaustive quantitative techniques to the many scores of registers surveyed here. For other, more sophisticated, methods of detecting and measuring mortality crises, see E.A. Wrigley and R.S. Schofield, *The Population History of England 1541–1871: A Reconstruction* (1981), Appendix 10; M.P. Gutmann, *War and Rural Life in the Early Modern Low Countries* (Princeton, 1980), pp. 231–2.
5 Wrigley and Schofield, *Population History of England*, pp. 311, 528.
6 On the problem of identifying plague more generally, see pp. 64–5; for register references to 'plague' in Essex, see Slack, thesis, pp. 82–3; and for the period 1637–40, Wrigley and Schofield, *Population History of England*, p. 679.
7 ERO, T/R 109; D/P 111/1/1, f. 1r.
8 In fact we would expect registration to be less complete in epidemic than in other years.
9 For a more detailed account of epidemics in Devon and Essex, see Slack, thesis, ch. 2; and for Devon, W.G. Hoskins, *Old Devon* (Newton Abbot, 1966), ch. 7; N.C. Oswald, 'Epidemics in Devon, 1538–1837', *Trans. Devon Assoc.*, 109 (1977), 73–116.

10 Apart from these two cases, however, the registers do not suggest as great a mortality in the 1550s as that indicated by the diocesan probate evidence mentioned in the previous chapter (above, p. 57). Burials may have been under-registered in other parishes, or the socially selective probate evidence may exaggerate the extent of mortality. Cf. pp. 147–8.

11 ECA, Book 51, ff. 331r, 343v; *Letters and Papers of Henry VIII*, xi. 166, xiii (i). 80, 101. Epidemics in Exeter are considered in the next chapter; they will be referred to only briefly here.

12 W.G. Hoskins, 'Harvest Fluctuations and English Economic History, 1480–1619', *Agric. Hist. Rev.*, XII (1964), 35.

13 DRO, DD 1984, Dartmouth Court Book 1555–66, ff. 240–1.

14 See p. 115; Plymouth RO, Receivers' Accounts 1570–1, f. 8r; J. Yonge, 'Plymouth Memoirs', ed. R.N. Worth, *Annual Report of the Plymouth Institution*, V (iii) (1875–6), 524.

15 J.J. Keevil, *Medicine and the Navy I: 1200–1649* (1957), pp. 77–9. On plague in northern Spain in 1589, see J. Nadal and E. Giralt, *La Population catalane de 1553 à 1717* (Paris, 1960), pp. 39–40.

16 Richard Carew, *The Survey of Cornwall*, ed. F.E. Halliday (1953), p. 85.

17 DRO, Quarter Sessions Order Book 1608–13, f. 257r. On the 1620s, see pp. 267–8.

18 Eight cases of plague were reported in Plymouth in October 1666, probably from ships in the harbour: Oswald, 'Epidemics in Devon', p. 95.

19 DRO, DD 62652, 1636–7 acct; R. Polwhele, *History of Devonshire* (Exeter, 1797), I. 327–8.

20 *Cal. SP Dom. 1547–80*, p. 587.

21 Cf. R.M.S. McConaghey, 'Dartmouth Medical Records', *Medical History*, IV (1960), 98.

22 Sick soldiers were supported in Dartmouth in 1626: DRO, DD 62218, 62276, 62277. Cf. R.N. Worth, *History of Plymouth* (Plymouth, 1890), p. 90.

23 DRO, Quarter Sessions Bundles, 14 September 1625.

24 ECA, Commonplace Book of John Hooker, f. 363v, under 1588–9.

25 Cf. J.-N. Biraben, *Les Hommes et la peste en France et dans les pays européens et méditerranéens* (Paris, 1975–6), I. 298–302; J.-N. Biraben, 'Certain Demographic Characteristics of the Plague Epidemic in France, 1720–22', *Daedalus*, Spring 1968, pp. 536–45.

26 Cf. J.F.D. Shrewsbury, *A History of Bubonic Plague in the British Isles* (Cambridge, 1970), p. 61.

27 See Slack, thesis, pp. 62–6.

28 W.G. Hoskins, *Devon* (1954), pp. 21–3; H.H. Lamb, *The English Climate* (2nd edn, 1964), figs 14, 24.

29 Sheail, 'Distribution of Taxable Population', p. 120; L. Toulmin Smith (ed.), *The Itinerary of John Leland* (1906–8), I. 244.

30 Sheail, 'Distribution of Taxable Population', pp. 117, 118. Professor W.G. Hoskins informs me that similar conclusions about population density are indicated by the 1569 Muster Rolls and the Protestation Returns of 1642.

31 Market towns have been identified from the lists in J. Thirsk (ed.), *The*

Agrarian History of England and Wales. IV: 1500–1640 (Cambridge, 1967), pp. 471, 474.

32 Cf. DRO, Quarter Sessions Order Book 1618–25, p. 646, 1625–33, p. 21. Bridford was still regarded as a country haven for Exeter citizens during the Napoleonic Wars: Hoskins, *Devon*, p. 152.

33 Cheshire RO, QSF 1625 (ii), doc. 105.

34 H. Greenwood, *Epidemic and Crowd Diseases* (1935), pp. 300–1. Cf. Wrigley and Schofield, *Population History of England*, p. 691.

35 The sources for Fig. 4.2 are: transcript of Crediton register in the library of the Devon and Cornwall Record Society, Exeter; T. Wainwright (ed.), *Barnstaple Parish Register 1538–1812* (Exeter, 1903); original register of St Andrew's, Plymouth, in Plymouth RO. All years are calendar years, January to December.

36 J.R. Chanter and T. Wainwright, *Reprint of the Barnstaple Records* (Barnstaple, 1900), II. 244, 131, 132; J.B. Gribble, *Memorials of Barnstaple* (Barnstaple, 1830), p. 621; J.R. Chanter, *Sketches of the Literary History of Barnstaple* (Barnstaple, 1866), p. 113.

37 Population estimates for these three towns are drawn from baptisms, assuming (which is unlikely) a constant baptism rate of thirty-three per thousand. They are inevitably very imprecise. The Protestation Returns, kindly communicated to me by Professor W.G. Hoskins, help only in the case of Crediton, where 1,060 names were recorded, suggesting a population of 3,500–4,000 in 1642. Cf. Hoskins, *Devon*, p. 113.

38 There were gaps in the registration of burials in 1546, but the total was probably over 200.

39 DRO, Crediton wardens' accts, 1660A/30, 49.

40 Worth, *History of Plymouth*, p. 367; R.N. Worth, *Calendar of the Plymouth Municipal Records* (Plymouth, 1893), pp. 19, 21; Plymouth RO, White Book, f. 51r.

41 Worth, *History of Plymouth*, p. 90; Plymouth RO, Receivers' Accts 1580–1, f. 48.

42 Keevil, *Medicine and the Navy*, pp. 71, 72, 74–5, 77–9.

43 *Ibid.*, pp. 170–2, 175, 182–4; Plymouth RO, Receivers' Accounts 1625–6, f. 209v; Overseers Accounts 1611–42, 1625–7; *Cal. SP Dom. 1625–6*, p. 295; *The Diary of Walter Yonge Esq.*, ed. G. Roberts (Camden Soc., XLI, 1848), p. 89.

44 Plymouth RO, White Book, f. 96. Cf. *Cal. SP Dom. 1625–6*, pp. 350, 375.

45 Chanter and Wainwright, *Barnstaple Records*, II. 244.

46 Slack, thesis, pp. 104–11.

47 Cf. Gutmann, *War and Rural Life, passim*; I. Roy, 'England Turned Germany? The Aftermath of the Civil War in its European Context', *Trans. Roy. Hist. Soc.*, 5th ser., 28 (1978), 127–44. The relevance of military activity in Devon is well described in Oswald, 'Epidemics in Devon'.

48 Worth, *History of Plymouth*, ch. vi; BL, Add. MS. 35297, f. 10v; *Sir Thomas Fairfax Letter . . . relating to the Storming . . . of Dartmouth* (1645).

49 J. Cock, *Records of the Borough of South Molton* (South Molton, 1893), pp. 24–5; parish registers.

50 For Exeter, see below, p. 118; and for Colyton, the full analysis in R. Schofield, 'An Anatomy of an Epidemic: Colyton, November 1645 to November 1646', in *The Plague Reconsidered* (LPS Supplement, 1977), pp. 95–126. For references to 'plague' in 1646 see J.S. Cockburn (ed.), *Western Circuit Assize Orders 1629–48* (Camden Soc., 4th ser., 17, 1976), p. 240; DRO, Quarter Sessions Bundles 1646, QS Order Book 1640–51, July, September 1646, January, April 1647.

51 The title of a work by William Gouge, published in 1631.

52 The two early parish registers of Exeter, those of St Petrock's and St Mary Arches, which are used in the next chapter, have been excluded from this total.

53 ERO, Q/SR 129/66, 66a; Slack, thesis, pp. 79–82, 91–5.

54 Slack, thesis, ch. 2, graph VIII; C. Creighton, *History of Epidemics in Britain* (Cambridge, 1891–4), I. 288, 290–1.

55 I am grateful to Dr W.J. Petchey for providing me with total burials in the three parishes of Maldon from 1558 onwards.

56 These outbreaks all followed visitations of plague in London. In addition there are individual references to plague in other years in: ERO, Calendar of Queen's Bench Indictments, 619 I 104 (1566); 639 II 200 (1574), 652 II 331 (1580); D.H. Allen (ed.), *Essex Quarter Sessions Order Book 1652–61* (Essex Edited Texts I, 1974), p. 172 (? 1659).

57 PRO, SP 16/166/69; *Privy Council Acts 1629–30*, p. 398.

58 Colchester Archives, Sessions Book 9, exam. of 25 January 1603/4.

59 ERO, D/B 3/3/207, docs 8, 9; J.C. Cox, *The Parish Registers of England* (1910), p. 171; Colchester Archives, Assembly Book I 1576–99, f. 13r.

60 ERO, Great Coggeshall register 1578; D/Y 2/46, p. 97; Q/SBa 2/34 Epiph. 1638/9, doc. 10; Q/SBa 2/46, Easter 1642, petition of John Conzin of Braintree.

61 ERO, D/P 135/1/1, f. 45r.

62 Cf. R. Pollitzer, *Plague* (WHO, Geneva, 1954), p. 327; Hoskins, *Devon*, pp. 21–3. Wrigley and Schofield also found that the South-West was more prone to mortality crises than other parts of England: *Population History of England*, p. 692.

63 F. Hull, 'Agriculture and Rural Society in Essex 1560–1640' (London Univ. PhD thesis, 1950), p. 156 and *passim*; J.E. Pilgrim, 'The Rise of the "New Draperies" in Essex', *Univ. Birmingham Hist. J.*, VII (1959–60), 36–59.

64 Cf. J.T. Alexander, 'Catherine II, Bubonic Plague and the Problem of Industry in Moscow', *American Hist. Rev.*, 79 (1974), 661.

65 Bodl., MS. Firth c. 4, pp. 189, 166–7. Cf. B.E. Supple, *Commercial Crisis and Change in England 1600–1642* (Cambridge, 1964), p. 57.

66 ERO, Q/SBa 2/28, doc. 35, 2/27 doc. 15; *Cal SP Dom. 1637*, p. 164; Colchester Archives, Assembly Book III 1620–46, f. 200r; ERO, Q/SBa 2/30, doc. 45, 2/31, doc. 2, 2/43, doc. 1. On economic and social problems in the county generally at this time, see J.A. Sharpe, *Crime in Seventeenth-Century England: A County Study* (Cambridge, 1983), p. 205;

W. Hunt, *The Puritan Moment: The Coming of Revolution in an English County* (Cambridge, Mass., 1983), chs 3, 8; J. Walter, 'Grain Riots and Popular Attitudes to the Law: Maldon and the Crisis of 1629', in J. Brewer and J. Styles (eds), *An Ungovernable People* (1980), pp. 65–70.

67 On the local economy of Terling, see K. Wrightson and D. Levine, *Poverty and Piety in an English Village: Terling 1525–1700* (1979).

68 Cf. Supple, *Commercial Crisis*, p. 57; W.B. Stephens, *Seventeenth-Century Exeter* (Exeter, 1958), pp. 14–22.

69 The parishes are Bocking, Great Chesterford, Chipping Ongar, Great Oakley, East Tilbury, Waltham Holy Cross, Widford and Wix. I am grateful to Dr Mary Dobson for figures for burials from the Bocking register. For Great Oakley, see R. Barker, 'The Local Study of Plague', *Local Historian*, 14 (1981), 332–40.

70 ERO, D/P 115/5/1, pp. 403–6; Q/SBa 2/105, 107, petitions from Chelmsford, Danbury and Horndon. Cf. D/P 81/8/1 (Barking); Q/SR 406/58, 106 (Leigh, Woodford).

71 A. Macfarlane (ed.), *The Diary of Ralph Josselin 1616–1683* (British Academy, Records of Social and Economic History, new ser., III, 1976), pp. 521, 530; Barker, 'Local Study of Plague', p. 338.

72 Lambeth Palace Library, Carte Misc. VI, 31. The hearth tax of 1670 listed 361 households in Bocking: K.H. Burley, 'The Economic Development of Essex in the Later 17th and Early 18th Centuries' (London Univ. PhD thesis, 1957), p. 394. This suggests a population of no more than 2,000 even before the epidemic.

73 H.J. Cunnington, *An Account of the Charities and Charitable Benefactions of Braintree* (1904), pp. 60–5. There were 286 households in 1670: Burley, 'Economic Development of Essex', p. 394.

74 I.G. Doolittle, 'The Plague in Colchester, 1579–1666', *Trans. Essex Arch. Soc.*, IV (1972), 137–8; *idem*, 'The Effects of the Plague on a Provincial Town in the Sixteenth and Seventeenth Centuries', *Medical History*, XIX (1975), 333–4; BL, Stowe MS. 840, ff. 44–5. I suspect that Dr Doolittle's estimate of 10,305 for the population in 1662 and his figure for the number of those exempted in that year from the hearth tax are both a little too low. I am grateful to him for discussing his conclusions with me.

75 *Diary of Josselin*, p. 524.

76 Burley, 'Economic Development of Essex', pp. 394, 361. It should be noted, however, that the proportions exempted from the hearth tax were only a little less than half in Chelmsford and Saffron Walden: *ibid.*, pp. 393–4.

77 ERO, D/P 94/5/1, f. 396r; Q/SR 406/104. See also pp. 267–8, 296.

78 *Diary of Josselin*, pp. 520–3, 532.

79 I.e. those with at least seventy-five years with recorded burials in that century.

80 It is possible to calculate the average expectation of a crisis in all the parishes with surviving registers which have been examined. If we divide the total number of years in which these parishes were in observation by the number of mortality crises (producing ratios of 2.0 or more) which

they suffered, we find that on average a parish in Devon or Essex could expect to experience a mortality crisis once every sixty years.

81 One such reference occurs in the court rolls of a manor of White Colne, Essex: ERO, D/DBm M65, 12 Sep. 1638.

Chapter 5 The urban impact

1 Bristol Reference Library, Braikenridge Collection, MS. B9076; F.F. Fox (ed.), *Adams' Chronicle of Bristol* (Bristol, 1910), p. 100; A.E. Hudd, 'Two Bristol Calendars', *Trans. Bristol and Gloucs. Arch. Soc.*, XIX (1894), 134, 138, 141; R. Ricart, *The Maire of Bristowe is Kalendar*, ed. L. Toulmin Smith (Camden Soc., NS, V, 1872), p. 59.

2 ECA, Act Book 3, pp. 123, 127, 129–32, 135–6; Act Book 6, ff. 53r, 63r, 67r. Cf. Slack, thesis, pp. 115, 120–1; below, pp. 257, 317–19.

3 ECA, Sessions Minute Books 1621–30, ff. 277, 281v, 1642–60, f. 80r.

4 BAO, SS. Philip and Jacob register, 12 August 1603. In 1625 a Bristol councillor was fined for receiving suspect goods from London: BAO, Common Council Proceedings 1608–27, f. 134v.

5 *Adams' Chronicle*, pp. 216–17; BAO, Mayors' Audits 1626–7, pp. 104, 108, 165; Common Council Proceedings, 1608–27, f. 128v; S. Seyer, *Memoirs Historical and Topographical of Bristol* (Bristol, 1821–3), I. 274–5.

6 ECA, Book 51, ff. 331, 343v; Receivers' Account Rolls, 19–20 Henry VII; Act Book 2, f. 40v.

7 The parishes whose registers have been used are listed in Table 5.1. One of them, St Thomas's, was technically outside the limits of the city; one further parish, Allhallows on the Walls, has a register dating from 1614, but it is incomplete. Transcripts of all the registers are in the Library of the Devon and Cornwall Record Society, Exeter, and they have been used to supplement the figures given in R. Pickard, *The Population and Epidemics of Exeter in Pre-Census Times* (Exeter, 1947). Where my own arithmetic differs from Pickard's, I have used my own totals.

8 ECA, Act Book 2, f. 76r.

9 According to the register, the rise in St Mary's occurred in 1547, but it is possible that the dating is mistaken: the original register, in ECA, is a transcript made later in the century.

10 Slack, thesis, pp. 114–15; ECA, Act Book 2, f. 179r.

11 W.G. Hoskins, 'Harvest Fluctuations and English Economic History, 1480–1619', *Agric. Hist. Rev.*, XII (1964), 35.

12 W.B. Stephens, *Seventeenth-Century Exeter* (Exeter, 1958), pp. 13–14, 17–19; below, p. 258.

13 The ratios have been calculated by dividing the number of burials in each parish in the years given by the annual average for the previous decade. All are calendar years, January to December, except in 1590–1 when the months from August to July have been taken. Under 1625, the ratio for St Thomas's is in fact for 1626, when plague was worst in this parish.

14 The ranking has been based on the following sources: PRO, E179/98/247 (1544); W.G. Hoskins (ed.), *Exeter in the Seventeenth Century* (Devon

and Cornwall Rec. Soc., II, 1957), pp. 1–6, 123 (1602); ECA, subsidy assessments, nos 2 and 3 (1641); W.G. Hoskins, *Industry, Trade and People in Exeter 1688–1800* (Manchester, 1935), p. 113 (hearth tax). For full details of the calculations, see Slack, thesis, p. 118. The poorest parishes and the richest parishes in 1602 are shaded on Fig. 5.1.

15 There are no comparable tax data for St Thomas's, which was outside the city, but it is likely to have shared the social characteristics of the other suburbs of the town.

16 W.T. MacCaffrey, *Exeter 1540–1640* (Cambridge, Mass., 1958), pp. 112–13; Hoskins (ed.), *Exeter in the Seventeenth Century*, pp. xvii–xix; W.G. Hoskins, 'The Population of Exeter', *Devon and Cornwall Notes and Queries*, XX (1938–9), 243. Conditions here must have been like those later described in Salisbury: see J. Winzar, *Vital Statistics of the City of Salisbury* (Salisbury, 1850), p. 6.

17 Slack, thesis, pp. 122–5; P. Slack, 'Mortality Crises and Epidemic Disease in England 1485–1610', in C. Webster (ed.), *Health, Medicine and Mortality in the Sixteenth Century* (Cambridge, 1979), pp. 37–8.

18 Clarendon, *History of the Rebellion and Civil Wars*, ed. W.D. Macray (Oxford, 1888), III. 163; ECA, Act Book 8, f. 151r; Pickard, *Population and Epidemics of Exeter*, pp. 44–5. Cf. M. Coate, 'Exeter in the Civil War and Interregnum', *Devon and Cornwall Notes and Queries*, XVIII (1934–5), 338–52.

19 ECA, subsidy assessments, nos 2 and 3; Slack, thesis, pp. 128–9. Estimates for the total population of Exeter at this time are given in MacCaffrey, *Exeter*, pp. 11–13; W.G. Hoskins, *Two Thousand Years in Exeter* (1960), p. 51; Stephens, *Seventeenth-Century Exeter*, p. 40.

20 These proportions assume a 'normal' death rate of twenty-six per thousand, but we have no reliable means of assessing the accuracy of this assumption.

21 See the references in n. 19 above. The Protestation Return enumerated 2,982 adult males in Exeter in 1642, which may suggest a population of *c.* 10,000 if children were 40 per cent of the total: House of Lords RO, Main Papers, Protestation Returns, BC 9–29.

22 Totals of baptisms and burials are given in Pickard, *Population and Epidemics of Exeter*, pp. 14–15. For a similar correlation between mortality and poverty in Exeter between 1690 and 1770, see M. Griffiths, 'The Association between Mortality and Poverty in Exeter from the 17th Century to the Present', *Exeter Papers in Economic History*, 11 (1976), 31–47.

23 ECA, Act Book 6, f. 198 r.

24 See the references in n. 1 above. A somewhat fuller account of Bristol's epidemics will be found in my 'The Local Incidence of Epidemic Disease: The Case of Bristol 1540–1650', in *The Plague Reconsidered* (Local Population Studies, Supplement, 1977), pp. 49–62.

25 The original registers of twelve of the eighteen parishes of the town, now in BAO, have been used. The parishes are listed in Table 5.2. One register has been printed: *The Registers of St. Augustine the Less, Bristol*, ed. A. Sabin (Bristol and Gloucs. Arch. Soc., Records Section, III, 1956).

26 BL, Lansdowne MS. 2, f. 91; Hoskins, 'Harvest Fluctuations', p. 36.

27 Hudd, 'Two Bristol Calendars', p. 134; *Adams' Chronicle*, p. 178; Ricart, *Kalendar*, p. 59.

28 E.E. Williams, *The Chantries of William Canynges in St. Mary Redcliffe Bristol* (Bristol, 1950), App., pp. 32–41.

29 J.C. Russell, *British Medieval Population*, (Albuquerque, 1948), pp. 296–7; B. Little, *The City and County of Bristol* (1954), p. 325; J. Latimer, *Annals of Bristol in the Seventeenth Century* (Bristol, 1900), p. 34.

30 D.V. Glass, 'Two Papers on Gregory King', in D.V. Glass and D.E.C. Eversley (eds), *Population in History* (1965), p. 192n.

31 On these outbreaks, see, besides the parish registers, BAO, Mayors' Audits 1624–5, p. 35; Temple Wardens' Accounts 1625, 1637; Common Council Proceedings 1627–42, f. 84r; St Mary Redcliffe Churchwardens' Accounts, May 1637; Common Council Proceedings 1649–59, pp. 31, 41, 1659–75, pp. 125, 129, 130, 133–6; Great Audit Book 1665–6, pp. 42–3, 46–8, 50; and on 1666, below, pp. 317–18.

32 BAO, Mayors' Audits 1640–1, pp. 109–11, 1641–2, pp. 161–3, 1642–3, p. 243; Common Council Proceedings 1627–42, f. 123v; *The Tragedy of the Kings Armies Fidelity since their entring into Bristol* (1643), p. 6. Military events are described in P. McGrath, *Bristol and the Civil War* (Bristol Historical Association, 1981).

33 R.E. Hemphill, 'Society, Artists and the Plague, with an Account of the Plague in Bristol', *Bristol Medico-Chir. Journal*, LXXXI (1966), 1. Three parish registers referred to 'plague' in 1645; they had not done so in 1643.

34 These parishes probably contained roughly two-thirds of the town's population in the 1630s. There were said to be 2,500 families in Bristol in 1645, of which 1,500 were indigent: *A Declaration of His Highness Prince Rupert with a Narrative of the state . . . of Bristol* (1645).

35 The data from which the Mortality Ratios and the ranking of the parishes have been derived are given in Slack, 'Local Incidence of Epidemic Disease', pp. 53, 54, 58. Since the subsidy assessments are arranged by ward and not by parish, the ranking may be less accurate than that for Exeter. Nevertheless, the poverty of Redcliffe, Temple and St James's can be confirmed from other sources: all three parishes were granted rates in aid from other parts of the town, for example: BAO, Sessions Minute Book 1653–71, ff. lv. 6v.

36 Slack, 'Local Incidence', p. 57.

37 E.M. Carus-Wilson, *Medieval Merchant Venturers* (2nd edn, 1967), p. 4. I have been unable to see the register of St Thomas's, but it seems to have been severely affected by plague: D.K. Gosling, 'The Parish Registers of the Churches of SS. Philip and Jacob and S. Thomas in Bristol' (Bristol Univ. MA thesis, 1934), p. 65.

38 See also, pp. 314–15.

39 E. Ralph and M.E. Williams (eds), *The Inhabitants of Bristol in 1696* (Bristol Rec. Soc., XXV, 1968), p. xxii; J. Dallaway (ed.), *Antiquities of Bristow in the Middle Centuries* (1834), p. 145; Carus-Wilson, *Merchant Venturers*, p. 75; M.D. Lobel (ed.), *Historic Towns*, II (1975), 'Bristol', p. 17. Cf. the

large amounts spent annually on the poor in Redcliffe parish: St Mary Redcliffe Church, Churchwardens' Accounts 1588–98, *passim*; BAO, Sessions Book 1642–3, f. 201r.

40 W. Camden, *Britannia*, ed. E. Gibson (1722), I. 94; Ricart, *Kalendar*, p. 47; BAO, Grand Jury Presentments 1628–66, 28 April 1629 and *passim*.

41 BAO, Easter Books of Christ Church. Since it is not always possible to tell at which end of the street the enumerators began, some of the figures in Fig. 5.3 may be in the wrong order. The sketch map is based on Millerd's plan of 1673.

42 P. Clark and P. Slack, *English Towns in Transition* (Oxford, 1976), p. 83.

43 The registers of eighteen parishes are available on microfilm or in the original in NNRO. Two have been consulted in the parish churches, and there are transcripts of seven in the library of the Society of Genealogists. These come from the parishes listed in Table 5.4 and in addition from St Peter Hungate. A further register has been printed: *The Register of St. George Tombland*, transc. G.B. Jay (Norwich, 1891).

44 Cf. W.J.C. Moens, *The Walloons and Their Church at Norwich 1565–1832* (Huguenot Soc. of London, Publications, I, 1887–8); B.H. Allen, 'The Administrative and Social Structure of the Norwich Merchant Class 1485–1660' (Harvard Univ. PhD thesis, 1951), pp. 3–11; M. Pelling and C. Webster, 'Medical Practitioners', in C. Webster (ed.), *Health, Medicine and Mortality in the Sixteenth Century* (Cambridge, 1979), pp. 207–22; J.F. Pound, 'An Elizabethan Census of the Poor', *Univ. Birmingham Hist. J.*, VIII (1962), 135–61; P. Collinson, *The Elizabethan Puritan Movement* (1967), pp. 141, 186–8.

45 Above, p. 16; Slack, thesis, ch. 4, graph I.

46 *Ibid.*, pp. 155–61.

47 For the age-incidence of plague, see pp. 181–3; and for the deficiencies of wills as indicators of mortality, pp. 55–6, 147–8.

48 NNRO, Mayor's Book, p. 18; W. Hudson and J.C. Tingey (eds), *Records of the City of Norwich* (1906–10), II. cxxiv–cxxv; NNRO, Court Book 1555–62, p. 252.

49 J.F. Pound, 'The Social and Trade Structure of Norwich 1525–75'. *P&P*, 34 (1966), 50, 58–9; NNRO, Assembly Book 1549–53, f. 211r; *Records of the City of Norwich*, II. 332–3.

50 Moens, *Walloons*, p. 34; R.W. Ketton-Cremer, *Norfolk Assembly* (1957), p. 120.

51 NNRO, Mayor's Book, p. 24.

52 The brief original order for the provision of these figures is printed in *Records of the City of Norwich*, II. 187. Fig. 5.4 is based on the figures given in the Court Books from 1579 to 1610, and on the totals given in K.J. Allison, 'The Wool Supply and the Worsted Cloth Industry in Norfolk in the 16th and 17th Centuries' (Leeds Univ. PhD thesis, 1955), Table 26, p. 607, after that date. I am grateful to Dr Allison for permission to use his findings. In the few cases where no weekly figures are given, the average of the weeks before and after the lacuna has been used to fill the gap.

53 F. Blomefield, *An Essay Towards a Topographical History of the County of*

Norfolk (2nd edn, Norwich, 1805–10), III. 354; register of St Martin at Palace; NNRO, Court Book 1576–81, p. 361; *Records of the City of Norwich*, II. 335.

54 The very slow decline of mortality in the winter of 1579–80 may partly have been caused by an epidemic of influenza adding to the toll taken by plague: Slack, thesis, pp. 165–6.

55 J.F. Pound, 'Government and Society in Tudor and Stuart Norwich 1525–1675' (Leicester Univ. PhD thesis, 1974), p. 3; Slack, thesis, pp. 166–7, 194–6.

56 *Ibid.*, pp. 168–9. The reported cases of plague may in fact had been of typhus, which was sometimes confused with it: below, pp. 275–6.

57 Above, p. 66.

58 Cf. R. Hughey (ed.), *The Correspondence of Lady Katherine Paston 1603–27* (Norfolk Rec. Soc., XIV, 1941), pp. 76, 77, 80; C. Creighton, *A History of Epidemics in Britain* (Cambridge, 1891–4), I. 504–5.

59 St Benedict's and St Saviour's.

60 Cf. NNRO, Court Book 1634–46, ff. 137r, 217r, 219r; Sessions Minute Book 1630–8, ff. 3v–5r; W.L. Sachse (ed.), *Minutes of the Norwich Court of Mayoralty 1630–1* (Norfolk Rec. Soc., XV, 1942), pp. 32–6, 60, 132ff. Plague also coincided, in mild form, with food shortage in 1647: cf. the provision of corn for the poor in NNRO, Corn Stock Accounts 1644–62.

61 The total burials for each parish are given in *The Records of Norwich* (1736–8), II. 6–7. For examples of the bills, see *Cal. SP Dom. 1666–7*, pp. 393–4. The total population was still around 20,000: P.J. Corfield, 'A Provincial Capital in the Late Seventeenth Century: The Case of Norwich', in P. Clark and P. Slack (eds), *Crisis and Order in English Towns 1500–1700* (1972), p. 266.

62 NNRO, Court Book 1603–15, f. 7v; Court Book 1624–34, ff. 57v, 58r, 59r, 61v.

63 Pound, 'An Elizabethan Census of the Poor', p. 161. Dr Pound informs me that he now considers his estimates of parish population to have been too low, and hence the proportions are all too large; but the original figures still show the relative poverty of different parishes. Much the same ranking of parishes may be obtained from the 1624 subsidy (Slack, thesis, p. 177) and from the poor rate assessment of 1633 (W. Rye (ed.), *The Norwich Rate Book* (1903)), though there were some individual alterations: St John Timberhill, for example, rose in ranking over the period. Full information about the number of burials from which the ratios are derived may be found in Slack, thesis, pp. 174–5, 177.

64 In addition to the sixty-three burials in St Lawrence's in 1579 which have been used in calculating the ratio in Table 5.4, there were another ninety-five burials, all of them of Strangers, registered. If they had been included the ratio would have risen to an impossible 34.3. They were excluded because it seems likely that foreign burials in this parish were not registered before 1579. It is possible that the sixty-three burials noted include additional Strangers who have not been detected.

65 There is space here only to deal in a crude comparison between extremes of this kind. The sources are, however, good enough to permit a more

detailed comparison between epidemic mortality and social topography in Norwich, and Dr Paul Laxton is at present undertaking such an analysis.

66 SS. Martin at Oak, Swithin, Helen, Peter Hungate, George Tombland, Martin in the Bailey, Michael at Thorn, and John de Sepulchre.

67 The other two were St Augustine and St Saviour, the latter being among the eight richest parishes.

68 *Records of Norwich*, II. 6–7; C. Parkin, *The History and Antiquities of the City of Norwich* (Lynn and London, 1783), p. 178. According to the latter the total population in 1693, excluding hamlets and the close, was 26,139. This has been reduced by 30 per cent to reach a total closer to the estimate of 20,000 for the whole town in the 1660s: above, n. 61.

69 Excluding St Martin in the Bailey, for which no figures are given. Burials which were recorded in 1665–6 for Heigham (17) and 'at the pesthouse' (217) have not been included in Table 5.5.

70 PRO, E179/154/701, 179/336–8. The parishes have been ranked in descending order of wealth according to the number of hearths per household (see Slack, thesis, pp. 192–3), or in the few cases where this figure is not available, according to the proportions of households exempted on the grounds of poverty in 1671 or the evidence of the 1624 subsidy (*ibid.*, p. 177).

71 For the poverty of this area as late as 1696, see J.T. Evans, *Seventeenth-Century Norwich* (Oxford, 1979), fig. 3, p. 17.

72 M.D. Lobel (ed.), *Historic Towns*, II (1975), 'Norwich', pp. 17, 19, and the maps there. See Slack, thesis, pp. 192–3, for the number of adults per acre, calculated from the 1580 Muster Rolls, and the number of hearths per household in 1671 in each parish. For seventeenth-century complaints of poor overcrowded tenements, see NNRO, Sessions Indictments and Recognisances, vol. 29, no. 6, vol. 37, no. 10; overcrowding was probably less severe in the sixteenth century, but for some conspicuous examples, see J.F. Pound (ed.), *The Norwich Census of the Poor 1570* (Norfold Rec. Soc., XL, 1971), pp. 13–14.

73 Moens, *Walloons*, p. 262; *Records of the City of Norwich*, II. 335. There is evidence of overcrowding among the Dutch in Colchester in a 1573 census of aliens: ERO, T/A 66, and there were complaints about the same thing in London: *Privy Council Acts 1571–5*, p. 135.

74 *Records of the City of Norwich*, II. 192.

75 Moens, *Walloons*, pp. 34, 162–73.

76 For the existence of both at a later date, see Moens, *Walloons*, ii–iii, 55–6.

77 *Ibid.*, pp. 55, 306–7. Cf. *Minutes of Norwich Court*, pp. 108, 110; below, pp. 272–3.

78 For heavy mortality among the Walloons in Southampton in the plague of 1604, see T.B. James (ed.), *The Third Book of Remembrance of Southampton 1514–1602*, vol. IV (Southampton Rec. Ser., XXII, 1979), xx.

79 PRO, E 179/150/218 (Norwich), 113/192 (Bristol); MacCaffrey, *Exeter*, p. 248.

80 Corfield, 'Provincial Capital', p. 266; W.G. Hoskins, *Industry, Trade and People*, pp. 115–16; PRO, E 179/116/541 (Bristol). The Bristol return

does not include St Philip's parish, however, which may distort the proportion.

81 Cf. R. Pollitzer, *Plague* (Geneva, 1954), p. 501.
82 R.H. Hill (ed.), *The Correspondence of Thomas Corie 1664–87* (Norfolk Rec. Soc., XXVII, 1956), pp. 18, 20.

Chapter 6 Metropolitan crises

1 F.P. Wilson (ed.), *The Plague Pamphlets of Thomas Dekker* (Oxford, 1925), pp. 31–2.
2 John Graunt, *Natural and Political Observations upon the Bills of Mortality* (1662). A convenient modern edition, reprinting the fifth edition of 1676, is contained in C.H. Hull (ed.), *The Economic Writings of Sir William Petty*, 2 vols (Cambridge, 1899), II. 314–435.
3 See especially F.P. Wilson, *The Plague in Shakespeare's London* (Oxford, 2nd edn, 1963); W.G. Bell, *The Great Plague in London in 1665* (2nd edn, 1951); J.F.D. Shrewsbury, *A History of Bubonic Plague in the British Isles* (Cambridge, 1970), *passim*; I. Sutherland, 'When Was the Great Plague? Mortality in London, 1563 to 1665', in D.V. Glass and R. Revelle (eds), *Population and Social Change* (1972), pp. 287–320; R.A.P. Finlay, *Population and Metropolis: The Demography of London 1580–1650* (Cambridge, 1981); T.R. Forbes, *Chronicle from Aldgate* (New Haven, 1971); and for earlier publications, 'A List of Works in Guildhall Library Relating to the Plague in London, Together with the Bills of Mortality 1532?–1858', *Guildhall Misc.*, II (1965), 306–17.
4 C. Read, *Mr. Secretary Cecil and Queen Elizabeth* (1965), p. 115; *Letters and Papers of Henry VIII*, XIII (i), 520.
5 The data in Fig. 6.1 are drawn from: I. Sutherland, 'A Summary Tabulation of Annual Totals of Burials, Plague Deaths and Christenings in London Prior to 1666' (typescript in Bodl.), and for the years 1666–79 from *Economic Writings of Petty*, II. 458. Until 1665 the totals used are those for the 113 parishes in the city and liberties and the 9 (after 1647, 10) outparishes. In the period 1666–79 they also include the 7 'distant' parishes. The annual bills normally covered the twelve months beginning with the last week in December of the previous year.
6 Shrewsbury, *Bubonic Plague*, pp. 191–2, 226–7; Sutherland, 'Summary Tabulation'; Sutherland, 'When Was the Great Plague?', p. 314; John Stow, *A Summarie of Englyshe Chronicles* (1565), f. 244; GL, MS. 1278/1, *sub* 1563; Lambeth Palace, MS. 306, ff. 62v, 69v.
7 Shrewsbury, *Bubonic Plague*, pp. 203–4, 214–18; Creighton, *History of Epidemics*, I. 341–4; GL, MS. 4507/1, burials 1569–71.
8 The data in the lower part of Fig. 6.2 have been calculated from M. Fitch (ed.), *Testamentary Records in the Commissary Court of London, I: 1374–1488, II: 1489–1570* (British Record Soc., Index Library, vols 82, 86, 1969, 1974).
9 For references to plague in London in 1479, 1499–1500, 1504, 1513, 1517–18, and 1521, see R.S. Gottfried, *Epidemic Disease in Fifteenth*

Century England (Leicester, 1978), pp. 144–5; Creighton, *History of Epidemics*, I. 287–92; J.B. Williamson, *The History of the Temple, London* (2nd edn, 1925), p. 128. There was said to be plague in Watford in 1540 and the chronology of burials in some of the London parish registers suggests that the disease was also in London in that year: Creighton, *History of Epidemics*, I. 302; Shrewsbury, *Bubonic Plague*, p. 175; G.L, MSS. 10212, 11367, 4429, *sub* 1540.

10 Burials have been aggregated from the following parishes: Allhallows Bread Street, SS. Antholin, Clement Eastcheap, Dionis Backchurch, Lawrence Jewry, Mary le Bow, Michael Bassishaw and Peter Cornhill, whose registers have been published by the Harleian Society; and SS. Andrew Hubbard, Lawrence Pountney, Martin Ludgate, Martin Pomeroy, Mary Bothaw, Mary Woolnoth, Michael Crooked Lane, Nicholas Cole Abbey, Olave Jewry and Stephen Coleman Street, whose registers have been consulted in the Guildhall Library. For further discussion of these sources, see P. Slack, 'Mortality Crises and Epidemic Disease in England, 1485–1610', in C. Webster (ed.), *Health, Medicine and Mortality in the Sixteenth Century* (Cambridge, 1979), pp. 12–14.

11 Creighton, *History of Epidemics*, I. 297–303. The chronological distribution of burials in 1543 and 1548 is consistent with plague.

12 Wilson, *Plague in Shakespeare's London*, pp. vi, 189–208; Sutherland, 'When Was the Great Plague?', pp. 289–92; J. Christie, *Some Account of Parish Clerks* (1893), pp. 132–9; R.H. Adams, *The Parish Clerks of London* (1971), pp. 48–9; A.B. Appleby, 'Nutrition and Disease: The Case of London 1550–1750', *J. Interdisc. Hist.*, VI (1975), 6–7; *Economic Writings of Petty*, I. lxxx–xci. The earliest surviving bill, BL, Egerton MS. 2603, f. 4, is undated; it may come from 1532 or even earlier.

13 Christie, *Parish Clerks*, pp. 136–7; *Economic Writings of Petty*, II. 333.

14 *Economic Writings of Petty*, II. 347, 365. Cf. below, pp. 275–6. For a suspected plague death not returned by the searchers as such, see H. Ellis (ed.), *The Obituary of Richard Smyth* (Camden Soc., OS, 1849), p. 63.

15 Wilson, *Plague in Shakespeare's London*, pp. 205–8; W. Ogle, 'An Inquiry into the Trustworthiness of the Old Bills of Mortality', *J. Roy. Stat. Soc.*, 55 (1892), 443–4; Sutherland, 'When Was the Great Plague?', p. 291; Finlay, *Population and Metropolis*, pp. 53–5. A comparison of the entries of burials in ten parish registers with those given in the bill for 1603 printed in Wilson, facing p. 114, shows rather larger discrepancies, which suggest that that bill recorded registered burials less completely than its successors.

16 Bell, *Great Plague*, pp. 18, 39, 180–1, 211, 286–7; BL, Harl. MS. 3785, f. 35v. For earlier new churchyards made necessary by plague, see GL, MSS. 2968/1, ff. 314r, 390; 4251/1, p. 7.

17 GL, MS. 4458/1, p. 295; A.W.C. Hallen (ed.), *The Registers of St. Botolph, Bishopsgate, London* (1889), p. 262; W. Caldin and H. Raine, 'The Plague of 1625 and the Story of John Boston, Parish Clerk of St. Saviour's Southwark', *Trans. London and Middx. Arch. Soc.*, 23 (1971), 94.

18 Sutherland, 'When Was the Great Plague?'.

19 *Ibid.*, tables 3 and 4, pp. 300, 303.
20 The population totals have been taken from the middle estimates for the nearest appropriate dates in *ibid.*, table 6, p. 310. The percentages are my own calculations. There are slightly different calculations from the bills in Finlay, *Population and Metropolis*, pp. 118, 155–7.
21 Crisis Mortality Ratios, calculated from totals in the bills of mortality (given in Sutherland, 'Summary Tabulation') by dividing the number of burials in each epidemic year by the annual average for the previous decade (except 1603) are: 1603 – 7.53 (for city and liberties only; average taken from 1597–1600); 1625 – 5.98 (city, liberties and outparishes); 1636 – 2.59 (city, liberties and outparishes); 1665 – 5.86 (city, liberties, outparishes and 'distant' parishes). Crisis Mortality Ratios for the aggregate burials of forty-seven parishes in the city and liberties (see Table 6.2) give very similar results for these epidemics. For 1563 they give a low result (6.1), but this is due to the average being taken from the years after the plague when the population was growing. For those eighteen parishes where averages can be taken from the decade before 1563, the ratio in 1563 was 7.8. It appears therefore that the indices in Table 6.1 are a fair reflection of the relative severity of the various epidemics, except that the outbreaks of 1625 and 1665 may have been more alike than is there implied.
22 *Economic Writings of Petty*, II. 475.
23 Wilson, *Plague in Shakespeare's London*, pp. 87, 131, 173; N.G. Brett-James, *The Growth of Stuart London* (1935), p. 205; Bell, *Great Plague.*
24 GL, MSS. 1432/4, 1665–6 acct; 593/2, f. 148v. Cf. MSS. 2089/1, 1636 acct; 1176/1, 1578–9 acct; 942A, ff. 15v, 24r.
25 GL, MSS. 12806/2, 28 June, 6 November 1563, 29 April 1564, 28 March 1582; 12818/1, deaths in 1563; 12806/3, ff. 68r, 70v; 12806/6, pp. 187, 210, 223 (Christ's Hospital); GLCRO, H1/ST/A1/3, ff. 182r, 185v (St Thomas's); St Bartholomew's Hospital, Board of Governors' Minutes 1647–66, ff. 372r, 373v–4, 376r; Bridewell records quoted in *Under the Dome*, XII (1903), 110.
26 E. Freshfield (ed.), *The Vestry Minute Books of the Parish of St. Bartholomew Exchange* (1890), pp. xlv–xlix; *idem* (ed.), *The Vestry Minute Book of the Parish of St. Margaret Lothbury 1571–1677* (1887), p. xxxiii; W.H. Overall (ed.), *Accounts of the Churchwardens of . . . St. Michael Cornhill* (1871), pp. 193, 255; GL, MS. 2968/3, ff. 511v, 512r; GLCRO, P92/SAV/1405, 1636 acct.
27 A. Plummer, *The London Weavers' Company 1600–1970* (1972), p. 4; C.M. Clode, *The Early History of the Guild of Merchant Taylors* (1888), I. 295–6. Cf. J.W. Sherwell, *A Descriptive and Historical Account of the Guild of Saddlers of the City of London* (1889), p. 74; LCRO, Quarter Sessions File, February 1665/6, prosecution of 7 August 1665; R.H. Tawney and E. Power (eds), *Tudor Economic Documents* (1924), III. 437–8.
28 J. Hawarde, *Les Reportes del Cases in Camera Stellata 1593–1609* (1894), p. 329; J.F. Larkin and P.L. Hughes (eds), *Stuart Royal Proclamations*, I. (Oxford, 1973), pp. 47–8. Cf. S. Young, *Annals of the Barber-Surgeons* (1890), pp. 121–3.

29 The growth of London is described in E.J. Davis, 'The Transformation of London', in R.W. Seton-Watson (ed.), *Tudor Studies Presented to A.F. Pollard* (1924), and Brett-James, *Growth of Stuart London*; and the problems it raised are perceptively discussed in V. Pearl, *London and the Outbreak of the Puritan Revolution* (Oxford, 1961), ch. I.

30 BL, Add. MS. 29597, f. 13; Add. MS. 35331, f. 37r; *Plague Pamphlets of Dekker*, p. 187; *The Newes*, 20 July 1665, p. 616.

31 The annual bills used for the epidemic years are: 1625: reproduced in Wilson, *Plague in Shakespeare's London*, facing p. 174; 1636: in GL; 1665: reproduced in Bell, *Great Plague*, facing p. 320. The average 'normal' burials have been taken from the bills for 1629–35 in GL, for comparison with 1625 and 1636; and from the bills for 1655–6 and 1658–64 in GL and for 1657 in Bodl., for comparison with 1665.

32 The original registers of St Leonard Shoreditch in GL, SS. Saviour Southwark, Mary Whitechapel and Dunstan Stepney in GLCRO, and SS. Clement Danes and Mary le Strand in Westminster City Library; the registers of St Martin-in-the-Fields and St James Clerkenwell, published by the Harleian Society; and the register printed in A.M. Burke (ed.), *Memorials of St. Margaret's Church, Westminster* (1914).

33 The original registers of SS. Andrew Holborn, Dunstan in the West, and Giles Cripplegate in GL; A.W.C. Hallen (ed.), *Registers of St. Botolph Bishopsgate*; and the annual figures from the register of St Botolph without Aldgate given in Forbes, *Chronicle from Aldgate*.

34 In addition to the eighteen parish registers listed in n. 10 above, these are: original registers in GL of Allhallows the Less, SS. Andrew by the Wardrobe, Benet Fink, James Garlickhithe, Mary Magdalen Old Fish Street, and Mildred Poultry; registers published by the Harleian Society of Allhallows Honey Lane, SS. Dunstan in the East, Margaret Moses, Mary Aldermanbury, Mary Aldermary, Mary Magdalen Milk Street, Mary Somerset, Matthew Friday Street, Michael Cornhill, Olave Hart Street, Pancras Soper Lane, Stephen Walbrook, Thomas the Apostle, and Vedast; E.B. Jupp and R. Hovenden (eds), *The Registers of Allhallows London Wall* (1878); E. Freshfield (ed.), *The Register Book of the Parish of St. Christopher le Stocks* (1882); J.M.S. Brooks and A.W.C. Challen, *The Transcript of the Register of . . . S. Mary Woolchurch Haw* (1886); and W. Brigg (transc.), *The Register Book of the Parish of St. Nicholas Acons* (1890).

35 It should be noted that the difference between worst- and least-affected parishes was smaller in 1563 than in later epidemics. As Table 6.2 also suggests, mortality was more evenly distributed in the earlier epidemic. Nevertheless, even in 1563 the ten most fortunate parishes all recorded ratios of less than 5.6 while those worst hit had ratios of more than 8.0.

36 The Crisis Mortality Ratios in St Stephen Coleman Street were: 1543 – 2.6, 1548 – 2.7; and in St Lawrence Jewry: 1543 – 5.9, 1548 – 6.3.

37 The epidemic of 1578 did not produce any very clear geographical pattern, largely because several parishes almost entirely escaped in that year, although some of them suffered from plague in 1569–70 or 1581–2.

38 R.W. Herlan, 'Social Articulation and the Configuration of Parochial Poverty in London on the Eve of the Restoration', *Guildhall Studies*, II

(1976), 43–53; D.V. Glass, *London Inhabitants Within the Walls 1695* (London Rec. Soc., II, 1966), map p. xxiii; P.E. Jones and A.V. Judges, 'London Population in the Late Seventeenth Century', *Ec. HR*, VI (1935–6), 45–63; D.V. Glass, 'Socio-Economic Status and Occupations in the City of London at the End of the Seventeenth Century', in A.E.J. Hollaender and W. Kellaway (eds), *Studies in London History presented to P.E. Jones* (1969), 373–89.
39 See the Appendix to this chapter, pp. 170–2.
40 The forty-seven parishes are those identified in nn. 10, 33, and 34 above. The poor and rich parishes are italicised in the Appendix, Table 6.4, p. 171.
41 If the minor outbreaks of plague between 1568 and 1571 had hit the poor parishes more than the rich, they would have seriously distorted the ratios of the two groups and made comparison between them misleading in 1563: inspection of the registers suggests, however, that this was not the case.
42 The important research being undertaken by Dr Derek Keene shows, for example, that there was no significant increase in demand for housing in the Cheapside area before 1580: 'Did London Grow during the Sixteenth Century?' (unpublished paper to the London History Conference, 25 June 1983).
43 Davis, 'The Transformation of London', pp. 294, 298–301, 304, 307–8; Brett-James, *Growth of Stuart London*, pp. 33, 74, 76; LCC, *Survey of London* (1900–), XII. 40–1, XV. 51–4; Pearl, *London and the Outbreak*, pp. 9–23.
44 J. Stow, *A Survey of London*, ed. C.L. Kingsford (Oxford, 1908), I. 165, 211, II. 4, 21, 71–2.
45 P.V. McGrath, 'The Marketing of Food, Fodder and Livestock in the London Area in the Seventeenth Century' (London Univ. MA thesis, 1948), pp. 135–6, 139–40. For the problem of rats in the granaries of the Livery Companies, many of which were at Bridewell, see J.T. Lambert (ed.), *Records of the Skinners Company of London* (1933), p. 359. Leadenhall was one exception to the peripheral location of markets and granaries, and its proximity may help to account for heavy mortality in St Peter's Cornhill in 1563. The corporation's own granary was at the Bridgehouse in Southwark, another unhealthy area: Stow, *Survey*, I. 156–7, II. 65.
46 R.E.G. Kirk and E.F. Kirk, *Returns of Aliens dwelling in the City and Suburbs of London* (Huguenot Soc. of London Publications, X, 1900–8), *passim*, and III. 439 on overcrowding; I. Scouloudi, 'Alien Immigration and Alien Communities in London 1558–1640' (London Univ. M.Sc. thesis, 1936), pp. 54, 60, App. I (I am grateful to Miss Scouloudi for permission to use her thesis); Stow, *Survey*, I. 124, 208.
47 Finlay, *Population and Metropolis*, pp. 16, 88–9, 100–5.
48 T.C. Dale, *The Inhabitants of London in 1638* (1931), pp. 201, 224, 238; GL, MSS. 5090/2, *passim*, 4524/2, f. 47v.
49 D.J. Johnson, *Southwark and the City* (Oxford, 1969), pp. 225, 324–6; M.J. Power, 'The East and West in Early-Modern London', in E.W. Ives, R.J. Knecht and J.J. Scarisbrick (eds), *Wealth and Power in Tudor England:*

Essays Presented to S.T. Bindoff (1978), pp. 167–85; M. Power, 'East London Housing in the Seventeenth Century', in P. Clark and P. Slack (eds), *Crisis and Order in English Towns 1500–1700* (1972), pp. 237–62; Brett-James, *Growth of Stuart London*, pp. 109, 116, 164–5, 216–17.'

50 As in Table 6.2, the ratios in Table 6.3 have been calculated from parish registers for the epidemics of 1563, 1593 and 1603, and from bills of mortality for 1625, 1636 and 1665, except in the case of Stepney where the register has also been used for 1625.

51 Westminster City Library, MS. 4514.

52 Bell, *Great Plague*, pp. 270, 274.

53 See pp. 117, 123, 134.

54 See pp. 127, 148.

55 See pp. 114, 193.

56 Some of the complexities of this subject are well discussed in J. Langton, 'Residential Patterns in Pre-industrial Cities: Some Case Studies from Seventeenth-Century Britain', *Trans. Inst. Brit. Geog.*, 65 (1975), 1–27; and in E. Jones, 'London in the Early Seventeenth Century: An Ecological Approach', *London J.*, 6 (1980), 123–33. See also N. Goose, 'Household Size and Structure in Early Stuart Cambridge', *Social History*, 5 (1980), 354–5, 369–70.

57 Cf. Brett-James, *Growth of Stuart London*, pp. 36, 40; Freshfield, *Minute Books of St. Bartholomew Exchange*, p. xlix; below, p. 322. There was certainly some sixteenth-century rebuilding in the centre of London for the well-to-do, and the destruction of alleys in order to build the Exchange in 1566 must have improved conditions in St Michael's Cornhill, where plague had been serious in 1563: Stow, *Survey*, I. 192.

58 P. Clark and P. Slack, *English Towns in Transition 1500–1700* (Oxford, 1976), pp. 83–4, 49; P. Corfield, 'A Provincial Capital in the Late Seventeenth Century: The Case of Norwich', in Clark and Slack (eds), *Crisis and Order in English Towns*, p. 270.

59 J.F. Pound, 'An Elizabethan Census of the Poor', *Univ. Birmingham Hist. J.*, VIII (1962), 158; W. Rye (ed.), *The Norwich Rate Book* (1903). After the 1630s the distribution of wealth in Norwich changed slightly (in favour of Ultra Aquam Ward), but Conesford retained its poor position: J.T. Evans, *Seventeenth-Century Norwich* (Oxford, 1979), pp. 36–9.

60 ECA, Book 157, f. 42; D2/159b(2). Unfortunately, there are no complete figures for any intermediate date. Conditions in St Sidwell's were probably very like those in a Worcester suburb described in I. Roy and S. Porter, 'The Social and Economic Structure of an Early Modern Suburb: The Tything at Worcester', *Bull. Inst. Hist. Res.*, LIII (1980), 203–17. Cf. P. and J. Clark, 'The Social Economy of the Canterbury Suburbs', in A. Detsicas and N. Yates (eds), *Studies in Modern Kentish History Presented to F. Hull and E. Melling* (Kent Arch. Soc., 1983), pp. 65–86.

61 Cf. W.G. Hoskins, 'The Elizabethan Merchants of Exeter', in S.T. Bindoff, J. Hurstfield and C.H. Williams (eds), *Elizabethan Government and Society: Essays Presented to Sir John Neale* (1961), pp. 178–9; D. Portman, *Exeter Houses 1400–1700* (Exeter, 1966), pp. 59–60; M.D. Lobel (ed.), *Historic Towns*, II (1975), 'Bristol', pp. 17–19; E. Ralph and M.E.

Williams (eds), *The Inhabitants of Bristol in 1696* (Bristol Rec. Soc., XXV, 1968), p. xxii; V. Parker, *The Making of King's Lynn* (1971), p. 79. Regulations for street-cleaning are surveyed in J.H. Thomas, *Town Government in the Sixteenth Century* (1933), ch. 6.

62 W. Rye, *Depositions Taken Before the Mayor and Aldermen of Norwich 1549–67* (Norwich, 1905), p. 70; J.F. Pound, 'The Social and Trade Structure of Norwich 1525–75', *P&P*, 34 (1966), 62; information on residences of mayors from Mr A. Baggs. Country gentry, as opposed to the mercantile elite, often had houses in Conesford in the early sixteenth century; but the move of the duke of Norfolk's palace from that outer ward to St John Maddermarket in mid-century must have had a centripetal social effect: *Historic Towns*, II. 'Norwich', pp. 18–20.

63 See Table 5.3, p. 124.

64 See pp. 27, 195, 305–6.

65 Above, pp. 41–4.

66 H.E. Malden (ed.), *The Cely Papers* (Camden Soc., 3 ser., I, 1900), p. 158; A. Taylor (ed.), *The Works of Symon Patrick* (1848), IX. 446. Cf. *Letters and Papers of Henry VIII*, XIII (i), p. 374; HMC, *Gawdy*, p. 9.

67 I.G. Doolittle, 'The Plague in Colchester 1579–1666', *Trans. Essex Arch. Soc.*, IV (1972), 145; Plymouth RO, W361/53/1; *Cal. SP Dom. 1665–6*, p. 523; Lambeth Palace, Carte Misc. VI, 42–3.

68 BL, Harl. MS. 3785, f. 20; GL, MS. 3570/2, f. 21r. Cf. *The Intelligencer*, 20 November 1665; *Plague Pamphlets of Dekker*, p. 147. In 1636, 155 householders left St Martin-in-the-Fields parish: Westminster City Library, MS. 3356.

69 The parishes are: Allhallows Bread Street, Allhallows Honey Lane, SS. Antholin, Mary le Bow, Matthew Friday Street, Michael Bassishaw, and Stephen Walbrook.

70 PRO, E179/251/15B. Cf. J. Cornwall, 'A Tudor Domesday: The Musters of 1522', *J. Soc. Archivists*, III (1965), 22.

71 GL, MS. 2942.

72 T.C. Dale, *The Inhabitants of London in 1638* (1931). For recent and comparable manipulations of the same source, see Finlay, *Population and Metropolis*, ch. 4; Jones, 'London in the Early Seventeenth Century'.

73 From Jones and Judges, 'London Population in the Late Seventeenth Century', table 3.

Chapter 7 Counting the costs

1 Quoted in D. Defoe, *A Journal of the Plague Year* (Everyman edn, 1908), pp. 285–6.

2 Estimates of total plague deaths in Exeter and Bristol have been based on the excess number of burials above the normal annual average in plague years in the parish registers, with upward adjustment to account for parishes with no surviving registers. In the case of parishes in Devon and Essex, all excess burials in obvious plague years have been counted and also all contemporary references to 'plague' casualties in the surviving

registers in years when no major epidemic developed. In all these instances the totals are likely to be minima, and less close to the truth than the more complete, but still doubtless inaccurate, records of plague burials compiled in London and Norwich.

3 M. Pelling, *Cholera, Fever and English Medicine 1825–1865* (Oxford, 1978), p. 2.

4 Although there are surviving registers for only one-third of the parishes, they probably contain the majority of plague deaths since they include most of the larger towns and many of the most populous rural parishes. Only 7,000 deaths have therefore been added to the total as an estimate for parishes without surviving registers.

5 Assuming the population of England to be 5 million and that of London 500,000 in 1670, the hearth tax returns suggest that Devon and Essex contained 6.6 per cent of the population of England outside the capital: K.H. Burley, 'The Economic Development of Essex in the later 17th and 18th Centuries' (London Univ. PhD thesis, 1957), pp. 10–11; W.G. Hoskins, *Devon* (1954), p. 172. The muster returns of 1569–70, however, would suggest that the proportion was less than 5 per cent a century earlier: E.E. Rich, 'The Population of Elizabethan England', *Ec. HR*, 2nd ser., II (1950), 251, 253. The growth of Plymouth and Colchester helps to explain the difference. I have therefore preferred to take 6 per cent as a maximum proportion for the whole century.

6 PRO, SP 16/349/70; SP 16/200/14.

7 J.F.D. Shrewsbury, *A History of Bubonic Plague in the British Isles* (Cambridge, 1970), p. 5; T.H. Hollingsworth, *Historical Demography* (1969), pp. 357, 365; R. Pollitzer, *Plague* (Geneva, 1954), p. 32; J.-N. Biraben, *Les Hommes et la peste en France et dans les pays européens et méditerranéens* (Paris, 1975–6), I. 10, 303; C.M. Cipolla, *Cristofano and the Plague* (1973), p. 103; B. Bennassar, *Recherches sur les grandes épidémies dans le nord de l'Espagne à la fin du XVIᵉ siècle* (Paris, 1969), pp. 142 ff.

8 Cf. *Cal. SP Dom. 1666–7*, pp. 26, 70.

9 J. Hughes, 'The Plague in Carlisle 1597/98', *Trans. Cumb. and Westm. Antiq. and Arch. Soc.*, NS, LXXI (1971), 53.

10 SCA, S161. The average number of people per household was 3.2: a low figure probably to be explained by the death of some inmates and the flight of others before the houses were shut up. The numbers are, however, recorded only in three of the thirteen months in the accounts.

11 A.L. Rowse, *Simon Forman* (1974), p. 287. Forman's household was infected again in 1603: Bodl., Ashm. MS. 802, f. 133r. For cases of rapid death, see William Worcestre, *Itineraries*, ed. J.H. Harvey (Oxford, 1969), p. 255; *Cal. SP Dom. 1625–6*, p. 307.

12 Cf. Shrewsbury, *Bubonic Plague*, p. 425.

13 Kent AO, PRC 2/34, acct no. 275.

14 For some instances, see Slack, thesis, p. 203. The family incidence of other diseases deserves further study, however.

15 The sources for Table 7.1 are: NNRO, register of St Peter Mancroft; BAO, register of SS. Philip and Jacob; Salisbury Diocesan RO, registers of SS. Edmund, Martin and Thomas, Salisbury, compared with SCA,

S161 for the second set of figures; R. Schofield, 'An Anatomy of an Epidemic: Colyton, November 1645 to November 1646', and L. Bradley, 'The Most Famous of All English Plagues: A Detailed Analysis of the Plague at Eyam 1665–6', in *The Plague Reconsidered* (Local Population Studies Suppl., 1977), pp. 106, 92; H.J. Cunnington, *An Account of the Charities and Charitable Benefactions of Braintree* (1904), pp. 60–5. In the cases of Norwich, Bristol and Salisbury burials have been taken only for the successive months when plague was clearly present in the parish. Their arrangement in household groups presents obvious difficulties, but wherever possible common surnames have been broken up into separate families, and servants and apprentices have been included in the households of their masters.

16 Schofield, 'Anatomy of an Epidemic', pp. 107–8.

17 For the epidemiological questions which arise from the household concentration of plague mortality, see above, p. 10.

18 *The Plague Reconsidered*, pp. 75, 119.

19 Pollitzer, *Plague*, pp. 503–4; Biraben, *Les Hommes et la peste*, I. 166, 222–5.

20 C.M. Cipolla and D.E. Zanetti, 'Peste et mortalité différentielle', *Annales de Demog. Hist.* (1972), 198, 200; F. Lebrun, *Les Hommes et la mort en Anjou aux 17ᵉ et 18ᵉ siècles*, (Paris, 1971), p. 306.

21 F. Herring, *A Modest Defence* (1604), sig. A4; M.F. and T.H. Hollingsworth, 'Plague Mortality Rates by Age and Sex in the Parish of St. Botolph's without Bishopsgate, London, 1603', *Pop. Studies*, XXV (1971), 135, 145.

22 R. Thompson, 'Seventeenth-Century English and Colonial Sex Ratios: A Postscript', *Pop. Studies*, XXVIII (1974), 164. Emigration of males provides a better explanation for a surplus of women: E.A. Wrigley and R.S. Schofield, *The Population History of England 1541–1871: A Reconstruction* (1981), pp. 224–6.

23 Bradley and Schofield in *The Plague Reconsidered*, pp. 93, 109.

24 R.A.P. Finlay, *Population and Metropolis: The Demography of London 1580–1650* (Cambridge, 1981), pp. 130–1. In 1665 male and female burials were almost equal: see n. 29 below.

25 Fig. 7.1 is based on Hollingsworths, 'Plague Mortality Rates', p. 135; and on the ratios given in Slack, thesis, pp. 208, 210 (with the addition of sex ratios for burials in Plymouth 1582–5 (127) and in Chelmsford in 1624 (118) from the parish registers). Because of the uncertainties referred to in the text, it has not been thought appropriate to present a more detailed analysis of this material here.

26 Hollingsworths, 'Plague Mortality Rates', p. 145.

27 Cf. Shrewsbury, *Bubonic Plague*, p. 235; Bennassar, *Recherches*, p. 70; P. Deyon, *Amiens, capitale provinciale* (Paris, 1967), pp. 32–3.

28 In the small town of Tiverton the sex ratio appears, from Graunt's figures, to have risen in some plague years: C.H. Hull (ed.), *The Economic Writings of Sir William Petty* (Cambridge, 1899), II. 416–17. But Tiverton was a predominantly industrial town and may have contained many labourers and apprenticies: Hoskins, *Devon*, p. 495.

29 After the 1650s, however, large towns may also have had a surplus of

women at the relevant ages. In the case of London, a change in the sex structure of the population affected the sex ratios in the final outbreak of plague. The surplus of men in the population disappeared in the course of the seventeenth century as the proportion of apprentices declined and that of maidservants rose (Finlay, *Population and Metropolis*, p. 19); and the sex ratio of burials seems to have been slightly lower in 1665 (100) than in 1657–64 (109): *Economic Writings of Petty*, II. 411; Bell, *Great Plague*, p. 245n, opp. p. 320. See also D. Souden, 'Migrants and the Population Structure of Later Seventeenth-Century Provincial Cities and Market Towns', in P. Clark (ed.), *The Transformation of English Provincial Towns* (1984), pp. 158–9.

30 BAO, Christ Church Easter Book, 1575. The sex ratio of burials in the parish in 1570–4 was 108, although the number of burials was then small.

31 The Hollingsworths argue that there was not a surplus of men in the population of St Botolph's: 'Plague Mortality Rates', p. 144.

32 Fig. 7.2 is based on *The Plague Reconsidered*, pp. 113–14, for Colyton and Eyam; on calculations from burials for 1587–93 in *The Register of St. Peter Cornhill* (Harl. Soc., 1877) and *The Registers of Allhallows London Wall* (1878); and on the figure and table in T.R. Forbes, *Chronicle from Aldgate* (New Haven, 1971). In St Botolph's Bishopsgate, 45 per cent of those buried in 1603 were aged five to twenty-four, compared with 13 per cent before the epidemic: Hollingsworths, 'Plague Mortality Rates', p. 135. For more precise computations of age-specific mortality in London, see Finlay, *Population and Metropolis*, pp. 121–30.

33 Pollitzer, *Plague*, pp. 503–4; L.F. Hirst, 'Plague', in *British Encyclopedia of Medical Practice* (2nd edn, 9, 1952), p. 61.

34 See Schofield, 'Anatomy of an Epidemic', pp. 109–18, for an excellent discussion of this subject; and Hollingsworths, 'Plague Mortality Rates', *passim*. In Colyton, though not in St Botolph's Bishopsgate, the decline in plague mortality stopped at age 50: the 50+ group in fact experienced greater excess mortality than that aged 20 to 49.

35 Infants appear to have suffered lower plague mortality than older children in Ludlow in 1609, in some London parishes, and in plagues in Geneva: R. Schofield and E.A. Wrigley, 'Infant and Child Mortality in England in the Late Tudor and Early Stuart Period', in C. Webster (ed.), *Health, Medicine and Mortality in the Sixteenth Century* (Cambridge, 1979), p. 86; Finlay, *Population and Metropolis*, p. 129; A. Perrenoud, *La Population de Genève du XVI⁰ au début du XIX⁰ siècle*, I (Geneva, 1979), pp. 450–1.

36 Cf. Schofield and Wrigley, 'Infant and Child Mortality', pp. 86–8; Slack, thesis, p. 212n.

37 Bodl., Ashm. MS. 384, f. 176v; above, p. 34; J. Balmford, *A Short dialogue concerning the Plagues Infection* (1603), p. 50.

38 Bradley and Schofield in *The Plague Reconsidered*, pp. 74–7, 90, 119–20. For a nice example of rapid remarriage in London, see H. Ellis (ed.), *The Obituary of Richard Smyth* (Camden Soc., OS, XLIV, 1849), p. 70.

39 P. Slack, 'Poverty and Politics in Salisbury, 1597–1666', in P. Clark and P. Slack (eds), *Crisis and Order in English Towns 1500–1700* (1972), pp. 166, 172; A.L. Beier, 'The Social Problems of an Elizabethan Country

Town: Warwick, 1580–90', in P. Clark (ed.), *Country Towns in Pre-Industrial England* (Leicester, 1981), pp. 60–1. On the problems of widows in early modern towns, see S.J. Wright, 'Family Life and Society in Sixteenth and Early Seventeenth Century Salisbury' (Leicester Univ. PhD thesis, 1982), ch. V; B.H. Todd, 'Widowhood in a Market Town: Abingdon 1540–1720' (Oxford Univ. D.Phil. thesis, 1983).

40 Cf. E.A. Wrigley, 'A Simple Model of London's Importance in Changing English Society and Economy 1650–1750', *P&P*, 37 (1967), 47; P. Clark, 'The Migrant in Kentish Towns 1580–1650', in Clark and Slack (eds), *Crisis and Order in English Towns*, pp. 124, 129–31; P. Slack, 'Vagrants and Vagrancy in England, 1598–1664', *Ec. HR*, 2nd ser., XXVII (1974), 365–6.

41 For the migration of parents with young children into London even before the 1603 plague, see Hollingsworths, 'Plague Mortality Rates', pp. 139, 141. Cf. Finlay, *Population and Metropolis*, p. 130.

42 D.V. Glass and D.E.C. Eversley (eds), *Population in History* (1965), p. 182; T. Harwood, *The History and Antiquities of the Church and City of Lichfield* (Gloucester, 1806), p. 306.

43 Biraben, *Les Hommes et la peste*, I. 310–11.

44 BL, Sloane MS. 1821, f. 263v; A. Paré, *A Treatise of the Plague* (1630), p. 9.

45 Salisbury Diocesan RO, registers of SS. Edmund and Thomas (that for St Martin's parish is incomplete for these years); Plymouth RO, register of St Andrew's Plymouth. Cf. E.A. Wrigley, *Population and History* (1969), pp. 113–15; Forbes, *Chronicle from Aldgate*, p. 60; Perrenoud, *Population de Genève*, pp. 402–7.

46 *Economic Writings of Petty*, II. 367–8; Wrigley, 'Simple Model of London's Importance', *passim*.

47 Above, pp. 96, 118–19; R. Finlay, 'Natural Decrease in Early Modern Cities', *P&P*, 92 (1981), 169–74.

48 Cf. Perrenoud, *Population de Genève*, pp. 357–9; M. Terrisse, 'Le Rattrapage de nuptialité d'après peste à Marseille (1720–1)', in J. Dupâquier (ed.), *Hommage à Marcel Reinhard: Sur la population française au XVIIIe et au XIXe siècles* (Paris, 1973), pp. 56–79; A. Bideau, 'Les Mécanismes autorégulateurs des populations traditionelles', *Annales ESC*, 38 (1983), 1050–2.

49 Quoted in G. Oliver, *The History of the City of Exeter* (Exeter, 1861), p. 109.

50 Wrigley and Schofield, *Population History*, pp. 244, 354; Wrigley, *Population and History*, pp. 108–13.

51 Wrigley and Schofield, *Population History*, pp. 311n, 176–8, 234, 334. Cf. P. Slack, 'Mortality Crises and Epidemic Disease in England 1485–1610', in Webster (ed.), *Health, Medicine and Mortality*, pp. 15–16, 19, 27–32.

52 Wrigley and Schofield, *Population History*, pp. 322, 654, 179, 316–18. Cf. Finlay, *Population and Metropolis*, pp. 111–12, 132.

53 The problems are discussed in A. Sharlin, 'Natural Decrease in Early Modern Cities: A Reconsideration', *P&P*, 79 (1978), 126–38, and in the debate between Sharlin and R. Finlay, *ibid.*, 92 (1981).

54 *Cal. SP Dom. 1637*, p. 256; HMC, *Shrewsbury and Talbot*, I. 92; PRO, SP 16/200/14.
55 For reduced income from fairs and markets, see GL, MS 1454/95; Winchester City Records, Proceedings in Boroughmote 1552–75, f. 56r; BAO, Mayor's Audits, 1624–5, p. 45; S. Bond, 'The Plague at Northampton', *Northants Past and Present*, III (1965–6), 236–7; J. Dennett (ed.), *Beverley Borough Records 1575–1821* (Yorks. Arch. Soc., Rec. Ser., LXXXIV, 1933), p. 136. Cf. A. Fletcher, *A County Community in Peace and War: Sussex 1600–1660* (1975), p. 237.
56 Northants RO, Cockayne Papers C2711; M.M. Verney, *Memoirs of the Verney Family* (1892–9), IV. 116–17.
57 *Cal. Treasury Books 1660–7*, pp. 710, 730–2, *1669–72*, pp. 147, 151, 531, 970, *1679–80*, pp. 841, 845; *Cal. SP Dom. 1665–6*, p. 66, *1667–8*, pp. 181, 229, *1668–9*, p. 134. Cf. C.D. Chandaman, *The English Public Revenue 1660–1688* (Oxford, 1975), pp. 23, 55, 91; and for the effects of plague on the assessment in the 1650s, *Cal. Committee for Compounding*, IV. 2590.
58 B.E. Supple, *Commercial Crisis and Change in England 1600–42* (Cambridge, 1964), pp. 26, 99–102; W.B. Stephens, *Seventeenth-Century Exeter* (Exeter, 1958), pp. 14–15, 167.
59 *Cal. SP Dom. 1666–7*, p. 53; GL, MS. 2089/1, 1636 acct.
60 Above, p. 143; Winchester City Records, Coffer Accounts 1589–1627, 27 August 1625; *Bibliotheca Phillippica*, NS, part 19 (Sotheby Catalogue), lot 4874; P. Slack (ed.), *Poverty in Early Stuart Salisbury* (Wilts. Rec. Soc., XXXI, 1975), p. 7; J.S. Davies, *History of Southampton* (1883), p. 496; Cheshire RO, Quarter Sessions File 1604 (iii), doc. 29; HMC, *Portland*, I. 279.
61 Slack, 'Mortality Crises and Epidemic Disease', p. 59; P. Wynter (ed.), *Works of the Right Reverend Joseph Hall*, V (Oxford, 1863), 258; J. Toy, *Worcester's Elegie and Evlogie* (1638), p. 9; R.C. Latham and W. Matthews (eds), *The Diary of Samuel Pepys*, VI (1972), p. 233. R. Milton, *Londons Miserie, The Countryes Crueltie* (1625), p. 29, denied it was true in London in 1625.
62 I.G. Doolittle, 'The Effects of the Plague on a Provincial Town in the Sixteenth and Seventeenth Centuries', *Medic. Hist.*, 19 (1975), 335–6; K.J. Allison, 'The Wool Supply and the Worsted Cloth Industry in Norfolk in the 16th and 17th Centuries' (Leeds Univ. PhD thesis, 1955), pp. 569, 576, tables 20–2.
63 Allison, 'Wool Supply', Appendix; D.M. Palliser, 'Epidemics in Tudor York', *Northern History*, VIII (1973), 57.
64 Slack, 'Poverty and Politics in Salisbury', pp. 164–203. Circumstances appear to have been similar in Gloucester: W.B. Willcox, *Gloucestershire: A Study in Local Government 1590–1640* (New Haven, 1940), p. 176; P. Clark, ' "The Ramoth-Gilead of the Good": Urban Change and Political Radicalism at Gloucester 1540–1640', in P. Clark, A.G.R. Smith and N. Tyacke (eds), *The English Commonwealth 1547–1640* (Leicester, 1979), pp. 167–87.
65 K.R. Adey, 'Seventeenth-Century Stafford: A County Town in Decline',

Midland History, II (1974), 152–67; C.J.M. Moxon, 'Ashby-de-la-Zouche, a Social and Economic Survey of a Market Town 1570–1720' (Oxford Univ. D.Phil. thesis, 1971), pp. 41, 105–7, 131–2 (I am grateful to Dr Moxon for permission to refer to his thesis); J. Aubrey, *The Natural History of Wiltshire* (1847), p. 115.

66 Schofield, 'Anatomy of an Epidemic', pp. 120–1; E.A. Wrigley, 'Family Limitation in Pre-industrial England', *Ec. HR*, 2nd ser., XIX (1966), 82–109; *idem*, 'Marital Fertility in Seventeenth-Century Colyton: A Note', *ibid.*, XXXI (1978), 433–5; *idem*, 'The Changing Occupational Structure of Colyton over Two Centuries', *Local Pop. Studies*, 18 (1977), 9, 16–17.

67 Salisbury Diocesan RO, registers of St Edmund's and St Thomas's parishes and the bishops transcripts for St Martin's; Slack, *Poverty in Early Stuart Salisbury*, pp. 65–82.

68 PRO, SP 16/349/70; W. Le Hardy (ed.), *Hertfordshire County Records: Calendar to the Sessions Books 1619–57*, V (Hertford, 1929), 231–2. The high costs of keeping and nursing an infected family can be illustrated from probate administrators' accounts: e.g. LCC, *Survey of London*, XII (i), 41; Kent AO, PRC 2/34, no. 275.

69 Lincs RO, Red Book of Lincoln, f. 151r; Lambeth Palace, Carte Misc. VI, no. 15. For similar complaints, see SCA, N100, petitions to Sessions 1629; Hull Corporation Records, Bench Book 5, f. 237r (1638).

70 Kent AO, NR/ZPa 4/5; S. and B. Webb, *The Old Poor Law* (1927), pp. 82–3; SCA, Box 4, File 'Various 1600–30', doc. 65a.

71 Winchester City Records, Fourth Book of Ordinances 1617–47, f. 42v; H.S. Scott (ed.), 'The Journal of Sir Roger Wilbraham', *Camden Misc.*, X (Camden Soc., 3 ser., IV, 1902), 63; J.E. Cussans, *History of Hertfordshire: Hundred of Dacorum* (1879), pp. 276–7.

72 E.g. ERO, register of West Hanningfield, 1609; Devon and Cornwall Record Society Library, Exeter, register transcript of Cruwys Morchard, 1646.

73 E.g. BAO, registers of SS. Nicholas and John Baptist, 1645; Salisbury Diocesan RO, registers of SS. Thomas and Edmund, Salisbury, 1604.

74 E.g. Salisbury Diocesan RO, register of St Edmund's, 1604; Worcs. RO, register of Claines, 1612, register of St John in Bedwardine, 1610; BAO, SS. Philip and Jacob and St Nicholas registers, 1603; *Privy Council Acts 1626*, p. 21.

75 A. Plummer, *The London Weavers' Company 1600–1970* (1972), p. 189; G.E. Trease, 'Devon Apothecaries in Seventeenth-Century Barnstaple', *Devon and Cornwall Notes and Queries*, XXXII (1971), 41.

76 Palliser, 'Epidemics in Tudor York', p. 47; W.J. Harte, *Gleanings from the Common Place Book of John Hooker* (Exeter, n.d.), p. 30.

77 *Obituary of Richard Smyth*, p. 67; E. Freshfield (ed.), *The Register Book of St. Christopher le Stocks* (1882), p. iv (1665); C. St. Barbe (ed.), *Records of New Lymington* (1848), p. 32; *Cal. Assize Records: Sussex Indictments, James I* (1975), p. 25; D. Pennington and K. Thomas (eds), *Puritans and Revolutionaries* (Oxford, 1978), p. 111; above, p. 18. Cf. Hughes, 'Plague in Carlisle', p. 56.

78 M. Fuller, *The Life, Letters and Writings of John Davenant 1572–1641* (1897), p. 256.
79 Above, pp. 76–7; Slack, 'Mortality Crises and Epidemic Disease', pp. 53–5.
80 See pp. 275–6.
81 Above, pp. 63–4, 99.
82 Above, pp. 164–5.
83 Based on subsidy assessments and the parish registers: see Slack, thesis, pp. 213–14.
84 PRO, SP 29/129/26. Cf. Bennassar, *Recherches*, p. 54, for a Spanish observation on the possibility of avoiding plague in Valladolid.
85 Hughes, 'Plague in Carlisle', p. 57; M. Bateson and H. Stocks (eds), *Records of the Borough of Leicester* (Cambridge, 1899–1923), IV. 232; BL, Sloane MS. 3723, f. 67r; *Intelligencer*, 23 October 1665, p. 1022. Cf. T.T. Wildridge (ed.), *The Hull Letters* (Hull, 1888), p. 16. For literary observations of a similar kind, see J. Jones, *A Diall for all Agues* (1566), sig. Fviiiᵛ; Herring, *Modest Defence*, sig. Bl.
86 PRO, SP 16/349/70; Sheffield City Library, Strafford Correspondence, 12/236.

Chapter 8 Public authority and a policy for control

1 PRO, SP 16/533/17, f. 37v.
2 Cf. E.M. Leonard, *The Early History of English Poor Relief* (Cambridge, 1900), pp. 61–2.
3 See above, pp. 61–2.
4 Above, pp. 44–7.
5 *Letters and Papers of Henry VIII*, II (ii), p. 1133. Cf. C. Creighton, *A History of Epidemics in Britain* (Cambridge, 1891–4), I. 328–9, 312.
6 LCRO, Journal xi, ff. 318v–319r; F.P. Wilson, *The Plague in Shakespeare's London* (2nd edn, Oxford, 1963), pp. 56–7; P.L. Hughes and J.F. Larkin (eds), *Tudor Royal Proclamations* (New Haven, 1964–9), III. 269–70.
7 J.J. Scarisbrick, 'Cardinal Wolsey and the Common Weal', in E.W. Ives, R.J. Knecht and J.J. Scarisbrick (eds), *Wealth and Power in Tudor England: Essays Presented to S.T. Bindoff* (1978), pp. 45–67; Hughes and Larkin, *Tudor Royal Proclamations*, I. 127–9; R.W. Heinze, *The Proclamations of the Tudor Kings* (Cambridge, 1976), p. 17; LCRO, Journal xi, ff. 305r, 337–8; M.D. Harris (ed.), *The Coventry Leet Book* (Early English Text Soc., 1907–13), p. 652.
8 C. Webster, 'Thomas Linacre and the Foundation of the College of Physicians', in F. Maddison, M. Pelling and C. Webster (eds), *Essays on the Life and Work of Thomas Linacre c. 1460–1524* (Oxford, 1977), pp. 198–222; E.F. Rogers (ed.), *The Correspondence of Sir Thomas More* (Princeton, 1947), pp. 135–6; *idem* (ed.), *St. Thomas More: Selected Letters* (New Haven, 1961), pp. 110–11.
9 Thomas More, *Utopia* (ed. G. Sampson, 1910), pp. 104–5; G.R. Elton, *Studies in Tudor and Stuart Politics and Government* (Cambridge, 1974), I.

130; J.H. Hexter, *More's Utopia: The Biography of an Idea* (New York, 1965), pp. 152–3.
10 Creighton, *History of Epidemics*, I. 247–8, 290–1; above, pp. 70–1. A riot against foreigners like that on Evil May Day 1517 was expected in September: *Letters and Papers of Henry VIII*, II (ii), p. 1166.
11 J.J. Scarisbrick, *Henry VIII* (1968), p. 501.
12 A. Chereau (ed.), *Les Ordonnances faictes et publiées a son de trompe par . . . ceste Ville de Paris pour éviter le dangier de Peste 1531* (Paris, 1873), pp. 20, 24; S. Guilbert, 'Un Conseil municipal face aux épidémies', *Annales ESC*, 23 (1968), 1293, 1295. Cf. S.J. Chadwick, 'Some Papers Relating to the Plague in Yorkshire', *Yorks. Arch. and Top. J.*, XV (1900), 467–75, nos 3, 10.
13 LCRO, Rep. ix, ff. 191r, 187r, 190v, 193. Cf. Rep. v, f. 142v; viii, f. 64v; xi, f. 387r.
14 LCRO, Rep. iv, f. 142v; Journal xv, f. 55; above, pp. 148–9.
15 LCRO, Rep. iii, f. 185r; Journal xi, f. 346v, xiii, f. 459, xv, ff. 48v–49r; Wilson, *Plague in Shakespeare's London*, pp. 61–4.
16 LCRO, Journal xv, ff. 47v–48r, xv, f.
17 *Letters and Papers of Henry VIII*, XIII (ii), pp. 153, 257, XIV (i), p. 14; W.H. Turner (ed.), *Selections from the Records of the City of Oxford 1509–1583* (Oxford, 1880), pp. 104–5; Beverley Corporation Records, Keepers' Account Rolls, 1520–1, 1522–3.
18 HMC, *15th Report App. X*, p. 34 (Shrewsbury); A. Raine (ed.), *York Civic Records* (Yorks. Arch. Soc., Record Ser., 1939–53), IV. 30; R.R. Tighe and J.E. Davis, *Annals of Windsor* (1858), I. 566–7; *Letters and Papers of Henry VIII*, XX (i), p. 363. For the activity of the prerogative Councils, see *ibid.*, XII (ii), p. 288; *York Civic Records*, IV. 22; York Corporation Records, E40, no. 77.
19 W.H. Stevenson (ed.), *Records of the Borough of Nottingham* (1882–1914), III. 374–6, 390; J. Raine (ed.), *The Durham Household Book* (Surtees Soc., 1844), p. 337; G.B. Richardson, *Plague and Pestilence in the North of England* (Newcastle, 1852), p. 51 (clearly referring to 1545); J.A. Twemlow (ed.), *Liverpool Town Books* (Liverpool, 1918), I. 16–17, 104–5, 108.
20 *York Civic Records*, V. 23, 28, 49, 82. Cf. BAO, 'Book of Ordinances and Acts of Common Council', f. 17v; NNRO, Assembly Book 1491–1553, ff. 139r, 202r.
21 *York Civic Records*, V. 29–36, 50–1, 57, 68, 71–2, 74–5.
22 York Corporation Records, House Book 13, f. 127; Lincolnshire RO, Lincoln Entries of Common Council 1541–64, f. 69v; E.M. Hampson, *The Treatment of Poverty in Cambridgeshire 1597–1834* (Cambridge, 1934), p. 6.
23 Winchester City Records, Chamberlains' Accounts, 1563–4; P. and J. Clark, 'The Social Economy of the Canterbury Suburbs: The Evidence of the Census of 1563', in A. Detsicas and N. Yates (eds), *Studies in Modern Kentish History Presented to Felix Hull and Elizabeth Melling* (Kent Arch. Soc., 1983), pp. 67–8; Lambeth Palace, MS. 306, f. 70r.
24 ECA, Act Book 4, f. 130v; Act Book 3, pp. 147, 244–5; M. Bateson and

H. Stocks (eds), *Records of the Borough of Leicester* (Cambridge, 1899–1923), III. 110; DRO, Crediton Wardens' Accounts, 1660A/30.

25 DRO, Dartmouth Court Book, DD1984, ff. 240–41r.

26 LCRO, Rep. xv, ff. 259v, 263r, 277v–279; Journal xviii, ff. 123v, 136, 142r, 184, 189v–190r. Cf. above, p. 154.

27 GL, MSS. 4810/1, ff. 18v, 20v; 4956/1, f. 93v; 9235/1, 1562–3; 645/1, f. 67v; 4956/2, f. 93v; W.H. Overall (ed.), *Accounts of the Churchwardens of the Parish of St. Michael Cornhill* (1871), p. 157. The only special payments to the sick I have discovered were in Southwark: GLCRO, P92/SAV/1387.

28 A.A. Van Schelven (ed.), *Kerkeraads-Protocollen der Nederduitsche Vluchtelingen-Kerk te Londen 1560–3* (Historisch Genootschap, Utrecht, 3 ser., 43, 1921), pp. 429–32. Cf. below, pp. 272–3.

29 LCRO, Journal xix, ff. 129r, 186r, 191r, 197, 198r, 216v; Journal xx (i), f. 2v.

30 Cf. LCRO, Rep. xvi, f. 112r, xvii, ff. 109v–110r, xix, f. 25v; Journal xx (i), ff. 42, 119r, xx (ii), ff. 323, 483r, 499v–503; below, pp. 281–2. I have discussed some of the problems of government in London during epidemics in 'Metropolitan Government in Crisis: London's Response to Plague', in A.L. Beier and R. Finlay (eds), *London 1500–1700: The Making of the Metropolis* (1985).

31 C.H. Cooper, *Annals of Cambridge* (Cambridge, 1842–53), II. 321, 335–6; HMC, *15th Report App. X*, pp. 18, 52; Richardson, *Pestilence in the North*, p. 14; R.H. Morris, *Chester in the Plantagenet and Tudor Reigns* (Chester, 1893), p. 78; Hull Corporation Records, Bench Book 4, ff. 138–44; *Records of Maidstone* (Maidstone, 1926), p. 198.

32 Wilson, *Plague in Shakespeare's London*, p. 15; E. Freshfield (ed.), *The Vestry Minute Books of St. Bartholomew Exchange* (1890), p. 3; *idem* (ed.), *The Vestry Minute Book of the Parish of St. Margaret Lothbury* (1887), pp. xxi, 6–7.

33 ERO, D/Y 2/41, p. 42, 2/42, p. 23 (Colchester); J.C. Cox (ed.), *The Records of the Borough of Northampton* (1898), II. 233–4; W. Hudson and J.C. Tingey, *The Records of the City of Norwich* (1906–10), II. 187; J. Webb (ed.), *Poor Relief in Elizabethan Ipswich* (Suffolk Records Soc., IX, 1966), p. 110; *Records of Leicester*, III. 179; HMC, *13th Report App. IV*, p. 66 (Rye); W.J. Hardy, *Calendar to the Records of the Borough of Doncaster* (Doncaster, 1899–1903), IV. 59; C. Bailey, *Transcripts from the Municipal Archives of Winchester* (Winchester, 1856), pp. 106–7; HMC, *9th Report Pt. 1*, App., p. 317 (Yarmouth); Hampson, *Poverty in Cambridgeshire*, p. 9 (Wisbech); J.L. Glasscock (ed.), *The Records of St. Michael's Church Bishop's Stortford* (1882), p. 62. Other possible instances are: Plymouth RO, Receivers' Accounts 1580–2; A.L. Merson (ed.), *The Third Book of Remembrance of Southampton 1514–1602, III: 1573–89* (Southampton Rec. Soc., VIII, 1965), pp. 18n, 24n, 58n.

34 *Tudor Royal Proclamations*, II, p. 466.

35 T. Wright, *Queen Elizabeth and Her Times* (1838), II. 62–4, 67; *Tudor Royal Proclamations*, II. no. 649; T.G. Barnes, 'The Prerogative and Environmental Control of London Building in the Early Seventeenth

Century: The Lost Opportunity', *California Law Review*, LVIII (1970), 1343–9; W.H. and H.C. Overall (eds), *Analytical Index to the Remembrancia* (of London) (1878), pp. 331–2. Cf. LCRO, Journal xix, ff. 171v–172r; Rep. xvii, f. 261v, xviii, f. 76r. On Cecil's interest in projects, see J. Thirsk, *Economic Policy and Projects* (Oxford, 1978), pp. 68–9, 86–8.

36 Creighton, *History of Epidemics*, I. 341–6; above, p. 147; T.T., *A view of certain wonderful effects . . . of the comete* (1578), sig. A4v; R. Flenley (ed.), *A Calendar of the Register of the Queen's Majesty's Council in . . . Wales 1569–91* (Cymmrodorion Rec. Ser., VIII, 1916), pp. 171–2.

37 PRO, SP 12/75/52. That Adelmare, father of Sir Julius Caesar, was the author is suggested by BL, Lansdowne 157, f. 344.

38 Above, pp. 45–6; B. Pullan, *Rich and Poor in Renaissance Venice* (Oxford, 1971), pp. 315–19; L.F. Hirst, *The Conquest of Plague* (Oxford, 1953), p. 52.

39 A. Croix, *Nantes et le pays Nantais au XVIᵉ siècle* (Paris, 1974), pp. 146–7; Chadwick, 'Papers Relating to Plague in Yorkshire', pp. 467–75 (Hague regulations 1557); Rodericus a Castro, *Tractatus Brevis de Natura et Causis Pestis* (Hamburg, 1596), sig. C4r; J.T. Alexander, *Bubonic Plague in Early Modern Russia* (Baltimore, 1980), pp. 30–1.

40 BL, Cotton MS. Vesp. F. xii, ff. 207–8 (n.d. but the content indicates 1578).

41 Heinze, *Proclamations of Tudor Kings*, pp. 228–9, 252; *Tudor Royal Proclamations*, II. no. 510.

42 Below, p. 229; *An admonition to be redde in the Churches of . . . London* (4 March 1564; *STC* 16704.7); *Willyam Cecill, knight, high Stewarde of . . . Westminster . . . To the Baylyffe* (12 March 1564; *STC* 16704.9).

43 HMC, *Salisbury*, II. 106; PRO, SP 12/103/3; *Privy Council Acts 1575–7*, p. 14.

44 PRO, SP 12/45, p. 27. (Like many documents of the period concerning plague, this is undated: the editor of the *Calendar* suggests September 1577 and it is certainly earlier than December 1578.)

45 *Privy Council Acts 1577–8*, pp. 387–8, 413.

46 C. Drew (ed.), *Lambeth Churchwardens' Accounts 1500–1645* (Surrey Rec. Soc., XVIII, 1941), p. 133; *Privy Council Acts 1578–80*, p. 211; *Poor Relief in Elizabethan Ipswich*, p. 110. The same publication may be referred to in *Records of St. Michael's Bishop's Stortford*, p. 59.

47 *STC* 9195; not dated, and suggested by *STC* as 1588, but it seems highly probable that this is the first printing of late 1578 or early 1579. The second edition of 1592 (*STC* 9199) is printed in *Present Remedies Against the Plague*, with an intro. by W.P. Barrett (Shakespeare Assoc., Facsimile no. 7, 1933).

48 *Orders thought meet . . .* (*STC* 9199, 1592; 9200, 1593; 9209, 1603; 9244–5, 1625); *Foure Statutes specially selected . . .* (1609; *STC* 9341), pp. 57–82; *Certaine Statutes especially selected . . .* (1630; *STC* 9342); *Certaine Necessary Directions* (1636; *STC* 16769), sig. Fl *et seq.*; *Orders Formerly Conceived . . .* (1646), sig. B4 *et seq.*; *Rules and Orders* (1666); below, pp. 222–3.

49 On the dearth orders, see P. Slack, 'Books of Orders: The Making of

English Social Policy, 1577–1631', *Trans. Roy. Hist. Soc.*, 5 ser., XXX (1980), pp. 1, 3.
50 J.-N. Biraben, *Les Hommes et la peste* (Paris, 1975–6), II. 155–7; Pullan, *Rich and Poor in Venice*, p. 319; P. Deyon, *Amiens, capitale provinciale* (Paris, 1967), p. 25.
51 M.A. Van Andel, 'Plague Regulations in the Netherlands', *Janus*, XXI (1916), 412, 414, 416; Chadwick, 'Papers Relating to Plague in Yorkshire', pp. 467–75, items 1, 9, 10, 13 (Hague regulations, 1557). In the larger Italian towns, only the contacts of the infected were generally isolated at home; the infected themselves were removed to pesthouses. Cf. C.M. Cipolla, *Cristofano and the Plague* (1973), pp. 167–8; Biraben, *Les Hommes et la peste*, II. 169–70.
52 1 James I, c. 31; W. Notestein, *The House of Commons 1604–10* (New Haven, 1971), pp. 52–3.
53 HMC, *Salisbury*, XV. 189–90; J.F.D. Shrewsbury, *A History of Bubonic Plague in the British Isles* (Cambridge, 1970), pp. 186, 262.
54 Renewals in 21 James I. c. 28; 1 Charles I, c. 7; 3 Charles I, c. 5; 16 Charles I, c. 4, sect. xxxi. For doubts in 1666, see A.H.A. Hamilton, *Quarter Sessions from Queen Elizabeth to Queen Anne* (1878), p. 219. Cf. S. Lambert, 'Procedure in the House of Commons in the Early Stuart Period', *Eng. Hist. Rev.*, XCV (1980), 780.
55 E. Coke, *The Third Part of the Institutes of the Laws of England* (1817), p. 90. For references to the statute, see W. Lambard, *Eirenarcha* (1619), pp. 197, 337–8, 609–10 (also in the 1607 edition, but not in that of 1602); *idem, The Duties of Constables, Borsholders, Tythingmen* (1606), p. 24; Balliol College, Oxford, MS. 331, memo. book of a JP *c.* 1628, ff. iir, 16r, 26; G. Leveson-Gower, 'Note Book of a Surrey Justice', *Surrey Arch. Coll.*, IX (1885–8), 181; Bodl., Rawlinson MS. B431, ff. llv, 14v, 16r (notes of a Sussex JP); R.D. Hunt (ed.), 'Henry Townshend's "Notes of the office of a Justice of the Peace", 1661–3', *Miscellany II* (Worcs. Hist. Soc., NS, V, 1967), p. 105.
56 Kent AO, Sa/AC6, f. 207v; W.B. Willcox, *Gloucestershire: A Study in Local Government 1590–1640* (New Haven, 1940), p. 225 n. 66; A.D. Dyer, 'The City of Worcester in the Sixteenth Century' (Birmingham Univ. PhD thesis, 1966), p. 282; SCA, Ledger C, ff. 176v, 178r; BAO, Common Council Proceedings 1598–1608, pp. 81, 83, 92; J.W. Horrocks (ed.), *The Assembly Books of Southampton* (South. Rec. Soc., 1917–25), I. xxxviii; ERO, D/B 3/3/207, docs 3–5 (Maldon).
57 HMC, *Rutland*, I. 217; Willcox, *Gloucestershire*, p. 225 n. 65; J. Lister (ed.), *West Riding Sessions Rolls 1597/8–1602* (Yorks. Arch. Soc., Record Ser., III, 1888), pp. 72–3; HMC, *10th Report App. IV*, p. 5 (Kent); DRO, Devon QS Order Book 1600–7, April 1604 order for Kingswear; J.H.E. Bennett and J.C. Dewhurst (eds), *Quarter Sessions Records for the County Palatine of Chester 1559–1760* (Lancs. and Ches. Record Soc., XCIV, 1940), p. 52: *Sir Henry Whithed's Letter Book, I. 1601–1614* (Hants Record Ser., I. 1976), p. 21. However, there is no sign of activity against plague like that against dearth in the late Elizabethan correspondence of the Kentish justices in the Leveson-Gower papers in the Staffs RO.

58 J. Tait (ed.), *Lancashire Quarter Sessions Records 1590–1606* (Chetham Soc., NS, LXXVII, 1917), pp. 274–6; H.H. Copnall (ed.), *Nottinghamshire County Records: Notes and Extracts, 17th Century* (Nottingham, 1915), p. 102; S.A.H. Burne (ed.), *Staffordshire Quarter Sessions Rolls 1581–1606* (William Salt Arch. Soc., 1929–40), V. 176; J.C. Atkinson (ed.), *North Riding Quarter Sessions Records* (North Riding Record Soc., I–IX, 1884–92), II. 3; Wilts. RO, QS Roll, Trinity 1604, doc. 120; BL, Add. MS. 29975, f. 25 (Dorset); E.H. Bates-Harbin (ed.), *Quarter Sessions Records for the County of Somerset* (Somerset Record Soc., XXIII–XXXIV, 1907–19), I. 66; J.W. Willis Bund (ed.), *Worcester County Records: The Quarter Sessions Rolls*, Part I (Worcester, 1899), pp. 152–4.

59 Kent AO, PRC 2/13, f. 137v; Lincs. RO, Ad. Ac. 6, f. 77 (I owe these references to Clare Gittings); Staffs. RO, QS Rolls Epiph. 1609–10, no. 57; Hants RO, Jervoise MSS., box 44M69/012, 30 October 1603; *Nottinghamshire County Records*, p. 102.

60 Cheshire RO, QS File 1603, no. 3, doc. 100; QS Book 4A 1593–1608, f. 196v. Towns also became accustomed to cite both the book of orders and the statute: e.g. Reading Corporation Records, box 39, plague documents, warrant of September 1625.

61 Below, Chs 10, 11.

62 PRO, SP 16/175/3 (i). Cf. Wilts. RO, QS Roll, Easter 1637, presentment of 8 April; Chester Corporation Records, M/B/28b, f. 146r; Leicester Corporation Records, Hall Papers Bound, II/18/16, 108; Kent AO, Sa/AC7, f. 322v.

63 W.A. Leighton, 'The Early Chronicles of Shrewsbury', *Trans. Salop Arch. and Nat. Hist. Soc.*, III (1880), 326; HMC, *Salisbury*, XXIII. 112; PRO, SP 16/6/114.

64 *Tudor Royal Proclamations*, II. 420n; *Privy Council Acts 1577–8*, pp. 326, 387; LCRO, Journal xx (ii), ff. 441v–442r, 450v, 451v, 455r; Rep. xix, f. 395r, xx, ff. 136r, 137r.

65 PRO, SP 12/98/38 (dated 1574 by editors of the *Calendar*, but it certainly belongs to 1578). The orders of 1583 are printed in C.F. Mullett, *The Bubonic Plague and England* (Lexington, Kentucky, 1956), pp. 380–3.

66 See, for example, Royal College of Physicians, Annals II, f. 26, III, ff. lv, 63, 99. I am grateful to the Registrar of the College for permission to consult and cite these records.

67 Below, p. 276.

68 Wilson, *Plague in Shakespeare's London*, pp. 76–80; LCRO, Rep. xx, ff. 136r, 414–15; Journal xxi, ff. 278v, 283v; BL, Lansdowne MS. 38, f. 23, MS. 74, f. 75; below, p. 277.

69 LCRO, Journal xxiii, f. 126, xxvi, f. 115v; *Present Remedies*, pp. viii–xiii; *Orders conceiued and thought fit* (1608; *STC* 16723); *Foure Statutes* (1609; *STC* 9341), pp. 83–95.

70 Below, pp. 281–2; *Certaine Statutes* (1630), sig. O1 *et seq.*; *Certaine Necessary Directions* (1636), sig. G3 *et seq.*; *Orders Formerly Conceived* (1646), sig. A3 *et seq.*; *Orders Conceived and Published* (n.d., but 1665: Wing 0397). For publications of other, more select orders in London, see *STC* 16729.1,2,3 (1625); 16731 (1630).

71 PRO, SP 12/98/38, f. 167r. Cf. V. Pearl, 'Change and Stability in Seventeenth-Century London', *London Journal*, V (1979), 14–25; *idem*, 'Social Policy in Early Modern London', in H. Lloyd-Jones, V. Pearl and B. Worden (eds), *History and Imagination: Essays in Honour of H.R. Trevor-Roper* (1981), pp. 116–17.

72 HMC, *Salisbury*, II. 224.

73 BL, Lansdowne MS. 74, ff. 75–6 (dated 1593 by the *Catalogue*, but it probably belongs to 1583 like the summary of the orders on f. 69). For later variations on this theme, see pp. 217, 223, 250–2.

74 C. Russell, *Parliaments and English Politics 1621–9* (Oxford, 1979), ch. iv; N.E. McClure (ed.), *The Letters of John Chamberlain*, II (Philadelphia, 1939), p. 623; BL, Add. MS. 36825, f. 22v. I am grateful to Professor Russell for this last and other references to this parliament.

75 *Lords Journals*, III. 473, 475, 486, 488; HMC, *Buccleuch*, III. 248; ERO, D/DMZ 10 (summary of Lords' orders). The activity of the Lords may partly be explained by the fact that they had little else to do: Russell, *Parliaments and Politics*, p. 239.

76 F.H. Relf (ed.), *Notes of the Debates in the House of Lords* (Camden Soc., 3 Ser., XLII, 1929), p. 62; below, pp. 281–2; W.A. Bewes, *Church Briefs* (1896), p. 126. The Crown's legal officers had ordered an extra rate for the poor in the suburbs of London in July 1625: BL, Add. MS. 40630, f. 78.

77 *Lords Journals*, III. 509, 526, 539–40, 572–3, 628; *Commons Journals*, I. 851; HMC, *Lonsdale*, p. 10; Cambridge University Library, MS. Dd 12/21, f. 167 (I owe this reference to Conrad Russell). On Carleton, see also *Letters of Chamberlain*, II. 97, 107.

78 For a full discussion of social policies and their context in 1630–1, see Slack, 'Books of Orders', pp. 1–22.

79 *Privy Council Acts 1629–30*, pp. 306, 310, 312–14, 347, 356; LCRO, Remembrancia, vii. nos 18, 19; Rep. xliv, f. 228r; Journal xxxv, ff. 169r, 180v, 187r. On Henry IV in Paris, see M. Fosseyeux, *L'Hôtel-Dieu au XVIIe et au XVIIIe siècles* (Paris, 1912), pp. 39–40, 216–33, 300–3.

80 College of Physicians, Annals III, ff. 97r, 98, 99r; G. Keynes, *The Life of William Harvey* (Oxford, 1966), pp. 189–91; *Certaine Statutes* (1630), sigs K2–4v. The separation of the sick and the whole was recommended more explicitly when the Advice was reprinted in 1636: *Certaine Necessary Directions* (1636), sig. B3v.

81 PRO, SP 16/187/60: signed by all the king's physicians, but in French and (Hugh Trevor-Roper kindly confirms for me) in Mayerne's hand. A contemporary English translation in SP 16/533/17 has been used for quotation here. Cf. *Privy Council Acts 1630–1*, p. 274.

82 *Privy Council Acts 1630–1*, p. 257. Dr Richard Palmer informs me that Mayerne's recommendations on isolation closely followed contemporary practices in Venice.

83 College of Physicians, Annals III, ff. 108–109r; PRO, SP 16/25/97. Cf. above, pp. 207–8.

84 BL, Egerton MS. 2623, f. 30; PRO, PC 2/47, pp. 227, 232, 284, 331–2; SP 16/175/3, 22, 24, 94; 184/32; 185/35; 187/50, 57; 355/130. For

activity on the ground in London, see GL, MSS. 942A, f. 24v; 2088/1, 1636–7; 2593/1, f. 364v; 4524/2, ff. 39, 41r, 48v; 4810/2, f. 76; 9237, ff. 70v–71r; GLCRO, P92/SAV/1405.

85 PRO, PC 2/48, p. 125; V. Pearl, *London and the Outbreak of the Puritan Revolution* (Oxford, 1961), pp. 23–37; R. Ashton, *The City and the Court 1603–1643* (Cambridge, 1979), pp. 163–7.

86 *Privy Council Acts 1629–30*, pp. 383–4, 407, *1630–1*, pp. 14–15; *Cal. SP Dom. 1629–31*, p. 258; PRO, SP 16/192/83; Cooper, *Annals of Cambridge*, III. 227–9; R. Masters, *The History of the College of Corpus Christi* (Cambridge, 1753), App., p. 71. Records of business at the weekly meetings are in Cambridge University Library, University Archives, 'Town' 36 and 37 *passim*. (I owe these references to the kindness of Dr Dorothy Owen.)

87 *Orders Agreed upon, and published by the Vicechancellour and Maior . . .* (n.d; *STC* 4490). *STC* suggests 1625, but this belongs to 1630, unlike *STC* 4476.

88 PRO, SP 16/200/14; York Corporation Records, House Book 35, ff. 105–73 (quotation from f. 117r); Sheffield City Library, Strafford Correspondence, 12/236, 255. For activity in the West Riding, see Yorks. Arch. Soc. Library, Leeds, Bretton Hall Archives, DD70/1 and box BEA/C2/33 (I owe these references to Dr John Addy). Cf. below, pp. 318–19.

89 F.N.L. Poynter, 'A Seventeenth-Century London Plague Document', *Bull. Hist. Med.*, XXXIV (1960), 365–72; College of Physicians, Annals III, ff. 212r, 213r; *Lords Journals*, IV. 388, 391, 396, 397; *Commons Journals*, II. 273, 275, 280, 284, 286, 295, IV. 649.

90 *Certain Orders thought meet to be put put in execution* (1641, reprinted 1646); *Orders Formerly Conceived and Agreed to be published* (1646); *Lords Journals*, IX. 371, 400–1; J.P. Earwaker (ed.), *Court Leet Records of the Manor of Manchester* (Manchester, 1884–90), IV. 24; H. Owen and J.B. Blakeway, *A History of Shrewsbury* (1825), I. 465.

91 *By the Lords and others his Majesties Commissioners. An order for . . . the plague* (Oxford, 1644, 1645); *An Order of the Lords . . . against the spreading of the Infection of the Plague* (Oxford, 1645, 1646).

92 For examples of rates and arrears, see PRO, Asz 24/21, ff. 64v–65r; B.H. Cunnington (ed.), *Records of the County of Wiltshire* (Devizes, 1932), pp. 172, 174, 175–6, 191; *North Riding Quarter Sessions Records*, IV. 243, 250, 251, 253; W.Le Hardy and G.L. Reckitt (eds.) *County of Buckingham. Calendar to the Sessions Records*, III (Aylesbury, 1939), p. 315; Staffs. RO, Q/SR Mich. 1647, no. 42.

93 *Cal. SP Dom. 1547–80*, p. 320; *Privy Council Acts 1580–1*, p. 61; *Remembrancia*, pp. 329–30; *Tudor Royal Proclamations*, II, no. 677; HMC, *Salisbury*, XII. 247, 428–9, 438, 703; Staffs RO, D593/S/4/52/9. Cf. Wilson, *Plague in Shakespeare's London*, pp. 85, 122–3; above, p. 46.

94 *Remembrancia*, pp. 339, 345; *Privy Council Acts 1629–30*, p. 160; J.F. Larkin (ed.), *Stuart Royal Proclamations*, II. *1625–46* (Oxford, 1983), no. 207; *Cal. SP Dom. 1655*, pp. 322–3, 381, 598. For local activity, see

Hull Corporation Records, Bench Book 5, ff. 120, 136, 191v; *Cal. SP Dom. 1635*, p. 559; *1635–6*, p. 185.

95 *Remembrancia*, pp. 348–9; PRO, PC 2/56, pp. 592, 607, 610–11, 624, 676, 688; PC 2/57, pp. 89, 93, 104, 126–8, 139, 164, 177, 186, 199–200; SP 29/109/108, 117 (Chiffinch); HMC, *8th Report* (Chester), p. 387.

96 PRO, PC 2/58, pp. 135, 141–2; College of Physicians, Annals IV. f. 88r; *Certain necessary Directions* (1665).

97 PRO, SP 29/122/123, 131/12, 157/87. The first is anonymous, but the other documents suggest that the author was Hugh Chamberlen, son of the more famous projector, Peter. On Hugh, see P. Gibbons, 'The Medical Projectors, 1640–1720', *J. Hist. Med.*, XXIV (1969), 252–4.

98 PRO, PC 2/58, pp. 141–2, 167, 170–1, 187, 207, 345–7; *Cal. SP Dom. 1664–5*, p. 432; *Orders Conceived and Published by the Lord Major . . . concerning . . . Plague* (n.d., but clearly 1665). For shutting up in the parishes, see GL, MSS. 877/1, p. 236; 2088/1, 1665–6; 4956/3, p. 270; 1432/4, 1665–6.

99 PRO, PC 2/58, pp. 199, 201, 207; *Cal. SP. Dom. 1664–5*, p. 466; below, p. 282. There are accounts relating to the collections in Lambeth Palace, Carte Misc. VI, nos 4–45.

100 W.G. Bell, *The Great Plague in London in 1665* (2nd edn, 1951), pp. 69–70 and *passim*.

101 *Ibid.*, pp. 315–18; BL, Stowe MS. 152, ff. 112–13.

102 PRO, SP 29/148/8, 29/155/102; *Rules and Orders* (1666), printed in Bell, *Great Plague*, pp. 333–5.

103 T. Cock, *Hygiene; or A Plain and Practical Discourse upon . . . Air* (1665), sig. Blv.

104 *Commons Journals*, VIII. 614, 616, 623–4, 687; *Lords Journals*, XI. 689, 694, 697–8, XII. 10, 52, 76, 101–2; House of Lords RO, Lords Committee Minute Book 1664–71, ff. 85, 96r, 99v, 156r, 157r; C. Robbins (ed.) *The Diary of John Milward* (Cambridge, 1938), pp. 38, 45, 98, 154, 158–9. There were other disputes between the Houses in 1666: D.T. Witcombe, *Charles II and the Cavalier House of Commons 1663–1674* (Manchester, 1966), pp. 48–51.

105 BL, Stowe MS. 152, f.112r. For other uncertainties which may have influenced the bill, see above, p. 211; PRO, SP 29/149/88; PC 2/58, pp. 278–9.

106 *Commons Journals*, VIII. 624; *Lords Journals*, XI. 698, XII. 101; House of Lords RO, Lords Committee Minute Book 1664–71, f. 86v.

107 Below, pp. 331–4.

108 *North Riding Quarter Sessions Records*, VI. 90–3, 95; York Corporation Records, House Book 38, ff. 16v. 17, 21v; *Rules and Orders made by the Vice-Chancellor of the University of Oxford, and Justices of Peace* (1665).

109 *Cal. SP Dom. 1664–5*, p. 449; *1665–6*, p. 568; BAO, Great Audit Book 1665–6, pp. 42, 43; NNRO, Mayor's Court Book 24, f. 5v.

110 *Schedule of the Records and Other Documents of the Corporation of Bedford* (1883), p. 86; ECA, Act Book xi, ff. 30r, 31v; HMC, *9th Report Pt 1*, App., p. 321; M.G. Hobson and H.E. Salter (eds.), *Oxford Council Acts 1626–1665* (Oxford Hist. Soc., XCV, 1933), p. 341; C.H. Mayo (ed.),

The Municipal Records of the Borough of Dorchester (Exeter, 1908), pp. 536–7; PC 2/58, p. 246 (Salisbury); BAO, Common Council Proceedings 1659–75, pp. 129, 150; W.M. Palmer, 'The Reformation of the Corporation of Cambridge', *Camb. Antiq. Soc. Proc.*, XVII (1914), 121–2; J. Dennett (ed.), *Beverley Borough Records* (Yorks. Arch. Soc., Record Ser., LXXXIV, 1933), p. 139; NNRO, Mayor's Court Book 24, f. 1r.

111 PRO, SP 29/129/26; *The Intelligencer*, 14, 21 August 1665, pp. 712, 754; *The Newes*, 27 July, 3 August, 19 October, 1665, pp. 647, 672, 679, 1015.

Chapter 9 Controversy and compromise

1 'Paracelsus', *A hundred and foureteene Experiments and Cures*, trans. J. Hester (1596), sig. B1v; *Certaine Prayers* (1603), sig. D1.
2 See above, pp. 41–3.
3 *The First and Second Prayer Books of King Edward VI* (Everyman, 1910), p. 423; J. Strype, *Historical Collections of the Life and Acts of John Aylmer* (1701), pp. 44–5; *Constitutions and Canons Ecclesiastical* (1604), LXVII.
4 W. Nicholson (ed.) *The Remains of Edmund Grindal* (Parker Soc., 1843), pp. 258–70; J. Strype, *The Life and Acts of Matthew Parker* (1711), pp. 131–2; *idem, The History of the Life and Acts of . . . Edmund Grindal* (1710), pp. 70–3: P. Collinson, *Archbishop Grindal* (1979), pp. 164–5.
5 The first form of prayer for plague of 1563 is printed in W.K. Clay (ed.), *Liturgies and Occasional Forms of Prayer set forth in the Reign of Queen Elizabeth* (Parker Soc., 1847), pp. 478–502. This and later editions are STC 16505–6, 16524, 16532, 16540–1, 16553. The 1665 form, *A Form of Common Prayer together with an Order of Fasting*, is in PRO, SP29/126/44.
6 *Liturgies*, pp. 513–18. This and later forms of thanksgiving are *STC* 16507, 16533, 16542.
7 P. Collinson, 'The Puritan Classical Movement in the Reign of Elizabeth I' (London Univ. PhD thesis, 1957), pp. 323–46. For examples of long fasts, see D.M. Meads (ed.), *Diary of Lady Margaret Hoby 1599–1605* (1930), p. 206; J.C. Walter, *Records of Woodhall Spa* (1899), p. 193; BL, Add. MS. 5830, f. 187r; and for justification of them, A. Peel and L.H. Carlson (eds.), *Cartwrightiana* (1951), pp. 140–1.
8 *Liturgies*, p. 490.
9 *Remains of Grindal*, p. 259; *Liturgies*, pp. 479, 503–7 (*STC* 16504.5).
10 *Remains of Grindal*, pp. 270–1.
11 *Certaine Prayers . . . to be vsed in the present Visitation* (1603), sigs C2–D4.
12 *Orders thought meet . . .* (1578 and later), no. 16; above pp. 43, 210; T. White, *A Sermon preached at Pawles Crosse* (1578), pp. 78–9; T. Beza, *A shorte learned and pithie Treatize* (1580), sig. A1r; J. Ewich, *Of the duetie of a faithfull and wise Magistrate . . . in the time of the Plague* (1583), dedication by the translator, J. Stockwood.
13 *Remains of Grindal*, p. 270.
14 *Privy Council Acts 1578–80*, p. 437 (for a similar suspicion of some of

the rulers of London, see *Cal. SP Dom. 1637*, pp. 506–7); F.J. Barton (ed.), *The Registrum Vagum of Anthony Harison I* (Norfolk Rec. Soc., XXXII, 1963), pp. 163, 36–7; A. Hassell Smith, *County and Court: Government and Politics in Norfolk 1558–1603* (Oxford, 1974), pp. 208–23.

15 Luisa de Carvajal y Mendoza, *Epistolario y poesias* (Biblioteca de Autores Españoles, 179, Madrid, 1965), pp. 281–2. I am indebted to Professor E.M. Wilson for this reference and for the translation.

16 N. Bownd, *Medicines for the Plague* (1604), p. 90 and cf. above, p. 22, below, p. 261.

17 J. Balmford, *A Short Dialogue concerning the Plagues Infection* (1603), sig. A2v; S. Bradwell, *Physick for the Sicknesse commonly called the Plague* (1636), p. 6; idem, *A Watchman for the Pest* (1625), p. 43; G. Wither, *The History of the Pestilence*, ed. J. Milton French (Cambridge, Mass., 1932), p. 61.

18 BL, Lansdowne MS. 19, no. 20, f. 38; HMC, *Gawdy*, p. 163; J. Squier, *A Thankesgiving for the decreasing . . . of the plague* (1637), p. 11.

19 Balmford, *Short Dialogue*, p. 38. Cf. below, pp. 292–3, 298.

20 For the ways in which Clapham's writings, described below, evaded censorship, see H. Clapham, *Doctor Andros, His Prosopopeia answered* ('Middelburg', 1605), p. 6.

21 T. Lodge, *A Treatise of the Plague* (1603), sigs. F3–4r.

22 T. Darling, *A Potion for the Heart-Plague* (1603), sig. A6v.

23 C. Burrage, *The Early English Dissenters* (Cambridge, 1912), I. 194–200; H. Clapham, *A Chronological Discourse touching the Church* (1609), sigs B2r, O3v; idem, *Errour on the Right Hand* (1608); idem, *Error on the left hand* (1608); idem, *A Manual of the Bibles Doctrine* (1606), sigs A4–5; idem, *Doctor Andros*, sig. A2v.

24 H. Clapham, *An Epistle Discovrsing vpon the present Pestilence* (2nd edn, 1603), sig. Blv. Cf. above, p. 26. The skin lesions and nervous symptoms of plague which may have given rise to this interpretation are described in R. Pollitzer, *Plague* (Geneva, 1954), pp. 415–16, 425.

25 H. Clapham, *His Demaundes and Answeres touching the Pestilence* (1604), pp. 3–4; HMC, *Salisbury*, XV. 266; below, p. 297.

26 P.A. Welsby, *Lancelot Andrewes 1555–1626* (1964), p. 78.

27 Clapham, *Demaundes and Answeres*, pp. 3–4 and *passim*; idem, 'A Petition Discoursory' in BL, Royal MS. 18A.XIX, ff. lr, 5r; idem, *Doctor Andros*, sigs A2–3; G.N. Clark, *A History of the Royal College of Physicians of London*, I (Oxford, 1964), 214.

28 F. Herring, *A Modest Defence* (1604), sigs A3, Blr. Herring thus contradicted his own earlier statement that flight might be useless: idem, *Certaine Rules* (1625, but written *c.* 1603), sig. A3.

29 Balmford, *Short Dialogue*, pp. 25, 32–8, 45, 66.

30 W.T., *A Casting Vp of accounts of certain Errors* (1603), sigs B2v, B4r, C2–3. I have been unable to identify the author. Might it have been Walter Travers, whose career after 1598 is obscure: S.J. Knox, *Walter Travers* (1962), ch. ix?

31 Clapham, *Doctor Andros*, p. 8.

32 *Ibid.*, pp. 35–7.

33 Ewich, *Duetie of a Magistrate*, sig. xxx3r; W. Cary, *A Briefe Treatise called Caries Farewell to Physick* (1587), pp. 46–8; W. Cupper, *Certaine Sermons concerning Gods late visitation* (1592), pp. 101–2; S. Forman, 'Of the plague', Bodl., Ashm. MS. 1436, f. 106.

34 Clapham, *Demaundes and Answeres*, pp. 3–4, 6, 10, 12, 14–15.

35 E.g. Bradwell, *Physick for the Sicknesse*, pp. 2–3; W. Boraston, *A Necessarie and Briefe Treatise of the Contagious disease of the pestilence* (1630), p. 2.

36 R. Abbot, *Bee Thankfull London and her sisters* (1626), p. 20.

37 S. Rowlands, *A Terrible Battell* (?1606), sig. D2r. Cf. B. Spenser, *Vox Civitatis* (1625), pp. 6–7, 13, 23; I.D., *Salomons Pest-House or Towre-Royall* (1630), p. 66; F.P. Wilson (ed.), *The Plague Pamphlets of Thomas Dekker* (Oxford, 1925), pp. 148–9.

38 Wither, *History of the Pestilence*, pp. 59, xiii.

39 *Ibid.*, pp. 56–7; R. Milton, *Londons Miserie, The Countryes Crueltie* (1625), p. 24.

40 *Privy Council Acts 1625–6*, p. 125; Bodl., Oxford Archdeaconry Papers, Berks. b. 5*, ff. 390–1; J. Rushworth, *Historical Collections*, III (1721), App., p. 119. The initial change in 1625 may have been prompted by Charles I himself: HMC, *Buccleuch*, III. 251.

41 PRO, SP 16/362/106; H. Burton, *A Divine Tragedie Lately Acted* (Amsterdam, 1636), p. 46; *The Letany of John Bastwick* (1637), p. 14. Cf.W.C., *Londons Lamentation for her Sinnes* (1625), sig. A3.

42 Milton, *Londons Miserie*, pp. 23–4; F. Rous, *The Onely Remedy, That Can Cvre a People* (1627), pp. 212–13; Squier, *A Thanksgiving*, pp. 20–8; T. Jackson, *Diverse Sermons* (Oxford 1637), treatise, pp. 95–6.

43 PRO, SP 16/350/54; H. Smith, 'An Objectionable Sermon', *Essex Review* (1927), pp. 202–4; Jackson, *Diverse Sermons*, treatise, p. 27. Another attack like Jackson's on the predestirarian view is in Emmanuel College, Cambridge, MS.44. (I am grateful to Dr N. Tyacke for this reference.) Cf. K. Thomas, *Religion and the Decline of Magic* (1971), p. 88 and n.4.

44 PRO, SP 16/174/45, 178/29; Bodl., Oxford University Archives, Register of Congregation 1630–4, f. 274v. This seems to have been a favourite topic at Oxford Acts: cf. Bodl., Tanner MS. 75, ff. 138v–139 (I owe this reference to Dr Tyacke).

45 T[homas] S[wadling], *Sermons, Meditations and Prayers upon the Plague. 1636* (1637), p. 27; D.A. Williams, 'London Puritanism: The Parish of St. Botolph without Aldgate', *Guildhall Misc.*, II (1960), 30.

46 Swadling, *Sermons*, pp. 6, 9, 30, 64, 76, 184–91, 207–8.

47 W. Gouge, *Gods Three Arrowes: Plague, Famine, Sword* (1631), pp. 22–4, 101–4.

48 R. Jenison, *Newcastles Call to her Neighbour and Sister Townes* (1637), pp. 35, 222–6; T. Fuller, *A Sermon . . . Upon the late Decrease . . . of GODs heavie Visitation* (1625), p. 29; Swadling, *Sermons*, p. 28; W. Warde, *Gods Arrowes or Two Sermons* (1607), f. 33v. M.M., *An Ease for a diseased Man* (1625), was written specifically for those infected barred from 'the comfortable society of their brethren': title-page.

49 See above, pp. 32–3.

50 Bradwell, *Physick for the Sicknesse*, p. 48; A. Paré, *A Treatise of the Plague*

(1630), pp. 87–8; J. Godskall, *The Kings Medicine for this present yeere 1604* (1604), sig. G2; MS. notes in Bodl., Gough London 154; R. Mohl, *John Milton and His Commonplace Book* (New York, 1969), pp. 300–1.
51 T. Cogan, *The Hauen of Health* (1584), pp. 261, 265; T. Brasbridge, *The Poore Mans Iewel* (1578), sig. Clr; Kent AO, Sa/Ac7, f. 301r; L.J. Ashford, *History of the Borough of High Wycombe* (1960), p. 124; D.C. Coleman, *The British Paper Industry 1495–1860* (Oxford, 1958), p. 37.
52 *The Red-Crosse: or Englands Lord have Mercy Vpon Vs* (1625).
53 PRO, SP 16/533, f. 44r (Mayerne); Lodge, *Treatise*, sig. C2v; Bodl., Ashm. MS. 1436, f. 42. For recipes for rat poison, see BL, Lansdowne MS. 75, no. 78, f. 168r; BL, Lansdowne MS. 223, f. 96r; and for observation of dead rats in plague-time: T.D. Whitaker, *Loidis and Elemete* (Leeds, 1816), p. 76
54 BL, Add. MS. 34274, f. 136v. For a possibly unique case of contemporary association of rats with human sickness in 1661 (not a plague year), see J. Crossley (ed.), *Diary and Correspondence of Dr. John Worthington*, I (Chetham Soc., OS, XIII, 1847), 352.
55 *Diary of Margaret Hoby*, pp. 204, 208.
56 Above, pp. 120, 128–9; BL, Harl. MS. 1929, f. 36 (Chester); York Corporation Records, House Book 32, f. 316r; Jenison, *Newcastles Call*, near p. 250 (pagination confused); Bodl., Wood 507 (49), 514 (15a) (Oxford); C. Webster, *The Great Instauration* (1975), p. 268.
57 W. Clever, *The flower of phisicke* (1590), p. 19; J. Spedding, R.L. Ellis and D.D. Heath (eds), *The Works of Francis Bacon*, II (1870), p. 646; Bradwell, *Watchman*, pp. 46–7; Ewich, *Duetie of a Magistrate*, f. 29v; S. Kellwaye, *A Defensative against the Plague* (1593), f. 2v; Godskall, *Kings Medicine*, sig. G4r.
58 See pp. 275–6.
59 S. Price, *Londons Remembrancer* (1626), pp. 18–19; Milton, *Londons Miserie*, pp. 30–2; BL, Egerton MS. 2978, ff. 1–2; BL, Add. MS. 42849, f. 76.
60 H. Burton, *A Most Godly Sermon . . . shewing the necessity of selfe-denyall* (1641), sig. A5.
61 B. Capp, *Astrology and the Popular Press* (1979), p. 112; *Plague Pamphlets of Dekker*, pp. 102–3, 142–3; Gouge, *Gods Three Arrowes*, p. 25; R. Harris, *Hezekiah's Recovery* (1626), p. 42. Cf. B. Spenser, *Vox Civitatis* (1625), p. 14; W. Simpson, *Zenexton Ante-Pestilentiale* (1665), p. 99.
62 Ewich, *Duetie of a Magistrate*, sig. xx4r. On familiar diseases being given natural explanations, see E.E. Evans-Pritchard, *Witchcraft, Oracles and Magic among the Azande* (Oxford, 1937), pp. 509–10; E.H. Ackerknecht, 'Natural Diseases and Rational Treatment in Primitive Medicine', *Bull. Hist. Med.*, XIX (1946), 472.
63 Cf. Swadling, *Sermons*, pp. 4, 157; Price, *Londons Remembrancer*, p. 19; *Plague Pamphlets of Dekker*, pp. 205–13.
64 Twenty-one out of thirty-six publications on plague between 1625 and 1627 were sermons or devotional tracts, and twelve out of twenty-two in 1636 and 1637. See also above, pp. 23–4,
65 Jenison, *Newcastles Call*, pp. 5, 178, and figures at *c.* p. 250; T. Brewer,

Lord Have Mercy Upon Vs (1636), p. 17. Cf. Gouge, *Gods Three Arrowes*, pp. 117–19.

66 J. Hall, *A Sermon of Publike Thanksgiving* (1626), pp. 10–11; W.C., *Londons Lamentation for her Sinnes* (1625), sig. B4r; Warde, *Gods Arrowes*, f. 40r; M.M., *Ease for a diseased man*, p. 2; R. W[right], *A. Receyt to stay the Plague* (1630), f. 14v; Swadling, *Sermons*, pp. 157–8; above, p. 39.

67 Harris, *Hezekiah's Recovery*, p. 42.

68 J. Birch, *The Court and Times of Charles I* (1848), I. 39, 43, 46, 59.

69 Kent AO, Sa/AC 6, f. 207v; PRO, SP 16/12/85; Kent AO, NR/AZ 37, 9 September, 14 November 1615. For a more absolute acknowledgment of providence (albeit in a different hand from the original order), see Berkshire RO., Wallingford Council Minutes, f. ll4v.

70 Above, pp. 32–5.

71 *Plague Pamphlets of Dekker, passim*; C.S. Hensley, *The Later Career of George Wither* (The Hague, 1969), pp. 53–5; and for Bullein and Defoe, see pp. 41, 335–7.

72 Cupper, *Certaine Sermons*, p. 51; *Lachrymae Londinenses* (1626?), 'To the Reader'.

73 B.V., *The Run-awayes Answer* (1625), sig. B3v; *Plague Pamphlets of Dekker*, pp. 41–2, 169–70.

74 *Ibid.*, pp. 59, 117, 157, 161–4; R. Milton, *Londoners their Entertainment in the Countrie* (1604), *passim*; H. Petowe, *The Countrie Ague, or, London, her welcome home to her retired children* (1626), p. 13; T. B[rewer], *The Weeping Lady: Or, London like Ninivie in Sack-Cloth* (1625); Wither, *History of the Pestilence*, pp. 73–7; Milton, *Londons Miserie*, p. 25. For the role of fiction in dealing with disaster, see R.J. Lifton, *Death in Life: The Survivors of Hiroshima* (1968), pp. 397–8.

75 There were four different broadsides with this title published in 1636 and 1637, one of which – no doubt the model for the rest – had appeared first in 1625: STC 4273, 19251.3, 20206, 20823–4, 20875. The second of these is reproduced in T.R. Forbes, *Chronicle from Aldgate* (New Haven, 1971), opposite p. 141.

76 Contemporaries made this point: Cupper, *Certaine Sermons*, p. 51; Bodl., MS. Gough Eccl. Top 7, f. lv, sermon on plague c. 1600.

77 *A Forme of Common Prayer . . .* (1640: 2 edns, STC 16557, 16559).

78 BAO, Common Council Proceedings 1649–59, p. 8; R. Steele, *A Bibliography of the Royal Proclamations of Tudor and Stuart Sovereigns* (1910), I. nos 3084, 3086, 3093; *By the Protector: A declaration of his highness for a day of Publique Fasting* (24 September 1658); A. Macfarlane (ed.), *The Diary of Ralph Josselin 1616–1683* (British Academy, Records of Social and Economic History, NS, III, 1976), p. 407.

79 *A Declaration and Prolcamation* [sic] *of the Deputy-General of Ireland concerning . . . the Plague* (Cork, 1650), sigs A2v, A4v.

80 *Five Wonders Seene in England* (1646), *passim*.

81 L. Gatford, *Hyperphysicall Directions in time of Plague* (Oxford, 1644), pp. 13, 16, 19–20; *DNB, sub* Gatford.

82 Webster, *Great Instauration*, pp. 30–1 and ch. IV.

83 L.G. Stevenson, 'New Diseases in the Seventeenth Century', *Bull. Hist.*

Med., 39 (1965), 1–21; H. Isler, *Thomas Willis 1621–75* (New York, 1968), pp. 69–83; D.G. Bates, 'Thomas Willis and the Epidemic Fever of 1661', *Bull. Hist. Med.*, 39 (1965), 393–407; L.S. King, *The Road to Medical Enlightenment 1650–95* (1970), pp. 113–33.

84 Graunt, 'Observations' in C.H. Hull (ed.), *The Economic Writings of Sir William Petty* (Cambridge, 1899), II. 319–97 (reference to God, p. 369). Cf. Webster, *Great Instauration*, pp. 293–6, 444–6; Marquis of Lansdowne (ed.), *Petty Papers* (1927), I. 7, 36–40, 274.

85 W. Keeling, *Liturgiae Britannicae* (1842), pp. 66–7; *A Form of Common Prayer together with an Order of Fasting for the Averting of God's heavy Visitation* (1665); PRO, SP 29/157/87, no. 3,

86 *Reflections on the Weekly Bills of Mortality* (1665); J. Bell, *Londons Remembrancer* (1665).

87 T. Cocke, *Advice for the Poor by way of Cure and Caution* (1665). Cf. *The Observations of Mr. Lillie and many Famous and Learned Divines* (1665); J. Belson, *Remedies against the Infection of the Plague* (1665).

88 *The Intelligencer*, 3, 10, 17 July 1665, pp. 535, 557, 592–3.

89 *Intelligencer*, 25 September, 9 October; *Newes*, 21 December, 17 August, 31 August 1665.

90 *Oxford Gazette*, 4–14 December 1665; *London Gazette*, 8–12, 22–26 February, 19–22 March, 12–16 April 1666. For sources of information for the *Gazette*, see *Cal. SP Dom. 1667*, p. 393; PRO, SP 29/173/77, 176/62, 185/119–61.

91 *Newes*, 9 March, 30 March, 18 May, 19 June, 6 July, 24 August, 21 September; *Intelligencer*, 26 June 1665; W.G. Bell, *The Great Plague in London in 1665* (2nd edn, 1951), pp. 35–6.

92 *Intelligencer*, 31 July, 7 August 1665.

93 P.M. Rattansi, 'The Helmontian-Galenist Controversy in Restoration England', *Ambix*, XII (1964), 19; Clark, *History of Royal College of Physicians*, I. 322; Bell, *Great Plague*, pp. 86–8. Cf. below, p. 276.

94 Bell, *Great Plague*, pp. 203–7, 340.

95 J.W., *A Friendly Letter to the Flying Clergy* (1665), p. 2; BL, Harl. MS. 3785, f. 26.

96 T. Vincent, *God's Terrible Voice in the City* (5th edn, 1667), pp. 27, 41–4. Cf. *Lamentatio Civitatis or Londons Complaint against her Children in the Countrey* (1665), p. 20.

97 S. Patrick, *A Brief Exhortation to those who are shut up from our society* (1665), pp. 1, 13; R. Baxter, *Short Instructions for the Sick especially who by Contagion or otherwise are deprived of the Presence of a Faithfull Pastor* (broadsheet, 1665). Cf. *The Autobiography of Symon Patrick, Bishop of Ely* (Oxford, 1839), pp. 52–6. I have traced seventeen religious works on plague published in 1665–6, out of a total of forty-six. It is possible that not all the sermons on the subject have been unearthed.

98 R. Kingston, *Pillulae Pestilentiales or a Spiritual Receipt for Cure of the Plague* (1665), pp. 30, 35; *The Prophecie of one of his Maiesties Chaplains Concerning the Plague and Black-patches* (1665), p. 2; M[atthew] M[ead], *Solomon's Prescription for the Removal of the Pestilence* (1665), p. 38.

99 R. Perrinchief, *A Sermon Preached before the Honourable House of Commons*

(1666), p. 21; Bell, *Londons Remembrancer*, sig. D3r; J. Dodson, *The Preachers Precept of Consideration* (1665), pp. 24, 36; J. Cade, *London's Disease and Remedie* (1665), pp. 8, 29; Mead, *Solomon's Prescription*, pp. 40–5; T. Salthouse, *A Brief Discovery of the Cause for which this Land Mourns* (1665), pp. 3–5; M. Sylvester (ed.), *Reliquiae Baxterianae* (1696), pt ii, p. 448, pt iii, p.l.

100 R. Kephale, *Medela Pestilentiae* (1665), pp. 34, 49–50; *Reliquiae Baxterianae*, pt iii, pp. 1–2.

101 For other comments on the same theme, see S. Patrick, *A Consolatory Discourse* (1665), p. 11; W. Bridge, *The Righteous Man's Habitation in the time of Plague* (1665), pt i, pp. 14–15, pt ii, p. 17; T. Doolittle, *A Serious Enquiry for a Suitable Return* (1666), p. 87.

102 Vincent, *God's Terrible Voice*, pp. 34, 37, 227; *Reliquiae Baxterianae*, pt iii, p. 2. Cf. Perrinchief, *A Sermon*, pp. 19–20.

103 *The Works of Thomas Sydenham*, trans. R.G. Latham (1848–50), I. 102, 108; T. Willis, *The Remaining Medical Works*, trans. S. Pordage (1681), pp. 123, 128.

104 P. Shaw (ed.), *The Philosophical Works of the Honourable Robert Boyle* (2nd edn, 1738), III. 533–4, 536. Cf. J.R. Jacob, *Robert Boyle and the English Revolution* (New York, 1977), pp. 159–69; King, *Road to Medical Enlightenment*, pp. 66–70, 126–8.

105 Webster, *Great Instauration*, pp. 276 *et seq.*; above, pp. 31–2; *Certain necessary Directions* (1665), p. 35.

106 C. Webster, 'English Medical Reformers of the Puritan Revolution: A Background to the "Society of Chymical Physitians"', *Ambix*, XIV (1967), 16–41; Rattansi, 'Helmontian-Galenist Controversy', pp. 1–23; H. Thomas, 'The Society of Chymical Physitians', in E.A. Underwood (ed.), *Science, Medicine and History*, II (Oxford, 1953), 56–71.

107 W. Pagel, *Paracelsus* (New York, 1958), pp. 185–7; G. Thomson, *Loimologia: a Consolatory Advice and some brief Observations concerning the Present Pest* (1665), p. 9; above, p. 28. For an earlier reflection of the Paracelsian view, see Boraston, *A Necessarie and Briefe Treatise*, p. 3.

108 G. Thomson, *Loimotomia or the Pest Anatomized* (1666), pp. 8, 36, 136; M[archamont] N[eedham], *Medela Medicinae* (1665), pp. 111–12; Simpson, *Zenexton Ante-Pestilentiale*, pp. 8, 15; H. Stubbe, *The Lord Bacon's Relation of the Sweating-Sickness Examin'd* (1671), p. 63. For a confusing mixture of old and new terminology, see Theophilus Garencieres, *A Mite Cast into the Treasury of the famous City of London* (1665), pp. 5–6 and *passim*.

109 G. Castle, *The Chymical Galenist* (1667), pp. 10, 119, 122–3; W. Boghurst, *Loimographia: An Account of the Great Plague of London in the year 1665*, ed. J.F. Payne (1894), p. 10 (atoms); Needham, *Medela Medicinae*, ch. V; *Petty Papers*, II. 29 (worms); Thomson, *Loimotomia*, p. 8 (gases); G. Harvey *A Discourse of the Plague* (2nd edn, 1673), p. 132 (but cf. pp. 134, 136, 138); Simpson, *Zenexton*, p. 23; BL, Sloane MS. 1821, f. 253v. ('miasmes'); N. Hodges, *Loimologia: or an Historical Account of the Plague in London in 1665*, trans. J. Quincy (1720), pp. 52, 56–7 (particles and miasma).

110 Needham, *Medela Medicinae*, p. 294 and ch. III; Simpson, *Zenexton*, p. 12; Thomson, *Loimologia*, pp. 6–7; Castle, *Chymical Galenist*, pp. 70, 99–100.
111 Rattansi, 'Helmontian-Galenist Controversy', p. 20; Stubbe, *Lord Bacon's Relation*, pp. 68–9; I. Diemerbroeck, *Several Choice Histories of . . . the Cure of the Plague* (1666), p. 43; Thomson, *Loimologia*, pp. 18–21; idem, *Loimotomia*, p. 147; above, p. 35.
112 R. Sprackling, *Medela Ignorantiae, or a Just and plain Vindication of Hippocrates and Galen* (1665), p. 46.
113 J.B. van Helmont, *Oriatrike or Physick Refined* (1662), p. 1142; Thomson, *Loimologia*, pp. 9–10: idem, *Loimotomia*, p. 136.
114 *The Prophecies and Predictions for Londons Deliverance* (1665), p. 5.
115 Thomson, *Loimologia*, p. 2; J.V., *Golgotha; or A Looking-Glass for London and the Suburbs thereof* (1665), pp. 8–9.
116 Hodges, *Loimologia* (1720 English edn; first published in Latin, 1672), pp. 7, 9, 11. Cf. C.F. Mullett, *The Bubonic Plague and England* (Lexington, Kentucky, 1956), pp. 236–8. Although Hodges defended the College against the chemists, his work clearly owed much to iatrochemical ideas: e.g. pp. 37, 46, 74, 172. Cf. Pagel, *Paracelsus*, p. 188.
117 Boghurst, *Loimographia*, pp. 25, 27, 57, 99 (written in 1666).
118 *The Shutting Up Infected Houses* (1665), pp. 4–11, 18, 19.
119 Graunt, 'Observations' in *Writings of Petty*, II. 320; *Petty Papers*, I. 38–9, 274; Hodges, *Loimologia*, pp. 205–9; H. Brooke, *Cautionary Rules for preventing The Sickness* (1665), pp. 1–2.
120 W. Kemp, *A Brief Treatise of the . . . Pestilence* (1665), pp. 15–16. Cf. *The Run-awayes safe Refuge* (broadsheet, 1665); Hodges, *Loimologia*, p. 36.
121 J. Gadbury, *London's Deliverance predicted* (1665), pp. 25–7, 29, 40.
122 R. Latham and W. Matthews (eds.), *The Diary of Samuel Pepys* (1970–83), VI. 108, 125, 142, 145, 171, 191, 246. Cf. *ibid.*, X. 177 on Pepys' sexual appetite in times of crisis.
123 *Ibid.*, VI. 128, 149, 174, 199, 203, 207, 225, 253, 256.
124 *Ibid.*, VI. 181, 200–6, 211–12, 224–5, 283.
125 *Ibid.*, VI. 131, 145, 155, 179, 189, 219, 268, 294.
126 W.D. Cooper, 'Notices of the Last Great Plague 1665–6 from the Letters of John Allin', *Archaeologia*, XXXVII (1857), 7–10, 14, 16, 18. Cf. Bell, *Great Plague*, pp. 255–65. For emphasis on religious submission from a Catholic in London in 1665, see M. Blundell (ed.), *Cavalier: Letters of William Blundell* (1933), p. 108.
127 A.R. and M.B. Hall (eds.), *The Correspondence of Henry Oldenburg* (Madison, Wisconsin, 1965–73), II. 241–2, 402–3, 449, 479, 506, 523, 526–7, 531, 536, 574; III. 602–3.
128 *Ibid.*, II. 449, 479, 527.

Chapter 10 Towns under stress

1 T. Pullein, *Ieremiah's Teares* (1608), sig. Flv.
2 Above, pp. 22, 203, 205, 208.

3 BAO, Common Council Proceedings 1598–1608, p. 79; NNRO, Assembly Book 1553–83, f. 276; Court Book 1576–81, pp. 361, 372; W. Hudson and J.C. Tingey (eds.), *The Records of the City of Norwich* (1906–10), II. 187.

4 NNRO, Court Book 1654–66, ff. 264r, 269r; *Cal. SP Dom. 1666–7*, p. 359.

5 T. Lodge, *A Treatise of the Plague* (1603), sig. Flv. For similar secrecy in modern epidemics, see D. Scott, *Epidemic Disease in Ghana* (Oxford, 1965), p. 5.

6 Chester Corporation Records, exhibition item 72, letter of 23 October 1610; W.H. Stevenson (ed.), *Records of the Borough of Nottingham* (1882–1914), IV. 238; *Cal. SP Dom. 1664–5*, p. 505. Cf. above, pp. 188–9.

7 York Corporation Records, House Book 35, f. 320v, 337v, 344r; NNRO, Court Book 1654–66, ff. 253, 257r, 258v, 259v.

8 BAO, Common Council Proceedings 1598–1608, p. 78, 1608–27, ff. 9r, 126v, 128–9, 131v–5r, 1627–42, ff. 25, 68–70, 72v, 77r, 1642–9, p. 103; Quarter Sessions Book 1634–47, f. 60r. Cf. below, pp. 317–19.

9 Letter of John Barnard of Hull, 1637, in my possession.

10 R.G. Lang, 'Social Origins and Social Aspirations of Jacobean London Merchants', *Ec. HR*, 2 ser., XXVII (1974), 41.

11 ECA, Act Books, *passim*; BAO, Common Council Proceedings 1598–1608, p. 81; SCA, Ledger C, f. 178.

12 Hull Corporation Records, Bench Book 4, f. 138v; D. and S. Lysons, *Magna Britannia*, VI. *Devonshire* (1822), p. 51; J.S. Davies, *History of Southampton* (1883), p. 497; Colchester Corporation Records, Assembly Book 1646–66, f. 355r. Cf. *Privy Council Acts 1625–6*, pp. 184, 244.

13 *Ibid.*, pp. 217–18, 312–14; PRO, SP 16/7/67; ECA, Act Book 7, ff. 312r, 314r; Sessions Minute Book 1621–30, f. 272r.

14 PRO, SP 16/12/68, 16/26/14, 16/81/45.

15 P. Slack (ed.), *Poverty in Early Stuart Salisbury* (Wilts. Rec. Soc., XXXI, 1975), pp. 117, 118; P. Slack, 'Poverty and Politics in Salisbury 1597–1666', in P. Clark and P. Slack (eds.), *Crisis and Order in English Towns 1500–1700* (1972), p. 171; Hants RO, Jervoise MSS. (Sherfield Papers), 44M69/S6/XXXVII. 29, 30. Cf. *ibid.*, 44M69/012, 2 October 1627.

16 *Poverty in Salisbury*, pp. 109–34; F. Nicolls, *The Life and Death of Mr. Ignatius Jurdain* (2nd edn, 1655), *passim*.

17 W.E.A. Axon (ed.), 'Documents Relating to the Plague in Manchester in 1605', *Chetham Misc.*, III (Chetham Soc., NS, LXXIII, 1915), 7–11, 17–19, 24; J.P. Earwaker (ed.), *The Court Leet Records of the Manor of Manchester* (Manchester, 1884–90), II. 210; *idem* (ed.), *The Constables Accounts of the Manor of Manchester* (Manchester, 1891–2), II. 119, 121, 125, 155, 157, 159; T.S. Willan, *Elizabethan Manchester* (Chetham Soc., 3 ser., XXVII, 1980), pp. 11–14.

18 The following paragraphs are based on LCRO, Repertories and Journals, and NNRO, Assembly Books and Mayor's Court Books.

19 Lambeth Palace, Carte Misc. VI, no. 14.

20 NNRO, Assembly Book 1585–1613, f. 300r; Court Book 1624–34, f. 12.

21 E.g. NNRO, Yarmouth Borough Court Roll, 1578–9; HMC, *15th Report App. X*, p. 40; PRO, PC 2/59, pp. 22–3; *The Newes*, 2 November 1665.

22 Hants RO, Jervoise MSS., 44M69/S6/XXXVII.29; F.F. Foster *The Politics of Stability: A Portrait of the Rulers in Elizabethan London* (1977), p. 146; York Corporation Records, House Book 35, ff. 117r, 335r. Cf. above, p. 193.

23 Above, p. 206; NNRO, Court Book 1582–7, p. 463, 1587–95, pp. 472, 476, 1603–15, p. 53; Asssembly Book 1585–1613, f. 300r. Payments to the infected were larger in 1589–92 than in 1579: Clavors' Accounts 1555–1646, f. 62r; 1550–1601, f. 94r.

24 Slack, 'Poverty and Politics', p. 171.

25 Above, pp. 231–2, 237–8.

26 Nicolls, *Jurdain*, sig. B3v, pp. 34–5, 44–5, 65; ECA, Receivers' Account Rolls, 1625–6. Cf. W.T. MacCaffrey, *Exeter 1540–1640* (Cambridge, Mass., 1958), pp. 199, 234, 273; C. Russell, *Parliaments and English Politics 1621–9* (Oxford, 1979), pp. 29, 222.

27 *Poverty in Salisbury*, pp. 109, 123, 124, 126. Cf. P. Slack, 'Religious Protest and Urban Authority: The Case of Henry Sherfield, Iconoclast, 1633', *Studies in Church History*, IX, ed. D. Baker (Cambridge, 1972), pp. 295–302.

28 PRO, SP 16/527/4; Slack, 'Poverty and Politics', *passim*.

29 Hants RO, Jervoise MSS., 44M69/S6/XXXVIII.54. On this kind of Puritan activism, see C. Hill, *God's Englishman* (1970), ch. ix; P. Collinson, *The Religion of Protestants* (Oxford, 1982), ch. 4.

30 Above, pp. 28–9; below, pp. 304–5.

31 B.G. Charles (ed.), *Calendar of the Records of the Borough of Haverfordwest 1539–1660* (Board of Celtic Studies, Univ. of Wales, History and Law Ser., 24, 1967), pp. 112, 119.

32 J.T. Evans, *Seventeenth-Century Norwich* (Oxford, 1979), pp. 97, 148; W.L. Sachse (ed.), *Minutes of the Norwich Court of Mayoralty 1630–1* (Norfolk Rec. Soc., XV, 1942), p. 143; NNRO, Court Book 1634–46, f. 147v; Bodl., Tanner MS. 68, ff. 153, 162. It may be significant that the Norwich plague regulations mentioned divine will in 1579 but not in 1637: NNRO, Assembly Book 1553–87, f. 276r; *Minutes of Norwich Court*, pp. 253–4. Private citizens of Norwich continued to appeal to providence, however: NNRO, Bills and Accounts, 1626 bundle, 22 December 1625.

33 Bernard Church, John Rayley and Richard Wenman. The mayor was Henry Woods. For their careers, see Evans, *Seventeenth-Century Norwich*, pp. 139n, 164n, 190, 225, 292–3, 276–7.

34 J. Fairfax, *The True Dignity of St. Paul's Elder exemplified in the Life of . . . Mr. Owen Stockton* (1826), pp. 34–5, 37–8.

35 York Corporation Records, House Book 32, ff. 339r, 340; 35, ff. 107v, 125r; 36, f. 157r; below, p. 304.

36 Hants RO, Jervoise MSS., 44M69/S6/XXXVII.31.

37 D. Hirst, *The Representative of the People?* (Cambridge, 1975), pp. 203–4.

38 Active aldermen have been identified from LCRO, Reps, and A.B. Beaven, *The Aldermen of the City of London* (1908, 1913).

39 LCRO., Rep. xvi, ff. 530v–531r. Cf. Foster, *Politics of Stability*, pp. 73–4.

40 V. Pearl, *London and the Outbreak of the Puritan Revolution* (Oxford, 1961), pp. 295, 297; Beaven, *Aldermen*, II. lvi; W.G. Bell, *The Great Plague in London in 1665* (2nd edn, 1951), pp. 82–3.

41 Evans, *Seventeenth-Century Norwich*, ch. iii.

42 PRO, SP 16/27/7, 19; SP 16/168/15; *Privy Council Acts 1625–6*, pp. 478, 494, *1629–30*, pp. 398–9.

43 *Minutes of Norwich Court*, pp. 14, 21, 22, 67, 161, 253 art. 1; Bodl., Tanner MS. 68, f. 238v.

44 BAO, Vetus Liber Ordinacionium, f. 18r; Common Council Proceedings 1627–42, f. 84r; Lincs. RO, Lincoln Entries of Common Council III, f. 165v; M.J. Groombridge (ed.), *Calendar of Chester City Council Minutes 1603–42* (Lancs. and Cheshire Rec. Soc., CVI, 1956), p. xi.

45 York Corporation Records, House Book 35, ff. 113v *et seq.*

46 F.W. Maitland and M. Bateson (eds), *The Charters of the Borough of Cambridge* (Cambridge, 1901), pp. xxxiii, 143; Hants RO, Jervoise MSS., 44M69/S6/XXXVIII.20.

47 B. Bennassar, *Recherches sur les grandes épidémies dans le nord de l'Espagne à la fin du XVIᵉ siècle* (Paris, 1969), p. 25; E. Carpentier, *Une Ville devant la Peste: Orvieto et la Peste Noire* (Paris, 1962), p. 139.

48 E.g. *Records of the City of Norwich*, II. 336; P.L. Hughes and J.F. Larkin, *Tudor Royal Proclamations* (New Haven, 1964–9), III. no. 757; J. Latimer, *The Annals of Bristol in the Seventeenth Century* (Bristol, 1900), pp. 137–8.

49 DRO, QS Order Book 1625–33, pp. 21, 30; 1640–51, September 1646; ECA, Act Book 8, f. 181v.

50 Chester Corporation Records, M/L/2/173; J.H.E. Bennett and J.C. Dewhurst (eds), *Quarter Sessions Records . . . for the County Palatine of Chester* (Lancs. and Cheshire Rec. Soc., XCIV, 1940), pp. 53–4; J.C. Atkinson (ed.), *North Riding Quarter Sessions Records* (North Riding Record Soc., I–IX, 1884–92), IV. 88–94; letter of John Barnard of Hull, in my possession.

51 Wilts. RO, QS Roll, Trinity 1604, doc. 120; QS Minute Book 1626–31, Trinity, Michaelmas 1627, Hilary 1628.

52 SCA, N101, 1627, 1628; Wilts. RO, QS Roll, Hilary 1628, doc. 121; QS Minute Book 1626–31, indictment of Hilary 1628.

53 Cheshire RO, QS Book 4A 1593–1608, ff. 182v, 184, 213v; QS File 1603 (iv), docs 19, 20, 1605 (i), doc. 24.

54 DRO, QS Order Book 1600–7, January 1604/5; 1625–33, pp. 9, 19, 30, 45, 47, 70–85, 101–2, 113, 160, 266, 427; 1640–51, September 1640, July, August 1646.

55 *Records of Maidstone* (Maidstone, 1926), p. 256; Kent AO, Sa/ZB2/56, 99, 101; BL, Add. MS. 29975, f. 25 (Dorset); *Somerset and Dorset Notes and Queries*, XXIV (1943–6), 180, XXVI (1951–4), 104–6; BL, Egerton MS. 2986, f. 231 (Rutland); W.B. Stephens (ed.), *History of Congleton* (Manchester, 1970), p. 57; H.H. Copnall (ed.), *Nottinghamshire County Records: Notes and Extracts 17th Century* (Nottingham, 1915), p. 103.

56 BL, Loan MS. 29/172, ff. 123, 128, 130, 132, 136; Notts. RO, Portland Loan DD4P, 68/103. I am grateful to Jacqueline Levy for these references to Harley's correspondence.
57 G.R. Batho, 'The Plague of Eyam: A Tercentenary Re-evaluation', *J. Derbyshire Arch. and Nat. Hist. Soc.*, LXXXIV (1964), 88–90; L. Bradley, 'The Most Famous of All English Plagues ... Eyam 1665–6', in *The Plague Reconsidered* (Local Pop. Studies, Supplement, 1977), pp. 65, 76–7, 80; W. Wood, *The History and Antiquities of Eyam* (6th edn, Derby, 1865), pp. 83, 98–102, 109–10. Mortality was greater in the village than in the parish as a whole. Cf. above, pp. 20–1; below, p. 320.
58 ERO, Q/SBa 2/28, doc. 35, 2/31, doc. 2, 2/43, doc. 1; Cheshire RO, QS File 1604 (iii), doc. 18, (iv) docs 18–21, 1605 (iv), doc. 17; HMC, *Kenyon*, p. 46.
59 For examples, see D.L. Powell and H. Jenkinson (eds), *Surrey Quarter Sessions Records* (Surrey County Council, 1931–51), VIII. 70–1; W.H. and H.C. Overall, *Index to the Remembrancia ... of the City of London* (1878), p. 339; *Privy Council Acts 1625–6*, pp. 128–9. Cf. above, p. 242.
60 *Intelligencer*, 25 September 1665.
61 Leicester Corporation Records, Hall Papers Bound, II/18/16: 107, 108.
62 1 James I, c. 31, sect. 4; *Lords Journals*, II. 325, 334, 338; *Commons Journals*, I. 251.
63 Wilts. RO, QS Roll, Trinity 1604, doc. 120; ECA, Act Book 8, f. 118v; NNRO, Assembly Book 1613–42, ff. 283v, 284, 288; *Minutes of Norwich Court*, pp. 207–8. For the similar reactions of University Colleges see BL, Add. MS. 24064, f. 10.
64 SCA, Z236, under 1627; NNRO, Court Book 1634–46, ff. 162v, 174r; S. Bond (ed.), *The Chapter Acts of the Dean and Canons of Windsor 1430, 1523–1672* (Windsor, 1966), p. 176.
65 Bristol Reference Library, Braikenridge Collection, MS. B9076, under 1575; Exeter Cathedral Library, Chapter Act Book 1622–30, p. 53; ECA, Act Book 5, f. 99v. For gifts to the infected, see *Windsor Chapter Acts*, p. 256; F.R. Goodman (ed.), *The Diary of John Young, Dean of Winchester* (1928), p. 78.
66 *Privy Council Acts 1578–80*, p. 211; Wilts. RO, QS Roll, Epiphany 1604, doc. 154.
67 E.g. ECA, Tailors' Act Books 1478–1600, 1600–1715, Merchant Adventurers' Act Book 1560–1602, *passim*; SCA, E1/246/3, f. 163v; W. McMurray (ed.), *The Records of Two City Parishes* (1925), p. 282; G. Parsloe (ed.), *Warden's Accounts of the Worshipful Company of Founders 1497–1681* (1964), p. 305.
6 ERO, D/Y 2/42, p. 23; *Records of the City of Norwich*, II. 189–90.
69 St Mary Redcliffe Church, Bristol, Churchwardens' Accounts, 1 December 1603. These uniforms were also recommended by Mayerne in 1631: PRO, SP 16/533, f. 45v.
70 GL, MS. 4249, pp. 6, 12, 116; above, p. 214.
71 GLCRO, P92/SAV/450, p. 279 (provider); GL, MSS. 593/2, ff. 67r, 69r; 1016/1, f. 91r; 1279/2, 1592–4; 1431/1, p. 33; 1432/3, f. 45v; 2088/1, f. 32v; 2593/1, f. 63v; 3570/1, f. 61r; 4165/1, p. 88; 4415/1,

ff. 17r, 31v; 4810/1, f. 137r; E. Freshfield (ed.), *The Vestry Minute Books of the Parish of St. Bartholomew Exchange* (1890), pp. xlii–xliii, 3, 5; *idem* (ed.), *Vestry Minute Book of St. Margaret Lothbury* (1887), p. xxi; W.H. Overall (ed.), *Accounts of the Churchwardens of St. Michael Cornhill* (1871), pp. 196–7, 250.

72 E.g. GL, MS. 1432/3, 1625–6 acct; E. Freshfield (ed.), *Minutes of the Vestry Meetings . . . of St. Christopher le Stocks* (1886), pp. 48–9; PRO, SP 16/175/24.

73 E.g. GL, MSS. 593/2, f. 149r; 942A, ff. 15v, 24r; 1176/1, 1578–9 acct; 12792/2, 1603–5 acct; 1432, f. 80.

74 PRO, SP 16/329/65.

75 *Accounts of St. Michael Cornhill*, pp. 193, 255; E. Freshfield (ed.), *Accomptes of the Churchwardens of the Paryshe of St. Christofer's* (1885), p. 40; GL, MSS. 1016/1, f. 91v; 1176/1, 1603–4; 1432/3, f. 45v; 2968/1, f. 482v; 3556/1, f. 98r; 4415/1, ff. 31v–32r; 4457/2, ff. 75v, 76r; 4810/1, f. 137r; 4824, ff. 21–22r, 26v.

76 SCA, S161; Reading Corporation Records, box 39, plague accounts. Cf. Westminster City Library, MSS. 4512, 4514, 4516, E47, E152.

77 W.J.C. Moens (ed.), *The Walloons and their Church at Norwich 1565–1832* (Huguenot Soc. of London, Publications, I, 1887–8), ch. viii; LCRO, Rep. xvi, f. 534r; W.J.C. Moens (ed.), *Register of Baptisms in the Dutch Church at Colchester* (Hug. Soc. of London, Publications, XII, 1905), p. xxv; F.W. Cross, *History of the Walloon and Huguenot Church at Canterbury* (*ibid.*, XV, 1898), p. 235.

78 Above, p. 140; *Records of the City of Norwich*, II. 335–7, 187; NNRO, Court Book 1582–7, pp. 313–14, 463.

79 A.A. Van Schelven (ed.), *Kerkeraads-Protocollen der Nederduitsche Vluchte-lingen-Kerk te Londen 1560–3* (Historisch Genootschap, Utrecht, 3 ser., 43, 1921), pp. 428–35. Cf. Cross, *Walloon Church at Canterbury*, pp. 69–70. Two ministers of the Dutch Church in London died during the 1563 epidemic: A. Pettegree, 'The Strangers and Their Churches in London, 1550–1580' (Oxford Univ. D.Phil. thesis, 1983), p. 238.

80 Moens, *Walloon Church at Norwich*, p. 298; NNRO, Court Book 1576–81, p. 488.

81 NNRO, Assembly Book 1585–1613, f. 283r; Cross, *Walloon Church at Canterbury*, p. 96; Kent AO, Sa/AC8, f. 43v; PRC 2/34, nos 269, 275, 297, 298.

82 Moens, *Walloon Church at Norwich*, pp. 70, 79, 80; NNRO, Court Book 1582–7, p. 504; Norwich QS Minute Book 1581–91, f. 125v; Strangers Order Book 1564–1643, ff. 97v, 106v.

83 SCA, N101, doc. 79; BL, Stowe MS. 840, f. 46; *Records of Maidstone*, pp. 257–8.

84 E.g. *Records of Maidstone*, p. 20; GL, MS. 1264/1, f. 35v.

85 *Poverty in Salisbury*, p. 121; NNRO, Court Book 1582–7, p. 323, 1587–95, p. 476, 1634–46, f. 228r; G.W. Hill and W.H. Frere (eds), *Memorials of Stepney Parish* (Guildford, 1890–1), pp. 107–8.

86 Bell, *Great Plague*, p. 56. For negligence and uncertainty about death,

see *Cal. SP Dom. 1664–5*, p. 551; LCRO, QS File, February 1665/6, indictment of 23 October 1665.

87 SCA, N101, docs 76, 79, 86–8.

88 NNRO, Court Book 1624–34, ff. 279v, 283r.

89 Bodl., Tanner MS. 68 , f. 238v; NNRO, Court Book 1634–46, f. 126v. For similar doubts about diagnosis of spotted fevers, see B. Schofield (ed.), *The Knyvett Letters 1620–1644* (Norfolk Rec. Soc., XX, 1949), pp. 67–8; HMC, *Gawdy*, p. 161; Hull Corporation Records, Bench Book 5, f. 213v.

90 For an excellent case study, see M. Pelling, 'Healing the Sick Poor: Social Policy and Disability in Norwich 1550–1640', *Medical History*, 29 (1985).

91 York Corporation Records, House Book 32, f. 323v; M. Bateson and H. Stocks (eds), *Records of the Borough of Leicester* (Cambridge, 1899–1923), IV. 100; J.E.O. Wilshere, 'Plague in Leicester 1558–1665', *Trans. Leics Arch. and Hist. Soc.*, XLIV (1968–9), 54; HMC, *15th Report App. X*, p. 52.

92 PRO, PC 2/52, 14 June 1640. Cf. *Cheshire Quarter Sessions Records*, pp. 145–6, and on provincial medical practice generally, M. Pelling and C. Webster, 'Medical Practitioners', in C. Webster (ed.), *Health, Medicine and Mortality in the Sixteenth Century* (Cambridge, 1979), pp. 165–235.

93 H.F. Westlake, *St. Margaret's Westminster* (1914), pp. 209, 216; GL, MS. 4457/2, f. 249v; F.P. Wilson, *The Plague in Shakespeare's London* (Oxford, 1963), pp. 82–3.

94 Wilson, *Plague in Shakespeare's London*, pp. 21–2; College of Physicians, Annals II, f. 26, III, ff. lv, 63; G.N. Clark, *History of the Royal College of Physicians*, I (Oxford, 1964), 138–9, 191.

95 NNRO, Court Book 1666–77, ff. 6r, 13v, 16v, 17r; above, p. 246. Cf. PRO, PC 2/58, p. 209; Colchester Corporation Records, Assembly Minute Book 1646–66, f. 339r; HMC, *9th Report, Pt. 1*, App., p. 321.

96 *Poverty in Salisbury*, p. 125; BAO, Common Council Proceedings 1627–42, f. 84r. For other examples, see H.E. Salter (ed.), *Oxford Council Acts 1583–1626* (Oxford Hist. Soc., LXXXVII, 1928), pp. 153, 186, 387; R. Welford, *History of Newcastle and Gateshead* (1883–7), III. 123; R.R. Tighe and J.E. Davis, *Annals of Windsor* (1858), II. 52–3.

97 P. Tinker, *Worcester's Affliction* (Worcester, n.d., *c.* 1638); *The Records of Norwich* (1736–8), II. 6–7.

98 Wilson, *Plague in Shakespeare's London*, pp. 77–84, 181–3; J.E. Smith, *A Catalogue of Westminster Records* (1900), p. 104; Westminster City Library, MS. 4514; Bell, *Great Plague*, pp. 37–9, 47–8, 192–3; above, p. 214.

99 Wilson, *Plague in Shakespeare's London*, p. 183; BAO, Common Council Proceedings 1642–9, p. 103.

100 *Present Remedies against the Plague*, intro. by W.P. Barrett (Shakespeare Assoc. Facsimile, 7, 1933), p. xii, sig. Aiiᵛ; Bell, *Great Plague*, pp. 76, 334. As little as twenty-one days' isolation was required in one London liberty: R. Somerville, *The Savoy* (1960), pp. 259–60.

101 Kent AO, PRC 2/34, accounts nos 269, 275; PRC 2/17, f. 13v; Lincs. AO, Ad. Ac. 6, ff. 77, 93 (I owe these references to Clare Gittings);

R.L. Kenyon and O. Wakeman (eds), *Shropshire County Records*, no. 12 (Shrewsbury, 1908), p. 94.

102 *Minutes of Norwich Court*, p. 60; NNRO, Court Book 1666–77, f. 5v; York Corporation Records, House Book 32, f. 332v; 35, f. 117v.

103 *Poverty in Salisbury*, p. 126; Westminster City Library, MS. 4514.

104 Bodl., Ashm. MS. 1436, f. 72.

105 GL, MSS. 4810/2, f. 76r; 5090/2, 1636–7 acct; 4524/2, ff. 41r, 49r; 2088/1, 1636–7 acct; 9237, ff. 70v–71r; 645/2, 1636–7 acct; *Minutes of Norwich Court, passim*; York Corporation Records, House Book 35, ff. 121v, 123v, 127v–128r, 307v, 315r, 336r.

106 Slack, 'Poverty and Politics', pp. 169–71; Westminster City Library, MS. E47.

107 PRO, SP 16/175/3; *By the Major. Whereas the infection of the plague . . .* (1625; *STC* 16729.2).

108 HMC, *Mar and Kellie*, II. 230. Cf. BL, Harl. MS. 3785, f. 31; HMC, *Cowper*, I. 209; R. Milton, *Londons Miserie, The Countryes Crueltie* (1625), p. 21; R. Latham and W. Matthews (eds), *The Diary of Samuel Pepys* (1970–83), VI. 224.

109 D.M. Meads (ed.), *Diary of Lady Margaret Hoby* (1930), p. 207. Cf. R. Spalding, *The Improbable Puritan: A Life of Bulstrode Whitelocke* (1975), p. 33.

110 BAO, Common Council Proceedings 1598–1608, p. 79; *Records of the City of Norwich*, II. 187; NNRO, Assembly Book 1585–1613, f. 107v; SCA, Ledger C, f. 179v.

111 BAO, Common Council Proceedings 1598–1608, pp. 79, 81, 83, 92; 1608–27, ff. 1r, 11r, 12r; Mayor's Audits, 1608–9, 1609–10. Cf. the confusion in the Exeter accounts in 1571: ECA, Book 157, poor accounts 1563–72.

112 For different bases for early plague rates, see: Reading Corporation Records, box 39, plague documents, 20 July 1603; S. Bond (ed.), *The Chamber Order Book of Worcester 1602–50* (Worcs. Hist. Soc., NS, VIII, 1974), pp. 80–2 (fifteenths); BL, Add. MS. 29975, f. 25; Cheshire RO, QS File 1603 (iv), doc. 10; M.A. Faraday (ed.), *Herefordshire Militia Assessments of 1663* (Camden Soc., 4 ser., X, 1972), p. 14n (gaol and purveyance rates); York Corporation Records, House Book 32, ff. 330r, 342r (*ad hoc* assessment); Cheshire RO, QS File 1604 (iii), docs 17, 20, 21, 1606 (ii), doc. 3 (county mise); Reading Corporation Records, box 39, plague documents, 26 February 1606/7 (poor rate).

113 E.g. Cheshire RO, QS File 1606 (i), doc. 17; 1604 (iii), doc. 15; 1604 (iv), doc. 10; B.C. Redwood (ed.), *Sussex Quarter Sessions Order Book 1642–9* (Sussex Record Soc., LIV, 1954), p. 19; S.C. Ratcliff and H.C. Johnson (eds), *Warwick County Records*, II (Warwick, 1936), pp. 34, 58; J.S. Cockburn (ed.), *Western Circuit Assize Orders 1629–48* (Camden Soc., 4 ser., XVII, 1976), pp. 134–5, 221–2, 243, 286–7, 289–90. Cf. E. Cannan, *The History of Local Rates in England* (1912), pp. 46–7.

114 Cheshire RO, QS File 1604 (iii), doc. 18; 1604 (iv), docs 18–21.

115 Northants RO, Cockayne Papers, C2576, 2714; BL, Harl. MS., 3785, f. 20.

116 Kent AO, Sa/AC8, ff. 44v, 45r, 47v–49r.
117 Plymouth Corporation Records, W361/53/1, rate for Venner's ward; Overseers' Accounts 1611–42, 1625–6 and 1625–7 accounts. For similar support from one town to another, see ECA, letter 310; Act Book 7, f. 340r; SCA, N101, letter of Mayor of Bristol, 7 November 1627; BAO, Christ Church Churchwardens' Accounts 1627–8; *Remembrancia*, pp. 347, 348.
118 Above, p. 216; 22 and 23 Charles II, c. 16; Lambeth Palace, Carte Misc. VI, docs 7, 8 and 4–45 *passim*; *The Newes*, 24 August 1665; *Intelligencer*, 28 August, 16 October 1665.
119 Colchester Corporation Records, Assembly Book 1646–66, ff. 315v–46v *passim*.
120 R.H. Hill (ed.), *The Correspondence of Thomas Corie 1664–87* (Norfolk Rec. Soc., XXVII, 1956), p. 20.
121 Kent AO, Sa/AC8, f. 44. For burials in Colchester and Plymouth see above pp. 97, 107.
122 NNRO, Court Book 1666–77, ff. 9v, 11; Assembly Book 1642–69, f. 277r; Norfolk QS Order Book 1657–68, October 1665; PRO, PC 2/59, pp. 125–6.
123 NNRO, Assembly Book 1585–1613, ff. 278v, 283v, 286v, 288v; *Minutes of Norwich Court* and Court Book 1624–34 *passim*; Slack, thesis, pp. 326–8.
124 NNRO, Court Book 1654–66, ff. 261–3, 270A, 280r; Court Book 24, ff. 5–7, 12, 15r; *Cal. SP Dom. 1666–7*, pp. 101, 119, 141, 191.
125 *Minute Book of St. Margaret Lothbury*, pp. xxii–xxiv, 6–7; GL, MS. 3570/1, 21 January 1593; J.V. Kitto (ed.), *St. Martin-in-the-Fields: The Accounts of the Churchwardens 1525–1603* (1901), p. 570.
126 Wilson, *Plague in Shakespeare's London*, pp. 91–2, 105; E.B. Jupp and W.W. Pocock, *An Historical Account of the Worshipful Company of Carpenters* (1887), p. 68; J.J. Lambert (ed.), *Records of the Skinners of London* (1933), p. 288; GLCRO, P92/SAV/450, p. 372.
127 GL, MS. 4524/1, 1592–3, 1602–3. Cf. *St. Martin-in-the-Fields Accounts*, p. 577; and for rich parishes with large poor stocks and benevolences: GL, MSS. 1432/3, f. 45v; 2968/1, ff. 482–3; 4457/2, f. 39v; 4824, f. 20v.
128 Wilson, *Plague in Shakespeare's London*, pp. 166–7; GL, MSS. 4813/1, f. 27; 4165/1, p. 183; 1279/3, p. 8.
129 LCRO, Cash Account Book 1/2, 1636–7 acct, ff. 122v–123r.
130 Bell, *Great Plague*, pp. 196–9; PRO, PC 2/58, pp. 199, 201, 207; LCRO, Rep. lxx, ff. 156v–157r; Journal xlvi, f. 98r; Sessions Minute Book 16, 9 December 1665.
131 See the references in Chapter 8 n. 98, above, p. 395.
132 Westminster City Library, MS. E47; BL, Harl. MS. 3785, f. 31.
133 NNRO, Court Book 1624–34, ff. 68r, 282v; Clavors' Accounts 1625–48, f. 17r; Misc. Bills and Accounts 1626–7, payments to keeper of the 'Blacke Tower'; York Corporation Records, House Book 35, f. 134r; PRO, PC 2/58, pp. 187, 207; BAO, Common Council Proceedings 1618–27, f. 18v.

Chapter 11 Police and people

1 M. Sylvester (ed.), *Reliquiae Baxterianae* (1696), pt ii, p. 448.
2 William Lilly, *History of His Life and Times* (1822), p. 214; T. Vincent, *God's Terrible Voice in the City* (5th edn, 1667), p. 39.
3 SCA, SSMII/I, accts of November 1627; W.D. Cooper, 'Notices of the Last Great Plague 1665–6 from the Letters of John Allin', *Archaeologia*, XXXVII (1857), 9. Cf. GL, MS. 2968/1, f. 157v; H.J.F. Swayne (ed.), *Churchwardens' Accounts of S. Edmund and S. Thomas Sarum* (Salisbury, 1896), pp. 239, 317.
4 NNRO, Norwich Consistory Court Deposition Book 18, 1579–80, ff. 281v, 284r; T.F. Barton (ed.), *The Registrum Vagum of Anthony Harison*, I (Norfolk Record Soc., XXXII, 1963), p. 94.
5 G.B. Richardson, *Plague and Pestilence in the North of England* (Newcastle on Tyne, 1852), pp. 12–13.
6 Above, pp. 176, 277–8; Bodl., MS. Wills Oxon, 169/3/15.
7 Cf. L. Stone, *The Family, Sex and Marriage in England 1500–1800* (1977), p. 70. Agnes, daughter of John Steven, for example, died at the age of four at the end of the 1546–7 plague in Barnstaple; in November 1547 a new baby was christened Agnes: T. Wainwright (ed.), *Barnstaple Parish Register* (Exeter, 1903), baptisms, p. 6, burials, p. 5.
8 Vincent, *God's Terrible Voice*, p. 32; R. Boyle, *The Philosophical Works*, ed. P. Shaw (2nd edn, 1738), III. 539; P. Slack (ed.), *Poverty in Early Stuart Salisbury* (Wilts. Rec. Soc., XXXI, 1975), p. 126; E.B. Jupp and R. Hovenden (eds), *The Registers of the Parish of Allhallows London Wall* (1878), p. 120.
9 E.g. ECA, Act Book 5, f. 99v; Commonplace Book of John Hooker, f. 356r; *The Autobiography of Symon Patrick* (Oxford, 1839), p. 54; *Cal. SP Dom. 1667–8*, p. 125.
10 BL, Harl. MS. 3785, ff. 24, 50; Westminster City Library, MS. E47; GL, MSS. 642/1, 6 July 1625; 2590/1, p. 254; 4457/2, f. 250r.
11 Lambeth Palace, Carte Misc. VI, nos 38, 42–3; *Cal. SP Dom. 1664–5*, p. 524; J. Owen and J.B. Blakeway, *A History of Shrewsbury* (1828), I. 404–5; Lilly, *Life and Times*, p. 48. Cf. J. Balmford, *A Short Dialogue* (1603), sig. A4r; R. Milton, *Londons Miserie* (1625), p. 18; E. Freshfield (ed.), *Minutes of the Vestry Meetings of St. Christopher le Stocks* (1886), p. 48; W.G. Bell, *The Great Plague in London in 1665* (2nd edn, 1951), pp. 94–5.
12 M. Vovelle, *Piété baroque et déchristianisation en Provence au XVIIIᵉ siècle* (Paris, 1973), pp. 366–9; J.D. Walsh, 'Eli Halevy and the Birth of Methodism', *Trans. Roy. Hist. Soc.*, 5 ser., 25 (1975), 10–11.
13 ECA, Sessions Minute Book 1621–30, f. 277v; PRO, SP 16/175/3; BL, Add. MS. 33512, f. 91.
14 Vincent, *God's Terrible Voice*, p. 42; P. Caraman, *Henry Morse* (1962), pp. 87, 92, 98; E.B. Underhill (ed.), *The Records of a Church of Christ meeting in Broadmead Bristol 1640–1687* (1847), p. 87.
15 J. Dod and R. Cleaver, *Three Godlie and Frvitfvl Sermons* (1610), p. 94; F.G. Emmison, *Elizabethan Life: Morals and the Church Courts* (Chelms-

ford, 1973), pp. 107, 108; NNRO, Norwich Archdeacon's Court, Act Book 4, 1604–10, presentments of SS. Stephen's and Saviour's Norwich; F.P. Wilson, *The Plague in Shakespeare's London* (Oxford, 1961), p. 154.

16 A. Macfarlane (ed.), *The Diary of Ralph Josselin 1616–1683* (British Academy, Records of Social and Economic History, NS, III, 1976), pp. 520, 523, 528.

17 Salisbury Diocesan RO, Consistory Court Depositions, vol. 59, 3 May 1667; A. Green, 'Essex Wills before and after the Reformation', *Essex Review*, 258 (1957), 73; Kent AO, Register of Wills 194/xvi, William Staunton (I owe this reference to Peter Clark); J.R. Beresford, 'Churchwardens' Accounts of Holy Trinity Chester 1532–1633', *J. Chester Arch. Soc.*, NS, XXXVIII (1951), 133; D.G. Vaisey (ed.), *Probate Inventories of Lichfield and District 1568–1680* (Staffs. Rec. Soc., 4 ser., V, 1969), p. 73.

18 For a good example see York Corporation Records, E40, no. 76, 4 February 6 Edward VI.

19 York Corporation Records, House Book 32, f. 372v.

20 *VCH Wilts*, V. 319; Sheffield City Library, Strafford Correspondence, 12/136.

21 PRO, SP 16/164/35. For similar cases, see SP 16/400/98; *Privy Council Acts 1629–30*, p. 346; NNRO, Court Book 1576–81, p. 472; LCRO, QS File, February 1665/6, recogs of 29 July, 3 August, 8 September; C. Bailey, *Transcripts from the Municipal Archives of Winchester* (Winchester, 1856), pp. 91–3; H.H. Copnall (ed.), *Nottinghamshire County Records: Notes and Extracts . . . of the 17th Century* (Nottingham, 1915), p. 67.

22 Cheshire RO, QS File 1604 (iii), doc. 18; Plymouth Corporation Records, Overseers' Accounts 1611–42, 1626 acct.

23 Kent AO, PRC 2/15, ff. 278r, 357v; Lincs. RO, Ad. Ac. 25, f. 159. I owe these references to Clare Gittings.

24 Kent AO, PRC 2/34, nos 269, 298; Salisbury Diocesan RO, Dean's Court Act Book 20, f. 86r. A more romantic encounter due to plague is described in R. Parkinson (ed.), *The Life of Adam Martindale* (Chetham Soc., OS, IV, 1845), pp. 7–8.

25 ERO, Q/SBa 2/105, Epiphany 1665/6, petition of John Foster; H.E. Nott and E. Ralph (eds), *The Deposition Books of Bristol, II: 1650–1654* (Bristol Rec. Soc., XIII, 1948), pp. 164–5.

26 A.J. Willis (ed.), *Winchester Consistory Court Depositions 1561–1602* (Winchester, 1960), p. 31; S. Tymms, 'Notes towards a Medical History of Bury', *Procs Suffolk Arch. Institute*, I (1853), 41. Cf. Lincs. RO, Ad. Ac. 39, f. 325.

27 Hants RO, QS Order Book 1658–72, p. 321; *Archives of Winchester*, pp. 91–2. Cf. PRO, SP 16/175/24.

28 A.J. Jewers, 'The Will of a Plague-Stricken Londoner', *Home Counties Magazine*, III (1901), 109–10; Hants RO, Jervoise MSS., 44M69/S6/XXXVIII. 16.

29 T. Beza, *A shorte learned and pithie Treatize* (1580), sigs D3–4r.

30 W. Wood, *The History and Antiquities of Eyam* (6th edn, Derby, 1865), p.

100; D.G. Greene (ed.), *The Meditations of Lady Elizabeth Delaval* (Surtees Soc., CXC, 1978), p. 85; J.C. Jeaffreson (ed.), *Middlesex County Records* (1886–92), II. 50, III. 375; Bodl., typescript calendar of Middlesex QS Rolls, 1610, p. 28, 1610–11, p. 110.

31 Chester Corporation Records, M/B/28, f. 152; Westminster City Library, MS. F4516, f. 15v.

32 *Certaine Prayers . . . to be vsed in the present Visitation* (1603), sig. D3.

33 J.C. Atkinson (ed.), *North Riding Quarter Sessions Records* (North Riding Rec. Soc., I–IX, 1884–92), IV. 69; W.J. Thoms (ed.), *Anecdotes and Traditions Illustrative of Early English History* (Camden Soc., OS, 1839), p. 33; York Corporation Records, House Book 35, ff. 150v, 126r; *Poverty in Salisbury*, pp. 121–2. Cf. Robert Graves' comment on First World War trenches which 'made us feel larger than life: only there was death a joke, rather than a threat': R. Graves, *Difficult Questions, Easy Answers* (1972), p. 151.

34 J. Raine (ed.), *Depositions from the Castle of York* (Surtees Soc., XL, 1861), p. 134; *Cal. SP Dom. 1664–5*, p. 529 (but contrast Charles' view in *ibid.*, p. 499).

35 NNRO, Court Book 1540–9, pp. 268–9; R.H. Tawney and E. Power (eds), *Tudor Economic Documents* (1924), I. 50–1; *Cal. SP Dom. 1666–7*, p. 313. Cf. K. Thomas, *Religion and the Decline of Magic* (1971), p. 508; Hull Corporation Records, Bench Book 4, f. 226v; E.R. Brinkworth (ed.), *The Archdeacon's Court: Liber Actorum, 1584*, I (Oxfordshire Rec. Soc., XXIII, 1942), p. 9.

36 Above, p. 273; W.J.C. Moens, *Registers of the Dutch Reformed Church Austin Friars, London* (Lymington, 1884), p. xxvi; LCRO, Rep. 1, f. 294r; Journal xxi, f. 5r; *Cal. SP Dom. 1636–7*, pp. 170–1.

37 J.A. Twemlow (ed.), *Liverpool Town Books* (Liverpool, 1918, 1936), I. 104–5.

38 Hants RO, QS Order Book 1628–49, ff. 133v–134; SCA, EI/253, f. 22v; York Corporation Records, E40, no. 76, 26 November, 5 Edward VI.

39 J.W. Willis Bund (ed.), *Worcester County Records. Quarter Sessions Rolls 1591–1643* (Worcester, 1899–1900), II. 622. Cf. PRO, PC 2/48, p. 371; Lincs. RO, Lindsey QS File, A4, 1631, doc. 67; GLCRO, P92/SAV/1387 (dorse).

40 NNRO, Sessions Indictments and Recognizances, xx, doc. 14; York Corporation Records, House Book 35, f. 121r; *Poverty in Salisbury*, p. 42.

41 *Worcester County Records*, I. 307; J. Colbatch, *Observations upon the Scheme lately Published* (1721), p. 22; R. Latham and W. Matthews (eds), *The Diary of Samuel Pepys* (1970–83), VII. 40–1; J.S. Cockburn (ed.), *Western Circuit Assize Orders 1629–48* (Camden Soc., 4 ser., XVII, 1976), p. 243; *Cal. SP Dom. 1665–6*, p. 389; W.H. Coates (ed.), *Journal of Sir Simonds D'Ewes from the First Recess of the Long Parliament* (New Haven, 1942), p. 37.

42 European scares and suspicions are referred to in: J. Bonnet (ed.), *Letters of John Calvin* (Edinburgh, 1858), p. 452; E.W. Monter, *Calvin's Geneva*

(New York, 1970), p. 72; G. Parker, *The Army of Flanders and the Spanish Road 1567–1659* (Cambridge, 1972), p. 66; H.C.E. Midelfort, *Witch-Hunting in Southwestern Germany 1562–1684* (Stanford, 1972), pp. 122–3; HMC, *Denbigh*, V. 6. Cf. Thomas, *Religion and the Decline of Magic*, p. 559.

43 Cf. R. Baehrel, 'Épidémie et terreur; histoire et sociologie', *Annales historiques de la Révolution française*, XXIII (1951), 113–46; *idem*, 'La Haine de classe en temps d'épidémie', *Annales ESC*, 7 (1952), 351–60; and for a brief survey of collective reactions to plague in Europe, J. Delumeau, *La Peur en Occident* (Paris, 1978), pp. 131–6. I suspect, however, that these works exaggerate the long-term, as distinct from the short-term, impact of fear of plague on popular mentality. Cf. the comments on Baehrel in R. Cobb, *Terreurs et Subsistances 1793–1795* (Paris, 1964), pp. 31–2.

44 R. Parkinson (ed.), *The Autobiography of Henry Newcome* (Chetham Soc., OS, 26, 27, 1852), I. 151.

45 Above, pp. 37, 237, 244; C.A. Markham and J.C. Cox (eds), *Records of the Borough of Northampton* (Northampton, 1898), II. 238; Hull Corporation Records, Bench Book 5, ff. 224r, 246r.

46 *Vestry Minutes of St. Christopher le Stocks*, p. 48; Bell, *Great Plague*, p. 221. Cf. J. Horsfall Turner (ed.), *Reverend Oliver Heywood 1630–1702. His Autobiography* ... (Brighouse, 1880–5), I. 197, 199. The social importance of religious ceremonies in a modern epidemic in China is described in F.L.K. Hsu, *Religion, Science and Human Crises* (1952), pp. 66–72.

47 Winchester City Records, 6th Book of Ordinances 1663–83, f. 26. Cf. York Corporation Records, House Book 35, ff. 128r, 336v; NNRO, Court Book 1654–66, f. 280r.

48 C. Mackay, *A Collection of Songs and Ballads Relative to the London Prentices and Trades* (Percy Soc., I, 1841), pp. 28–31; J.F. Larkin and P.L. Hughes, *Stuart Royal Proclamations*, I (Oxford, 1973), no. 19.

49 *Nottinghamshire County Records*, p. 52; *Archives of Winchester*, p. 118; NNRO, Court Book 1624–34, ff. 45v, 91v, 92r, 285v, 1634–46, ff. 200r, 219v.

50 NNRO, Court Book 1654–66, f. 280r, 1666–77, f. 3v; York Corporation Records, House Book 35, f. 116v; above, p. 34.

51 York Corporation Records, House Book 35, f. 127v. For other orders against assemblies and drinking during epidemics, see C.F. Mullett, *The Bubonic Plague and England* (Lexington, Kentucky, 1956), p. 383; SCA, N101, doc. 89; York Corporation Records, House Book 35, ff. 114r, 116r, 130r, 132v.

52 SCA, N101, doc. 88.

53 GL, MS. 4887, p. 278; J.E. Cox, *Annals of St. Helen's Bishopsgate* (1876), p. 103; S. Rudder, *A New History of Gloucestershire* (Cirencester, 1779), p. 737.

54 GL, MSS. 4251/1, p. 7; 2968/1, f. 390; 4256/1, f. 127r; 4458/1, p. 295; LCRO, Rep. lxx, ff. 153v, 156r. Cf. W.H. and H.C. Overall, *Index to the Remembrancia ... of the City of London* (1878), pp. 332–3.

55 ERO, D/P 94/5/1, f. 396r. Cf. Chester Corporation Records, M/B/28, f. 152r.
56 W.H. Frere and W.M. Kennedy (eds), *Visitation Articles and Injunctions*, II, *1536–58* (1910), pp. 17–18, 87; Bell, *Great Plague*, p. 334.
57 *Orders thought meet . . .* (?1578), no. 10; G. Oliver, *The History and Antiquities of the Town and Minster of Beverley* (Beverley, 1829), p. 234 n. 12; J. Dennett (ed.), *Beverley Borough Records* (Yorks. Arch. Soc., Rec. Ser., LXXXIV, 1933), p. 138; Hull Corporation Records, Bench Book 5, f. 216. Cf. NNRO, Court Book 1624–34, ff. 395v–396, 1654–66, f. 268v; BAO, Common Council Proceedings 1627–42, f. 69r; LCRO, Journal xxiii, f. 132v.
58 HMC, *Salisbury*, XV. 266. Cf. W.H. Stevenson (ed.), *Records of the Borough of Nottingham* (Nottingham, 1882–1914), IV. 297. On Clapham, see above, pp. 233–6.
59 J. Balmford, *A Short Dialogue* (1603), p. 32; H. Petowe, *The Countrie Ague* (1626), pp. 19–21. On the functions of funerals, see Clare Gittings, *Death, Burial and the Individual in Early Modern England* (1984).
60 PRO, SP 16/531/81; 16/175/3,22; *Middlesex County Records*, III. 62.
61 PRO, PC 2/59, pp. 123, 135; BL, Harl. MS. 3785, f. 32; Pepys, *Diary*, VI. 211; Bell, *Great Plague*, p. 258; *Middlesex County Records*, III. 383. Cf. P. Clark, '"The Ramoth-Gilead of the Good": Urban Change and Political Radicalism at Gloucester 1540–1640', in P. Clark, A.G.R. Smith and N. Tyacke (eds), *The English Commonwealth 1547–1640: Essays Presented to Joel Hurstfield* (Leicester, 1979), p. 175.
62 Hull Corporation Records, Bench Book 4, f. 139v.
63 J.S. Davies, *History of Southampton* (1883), p. 499.
64 NNRO, Court Book 1582–7, p. 33, 1624–34, ff. 113v; 121r. For similar Norwich cases, see QS Minute Books 1630–8, 28 March 1638, 1654–70, 11 July 1666; Court Book 1582–7, p. 440, 1603–15, ff. 16v, 51v, 1624–34, ff. 70v, 79r, 1654–66, f. 281v.
65 ECA, Sessions Minute Book 1621–30, ff. 277, 281v, 282r, 302r; BAO, Mayor's Audits 1575–6; Beverley Corporation Records, Keepers' Account Rolls, 1603–4; ERO, QS Rolls, 407, doc. 62; *Cal. SP Dom. 1664–5*, pp. 512–3; PRO, PC 2/58, p. 118.
66 W.L. Sachse (ed.), *Minutes of the Norwich Court of Mayoralty 1630–1* (Norfolk Rec. Soc., XV, 1942), p. 177; *Poverty in Salisbury*, p. 126.
67 PRO, SP 16/175/3, 24; LCRO, Sessions File, February 1665/6, 22 August 1665.
68 J. Hawarde, *Les Reportes del Cases in Camera Stellata 1593–1609* (1894), p. 168; LCRO, Lord Mayor's Waiting Book, ii, 22 September 1665 (I owe this reference to Stephen Macfarlane).
69 S. Bond (ed.), *The Chamber Order Book of Worcester 1602–50* (Worcs. Hist. Soc., NS, VIII, 1974), p. 321; F.P. and M.M. Verney, *Memoirs of the Verney Family* (1892–9), IV. 125.
70 *Poverty in Salisbury*, pp. 125, 120–1.
71 Colchester Corporation Records, Sessions Book of Examinations and Recognizances, 1619–45, 11 July, 23 July 1631. 'Some evil disposed persons' destroyed the lodges built for the sick in Carlisle: T. Hughes,

'The Plague in Carlisle 1597/98', *Trans. Cumb. and Westm. Antiq. and Arch. Soc.*, NS, LXXI (1971), 61.
72 ERO, QS Rolls, 406, Michaelmas 1665, doc. 104; *Cal. SP Dom. 1635*, p. 559; *1635–6*, p. 185; Colchester Corporation Records, Sessions Book of Examinations and Recognizances 1619–45, 7 June 1626. For other disturbances during epidemics, see ECA, Sessions Minute Book 1621–30, f. 287v; *Cal. SP Dom. 1636–7*, p. 108; HMC, *Cowper*, II. 139–40; W.B. Willcox, *Gloucestershire: A Study in Local Government 1590–1640* (New Haven, 1940), p. 225 n. 67; NNRO, Court Book 1666–77, f. 5r; LCRO, Sessions File, February 1665/6, 2 September 1665.
73 E.g. BAO, Common Council Proceedings 1608–27, f. 37v; ECA, Act Book 3, p. 244.
74 NNRO, Assembly Book 1585–1613, ff. 285v–286, 301v; PRO, SP 14/12/3.
75 ECA, Sessions Minute Book 1621–30, ff. 262v, 271r; J.C. Cox, *Three Centuries of Derbyshire Annals* (1890), I. 151–2n.
76 *Poverty in Salisbury*, p. 120; York Corporation Records, House Book 35, f. 118r; ECA, Sessions Minute Book 1621–30, f. 277v; PRO, SP 16/345/1; PC 2/47, p. 98; G. Ormerod (ed.), *Tracts Relating to Military Proceedings in Lancashire during the Great Civil War* (Chetham Soc., OS, II, 1844), pp. 232–3.
77 *Poverty in Salisbury*, p. 121; PRO, SP 16/175/3; ECA, Sessions Minute Book 1621–30, f. 264.
78 Cf. E.P. Thompson, 'The Moral Economy of the English Crowd in the Eighteenth Century', *P&P*, 50 (1971), 115–16.
79 York Corporation Records, House Book 35, ff. 143r, 146v.
80 Above, pp. 231–2.
81 NNRO, Court Book 1587–95, p. 423; QS Minute Book 1630–8, 28 June, 9 August 1637; ERO, QS Rolls, 412, Easter 1667, doc. 47; *Cal. SP Dom. 1665–6*, p. 79.
82 F.S. Boas (ed.), *The Diary of Thomas Crosfield* (1935), p. 93; *Middlesex County Records*, III. 368, 375, 377; NNRO, Court Book 1666–77, f. 13r.
83 *Middlesex County Records*, III. 377–8; B.H. Cunnington (ed.), *Records of the County of Wiltshire* (Devizes, 1932), p. 115; Lincs. RO, Ad. Ac., 6, f. 85.
84 York Corporation Records, E40, no. 76, 26 November, 5 Edward VI.
85 *The Intelligencer*, 24 July 1665.
86 York Corporation Records, House Book 35, f. 117v. Antagonism towards bureaucracy often occurs when catastrophe seems to demand generosity: A.H. Barton, *Communities in Disaster* (1969), pp. 299–300.
87 LCRO, Journal xi, f. 330r; Rep. iii, ff. 189v, 191r, 192r. Cf. *Letters and Papers of Henry VIII*, II (ii), p. 1276.
88 *Verney Memoirs*, IV. 136.
89 *York Castle Depositions*, p. 134; *Cal. SP Dom. 1664–5*, pp. 484, 486–90, *1666–7*, pp. 179, 245, 530; BL, Harl. MS. 3785, ff. 29, 35v. For rumours of plots, see Pepys, *Diary*, VI. 209.
90 *Orders thought meet* (?1578), no. 17; Mullett, *Bubonic Plague*, p. 383; T.

Lodge, *A Treatise of the Plague* (1603), sig. Fl; *Stuart Royal Proclamations*, I, p. 44. On concepts of order, see K. Wrightson, 'Two Concepts of Order', in J. Brewer and J. Styles (eds), *An Ungovernable People: The English and Their Law in the Seventeenth and Eighteenth Centuries* (1980), pp. 21–46.

91 *Diary of Crosfield*, p. 93; PRO, SP 16/200/14; *The Intelligencer*, 11 September 1665.

92 York Corporation Records, House Book 32, f. 340.

93 Sheffield City Library, Strafford Correspondence, 12/255; J.P. Earwaker (ed.), *Constables Accounts of the Manor of Manchester* (Manchester, 1891–2), II. 125, 155, 159.

94 Kent AO, transcript of Cranbrook parish register, 1597; PRO, SP 16/200/14; R.L. Hine, *Relics of an Uncommon Attorney* (1951), p. 71; *Sir Henry Whithed's Letter Book, I: 1601–14* (Hants Rec. Ser., I, 1976), pp. 39–40; *Western Circuit Assize Orders*, p. 206.

95 Examples of the commonplace link between plague and the sins of the poor are J. Squier, *A Thanksgiving for the decreasing . . . of the plague* (1637), p. 16; *Lachrymae Londinenses* (1626), pp. 7–8; R. Harris, *Hezekiah's Recovery* (1626), pp. 32–3; J. Donne, *XXVI Sermons. The Third Volume* (1661), p. 294; *Lamentatio Civitatis* (1665), pp. 27–8; Vincent, *God's Terrible Voice*, p. 95.

96 Cf. L. Chevalier (ed.), *Le Choléra* (La Roche-sur-Yon, 1958), pp. 15–17; D. Apple (ed.), *Sociological Studies of Health and Sickness* (New York, 1960), p. 72; R. and E. Blum, *Health and Healing in Rural Greece* (Stanford, 1965), p. 125.

97 Cf. Gittings, *Death, Burial and the Individual*, pp. 49–50; J.S. Purvis, *Tudor Parish Documents of the Diocese of York* (Cambridge, 1948), pp. 160, 229; Thomas, *Religion and the Decline of Magic*, pp. 604–5.

98 Above, pp. 262–3; ECA, letter 288, 8 January 1627; R. Jenison, *The Cities Safetie* (1630), pp. 28, 147–8. Cf. J. Godskall, *The Kings Medicine* (1604), sig. N4v; W. Cupper, *Certaine Sermons concerning Gods late visitation* (1592), pp. 341–4.

99 *Privy Council Acts 1595–6*, p. 230; PRO, SP 16/533/17, ff. 35r, 37r, 38v–40r, 43v; *Poverty in Salisbury*, p. 122. Cf. Laud's view, quoted above, p. 22.

100 A. Wood, *The History and Antiquities of the University of Oxford* (Oxford, 1792–6), II. 279–80; R.H. Morris, *Chester in the Plantagenet and Tudor Reigns* (Chester, 1893), pp. 78–9.

101 HMC, *Salisbury*, XV. 227–8; PRO, SP 16/398/138. Cf. *Cal. SP Dom. 1595–7*, p. 310.

102 *Verney Memoirs*, IV. 130; *The Newes*, 31 August 1665; *Cal. SP Dom. 1664–5*, pp. 504–5. On victims being blamed for disasters, see A.H. Barton, *Social Organization under Stress: A Sociological Review of Disaster Studies* (Washington, DC, 1963), p. 141.

103 NNRO, Assembly Book 1585–1613, f. 286r.

104 E.g. Cheshire RO, QS File 1604 (iii), doc. 19; Sheffield City Library, Spencer-Stanhope Collection, 60232, orders for restraint of the poor, 1636; York Corporation Records, House Book 35, f. 134r; NNRO, Court Book 1666–77, f. 12r.

105 York Corporation Records, House Book 35, f. 116r; BL Sloane MS. 3267, f. 10r.
106 *Beverley Borough Records*, p. 140.
107 This problem is considered in Thomas, *Religion and the Decline of Magic*, pp. 656–63.
108 For an excellent demonstration of the connection in Venice, see B. Pullan, *Rich and Poor in Renaissance Venice* (Oxford, 1971). Cf. J.T. Alexander, *Bubonic Plague in Early Modern Russia* (Baltimore, 1980), pp. 277–8; P. Slack, 'Social Policy and the Constraints of Government', in J. Loach and R. Tittler (eds), *The Mid Tudor Polity c. 1540–1560* (1980), pp. 107–8.
109 Thompson, 'Moral Economy of the English Crowd', pp. 83–8, 109–12; J. Walter and K. Wrightson, 'Dearth and the Social Order in Early Modern England', *P&P*, 71 (1976), 22–42; P. Slack, 'Books of Orders: The Making of English Social Policy, 1577–1631', *Trans. Roy. Hist. Soc.*, 5 ser., XXX (1980), 3, 17.
110 P. Slack, 'Vagrants and Vagrancy in England, 1598–1664', *Ec. HR*, 2 ser., XXVII (1974), 367–8.
111 M. Foucault, *Madness and Civilization* (1965), esp. ch. II. Cf. H.C.E. Midelfort, 'Madness and Civilization in Early Modern Europe: A Reappraisal of Michel Foucault', in B. Malament (ed.), *After the Reformation: Essays in Honor of J.H. Hexter* (Manchester, 1980), pp. 247–65.
112 P. Razzell, *The Conquest of Smallpox* (Firle, 1977), pp. 28, 87, 114–15. For examples, see above, p. 241; ERO, Q/SBa 2/39, doc. 1 (I owe this reference to J.A. Sharpe); Kent AO, PRC 2/34, acct no. 47. For isolation against dysentery, see BAO, SS. Philip and Jacob register, 20 September 1603.
113 R.J. Morris, *Cholera 1832* (1976), pp. 112–13. This work, and M. Durey, *The Return of the Plague: British Society and the Cholera 1831–2* (Dublin, 1979), show many parallels with the history of reactions to plague.
114 M. Pelling, *Cholera, Fever and English Medicine 1825–65* (Oxford, 1978), pp. 2–3.
115 *Liverpool Town Books*, I. 108; Lincs. RO, Lincoln Entries of Common Council 1541–64, f. 131v.
116 Above, p. 205.
117 T.S[wadling], *Sermons, Meditations and Prayers upon the Plague* (1637), pp. 27–8.
118 B. Spenser, *Vox Civitatis* (1625), p. 23; H. Holland, *Spirituall Preseruatiues against the pestilence* (1603 edn), p. 173.

Chapter 12 The end of plague 1665–1722

1 W. Hendley, *Loimologia Sacra* (1721), p. 59.
2 For recent discussion of the problem, see M.W. Flinn, 'Plague in Europe and the Mediterranean Countries', *J. European Economic Hist.*, VIII (1979), 131–48; A.B. Appleby, 'The Disappearance of Plague: A Continuing Puzzle', *Ec. HR*, 2 ser., XXXIII (1980), 161–73; P. Slack, 'The Disappear-

ance of Plague: An Alternative View', *ibid.*, XXXIV (1981), 469–76; W.H. McNeill, *Plagues and Peoples* (Oxford, 1976), pp. 172–4.

3 What follows is a revised version of my 'The Response to Plague in Early Modern England: Public Policies and their Consequences', in R.S. Schofield and J. Walter (eds), *Death and the Social Order* (Cambridge, forthcoming).

4 See above, pp. 9–11.

5 Above, pp. 66–9.

6 Above, pp. 12, 86; R. Pollitzer, *Plague* (Geneva, 1954), pp. 330–1; L.F. Hirst, *The Conquest of Plague* (Oxford, 1953), pp. 303–9.

7 Above, p. 10; Hirst, *Conquest*, pp. 238–46; Pollitzer, *Plague*, pp. 378–81; L. Bradley, 'Some Medical Aspects of Plague', in *The Plague Reconsidered* (Local Population Studies, Supplement, 1977), pp. 13–15. A recent argument for the importance of human fleas in medieval epidemics, which also summarises the modern medical literature, is S.R. Ell, 'Interhuman Transmission of Medieval Plague', *Bull. Hist. Med.*, LIV (1980), 497–510.

8 T. Willis, *The Remaining Medical Works*, trans. S. Pordage (1681), pp. 124, 131. Cf. above, p. 101.

9 Above, pp.123–4, 10.

10 Above, p. 67. For a similar modern incident, see F.M. Laforce *et al.*, 'Clinical and Epidemiological Observations on an Outbreak of Plague in Nepal', *Bull. WHO*, XLV (1971), 693–706.

11 Cf. J. Norris, 'East or West? The Geographic Origin of the Black Death', *Bull. Hist. Med.*, LI (1977), 16–17, and *idem*, 'Geographic Origin of the Black Death: A Response', *ibid.*, LII (1978), 117–19.

12 Slack, 'Disappearance of Plague: An Alternative View', p. 471; above, pp. 132, 146.

13 For examples, see above, p. 112; *Cal. SP. Dom. 1665–6*, p. 568; NNRO, Court Book 1654–66, f. 259r; York Corporation Records, House Book 32, f. 305v.

14 ECA, Act Book 11, ff. 31–39r. One suspect from an infected town did get into Exeter, however: Strangers' Book 1621–68, p. 183.

15 NNRO, Court Book 1654–66, ff. 253, 257–61, 268v, 276v; 1666–77, f. 6v; Assembly Book 1642–68, f. 267v; above pp. 137–9.

16 Cf. J. Cornwall, *Revolt of the Peasantry 1549* (1977), pp. 100–2, 151.

17 Above, p. 115.

18 BAO, Orders of Mayor and Aldermen 1660–6, 19 June 1665, 13 January 1666; Sessions Minute Book 1653–71, f. 64r; Common Council Proceedings 1659–75, pp. 130, 133–4; Great Audit Book 1665–6, pp. 42–3; J. Latimer, *Annals of Bristol in the Seventeenth Century* (Bristol, 1900), p. 333; *Cal. Treasury Books 1660–7*, p. (731).

19 Above, p. 220; York Corporation Records, House Book 35, ff. 105–13, 115v–117r (Wentworth's letter), 118–52 *passim*; PRO, SP 16/200/14; parish registers of St Michael-le-Belfrey, Holy Trinity and St Martin cum Gregory, published by the Yorkshire Parish Register Society.

20 ERO, D/B 3/3/207 (Maldon); York Corporation Records, House Book 35, f. 335r; Book 36, f. 10r (1637–8).

21 T.F. Sheppard, *Lourmarin in the Eighteenth Century* (Baltimore, 1971), pp.

118–27; J.-N. Biraben, *Les Hommes et la peste* (Paris, 1975–6), I. 198, 205–6; J. Revel, 'Autour d'une épidémie ancienne: la peste de 1666–70', *Revue d'hist. moderne et contemp.*, XVII (1970), 967–71; G.E. Rothenburg, 'The Austrian Sanitary Cordon and the Control of the Bubonic Plague, 1710–1871', *J. Hist. Med.*, 28 (1973), 15–23.

22 Above, pp. 68–9, 224–5.

23 Above, Table 7.1, p. 177. Table 7.1 shows that Braintree also registered a high household concentration of mortality in 1666: unfortunately, we do not know whether isolation was strictly enforced there; it may have been.

24 Cf. above, pp. 112, 224–5, 257; and for Italy, C.M. Cipolla, *Public Health and the Medical Profession in the Renaissance* (Cambridge, 1976), pp. 28–9, 47–57.

25 The argument which follows is based on my 'Disappearance of Plague: An Alternative View'; for other discussion of the various hypotheses, see Appleby, 'Disappearance of Plague'.

26 For extensive, but not complete or infallible, information on the chronology of European epidemics, see Biraben, *Les Hommes et la peste*, I. 118–29, 375–449.

27 *Cal. SP Dom. 1651–2*, pp. 197, 198.

28 Above, Chs 5, 6; E. Freshfield (ed.), *The Vestry Minute Books of the Parish of St. Bartholomew Exchange* (1890), p. xlix.

29 Plague epidemics continued in Smyrna in the eighteenth century: D. Panzac, 'La Peste à Smyrne au XVIIIᵉ siècle', *Annales ESC*, 28 (1973), 1071–93. Since English commerce with that port was heavy, I am not persuaded that any change in the pattern of international trade can account for England's escape from plague, as has been suggested: J.F.D. Shrewsbury, *A History of Bubonic Plague in the British Isles* (Cambridge, 1970), pp. 485–6; F. Braudel, *Capitalism and Material Life* (1967), p. 47.

30 Cf. Biraben, *Les Hommes et la peste*, II. 86–90, 173–5; Flinn, 'Plague in Europe', pp. 139–46.

31 Above, pp. 221–2. Cf. *Cal. SP Dom. 1655–6*, pp. 176, 200.

32 Hull Corporation Records, Bench Book 6, pp. 545, 548, 591–2; Book 7, pp. 21–5.

33 *Cal. SP Dom. 1667–8*, p. 580, *1668–9*, pp. 409–10, 413, 555, 577; PRO, PC 2/60, pp. 444–5, 2/62, p. 29; Wellcome Historical Medical Library, MS. 3109, 3 September–5 October 1668, 1 July 1669.

34 It took at least twenty-five days; fleas have been shown to be able to transmit plague after periods of starvation lasting up to twenty-nine days: *Parliamentary Papers*, 1824 (VI), *Minutes of Evidence, Quarantine*, p. 74; Pollitzer, *Plague*, p. 381.

35 *Cal. Treasury Books 1679–80*, p. 536; *1689–92*, pp. 1708, 1762; *1709*, pp. 357–8, 410, 425, 445; *1710*, p. 233; *1713*, p. 329; *Cal. Treasury Papers 1720–8*, p. 435; PRO, PC 2/87, pp. 15–16, 313–17; *Cal. Treasury Books and Papers 1729–30*, p. 206; *1731–4*, pp. 89, 141; *1739–41*, pp. 471–3; *1742–5*, pp. 295, 307–8.

36 *Cal. Treasury Books 1681–2*, p. 256; PRO, PC 1/2/232, 2/87, p. 324.

37 C.F. Mullett, 'A Century of English Quarantine (1709–1825)', *Bull. Hist. Med.*, XXIII (1949), 527–45; *Cal. Treasury Books 1713*, p. 186.
38 PRO, SP 35/23/124, 126, 127, 133, 145, 153; PC 2/87, pp. 24–5, 391.
39 PRO, SP 35/23/90; PC 1/3/89.
40 PRO, SP 35/23/126, 35/28/26, 33, 36. Cf. *London Gazette*, 16–20 April, 30 April–4 May 1668; W. Lee, *Daniel Defoe: His Life and Recently Discovered Writings 1716–29* (1869), II. 142, 277–8, 464–5.
41 PRO, SP 35/24/3, 6–8; 35/25/101, 102, 107; 35/28/85, 86. Cf. PC 2/87, p. 167.
42 Biraben, *Les Hommes et la peste*, I. 231–2.
43 Mullett, 'Century of English Quarantine', pp. 538, 544.
44 Hirst, *Conquest of Plague*, pp. 334–5; W.G. Liston, 'The Milroy Lectures, 1924, on the Plague', *British Medical Journal*, I (1924), 951; D. Van Zwanenberg, 'The Last Epidemic of Plague in England? Suffolk, 1906–18', *Medical Hist.*, XIV (1970), 63–74.
45 *Parl. Papers*, 1824 (VI), *Minutes of Evidence, Quarantine*, pp. 47, 51; T. Short, *New Observations on City, Town and Country Bills of Mortality* (1750), pp. 240–1. For further diverse views on the nature of plague, see J. Howard, *An Account of the Principal Lazarettos in Europe* (Warrington, 1789), pp. 32–41; C.F. Mullett, *The Bubonic Plague and England* (Lexington, Kentucky, 1956), chs 13, 14.
46 E. Gibbon, *The Decline and Fall of the Roman Empire* (Everyman edn, 1910), IV. 373.
47 E.g. *A Weekly Review of the Affairs of France* (9 vols, 1704–13), VIII. 297–300; *Philosophical Trans. of the Royal Society of London*, 28 (1713), 101–44, 279–81; S. Gough, *A Discourse Occasion'd by the Small-Pox and Plague now reigning in Europe* (1711), p. 27; ECA, Act Book 13, p. 129; B. Stitt (ed.), *Diana Astry's Recipe Book 1700* (Beds. Hist. Rec. Soc., 37, 1957), pp. 112, 155–6.
48 Lee, *Defoe: Recently Discovered Writings*, II. 142, 277 *et seq.*; HMC, *Carlisle*, p. 36. There is a good general discussion of the literature relating to the scare in Mullett, *Bubonic Plague*, ch. 12, and in C.F. Mullett, 'The English Plague Scare of 1720–3', *Osiris*, II (1936), 484–516. On Marseilles itself, see Biraben, *Les Hommes et la peste*, I. 230 *et seq.*
49 *Bibliotheca Lindesiana*, VIII, *Handlist of Proclamations 1714–1910*, 25 August, 3 September, 12, 27 October, 15 November 1720; PRO, PC 2/87, pp. 50–2 (there was another similar fast in 1721: *ibid.*, pp. 335–7); 7 George I, c. 3.
50 R. Mead, *A Short Discourse concerning Pestilential Contagion* (8th edn, 1722), pp. 21, 72, 85–8, 90–5, 98, 128, 135–6. (The first edition appeared in 1720.)
51 F. Chicoyneau, *A Succinct Account of the Plague at Marseilles* (1721); anon., *The Late Dreadful Plague at Marseilles* (1721); R. Bradley, *The Plague at Marseilles Consider'd* (1721).
52 *A Collection of very Valuable and Scarce Pieces relating to the last Plague in the Year 1665* (1721) included, besides the orders, an essay by Nathaniel Hodges, whose *Loimologia* was first published in English in 1720, and an introduction criticising Mead.

53 N. Carter, *A Sermon preach'd at the Chapel at Deal in Kent* (1721), pp. 5, 16, 19–20; T. Wise, *A Sermon Preach'd at . . . St. Alphage in Canterbury* (1721), pp. 6–7; J. Norman, *Seasonable Advice to a Sinful Nation* (1721), pp. 7–9, 16, 20; T. Newlin, *God's gracious Design in inflicting National Judgments* (Oxford, 1721), p. 22; J. Barker, *Preparations to meet God in the Way of his Judgments* (1720), pp. 7–11. Cf. J.D. Walsh, 'Eli Halevy and the Birth of Methodism', *Trans. Roy. Hist. Soc.*, 5 ser., 25 (1975), 5.

54 E. Massey, *The Signs of the Times* (1722), pp. 28 *et seq.* Massey's implications were spelled out in James Smith's reply: *An Examination of the Signs of the Times* (1722). On the South Sea Bubble, see also E. Saunders, *A Discourse of the Dangers of Abusing the Divine Blessings* (?1722), p. 27.

55 P. Razzell, *The Conquest of Smallpox* (Firle, Sussex, 1977), p. 42; Massey, *Signs of the Times*, pp. 17–18, 28. Cf. Saunders, *A Discourse*, p. 26; Hendley, *Loimologia Sacra*, pp. 37–9.

56 See, for example, Sir Richard Blackmore, *A Discourse upon the Plague* (1721); J. Browne, *Antidotaria* (1721); R. Boulton, *An Essay on the Plague* (Dublin, 1721); T. Willis, *A Preservative from the Infection of the Plague* (1721); Eugenius Philalethes [Robert Samber], *A Treatise of the Plague* (1721).

57 G. Pye, *A Discourse of the Plague wherein Dr Mead's Notions are Consider'd and Refuted* (1721); 'The Free-Thinker', *Considerations on the Nature, Causes, Cure and Prevention of Pestilences* (1721); 'The Explainer', *Doctor Mead's Short Discourse Explain'd* (2nd edn, 1722); *idem, Distinct Notions of the Plague* (1722); anon., *The Remarks lately published on Three Treatises of the Plague* (1722). The latter seems from its content (p. 6) to have been by 'The Explainer'. Margaret Pelling informs me that Pye took his MD at Leyden in 1714, when he was twenty-seven.

58 Pye, *Discourse*, pp. 2–3, 22–3, 33–7, 60–3; 'Free–Thinker', *Considerations*, pp. 11, 107–8, 110–13.

59 Cf. above, pp. 27–8, 203, 208, 249–52.

60 Cf. Mead, *Short Discourse*, p. ii; Pye, *Discourse*, p. x; *The Remarks lately published*, p. 6.

61 J. Ehrard, 'La Peste et l'idée de contagion', *Annales ESC*, 21 (1957), 46–59. Cf. Mead, *Short Discourse*, pp. ii–iii.

62 'The Explainer', *Distinct Notions*, p. 105; *idem, Doctor Mead's Short Discourse*, pp. 33–4. Most writers continued to combine 'foreign' and 'domestic' causes of plague, however, although only one was as lucid on the subject as Mead: P. Rose, *A Theorico-Practical Miscellaneous and Succinct Treatise of the Plague* (1721), pp. 9 *et seq.*

63 Pye, *Discourse*, pp. v–vii, 48, 51, 53, 66, 72. Cf. 'Free-Thinker', *Considerations*, pp. 154, 163; 'The Explainer', *Doctor Mead's Short Discourse*, p. 53.

64 Mead, *Short Discourse*, pp. xiv–xxix.

65 8 George I, c. 10. The political controversy and its parliamentary history are fully described in A.J. Henderson, *London and the National Government 1721–1742* (Durham, North Carolina, 1945), pp. 34–45, 49, 52–4. Cf. C.B. Realey, *The Early Opposition to Sir Robert Walpole 1720–1727* (Lawrence, Kansas, 1931), pp. 92, 112.

66 The two bills became 8 George I, cs 8, 18. For opposition to them, see

Reasons humbly offer'd by the Grocers of the City of London against Part of the Bill . . . to prevent . . . Infection [?1721]; *The Case of the Levant Company in relation to the Bill . . . for performing Quarentine* [?1721]. The influence of the trading interest can be seen in the modifications introduced into the second edition of J. Browne, *A Practical Treatise of the Plague* (2nd edn, 1720), p. 24.

67 LCRO, Rep. cxxv, pp. 283, 306, 553–4; *Lords Journal*, XXI.˙581–2; *The Case of the Inhabitants of the Liberty of Westminster against the Clauses . . . to a Bill . . . to require Quarentine* [?1721]. Cf. S. and B. Webb, *The Manor and the Borough* (1908), I. 225.

68 *Three Clauses in the Quarantine Act . . . The Petition of the City of London . . . Their Lordships Protest* [?1721], pp. 3–4; *Lords Journals*, XXI. 629–30; Henderson, *London and the National Government*, p. 40 and n. 80. The consistency between these attacks on the Quarantine Act and other criticisms of Walpole's administration can be seen from G.V. Bennett, 'Jacobitism and the Rise of Walpole', and Q. Skinner, 'The Principles and Practice of Opposition: The Case of Bolingbroke versus Walpole', in N. McKendrick (ed.), *Historical Perspectives: Studies in English Thought and Society in Honour of J.H. Plumb* (1974), pp. 77–8, 96, 98–9.

69 *Applebee's Original Weekly Journal*, 25 November, 2 December 1721; Lee, *Defoe: Recently Discovered Writings*, II. 450. The first articles, which may also have been by Defoe, were investigated by the government: PRO, SP 35/29/37–40.

70 [E. Gibson], *The Causes of the Discontents in Relation to the Plague* (1721), pp. 3, 12–13; N. Sykes, *Edmund Gibson* (1926), p. 81.

71 PRO, PC 2/87, pp. 320, 323–4, 329; College of Physicians, Annals V, ff. 179–89; BL, Sloane MS. 3984, ff. 101–3, 111–12, 116–21.

72 PRO, PC 2/87, pp. 324, 327, 341–3, 451; PC 1/3/95. Cf. above, p. 219.

73 Sir John Colbatch, *A Scheme for Proper Methods to be taken should it please God to visit us with the Plague* (1721), pp. 11, 13–14; idem, *Observations upon the Scheme lately Published* (1721), pp. 15, 17, 20; *Captain Dunning's Scheme for effectually preventing the Progress of the Plague* [?1721].

74 Lee, *Defoe: Recently Discovered Writings*, II. 285, 291–2, 378–9, 407–10, 429–30; Henderson, *London and the National Government*, pp. 43–5.

75 Lee, *Defoe: Recently Discovered Writings*, II. 436–8, 453–5; D. Defoe, *Due Preparations for the Plague as well for Soul as Body*, ed. G.A. Aitken (1895), pp. 8–13, 94–5, 193–4, 213–19; D. Defoe, *A Journal of the Plague Year*, ed. L. Landa (1969), pp. 94–5, 213–19.

76 *Due Preparations*, pp. 12, 15–16, 18–19.

77 M. Schonhorn, 'Defoe's *Journal of the Plague Year*: Topography and Intention', *Rev. Eng. Studies*, NS, 19 (1968), 393–7.

78 *Journal*, ed. Landa, pp. 48, 155–60, 198.

79 *Journal*, ed. Landa, pp. 53–5, 70–1, 74–5, 164–7, 170, 182–3; Lee, *Defoe: Recently Discovered Writings*, II. 378–9, 428.

80 Cf. Landa, 'Introduction' to *Journal*; F. Bastian, 'Defoe's *Journal of the Plague Year* Reconsidered', *Rev. Eng. Studies*, NS, 16 (1965), 151–73; Schonhorn, 'Defoe's *Journal*', pp. 387–99.

81 *Journal*, ed. Landa, p. 152.

Conclusion

1 Albert Camus, *The Plague* (trans. Stuart Gilbert, Harmondsworth, 1960), pp. 251–2.
2 K. Wrightson and D. Levine, *Poverty and Piety in an English Village. Terling 1525–1700* (1979), ch. 7; V. Skipp, *Crisis and Development: An Ecological Case Study of the Forest of Arden 1570–1674* (Cambridge, 1978), pp. 78–80.
3 For an attempt at a cost-benefit analysis, see C.M. Cipolla, *Public Health and the Medical Profession in the Renaissance* (Cambridge, 1976), pp. 57–66; and for some revision of it, *idem, Faith, Reason and the Plague in Seventeenth-Century Tuscany* (Ithaca, 1979), pp. 79–80.
4 *A mournfull Dittie on the death of certaine Judges . . . at Lincoln* (1590): BL, Huth 5 (62).

Index

Abbot, Robert, 236
absolute power, 219. *See also* arbitrary power; liberties; prerogative, royal
Adelmare, Cesare, 207, 222
adultery, 261
Africa, 9–10, 14, 323
age-groups, *see* plague: incidence by age
aldermen and mayors: deaths from influenza, 128; deaths from plague, 114, 164, 167, 193; duties during plague, 255–66; flight, 257–62, 280
alehouses and inns: control of, 29, 49, 262, 295, 305; infected, 291, 304, 314; keepers, 253; suspected, 19, 101, 189, 193
aliens, *see* Dutch and Walloon refugees
alleys, 123, 167, 291, 314; in London, 152, 159–61, 167, 322
Allin, John, 253–4
Amsterdam, 68, 233, 254, 324
amulets, 32, 253
Anabaptists, 237, 302
Andrewes, Lancelot, 234–6
angels, 26, 41, 236, 242, 247; destroying, 21, 243, 253. *See also* devils
Anguish, Alexander, 263
annals, civic, 111, 260
Antwerp, 68
apothecaries, 33, 193, 214, 218, 246, 276
Applebee's Journal, 332–3, 335
apprentices and servants, 181, 188, 190, 269, 275; deaths from plague, 126, 176, 178, 253, 274; relations with masters, 152, 288–9
arbitrary power, 331, 332. *See also* absolute power; liberties; prerogative, royal
Arbuthnot, John, 333, 334

Archeus, 248–9, 250
Ardleigh, Essex, 83
Armada, 97
Arminianism, 26, 237, 238. *See also* Laud, William
arsenic, 32, 35
arson, 299
Ashburton, Devon, 90, 98
Ashby de la Zouche, Leics., 190
Asia, 9–10, 14, 66, 311
assemblies: religious, 229, 231; unlawful, 49, 295–6
assessment, county, 268, 385. *See also* rates
Assizes, 18, 117, 207, 267
astrology, 26–7, 71, 252, 253. *See also* Forman, Simon; Gadbury, John; Napier, Richard
atheists, 233. *See also* deists; naturians
atoms, 249
Atterbury, Francis, 332
Aubrey, John, 190–1
Avicenna, 24
Axminster, Devon, 85
Aylesbury, Bucks., 299
Aylmer, John, 228, 229, 231, 237

Baker, John, 126
Balmford, James, 183, 235
Baltic, 322, 324, 326
Bancroft, Richard, 233, 234
Bangor, diocese, 280
baptisms, 117, 168, 412. *See also* fertility
Barcelona, 46
Barnard, John, 257
Barnstaple, Devon: epidemics, 84, 86, 88–9, 94–8, 412; Independents, 243; sex-ratio of burials, 179–81

426

fumigants, 30, 245, 249. *See also* perfumes
funerals, 17, 235, 253, 285; children playing at, 34; controls on, 210, 213, 234, 296–8. *See also* bell-ringing; burial; graveyards

Gadbury, John, 252, 254
Galen, 24, 27, 30, 35, 233, 248, 249
games, 29, 295–6, 304. *See also* children
gaol fever, 70, 117, 207
Gassendi, Pierre, 249
Gateshead, Durham, 285
Gatford, Lionel, 243
Geneva, 229
Georgeham, Devon, 90
Germany, 68, 73, 208
Gestingthorpe, Essex, 103
Gibbon, Edward, 326
Gibson, Edmund, 333, 334
Gibson, Robert, 300
Glasgow, 325
Gloucester, 47, 212
Gloucestershire, 212
God, parenthetical references to, 241
Gosfield, Essex, 103
Gosport, Hants, 245
Gouge, William, 238, 239
granaries, 160, 378
grass, in streets, 190
Graunt, John, 144, 149, 185, 244, 245, 251, 329
grave-diggers, 144, 205
graveyards, 17, 37, 79, 291; hazards to health, 27, 45; new, 141, 149, 224, 286, 296. *See also* burial; funerals
Great Chesterford, Essex, 101, 102
Great Coggeshall, Essex, 101, 102, 105, 106
Great Easton, Essex, 102
Great Oakley, Essex, 106
Great Sampford, Essex, 103
Greece, 245
Grenville, Lady, 186
grief, death from, 286
Grindal, Edmund, 228–9, 231
guilds and companies, 270. *See also* East India Company; feasts; Levant Company; London: livery companies

Halifax, Yorks., 188
Hall, Joseph, 25
Hamburg, 112

Hampshire, 212, 292, 304
Harley, Robert, 268
harlots, 29, 101
Harris, Robert, 239, 241
Hartlepool, Durham, 325
harvest, 189, 287. *See also* dearth; famine; subsistence crises
Harvey, William, 218
Harwich, Essex, 101, 104, 106, 110
Hatherleigh, Devon, 85, 90
Haverfordwest, Pemb., 263
hearth tax, 17, 107, 116, 137, 139, 142
Helion Bumpstead, Essex, 102
Helmont, J. B. van, 248, 250. *See also* chemical medicine
Hemyock, Devon, 98
hen, applied to buboes, 31
Hendley, William, 311
Henrietta Maria, Queen, 217
Henry, Prince of Wales, 234
Henry IV, of France, 218
Henry VII, 31
Henry VIII, 31, 160, 201, 202
Hereford, 70
Herefordshire, 188, 268
Herrick, Nicholas, 44
Herrick, William, 44
Herring, Francis, 41, 43, 179, 234
Heydon, Essex, 102
Heyward, Rowland, 264
High Commission, 234
High Laver, Essex, 83
Highworth, Wilts., 191
Hippocrates, 24, 245
Hitchin, Herts., 175, 191, 304
Hoby, Margaret, 239, 279
Hoby, Philip, 145
Hodges, Nathaniel, 246, 251, 252, 422
Holland, Henry, 309
Holsworthy, Devon, 90, 91
Honiton, Devon, 85, 86
Hooker, John, 114
Hooper, John, 29, 43
Hornchurch, Essex, 106
Horndon, Essex, 106
hospitals, private, 290. *See also* London: hospitals; pesthouses
House, Robert, 298
household, *see* family; plague: incidence by household; quarantine
household size, 178
housing conditions, 11–12, 143, 152, 166, 322, 379; of immigrants, 140,